# The Materials Sourcebook for Design Professionals

**Rob Thompson**
**Photography by Martin Thompson**
**Engineering calculations by Nigel Burgess**

# The Materials
# Sourcebook for
# Design
# Professionals

Thames & Hudson

Nigel Burgess researched and composed the
formulas needed to create the material comparison
charts on the opening page of each material.

First published in the United Kingdom in 2017
by Thames & Hudson Ltd, 181A High Holborn,
London WC1V 7QX

*The Materials Sourcebook for Design Professionals*
© 2017 Rob Thompson and Martin Thompson

Photographs © 2017 Martin Thompson save where
otherwise indicated

Designed by Christopher Perkins

British Library Cataloguing-in-Publication Data
A catalogue record for this book is available from
the British Library

ISBN 978-0-500-51854-0

Printed and bound in China by C & C Offset
Printing Co., Ltd

To find out about all our publications,
please visit **www.thamesandhudson.com**.
There you can subscribe to our e-newsletter,
browse or download our current catalogue,
and buy any titles that are in print.

# Contents

**How to use this book**     8
Providing an insight into the structure, format and content of the book's chapters

**Introduction**     10
Inspirational materials, processes and knowledge for design professionals

## 1 METAL

**Ferrous Metal**

Cast Iron     22
   Cookware
   Architecture
   Automotive

Steel     28
   Products, furniture and lighting
   Cookware and appliances
   Packaging
   Automotive
   Architecture and construction

**Non-Ferrous Metal**

Aluminium     42
   Packaging
   Cookware
   Textiles
   Products, furniture and lighting
   Automotive and aerospace
   Sports
   Architecture and construction

Magnesium     54

Titanium     58
   Aerospace
   Architecture and construction
   Medical

Copper, Brass, Bronze and
Nickel Silver     66
   Products, furniture and lighting
   Cookware
   Fashion and textiles
   Architecture and construction

Zinc     78
   Products and furniture
   Architecture and construction

**Precious metal**

Silver     84
   Fashion and textiles
   Jewelry

Gold     90
   Jewelry
   Food
   Textiles

## 2 PLASTIC

**Thermoplastic**

Polypropylene (PP)     98
   Products, furniture and lighting
   Packaging
   Technical textiles
   Automotive and transportation

Polyethylene (PE)     108
   Packaging
   Products, furniture and lighting
   Technical textiles and fashion

Ethylene Vinyl Acetate (EVA)     118

Polyvinyl Chloride (PVC)     122
   Products and industrial
   Architecture and construction
   Packaging and promotion
   Fashion and textiles

Acid Copolymers and Ionomers     130

Polystyrene (PS)     132

Styrene Acrylonitrile (SAN)
   and Acrylic Styrene
   Acrylonitrile (ASA)     136

Acrylonitrile Butadiene Styrene
   (ABS)     138
   Products, furniture and lighting

Polycarbonate (PC)     144
   Products, furniture and lighting
   Automotive and aerospace

Polyethylene Terephthalate (PET),
   Polyester     152
   Textiles
   Packaging
   Products, furniture and lighting

Polyamide (PA), Nylon     164
   Products, furniture and lighting
   Automotive and aerospace
   Fashion and textiles

Polymethyl Methacrylate (PMMA),
   Acrylic     174
   Products, furniture and lighting
   Architecture and construction

Polyacrylonitrile (PAN),
   Acrylic Fibre     180

Polyoxymethylene (POM),
   Acetal     184
   Automotive
   Products, furniture and lighting

Polyetheretherketone (PEEK)     188

Fluoropolymer     190

PLASTIC CONTINUED

**Thermoplastic Elastomer
(TPE)**                          194
Products and furniture
Fashion and textiles

**Thermoset**
Polyurethane (PU)                202
Products, furniture and lighting
Automotive and aerospace
Fashion and textiles

Polysiloxane, Silicone           212

Synthetic Rubber                 216
Automotive and transportation
Fashion and technical textiles

Formaldehyde-Based:
Melamine (MF), Phenolic (PF)
and Urea (UF)                    224

Unsaturated Polyester (UP)
Resin                            228

Polyepoxide, Epoxy Resin         232

**Super Fibre**
Carbon-Fibre-Reinforced
Plastic (CFRP)                   236
Automotive and aerospace

Aromatic Polyamide, Aramid       242

Polyphenylene Benzobisthiazole
(PBO)                            246

**Bio-Derived**
Natural Rubber and Latex         248

Cellulose Acetate (CA)
and Viscose                      252
Products and accessories
Fashion and textiles

Starch Plastic                   260

Polylactic Acid (PLA)            262

# 3 WOOD

**Wood Products**
Wood Pulp, Paper and Board       268
Packaging
Products and furniture

Bark                             280

Cork                             286

Veneer                           290

Engineered Timber                296
Products and furniture
Architecture and construction

**Softwood**
Spruce, Pine and Fir             304

Hemlock                          308

Larch                            310

Douglas-Fir                      314

Cypress Family                   318
Architecture and construction

**Hardwood**
Poplar, Aspen and Cottonwood     324

Willow                           328

Maple                            330

Birch                            334

Beech                            338

Oak                              342

Chestnut                         346

Walnut                           348

Hickory and Pecan                352

Ash                              354

Elm                              358

Cherry, Apple and Pear           360

**Tropical Hardwood**
Acacia                           364

Iroko                            366

Teak                             370

Mahogany Family                  372

Exotics                          374

Balsa                            378

# 4 PLANT

**Stem and Leaf**
Rattan                           382

Bamboo                           386
Architecture and construction
Products, furniture and lighting

Grass, Rush and Sedge            392

Leaf Fibres                      394
Fashion and textiles
Products, automotive and construction

**Bast Fibre**
Flax, Linen                      400
Fashion and technical textiles

Jute and Kenaf                   404

Hemp                             406

Ramie                            408

**Seed Fibre**
Cotton                           410
Fashion and textiles

Coconut coir                     416

## 5 ANIMAL

**Animal Fibres**

Silk 420
Fashion and textiles

Wool 426
Fashion and textiles
Furniture, lighting and interiors

Hair 434

**Bone and Horn**

Horn 440

Bone and Antler 442

**Leather and Fur**

Cowhide 444
Fashion and textiles

Sheepskin and Goatskin 452

Pigskin 456

Horsehide 458

Deerskin and Kangaroo Hide 460

Exotics 462

Fur 466

## 6 MINERAL

**Rock**

Stone 472

Diamond and Corundum 476

**Ceramic**

Clay 480
Products, furniture and lighting
Architecture and construction

Plaster 492

Cement 496

Technical Ceramic 502

**Glass**

Soda-Lime Glass 508
Packaging
Architecture and construction
Products, furniture and lighting

Lead Glass 518

High-Performance Glass 522

## DIRECTORY

Glossary and Abbreviations 528

Featured Designers, Artists and
Manufacturers 533

Selected Bibliography 536

Illustration Credits 537

Sources 538

Index 541

# How to Use this Book

> The knowledge in this book is fundamental to help designers choose the most appropriate materials. Getting it right not only leads to better design, but also means the least energy is consumed and waste produced. Regardless of application, the richness of information provides designers with endless possibilities to explore the most positive material experiences.

This book is divided into six chapters. Each represents a category of materials: Part 1: Metal; Part 2: Plastic; Part 3: Wood; Part 4: Plant; Part 5: Animal; and Part 6: Mineral. Each material within the chapter – there are 98 sections and hundreds of materials covered – is explored in relation to the industries where it is most commonly found. Exciting applications and beautiful design executions are included to demonstrate each material's qualities and opportunities for design.

To support the process of material selection, the book includes general notes on the compatibility of each material with manufacturing processes as well as with other materials. There are countless ways to interpret how to apply the information to a design project; the selected examples show the range of qualities and characteristics that makes each one unique. This is intended as a starting point, since how the material fits into a project depends on geometry, volumes, cost, availability and other factors.

While certain materials have an inherently design-compatible finish – glossy ionomer (page 130), colour-anodized aluminium (page 42), self-cleaning concrete (page 496) – others require protection. The ability to manipulate surface topography, tactility and materiality provides great scope for design projects. The various considerations for each, such as compatibility and recyclability, are presented and examples given.

Through design and technological development, the potential for materials to remain a precious commodity after their 'useful life' is increasing. As a result of legislation, directives and ingenious design and engineering, it is not uncommon for materials to be reused in the same application countless times. Concentrating resources and avoiding contamination helps to make this cycle more efficient and thus sustainable. This book gives the means to influence those decisions and so tip the balance in favour of continued progress.

**Introduction** Each of the material groups is defined and discussed in relation to design, architecture and fashion to provide insight into current and future trends. Our perception of materials is shaped as much by history and context as by the physical properties; this is something that is expanded on throughout the book.

**Chapter** Each of the six chapters, divided according to material group, is colour-coded for ease of reference: Part 1: Metal (blue-grey); Part 2: Plastic (teal); Part 3: Wood (green); Part 4: Plant (mustard); Part 5: Animal (orange); and Part 6: Mineral (red).

**Material** This book brings together inspiring content with technical information by combining rich imagery with a highly accessible approach to material science. Through collaboration with suppliers and a mechanical engineer, the technical overview of each material visualizes the data to make it easily understood.

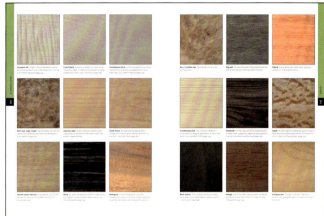

**Visual glossary** Throughout the book examples of finished articles show materials in all their glory. Where relevant, photographs of the types of colours, details and finishes that can be achieved are included. In the case of wood veneer (page 290) several types are included to demonstrate the potential for design.

**Curated content** The content has been carefully selected to demonstrate each material's most desirable properties. For example, in the case of Polypropylene (PP) (page 98) the examples have been chosen to demonstrate its impressive versatility, strength, formability and recyclability.

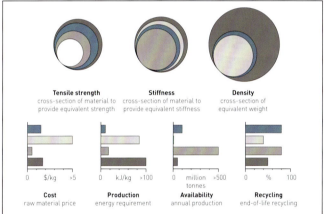

**Comparative analysis** Relevant properties of each material are compared – such as strength-to-weight and density – to show why some materials perform better than others for certain applications. The cost, embodied energy, availability and recycled percentage are also given. This information is intended as guidance.

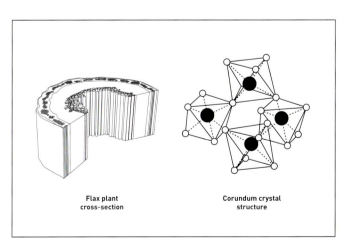

**Technical insight** Where necessary, the atomic structure, packing and other attributes are explored to show why a material behaves in the way that it does. In addition, cross-sections help to demonstrate how materials are constructed, or deconstructed, as the case may be.

**Glossary and sources** Key processes, technologies and principles are included in the glossary. This information helps to explain the range of opportunities and limitations of each material. Additionally, the best books and websites to consult to gain further knowledge in specific areas of technology are included.

# Introduction

Natural to synthetic, nano to macro, materials are a source of inspiration and excitement. Intrinsic to good design, material knowledge helps build the most successful and enduring objects, architecture and clothing. This book celebrates materials in all their guises, from hidden structures to worn exteriors, to demonstrate the incredible range of possibilities. New materials continually emerge, not only from laboratories but also through reinterpretation: while materials previously confined to industrial or high-performance applications are becoming more accessible, others are being reinvented through clever design and novel production techniques. These opportunities have been highlighted throughout the book to show where materials have come from and, ultimately, what could come next.

The wealth of our material world is the result of many millennia of development. From Roman concrete structures (see Cement, page 496) to precision-pressed zirconia ceramic (see Technical Ceramic, page 502), materials have continually been pushed to their limits through ingenuity and creativity. We now understand material properties better than ever before, so much so that it is possible to predict the exact point of failure in critical structures and adjust the design accordingly.

While innovation and development open up new areas of exploration, the fundamental characteristics that make materials what they are remain unchanged. In some cases the range of use is so diverse that it is hard to imagine how a single material can perform so many different functions. For example, polyethylene terephthalate (PET, polyester) (page 152) is one of the most widely used plastics, and applications range from humble textiles to enabling flexible screens in wearable technology, and from metallized packaging to one-piece molded chairs. The building blocks for each material are explained – from atomic structure to crystallinity – to allow an understanding of how materials meet the needs of such diverse criteria.

The book celebrates the material groups most relevant to design, comprising metal, plastic, wood, plant, animal and mineral. Enclosed within are many subgroups, including established and emerging composite technologies, biobased plastics and engineered timbers. All have the potential to invigorate projects. The major applications for each material – leading examples are derived from design, fashion and architecture – are brought to the fore to show off their most inspiring qualities.

**Large-scale structural timber** Timber is a renewable and versatile material. The structure of the Metropol Parasol (2011) in Seville, Spain, consists of sheets of interlocked engineered timber rising from concrete platforms. Designed by Jürgen Mayer H. Architects, it is the largest wooden structure in the world and demonstrates the potential of engineering timber for sustainable architecture of the future.

## METAL
Held together by very strong internal bonds, metals are classified as conductive, hard, stiff, strong, opaque and reflective with a high melting point. The weighting of these properties depends on the composition of the metal; so while some are more efficient conductors, others have superior tensile strength.

Metals are crystalline and each atom is connected to its neighbour. When put under pressure, ductile metals such as steel (page 28) and aluminium (page 42) will bend before they break. This property means they are suitable for plastic-forming processes, such as bending, pressing and forging. Gold (page 90) is so malleable that it can be beaten into very thin sheets, a mere 4 microns thick.

The surface of all metals, except for gold, oxidizes when exposed to the atmosphere. In the case of steel, even stainless types, this process is degenerative (rusting). However, one type of steel – a type of high-strength low-alloy (HSLA) steel known as weathering steel – is designed to rust. A familiar-looking layer of brown-orange oxide develops on the surface, but instead of flaking off it stays and protects the base metal from further corrosion. Used in bridges, buildings and sculpture, the patina develops over time to a rich dark brown.

The oxide layer on aluminium, which is promoted through anodizing, offers a host of design opportunities. Consisting of alumina (aluminium oxide, $AlO$), one of the hardest materials known to man, which also exists in crystal form (see Diamond and Corundum, page 476) and as a technical ceramic, the thin translucent layer of protection may be dyed with colour. Taking advantage of the highly reflective and light surface quality of certain alloys, a range of bright metallic colours is possible. From vivid red to dark grey, anodized aluminium has become a staple of design, featuring in a wide range of situations.

Metals tend to be heavy owing to the densely packed structure. Even so, some of the non-ferrous alloys offer exceptional strength-to-weight. In other words, in applications where thinness is critical, metals outperform the other material

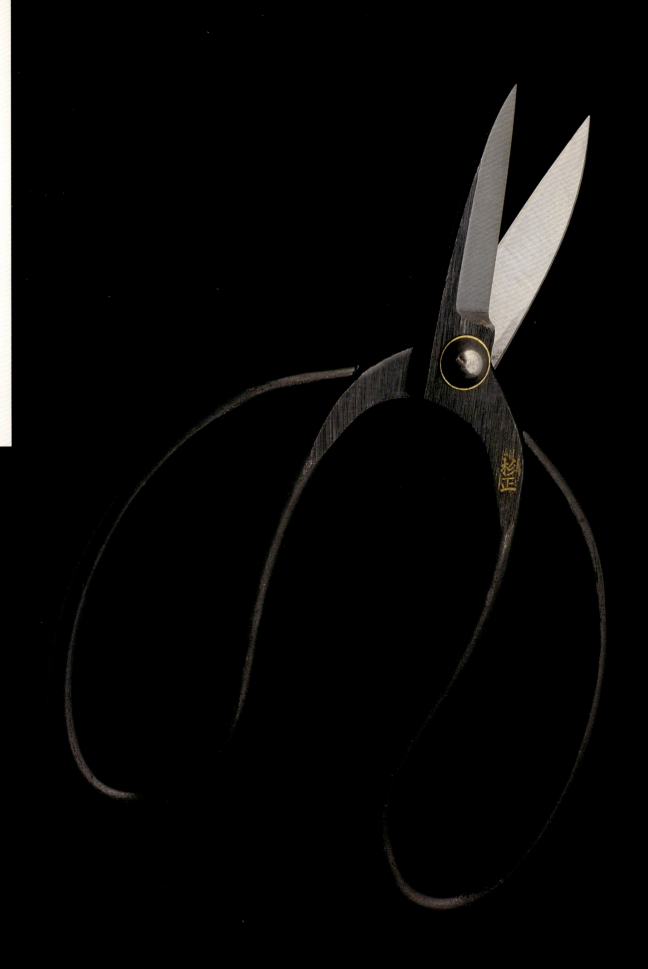

**Opposite**
**Perfecting steel** These Japanese Okubo-basami gardening shears from Banshu Hamono are crafted from a combination of two steels: hard carbon steel (known as hagane; there are several types including ki, shiro, ao and tama) for the edge and soft steel (low-carbon) for the core. This combination provides unrivalled performance and is the result of generations of bladesmithing in Japan. The steel industry in the region historically known as Banshu, in what is now the southwestern part of Hyogo Prefecture in Japan, is thought to have started as a katana (single-edged samurai sword) factory. For centuries, craftsmen in this region have been developing their compositions to serve a variety of needs.

**Right**
**High-performance coating** Conductive fabrics, sometimes referred to as smart textiles, are used for a range of technical applications such as heat shielding (firefighter uniforms), electromagnetic interference (EMI) shielding, radar reflection (survival suits), antimicrobial (shoes and medical), wearable electronics and flexible heater elements (seats, blankets, pocket linings and gloves). This example consists of woven polyester (page 152) fabric coated with a thin film of titanium.

groups. Titanium alloy (page 58), for example, performs well at reasonably high temperatures – although metals are prone to expansion and contraction, which can cause problems – and has excellent corrosion resistance. As a result, it is the material of choice for demanding aerospace applications and has found its way into consumer products, such as ultrathin eyewear and performance bicycles. It is biocompatible too, and so useful for medical applications.

## PLASTIC

The impact of these synthetic materials – comprising long chains of repeating monomers (polymers) made up of carbon, hydrogen, oxygen and other elements, such as chlorine and fluorine – on the modern world could not have been fully understood when Bakelite (phenol-formaldehyde resin, page 224) was invented in 1907. The first truly synthetic material, its invention marked the start of the modern plastics industry, and it remains in use to this day. Today there are countless different plastics, and new formulations, alloys and composites continually emerge, with each new grade claiming to outperform its predecessors. They are relatively inexpensive – although this is not always the case – and offer a high degree of moldability, colourability and customizability.

Plastics are either thermosetting or thermoplastic. The difference is that thermoset plastics form physical cross-links between the polymer chains in a one-way reaction. This means they are challenging, if not impossible, to recycle. Thermoplastics do not form permanent cross-links and so are, mostly, melt-processible. Thermosets generally have high-temperature resistance, good chemical resistance and a hard surface. Thermoplastics, by comparison, are tough, resilient, recyclable and have poor resistance to high temperature. Of course, there are many exceptions to this rule. With increased molecular weight (length of polymer chain) and crystallinity, thermoplastics become stiffer, stronger and more resistant to heat and chemicals. This is demonstrated by the so-called super fibres: polyphenylene benzobisthiazole (PBO) (page 246), aramid (page 242) and ultra-high-molecular-weight polyethylene (UHMPE) (page 108). These materials – more commonly known by trademark names, such as Zylon, Kevlar and Dyneema respectively – have exceptional strength; they outperform steel and even carbon fibre (page 236) for the same weight.

The majority of plastics are derived from oil in an energy-intensive process that results in high embodied energy. Several types are derived from renewable biobased ingredients, including natural rubber (page 248), semi-synthetics (cellulose acetate, CA, page 252) and bioplastics (see Starch Plastic, page

14

260, and Polylactic Acid, page 262). These materials have significantly lower environmental impact, can be recycled and, in some cases, are fully biodegradable.

It is also possible to produce certain 'conventional' plastics from monomers derived from natural sources, such as maize and potatoes. Examples include epoxy (page 232) and polyamide (PA, nylon) (page 164). Manufacturers claim that these plastics produce significantly fewer greenhouse gas emissions and consume less energy in production. However, there are other environmental issues to take into account, such as the use of farmland to grow crops for plastic instead of food and the widespread use of genetically modified (GM) ingredients.

Thermoplastic elastomers (TPE) (page 194) combine the mechanical performance of thermoset elastomers – polyurethane (PU) (page 202), silicone (page 212), synthetic rubber (page 216) – with melt-processability. This has many advantages, not least being able to recycle waste and scrap. Stiffness (flexibility) ranges from very low to high (hard), depending on the type, and they can be coloured, textured, printed and laminated. This makes them suitable for a wide range of applications, from technical components to sportswear.

The development of plastic composites has had a profound impact on design, from helping to make lightweight portable items to enabling new forms of

architecture. Continuous fibre-reinforced plastics – see Carbon-Fibre-Reinforced Plastic (CFRP) (page 236), Epoxy Resin (page 232) and Unsaturated Polyester (UP) (page 228) – offer superior strength-to-weight and dimensional stability. Utilized in both rigid and flexible structures, fibre-reinforced composites (FRP) comfortably outperform the strongest of the metal alloys in tensile applications.

The benefits of composites are not limited to low-volume and batch production. Short-fibre reinforcement is incorporated into mass-produced thermoplastic to enhance stiffness and strength. This practice is widespread throughout automotive and furniture design, because adding fibre helps to reduce weight and volume. There have been several significant developments in thermoplastic composites in recent years, because of the many advantages this matrix offers. One such development takes advantage of the versatility and range of formats possible with thermoplastic. So-called self-reinforced plastic (SRP) is made up of drawn fibres embedded in a resin matrix of the same material (typically polypropylene, PP, page 98). As well as the environmental benefits of using a single material throughout, SRP offers exceptional impact resistance, stiffness and strength-to-weight.

## WOOD
Wood and bark consist of cellulose, hemicellulose and lignin, as well as

**Above**
**Crafted materials** In the case of cellulose acetate (CA) spectacle frames, material quality is very much a combination of science and craftsmanship. Multicoloured CA – such as this Mazzucchelli tortoiseshell frame in the process of being CNC-milled – is the result of several stages of production. Blocks are molded and then sliced and diced. These small cubes are reassembled by hand in the desired pattern and pressed into a new block. This is sliced to produce the sheet that the frames are then cut from. Using this technique a huge array of different patterns and colour combinations is possible; it is up to the designer how the elements come together.

**Opposite**
**The beauty of commodity materials** Naoto Fukasawa designed this kettle for Muji and it was launched in Japan in 2014. Over the years Muji have made the most of the naked quality of PP in a plethora of products. Even though it is one of the least expensive plastics, it can be produced with a fine finish, from glossy to matt, as a result of its low melt viscosity. This is essential for items that will sit on the countertop alongside high-value materials such as copper (page 66), steel and beech.

waxes and tannins. These strong natural polymers are aligned with the direction of growth, providing impressive strength parallel to the grain like a highly engineered composite.

As well as providing lumber, trees are converted into a huge number of raw materials, in particular paper (page 268), cork (page 286), bark (page 280) veneer (page 290) and engineered timber (page 296). Lumber is classed as either softwood

or hardwood. This taxonomy does not help the designer much, because several types of softwood are harder, stronger and higher-density than some of the hardwoods. Nevertheless, the softwoods – spruce, pine and fir (page 304), hemlock (page 308), larch (page 310) and Douglas-fir (page 314) – are available from renewable sources and provide a valuable construction material. Larch is durable enough to be used outdoors unprotected.

Of the hardwoods, the most common are birch (page 334), beech (page 338) and oak (page 342). They are relatively slow-growing and have a fine, dense grain. This gives them a hard-wearing surface, which makes them suitable for applications spanning packaging, construction and furniture. Over time, we have learned to take advantage of timbers in different ways, depending on their unique qualities and characteristics. Chocolate-coloured walnut (page 348) is prized for its durability and mechanical properties; hickory and pecan (page 352) are some of the strongest and heaviest timbers; ash (page 354) is strong and flexible for its weight; elm (page 358) has an interlocked grain that makes it resistant to splitting; and cherry (page 360) is utilized in furniture and cabinetmaking for its ease of working and clean, straight grain.

Tropical hardwoods – timber derived from rainforests – are some of the most desirable timbers of all; they are prized for their rich colour and high strength. Demand from Europe, Asia and North America has consistently outstripped supply. As a result, tropical timbers have been overexploited and many are now considered vulnerable or endangered. There are, however, a few species of tropical wood – acacia (page 364), iroko (page 366) and plantation-grown teak (page 370) – that are available from certified and well-managed forests.

## PLANT
The cellulose-rich stems and leaves of a wide range of plants provide the raw materials for applications ranging from fine fabric to hardy construction material.

Fibres are extracted from the leaves and stems of grasses and flowering plants. Unlike synthetic fibres, their length is limited and the profile variable. This gives fabrics produced from these materials endearing qualities that synthetics can only mimic. That is not to say these fabrics cannot compete with synthetics in terms of strength and

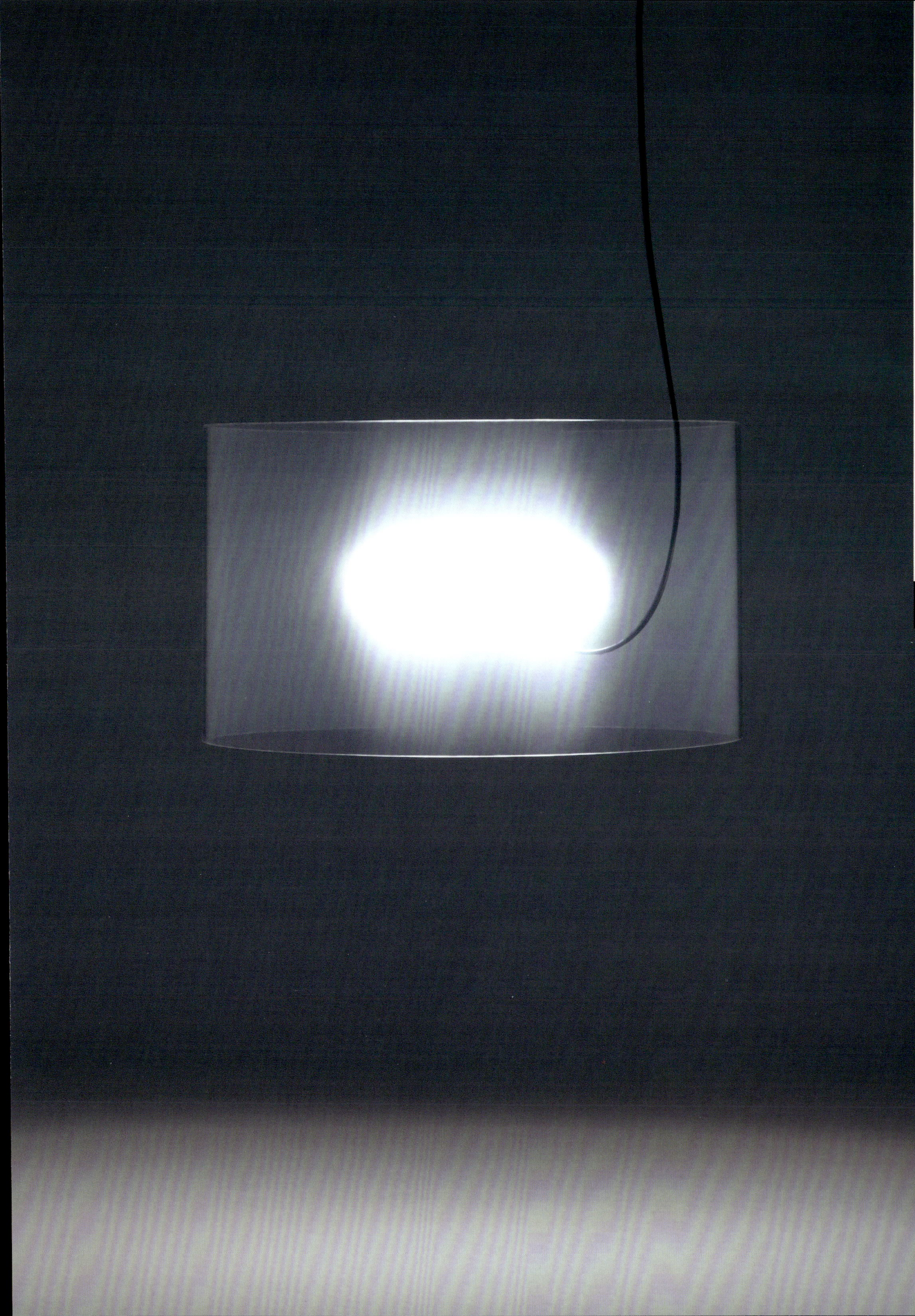

stiffness. Fibres such as flax (page 400) and hemp (page 406) have equivalent strength-to-weight to PP and comfortably outperform viscose (page 252). They are being explored as an alternative to glass fibre in the production of FRP.

Over the course of millennia, the tools and techniques for harvesting and processing these fibres have been optimized and refined. While some of the plants grow exceptionally well without the use of too many chemicals, cotton (page 410) dominates agrochemical consumption. Demand for this soft and versatile fibre has resulted in the growth of a highly polluting and environmentally damaging industry. Fair trade and organic cotton provides an alternative, albeit in very small quantities and at a premium.

## ANIMAL

From strong protein fibres – silk (page 420), wool (page 426) and hair (page 434) – to tough collagen-based leather, it is hard to imagine the fashion and furniture industries without animal products. Wherever meat and fish are consumed,

there is the potential to use the skin for leather. Wool and hair that are sheared or combed from animals are renewable and may be processed in a way that preserves them as natural materials. If chemicals are added during production (bleaches and dyes, for example), they may come to be considered hazardous waste at the end of their useful life.

Silk requires that the insect be killed so that a continuous filament can be obtained. Animals are also killed for fur (page 466); many consider this to be unethical and production is severely restricted as a result. Nowadays, faux fur (see Acrylic, page 174) is becoming increasingly popular, because it provides an ethical alternative.

## MINERAL

Stone, mud and clay may be older than humankind, but the industry that surrounds them is continually developing, innovating and opening up new areas for design. Spanning everything from bricks (see image, page 484) to ultra-tough glass (see image, page 526) on

**Computer-aided design (CAD) and manufacture (CAM)** The roof of the British Museum Great Court, London, covers an area of 6,000 m² (65,000 ft²) and is made up of 3,312 panels weighing a total of 315 tonnes (closer to 800 tonnes including the steel). The panels of glass were individually prepared, because no two holes are the same. The use of CAD CAM makes feats of design and engineering on this scale feasible; the components turn up on site and fit first time, because it has all been precisely calculated. They are screen printed with small dots of frit (glaze), which cover 50% of the surface. This is to help reduce solar gain. Designed by Foster & Partners, this impressive structure was completed in 2000.

mobile devices, minerals are fundamental to the progress of technology. They are crystalline, or partially crystalline, and held together by strong ionic and covalent bonds, which gives them exceptional hardness and resistance to high temperatures. However, they are brittle; tensile strength is typically in the region of one-tenth of compressive strength.

Diamond (page 476) is the hardest material of all and exceptionally strong. It has become such a valuable industrial material, as well as a jewel, that it has

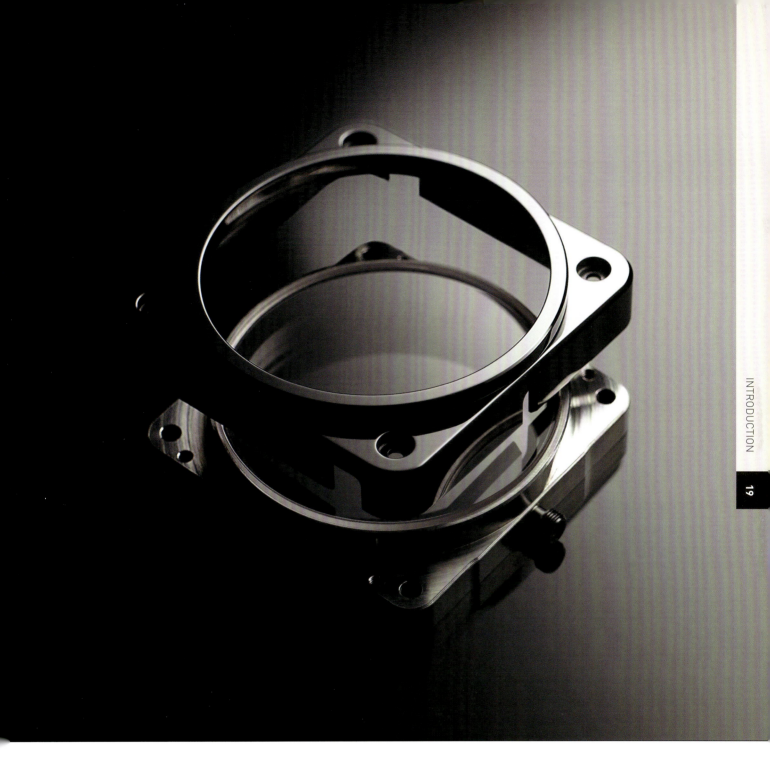

had to be synthesized to bolster supplies. Lab-made diamond is chemically identical to natural diamond, but with added versatility. Not only can it be produced as a large rock, but thin films of diamond may be applied onto another material to impart some of its impressive properties.

Clay-based ceramics (page 480) provide an important building material, as well as a medium for artistic expression. The colour and quality depend on geographical location, meaning that buildings and pottery evolved differently depending on locally available materials.

Glass (pages 508–527) has an amorphous structure, setting it apart from the other ceramics. It is not the only translucent mineral – diamond, sapphire and several other minerals exhibit exceptional optical properties. However, it is the only transparent mineral that can be produced on such an enormous scale. Ranging from small items of jewelry to façades hundreds of metres high, this versatile material has enchanted humankind since ancient Egypt.

**Advanced materials**
New material compositions are produced as a result of specific technical demands. Crossing over between jewelry and technology, the watch industry holds a unique position in the market and manufacturers use materials that remain unaffordable elsewhere. French watch company Bell & Ross is a market leader and material innovation plays a key role in its differentiation. This version of the BR 01-92 aviation watch features a technical ceramic case, CNC-milled steel housing and anti-reflective sapphire window. This combination of materials results in an extremely durable watch, highly resistant to wear and tear. Photo courtesy of Bell & Ross.

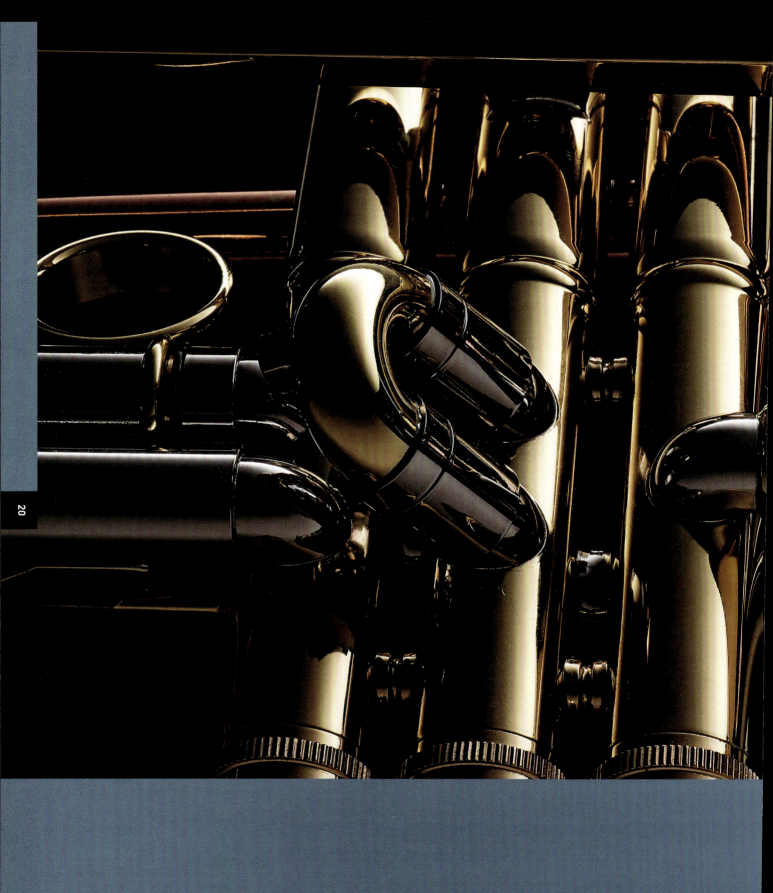

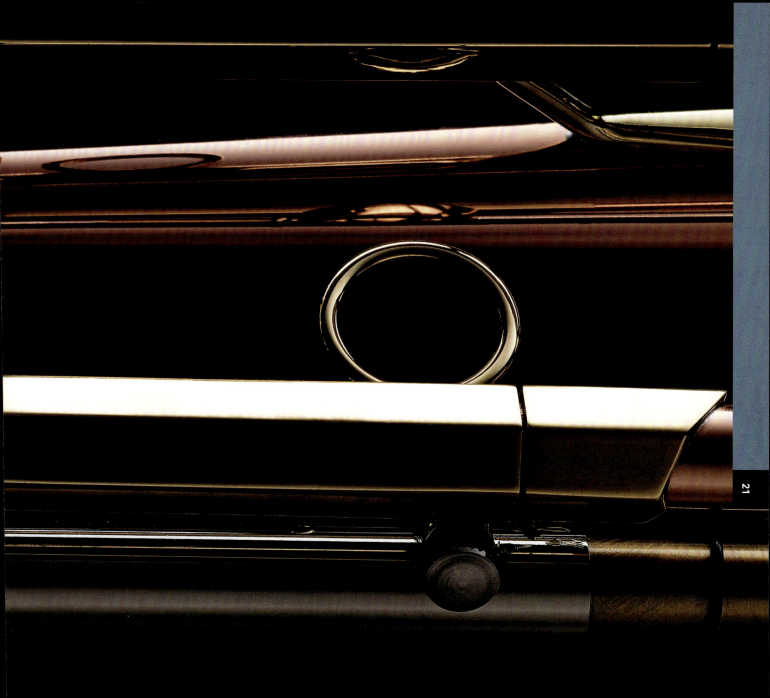

# METAL

**1**

# Cast Iron

**A common element and a historically significant material, iron remains an important metal in construction, engineering and cookware applications. Its mechanical properties depend on the exact ingredients, especially the proportion of carbon, silicon and manganese. While grey cast iron is stiff and brittle, the strength-to-weight of ductile cast iron is comparable with mild steel.**

| Types | Typical Applications | Sustainability |
|---|---|---|
| • Grey<br>• Ductile<br>• Compacted graphite (CGI)<br>• Alloy | • Cookware<br>• Construction<br>• Automotive | • Low embodied energy<br>• Very high end-of-life recycling rates |

| Properties | Competing Materials | Costs |
|---|---|---|
| • Ranging from brittle and dense to high-strength<br>• Surface properties depend on the alloy | • Steel, aluminium alloys, copper alloys, zinc alloys<br>• Pottery ceramics, brick, cement, stone<br>• Engineering thermoplastics, esp. PA | • Material cost is higher than steel but less than aluminium alloys<br>• Manufacturing cost is low |

## INTRODUCTION

The historical significance and use of iron in ornate applications makes it easy to overlook the critical role this metal plays in our modern world. It is used to make functional parts for the automotive industry, including engine blocks, chassis and brake assemblies that conform to strict performance criteria.

As a ferrous metal, it primarily consists of iron with carbon as the key alloying element. Whereas steel (page 28) consists of less than 2% carbon, and typically less than 1%, cast iron contains between 2 and 4%. The high carbon content, plus a little silicon, contributes to its excellent casting properties.

Iron is susceptible to corrosion in the atmosphere. A porous layer of oxide (rust) develops on the surface and gradually disintegrates to reveal underlying metal, albeit not as rapidly as steel. It is painted or enamelled to ensure a durable, long-lasting and hygienic surface. Iron alloyed with chromium or nickel has improved corrosion resistance and a harder surface.

Selection of casting method is determined by the application's requirements. Sand casting is used for all sizes from 0.1 kg (0.2 lb) to 5 tonnes. Investment casting is used for small to medium-sized parts (although all sizes of parts are possible it is not always practical). With both techniques the mold is expendable. In other words, a new mold is required for each casting.

Machining is used to finish parts to very accurate dimensions. The quality and speed of machining depends on the type of iron, in particular the graphite microstructure. Cast iron is not sufficiently ductile to be forged. In comparison with forged steel – common for structural applications – cast iron is brittle, and has lower fatigue strength and lower yield strength.

| | Tensile strength<br>diameter of bar required to provide equivalent strength | | Stiffness<br>diameter of bar required to provide equivalent stiffness | | Density<br>diameter of bar of equivalent weight | |
|---|---|---|---|---|---|---|
| | $\sigma_t$ (MPa) | % | E (GPa) | % | $\rho$ (kg/m³) | % |
| Grey cast iron | 362 | 1.0 | 145 | 1.0 | 7,200 | 1.0 |
| Ductile cast iron | 1,210 | 0.6 | 170 | 1.0 | 7,100 | 1.0 |
| Brass | 350 | 1.0 | 110 | 1.1 | 8,530 | 0.9 |
| Mild steel | 525 | 0.8 | 210 | 0.9 | 7,830 | 0.9 |
| Aluminium alloy | 310 | 1.1 | 69 | 1.2 | 2,700 | 1.6 |

Cast iron
Brass
Mild steel
Aluminium alloy

-500°C   0°C   500°C   1,000°C
-868°F   32°F   932°F   1,832°F

**Temperature**
minimum and maximum
service temperature

100   Electrical   0   Thermal   >250
%IACS   W/mK

**Conductivity**

Cast iron
Brass
Mild steel
Aluminium alloy

0   $/kg   >5

**Cost**
raw material price

0   kJ/kg   >100

**Energy**
energy requirement

0   million   >500
tonnes

**Availability**
annual production

0   %   100

**Recycling**
end-of-life recycling

## COMMERCIAL TYPES AND USES

There are several types of cast iron. Of these, the most important to design are grey, ductile, compacted graphite (CGI) and alloy types.

Grey cast iron is the least expensive and most common. It is distinguished by a microstructure of flake graphite. It

**Cast-iron teapot** Cast-iron teapots date back at least to 17th-century China and Japan: their exact origin is uncertain. They are suitable for boiling water as well as steeping tea. Considered the best

material in which to brew full-leaf green tea – the high heat retention helps to keep water hot for longer – cast-iron teapots became status symbols in Japan and their decoration evolved accordingly.

Traditionally, production started with the raw materials in a furnace and required several days to complete. In ancient times production was overseen by many highly skilled craftsmen and was a carefully

guarded secret. In some instances the inside surface of a cast-iron teapot may be enamelled to prevent the iron from corroding.

Flake

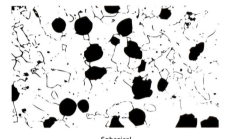

Spherical

Vermicular

**Graphite microstructure** The graphite microstructure of cast iron affects mechanical properties, since this is where failure occurs. The flakes of graphite that run through the ferrite and pearlite matrix of grey cast iron offer very little ductility, because high stress concentrations occur at the tips. However, grey iron does offer excellent damping and ease of machining. By contrast, ductile cast iron consists of graphite in the form of spherical nodules. Stress does not build up to the same level, which results in higher tensile strength and elongation. The vermicular microstructure of CGI is made up of blunt flakes that are interconnected, thus offering the beneficial mechanical properties of grey and ductile iron combined.

is a low-strength metal with high vibration-damping properties (automotive and machine applications), high resistance to thermal shock (molds) and high compressive strength (weight-bearing applications, such as machine stands and bases).

Ductile cast iron (also called spherical graphite iron) is produced with the addition of magnesium, which causes the graphite to form into tiny spheres. This change in morphology produces an iron with superior tensile strength and

elongation. As a result it is utilized in demanding applications, such as brake disks, gears and gearboxes, crankshafts and pressure-containing items (valves and pump bodies).

In the case of CGI, the graphite forms a vermicular pattern of interconnected blunt flakes, which produces an iron with improved strength-to-weight. In recent years, this has proved beneficial for automotive and locomotive engineering.

Alloy irons contain small amounts of other elements (in addition to carbon and silicon), such as chromium, molybdenum and nickel, to produce high-strength, wear-resistant, corrosion-resistant or heat-resistant parts.

## SUSTAINABILITY

Iron is mined and extracted from its ore in a blast furnace along with coke (carbon) and flux (limestone). Iron forms the basis and is the chief constituent of all ferrous metals, including steel. It is recyclable and widely collected and reprocessed.

Production uses only around two-thirds of the energy compared to steel, 10% compared to brass and 6% compared to aluminium. As well as consuming energy, production results in air emissions (such as carbon dioxide, sulphur oxide, nitrogen oxide and fine particulates), water contamination, hazardous waste and solid waste. There has been significant development in the production of iron in preparation for steelmaking. Direct-reduced iron, also called sponge iron owing to its porous nature, is more energy efficient than iron made by melting in a blast furnace.

## CAST IRON IN COOKWARE

Cast iron has been utilized in cooking for so long our habits have been shaped by its properties. It does not have very good thermal conductivity and so will develop hot spots (around 25% compared to aluminium alloy). However, it does have high heat capacity (retains heat over a relatively long period and is why cast iron cooks evenly) and heat emissivity (expels a lot of heat energy as radiation and is why cast iron cooks thoroughly even when frying and searing). It is a practical and versatile material, suitable for a

**COOKWARE**

Low cost
Cast iron is around three times more expensive than mild steel, but is much easier to cast, which can mean it is less expensive overall.

Heat retention
It has high thermal capacity – it takes more heat to get up to temperature than aluminium, but will stay hot for longer. Aluminium has higher thermal capacity per unit mass, but is much less dense.

Low distortion
It is used in thick sections and so does not warp or distort when heated, which makes cooking more consistent.

range of cookware, including oven dishes, skillets, griddles, pots and pans.

Several other materials are used to manufacture cookware – such as aluminium alloy (page 42), copper alloy (page 66) and ceramic (see Clay, page 480) – and it comes down to the type of cooking and individual taste to determine which is most suitable.

Cast iron is very fluid when molten and shrinks very little, if at all, as it cools. Therefore it is suitable for producing intricate parts with varying wall thickness, such as skillets, waffle irons and corn-shaped muffin pans. Casting allows complex parts to be formed in a single step and so helps to reduce weight while minimizing production time. In addition, it means intricate design details are reproduced at little or no extra cost.

A wide range of coatings is available, from black to bright colours, with a highly textured or glossy surface. Where coating is not practical or desirable, such as in the case of skillets (used for frying and roasting), the surface is protected by 'seasoning'. This is the process of heating the metal to around 250°C (480°F) with a thin coating of oil or fat on the surface. The process occurs naturally during cooking, supplemented

**Enamelled cooking pot** Designed by Timo Sarpaneva in 1960, this pot continues to be produced by Finnish company Iittala to this day. One advantage of cast-iron cookware is that it is compatible with all types of cooking appliance, including induction, gas and electric hobs. It is also suitable for use in the oven (with its wooden handle removed in this case), which makes these pots versatile. An enamelled surface prevents food sticking and makes it easier to maintain.

before use and after cooking for best results. The heat causes the oil to polymerize on the surface and form a strong bond with the iron. The coating is hydrophobic and so prevents food sticking (see also PTFE, page 190).

## CAST IRON IN ARCHITECTURE

Architecture was first influenced by the opportunities of cast iron centuries ago and its use proliferated up to the mid-19th century. The ease of casting complex shapes in a single material made cast iron useful for ornate work as well as for more functional elements. This approach to manufacturing proved less expensive than traditional stone carving (page 472) and so rapidly expanded into all areas of building.

Structural ironwork was first employed close to the end of the 18th century in the construction of railway bridges and industrial buildings. Multi-storey textile mills were among the earliest adopters, mainly because their timber post-and-beam construction was vulnerable to fire. Another notable example is the 31 m

### ARCHITECTURE

**Castability**
Its high fluidity when molten means intricate decorative and functional elements may be incorporated at little or no extra cost. In addition, casting multiple identical parts is far more cost-effective than fabricating individual pieces from steel, timber or stone.

**Strength-to-weight**
Grey cast iron, the most common type, is very strong in compression, but is brittle and has relatively poor tensile strength. Ductile cast iron is around three times stronger in tension.

**Consistency**
Mid-18th-century cast iron may seem rudimentary by modern standards, but the developments in production that occurred around this time led to more reliable and readily available material suitable for large-scale construction projects.

(100 ft) iron bridge that spans the river Severn in the UK. Completed in 1781, it was the first arch bridge of cast iron. The early success of these types of structure led to many more construction projects adopting cast iron, ranging from train stations to terraced housing.

Over-reliance on the strength of iron led to some catastrophic failures, with devastating consequences. Grey cast

**Cast-iron station roof**
Like many large buildings of the time, Liverpool Street Station in London utilizes iron in various forms. The Gothic-style train shed was designed by the engineer Edward Wilson. Since its opening in 1875, the station has seen many transformations, but the high iron and glass roof remains. The roof structure consists of wrought-iron spans on cast-iron columns. From the sturdy capitals to the highly figured roof supports, the elaborate detailing is accentuated with colour.

iron has high compressive strength but relatively low tensile strength, and so is prone to fail under bending. In addition, the mechanical properties of cast iron decrease at relatively low elevated temperatures and so load-bearing structures are vulnerable when exposed to fire. Nowadays, exposed ironwork can be protected with, for example, intumescent coating, which swells up to form a foam barrier when exposed to fire. This helps to slow the temperature rise of the structural element.

These limiting factors, along with the advent of affordable steel frame construction techniques towards the

**Castability**
The high fluidity and very low shrinkage of cast iron makes it cost-effective to cast intricate parts incorporating thick and thin wall sections. By comparison, steel is much more challenging and expensive to cast because it has a higher melting point.

**Damping capacity**
Grey iron quells vibrations much more effectively than steel or aluminium, by converting the mechanical energy into heat.

**Strength-to-weight**
Irons modified with alloying elements or by heat treatment have lower strength-to-weight than aluminium, but at around four times the density they offer weight savings in structural parts where a reduction in section thickness is desirable.

end of the 19th century, contributed to the decline of iron architecture.

## CAST IRON IN AUTOMOTIVE

Grey iron is the least expensive cast iron to manufacture. All types of grey iron machine very well. It is the best material where strength and toughness are not the main concern, such as brake drums, engine blocks, gears and valves.

The flake graphite acts like micro-notches, which can propagate cracks. As a result, grey iron is quite brittle and has low fatigue strength. This is especially critical for parts that need to withstand continual loading and unloading, such as camshafts and crankshafts. In such cases, ductile cast iron is preferable thanks to its spherical graphite microstructure, which is less prone to fail through fatigue.

Ductile irons consisting of silicon (SiMo ductile iron) and molybdenum are utilized in applications that require high heat resistance, such as turbochargers and exhaust manifolds. This alloy comfortably withstands continuous operating temperatures up to 600°C (1,110°F) or more and is a cost-effective alternative to high-alloy irons and steels.

The yield strength, toughness and fatigue characteristics of ductile iron are improved with heat treatment known as austempering. Austempered ductile iron (ADI) is around twice the strength of ductile iron, and has higher strength-to-weight than aluminium, with equivalent wear resistance to steel. It is used in

**Sand-cast ductile iron**
Produced by BAS Castings in the UK, this underground train gearbox part weighs 115 kg (254 lb). Ductile iron has a lower casting temperature than steel, which allows for superior surface finish and more complex shapes incorporating changes of wall thickness. Photo courtesy of BAS Castings.

high-load applications, such as chassis, suspension systems and gearboxes, where a reduction in section size is desirable.

CGI demonstrates a good balance of tensile strength (twice that of grey iron) with ease of casting. It is used in multiple applications – including flywheels, clutch components, turbo housings, exhaust manifolds and brake drums – as well as being the material of choice for modern, fuel-efficient diesel engine blocks.

High-chrome alloys are used in applications that require a high resistance to wear and abrasion. Owing to an increase in surface hardness, these irons are much more challenging to machine and require specialized tooling. Alloy irons offer many technical advantages, but tend to be more expensive to manufacture.

# Steel

As the most commonly used metal, steel has had a significant impact on design. Born out of the Industrial Revolution, steel rose to prominence following the development of an affordable mass-production technique. It has since been utilized at every conceivable scale, from micro medical components to packaging to skyscrapers and the longest suspension bridges.

| Types | Typical Applications | Sustainability |
|---|---|---|
| • Carbon<br>• Alloy<br>• Stainless | • Automotive<br>• Construction<br>• Packaging | • Additional energy input is required to convert iron into steel and more still to produce stainless steel<br>• Highly recycled |

| Properties | Competing Materials | Costs |
|---|---|---|
| • High tensile strength<br>• Work hardening<br>• Carbon steels are prone to corrosion (rust) | • Cast iron, aluminium, copper, zinc<br>• PA, PP and fibre-reinforced composites, such as GFRP and CFRP<br>• Lumber, engineered timber | • Relatively low material cost<br>• High manufacturing costs for complex parts |

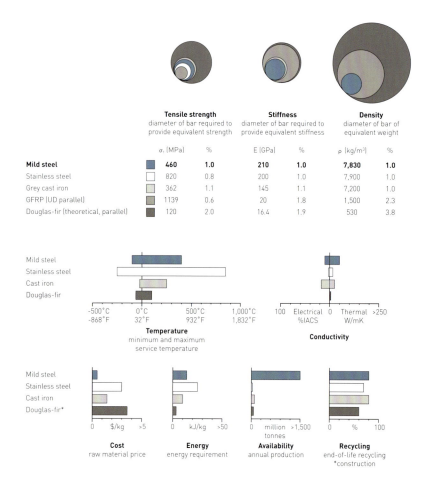

| | | Tensile strength<br>diameter of bar required to provide equivalent strength | | Stiffness<br>diameter of bar required to provide equivalent stiffness | | Density<br>diameter of bar of equivalent weight | |
|---|---|---|---|---|---|---|---|
| | | σ, (MPa) | % | E (GPa) | % | ρ (kg/m³) | % |
| Mild steel | | 460 | 1.0 | 210 | 1.0 | 7,830 | 1.0 |
| Stainless steel | | 820 | 0.8 | 200 | 1.0 | 7,900 | 1.0 |
| Grey cast iron | | 362 | 1.1 | 145 | 1.1 | 7,200 | 1.0 |
| GFRP (UD parallel) | | 1139 | 0.6 | 20 | 1.8 | 1,500 | 2.3 |
| Douglas-fir (theoretical, parallel) | | 120 | 2.0 | 16.4 | 1.9 | 530 | 3.8 |

Mild steel
Stainless steel
Cast iron
Douglas-fir

-500°C   0°C   500°C   1,000°C        100  Electrical  0  Thermal  >250
-868°F   32°F   932°F   1,832°F              %IACS        W/mK

**Temperature**
minimum and maximum service temperature

**Conductivity**

Mild steel
Stainless steel
Cast iron
Douglas-fir*

0   $/kg   >5        0   kJ/kg   >50        0   million   >1,500        0   %   100
                                                tonnes

**Cost**
raw material price

**Energy**
energy requirement

**Availability**
annual production

**Recycling**
end-of-life recycling
*construction

## INTRODUCTION

The potential of steel was well understood centuries before a cost-effective method of high-volume production was developed. The first major step towards affordable steel occurred around the mid-19th century. A process patented by Henry Bessemer in the UK – there is evidence of steelmaking using similar techniques in Asia much earlier, but not on an industrial scale – overcame the high cost of steelmaking by reducing the time taken and materials required. The invention uses pressurized air, which is blown through molten iron, to burn off the impurities and accelerate heating through the introduction of oxygen.

Bessemer's process revolutionized steelmaking and dominated production until the development of the basic oxygen technique in the mid-20th century. With this process, air is replaced with oxygen, which greatly increases efficiency. Fluxes (lime or dolomite) are mixed into the molten iron to absorb

**Laminated-steel Santoku knife** For this traditional Japanese all-purpose kitchen knife, thin sheets of stainless steel – one with more carbon and another with less, to make it softer – are folded together in alternating layers to create a flexible and very hard blade. The highest-quality modern kitchen knife blades consist of 60 or so layers. The pakka wood handle is injected or coated with silicone (page 212) to make it easier to maintain.

The folding technique was made famous two millennia ago by the blacksmiths of Damascus, Syria, who created impressively strong and sharp swords that became the envy of the world. Over time, the secret was passed on, eventually reaching Japan, where the technique was developed and turned to samurai swords. Each sword may have consisted of up to two million layers. Its characteristic curve and outstanding performance are the result of the combination of layering with a painstaking heat-treatment process, which took several weeks to complete.

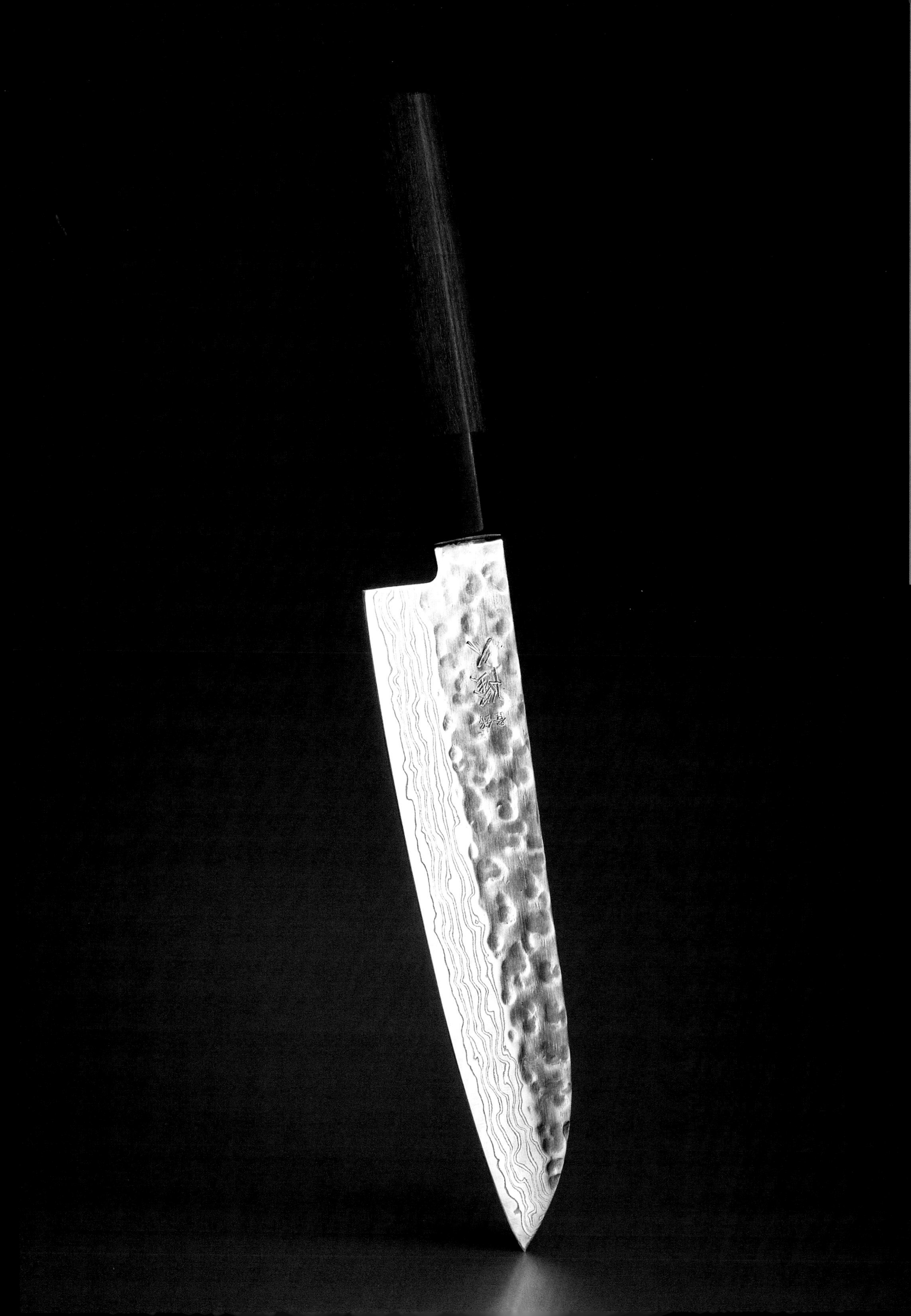

impurities and alloying elements are introduced as required.

The electric arc furnace technique – which has been under development since the beginning of the 19th century and uses an electric arc to provide heat – is not as widely used but is now gaining in popularity. It uses scrap steel as its principal input and so is speedier and more straightforward than basic oxygen steelmaking (the basic oxygen process uses only 10–15% scrap).

## COMMERCIAL TYPES AND USES

Steel is principally made up of iron (page 22) and carbon. The proportion of carbon and inclusion of alloying elements determine its specific properties. There are several thousand individual types; the three principal groups are carbon, alloy and stainless.

Carbon steels are the most common. These are broadly classed as low (less than 0.3% carbon), medium (around 0.3–0.6%) and high (more than 0.6%). Low-carbon types, commonly referred to as mild steel, are the least expensive and relatively soft (good formability). They are used in a variety of applications, including car body parts, packaging and construction. Medium-carbon steels are heat-treatable, which greatly increases strength and stiffness. They are used in more demanding applications, such as engines, shafts and springs. High-carbon steels are the strongest of these and used to make tools, cutters and knives, for example.

Alloy steels have a higher proportion of alloying elements such as chromium, copper (page 66), aluminium (page 42), nickel and molybdenum. Low-alloy steels include elements that affect the microstructure to improve the benefits of heat treatment. High-strength low-alloy types (HSLA) are stronger and stiffer than carbon steel per unit weight, with improved resistance to wear and corrosion. They are popular in construction and automotive parts, in particular large cross-sections.

Stainless steel covers a wide range of types applied to corrosion-resistant applications. Their brightness and superior surface properties derive from the addition of a minimum of 10.5%

**Weathering cycle of weathering steel**
Unlike unalloyed steel, the oxide that develops on this particular HSLA steel acts to protect the surface. It adheres firmly to the base metal, preventing further corrosion. Insoluble compounds produced by the copper, chromium and nickel alloys fill the porous surface of the rust, thereby ending regeneration. With exposure to atmosphere the surface develops a typical rust-like appearance. Over the course of a year or two, depending on the local climate, orange turns to brown. This gradually deepens to a very dark brown over the next decades.

chromium. In the presence of atmosphere, this element forms a passive layer on the surface to prevent further corrosion. This does not eliminate corrosion fully, but under normal conditions helps to maintain a clean and bright surface. Additional alloying elements, such as nickel, molybdenum and titanium, are combined to improve specific mechanical and physical properties, as well as enhancing formability.

Stainless steels are classed as being austenitic, ferritic, martensitic, duplex or precipitation hardening (PH). Austenitic types are the most common and have superior corrosion resistance combined with high toughness and durability. This makes them relatively easy to form and weld. They are normally non-magnetic, which helps to identify them. They are used to make cutlery, kitchen utensils and cookware, industrial equipment, parts used in marine environments, medical equipment, and car trim.

Ferritic types (less than 0.1% carbon) have lower corrosion resistance but improved formability (they are more ductile). They are used to make appliances and furniture, as well as car parts.

Martensitic types (up to 1% carbon) have the lowest corrosion resistance of the stainless steels, but are strong and hard. They are not so easy to form and so are typically used in sheet form to make parts that require high surface hardness, such as cutlery, knives, surgical instruments and aerospace parts.

The low-temperature properties of these three stainless steels are quite different. Whereas austenitic types are used at operating temperatures as low as -270°C (-454°F), ferritic and martensitic types exhibit fatal brittleness much earlier, typically above -100°C (-148°F).

Duplex stainless steel is a mix of ferritic with austenitic. This results in corrosion resistance combined with high strength. And precipitation hardening types include alloying elements that make them very strong following heat treatment (see page 88). This property means they are relatively cost-effective to shape into complex parts pre-treatment.

## SUSTAINABILITY

Recycling steel, as opposed to producing virgin material from iron ore, reduces the environmental impacts by around two-thirds. With steel, this process is infinite. What makes it easier is the fact that most steel is magnetic and so is easily separated from mixed waste streams. Steel of different composition should not be mixed to avoid downcycling (producing an inferior material), although in some cases, scrap may be upgraded through recycling.

It is estimated that around 80% of steel is recycled globally and more than one-third of new steel is produced from scrap. The highest recovery rates are in automotive, construction and machinery, where the flow of materials is more straightforward to control. It is more challenging to ensure that consumer products, such as white goods and electronics, are sent for recycling.

The basic oxygen process is fed with iron from a blast furnace (see page

**Weathering steel**
Pancras Square, London, seen here under construction, is due to be completed in 2017. Designed by Eric Parry Architects, the giant structural steel façade will remain exposed to the elements. Weathering steel, a type of HSLA steel often known under the trademark COR-TEN, protects itself when used outdoors by developing a durable layer of surface oxide (see box above). The combination of alloying elements results in a durable rust-like appearance when exposed to atmosphere. Unlike the iron oxide that develops on the surface of carbon steel, the layer of patina does not flake off weathering steel. When designed correctly – and in a suitable climate – it protects the base metal from further corrosion.

## PRODUCTS, FURNITURE AND LIGHTING

**Low cost**
Mild steel is the least expensive engineering material. Stainless steel is several times more expensive, but still very reasonable considering there is no need for a protective coating.

**Availability**
Steel is widely available in a range of formats and strengths. The different properties make it suitable

for diverse applications, from prototyping through to mass production.

**Toughness**
Steel does not damage easily, because it is harder, tougher and stronger than most other materials in common use.

24). Thus, it suffers from the same environmental impacts. The electric arc process cuts out the ironmaking and as a result is less polluting. Of course, electricity generation makes a significant difference on the overall impact.

### STEEL IN PRODUCTS, FURNITURE AND LIGHTING

Steel is best suited to parts that require a small cross-section. For example, cutlery needs to be comfortable in the hand and thin enough to cut, stab and scoop; the inner workings of electronic parts must be as thin as possible to maintain overall slimness; and pressed metal furniture must avoid taking up too much space while being able to take daily knocks.

It is used in heavier parts too, because steel is strong. However, it is heavier than aluminium alloy (page 42), as well as many engineering plastics, for the same strength. Even so, the price of steel is so much less that it still often works out more economical for equivalent parts. Aluminium alloy and engineering plastics present more of a challenge when lightness is critical, or for complex three-dimensional parts.

The majority of steel used in domestic and commercial situations is wrought. Available as sheet, bar and wire, it is sufficiently ductile to be formed with all forms of metal pressing. Whereas unidirectional bends and shallow parts are very straightforward, deeper parts are more challenging, because steel is stiff and there is a limit to how far it will stretch before breaking (around 35% for mild and alloy types, and 8% for stainless). Pressed steel is used to make a variety of products, from tableware and toaster housings to lampshades and dustbins.

Bending increases the strength of parts, and thus helps reduce weight. Long lengths, such as used to make structural frameworks, are relatively cheap to produce by roll forming or press braking and more expensive to extrude or hot roll (although more complex shapes are possible).

Carbon steels are coated to protect the surface from corrosion. The most commonly used is polyester (page 152) powder coating. It is tough and available in a wide range of colours and finishes, from high gloss to matt and textured to soft touch. A superior-quality colour finish is achieved with spray painting. This approach requires more careful surface preparation, and several layers may be needed if a high-quality finish is required, which greatly increases processing time and cost.

Galvanizing is the process of coating steel with a layer of zinc (page 78). A strong metallurgical bond is formed and the protective layer is self-healing. It is used for particularly demanding applications, such as when parts are destined for use outdoors. The finish starts off bright and gradually dulls over time. Galvanizing should be used to protect steelwork before other coatings are applied, to ensure the steel does not rust beneath.

Several other types of metal are suitable for plating onto steel, such as silver (cutlery) and tin (packaging). Chrome plating is used to produce a durable and bright finish. It was used a great deal in furniture and lighting, but has gradually been phased out because of the negative environmental impacts – in addition to all the water and waste, chrome plating uses highly polluting chromic acid.

Stainless steel provides an alternative to chrome plating. Its bright and corrosion-resistant surface is enriched through a process of electropolishing. Carried out in an acidic electrolytic solution, this simultaneously polishes, cleans and brightens the surface. Compared to plating, this process adds little to the base material cost (5% versus around 20%). However, a higher-quality base material is required to start with.

Physical vapour deposition (PVD) is used to create a very durable layer of oxide or nitride on the surface of steel (see Technical Ceramic, page 502). Borrowed from metal tooling (where a very hard surface is required for cutting), this technique is employed in consumer electronics. It takes place in a vacuum chamber, whereby elements are vaporized in the presence of a gas and condensed onto the surface of steel. The thin layer that is built up is incredibly tough. Its thinness helps to maintain a high-quality finish too, because the edges do not bulge (fat edge) as they do with painting. And it is possible to create colour, although this is limited to shades of grey, yellow, green, pink and blue.

Diamond-like carbon (DLC) (see Diamond, page 476) is similar to coatings produced with PVD. It is used in the watch and jewelry industry as the deep black finish is unparalleled for hardness, wear resistance and colour. The amorphous carbon layer is built up with chemical vapour deposition (CVD). The principal difference from PVD is that this technique uses chemical reactions during depositions, which presents additional material opportunities. Like PVD, this is

**Stainless-steel phone chassis** Through clever design and material selection, the bezel and chassis of the iPhone 4 are combined to produce a durable and elegant product that uses the minimum number of parts. First, the stainless-steel bezel is forged and machined to shape. An etched stainless-steel plate is laser welded with the utmost precision to hold the bezel in place and provide a surface on which the internal componentry can be mounted. Once assembled, the gaps (essential for the performance of the antenna) are over-molded with plastic. It is manufactured to an exceptionally high standard and as a result the unit cost is high.

a relatively expensive process and will increase unit cost several times over.

## STEEL IN COOKWARE AND APPLIANCES

A great deal of cookware makes use of the durability and strength of steel, such as trays, pots, pans and skillets. Steel does not have great thermal properties for cooker-top pans (it is several times less efficient than aluminium and copper). Therefore, high-quality steel pans are often combined with a base of aluminium or copper. This combines the benefits of both to produce cookware with the durability and longevity of steel and the thermal efficiency of aluminium or copper.

Virtually all types of appliance are manufactured from steel. Ranging from toasters to dishwashers, the structure and housings are manufactured with a combination of punching and pressing or drawing. Similar to the way car chassis and bodywork are assembled, the panels and structure are joined together by welding or riveting, or with mechanical fasteners. Using temporary fixings may not be aesthetically desirable, but the result is a product that can be more easily dismantled for maintenance and refurbishment. This helps to extend a product's useful life and thus reduce its overall environmental impact.

At a smaller scale, it is used to make utensils, kitchen knives, cutlery, presses and many of the other items to be found on counters and in drawers. Steel tableware including plates, bowls and cups is utilized in the kitchen as well as at work, outdoors and on the campsite.

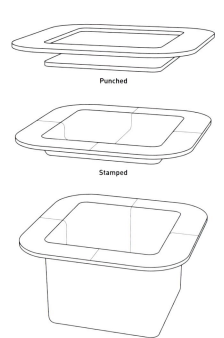

Punched

Stamped

Drawn

**Metal pressing** Sheet metal is shaped into a range of mass-produced products by punching, stamping and drawing. Holes are punched before or after forming, depending on the design, because, for example, holes cut into the side walls may become elongated during forming. Shallow profiles are stamped in a single operation between matched tools. Deeper profiles – where the depth is 0.5 times or more than the diameter – are shaped by drawing. Wall thickness stays more or less the same; as the metal is pressed downwards the sheet is drawn into the tool as well as stretching slightly. Multiple forming and punching operations are produced with progressive dies working in tandem.

Whereas stainless-steel items are left uncoated, carbon-steel tableware can be found enamelled, painted or plated.

Enamelware consists of glass frit fused onto steel. The coating provides steel with a smooth, resistant and colourful finish. Applications range from highly decorative pieces, like patterned teapots, through to industrial items. It is coloured with metal oxide and so will not fade like paint. However, like glass (page 508), it is brittle and so chips off the steel over time. While this distress (or character) is desirable in some applications, in others it is viewed as a technical flaw.

Stainless steel is prominent in application. It maintains its lustrous finish, even with heavy use, thanks to its high chromium content. Combined with its unique mechanical properties – high

stiffness and strength – stainless steel is a practical and desirable material for cutlery, utensils and knives. Even though relatively simple in appearance, its production is complex and involves punching, pressing, forging, grinding and polishing. The number of steps depends on cost, quality and volume.

High-quality items, including pots and pans as well as cutlery and flatware, are made from stainless steel that contains a high proportion of chromium and nickel. An example is austenitic 18/10 used for cutlery, which contains 18% and 10% respectively. The proportion of both these alloying elements is important: chromium and nickel combined provides the best resistance to corrosion and wear. Other types of stainless steel commonly used in the kitchen include austenitic 18/8 or ferritic 18/0 (referred to as 304 and 430 respectively in the American AISI grade designation system). Stainless steel with lower values of nickel is more vulnerable to corrosion (such as pitting), especially when put through repeated dishwasher cycles, because the detergents tend to be quite harsh.

These grades are not heat-treatable, which limits their ultimate hardness. High-carbon types that are suitable for heat treatment are preferable for applications that demand high surface hardness, such as knife blades (ability to maintain a sharp cutting edge, see also Technical Ceramic). Hard steels, such as those utilizing molybdenum, chromium and vanadium (labelled CroMoVa), will tend to be stiff but prone to corrosion owing to the relatively lower chromium content.

Laminated-steel knives overcome the problem of balancing hardness with flexibility by fusing very thin layers of high-carbon with low-carbon steel.

**Stainless-steel utensils** The Utensil Family was designed by Jasper Morrison in 2001 and is manufactured by Alessi, Italy. Punched and pressed from sheet, the family has a modern, functional aesthetic to match the impressive properties of stainless steel. While its high strength and stiffness helps to keep the parts as thin as possible, its superior surface properties ensure the utensils maintain a clean and bright finish even after years of bashing about the kitchen.

### COOKWARE AND APPLIANCES

**Durability**
Steel is a tough, strong and stiff material that can withstand the heaviest use in domestic and commercial cooking environments.

**Corrosion resistance**
Stainless steel has high resistance to wear and corrosion, and is used uncoated in the kitchen.

**Low cost**
It is the least expensive and most commonly used metal (more steel is produced each year than all other metals combined). High-performance steels, such as stainless, are more expensive but still relatively cheap compared to other metals.

## PACKAGING

**Low cost**
Combined with its impressive mechanical properties, steel is a cost-effective and reliable solution for many types of packaging – for the same weight it is around one-third cheaper than aluminium and polyethylene terephthalate (PET), polyester.

**Mechanical strength**
It has very high tensile strength and stiffness, superior to aluminium for the same wall thickness. This has many advantages, such as shipping without the need for secondary packaging.

**Barrier**
Tinplate containers offer a long-term and durable packaging solution for a variety of foodstuffs. Combined, steel and tin provides protection against insects, bacteria, gases, odours and ultraviolet light.

**Recyclable**
It is magnetic and so easily separated from mixed waste streams. As a result, it is the most widely recycled packaging material (70% in Europe, equal to around 2.6 million tonnes). Steel packaging, including tinplate, is fully recyclable without any loss of quality.

**Tinplate packaging**
Steel is printed in sheet form before pressing. The surface is coated with film to protect the graphics from contact with the metal press. Steel packaging is suitable for embossing and debossing. There is very little springback with steel so precise, and intricate designs are straightforward to reproduce and will hold their shape. As well as helping to differentiate packaging on the shelf, ridges, bends and raised graphics improve the rigidity and usability of packaging, which in turn helps to reduce the weight.

The combined properties provide the optimum balance, such as demonstrated by Japanese Damascus knives.

## STEEL IN PACKAGING

Steel cans have been in use for nearly two centuries. Processed food is sealed into a can and the temperature is raised to kill any potentially harmful bacteria inside. The hermetically sealed can helps to maintain the flavour and the nutritional value of the food without requiring refrigeration.

The majority of steel used in packaging is low carbon. It is electroplated with tin on both sides to produce a bright metallic finish, to protect the metal from corrosion and to maintain a hygienic surface. As well as providing a barrier, the thin layer of tin also provides excellent soldering and welding properties. It is fully recyclable.

Tinplate is drawn and rolled into a number of products, including two- and three-piece cans. Certain grades of tinplate are capable of stretching to one-third their original thickness when formed, which ensures an unbroken coating on the surface of finished items. Tinplate's versatility is also utilized in a range of applications outside packaging, such as toys and wiring connectors.

Steel sheet is supplied in thicknesses ranging from 0.15 to 0.6 mm (0.006–0.02 in). Tin thickness depends on the performance requirements and adds between 2 and 10 g/m² (0.05–0.2 lb/ft²). Thick coating is used for packaging that requires very high resistance to corrosion or is used without painting and printing.

Chrome plating adds only 50 to 150 mg/m² (0.0001–0.0004 lb/ft²) to steel. Known as tin-free steel when used for packaging, it is less expensive and provides an improved surface for painting. However, the use of chromic acid presents some environmental challenges, because it is very harmful if not managed properly. It is not so good for welding and so tends to be used in parts that only require forming, such as shallow food cans, bottoms, lids and closures.

Cans are sealed with paint, lacquer or enamel to ensure a safe and hygienic surface. Layers of decoration, such as printed graphics, are applied over the top. For high-volume production, the most commonly used technique is offset lithography. This is a very high-quality four-colour printing process used in a huge diversity of applications within packaging and other industries. As well as the four-colours used in conventional printing – cyan, magenta, yellow and key (black), abbreviated as CMYK – all manner of spot (additional) colours may be incorporated, ranging from fluorescent to metallic.

Printed graphics are typically applied over a white background to ensure optimum colour reproduction. The metallic quality is maintained by printing directly onto the surface of plated steel, or with a clear lacquer. Alternatively, decorated polyethylene terephthalate (PET, polyester) (page 152) or polypropylene (PP) (page 98) films are laminated onto the surface of tin-free steel to eliminate the coating and decorating steps.

Steel is a durable material, with high strength and stiffness. This has obvious benefits for consumers and also helps with production. Steel-can filling lines operate at speeds of up to 1,500 units per minute. Combined with high-volume production, such speeds offer financial benefits as well as reducing the potential for food spoilage.

## STEEL IN AUTOMOTIVE

Steels have undergone sophisticated development in recent decades. Through improvements in processing and control, higher-strength steels, with greater formability, are now manufactured at lower cost. Steels with tensile strength of more than 550 MPa are commonly referred to as advanced high-strength steel (AHSS). They are the result of carefully selected chemical compositions

and multiphase microstructures produced through precise heating and cooling cycles.

Specifying materials that have higher strength helps to reduce weight. For example, a material used in crash protection that has a 10% improvement in energy absorption means the part can be 10% lighter. This has helped to fend off competition from materials with higher strength-to-weight, such as aluminium alloy and fibre-reinforced composites (see Unsaturated Polyester Resin, page 228, Polyepoxide, page 232, and Carbon-Fibre-Reinforced Plastic, page 236).

**Polished stainless-steel container** Eva Solo's double-walled Thermo flask from 2008 utilizes the decorative and durable properties of stainless steel. Available in a polished or brushed finish, the hard surface easily withstands the wear and tear of daily use without the need for a protective case. The polyamide (PA, nylon) carry-strap adds a flash of colour.

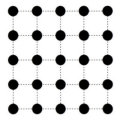

**Crystalline structure**

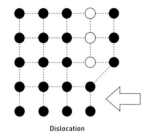

**Dislocation**

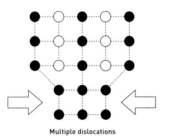

**Multiple dislocations**

### Work hardening

Metals become stiffer and harder as a result of work hardening. Metal is made of a crystalline structure whereby each atom is connected to its neighbours. Applying force, such as with stamping or drawing, causes plastic deformation. The atoms slip over one another and form dislocations. As the force increases, the dislocation can travel along the slip plane; as different forces are introduced, more dislocations occur. Dislocations in the same slip plane will repel one another. As they pile up and entangle, movement becomes more and more difficult. This results in a harder and more brittle structure. Alloying has a similar effect, by which the additional ingredients interact with the crystal lattice, blocking the movement of dislocations (see page 40). The process of work hardening is reversed with heat treatment (annealing). This provides the atoms with enough energy to break their bonds and return to their equilibrium position.

With regard to aluminium alloy, it is important to consider that even though the potential mass saving is up to around 20% compared to steel, it works out more expensive in mass production. However, for certain parts, in particular in low-volume production, aluminium

is cost-comparable. While steel has higher tensile strength, aluminium is more straightforward to extrude in long lengths – so the profile can compensate for the difference in tensile strength and thus the trade-offs will balance out.

An advantage of steel is that it can tolerate infinite cyclic loads up to around 10% of its tensile strength. Below this the steel remains undamaged. Therefore, it can be given a lifetime guarantee. By contrast, aluminium will fatigue no matter how insignificant the load.

For passenger safety, the two most demanding areas are crumple zone and passenger compartment. Whereas the crumple zone is required to absorb as much energy as possible over the greatest distance, the passenger compartment should distort very little. Thus the types of steel used are different. For the crumple zone, materials with high strength and ductility are required. The added benefit of steel is that it work hardens (becomes tougher through deformation). For the passenger compartment, materials with high tensile strength are required. AHSS has exceptional strength, outperforming aluminium alloy in parts with equivalent cross-section.

The bodywork is constructed from steels with high formability, typically plain carbon or HSLA. These steels require a protective coating. Modern zinc coatings are alloyed with aluminium and magnesium. This development provides many advantages over conventional zinc galvanizing. The excellent corrosion resistance is combined with improved forming properties and resistance to stone chipping. These improvements mean that the coating thickness has been reduced to around half that of conventional galvanizing.

In addition to developments in materials and finishes, there has been a great deal of improvement in forming technologies. One such example is hydroforming (see image, page 62). Tubular sections, or sheets, of steel are placed into a mold and liquid pressure is applied to force the steel to the contours of the mold. Using liquid pressure, as opposed to matched tooling (used for stamping), means that different types of

geometry can be achieved at lower cost. For example, entire structural parts, which may previously have been fabricated from several pieces, can be produced in a single hydroforming cycle.

Conventional forming techniques, such as stamping, deep drawing and roll forming, continue to be important in automotive manufacture. Typically, a combination of these processes is used, depending on the material and geometry required. Forging is used to shape parts that require very high strength and toughness in the powertrain, steering and suspension. It is expensive in steel, owing to the high forces required, and so is only used when absolutely necessary.

**Painted steel car body panel** A typical front wing stamped from plain carbon steel, which has been galvanized and primed in readiness for the top coat. The ridges and curvature – following the styling of the vehicle – improve the stiffness of the part, which helps to keep weight to a minimum without sacrificing strength and safety. Lugs and other fixing points are integrated into the design for ease of assembly and maintenance.

## AUTOMOTIVE

**Stiffness**
Steel is very stiff. Its elastic modulus (201 GPa) is higher than that of aluminium alloy (69 GPa) or titanium alloy (107 GPa).

**Strength**
Cars made of steel are getting lighter and stronger: newly developed grades are emerging that are around one-third lighter than their predecessors.

**Low cost**
It makes up roughly 60% of the average car because it is the least expensive mass-produced engineering material and the most straightforward to convert into automotive parts.

**Versatility**
The majority of parts are formed from standard sheet materials, of which there are many, to keep costs down. Owing to the scale of production in the automotive industry many grades of material have been specially developed with the optimum balance of properties required for different aspects of car design.

**Formability**
Its high stiffness and malleability provide superior pressing properties compared to aluminium alloy, magnesium alloy and titanium alloy.

**Recyclability**
Thanks to stringent legislation, automobiles now have the highest recycling rates of any consumer product. Steel is infinitely recyclable and straightforward to separate, which makes it rewarding for manufacturers.

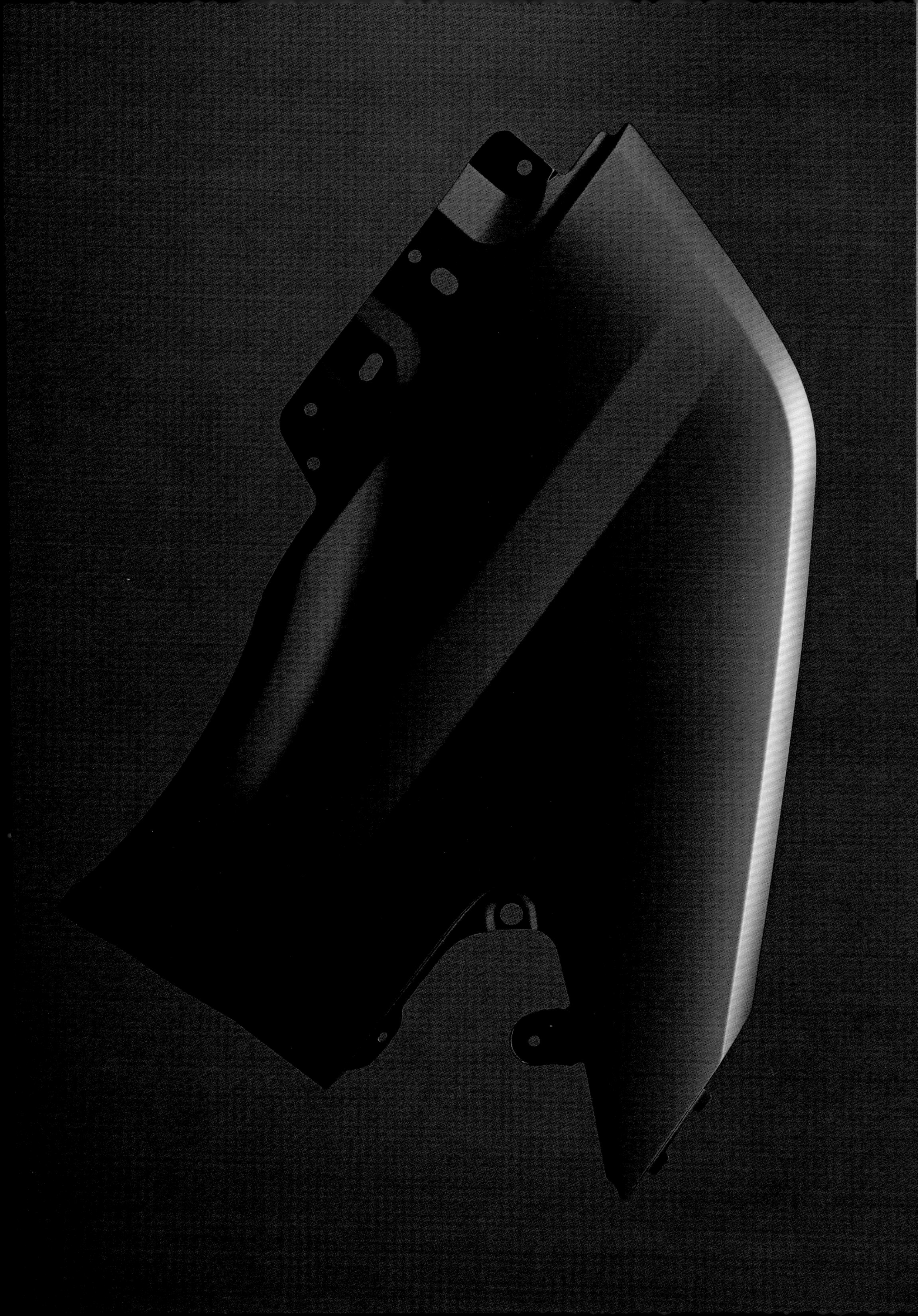

**Low cost**
Steel is produced in huge quantities around the world and so readily available and competitively priced. A wide variety of types is available, which helps to engineer cost-effective and mechanically optimized structures.

**High strength**
Through decades of development the strength-to-weight of steel has been greatly improved. It remains heavier than aluminium for the same strength, but is stiffer and stronger in parts with equivalent cross-section.

**Corrosion resistance**
The majority of steel used in construction is protected with paint or galvanizing or both. With proper maintenance, coated structures have an indefinite lifespan. There are grades of corrosion-resistant steel, including stainless steel and weathering steel, that virtually eliminate the need for paint and maintenance.

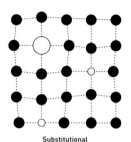

**Substitutional**

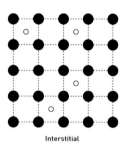

**Interstitial**

**Alloys** Individual atoms of the alloying element dissolve into the crystal structure. The defects caused by their inclusion introduce stresses that reduce the motion of dislocations (see page 38) and so act to strengthen the material. When they take the place of a normal atom in the lattice structure they are referred to as substitutional. Large atoms put the structure into compression and smaller ones cause tension, helping it resist plastic deformation. Atoms much smaller than those of the base metal sit in between the lattice structure and are referred to as interstitial. The extra bonds formed result in a harder, stronger and stiffer metal. For example, stainless steel is both substitutional (nickel and chromium) and interstitial (carbon).

## STEEL IN ARCHITECTURE AND CONSTRUCTION

Steel has shaped modern architecture more than any other metal. Its unique blend of mechanical properties has made previously inconceivable structures possible, from vast roofs to skyscrapers to the longest spanning bridges.

The mechanical properties of steel for large-scale structures are determined by a combination of chemical composition, heat treatment and method of manufacture. As-rolled steel has been allowed to cool naturally (tempered) after hot forming. Toughness is improved through refining the grain size. Known as 'normalizing' (designated by 'N'), the process involves reheating the steel and holding it at elevated temperature for a specific period of time. Quenched steel (designated by 'Q'), has been heated up and then cooled very quickly to increase strength and stiffness. Toughness is restored through a process of tempering.

The properties of high-strength low-alloy (HSLA) steel are optimized with thermomechanical treatment. Alloying elements in the steel reduce the critical rate of cooling, which allows thick sections to be more effectively hardened and tempered. The result is stronger steel, even at thick sections, with improved toughness and sufficient ductility to withstand crack propagation.

Certain alloying elements included to improve strength have an adverse impact on other properties such as ductility, toughness and weldability. This affects which type of steel is best suited to each high-strength application. For example, all steels are suitable for welding. However, the affect that melting and cooling has on strength will differ depending on the type of steel and section thickness. The quicker a material conducts heat away from the weld zone, the greater the hardening affect on the heat-affected zone (HAZ), which leads to reduced toughness.

Mechanical fasteners are preferred for parts assembled on-site. Welding outside the workshop is more expensive. Bolts and rivets transfer the loads between structural members through friction (between the adjoining surfaces) or shear (shank of the bolt or rivet). A friction type provides the greatest strength and is preferable for permanent structures. This requires a substantial overlap and is why joins are covered with several bolts (to spread the load across the surface).

When combining two dissimilar metals there is a danger of galvanic corrosion. This occurs when metals of contrasting nobility are placed together and in contact with an electrolyte. The metal that acts as the anode (more active) will thus be more prone to corrosion. For example, zinc, aluminium alloy and magnesium alloy (page 54) will corrode preferentially when placed in contact with steel. Insulating the metals from one another helps to prevent this.

There are several grades of corrosion-resistant steel used in construction, including stainless steel. However, the majority require protection when exposed to the elements. In what is referred to as a duplex coating, structural steel is typically coated with a metallic base layer (galvanizing, electroplating or thermal spraying) and painted. The metallic layer forms a durable metallurgical bond with the steel, providing superior corrosion resistance and a strong foundation for the paint layer.

Alternatively, weathering steel is used. This is HSLA steel with similar mechanical properties to conventional structural steel – designated as A 242, A 588 and A 606 by the American Society for Testing and Materials (ASTM). Capable of surviving more than 100 years with minimal maintenance, it is used in large, hard-to-reach structures, such as bridge decks, buildings and sculpture. However, it is not suitable for all locations, in particular near the coast or permanently damp environments. In such cases the steel may corrode as rapidly as plain carbon steel.

**Steel structure of the Centre Pompidou**
Designed by Richard Rogers and Renzo Piano, the Centre Pompidou in Paris, completed in 1977, marked a turning point in modern architecture. The strength and durability of steel is fundamental to the appearance of the building. Its exposed tubular structure – including services, lifts, stairwells and escalators – meant that vast uninterrupted spaces were created within the building.

# Aluminium

**Also known as**
Chemical symbol: Al

From pure aluminium to high-strength alloys utilized in aerospace, this is a versatile material suitable for an ever-increasing range of applications. It is lightweight and an efficient conductor. The durable oxide layer that develops on its surface is enhanced with anodizing. Synonymous with high-value consumer products, it is dyed a range of sophisticated metallic colours.

| Types | Typical Applications | Sustainability |
|---|---|---|
| • Pure aluminium<br>• Several hundred alloys, including cast and wrought types, that are either heat-treatable or not. | • Packaging and cookware<br>• Products, furniture and lighting<br>• Automotive and aerospace | • Energy-intensive to produce<br>• Efficient to recycle – although different grades should be kept separate |

| Properties | Competing Materials | Costs |
|---|---|---|
| • Good strength-to-weight, excellent thermal conductor, malleable, ductile, reflective and non-toxic | • Steel, magnesium and titanium<br>• PVC, PC and PA<br>• Fibre-reinforced composites: GFRP and CFRP | • Material cost is higher than steel, but lower than titanium and high-performance plastics<br>• Manufacturing costs vary |

42

## INTRODUCTION

Aluminium is a widely used metal, second only to steel (page 28). Extracting it from bauxite ore is very energy-intensive, making aluminium more expensive than steel.

Pure aluminium is relatively soft. During production it is alloyed to improve its mechanical properties or formability. High-strength grades are utilized for engineering applications in the furniture, automotive and aerospace industries. Aluminium has very good surface properties too: it is smooth and non-toxic (it has no known biological function), and provides a very effective barrier layer – it does not allow gas, water or light to pass through, even when applied as a very thin film. These properties are particularly exploited in packaging, to protect the contents, in the food, beverage and pharmaceutical industries.

It is an efficient conductor of heat, especially considering its low density. While this has obvious benefits for food and drink packaging as well as cookware, the high thermal conductivity means it feels cold to the touch: a quality that helps to reassure users that they are holding a 'valuable' metal object.

## COMMERCIAL TYPES AND USES

There are two main types: wrought and cast. While they share many of the same characteristics, wrought alloys are limited to sheet and extrusion

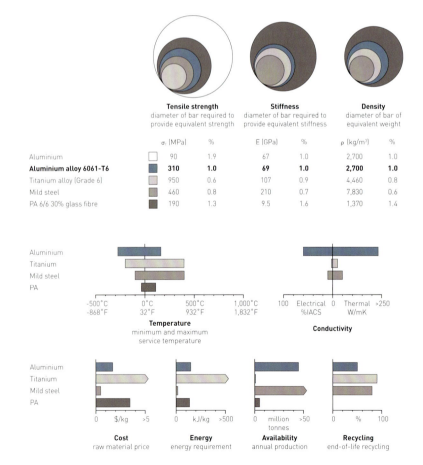

| | Tensile strength<br>diameter of bar required to provide equivalent strength | | Stiffness<br>diameter of bar required to provide equivalent stiffness | | Density<br>diameter of bar of equivalent weight | |
|---|---|---|---|---|---|---|
| | $\sigma_t$ (MPa) | % | E (GPa) | % | $\rho$ (kg/m³) | % |
| Aluminium | 90 | 1.9 | 67 | 1.0 | 2,700 | 1.0 |
| **Aluminium alloy 6061-T6** | **310** | **1.0** | **69** | **1.0** | **2,700** | **1.0** |
| Titanium alloy (Grade 6) | 950 | 0.6 | 107 | 0.9 | 4,460 | 0.8 |
| Mild steel | 460 | 0.8 | 210 | 0.7 | 7,830 | 0.6 |
| PA 6/6 30% glass fibre | 190 | 1.3 | 9.5 | 1.6 | 1,370 | 1.4 |

**Danzka vodka bottle**
Aluminium bottles are slimmer and around one-tenth lighter than glass (page 508) equivalents. It remains a premium option because of the high price of the aluminium and relatively limited production. Formed by impact extrusion, the bottles are manufactured at breathtaking speed. The incredible versatility of aluminium alloy helps to differentiate products by providing the ability to combine bright, metallic graphics with novel forms.

processes; and casting alloys are shaped in molds. Wrought alloys are designated by a four-digit code – assigned by the US-based Aluminum Association – where the first digit identifies the major alloying element: 1-series are virtually pure aluminium and have low mechanical properties so are the most easily formed, and they have excellent corrosion resistance; 2-series (copper) have high strength-to-weight and are good for machining so are commonly used in aerospace applications as well as for sports equipment (page 52), but they are not so easy to form or weld and have lower corrosion resistance; 3-series (manganese) have good strength-to-weight and are formable; 4-series (silicon) have a good balance of strength and formability, and contain silicon, producing a darker-coloured metal when oxidized, which is popular for architectural applications; 5-series (magnesium) also have a good balance of strength and formability, with improved corrosion resistance, which makes them useful for application in marine environments; 6-series (magnesium and silicon) are not as strong as 2-series and 7-series but have mechanical properties suitable for application in automotive parts and consumer electronics; 7-series (zinc) have very good mechanical properties suitable for aerospace, consumer electronic and sports equipment that have high performance requirements; and certain grades of 8-series (other elements) have high strength, but are less widely used.

Subsequent digits identify specific modifications to the alloy, as well as helping to identify each alloy within the series. For example, 7129 designates an aluminium alloy that has zinc as the main alloying element. The '1' indicates that it is the first modification to the original 7029, and the '29' identifies it in the series. The only exception to this rule is 1-series, where the last two digits represent the minimum aluminium percentage.

Casting alloys are identified using a similar numbering system – three digits followed by a decimal – where the first digit designates the major alloying element. The second and third digits identify the alloy in the series and the

(page 52)

## PACKAGING

**Barrier**
Even ultra-thin aluminium provides a very effective barrier against gas, water and light. This helps preserve the contents.

**Strength-to-weight**
The high strength of aluminium means packaging is lightweight (a 330 ml [11 fl oz] can weighs around 15 g [0.5 oz]), which helps minimize the energy used in transportation.

**Formability**
It is suitably ductile to be formed into very thin-walled containers, such as cans with sidewalls approximately 0.2 mm (0.08 in) thick.

**Print and finish**
The smooth and bright surface of aluminium provides the ideal base for applying point-of-sale graphics.

**Thermal conductivity**
It is a very efficient conductor (around four times more than steel and incomparable with glass) and so minimizes the amount of energy required to heat or chill the container and its contents.

**Recyclability**
Collection and recycling has become so efficient that in the USA and Europe a beverage can is produced, consumed and converted back into a new can within around 60 days.

**Hygienic**
It is harmless, non-toxic and does not affect the taste of food or drink. The surface is smooth and can be sterilized.

decimal indicates whether it is a casting (.0) or ingot (.1 or .2).

The series classification is followed by temper designation to indicate an alloy's hardness (or elasticity). Whereas heat-treatable alloys acquire their optimal mechanical performance through a process of thermal treatment, non-heat-treatable alloys are strengthened by strain hardening (cold working). The five categories are identified as follows: H denotes non-heat-treatable alloys; T denotes heat-treatable alloys; W denotes solution heat-treated alloys; O denotes annealed alloys that have been heat-treated to improve ductility (lowest strength condition); and F denotes untreated alloys, called 'as fabricated'.

## SUSTAINABILITY

Aluminium production requires so much energy that it is only economically viable in locations where electricity is abundant and cheap. The process involves heating mined bauxite ore to form aluminium oxide (alumina). Through a process of electrolysis – developed towards the end of the 19th century and known as the Hall–Héroult technique – pure aluminium is separated from the oxygen (collects on the anode to form carbon dioxide).

It is much more efficient to recycle aluminium than use virgin material. It requires only 5% of the energy, is carried out at lower temperatures – the melting point of aluminium is 660°C (1,220°F) – and produces only 5% of the carbon dioxide of primary aluminium production.

The drawback of its versatility when alloyed with different ingredients is that mixed recycled aluminium will have inferior properties to the virgin material. To maintain optimum properties different grades of aluminium should be kept separate prior to recycling.

## ALUMINIUM ALLOY IN PACKAGING

Aluminium is synonymous with high-quality packaging for food, drink and pharmaceuticals. It is utilized in a wide range of these products, from the iconic drinks can, aerosols, squeezable tubes, blister packs and foil wrap to take-away food trays. This is in part thanks to the versatility of aluminium and the ease with which it can be converted into a wide range of shapes and formats.

Beverage cans and aerosol cans are deeper than they are wide: they are manufactured with deep drawing and impact extrusion respectively. Aluminium plates, trays and dishes are stamped

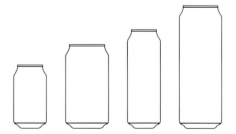

**Beverage cans** All sizes of two-piece beverage cans are produced by deep drawing. Additional features, such as necks, embossing and screw threads for the cap, require additional forming operations.

from a sheet in a continuous process. Using techniques similar to automotive engineering (see page 50), designing in ribs and other stiffening elements improves sturdiness without adding thickness.

Very thin foils, less than 0.05 mm (0.02 in) thick, are used to make flexible items such as tubes (see image, right) and blister packs. The foil is used alone, or laminated with plastic (drinks pouches and foil crisp packets) to create tough and tear-resistant barrier-films. The air-, gas-and light-tight properties of aluminium are maintained in foils as thin as 0.007 mm (0.003 in.).

Very thin films of aluminium, applied by vacuum deposition or lamination onto plastic or other suitable material, utilize the bright, reflective and protective properties of metal at a fraction of the cost. This technique is utilized for both decorative and technical purposes (see image, page 159). Examples include metallic-looking perfume packaging, laminated crisp packets and reflective labels.

Graphics and colour are most commonly applied by offset lithographic printing (often referred to as offset litho). This process is capable of very accurately applying four or more colours at high speed and in-line with fabrication. Packaging is often finished with a layer of varnish to protect the surfaces from abrasion. Recently, digital printing has been adopted for prototyping, mass customization and low volumes of identical parts. With this technique, multiple colours are applied wet-on-wet with high resolution.

Another significant benefit of aluminium packaging is that it is widely collected and recycled. A major advantage of having a consistent single source of waste, such as beverage cans, which can be readily distinguished and separated from mixed waste, is that the material can be repeatedly recycled and made into new containers of the same value. This is important, because if different grades of aluminium are mixed, such as beverage cans with automotive scrap, then the recycled material will not be suitable for converting back into new cans. This is because of the various ingredients used

**Aluminium cosmetics tube** Aluminium tubes, such as used to package liquids and pastes, are produced by impact extrusion. Aluminium tubes do not spring back like plastic types, which avoids atmosphere mixing with the remaining contents during use. This reduces the risk of contamination as well as helping to maintain the shelf life of the contents.

in different alloys to fulfil contrasting performance requirements.

## ALUMINIUM ALLOY IN COOKWARE
Aluminium alloy overlaps with several other metals in the kitchen, including cast iron (page 22), steel (page 28) and copper alloy (page 66). Preference comes down to individual taste and cooking methods. After all, high-quality pots, pans and skillets are fabricated from all of the above metals.

Aluminium has several key assets. It is a much more efficient conductor than steel (this is why high-quality steel pans are fabricated with an aluminium or copper base). However, it is compatible only with gas and electric cooker tops, not inductive. Like steel, it is formed by pressing, deep drawing and metal spinning. These techniques are used to produce trays and pans, for example. Unlike steel, it is relatively easy to cast into complex shapes, because it has a lower melting temperature and has higher fluidity when molten.

Iron is relatively inexpensive and is

### COOKWARE

**Thermal conductivity**
It is a very efficient conductor (around four times more than iron or steel, but slightly less than copper alloy), which helps to accelerate the cooking process.

**Lightness**
It is around one-third the weight of steel and iron, making skillets fabricated from aluminium lighter and easier to handle in the kitchen.

**Formability**
It is suitable for casting, as well as forming from sheet, so a wide range of geometries are possible in a single piece of material.

**Hygiene**
It does not affect the taste of food and drink, and hard-anodized surfaces are easily maintained.

cast to make skillets, pots and pans. It is much heavier than aluminium and the surface requires coating or careful 'seasoning' to ensure that it does not corrode. Copper alloy performs better than aluminium in thermal and conductive applications. However, it has significantly lower strength-to-weight, making copper pans more cumbersome than aluminium equivalents.

**Die-cast citrus press**
The Divertimenti juicer is formed of two halves that rotate around a pivot to apply squeezing pressure. The surface is protected with a durable and brightly coloured powder coating to prevent the acidic juices coming into contact with the base metal. Without protection the aluminium alloy would become tarnished.

The surface of aluminium is hard anodized or coated to produce a durable and long-lasting finish. It is extremely durable and scratch-resistant and will not peel. Unlike the anodizing commonly used to finish consumer products (known as dip and dye), hard anodizing cannot be dyed. The colour comes from light interference on the surface.

Coatings are bonded onto the surface and are durable, but not quite as tough as anodizing. In addition, a non-stick coating (see PTFE, page 190) may be applied to the inside surface. As well as aiding cooking and cleaning, a non-stick coating provides an impenetrable barrier between the food and the metal. However, it is not as durable as the base metal and so care needs to be taken to avoid scratching it.

## ALUMINIUM ALLOY IN TEXTILES

Bright and metallic fabrics, such as used to make decorative fashion apparel and fire proximity suits, typically consist of a base material combined with a thin layer of aluminium. Whereas traditional and high-value metallic fabrics are manufactured from gold (page 90) or silver (page 84), tough and abrasion-resistant types (such as shark-protection suits) are produced with drawn steel wire.

In the case of aluminium-coated fabric, the metal is combined with the

## TEXTILES

**Reflective**
Aluminium is one of the most highly reflective metals to light (around 90%) and radiant heat (around 95%). The exact properties depend on the grade of aluminium and surface finish.

**Lightweight**
An aluminized film increases the weight of the base fabric by up to only 1–2%.

**Barrier**
Even a very thin film of aluminium prevents gases, vapour and chemicals from passing through.

**Aluminized protective clothing** Lightweight and flexible aluminized apparel such as this insulated proximity jacket manufactured by Newtex Industries in the United States provides workers with comfortable protection against ambient temperatures of up to 93°C (200°F). A full suit is capable of resisting short bursts of radiant heat (given off by the heat source in proximity) of up to 1,650°C (3,000°F). And insulated suits, which incorporate a 25 mm (1 in) thick glass-fibre lining, are suitable for ambient temperatures up to 430°C (800°F) with a flame rating up to 1,095°C (2,000°F).

base layer by vacuum deposition or lamination. Vacuum deposition is the process of heating the metal until it vaporizes and then condensing it under pressure onto the fabric. This results in a thin and flexible coating, which will feel more comfortable in apparel. Lamination combines thin metal foils with plastic film at high pressure. This process is used to incorporate thicker layers of aluminium, for functional purposes, such as to provide a complete barrier to light, gases and moisture in packaging applications. When flexed, vacuum-metallized coatings will spring back, whereas laminated foils permanently deform – a good way to distinguish the two.

Metallic yarn for fashion fabrics is produced using vacuum-metallized polyethylene terephthalate (PET, polyester) (page 152) film. Produced as a roll of film, it is cut into thin strips to make it suitable for knitting, weaving or embroidery. Survival suits are used to protect people against temperatures as low as -30°C (-22°F). The aluminized coating, which is applied by metallization to lightweight polyethylene (PE) (page 108), helps to maintain body temperature by reflecting radiant heat (up to 95%) back towards the user.

At the other end of the spectrum, aluminized textiles are used to provide protection from sources of extreme heat, such as fires, furnaces and foundries. High-performance base fabrics are able to withstand ambient temperatures up to 1,095°C (2,000°F). The maximum service temperature depends on the choice of yarn. Commonly used types include acrylic (page 174), aramid (page 242), rayon (page 252) and glass (page 508).

## ALUMINIUM ALLOY IN PRODUCTS, FURNITURE AND LIGHTING

Employed for its bright metallic-grey appearance and impressive mechanical properties, aluminium features in high-end products, furniture and lighting. It is equally suited to load-bearing structures – tables, chairs and desk lighting – as it is to sculptural items, such as those designed by Ross Lovegrove (Liquid Bench, 2005, and Liquid Bioform, 2008), Zaha Hadid (Bench, 2003), Marc Newson

(Orgone Stretch Lounge and Alufelt Chair, both 1993) and Thomas Heatherwick (Extrusion series, 2009).

It is sufficiently durable to be used outdoors and in public spaces. Likewise, its lightness makes it an ideal material for items that will be moved around a lot. In recent years, largely thanks to the success of Apple, the use of aluminium in consumer products has exploded. 6-series is the most common owing to its balance of strength and formability. Utilized in the housing of laptops, tablets, mobile phones and a plethora of accessories, aluminium alloy has in some cases superseded engineering plastics, such as polycarbonate (PC) (page 144) and polyamide (PA, nylon) (page 164). While it does not have the moldability of plastic – the manufacturing of aluminium alloy parts is typically more time-consuming and costly than equivalent plastic parts – it is considerably stronger and stiffer for the same cross-section.

A range of forming processes is employed. Extrusion produces long lengths with a continuous cross-section. It is used to make beams to carry table tops or multiple seats in a straight line, as well as tubes that are bent to form one-piece looping structures. One-piece laptop, tablet and phone housings are extruded near net shape and finished with CNC machining.

Several grades of aluminium are suitable for machining. Aluminium is much more efficient to shape in this way than, for example, steel and titanium (page 58), because it is softer. Machining is used to produce complex and accurate parts ranging from one-offs to mass production. The number of axes that the machine operates on determines

**Strength-to-weight**
For structural parts the same strength can be achieved with roughly half the amount of aluminium compared to steel.

**Bright colour**
Its highly reflective surface gives translucent colour – such as produced by dip-and-dye anodizing or spraying with a tinted top coat – a luminous metallic backdrop.

**Durable**
The surface of aluminium oxidizes to form a protective ceramic layer (aluminium oxide is one of the hardest substances known), which makes it virtually maintenance-free.

**Recyclable**
At the end of its useful life, aluminium is fully recyclable. Non-critical parts are manufactured from recycled aluminium derived from mixed waste streams, providing a valuable outlet for lesser-quality material.

**Coloured anodizing**
A wide range of shades and colours is possible with dip-and-dye anodizing, ranging from its natural

silvery-grey through yellow, red, blue, green and black. The exact colour will vary slightly according to the processing parameters.

the angles of geometry that can be reproduced. Simple two-axis machines operate on an x- and y-axis (width and length); three-axis machines have the addition of a z-axis (depth); four-axis types include an axis of rotation; five-axis have two perpendicular axes of rotation to allow 360° of possible movement.

Die casting produces complex geometries in a single process. In terms of scope of design, it is comparable with injection molding plastic and is used to produce chair seats (such as integrated seat with back), spoke chair bases, and light housings and fixings. Cast aluminium is not as strong and flexible as wrought and so this technique is limited to parts where section thickness is not critical. The surface quality will not be as good either, owing to the porosity of cast metal.

**CNC-machined aluminium housing**
The aluminium alloy housing of the Google Nexus One phone is sculpted from a single piece of metal. Its sideways profile is extruded in long lengths, cut to width and CNC machined (milled) to the final shape. Techniques have evolved to reduce the

cost and complexity of fully CNC-machined parts. Undercuts, fixings and variously shaped details are produced with an array of cutting tools. While milling is a reductive method, all of the waste is recyclable. The finished part is abrasive blasted to an even matt texture followed by dip-and-dye anodizing.

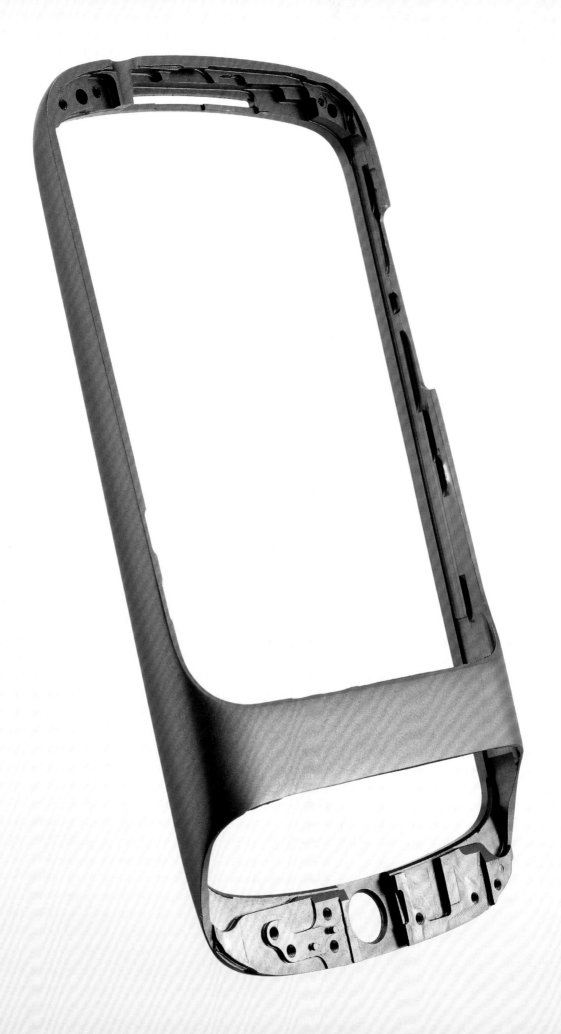

Shallow sheet profiles are produced using stamping (see diagram, page 34). Deep profiles are fabricated from sheet material, or formed from a single piece by deep drawing or metal spinning. Examples include containers and light shades. For low volumes spinning is by far the cheaper of the two, mainly because it needs only a single-sided tool.

A very good surface finish is achieved with blasting, polishing or cutting. As a result of its versatility there are teams dedicated to perfecting aluminium finishes. Blasting produces a uniform matt finish: media selection, pressure and time determine the depth and topography (roughness) of finish. Smooth to reflective surfaces are created with polishing. Smooth surfaces can highlight defects, making this a more expensive option. Surfaces that have gloss and matt areas are typically polished first, then masked and blasted (such as to incorporate a logo). Bright edges and chamfers are produced last of all, using a diamond-coated (see Diamond, page 476) cutting tool. The smooth and reflective finish obtained is known as 'diamond cut'.

## ALUMINIUM ALLOY IN AUTOMOTIVE AND AEROSPACE

Around the mid-20th century, aluminium alloy became the most important material in modern aviation. High-strength alloys, including 2- and 7-series, are used for demanding applications such as chassis, covering, brackets and seating. Less critical parts utilize 3-, 5- and 6-series.

The dominance of aluminium in passenger aircraft – around two-thirds by weight on average – has only recently been challenged by fibre-reinforced composites. Through developments in materials and manufacturing, the cost of composites has decreased to the point where their application, and impact on fuel efficiency, has become cost-effective. These materials, in particular carbon-fibre-reinforced plastic (page 236) and polyetheretherketone (PEEK) (page 188), have superior mechanical properties that are tailored to the application through material selection and fibre orientation.

Aluminium alloy is suitable for many

parts of an automobile. Whereas cast-aluminium alloy has been employed in wheels (magnesium, page 54, is lighter but more expensive), petrol engine blocks (see also Cast Iron), transmission parts and suspension systems, wrought aluminium is used in the chassis and the bodywork.

Replacing cast iron, mild steel or copper alloy with aluminium alloy helps to reduce the total weight of a vehicle. As well as the obvious efficiency benefits (fuel, tyres and so on), removing weight helps to make vehicles safer by reducing the energy required to stop.

Chassis and panels are joined with conventional welding techniques, including metal inert gas (MIG), tungsten inert gas (TIG) and laser. Aluminium alloy

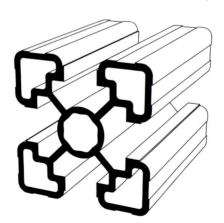

**Extruded profile**
Aluminium alloy is relatively easy to extrude, in particular 6-series. With this process, thick and thin sections are combined to provide strength where it is needed most. In conjunction with secondary pressing and forming operations, complex parts can be created from a single piece of material. Compared to pressing from sheet (stamping) this approach is more cost-effective because tooling and assembly costs are reduced. It is for this reason that extruded aluminium is utilized for low-volume production cars.

is an efficient conductor and therefore requires higher thermal input than steel to form a strong join. Friction-stir welding utilizes the ductility and low melting point of aluminium alloy to form seamless, high-strength joins without adding heat. Used in only a few applications so far, this relatively new technique has the potential to revolutionize assembly practices.

Where thermal joining techniques are not practical or desirable (for example, with heat-sensitive alloys or thin sections prone to warp), adhesive bonding or riveting may be considered. These techniques have many advantages. They are 'cold' and so do not cause the material to distort. This is especially important for thin sheet materials and critical for parts of vehicles that are associated with on-road handling. They do not rely on the thermal or metallurgical compatibility of the material and so are suitable for joining dissimilar materials. Additional opportunities of adhesive bonding include spreading the load of the join (strength advantages) and providing secondary functions, such as sealing, insulating and damping. A nice example of adhesive bonding is the Lotus Elise chassis, which combines extruded lengths of 6-series alloy with 3-series panels. The chassis weighs just 68 kg (150 lb), which is around half the weight of the steel equivalent.

A disadvantage of aluminium alloy is that it will always fatigue (develop cracks over time) under cyclic loads (repetitive stresses). Whereas steel can tolerate cyclic loads up to around 10% of its strength, aluminium alloy does not have such a limit. Therefore, it is not suitable for applications that involve vibration or rotation and require an infinite fatigue lifespan. Cracks start slowly, but accelerate rapidly as they increase in size, owing to the decrease in cross-section of the supporting material. Lack of knowledge in this area has led to some catastrophic failures in the past.

Designers can minimize the impacts of fatigue by avoiding stress-raisers, in particular corners. This is why the windows in aircraft are rounded rather than square. In practice, a margin of safety is used so that a crack becomes detectable before it causes structural failure. Known as factor of safety (FoS), the amount depends on the application and ranges from 3.0 for automobiles to as low as 1.5 for certain parts of aircraft (increasing the FoS increases weight). Quality control and material inspection help to minimize the necessary FoS.

## ALUMINIUM ALLOY IN SPORTS

High-strength alloys offer a near-perfect balance of mechanical properties suitable for a range of sports equipment. The benefits of aluminium for sports products, along with many others, are tied to developments in automotive and aerospace. Within these industries there is budget and scope to develop the material technology in the pursuit of increasingly lightweight and reliable structures. In return, the sports industry pushes aluminium alloy to its limits, revealing new possibilities for future development.

The lightness of aluminium alloys is utilized in a range of equipment. 2-series and 7-series alloys are heat-treatable and have exceptional strength-to-weight;

**Aluminium alloy architecture of the Jaguar XE** Launched in 2014, the Jaguar XE has a stiff and lightweight chassis combined with an aerodynamic aluminium alloy body. The Jaguar XE is the first car to be built around an alloy-intensive monocoque. A mix of virgin and recycled aluminium alloy is used in conjunction with cast magnesium and high-strength steels for optimum strength and performance. In addition, rivets and adhesives have been utilized in place of welding in order to allow greater freedom of joint design. Photo by FP Creative, London; courtesy of Jaguar.

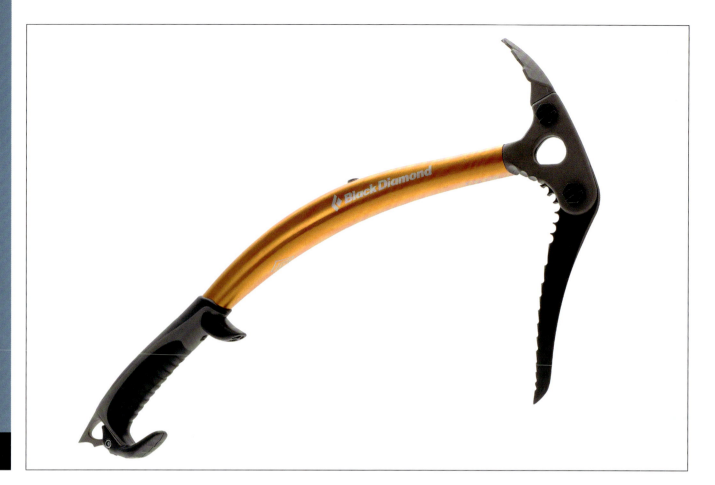

**Strength-to-weight**
For its weight, aluminium is one of the highest-performing materials, outstripping both steel and engineering plastics.

**Corrosion resistance**
The naturally occurring oxide layer that develops on the surface of aluminium, which may be enhanced with anodizing, provides excellent resistance to corrosion for outdoor applications.

**Formability**
The high ductility of aluminium means that it can be formed using a range of processes to maximize strength, such as bending, forging and hydroforming.

**Weldability**
MIG and TIG welding produce high-strength and reliable joins.

they include some of the highest-performing alloys. Their strength and stiffness are utilized in tubular bicycle frames, for example. They compete directly with steel (mild and alloy), titanium and carbon-fibre-reinforced plastic (CFRP). Each offers a trade-off in terms of strength and weight. CFRP is the strongest, but it is also the most expensive.

6-series is a medium-strength aluminium alloy. It is bright with an excellent surface finish. This is the alloy most commonly used in conjunction with coloured anodizing.

Aluminium alloy is extruded as a continuous shape. With this process it is relatively inexpensive to produce complex geometries. Available as closed tube or open profile, extrusions are used to make frames (such as for gliders and bicycles), wheels, handles (bicycle and climbing equipment) and poles (skiing and walking) .

Casting is used for large or complex geometries that are impractical to make from sheet or tube, such as bicycle componentry, boot studs, fishing reels and knuckles (joints). It is suitable for producing low to high volumes of parts and is relatively cost-effective in mass production. Forging is capable of producing similar geometries to casting, with the advantage of improved strength. Examples include strength-critical parts such as karabiners, pedals, gears, hubs and levers.

**Hydroformed aluminium alloy ice axe** Used by mountaineers, ice climbers, alpinists and high-country trekkers, ice axes must be light and practical. The handle of this Black Diamond Viper ice axe is shaped by hydroforming. With this process, extruded aluminium (it is also possible to form sheets with hydroforming) is placed into a closed mold and liquid pressure is applied internally. Shaping tubular parts in this way helps to reduce weight, by increasing stiffness, while maintaining the ergonomics. In this ice axe, the head is made of stainless steel, the pick is alloy steel (consisting of chromium and molybdenum) and the handle is thermoplastic polyurethane (TPU) (page 196).

## ALUMINIUM ALLOY IN ARCHITECTURE AND CONSTRUCTION

Since the early 20th century, aluminium alloy has been utilized in the structure and embellishment of buildings. Adoption was slow to begin with – it was initially used for decoration, and the first major structural use was in New York's Empire State Building, completed in 1931 – and gradually expanded. Nowadays, 20–30% of aluminium alloy produced

## ARCHITECTURE AND CONSTRUCTION

### Recyclability
A high proportion of aluminium alloy is collected and recycled (up to 95% in the construction sector). Architectural projects provide a valuable outlet for a range of recycled grades containing up to 85% reused material.

### Weatherproof
Even though aluminium alloy builds up a natural layer of protection, it is typically protected with anodizing, paint or powder coat.

### Colour
Anodized aluminium is dyed a range of metallic colours, from gold to blue, and the widest range of surface finishes is possible with painting and powder coating.

### Reflective
When used as a coating or lining on insulation panels and roofs, its high reflectivity helps to maintain temperature and thereby qualify projects for green building status under the certification programme LEED (Leadership in Energy and Environmental Design).

### Strength-to-weight
Structures fabricated using aluminium alloy can be easily half the weight of steel equivalents. Examples include roofs, sidings, curtain walls, façades and frames for windows and doors.

### Low cost
It is more than three times the price of mild steel, but relatively easy to manufacture into complex parts. Modular systems take advantage of this, whereby the parts are manufactured off-site with precise and highly automated computer-guided processes.

**Aluminium louvres in Beijing Airport's Terminal 3** Nearly 3 km (1.9 miles) long, Terminal 3 at Beijing Airport is one of the world's largest buildings. Designed by Foster + Partners and engineered by Arup, it was finished in 2008 and took just four years from brief to completion. Steel columns support the vast 28 m (92 ft) high roof canopy. The underside of the trussed steel roof is clad with aluminium louvres. They partially conceal the roof (whose colour changes from yellow to red depending on where you are) and skylights above, while casting light back into the building.

goes into architectural projects. Steel is the only metal that is used in greater quantities. The use of aluminium alloy stretches from lightweight load-bearing structures, façades, interiors and trim, to the reflective coating on roofs and insulated panels. Aluminium alloy is as well suited to commercial projects, including large-scale structures, as it is to domestic dwellings.

The most commonly specified types are 3-, 5- and 6-series. While the former are applied in sheet form, 6-series is well suited to extrusion. This provides many design opportunities and as a result profiles have become ubiquitous in modern architecture (window frames, louvres and so on).

Aluminium alloy is used alongside, and in direct competition with, steel,

timber and polyvinyl chloride (PVC) (page 122). While these materials have many benefits, steel is heavier than aluminium and more vulnerable to corrosion; timber is more variable (less reliable in load-bearing structures) and less straightforward to produce in complex shapes; and PVC is less rigid, with lower strength-to-weight, and faces challenges in terms of its sustainability.

# Magnesium

It has very low density – one-third less than aluminium and roughly equivalent to engineering thermoplastic – making it desirable for physically demanding applications needing extreme lightness. Mainly used in aerospace and high-performance automotive parts, magnesium alloy is also useful for lightweight portable items, such as power tools and consumer electronics.

| Types | Typical Applications | Sustainability |
|---|---|---|
| • Pure magnesium<br>• Magnesium alloy | • Aerospace<br>• Automotive<br>• Portable equipment | • Energy-intensive to manufacture<br>• Fully recyclable |

| Properties | Competing Materials | Costs |
|---|---|---|
| • Lowest density of the structural metals<br>• Excellent damping<br>• Dull grey appearance | • Aluminium, titanium and steel<br>• Engineering thermoplastics such as PA, PC and PET | • Material cost is 2–3 times more than for aluminium alloy and equivalent to premium thermoplastics |

54

| | | Tensile strength<br>diameter of bar required to provide equivalent strength | | Stiffness<br>diameter of bar required to provide equivalent stiffness | | Density<br>diameter of bar of equivalent weight | |
|---|---|---|---|---|---|---|---|
| | | $\sigma_t$ (MPa) | % | E (GPa) | % | $\rho$ (kg/m³) | % |
| **Magnesium alloy** | | 240 | 1.0 | 45 | 1.0 | 1,740 | 1.0 |
| Titanium alloy | | 950 | 0.5 | 107 | 0.8 | 4,460 | 0.6 |
| Aluminium alloy | | 310 | 0.9 | 69 | 0.9 | 2,700 | 0.8 |
| Mild steel | | 460 | 0.7 | 210 | 0.7 | 7,830 | 0.5 |
| PC | | 69 | 1.9 | 2.2 | 2.1 | 1,200 | 1.2 |

Magnesium
Titanium
Aluminium
Mild steel

-500°C / -868°F    0°C / 32°F    500°C / 932°F    1,000°C / 1,832°F

**Temperature**
minimum and maximum service temperature

100   Electrical %IACS   0   Thermal W/mK   >250

**Conductivity**

Magnesium
Titanium
Aluminium
Mild steel

0   $/kg   >5

**Cost**
raw material price

0   kJ/kg   >500

**Energy**
energy requirement

0   million tonnes   >5

**Availability**
annual production

0   %   100

**Recycling**
end-of-life recycling

## INTRODUCTION

Magnesium has the unique combination of lightness coupled with damping capacity (the ability to absorb vibration energy), dimensional stability and impact resistance. And while its strength-to-weight is comparable with high-strength aluminium alloys and steel, magnesium is used in significantly lower quantities. This is partly because magnesium is more expensive – around 2.5 times more expensive than aluminium alloy (page 42) and one-third more expensive than stainless steel (page 28) – and partly because it presents some challenges in application.

Although the surface reacts to form a protective oxide layer, magnesium is prone to corrosion, especially in saline environments, so it is often painted. By contrast, anodized aluminium alloy is available in a range of durable colour finishes, and the surface of stainless steel can be polished to a very bright natural (or electrochemically coloured) finish. Magnesium is highly flammable in foil, flake or powdered form – a quality that features in bright white-coloured fireworks and flares – and this can present a challenge during manufacture.

As a result of these drawbacks, magnesium tends to be used where its extreme lightness is critical to performance, in particular for parts that require high stiffness and damping capacity. Examples from the automotive industry, where magnesium is used for lightweighting, include chassis parts, engine blocks, seats, gearbox enclosures and wheels.

Magnesium alloy has significantly higher tensile strength than engineering thermoplastics, even when considering fibre-reinforced types. Furthermore, the base material cost is comparable with certain grades of polyamide (PA,

nylon) (page 164) and polycarbonate
(PC) (page 144), although manufacturing
costs tend to be higher owing to the
complexities involved.

### COMMERCIAL TYPES AND USES

The majority of magnesium comes
from China, where it is produced using
the Pidgeon process. In this process,
mined dolomite (calcium magnesium
carbonate) is crushed and roasted to
remove the carbon dioxide. The remaining
mix is combined with reaction agents
(ferrosilicon and fluorite) and pressed into
briquettes. A second roasting cycle in a
vacuum chamber causes deoxidization
and crude magnesium crystallizes within.

From here it is refined and mixed
with alloys to improve its mechanical
properties. The ingredients are
identifiable by a short code, defined by
the American Society for Testing and
Materials (ASTM), such as AZ91. The letters
indicate the alloying elements and the
numbers specify the respective amounts
by weight. Thus, AZ91 contains 9%
aluminium and 1% zinc.

Aluminium is the principal alloying
element; it improves tensile strength,
corrosion resistance and castability.
However, as the proportion is increased,
ductility and fracture toughness are
reduced. Incorporating manganese
(M) reduces the quantity of aluminium

**Forged magnesium
alloy racing wheel**
Prodrive produce
world-leading race
and rally cars from
their headquarters
in Banbury, UK. Since
1984 the team has
won numerous titles,
including World Rally
and Le Mans. This is a
magnesium alloy wheel
from one of their Aston
Martin GTE endurance-
racing cars. The mass
of the wheels, tyres
and brake discs directly

affects performance,
because acceleration,
manoeuvrability and
braking improve as
un-sprung weight is
reduced. Magnesium
produces lighter wheels
than aluminium –
forged magnesium is
up to one-third lighter
than aluminium and
half the weight of cast
aluminium – but it is
more expensive and
not as resilient, so it
tends to be reserved for
racing applications.

required to achieve good elongation, toughness and impact resistance, while helping to control iron content. However, castability and tensile strength are reduced as the aluminium content decreases. Silicon (S) is added to improve high-temperature properties of the alloy. It provides excellent ductility and corrosion resistance. Some other elements include zirconium (K), rare earth (E) and yttrium (W).

Magnesium's hexagonal crystal structure makes it challenging to form at room temperature. In recent years, casting developments have expanded the range of potential applications. The highest-quality results are achieved with semi-solid casting. One such process, known by the trade name Thixomolding, works in a similar way to injection molding plastic. In operation, magnesium alloy chips are heated and sheared to form a thixotropic (gel-like) consistency. Once

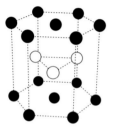

**Crystal structure – hexagonal close-packed (HCP)**
Consisting of an atom at each corner of the hexagonal structure, one in the middle of each hexagonal plane and three in the centre, arranged as a triangle to fit between the corner atoms. It has the same packing density as the cubic crystal structure (see page 68).

Basal          Prismatic          Pyramidal

**Slip systems** The limited formability of magnesium at room temperature is a result of the HCP crystal structure and its resistance to twinning (crystal deformation). The plastic deformation of magnesium occurs when enough force is applied to cause dislocations in the crystal lattice. For magnesium, basal slip requires the least energy. Heating reduces the energy needed to engage the remaining slip systems, improving formability. Magnesium is best suited to simple geometries that do not require significant metal flow to fill all the features.

up to temperature an exact measure of material is injected under high pressure into the mold cavity protected within an argon gas atmosphere. The gel-like consistency ensures it flows without turbulence to produce parts with improved uniformity and lower porosity than die-cast equivalents. The design needs to allow the metal to flow smoothly; with certain geometries it is possible to produce parts with wall thicknesses down to 0.5 mm (0.02 in).

Die casting and sand casting are also suitable. Examples range from gearbox housings and engine parts to power tools and cameras. AZ91 is the most commonly used alloy for casting applications and offers good strength-to-weight (up to 25% lighter than an aluminium alloy equivalent) and corrosion resistance.

AM20, AM50 and AM60 have excellent ductility, elongation and energy absorption at the expense of castability and strength. These alloys are utilized, for example, in automotive safety components, instrument panels and steering components.

ZM21, ZK60, AK60, AZ31, AZ61 and AZ80 are suitable for extrusion. However, the speed, efficiency and design considerations vary. For example AZ31 has very good extrudability for complex shapes, but is only medium strength; and AZ80 is the strongest of the AZ family but is very challenging and slow to extrude.

Forging minimizes porosity and optimizes grain structure, resulting in the strongest and most reliable parts. For example, ZK60 is used to make rotors and racing wheels. However, it is significantly more expensive than casting owing to the length and complexity of the process. As a result, mass-production parts are often produced using a hybrid, such as flow forming. With this process, a cast semi-formed part is rolled under high pressure, causing the metal to 'flow' into the final shape. This improves the grain structure in a similar way to forging and yields wheels up to 15% lighter than cast equivalents.

Magnesium alloys have the best machinability of the structural metals. This allows for deeper cuts and higher feed rates, which minimizes cost – time is

the critical factor used to determine the price of machining.

Coatings are not sufficient to stop galvanic corrosion, which is of particular concern because magnesium is the least noble of the structural metals. Facilitated by an electrolyte, such as water or moisture in the atmosphere, magnesium acts as the anode. Thus when in contact with other metals, most notably iron, nickel and copper, the surface of magnesium is dissolved. Insulation helps to prevent damage. However, care must be taken to ensure problems do not arise from elsewhere, such as metal fasteners and metallic pigments.

## SUSTAINABILITY
Magnesium's strength-to-weight is helping to progress the fuel efficiency of automobiles and aircraft. So while the embodied energy of magnesium is higher than that of competing metals, such as steel and aluminium, this is offset or even cancelled by savings made throughout its useful life.

Scrap produced during casting, which can be 50% or more of the cast weight, is directly recycled in a closed-loop process. This reduces the amount of primary material needed.

While re-melting uses significantly less energy than raw material production, recycling from mixed waste streams is far less rewarding. Metal from end-of-life vehicles (ELV) – the predominant source of post-consumer scrap magnesium – contains lots of iron, nickel and copper, all of which corrode magnesium. Coupled with magnesium's propensity to oxidize, the quality of scrap magnesium is often unsuitable for the sort of critical applications to which it is so well suited.

**Thixomolded magnesium alloy laptop cover** The cover of Panasonic's Toughbook, a rugged computer designed to survive extreme conditions, features a Thixomolded AZ91 outer case. The same technique is used in the production of cameras, mobile phones and large-screen televisions alike. The underside reveals the engineering required to maximize stiffness and strength in such a thin part; the ribs also assist with the flow of metal during casting. The outward-facing surface is painted to increase resistance to corrosion and abrasion.

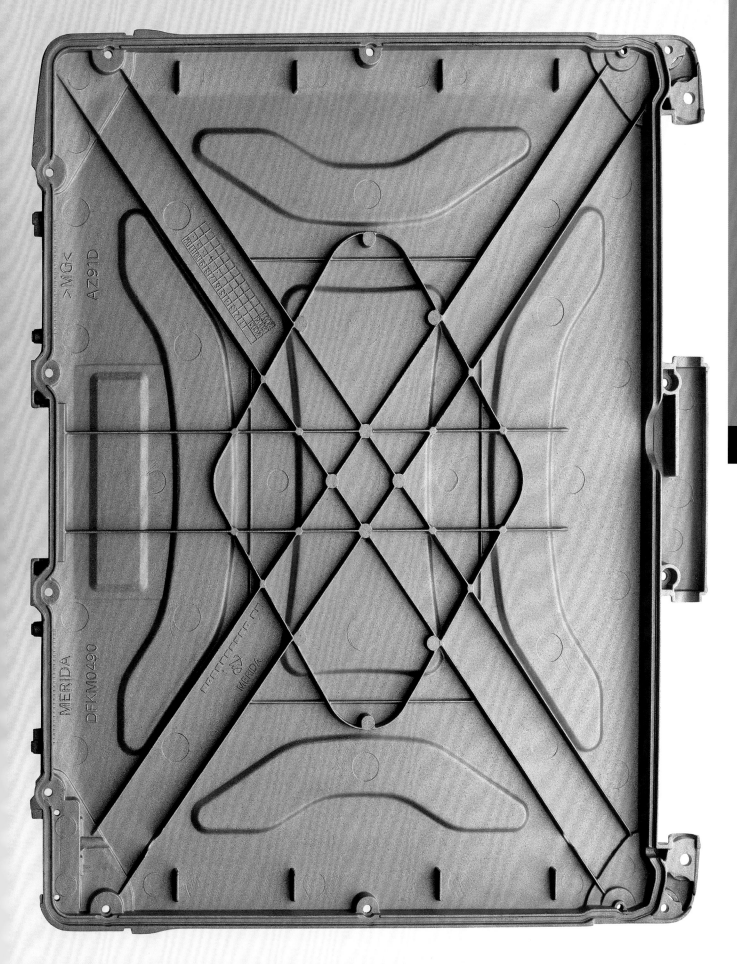

# Titanium

Although the process of extracting titanium from its ore is costly, designers consider it a valuable enough material to specify. Principally used in aerospace, where its combination of strength-to-weight and corrosion resistance is unrivalled, it is found in a variety of high-performance industrial and consumer products. It is biocompatible and so useful for medical applications.

| Types | Typical Applications | Sustainability |
|---|---|---|
| • Pure titanium<br>• Titanium alloy | • Aerospace, marine and automotive<br>• Construction<br>• Medical and dental | • Raw material production is energy-intensive and polluting<br>• Fully recyclable |

| Properties | Competing Materials | Costs |
|---|---|---|
| • High strength-to-weight<br>• Superior corrosion resistance<br>• Biocompatible | • Aluminium and magnesium<br>• Fibre-reinforced plastics, in particular CFRP and GFRP | • High material cost<br>• High manufacturing costs |

## INTRODUCTION

Titanium is often compared to aluminium (page 42) and magnesium (page 54). Like these two, it develops a protective oxide film. It is slightly heavier, but has far higher tensile strength, which is improved through alloying. It can operate at higher temperatures too, typically up to 350°C (660°F) and as high as 650°C (1,200°F) for certain alloys. It has a desirable balance of stiffness and elasticity; its elastic modulus (stiffness) is higher than for aluminium and magnesium, but around half that of steel (page 28). It has excellent resistance to corrosion, especially in saline environments that would destroy steels, while pure titanium is sufficiently stable to be used for medical implants.

Its track record is testament to these impressive properties, from NASA spacecraft to Boeing and Airbus passenger jets, and from Apple's Titanium PowerBook G4 to custom-designed laser-sintered bone repair plates. A range of alloys has been developed, each one with particular characteristics suited to the needs of different applications.

## COMMERCIAL TYPES AND USES

Commercial production of titanium alloys began almost a century ago. Since the 1930s, a complex thermal treatment known as the Kroll process has remained the predominant method of production. It takes many days and yields small amounts of metal compared to other commercial foundry techniques. This makes titanium the most expensive structural metal, costing roughly four times more than aluminium alloy, twice as much as stainless steel and one-third more than magnesium alloy.

Titanium is used 'commercially pure' or alloyed to improve specific properties. The ingredients are identified by different grades, defined by the American Society

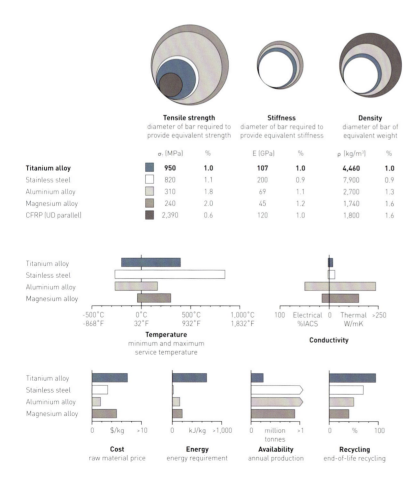

|  | Tensile strength<br>diameter of bar required to provide equivalent strength | | Stiffness<br>diameter of bar required to provide equivalent stiffness | | Density<br>diameter of bar of equivalent weight | |
|---|---|---|---|---|---|---|
|  | $\sigma_t$ (MPa) | % | E (GPa) | % | $\rho$ (kg/m³) | % |
| Titanium alloy | 950 | 1.0 | 107 | 1.0 | 4,460 | 1.0 |
| Stainless steel | 820 | 1.1 | 200 | 0.9 | 7,900 | 0.9 |
| Aluminium alloy | 310 | 1.8 | 69 | 1.1 | 2,700 | 1.3 |
| Magnesium alloy | 240 | 2.0 | 45 | 1.2 | 1,740 | 1.6 |
| CFRP (UD parallel) | 2,390 | 0.6 | 120 | 1.0 | 1,800 | 1.6 |

Temperature
minimum and maximum service temperature

Conductivity

Cost
raw material price

Energy
energy requirement

Availability
annual production

Recycling
end-of-life recycling

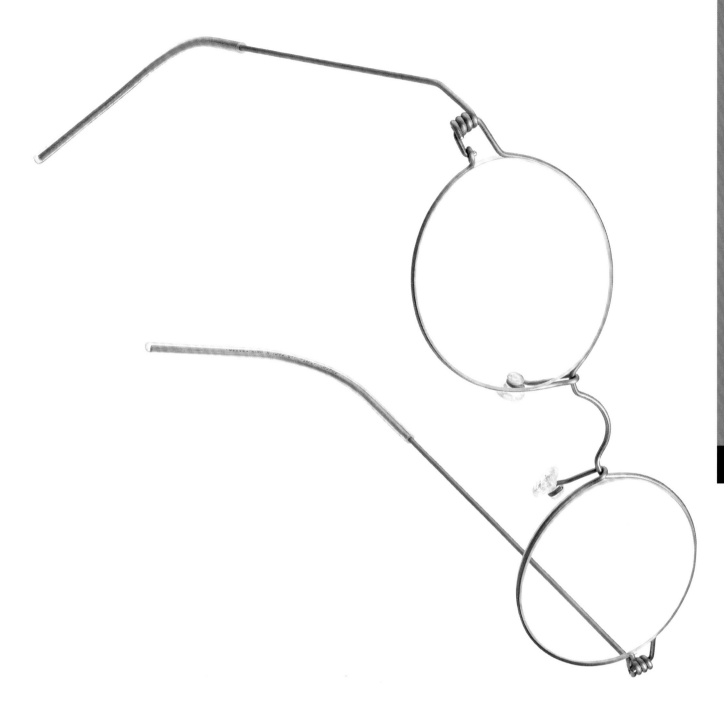

for Testing and Materials (ASTM), from 1 upwards. Alternatively, a short code is used to identify the type and proportion of ingredients. For example, grade 5, the most common titanium alloy, consists of 6% aluminium and 4% vanadium, and so is also known as Ti 6Al-4V (or Ti 6-4).

The commercially pure (unalloyed) grades are utilized for their corrosion resistance, formability (pressing, forging and machining) and weldability. Grades 1 through 4 are unalloyed; their mechanical properties are adjusted by varying the amount of contaminations, such as oxygen, nitrogen and carbon. Grade 1 is the 'purest' and has the highest formability, while grade 4 has the highest strength – similar to low-carbon steel – of these four, and moderate formability. These grades are used for airframe and aircraft engine parts, architecture, marine applications and orthopaedic applications such as implants and prostheses.

There is another group of almost pure alloys – although they do not follow numerically – that are modified

**Lightweight titanium glasses** The result of a collaboration between architects Dissing + Weitling and LINDBERG in 1983, the Air Titanium range transformed spectacle design. The lightweight frame – a mere 2.4 g (0.08 oz) – is fabricated from a specially developed grade of titanium, which provides the optimum balance of strength, spring tension and tenacity. All unnecessary details have been removed. There are no screws, rivets or solder holding the glasses together. Instead, the pivoting action is provided by the resilience of the titanium; a neatly formed coil ensures that the arms return to their correct place. Photo courtesy of LINDBERG.

with small amounts of palladium (Pd) or ruthenium (Ru). These elements significantly improve corrosion resistance. This includes grades 7, 11, 16, 17, 26 and 27. They are utilized in chemical processing, marine environments and manufacturing equipment.

Grade 7 includes a small amount of palladium, from 0.12 to 0.25%, and has superior corrosion resistance. Otherwise, its mechanical properties are similar to grade 2. Grade 11 is the same but with slightly less oxygen, so that, similar to grade 1, it has improved formability but reduced tensile strength. Grades 16 and 17 consist of less than 0.1% palladium, which means they are less expensive, but otherwise similar to grades 7 and 11 respectively. Grades 26 and 27 contain around 0.1% ruthenium, with standard and low levels of oxygen respectively. They are the least expensive of the group; with slightly reduced mechanical properties and corrosion endurance. The tensile strength of these grades ranges from around 290 to 550 MPa.

Titanium alloys have two different crystal forms, depending on ingredients and temperature. The alpha (α) phase is dominated by a hexagonal close-packed structure (page 56), and the beta (β) phase consists of a body-centred cubic structure (see page 68). Oxygen, carbon, nitrogen and aluminium (Al) stabilize the alpha phase. Those that promote the formation of the beta phase at a lower temperature are chromium (C), molybdenum (Mo), niobium (Nb) and vanadium (V). Neutral elements include tin (Sn) and zirconium (Zr).

There are three types of structural titanium alloys: alpha and near-alpha; alpha-beta; and beta.

Similar to commercially pure grades, the alpha alloys do not respond to heat treatment; they are easily welded, and have good ductility (even at low temperatures) and high corrosion resistance. Near-alpha alloys have improved high-temperature properties. They have higher tensile strength than unalloyed types (in the region of 500–900 MPa). Typified by grade 6 (Ti 5Al-2.5Sn), they are found in aircraft, spacecraft, sports equipment and machinery.

The alpha-beta alloys are susceptible to heat treatment. Quenching (heating followed by rapid cooling) the alloy suppresses the formation of the beta phase and so results in a much stronger structure. This group is characterized by the amount of beta present: as the proportion of body-centred cubic structure increases, tensile strength improves at the expense of ductility and toughness. So, while grade 5 (Ti 6AL-4V) has a tensile strength of 950 MPa and elongation at break of 15%, Ti 5Al-4Cr-4Mo-2Sn-2Zr has a tensile strength of around 1,150 MPa and elongation of only 11%. Such two-phase alloys are strengthened by heat treatment.

The beta alloys have the highest proportion of beta-stabilizing elements. Precipitation of fine alpha particles during heat treatment produces extensive strengthening. As a result, these alloys have roughly equivalent strength but with improved ductility, suitable even for forging. Examples include grades 19 to 21, which are used in applications ranging from landing gear to sports equipment.

## SUSTAINABILITY

Even though titanium is abundant in the earth's crust, mining and manufacturing is energy-intensive and produces a lot of waste, a problem reflected in the material's very high embodied energy. Compared to the smelting, flotation and refinement used in the production of other structural metals, the Kroll process is particularly slow, complex and inefficient. This is why titanium is such an expensive raw material.

The high price and energy requirements of titanium production mean recycling is economically very worthwhile. It is mainly used in aerospace and industrial products: such applications require careful dismantling and so titanium is straightforward to collect. Recyclers are capable of identifying the different grades so they can be reused for parts of more or less equal value.

While most safety-critical parts – such as in aircraft – are produced from virgin material to avoid problems from contamination, there is a healthy market for titanium scrap elsewhere.

**Electrolytically coloured titanium**
These colours are the result of light interference, not pigments or dyes. The naturally occurring oxide film that develops on the surface is enhanced electrolytically in a process akin to anodizing aluminium. Film thickness determines the visible colour, which will shift slightly depending on the angle of view. The range of colours progresses from its natural silver-grey, through brown, gold, purple, blue, teal, yellow, pink and green as film thickness increases. The film is very thin and so the range than can be achieved depends on the surface quality and grade of titanium. As an example, a broader colour range can be produced with grade 5 than is possible with grade 2. The colour is integral to the surface and provides a durable, wear-resistant and biocompatible finish to titanium. Multiple colours are produced by masking. As well as being used for decorative purposes, colour-coding ensures the correct parts are used in critical applications.

## TITANIUM IN AEROSPACE
Titanium and its alloys are used throughout passenger jets and military aircraft. The diversity of grades offers choice for a variety of applications. One of the major drivers is lightness: titanium's superior strength-to-weight helps to make aircraft safer and more fuel-efficient. In addition to its strength, titanium is highly compatible with carbon-fibre-reinforced plastic (CFRP) (page 236), which, like titanium, is growing in popularity thanks to its

**Titanium alloy road bike**  The Great Divide from No. 22 Bicycle Company demonstrates some of the best characteristics of titanium alloy while embracing the latest developments in bicycle design. The frame is constructed from grade 9 (Ti 3AL-2.5V), a high-strength titanium alloy typically utilized as tubing in aerospace as well as in sports equipment and bicycle frames. It can be formed and welded and has very good resistance to corrosion. Titanium alloy frames offer superior strength-to-weight compared to aluminium alloy or steel, resulting in a more efficient bicycle. In addition, the balance of stiffness and spring tension provided by titanium alloy offers a very smooth ride; a quality emphasized by the design and construction of the frame. The colour is applied electrolytically to ensure a high-quality finish that will last the life of the bicycle. Photo courtesy of No. 22 Bicycle Company.

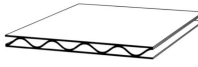

Wavy corrugate

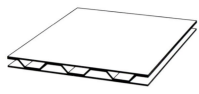

Straight corrugate

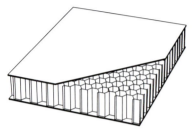

Honeycomb

**Structural panels**
Sandwich panels have far higher strength- and stiffness-to-weight than a simple sheet of material. The improvements in mechanical properties are the result of increasing thickness without adding significant weight. For example, increasing thickness by a factor of four using honeycomb core will yield a material nearly 10 times stronger and 35 times stiffer, and yet only a fraction heavier. Corrugates are manufactured as three separate sheets and joined by welding or adhesive bonding. The middle layer is formed by rolling or pressing; selection depends on the size and design.

Alternatively, the corrugate is formed and welded using a combination of superplastic forming and diffusion bonding. Increasing the size of the joint interface ensures a strong bond is achieved. Corrugates are anisotropic as a result of their configuration. Honeycomb turns corrugate on its side: each layer is pressed as a series of half-hexagons and welded or adhesive bonded to the next layer. Honeycomb distributes load more effectively than corrugated sheets and so offers superior mechanical properties in all directions. As it involves more steps in production it tends to be more expensive.

impressive strength. Unlike aluminium, titanium expands and contracts at the same rate as CFRP. Also, whereas titanium and CFRP do not corrode one another, aluminium is prone to severe galvanic corrosion in the presence of carbon.

Machining is very precise and so utilized a great deal in aerospace.

## AEROSPACE

**Strength-to-weight**
Titanium is around half the weight of steel for the same strength, and two-thirds heavier than aluminium but twice as strong.

**Resistance to corrosion**
The naturally occurring oxide film that develops on titanium improves surface durability. It is enhanced electrolytically and can be built up to provide colour through light interference.

**High-temperature performance**
It performs very well up to around 350°C (660°F) – comparable with carbon steel and around twice that of aluminium – and certain grades are capable of operating safely up to 650°C (1200°F).

While lathing and boring titanium is relatively straightforward, milling is quite challenging due to titanium's hardness and low heat conductivity. Water jet cutting does not heat up the metal and so allows for higher cutting speeds and produces a superior edge finish. Electrical discharge machining (EDM) provides another alternative. With this technique high-voltage sparks erode the surface or cut a profile. It is very precise and capable of applying a texture simultaneously during cutting.

Investment casting is utilized in the production of complex parts. This reduces machining time, which is especially useful for high volumes of parts.

Sheet formability depends on the choice of titanium. Commercially pure titanium and beta alloys tend to be the most ductile and so more easily formed by pressing and bending. Similar profiles to stainless steel can be achieved, but owing to the springback of titanium at room temperature – a property utilized in many applications – it is often warmed to reduce stress and ensure more accurate parts during forming. Deep drawing is possible for the most ductile grades, but requires generous bend radii to ensure the material does not crack. The minimum radius achievable depends on the grade, thickness and temperature.

Grade 5 (Ti 6AL-4V) and several other alloys – plus certain aluminium alloys and magnesium alloys – exhibit superplastic properties. They are therefore suitable for superplastic forming. This process is similar in many respects to vacuum forming plastic: the sheet is heated up

and then pressed onto the die cavity using gas pressure. Complex configurations are readily formed in a single operation, which makes lighter, more efficient structures possible. The tooling costs are high and cycle time is long, making this an expensive process.

Ultra-lightweight 'sandwich' structural panels and hollow parts are produced with a combination of superplastic forming and diffusion bonding. Multiple sheets are formed and held together under pressure. Over time, the atoms at the surface of the materials intermingle to form a strong join. While this process offers impressive weight savings, there are many geometry restrictions and it is very expensive owing to the skills required, complexity and cycle time.

Most welding techniques are suitable for titanium; however, it is not a straightforward material to join. Molten titanium reacts with the atmosphere and so – except for resistance and friction techniques – the weld zone must be shielded with an inert gas during and after welding.

### TITANIUM IN ARCHITECTURE AND CONSTRUCTION
Titanium is an expensive material to purchase and fabricate, but its value outweighs the project cost in many cases. Perhaps most famously, Frank Gehry's Guggenheim Museum Bilbao (1997) is clad with sheets of titanium, which

**Airframe** Aerospace pushes materials to their limits, within a safety margin of course, and the F-22 Raptor from Lockheed Martin is no exception. Titanium alloy and titanium composite materials are used in the frame, bulkheads and other components that require high strength-to-weight and heat resistance, giving the F-22's airframe the strength to conduct high-performance aerial manoeuvres without the added weight associated with other durable materials.

The properties of cast titanium parts are optimized with hot isostatic pressing (to minimize porosity), and fasteners have been reduced through the use of electron beam welding (superior weld quality even in thick parts). Parts of the frame, doors, wing spars and skin panels are fabricated from carbon fibre composite. There are also small amounts of aluminium alloy and steel. The canopy is produced from PC. Photo courtesy of Lockheed Martin Aeronautics.

**Ultralight spatula** This spatula is handmade in Wyoming by Mike Draper from grade 5 (Ti 6AL-4V) titanium alloy. A mere 0.5 mm (0.02 in) thick, the head is flexible enough to bend 90° and yet strong enough to spring back to its original shape. Titanium alloy is hypoallergenic, resistant to corrosion and a poor conductor of heat, all of which means it is well suited to cooking utensils.

shift colour and appearance according to changes in light and weather. Before this, it was already very popular in Japan, with applications ranging from industrial buildings to revered temples.

Titanium lasts a long time, even in industrial zones and coastal areas. This helps to offset the high price, because over 30 or more years the low running costs bring the life cycle total down considerably.

As a result of its very desirable properties, titanium's use in architecture stretches beyond exterior cladding. It can be found in the structure, interior and furniture of buildings. Commercially pure grades, such as 1 and 2, are most common in construction. Typically applied as sheet, it is fabricated through pressing or superplastic forming and welding.

The surface can be polished to a mirror-like finish, or blasted or etched to a soft matt texture. It can be coloured too. Without pigments or coatings, colour is created through light interference with the surface oxide film. By carefully controlling film thickness, a spectrum of vivid colours is produced.

Over time and with exposure to the atmosphere, the film will increase in thickness. Thus, the colour will gradually change. For example, natural silver-grey titanium will gradually become yellow-brown over time. Manufacturers have developed treatments to counteract this phenomenon, but it is not feasible to prevent it completely.

### TITANIUM IN MEDICAL
An expanding number of medical procedures have become reliant on titanium and its alloys. Applications include bone and joint replacement, dental implants, maxillofacial and craniofacial treatments, cardiovascular devices (such as pacemakers and

intravascular stents) and prostheses. In addition, titanium is utilized in the construction of surgical instruments, its lightness helping to improve the accuracy of surgeons and reduce fatigue.

Titanium is biocompatible and does not hinder osseointegration. In other words, it is accepted by human tissue and immune systems and so over time becomes fully integrated. When used as an orthopaedic implant, bone-forming cells grow on the surface of the titanium and thus create a structural and functional bridge to be formed between bone and implant. Parts inserted into the body can last upwards of 20 years and dental implants can last even longer.

Additive manufacturing (rapid prototyping) has many advantages for the medical industry, in particular the ability to produce parts tailored to the exact dimensions and needs of an individual. With electron beam melting (EBM) it is now possible to additive manufacture three-dimensional parts in titanium. Layers of titanium powder are fused together to form fully dense, complex geometries without the need for expensive tooling and lengthy lead-time. Combined with tomography-scan data, engineers are capable of producing implants that follow the contours of an individual's body.

The most commonly used types are the commercially pure grades and grade 5 (Ti 6AL-4V). Selection depends on the requirements of the application and whether formability (ductility) or tensile strength is required. Cobalt-chrome-molybdenum (CoCrMo) alloy is harder and so preferred for applications that require a highly polished surface, such as joint implants.

While titanium is often used in its natural silver-grey state, coloured finishes help to identify parts and reduce mistakes in medical procedures. The electrolytic process used to colour titanium does not add any coating or pigments and so retains titanium's non-toxic and biocompatible surface. Instruments are finished with a dull non-reflecting surface, which is essential for microsurgical tools.

**Custom lattice skull implant** Since it was founded in 1997, Arcam has revolutionized additive manufacturing solutions for metal components, leading to improvements in the orthopaedic and aerospace industries. With Arcam's EBM technology, patient-specific implants can be made using data from computer tomography (CT) scanning. The CT data creates an exact representation of the implant. The EBM machine uses this data to build the part, ensuring it fits exactly. Solid and porous sections are built in the same process – trabecular (rod-like) structures improve osseointegration – eliminating the need for expensive finishing. Photo courtesy of Arcam.

## ARCHITECTURE AND CONSTRUCTION

**Resistance to corrosion**
The formation of a very stable, protective oxide on the surface of titanium prevents corrosion in virtually every environment and minimizes maintenance.

**Low thermal expansion**
Titanium's coefficient of thermal expansion is more or less equivalent to that of concrete and glass, half that of stainless steel and copper, and one-third that of aluminium.

**Range of finishes**
Colour varies from its natural silver-grey through a spectrum of vivid colours; texture ranges from mirror-polished to dull matt.

**Lightweight**
With superior strength-to-weight, titanium reduces the load on building structures.

**Recyclability**
Grades of titanium used in architecture contain high levels of recycled content, up to around 75%.

## MEDICAL

**Biocompatibility**
Titanium is one of the few materials that are fully compatible with the human body. Once implanted it is not affected by bodily fluids or tissue and becomes fully osseointegrated.

**Strength-to-weight**
Titanium is lighter than cobalt-chrome alloy and stainless steel for the same strength.

**Range of grades**
As it ranges from the more ductile to tensile strengths over 1,000 MPa, selection depends on the needs of the individual and this allows medical professionals to match the part to the application.

# Copper, Brass, Bronze and Nickel Silver

**Also known as**
Chemical symbol: Cu
Nickel silver also referred to as: cupronickel

**Pure copper is used for its excellent conductivity and corrosion resistance. Incorporating alloys improves strength, but will inevitably reduce conductivity. Brass is produced with the addition of zinc; nickel silver is an alloy of copper and nickel; and all other alloys are categorized as bronze. Oxidization produces a rich surface patina; the colour depends on the alloy.**

| Types | Typical Applications | | Sustainability |
|---|---|---|---|
| • Copper<br>• Copper alloy: high copper, brass, bronze and nickel silver | • Electrical<br>• Roofing, cladding and sculpture<br>• Cookware | • Musical instruments<br>• Coinage and jewelry | • Mining is energy-intensive and it takes approximately 1 tonne of ore to yield 1 kg (2.2 lb) or so of copper<br>• Efficient to recycle |
| **Properties** | **Competing Materials** | | **Costs** |
| • Efficient conductor<br>• Good strength and fatigue resistance<br>• Develops surface patina | • Steel, aluminium and zinc<br>• PVC | | • Pure copper is relatively expensive<br>• Manufacturing costs depend on the alloy |

## INTRODUCTION

Copper owes its versatility to a unique combination of malleability, conductivity and corrosion resistance. It is utilized for a huge diversity of applications, from sculpture to coinage and from precision machine parts to imitation jewelry. It is the third most consumed metal – behind steel (page 28) and aluminium (page 42) – and is available in several hundred different alloy configurations and formats, including cast, wire, bar and powder.

Copper is inherently antimicrobial. Similar to silver (page 84), its ions inhibit or destroy a wide range of molds, fungi and other microbes. This action has proved to be very effective against microbes that pose a significant health risk, including *Escherichia coli* (*E. coli*), methicillin-resistant *Staphylococcus aureus* (MRSA) and *Clostridium difficile* (*C. difficile*).

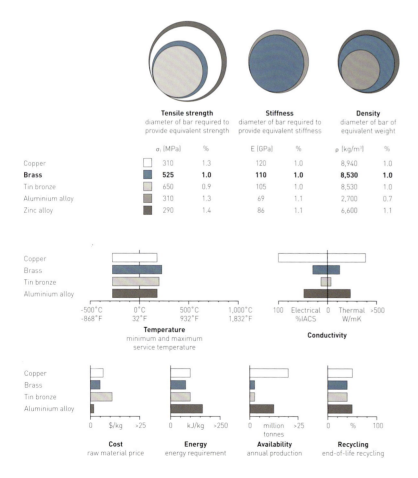

| | Tensile strength<br>diameter of bar required to provide equivalent strength | | Stiffness<br>diameter of bar required to provide equivalent stiffness | | Density<br>diameter of bar of equivalent weight | |
|---|---|---|---|---|---|---|
| | $\sigma_i$ (MPa) | % | E (GPa) | % | $\rho$ (kg/m³) | % |
| Copper | 310 | 1.3 | 120 | 1.0 | 8,940 | 1.0 |
| **Brass** | 525 | 1.0 | 110 | 1.0 | 8,530 | 1.0 |
| Tin bronze | 650 | 0.9 | 105 | 1.0 | 8,530 | 1.0 |
| Aluminium alloy | 310 | 1.3 | 69 | 1.1 | 2,700 | 0.7 |
| Zinc alloy | 290 | 1.4 | 86 | 1.1 | 6,600 | 1.1 |

Copper
Brass
Tin bronze
Aluminium alloy

-500°C  0°C  500°C  1,000°C
-868°F  32°F  932°F  1,832°F

**Temperature**
minimum and maximum service temperature

100  Electrical  0  Thermal  >500
%IACS  W/mK

**Conductivity**

Copper
Brass
Tin bronze
Aluminium alloy

0  $/kg  >25
**Cost**
raw material price

0  kJ/kg  >250
**Energy**
energy requirement

0  million  >25
tonnes
**Availability**
annual production

0  %  100
**Recycling**
end-of-life recycling

**Brass trumpet** Taylor Trumpets hand-craft brass instruments to the highest standards. Musicians come from around the world to their UK workshop to commission their ideal instrument. Several copper alloys are utilized in the Chicago Standard. Colour is a good indication of the amount of alloy present. Whereas high quantities of zinc (yellow brass contains around 30%) result in a bright and direct tone, increasing the amount of copper (red brass contains around 10% zinc) produces a warmer and mellower acoustic. Tubular and precision parts are typically leaded yellow brass (around 30% zinc), which has excellent machining properties. The bell is shaped with a combination of panel beating and spinning. In this case it is produced from red brass (around 10% zinc). A malleable yellow brass would be equally suitable. The tuning slides are produced from nickel silver for ease of fabrication, lightness and colour. The valves are machined from stainless steel. The trumpet is lacquered so that the surface does not oxidize and change colour. Of course, it can be left bare, and many musicians prefer it this way. The mouthpiece depends on the player and is often gold-plated for skin contact.

Its high resistance to corrosion means the surface may be left exposed, which maximizes the antimicrobial effect and so helps to maintain a hygienic surface. This is particularly useful for high-traffic applications, such as door furniture, as well as items associated with the storage and preparation of food and drink.

Copper and its alloys have a distinctive colour ranging from silvery-grey to yellow and gold through reddish-pink and brown. Surface oxidization results in a gradual change in colour. The rate of change depends on the local environment and alloy ingredients: copper turns green; brass turns a greenish-brown before becoming dark brown; tin-bronze gradually becomes deep brown; aluminium-bronze lightens, becoming reddish-brown; and nickel silver becomes brownish-green over an extended period of time.

## COMMERCIAL TYPES AND USES

The Unified Numbering System (UNS) created by the North American copper and brass industry helps to identify the different alloys. Each alloy has a unique code, starting with C. The first number designates the copper content, followed by four numbers that indicate other alloying elements in progressively smaller quantities. Numbers C1 through C7 denote a wrought alloy, and C8 through C9 are cast. Wrought products – sheet, rod, bar, tube, plate and wire produced by rolling and extrusion mills, as well as forging – have improved strength, hardness and stiffness, with reduced ductility, owing to cold working.

C1 identifies high copper. It is considered pure when it contains less than 0.7% debasement. It is very soft and ductile, with the highest conductivity of the engineering metals. It is used for wiring, electrical fittings, heating elements, water pipes, roofs and cladding.

Wrought brasses are designated as C2 through C4. Compared to high copper, these alloys have improved strength with excellent machinability and castability. The proportion of zinc determines the exact properties. Alloys that contain up to around one-third zinc maintain a face-centred cubic (FCC) crystal structure.

**Face-centred cubic (FCC)**

**Body-centred cubic (BCC)**

**Close-packed plane in the FCC structure**

**Lower packing density in the BCC structure**

**Crystal structure and atomic arrangement in metals** FCC consists of an atom at each cube corner and an atom in the centre of each cube face. This results in very closely packed planes, which can slide past one another more easily than in a BCC lattice structure. Thus,

FCC metals tend to be softer and more ductile. BCC consists of atoms at each cube corner and a single atom in the centre of the cube. The atoms are less closely packed on each plane than in the FCC lattice structure, which results in stronger, harder and more brittle metals.

Known as single-phase, or alpha (α), brasses, they are ductile and relatively easy to form and join. Examples include C21*** gilding (5% zinc), C22*** commercial bronze (10% zinc), C23*** red brass (15% zinc) and C24*** low brass (20% zinc).

As the amount of copper is reduced, the colour shifts from red to gold; a quality often reflected in the alloy's name. They have excellent formability and resistance to corrosion, properties that are employed in musical instruments, architectural façades, jewelry, door handles and packaging.

Alloys containing around one-third zinc, such as C26*** cartridge brass (30% zinc) and C27*** yellow brass (35% zinc), are characteristically bright yellow in appearance. They have the optimum balance of strength and ductility (useful for deep drawing and spinning) combined with corrosion resistance. They are used where a combination of formability and low cost is required, such as for musical instruments, architectural fittings, ammunition and plumbing hardware.

Brasses made up of more than around one-third zinc, and containing both FCC and body-centred cubic (BCC) crystal

structures, are harder and stronger than alpha types. They are known as alpha-beta (α-β) brasses, owing to their duplex structure. They are less easy to cold work and so tend to be formed by casting, extrusion and machining. Examples include C28*** Muntz metal (plate and sheet), C3**** leaded brasses (in particular C36*** free-cutting brass for machined parts), C37*** and C38*** forging brass, and C464** naval brass (high resistance to corrosion in sea water). C4 covers a broad range of brasses, some of which contain up to around 95% copper plus various alloying elements.

Bronzes include copper alloys in which the major alloying element is neither zinc nor nickel. They are utilized where greater hardness, strength and corrosion resistance are required. The main groups include tin bronze (copper-tin), aluminium bronze (copper-aluminium), phosphor bronze (copper-tin-phosphor) and manganese bronze (copper-manganese-aluminium), usually with various other alloying elements, such as phosphorus, lead and silicon.

Manganese bronzes (C66, C67 and C86) have excellent mechanical properties and corrosion resistance. As a result they can operate under very high speeds and loads, such as is required in gears, bearings and marine propellers.

Tin bronzes (C9) contain 4–8% tin and are utilized in the production of springs, masonry fixings, gears and bearings. Cast lead-tin bronzes (C92 through C94) contain an additional 7–15% lead, which improves machinability. They are used to make bearings and other sliding surfaces.

Bronze is very liquid when molten, which is useful for casting complex and intricate shapes. Statues, sculpture and bells continue to be produced in this way. While the surface of sculpture tends to be patinated for decorative effect, bells are cut and polished to exact dimensions to ensure the required note when struck.

Tin bronzes with the addition of phosphor, known as phosphor bronzes (C5), are used to make corrosion-resistant items such as propellers, automotive under-the-bonnet parts, springs and precision machine parts. They have desirable acoustic properties too, which

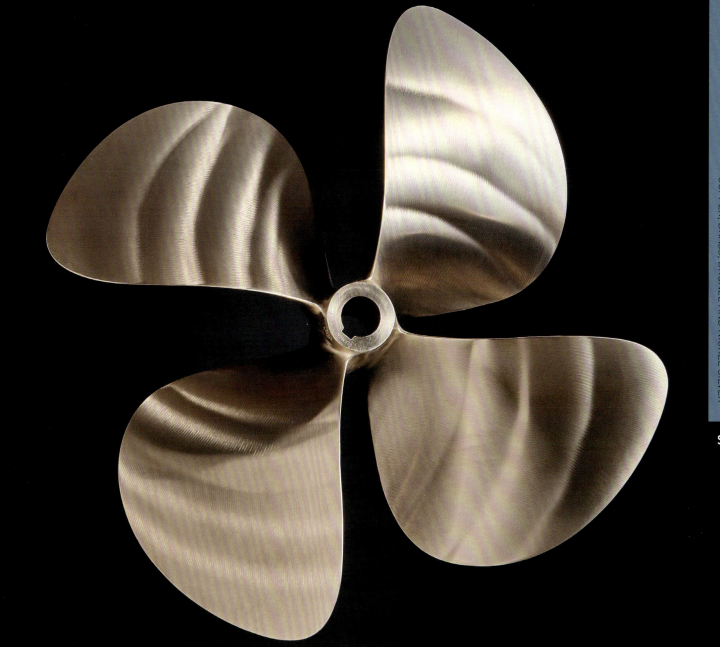

are utilized in cymbals as well as the bodies and bells of metal wind and reed instruments.

Aluminium bronzes (C95) contain up to 12% aluminium and are the strongest of the copper alloys, with excellent resistance to corrosion. Below 11% aluminium, the alloy retains an FCC structure, which helps to maintain ductility without loss of strength. Quenching (rapidly cooling) results in the formation of BCC structure, which is harder and more brittle. Tempering (heating and cooling) maintains the

FCC structure. The designation for wrought types is C61 to C64 and for cast types is C95. They have a bright golden colour and resist tarnishing thanks to the protective alumina layer that builds up on the surface through oxidization. They are used to make corrosion-resistant vessels and structural parts, propellers, pipe fittings and bearings, for example.

Nickel silvers (C7 through C79 and C96 through C97), also known as cupronickel, have good mechanical properties and excellent corrosion resistance. These properties improve as nickel content is

**Bronze marine propeller** This four-blade propeller, manufactured by Clements Engineering in the UK, is fabricated from AB2. This aluminium bronze alloy is the most commonly used for castings of this type, because it offers exceptional resistance to seawater corrosion and is known for its high strength, and shock and wear

resistance. Shaped by sand casting, it is machined and polished to precise tolerances to ensure maximum efficiency under water. Manganese bronze and stainless steel are used to a lesser extent. While these alternatives provide some benefits compared to aluminium bronze, they are less resistant to corrosion and so require more frequent maintenance.

**Left**
**Machined pencil sharpener** This pencil sharpener from M+R in Germany is cut from solid brass on a lathe. Long bars are produced, cut to length, and the holes and other details milled. The diamond- knurled edge finish is applied by cutting grooves into the surface as the part is rotated on the lathe. The blade is stamped from high-carbon steel, hardened through quenching and ground to a sharp edge.

**Opposite**
**Hand-beaten pendant light** This brass shade, created by British product design brand Tom Dixon, is spun to the correct shape and then hand-beaten. Using hammering to shape the item has three principal benefits: it strengthens the material, hides defects and creates an irregular surface pattern. Through the use of these techniques, the handicraft industry in Moradabad (Uttar Pradesh district, India), where these are produced, is responsible for much of India's brassware; the design makes reference to traditional brass pots and vessels. The inside is lacquered to retain a bright and lustrous colour, and the outside is blackened with patination.

increased. Nickel affects the colour: from around 15% the alloy becomes silvery-white and at 40% it is indistinguishable from silver, hence the name. Alloys with two-thirds copper retain an FCC structure and so are suitable for cold working; higher quantities of alloy result in the formation of a two-phase (duplex) structure. All types are suitable for casting and machining and they are straightforward to fabricate. Traditionally they have been used to make packaging, stationery, tableware, jewelry and other decorative items. Nowadays applications include food and beverage equipment, springs, musical instruments, marine parts and architectural sections.

## SUSTAINABILITY

Copper is derived from sulphide and oxide ores and the typical concentration is 0.5–1%. In other words, it takes 1 tonne or more of ore to produce 1 kg (2.2 lb) of copper. Through a series of grinding, floating, smelting and roasting processes the impurities are gradually removed and the concentration increased to

99%. Because of the large amount of waste produced, processing facilities are typically located near the mines and can have significant adverse impacts on air quality, surface and groundwater quality, and the land. Companies must follow strict guidelines, which helps to minimize pollution and loss of biodiversity.

Copper is fully recyclable and retains all of its properties. Furthermore, recycling copper saves around 85% of the energy needed to produce primary metal. However, it is often alloyed, which makes reuse a little more complicated, because many applications cannot tolerate any impurities. For example, electrical wiring and cables are produced from virgin copper to ensure the highest level of conductivity. For non-electrical applications, a higher proportion of recycled copper can be used.

In most cases it is not economically viable to remove alloyed elements and other impurities (such as solder). Therefore, virgin copper is mixed in during smelting to reduce the proportion of impurities to an acceptable level.

## COPPER, BRASS AND BRONZE IN PRODUCTS, FURNITURE AND LIGHTING

Whether in the form of wiring, connectors or heating elements, the majority of applications make use of the superior conductivity coupled with the very good corrosion resistance of copper. In the past, these functions have been largely hidden from view. Recent innovations in inkjet technology have made it possible to apply copper circuitry to transparent and flexible polyethylene terephthalate (PET, polyester) film (page 152). This solution is much more cost-effective than previous flexible circuit materials, such as polyimide. In addition, PET film coated with acrylic may be printed with graphics. This has created a wide range of design opportunities outside the conventional areas of application for copper circuitry, including wearable technology, disposable packaging and large area electronics.

Copper alloys can be shaped in a number of different ways, making them perhaps one of the most versatile metals. Copper retains its very good ductility until alloys account for one-third or more of

the metal. At this point, a two-phase structure is formed, which consists of face- and body-centred cubic arrangements. Up until this point, copper alloys are suitable for cold-working processes, such as spinning, pressing, bending and deep drawing. These techniques are widely used in the manufacture of products, furniture and lighting. For example, items with a constant wall thickness, such as plates, bowls, dishes, tumblers and light shades, are all made using these techniques.

Copper alloys are very efficient to shape by milling or lathing. While the primary metal can be several times more expensive than steel (pure copper is up to around 10 times more expensive than steel for the same weight), it is so much more efficient to machine than steel that the unit price can work out lower for copper alloy when large quantities are produced.

Casting is used to manufacture complex parts, and those with internal features, such as door handles, fixtures, faucets and other plumbing components. While low volumes of parts are sand cast, large volumes are manufactured by investment casting or pressure die casting. Brass and bronze are suitable for very high-quality items, because they are durable, strong and corrosion-resistant, and can be polished to a very good finish. Exposed surfaces are inherently antimicrobial, a property that is particularly beneficial in door handles. Alternatively, the surface is painted or plated to provide the desired physical and visual properties.

The price of bronze depends on the alloy: tin is much more expensive than aluminium. So, even though it has superior mechanical properties to brass in

## PRODUCTS, FURNITURE AND LIGHTING

**High perceived value**
While copper alloys provide a lower-cost alternative to gold and silver in certain applications, they are considered very desirable in their own right. Depending on the alloy, the colour ranges from red to silver to gold.

**Corrosion resistance**
Over time, the surface oxidizes and in doing so protects the metal below. The colour of the oxide layer depends on the alloy.

**Machinability**
Copper alloys are much quicker and more cost-effective to machine than steel. The addition of small amounts of lead in certain brasses, known as 'free-cutting', further improves this property.

**Conductivity**
Copper is a very efficient conductor, with twice the conductivity of aluminium alloy.

---

many respects, bronze is not economically viable in most cases. Tin bronze continues to be used for sculpture and statues, even though it is around twice as expensive, thanks to the desirable colour of patina that develops on its surface.

Zinc alloys (page 78) provide a less expensive alternative to brass and bronze in many cast applications, including household equipment, automotive parts, hardware and toys. It has excellent casting qualities, but lacks the tensile strength, stiffness and durability of copper alloy equivalents.

In the case of plumbing components, leaded brass has been largely replaced by lead-free brass (or alternative) to help improve water quality. For example, in the case of EnviroBrass (C89 through C95) lead is substituted with selenium and bismuth. Alloyed with copper, these provide many of the same benefits to production as lead.

## COPPER, BRASS AND BRONZE IN COOKWARE

While copper is an excellent conductor, the surface is prone to scratching and will dissolve in certain foods, which can affect taste. The cooking surface is therefore often tin-plated or laminated with stainless steel to prevent this. Alternatively, copper is used solely for

the base, where heat transfer efficiency is most important.

To make the most of copper in cookware, the wall thickness must be sufficient to allow heat to transfer. In other words, a plated-copper coating will not be as effective as sheet copper. This means that copper pots and pans tend to be quite heavy, because copper is around three times denser than aluminium and 25% denser than steel or cast iron. Heavy-use copper pans generally have a wall thickness of around 2.5 mm (0.1 in). For less demanding applications the wall thickness need be only around 1.5 mm (0.06 in).

Shallow and hemispherical parts are pressed from sheet. Deep parts, in particular where the height exceeds the diameter, such as pots and pans, are produced by spinning. Deep drawing is also suitable for straight-walled parts, but is rarely used in cookware because of the high volumes required to justify the tooling costs.

## COPPER, BRASS AND BRONZE IN FASHION AND TEXTILES

Copper is incorporated into textiles as a filament, as an electroplated coating or as an additive in synthetic fibres. Applications range from fashion to medical to architectural.

## COOKWARE

**Conductivity**
Copper has the highest heat transfer of any material used in cooking – twice that of aluminium and several times more efficient than steel or cast iron – and so is less prone to developing hot spots, thereby helping to cook evenly.

**Corrosion resistance**
The surface of copper oxidizes to form a protective layer that resists further corrosion. Over time, copper pans

will become reddish-brown – unless of course used with alkali or acidic ingredients, which will clean the copper to a bright reddish-pink.

**Durability**
It is robust and around twice as hard as and three times heavier than aluminium for the same cross-section. However, it is not as durable as stainless steel, which has higher strength-to-weight and surface hardness.

**Laminated copper cookware**
Established in 1830 in Normandy, France, Mauviel make some of the finest copper cookware. This robust saucepan, measuring 2.5 mm (0.1 in) thick, is lined with a thin layer of high-quality austenitic 18/10 stainless steel. The two metals are laminated prior to spinning. This provides the optimum cooking surface encapsulated within the highly conductive copper exterior. The bronze handles are joined with rivets. Bronze is not the most efficient conductor, and so heats up more slowly than the rest of the pan.

**Above**
**Bronze cladding**
The Archives départementales in Lyon, France, by Gautier+Conquet & associés, features a copper-aluminium alloy envelope. This cladding is well suited to large area applications thanks to its unique material properties. Completed in 2014, the bright golden surface has mellowed to a warm gold-coloured finish that is exceptionally durable. Photo courtesy of Gautier+Conquet & associés.

**Left**
**Brass dress**  The decorative properties of brass are used in embroidery, lace and upholstery. This dress by Pauline van Dongen is fabricated from Inntex knitted brass (Dream11). The wire has a rich gold colour that will darken with age; the knitted construction allows it to drape around the wearer. At 250 g/m² (10 oz/yd²), it is no heavier than regular garment fabric, but has a unique tactility. As well as being utilized in luxury fashion, it is suitable for interior fabrics and laminating with glass (page 508). Photo by Mike Nicolaassen; courtesy of Inntex.

fibres. Electroplating copper onto a base fabric takes advantage of many of the benefits while reducing the drawbacks. For example, copper-plated polyamide (PA, nylon) (page 164) is sufficiently conductive to provide a barrier against electrostatic charges and electromagnetic radiation, the predominant use of copper in textiles.

Copper textile is utilized in electrical circuitry, and just like wiring it can be soldered to form strong conductive joins. Bare copper tends to be avoided in applications that have close skin contact. This is mainly because copper oxidizes, eventually turning dark reddish-brown through green. When it comes into contact with sweat and lotions the tarnish will rub off on its surroundings. Therefore, copper textiles and finishes are often plated (such as with silver, tin or cobalt) or coated. Using a clear coating will maintain the characteristic reddish-pink colour of copper.

As an additive its antibacterial and antifungal properties are used in odour-free textiles and the treatment of wounds and skin diseases. In such applications copper is in direct competition with silver (page 84). Several companies have taken advantage of this fact and produce copper-impregnated fabrics including clothing, upholstery and bedding. However, copper is a broad-spectrum antimicrobial, and so even though it makes up a fundamental (albeit minute) part of our diet, the health implications of long-term exposure to copper in clothing and bedding are not yet fully understood. As a result, there are mixed opinions about whether copper fabrics should be used in skin-contact fabrics, in particular in hospitals, where they

Copper filament used in textiles typically ranges from 0.2 mm to around 1 mm (0.01–0.04 in) in diameter. It is incorporated as a continuous length, twisted with existing yarn, or chopped into shorter lengths and incorporated into staple yarn.

Metallic textiles have many advantages but tend to be much stiffer, heavier and more expensive than conventional flexible

## FASHION AND TEXTILES

**Conductive**
It is utilized in textiles designed to provide a barrier against electrostatic charges and electromagnetic radiation. And just like conventional wiring, it can be used as part of a circuit.

**Antimicrobial**
Like silver, copper demonstrates antibacterial and antifungal properties. Microbes are inhibited or destroyed through interaction with copper ions.

**Malleable**
While copper is soft and flexible enough to be woven, knitted and embroidered, its stiffness allows textiles to be shaped and creased.

**Decorative**
Newly formed copper has a distinctive reddish-pink lustre, which is maintained with the application of a clear coating. Alternatively, it is colour-coated or electroplated.

## ARCHITECTURE AND CONSTRUCTION

**Corrosion resistance**
Copper performs very well outdoors and in most climatic conditions, quickly developing a protective oxide film. The colour changes as the film progresses through its weathering cycle.

**Colour range**
Copper and its alloys are available in a variety of durable pre-patinated colours, from gold through black.

**Durability**
Copper has endured to become a familiar and characteristic part of the built environment.

**Ease of fabrication**
A wide variety of cold-working techniques is utilized, such as rolling, stamping and drawing. Hot forming processes include forging and extrusion. Parts are joined with soldering, brazing and welding.

**Conductivity**
Copper's high electrical conductivity is utilized in the construction of enclosures designed to reduce the transmission of electrical or magnetic fields.

could help reduce the spread of harmful microbes. Of course, this is not a concern for fabrics that do not have a great deal of skin contact, such as curtains, screens and cloths.

### COPPER, BRASS AND BRONZE IN ARCHITECTURE AND CONSTRUCTION

Copper, brass, bronze and nickel silver are utilized inside and outside. From skyscrapers to churches, copper is used for a variety of architectural elements, including roofs, cladding and drainage. Inside buildings it is used to decorate walls and ceilings, as well as for all the componentry of a building, such as plumbing, wiring and furnishing.

While the unit price of copper is comparable with titanium (page 58) and high compared to zinc, it has the advantage of a wide range of natural colours. Spanning from reddish-pink, through gold, brown and black, virgin metal has a bright finish that matures as the oxide layer develops. Clear coatings are used to maintain the original

colour. Alternatively, the natural patina is allowed to develop – through the natural weathering cycle – to form a tough corrosion-resistant surface that will last for decades, or even centuries, with minimal maintenance. Natural weathering is a gradual and predictable process that yields buildings with unique characteristics peculiar to their local environment.

This enduring characteristic has been employed by generations of architects, from ancient Egypt to some of the most dramatic new structures. Alloys with a high proportion of copper start out bright reddish-pink. This quickly darkens to shades of plum and chocolate-brown. It takes many years for untreated copper to develop its typically green patina. As a result, modern copper components are sometimes chemically treated to yield the desired colour from the outset. This is also useful for carrying out repairs to existing copper structures.

Brass has improved mechanical properties at a lower price than pure copper. Starting out bright gold – the exact colour depends on the alloy – it gradually develops a warm brown patina. Tin bronze gradually turns from its raw reddish-brown colour to a uniform dark brown. Aluminium bronze has perhaps the most striking colour: it starts bright gold and gradually turns to a warm golden colour. Compared to pure copper, the weathering cycle occurs much more slowly with certain alloys.

Copper is very malleable and so is easily formed, a useful property for intricate geometries. Cold rolling is used to increase stiffness and produce copper sheet suitable for roofs, cladding

and guttering. While alloys with a high proportion of copper are extremely ductile and easily formed, brasses and bronzes are stiffer and stronger, a property that improves as the proportion of alloyed elements is increased.

Copper alloys are available in rolled or extruded sections, as well as forged components, which extends application opportunities through the interior and exterior of buildings.

The choice of joining technique is determined by the requirements of the application. Copper alloys are versatile and compatible with thermal, mechanical and adhesive techniques. Soldering and brazing are popular, especially

**Weathering cycle of untreated copper**
With exposure to atmosphere, the surface of copper oxidizes and in doing so changes colour. The speed depends on acidity; the process is faster in some metropolitan, marine and industrial areas. Starting out a bright reddish-pink, in just a few months the colour turns to dark reddish-brown. Over the next 10 years or so, depending on the local climate, it will become a characteristic copper-green. The colour gradually lightens over time as the oxide layer reaches an equilibrium with the local conditions.

for plumbing and electrical work, because they form a strong watertight metallurgical bond. Construction methods rely on a combination of solder – for sealing – with mechanical fasteners. Long continuous seams of solder are best avoided, because they are prone to fracture when stressed by the expansion and contraction of the metalwork. In such cases, adhesive is preferable.

With careful planning, weathering is used to enhance a building's appearance over time. A major consideration for long-term applications is the potential for galvanic corrosion with neighbouring metals. Metals with a lower galvanic number – in particular aluminium and

zinc – will be eroded when in direct contact with copper. The electrochemical process is facilitated by rainwater, or even moisture in the air, which acts as an electrolyte. While the metal with the higher galvanic number acts as the cathode, the lower becomes the anode and is subsequently dissolved. When used together, metals with greater relative difference in nobility must be insulated to prevent this. Under most circumstances, it is not necessary to separate copper from stainless steel, tin or lead.

Rainwater run-off from copper surfaces affects neighbouring materials too. Copper salts are dissolved and then absorbed by porous materials further

**Lost-wax cast-bronze sculpture** Created by sculptor Alfred Hardiman in 1936, this is one of two heraldic lions that guard Norwich City Hall, England. Over the years a variegated green patina (verdigris) has developed on the surface of the bronze. The chemical reaction is driven by the local weather conditions. In another location, the colour, pattern and speed of change would be different.

down the building, such as marble (see Stone, page 482). In the case of pure copper this will result in green stains, which are particularly visible on light-coloured surfaces. Copper alloys will produce different effects. For example, leaded copper will result in black stains.

# Zinc

**Also known as**
Chemical symbol: Zn
Common alloy names: RHEINZINK, Zintek, VMZINC,
Zamak, ZA

**The metal of choice for many die-cast components, zinc offers a good combination of strength, ductility, impact resistance and finishing. Even though it is not the cheapest, its relatively low price means that it competes with aluminium, steel and even thermoplastics in some cases. Much zinc goes into galvanizing and plating for corrosion protection; and it is a useful alloy.**

| Types | Typical Applications | Sustainability |
|---|---|---|
| • Pure zinc or special high grade (SHG) <br> • Zinc alloy | • Consumer products, kitchenware and bathroom fittings <br> • Galvanizing and plating <br> • Cladding and worktops | • Mining is energy-intensive and polluting <br> • Construction material is often reused and it is efficient to recycle |
| **Properties** | **Competing Materials** | **Costs** |
| • High fluidity when molten <br> • High corrosion resistance <br> • Readily tarnishes | • Aluminium, copper, titanium and steel <br> • Engineering thermoplastics, in particular PP, PA and PC | • Low to moderate <br> • Manufacturing costs are low |

## INTRODUCTION

From its inclusion in brass (page 66) to its use in protecting steel (page 28) from corrosion, zinc has played an important supporting role in the history of civilization and of industry, and remains fundamental to the success of modern transportation and construction. It is also used as a metal in its own right, such as in die-cast consumer products, counter tops and cladding.

The metal starts out with a bright bluish-silvery-white appearance. The dark blue-grey tarnish that forms on the surface – zinc carbonate – is the result of the surface reacting with water and carbon dioxide and protects the metal beneath. In normal conditions zinc loses around 1 micron per year. Therefore, even zinc sheet less than 1 mm (0.04 in) thick will last more than half a century.

## COMMERCIAL TYPES AND USES

Sheet zinc is produced in a continuous casting and rolling process. Primary zinc is graded from Z1 through Z5 according to the proportion of other elements. Z1 is the highest grade and contains 99.995% zinc; Z5 consists of about 1.5% other elements.

It is often alloyed to improve specific properties and sold under trademark names. For example, VMZINC, RHEINZINK and Zintek consist of small amounts of other elements, such as copper, titanium and aluminium (ZN-Cu-Ti-Al), to improve strength and resistance to stress, as well as reducing the coefficient of thermal expansion (useful in cladding) – that

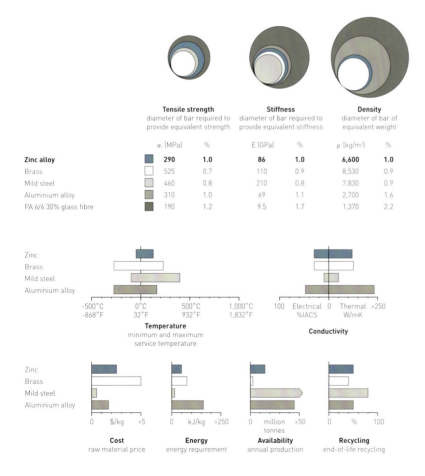

| | Tensile strength <br> diameter of bar required to provide equivalent strength | | Stiffness <br> diameter of bar required to provide equivalent stiffness | | Density <br> diameter of bar of equivalent weight | |
|---|---|---|---|---|---|---|
| | σ. (MPa) | % | E (GPa) | % | ρ (kg/m³) | % |
| Zinc alloy | 290 | 1.0 | 86 | 1.0 | 6,600 | 1.0 |
| Brass | 525 | 0.7 | 110 | 0.9 | 8,530 | 0.9 |
| Mild steel | 460 | 0.8 | 210 | 0.8 | 7,830 | 0.9 |
| Aluminium alloy | 310 | 1.0 | 69 | 1.1 | 2,700 | 1.6 |
| PA 6/6 30% glass fibre | 190 | 1.2 | 9.5 | 1.7 | 1,370 | 2.2 |

**Die-cast zinc handle**
The handle of the Stanley 99E retractable blade knife is zinc. The excellent castability of zinc means that fixtures, graphics and other details are incorporated; minimizing secondary processes. The design of the handle, combined with zinc's balance of strength and stiffness, means a single central fixing point is adequate to hold the two halves securely together.

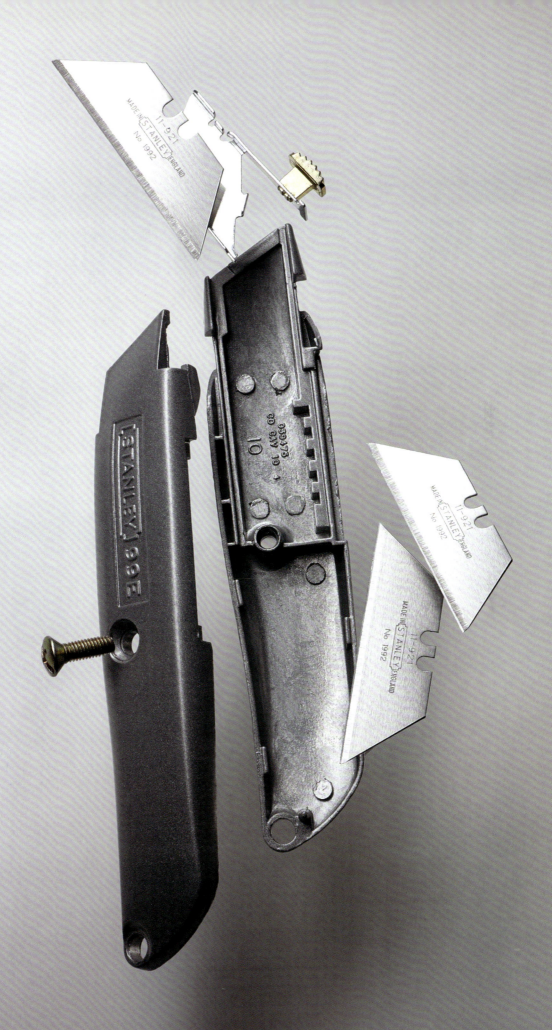

is, the change in length or volume of material per unit change in temperature.

There are two principal families of casting alloy: Zamak and ZA. While the former contains around 4% aluminium and has excellent castability, ZA alloys (also called Zn-Al) contain more aluminium and offer superior strength. The aluminium content for ZA-8, -12 and -27 is around 8.5, 11 and 26.5% respectively. Tensile strength and hardness are increased at the expense of elongation and impact strength. ZA-12 is comparable with cast iron (page 22): it has slightly lower strength and density. The advantage of zinc is that it has higher fluidity and so can be cast into parts with thinner wall sections and finer details.

Zamak 3 (or zinc alloy #3) is widely used thanks to its balance of strength and elongation. Zamak 7 (or zinc alloy #7) is a higher-purity version of #3 with improved castability, ductility and surface finish. However, this means it flashes more readily (the molten zinc flows into all the crevices of the mold, including through the gap between the mold halves). Zamak 5 (or zinc alloy #5) has higher copper content, which provides higher tensile strength. Compared to #3 it has lower ductility but improved finishing and machining properties.

Zinc's hexagonal close-packed crystal structure (similar to magnesium, see page 56) limits the amount of plastic deformation that can be achieved, such as through pressing and forging.

## SUSTAINABILITY

Zinc is mined in large quantities around the world. The principal ore is the zinc sulphide mineral called sphalerite. This is crushed into a fine powder and the minerals are separated from gangue (surrounding material) by froth flotation. Used in the processing of many metals, flotation relies on the different hydrophobicity of minerals. The zinc-bearing mineral forms froth on the surface, which is skimmed off. At this point, the concentrate contains around 50% zinc along with elements such as copper, lead and iron. It is roasted in a blast furnace (smelted) and the zinc extracted through chemical treatment

## PRODUCTS AND FURNITURE

### Castability
Zinc's relatively low melting point (420°C [788°F]) and low viscosity when molten make it an extremely efficient metal to cast. More complex geometries and thinner wall sections are achievable than with other structural alloys.

### Surface finish
As a result of its high fluidity and relatively low die shrinkage, zinc castings have superior surface finish, which helps to make preparation for painting and plating relatively easy.

### Impact strength
It has good ductility and elongation, which together provide very good resistance to impact.

(sulphuric acid) or by smelting with carbon (this is very energy-intensive and so not as common). Production results in air emissions, waste and hazardous by-products. While a great deal is collected, processed and repurposed, zinc mining overall has a detrimental effect on the environment.

Zinc is fully recyclable and is recovered wherever possible. High-quality scrap from die casting, cladding and other zinc-rich sources is relatively straightforward to identify and so can be directly reused. It is recaptured from industrial processes too, such as steel galvanizing furnaces.

The majority of industrial zinc goes into galvanizing and plating steel. Steel reclaimed from construction is often reused, and the zinc coating ensures its longevity. Where this is not practical the zinc and steel are separated electrochemically and recycled separately.

## ZINC IN PRODUCTS AND FURNITURE

As a result of its low viscosity and low die shrinkage, zinc castings are net shape (within precise tolerances) and require little or no machining. The excellent surface finish is enhanced with plating and painting. Zinc is commonly used for kitchen and bathroom parts that have the finished appearance of gold (page 90), brass or steel.

Zinc is compatible with virtually every casting process, the most commonly used being high-pressure die casting. This technique is only really suitable for high volumes owing to the cost of tooling. It is used to produce high-quality thin-walled precise parts, such as consumer

products, kitchen equipment, door and window hardware, and taps and bathroom fixtures.

Zinc's excellent castability, coupled with its mechanical properties, places it in direct competition with aluminium (page 42) as well as injection-molded engineering thermoplastics in many cases, in particular polyamide (PA, nylon) (page 164), polycarbonate (PC) (page 144) and polypropylene (PP) (page 98). However, it has relatively high density and so is not suitable for applications where lightness is critical.

Zinc cannot be used in applications that go much above 100°C (212°F) owing to loss of strength and hardness. In fact, zinc will creep (deform gradually under stress) even at room temperature.

## ZINC IN ARCHITECTURE AND CONSTRUCTION

Around half of all zinc goes into construction. It is mostly used for galvanizing and plating steel, the most commonly used metal in construction, followed by aluminium. Similar to copper (page 66) and titanium (page 58), and particularly in Europe, zinc is applied as cladding. With exposure to the atmosphere it develops a distinctive blue-grey finish. It is often alloyed with small amounts of copper, titanium and aluminium, which affect the colour of patina that develops on the surface.

Zinc is prone to corrosion in the presence of moisture when there is no carbon dioxide to help form the patina. Zinc hydroxide (also known as white rust) forms on the surface, which deteriorates the zinc much like rust

**Die-cast zinc kitchen appliance housing** The KitchenAid mixer, which is renowned for its durability and longevity, relies on a housing constructed primarily from die-cast Zamak #3 alloy. Zinc has many qualities that make it an ideal choice for such an application. It provides a good balance of mechanical properties, excellent castability and high- quality surface finish. Its density and vibration damping properties help to provide stability. Die casting ensures the minimum amount of machining (just critical parts and surfaces), which helps to keep down costs. And the cast surface is finished with a gloss coating, which provides functional benefits as well as aesthetic appeal.

## ARCHITECTURE AND CONSTRUCTION

**Corrosion resistance**
In the form of galvanizing, zinc provides a continuous impervious metallic layer on the surface of steel, which prevents it from corroding. If scratched, the steel continues to be protected, because the zinc will corrode preferentially – in other words, zinc in the vicinity will corrode in place of the exposed steel. This phenomenon is referred to as sacrificial or cathodic protection.

**Non-toxic**
Unlike copper, the run-off from zinc is completely clear and does not harm surrounding vegetation. It does not stain or corrode materials with which it is in contact.

**Formability**
Sheet materials are malleable and relatively easily formed. This is especially useful for cladding and guttering systems assembled on-site.

**Low cost**
As a building material it requires minimal maintenance and in normal conditions will last 80 to 100 years before it needs replacing.

**Reuse and recyclability**
It is estimated that around 95% of rolled zinc is recovered each year in Europe.

**Above and opposite**
**Zinc cladding** The Leaning House, located near Seoul in South Korea, was designed by PRAUD architects and completed in 2014. The tilted design offers the maximum exposure to daylight and surrounding views. All sides of the 'box' have been treated the same and clad with zinc. The strips are joined with a standing seam: the architects have made use of the functional and visual qualities of this lightweight construction method. The sides of each strip are closed with a mechanical seam over supporting halters, and so no external penetrations are required, which ensures superior weather protection. Photos by Kyungsub Shin.

does steel. To prevent this, the backside of panels, cladding and guttering is coated. Another consideration is that zinc expands considerably in warm weather, around twice as much as steel. Therefore, assembly systems such as the standing seam (in which sheets of zinc are joined along their edge by folding one over the other, resulting in a seam that stands perpendicular to the roof; see image above) are utilized to allow movement and so avoid the zinc bowing or buckling.

Zinc is prone to galvanic corrosion (corrodes preferentially in the presence of other metals) when used in contact with, or when receiving rainwater run-off from, copper alloys, iron or steel. (Galvanized steel will be not be affected.) It is also not recommended to use zinc in contact with materials that have a pH lower than 5 or above 7. This includes certain woods, such as larch (page 310), oak (page 342), chestnut (page 346), birch (page 334), cedar (Cypress, page 318), and Douglas-

fir (page 314), among others. Woods including pine and spruce (page 304) and poplar (page 324) are fine.

Zinc coating protects steel by providing an impervious barrier and through cathodic action (see box above). Coating selection depends on the part and application. The conventional process of hot-dip galvanizing is used for large parts and assemblies. It is used to produce a thick coating – upwards of 50 microns – and so is ideal for parts that will be

**Natural**    **Pre-weathered grey**    **Pre-weathered black**

**Examples of mineral pigment colours**

**Zinc colour options**

Zinc cladding is available with a natural colour finish (dull blue-grey) or pre-weathered. When used for counter tops and interior applications it is typically left un-weathered. On the outside of buildings, pre-weathering offers greater choice of colour and finish. Adding mineral pigments (for application inside or outside) creates an even broader range of colour options, which develop a unique appearance as their patina matures.

exposed outdoors for decades, or even centuries. The steel is passed through a series of baths to degrease and clean the surface in preparation. Galvanizing takes place in a bath of molten zinc, which flows around the details of the part to ensure a thorough coating. On contact the hot zinc forms a metallurgical bond with the steel that is impervious to moisture. It rapidly loses its shine through tarnishing, turning matt grey.

In a slightly modified version of this process, galvanized parts are spun in sieves to remove excess zinc. This technique is used to finish smaller items, in particular bolts and fixings.

Sheet steel (and wire) is coated in a continuous high-speed process. Lengths are fed through progressive baths at up to 200 m (655 ft) per minute. Coating thickness is precisely controlled using an air knife (formed by a high-pressure, uniform sheet of laminar airflow) as the steel exits the galvanizing bath. Galvanized sheet is cut, pressed and fabricated like uncoated steel. This makes it a very economical method of long-term

corrosion protection. High-aluminium zinc alloys (also known as Galvalloy and AX alloys) provide improved corrosion resistance at the expense of formability. These are used mainly in coastal areas and for automotive and transportation.

Thermal spraying is used for large structures unsuitable for dipping and can achieve coatings up to 200 microns thick. It is slightly porous, but very durable owing to the amount of zinc laid down. Electroplating or mechanical plating techniques are used for small parts, such as mechanical fasteners. In the case of mechanical plating, the parts are placed into a rotating drum with zinc powder and glass beads. As they are tumbled the zinc is hammered onto the surface.

In some cases, zinc powder is added to paint and applied by spraying. The metals do not form a metallurgical bond, but the zinc still provides cathodic protection. Alternatively, powder coating or painting is applied over hot-dip galvanizing. This two-layer system provides superior protection and allows a range of colours and finishes to be achieved.

# Silver

**Silver has many desirable properties that make it as valuable to industry as to silversmiths. It is malleable, reflective and highly conductive. In addition, it has inherent antimicrobial properties, which are utilized in applications ranging from odour-beating sportswear to hygienic surfaces. It is expensive and applied as plating to make use of its bright and beautiful appearance.**

| Types | Typical Applications | Sustainability |
|---|---|---|
| • Pure silver<br>• Sterling silver (92.5%), Britannia silver (95.8%), Mexican silver (95%), Argentium silver (93.5–96%) and coin silver (90%) | • Electronics<br>• Medical<br>• Jewelry and textiles<br>• Tableware and ornaments | • The majority of silver is produced as a by-product of copper, lead and gold extraction<br>• It is fully recyclable |

| Properties | Competing Materials | Costs |
|---|---|---|
| • Superior conductivity<br>• Highly reflective<br>• Malleable<br>• Resistant to corrosion | • Gold and platinum<br>• Copper and nickel silver<br>• Aluminized PET film | • Expensive, but still only a fraction of the cost of gold and platinum |

84

## INTRODUCTION

Silver has long played an important role in our lives. Like gold (page 90), it has historically been used for coinage and ceremonial items. In fact, the two were often mixed in the same alloy. It continues to be used for items of great significance and importance such as jewelry, tableware and ornaments. In recent years, the unique properties of silver have proved advantageous for a range of modern technologies, from photovoltaic cells to wearable sensors.

Silver is a noble metal, like gold and platinum. This means that it is relatively stable and resistant to corrosion. Over time and with exposure to the atmosphere, silver reacts to form a dark layer of silver sulphide. On bare surfaces the metal's bright lustre is maintained by polishing.

## COMMERCIAL TYPES AND USES

Silver that is 99.9% pure is designated as 999 and referred to as fine silver. It is very malleable – although not as soft as gold – and so alloys have been developed to make it stronger and suitable for a broader range of applications. Pure silver is applied as plating, such as onto cutlery, flatware and ornaments. It is highly reflective and silvery-white.

Sterling silver contains 7.5% copper (page 66). Silver is alloyed with other metals, but copper is most commonly used in jewelry, tableware and ornaments, because it provides the optimum balance of strength and formability. As a result of the copper content, polishing yields a greater depth of colour than pure silver, and over time the surface develops a patina of scratches and wear. For identification, the number of parts of fine silver per thousand indicates purity. Thus, sterling silver is marked 925 and one containing 80% would be marked 800.

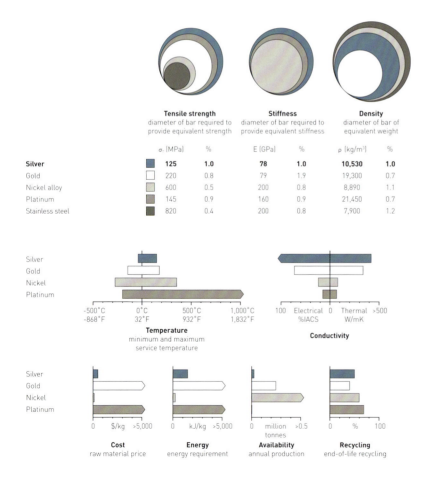

|  | Tensile strength<br>diameter of bar required to provide equivalent strength | | Stiffness<br>diameter of bar required to provide equivalent stiffness | | Density<br>diameter of bar of equivalent weight | |
|---|---|---|---|---|---|---|
|  | $\sigma$. [MPa] | % | E [GPa] | % | $\rho$ [kg/m³] | % |
| Silver | 125 | 1.0 | 78 | 1.0 | 10,530 | 1.0 |
| Gold | 220 | 0.8 | 79 | 1.9 | 19,300 | 0.7 |
| Nickel alloy | 600 | 0.5 | 200 | 0.8 | 8,890 | 1.1 |
| Platinum | 145 | 0.9 | 160 | 0.9 | 21,450 | 0.7 |
| Stainless steel | 820 | 0.4 | 200 | 0.8 | 7,900 | 1.2 |

**Temperature**
minimum and maximum service temperature

**Conductivity**

**Cost**
raw material price

**Energy**
energy requirement

**Availability**
annual production

**Recycling**
end-of-life recycling

Other than sterling silver, popular types include Britannia silver (95.84% fine silver), Mexican silver (the fine silver content has fluctuated over the years, but has always been above 92.5%), Argentium silver (a trademark name for a group of alloys manufactured from recycled content with 93.5 to 96% fine silver) and coin silver (around 90% fine silver). Like sterling silver, each type is identified by the fine silver content in parts per thousand, such as 958 for Britannia.

Silver's combination of corrosion resistance and high conductivity – its electrical conductivity surpasses that of copper – is utilized in rigid and flexible electronics alike. It is plated onto connectors and switches to improve efficiency, and integrated into textiles to allow them to sense and conduct electricity. Silver-palladium is screen-printed to make circuit paths (although the rising cost of palladium has reduced this type of application in recent years), while silver powder is the main precursor of the conductive paste used in photovoltaic cells.

As a coating its high reflectivity (95%), in particular of the infrared part of the spectrum, is utilized in telescopes and solar power collectors (the sun's rays are focused onto collectors containing salts,

**Repoussé and chasing**
Traditional silverware from Borneo is shaped by hand utilizing the metal's malleability and ductility. Repoussé is the art of hammering metal on the reverse side to form a relief design; and chasing is hammering from the front side to refine the design and sharpen the details. A pliable backing or support is sometimes used (known as chaser's pitch) to beat onto or into, and improves the accuracy of thin sheet work by reducing the area affected by each tap of the hammer. Repoussé and chasing are an ancient and slow process, but very economical and versatile. Depending on the skill of the silversmith, complex and delicate pieces can be achieved. As well as silver, metals including steel, copper alloy and gold are formed in this way.

which are then used to run generators). This same quality is utilized in window coatings, to reduce solar energy absorbed by modern buildings by up to 95%. In the past, mirrors were made by silver-coating glass (page 508). Known as silvering, it is still used today in the production of high-end mirrors and tableware. If left exposed to the atmosphere, silver quickly develops a dark tarnish. Therefore, it is coated on the backside of a transparent material or protected with a clear coating.

It is now much more common to use vacuum-deposited aluminium coatings (see page 45) for reflective surfaces, because it is much less expensive and the protective oxide that develops on the surface is transparent and so does not affect optical quality.

Like copper, silver is inherently antimicrobial: the ions interrupt bacteria cells' chemical bonds. On a practical level, this means food and liquid stored in silver containers will stay fresher for longer. There are medical benefits too. For example, silver is embedded in wound dressings to help with hygiene and promote healing. As well as a straightforward additive, it is used as a biocide against microbes that present a serious health risk, including the infamous methicillin-resistant *Staphylococcus aureus* (MRSA). In recent years, consumer product manufacturers have begun to incorporate silver nanoparticles in plastic, synthetic fibres and coatings to take advantage of the antibacterial and antifungal properties. Applications range from refrigerators and air-conditioning units to sportswear.

Sterling silver cutlery and flatware is fashioned from solid silver in much the same way as stainless steel (page 28). Nickel silver (copper alloy) is used as

**Silver-plated clothing**
Created by New York-based ARJUNA.AG, the hoodie was inspired by the multidimensional protective properties of silver. It is constructed from polyamide elastomer (page 164) and coated with 18% by weight silver.

While its conductivity shields against electromagnetic radiation, its antimicrobial properties defend against bacteria. The silver will tarnish over time, gradually becoming darker. Photo courtesy of ARJUNA.AG.

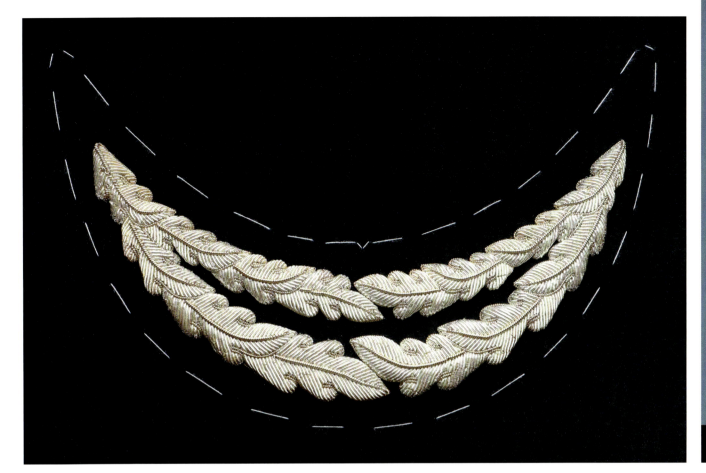

the base metal for plated-silver pieces, because its appearance closely matches that of sterling silver. While stainless-steel and nickel-silver cutlery is mass-producible, sterling silver items continue to be made by hand.

## SUSTAINABILITY
Silver occurs in many mineral forms, such as combined with lead, copper or gold. In the extraction of these metals silver is produced as a by-product. The method of separation depends on the type of ore and typically involves electrolysis or chemical reaction. Even though silver is a by-product, its embodied energy is largely determined by the negative impact of these metals, and several harmful chemicals are used, including mercury and cyanide. Process efficiency depends on the ore. For example, silver-bearing lead sulphide (galena) yields around 1 kg (2.2 lb) of silver for every tonne of ore.

As a result of its high value, silver is recycled where possible. This helps to reduce the overall impact. However, owing to the broad range of applications and

### FASHION AND TEXTILES

**Reflective**
Silver is one of the most highly reflective metals, with a silvery-white appearance. However, its shiny appearance is short-lived, because it readily tarnishes when exposed to sunlight and atmosphere.

**Formability**
It is malleable and so can be worked by hand without breaking.

**Conductivity**
Its superior conductivity is utilized in textiles to make an electrical circuit, and to shield against electromagnetic radiation and electrostatic charges.

variety of ways it is used – the majority of silver is used for industrial applications – it is not always practical to collect and separate for recycling.

## SILVER IN FASHION AND TEXTILES
Silver is utilized in textiles in a variety of forms. Traditionally, silver thread is used for embroidery, in particular laid work and couching. It is positioned on the surface of the fabric – usually held in place with a fine thread of silk – to make the most of its silvery-white lustre. Unlike gold,

**Embroidered silver**
This military cap detail, embroidered by Hand & Lock in London, is constructed from silver thread couched onto the surface of the fabric. The tack stitches around the perimeter are temporary and mark the edge of the cap. Similar to goldwork (see page 95), silver embroidery is used to add value to ceremonial and military outfits. It is raised into a three-dimensional profile to enhance the design. Over time, the surface will tarnish. With use the relief areas will become contrasted with the darker recesses, emphasizing the intricacies of the pattern.

it readily forms surface tarnish, which affects its lustre.

Because of the high price of silver, it is often applied as plating onto more economical metal or plastic yarn. In addition to providing the aesthetic and tactile benefits of silver, the thin coating is highly conductive. This quality is being utilized in a variety of ways. For example, silver-plated fabric gloves allow the wearer to operate a touch screen (capacitive sensors on touch screens respond to changes in electrical conductivity; that is how they sense a finger). The plating is very thin and so does not affect the drape and handle of textile significantly. It is also suitable for knitted and elastic fabrics (interestingly, the conductivity may go up or down depending on how the fabric is pulled). As input and output technologies are continually miniaturized, the potential for conductive garments expands into new fields, including medical, well-being, military and gaming.

Silver nanoparticles (1–100 nanometres) are incorporated in textiles to take advantage of their antimicrobial properties. Examples span from medical applications to sportswear and camping equipment. The antimicrobial effect helps reduce odour and maintain hygiene. However, it should be noted that although it is known that silver nanoparticles are highly effective against bacteria, fungi and other microorganisms, it is not known how damaging they may be to the broader environment. There is a great deal of research ongoing, and while several scientists argue that the use of silver nanoparticles should be curbed until we know more about their effects, others say there are no significant new risks.

Silver nanoparticles are conductive and are incorporated into ink to make printed flexible circuitry. Applied by inkjet printing, they are suitable for coating a range of materials, including plastic film (see Polyethylene Terephthalate, page 152).

### SILVER IN JEWELRY
Even though jewelry accounts for only a small proportion of total silver consumption, it is perhaps the most familiar. Silversmiths employ a range of techniques. The same processes are used to make tableware, ornaments and other silver items. Because silver is relatively easy to work by hand it can be bent, beaten and pressed into most shapes. Hammering is used to apply texture as well as shape. Silversmithing hammers come with a huge variety of different materials and textures, which allows for many different finishes to be achieved.

Where a continuous profile is needed, such as a ring, then rod is cut to size, bent and soldered. It will work

**Alloy heat treatment**

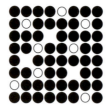 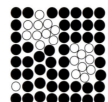

**Quenched** Heating duplex alloys to above a specific temperature (alloy-dependent) causes the beta-phase atoms to fully dissolve in the crystal lattice and become uniformly distributed. When this is followed by quenching, the beta atoms are locked in place and so the mechanical properties are maintained. It will stay that way as long as the temperature is low.

**Precipitation hardened** With prolonged heating at a lower temperature (or simply over a long time) the beta atoms will come out of solution and cluster. These groups impede the movement of the crystal lattice much more effectively and so result in a stronger alloy. Just the right temperature and time ensure optimum mechanical properties are achieved.

harden – dislocations form in the crystal structure (see page 38) – as it is pressed and shaped. Annealing (heating and cooling) allows the crystal structure to find its equilibrium and so regain malleability. Once forming is complete, certain geometries will benefit from work hardening, because it results in a stronger material with higher spring tension.

As a result of the copper content in sterling silver – they form a duplex, or alpha-beta, alloy (see page 68) – it is susceptible to precipitation hardening. This technique relies on the metal containing two crystal phases at room temperature. Hardening occurs when small crystals of the beta (β) phase are allowed to precipitate out of the alpha (α) phase when a specific heat treatment takes place. The separated beta-phase crystals block dislocations in the crystal lattice and so reduce the ease with which the metal can be deformed. This technique has major industrial application with alloys of steel, aluminium (page 42), magnesium (page 54) and titanium (page 58), for example.

Another benefit of having crystals in two phases is that annealing and quenching (very rapid cooling) does not allow the beta phase to form and so results in a very malleable metal. Thus

JEWELRY

### JEWELRY

**Formability**
Sterling silver typically contains copper, which provides the right balance of formability with strength for the majority of applications. Malleability increases as the proportion of copper, or other alloy, is reduced.

**Inert**
Silver is impervious to the elements. And while it readily tarnishes, it is not eroded through oxidization. It is non-toxic and hypoallergenic.

**Patina**
When in use, exposed surfaces remain lustrous. Recesses and undercuts gradually darken with time.

it can be shaped more easily. Over time (accelerated with heating) the beta-phase will form and harden the metal. This is why precipitation hardening is also referred to as age hardening.

As with gold and platinum, silver is expensive and so is applied as a finish on less expensive metals. Nickel silver is commonly used as the base metal for silver-plated items, because of its very similar appearance. As well as the obvious economic advantages, there are other benefits. For example, nickel silvers are suitable for casting and machining and are straightforward to fabricate. Mass production results in waste, which is not such a problem when working with nickel silver as it would be with silver alloy. The disadvantage of plating is that it is thin and so will eventually wear through.

Silver's propensity to tarnish is utilized in the finishing process. For example, whereas polishing produces a bright silvery-white and highly reflective finish, potassium sulphide treatment results in a dark grey-black tarnish. Through consideration for surface patina and by incorporating relief details into the design, the finished appearance will be enhanced by everyday use.

**Hammered silver pendant** Handmade by jeweller Stine Bülow in Luxembourg, the pendant is sterling silver. The shape is cut from sheet and dished by beating into a tin block. The texture is the result of hammering the surface, determined by the shape of the hammer's face and the strength and temper of the blows. Coupled with the reflective properties of silver, the texture scatters light from the surface to create a unique appearance. Work hardening affects the hammering process and is controlled with heating and cooling.

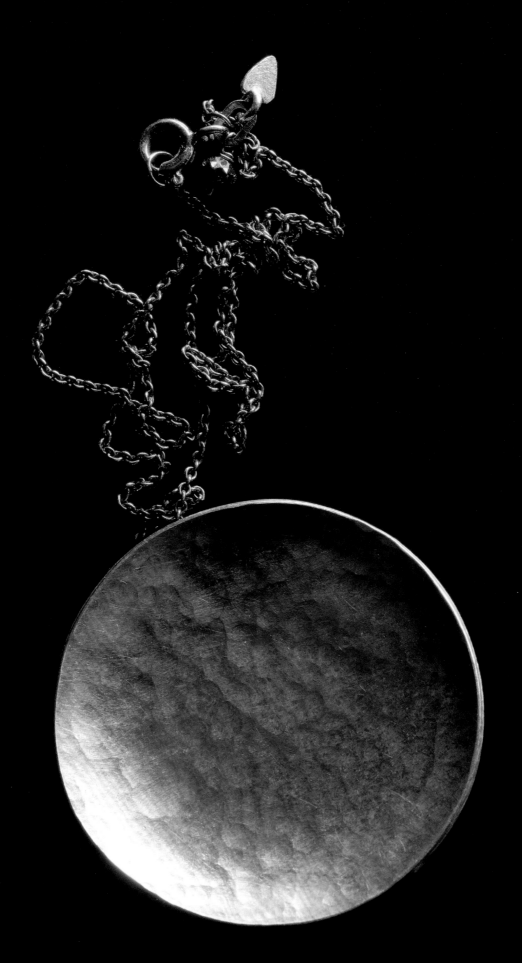

# Gold

Gold is on the one hand revered for its aesthetic and cultural value and on the other prized for its functional properties. It is an efficient conductor and does not tarnish or oxidize readily, so maintains its appearance. As one of the most expensive metals, partly because it is so challenging to mine, the price is governed by stock market trading.

| Types | Typical Applications | Sustainability |
|---|---|---|
| • Yellow (varying purity)<br>• White (alloyed with nickel, manganese or palladium)<br>• Rose (alloyed with copper) | • Jewelry<br>• Electrical connectors<br>• Food and drink<br>• Artwork | • Gold mining and extraction causes pollution and is energy-intensive<br>• It is highly recycled end-of-life |
| **Properties** | **Competing Materials** | **Costs** |
| • Ductile and malleable<br>• Good conductor of heat and electricity<br>• Resistant to corrosion | • Silver, platinum, copper and tin<br>• Porcelain, gemstone and technical ceramic<br>• Aluminized PET film | • Very high material cost<br>• Relatively low manufacturing cost |

## INTRODUCTION

Gold has enjoyed celebrity status since ancient times. It has been used throughout the world to make high-value items, such as currency, jewelry and adornment prized by emperors and laypeople alike. Its exceptionally high price means it is no longer suitable for currency, but is bought and sold as an investment.

It is estimated that half of all gold goes into jewelry and tableware. In addition, it is used for its excellent conductivity and corrosion resistance in the electronics of sound systems and telecommunications. In such cases it is plated onto connectors to ensure that performance is maintained over the long term.

Gold is equally well suited to being worked by hand as with machine. In contrast with other relatively soft metals (such as aluminium alloy, page 42), gold tends not to be formed using reducing processes such as machining, because it is too valuable. Instead, it is carefully cast, bent, pressed and stretched to the desired shape.

The exceptional malleability of pure gold allows it to be beaten into very thin sheets of leaf. Using a technique that has been around for millennia, these foils are traditionally employed to gild statues, engravings, artworks, frames

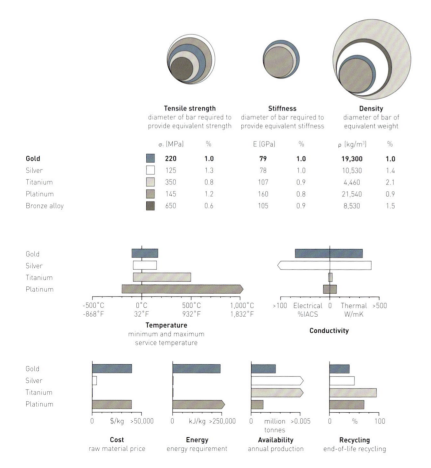

| | Tensile strength<br>diameter of bar required to provide equivalent strength | | Stiffness<br>diameter of bar required to provide equivalent stiffness | | Density<br>diameter of bar of equivalent weight | |
|---|---|---|---|---|---|---|
| | σᵣ (MPa) | % | E (GPa) | % | ρ (kg/m³) | % |
| **Gold** | **220** | **1.0** | **79** | **1.0** | **19,300** | **1.0** |
| Silver | 125 | 1.3 | 78 | 1.0 | 10,530 | 1.4 |
| Titanium | 350 | 0.8 | 107 | 0.9 | 4,460 | 2.1 |
| Platinum | 145 | 1.2 | 160 | 0.8 | 21,540 | 0.9 |
| Bronze alloy | 650 | 0.6 | 105 | 0.9 | 8,530 | 1.5 |

**Gilded china necklace**
The Hula necklace, designed and produced by Reiko Kaneko, is slip cast in fine bone china (see Clay, page 480). Long tubes are produced and cut by hand to length. Each one is carefully finished, fired and glazed. In preparation for gilding, pure gold is dissolved in acid and held suspended in a resinous solution along with a small amount of flux. The liquid gold is brushed onto the surface of the china hoop as it is turned on a rotating table. The decorated china is fired once more, this time at a much lower temperature, to burn off the resin and set the gold in place.

**Gold and its alloys** The colour depends on the type and proportion of alloyed ingredients. Left to right: 24 ct; 18 ct; 9 ct; 18 ct rose; 9 ct rose; 18 ct white; 9 ct white. Using silver-coloured alloying elements, such as zinc, silver, manganese and palladium, produces white gold. Nickel is also used for white gold, but is avoided in items placed close to the body, as it can cause skin irritation. White gold will be 18 ct (75% gold with 25% alloying elements) or less. In some cases, white gold is plated with rhodium to enhance its silvery colour. Alloying with copper produces rose gold. The more copper used, the lower the carat and the redder the colour. Depending on the amount of reddish-coloured alloying element, it may be referred to as pink through red.

**Cast white-gold ring** Made by Atelier Shinji Ginza, Japan, the Clover Ring is produced by investment casting from a hand-carved wax pattern. 18 ct white gold for applications like this, which require high strength and durability, is produced with palladium alloy. A member of the platinum family, it is relatively inert and does not produce any allergic reactions, making it an ideal alloy to combine with gold for fine jewelry.

and books. Nowadays, gold leaf can even be found decorating food and drink as well as their packaging.

## COMMERCIAL TYPES AND USES

The purity of gold is measured in carats (ct) (also spelled karat, kt): 24 ct is pure gold; 18 ct is 75% gold; 14 ct is 58.3% gold; and 10 ct is 41.1% gold by weight. Unlike many gold standards, the UK allows no negative tolerance.

Alloy content affects colour and is also adjusted for technical purposes. For example, including palladium increases the hardness of gold and so improves its durability and resistance to wear. The amount of palladium typically ranges from 10% to the full 15% (at which point it is referred to as high-palladium white gold).

Gold is applied as plating for less expensive parts. Plating is also useful in cases where gold is impractical as the base metal, for example because of forming or strength requirements of the application. Once the desired shape has been produced, a thin layer of gold is deposited onto the surface by electroplating. It is quite soft and so not very durable in application.

## SUSTAINABILITY

Gold is mined in relatively small quantities: 2,500 tonnes per annum worldwide compared to 20 million tonnes per annum for copper. In the past, gold was extracted using liquid mercury in a process of amalgamation. This is an extremely polluting process that has significant negative impacts on people and the environment. As a result, it has been phased out in many parts of the world, but unfortunately the process continues to play a role in developing countries.

Nowadays, the majority of gold is extracted from its ore by cyanidation. Worldwide, the mining of gold (and silver) accounts for around one-fifth of cyanide consumption. The process involves soaking crushed ore in aqueous sodium cyanide. The gold dissolves into the solution and is later recovered using complex electrochemical processes.

### JEWELRY

**High value**
Gold is one of the most expensive metals, equivalent to platinum, and around 20 times more than silver for the same weight.

**Inert**
It does not react with oxygen, unlike many other metals, including silver, and therefore retains a lustrous colour and appearance.

**Formability**
It is highly malleable and ductile, as well as very fluid when molten. These properties mean that gold can be produced in virtually any shape, from thin leaf through complex castings.

Cyanide is a naturally occurring chemical and is biodegradable but in high concentrations is extremely toxic. Therefore it requires very careful management to ensure it does not have negative impacts on people and the environment. The International Cyanide Management Code was established in 2005 following several cyanide spills that had devastating effects on the local environment. Companies that adopt the voluntary code are certified and inspected by a third party.

## GOLD IN JEWELRY

Gold is endowed with many positive metaphors. The ancient Egyptians associated its colour with the sun; in weddings rings its resistance to tarnishing and corrosion represents the eternal partnership; and its value corresponds to its use as currency. These factors all contribute to its very high perceived importance. This is reinforced by the use of gold in royal adornment, such as crowns and jewels, and religious symbols, including temples, sanctuaries, shrines and churches lavishly decorated with gold.

The type of gold used depends on the applications. The most commonly used is 14 ct gold, which has a desirable balance

**Gold leaf**  Gold is beaten into foil 2–4 microns thin. This makes it extremely delicate. It cannot be handled, because it will readily stick to skin. A special brush is used, or tweezers, to place the leaf and rub it onto the surface. It is so light that the smallest gust of air can blow it away before it is stuck down. As well as being used to decorate food, gold leaf is applied to artwork, picture frames, sculpture and interiors.

of properties. Fine jewelry tends to be produced in 18 ct gold. And 24 ct gold is so soft that it is typically only suitable for plating.

A hallmark identifies the material used – stamped onto gold, silver and platinum, it provides certification of their purity. This standard has been practised for centuries and represents one of the earliest forms of consumer protection. It is made up of three parts: the maker's mark; the millesimal fineness mark (this indicates the quantity of precious metal used in parts per thousand, so for example, 18 ct contains 75% gold and thus will be marked with '750'); and the location mark. Makers may include additions such as the date and a graphic to indicate the type of precious metal (a crown to indicate gold, for example).

Gold-plated items do not carry a hallmark. Instead, they are often stamped with the letters GP (gold plated), HGP (heavy gold plated), GEP (gold electroplated) or RGP (rolled gold plated), among others.

Jewellers employ a variety of forming techniques. Gold is shaped in solid state: manipulated by hand with hammering, bending and carving; or by machine pressing, drawing and forging. Its ductility and malleability mean that it is shaped relatively easily. These same characteristics mean it is quite delicate in application. For comparison, the elastic modulus (stiffness) (E) of platinum alloy (95% pure) is twice that of gold, which means that only half the cross-section is required to provide equivalent stiffness. Thin gold items, such as rings, will become deformed without sufficient thickness.

Gold is very fluid when molten, making a fine finish possible with all types of casting. A commonly used technique, for both one-offs and high-volume production, is investment casting. It is also known as lost-wax casting, because the process involves forming a wax pattern into an exact replica of the piece to be made in metal. The wax pattern is produced by carving, molding, machining or rapid prototyping with a specially formulated wax.

Once formed, the pattern is coated with several layers of ceramic slurry.

## FOOD

### Non-toxic
It is inert and safe to consume, without taste or smell. As a food colouring agent it is known as E175, as designated by the European Commission. As well as leaf, flake and dust are available in some countries.

### Malleable
It is soft enough to be beaten into very thin sheets of leaf that are safe to eat. The thin foil is applied to the surface of food for decoration. It is so thin it does not affect texture.

Progressing from very fine to coarse ensures the highest-quality reproduction of surface details and sturdy mold. The ceramic forms a hard shell, which is fired to remove the wax (melted out) and produce a durable mold for casting. The cavity within the ceramic shell is filled with molten metal. In this way, intricate and complex shapes are reproduced exactly without wasting any of the precious metal.

### GOLD IN FOOD
As a food additive gold is used for external decoration, in particular on chocolate. As one of the most expensive food additives, it is perceived as a sign of luxury and hospitality. High-purity gold (22–24 ct) is considered biologically inert and thus safe to consume in most countries. When eaten, the gold will pass through the digestive system without being absorbed. It is sometimes alloyed with small amounts of silver (page 84), which is also safe to consume.

Considered by some cultures to have mythical and medicinal properties, gold has been used to decorate food for centuries, reportedly as far back as the 16th century. The colour of gold works well in candlelight, which perhaps contributed to its success in the past.

### GOLD IN TEXTILES
Gold is a unique material suitable for a variety of textiles and apparel. It is very expensive and requires highly skilled embroiderers and weavers to incorporate it. This tends to limit is use to ceremonial accoutrements and haute couture.

Traditionally, it is used to decorate

## TEXTILES

### Inert
The surface does not react with the atmosphere and so remains bright and lustrous.

### Malleable
It is soft enough to be worked by hand without breaking. This allows for it to be integrated into complex fabric constructions, including woven and embroidered designs. In application, this quality helps it tolerate a certain amount of flexing.

### Dense
It is heavy and so affects the drape and appearance of fabrics. This helps reinforce its value and significance.

lampas (a type of drapery and upholstery fabric), brocade (highly figured fabric with discontinuous weft), lace (knitted or woven with an openwork structure) and embroidery (decorative thread applied onto a pre-woven fabric).

Gold thread comes in several different formats. Selection depends on the purpose and method of application. It is available in long thin strips – known as plate – used for embroidery or coiled around a thread to produce flexible gold-wrapped yarn. Alternatively, gold wire is wrapped around a rod (which is later removed) to produce a hollow wire coil, known as purl. There are several types, formats and shapes of purl, all of which are utilised in embroidery.

There are many less expensive alternatives to using gold. Plastic film – in particular polyethylene terephthalate (PET, polyester) (page 152) – is aluminized and coloured (any metallic colour is possible, from green to pink) to give the appearance of gold plate. Produced as a strip, it is applied directly, or wrapped around a core to make metallic-looking threads that are suitable for weaving and knitting. Alternatively, coloured foils are laminated onto the surface of fabric to give the appearance of foil or leaf.

**Goldwork embroidery**
This Serbian diplomatic uniform has been embroidered by Hand & Lock, London. The pattern is made up of twisted gold wire couched onto the surface of the fabric by hand. Goldwork is prized for its lustrous appearance; raising it off the fabric into a three-dimensional pattern emphasizes the rich colour.

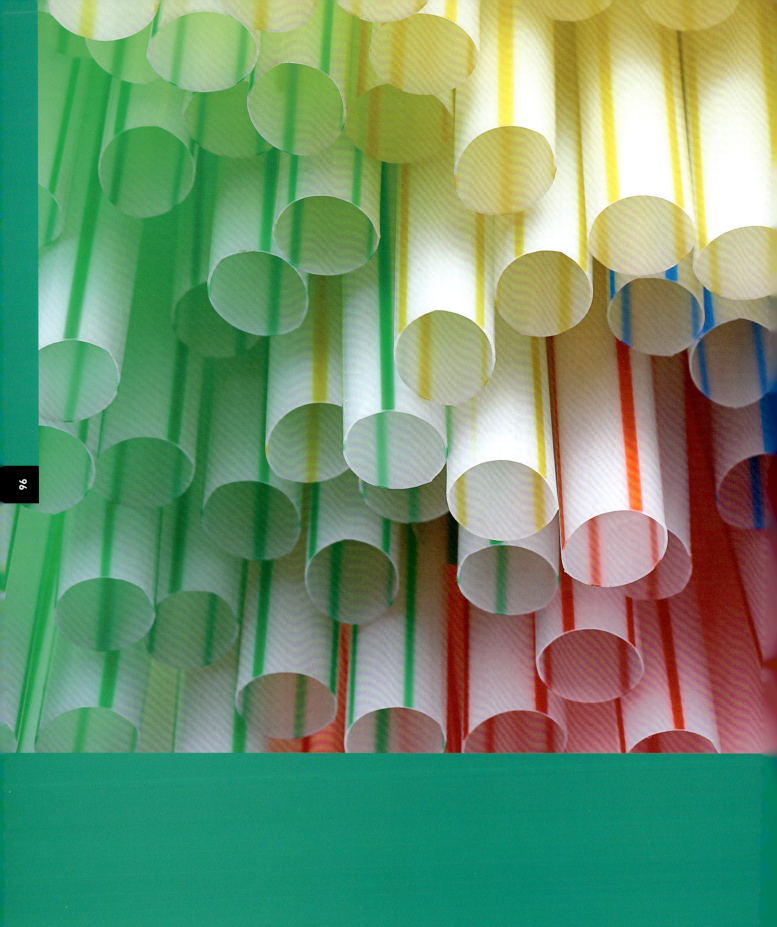

# PLASTIC

# 2

# Polypropylene (PP)

As one of the most versatile plastics, PP can be found in virtually every end use, from common household items to technical textiles and industrial products. Naturally translucent, lightweight and flexible, it is similar to polyethylene (PE) in many ways. The raw material is inexpensive and straightforward to manufacture as molding, film and fibre.

| Types | Typical Applications | Sustainability |
|---|---|---|
| • PP: homopolymer (PPH) and copolymer (PPC)<br>• Expanded PP (EPP)<br>• Biaxially oriented PP film (BOPP) | • Consumer and industrial products<br>• Packaging<br>• Automotive<br>• Carpets and apparel | • High embodied energy<br>• Recycling rates depend on application; it is identified by code #5 |
| **Properties** | **Competing Materials** | **Costs** |
| • Tough and resilient<br>• Translucent, but readily coloured<br>• Hydrophobic | • PE, PS, PET, ABS, PC and PA<br>• EPS and PU foam<br>• Steel and aluminium alloys | • Low total cost as a result of low material price and ease of manufacture |

## INTRODUCTION

Production began in 1950s and since then polypropylene (PP) has become one of the most widely used plastics. Applications span the industries, from automotive to appliance and furniture to apparel. Often compared to polyethylene (PE) (page 108), PP is set apart by being harder with higher tensile strength and being able to operate at slightly higher temperature.

PP owes its mechanical, chemical and thermal resistance to its semi-crystalline structure (see page 166). This structure is also the reason why PP appears milky white, not transparent, because the crystalline areas interact with the visible light. PP is made transparent – useful in packaging – through the introduction of a clarifier during polymerization. The additive stops the build-up of large crystalline areas and in doing so, reduces the effects of the plastic's crystallinity on its transparency.

## COMMERCIAL TYPES AND USES

PP is available as either homopolymer (one monomer type) or copolymer (contains two monomers). Homopolymer types (sometimes abbreviated as PPH) are suitable for general-purpose applications and compete with PE. Produced through the polymerization of propylene, copolymers (sometimes abbreviated as PPC) are created with the addition of ethylene. They are incorporated in the polymer chain randomly, or in blocks.

Random arrangement improves flexibility and clarity, two properties utilized in packaging bottles and films, for example. The improved mechanical properties of block copolymer types – improved toughness down to -20°C (-4°F) – puts them into competition with engineering thermoplastics, such as acrylonitrile butadiene styrene (ABS) (page 138) and polycarbonate

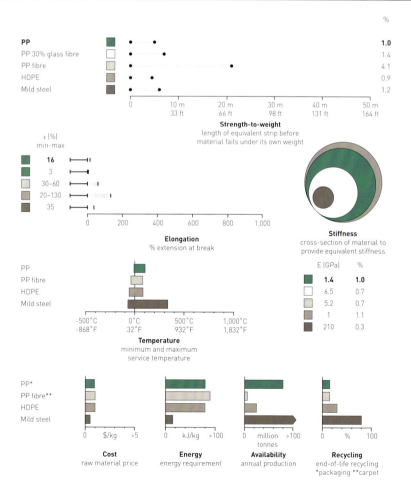

| | % |
|---|---|
| PP | 1.0 |
| PP 30% glass fibre | 1.4 |
| PP fibre | 4.1 |
| HDPE | 0.9 |
| Mild steel | 1.2 |

0   10 m / 33 ft   20 m / 66 ft   30 m / 98 ft   40 m / 131 ft   50 m / 164 ft

**Strength-to-weight**
length of equivalent strip before material fails under its own weight

ε [%] min-max

| 16 |
| 3 |
| 30–60 |
| 20–130 |
| 35 |

0   200   400   600   800   1,000

**Elongation**
% extension at break

**Stiffness**
cross-section of material to provide equivalent stiffness

| | E [GPa] | % |
|---|---|---|
| | 1.4 | 1.0 |
| | 6.5 | 0.7 |
| | 5.2 | 0.7 |
| | 1 | 1.1 |
| | 210 | 0.3 |

PP
PP fibre
HDPE
Mild steel

-500°C / -868°F   0°C / 32°F   500°C / 932°F   1,000°C / 1,832°F

**Temperature**
minimum and maximum service temperature

PP*
PP fibre**
HDPE
Mild steel

0  $/kg  >5      0  kJ/kg  >100      0  million tonnes  >100      0  %  100

**Cost**
raw material price

**Energy**
energy requirement

**Availability**
annual production

**Recycling**
end-of-life recycling
*packaging **carpet

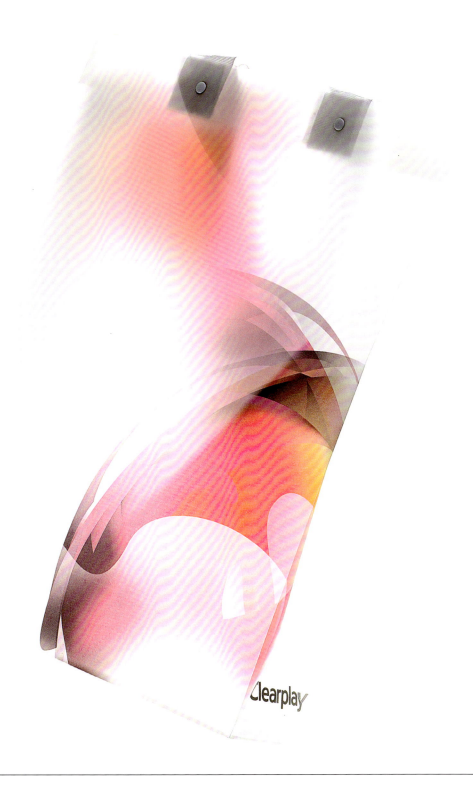

(PC) (page 144). They are utilized for everyday applications, such as furniture and toys, as well as more demanding products, such as protective packaging, car bumpers and crates. Compared to engineering thermoplastics, PP is less expensive, and easier to fabricate.

Increasing the ethylene content improves impact strength and flexibility. Through a modified manufacturing process, up to around 25% ethylene is incorporated, copolymerized with the PP as ethylene-propylene rubber (EPR or EPDM) (see Synthetic Rubber, page 216). The resultant material has two distinct phases: rigid homopolymer combined with dispersed particles of impact-absorbing EPR. By adjusting the proportion of EPR, a range of stiffness can be achieved. Thermoplastic elastomers

**Printed tote** Produced by Progress Packaging for graphic design company Roundel, this bag of translucent PP is printed, cut out, folded and heat welded. Offset lithography was selected for the printing, as it offers the best reproduction of toned images. The end result is precise, with a smooth contoured print that accurately reflects the original graphics. There are costs associated with set-up, so offset litho is generally only used for medium- to large-volume runs. Image courtesy of Progress Packaging.

(TPE) (page 194) based on PP contain up to around 50% rubber content. They are much more flexible and able to withstand significant impact. They are utilized mainly in automotive applications.

PP is stable up to a higher temperature than PE – it will not melt below 160°C (320°F) – and so is suited to a broader range of applications. This is important in food-related items, such as packaging and equipment where operating temperatures reach 100°C (212°F).

## SUSTAINABILITY

Along with PE, it has one of the highest rates of recycling of all the plastics. This is partly due to its widespread use in packaging, which makes it readily identifiable (resin identification code #5), and partly because it is used in applications where it is often the sole material. This makes it quite efficient to separate and so economical to process.

It floats on water and this helps to separate it from mixed waste. For example, packaging contains a lot of polyethylene terephthalate (PET, polyester) (page 152), PP and PE; the PP and PE will float and the PET will sink. Material that contains additives and fillers, such as glass fibre, will not float, making it more challenging to separate.

It is feasible to use 100% recycled PP, such as for injection molding or thermoforming, and it is estimated to reduce energy consumption by three-quarters or more. Separating colours prior to recycling increases the reuse value of the material. However, the polymer is broken down through heat and exposure to ultraviolet (UV), so this cannot go on indefinitely in a closed-loop process. Mixing recycled material with virgin PP helps to offset the embodied energy.

## PP IN PRODUCTS, FURNITURE AND LIGHTING

With applications ranging from one-piece chairs to delicate lightshades and translucent storage, it is clear there are many design opportunities associated with PP. It has excellent injection molding properties, even though it is semi-crystalline, thanks to its low melt viscosity. This means that it flows well in the mold,

which helps to make production efficient, accurately reproduce the mold (good for texture) and allow for relatively large parts to be produced in single molding.

The relatively high melting point and resistance to chemicals means that PP is well suited to kitchen appliances, including rice cookers, toasters and kettles. In such cases it sits alongside high-value materials such as steel (page 28) and aluminium (page 42). And recently developed transparent grades have put it into competition with the likes of styrene acrylonitrile (SAN) (page 136) and PC in some cases.

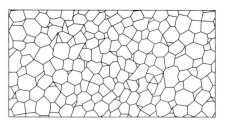

**EPP foam**

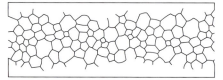

**Injection-molded foam**

**Foam molding** The properties of PP foam depend on the manufacturing method. EPP (expanded PP) is produced in a steam mold, whereby small beads of PP plus additive are fused with heat and pressure. The resulting foam structure is more or less consistent throughout. Injection-molded foam, on the other hand, consists of a core of foam surrounded by a much more dense skin layer. This is the result of the polymer cooling at different rates: a given thickness of the surface 'freezes' (solidifies) and so reduces the effect of the foaming agent. The density depends on the amount of polymer injected. Using less polymer will allow more space for the foam, thus reducing density.

Glass-fibre (GF) (see page 106) and other reinforcements are added to improve stiffness and tensile strength. Short glass fibres (SGF) are used for applications where surface quality is important, such as furniture. They increase cost slightly, so reinforcements are used only where necessary. However, if there is a choice between GF-reinforced PP (GFPP) and an engineering polymer, or even metal, then GFPP typically works out less expensive. Surface quality is affected by part design as much as mold finish. Textures help to mask defects caused by weld lines, ribs and bosses.

PP tends to retain static charges caused by processing and handling. This means the surface attracts dust and dirt. Additive is incorporated to alleviate the problem, but this has drawbacks, such as making printing on the surface near impossible and in some cases leading to white discoloration (bloom) on the surface, which worsens over time.

PP fibre-based textiles are utilized for a range of industrial applications for their strength, lightness and low cost. Self-reinforced PP (SrPP) makes use of the impressive properties of drawn fibre with the rigidity and stiffness of sheet material. A composite material made from 100% PP developed in the 1990s, SrPP is commonly referred to by trade names, such as Curv. The production process starts with the making of woven fabric. Through the application of precise heat and pressure, the outer layer of the fibres melts and coalesces to form a solid sheet material. Compared to extruded sheet it has higher strength-to-weight, impact resistance and stiffness. It has so far been successfully used to make suitcases, anti-ballistic panels, sports gear and automotive parts. It is shaped by thermoforming – like

## PRODUCTS, FURNITURE AND LIGHTING

**Lightweight**
PP is one of the lowest-density plastics and around half the weight of magnesium for the same thickness. Adding glass fibres enhances strength-to-weight.

**Impact strength**
Copolymer types are more flexible than homopolymer and have good impact strength, even at low temperatures.

**Colourful**
It is available in a wide range of colours with reasonable fastness. Colour intensity depends on the translucency of the base resin and consistency of pigment.

**Surface finish**
Molded surface quality is very good, from gloss to matt. And PP exhibits good resistance to abrasion and staining.

conventional sheet – and overmolded to conceal the cut edge and incorporate fixtures and features. Unlike conventional composites, such as glass-fibre-reinforced plastic (GFRP), it does not rely on a mix of dissimilar materials, which has several environmental advantages.

A similar self-reinforced composite is produced using high-strength PET. This alternative provides higher temperature resistance and impact strength, but is more expensive.

## PP IN PACKAGING

PP has several properties advantageous for packaging. While its translucent visual quality has defined high-street folded sheet packaging, high-strength PP filament dominates industrial sacking. As molding, fibre, film and foam, it provides lightweight and resilient protection in virtually every packaging end use.

Converted into trays, containers, lids and caps, PP has excellent injection-molding characteristics. It is inexpensive, so is cost-effective in most applications. A measure of its success is how its unique visual and tactile quality has become synonymous with global brands, such as Muji and Tupperware. It is naturally frosted; its transparency is enhanced with clarifying additives. Containers

**Lightweight, stackable one-piece chair** Don Chadwick's Spark Series stacking lounge chair for Knoll International (launched 2009) is molded from GFPP. Its lightness and high-quality finish is the result of co-injection molding a foamed glass-filled PP core with a prime grade, coloured, glass-filled PP outer. The core material is injected first and contains a small amount of foaming agent. This is followed by the colourful outer material, which encapsulates the foaming PP within. This allows for recycled content to be used in the core. As it cools, the foaming agent expands, which reduces the potential for voids and sink marks in thick sections. With the textile-covered polyurethane (PU) foam pad removed, the chair is suitable for outdoor as well as indoor use. Photo courtesy of Knoll, Inc.

made from PP can be virtually water-clear. This brings it into direct competition with packaging plastics including PET, polystyrene (PS) (page 132) and polyvinyl chloride (PVC) (page 122).

PP is utilized as sheet for bags, boxes and other items that can be folded from a die-cut net. Compared to PE, PVC and ethylene vinyl acetate (EVA) (page 118), which are used for similar applications, PP has higher rigidity (lower elasticity). Extruded with a gloss or textured finish, like molded PP it has a distinctive slippery feel. It is similar to PE and polyamide (PA) (page 164) in this respect, owing to its low coefficient of friction.

**Above**
**Super-tough luggage**
The Pelican case is injection molded from PP copolymer (PPC). It provides lightweight impact protection coupled with resistance to water and chemicals. These cases are destined for some of the most demanding end uses, including

military, fire safety, life sciences, film and aerospace. The indestructability of these products – users claim their Pelican cases have survived crashes, explosions and tsunamis – is testament to the impressive durability of PP.

**Opposite**
**Synthetic woven sack** PP is a low-cost packaging textile. In recent years it has been created to mimic hessian, which is traditionally produced from woven jute (page 404). This is because PP sacking is lighter (less energy to ship), less expensive and more predictable (highly engineered). However, it is not so desirable in some cases owing to its synthetic appearance. While this does not

matter for sandbags and agricultural sacking, it does have a bearing on coffee and other high-value goods. Therefore, PP is modified through spinning – the fibres are textured and cut into short staples – to produce a more 'natural' appearance. PP is fully recyclable; however, jute is a long-lasting natural fibre with very little negative impact if farmed and processed in a sustainable manner.

## PACKAGING

**Integral hinge**
As a result of its unique balance of fatigue resistance, ultimate tensile strength and elongation, thin sections of PP have a virtually unlimited flex life, making it an excellent material for integral hinges.

**Colour and translucency**
From naturally diffused to transparent, a wide range of low-cost visual effects is possible.

**Heat resistance**
It is able to resist higher temperatures than PE and suitable for hot filling, freezing and microwaving.

**Lightness**
Its low density means it adds the least weight possible to the contents it's protecting.

**Barrier**
It is resistant to many chemicals, inert and is hydrophobic.

Foamed PP, referred to as expanded (EPP), is gradually becoming more widespread in packaging. EPP provides lightweight impact protection and insulation with good structural integrity (properties also utilized in automotive parts, such as for crash protection). Its strength provides many design opportunities, including the ability to incorporate hinges, inserts, fasteners and snap fits. Compared to expanded polystyrene (EPS) (see page 134), it is more elastic and less rigid and so far more durable (better recovery), but it is also more expensive. Unlike EPS, production does not use blowing agent (pentane gas). EPP is produced as small closed-cell beads, which are injected into a steam chest mold and fused together with steam heat and pressure.

Similar to PET, the properties of PP film are improved with stretching. Stretching the film along its length and across its width during manufacture enhances strength, stiffness and clarity. Known as biaxially oriented (BOPP), it is widely used in point-of-sale packaging, such as for bakery products. It is stiff and glossy, which results in a characteristically smooth, shiny appearance.

It is hydrophobic and so inherently resistant to water. Where other barrier properties are required, such as for packaging applications, BOPP is metallized, coated, coextruded or laminated. Metallizing and coating are the least expensive and in some cases can

provide the same benefits as laminating or coextruding. Print presentation is improved through lamination: the ink is sandwiched between two layers of PP, giving a high-gloss and wear-resistant finish. Heat-sealable films are produced by coextruding PP with PP/PE outer layer.

Recently, PP films have been produced that are engineered to degrade after a period of time. The advantage is that oxydegradable films (contain photoactive or thermoactive ingredients) have the same physical properties as conventional BOPP, but will break down once disposed. However, even though they fragment into tiny particles, their biodegradability has not been scientifically proven.

PP is an important textile fibre in the packaging industry. It is utilized in a range of different fabric constructions, including woven (sacks and sheets), knitted (nets to provide air circulation), braided (tapes and ropes) and nonwoven (tote bags). The fibres are produced from extruded film (slit to width) or spun filament, both of which are drawn to enhance tensile strength and stiffness. It is inexpensive and so popular for industrial and promotional applications.

## PP IN TECHNICAL TEXTILES

PP textile is fabricated from woven strips of film, filament or staple yarn. Filaments are spun and drawn to enhance physical properties. It has relatively low density and is the lightest fibre for its size. It is unaffected by moisture and so suitable for outdoor applications. However, it is affected by UV and will eventually degrade outdoors, even when UV stabilizer is added.

Ropes braided from PP are low-cost and suitable for a range of everyday applications, from marine through transportation. One of the biggest advantages of PP is that its low density means it floats on water. Therefore, it is utilized in towing ropes and safety lines (especially for dinghies and water skis). PP rope is not as strong as rope produced with PET, PA or ultra-high-molecular-weight PE (UHMWPE) (see Polyethylene, page 108). But where a large diameter is required, such as for ease of handling, PP is the lightest thanks to its low density

## TECHNICAL TEXTILES

**Lightness**
It is the lightest fibre for its size, around one-third lighter than PET and one-fifth lighter than PA.

**Hydrophobic**
PP is unaffected by water and so the physical properties remain constant in wet and dry conditions.

**Colourful**
It is available in a wide range of saturated colours with good fastness. High-performance textiles are produced in lower quantities and so are available in fewer colours. Films range from water-clear to hazy, depending on the grade and thickness.

**Inexpensive**
PP is one of the least expensive and most versatile plastics. Like PE, it is utilized in textiles as film and fibre and is suitable for all types of manufacturing.

and hydrophobicity. It is produced as a textured staple and spun into rope that mimics traditional hemp (page 406), jute and burlap.

As a woven textile it is used a great deal in carpet, packaging and agriculture.

Its hydrophobicity makes it uncomfortable close to the skin and so it is rarely used in apparel.

The largest area of application is in nonwovens, such as teabags, nappies and surgical masks. These textiles are inexpensive: they are produced by laying freshly spun fibres together on a collection surface where they bond

**Polymer bank note**
Following unsuccessful attempts to use DuPont Tyvek (a nonwoven HDPE) for banknotes in the 1980s, BOPP proved to be a more suitable material. Introduced in 1988 and manufactured by Securency International of Australia under the trade name Guardian, the polymer banknotes are now used in more than 20 countries. Produced using the bubble process (by which a tube is extruded and inflated with air to cause bubble-like expansion), the film is combined with opacifying layers and embedded security features prior to printing. Tactility is provided by raised print on the surface. The notes feature many innovations unique to plastics, designed mainly to prevent counterfeiting, including clear windows and very fine printing. The security features have proved so difficult to reproduce that in countries where polymer banknotes have replaced paper types counterfeit rates have dropped by 80–90%. They are also cleaner and more durable than paper types, so work out longer-lasting and thus less expensive. Like paper notes, they are recyclable.

together. Additional layers of material are introduced by laminating or needle punching to the spun-bonded base layer. Density ranges from sheer (see-through) to heavy-duty geotextiles. It is much more straightforward to recycle end-of-life if only PP is used.

As with packaging, the properties of film are tailored to the needs of the application. High-strength BOPP outperforms other plastics films where a combination of printability, durability and transparency are required at low cost. It is utilized in polymer banknotes, which were developed in Australia in 1988 and are now used worldwide.

## PP IN AUTOMOTIVE AND TRANSPORTATION

The automotive industry has pioneered a variety of injection-molding grades and techniques that take advantage of PP's lightweight and resilient character.

Molding with short glass fibres (SGF) provides PP with improved strength-to-weight and stiffness. The plastic is typically supplied already mixed; the proportion of GF ranges from around 10 to 40% by weight. Far higher concentrations are possible, up to around 60%, at the expense of notched impact strength (toughness): increasing GF content reduces ductility. Applications include fans, housings, engine covers, seat carriers, instrument panel carriers and other thin-walled structural parts.

GF affect the surface finish and are visible, especially in dark-coloured plastic. Where visual quality is important various finishing techniques are used to conceal them, from heavy texture (effectiveness depends on proportion of fibre content) to coating. Alternatively, parts are co-injection molded with an outer skin of higher-quality PP to conceal the high-strength core within (see image, page 101).

Long glass fibres (LGF), from 12 to 25 mm (0.5–1 in), provide significant mechanical advantages, even at high temperatures, including minimizing shrinkage, maximizing strength and stiffness, and improving energy absorption. Impact resistance is improved five-fold. The same strength can be achieved as SGF using lower

concentrations of LGF, meaning a lighter part. It is more expensive owing to the raw material production (pultrusion) and more challenging to injection mold (SGF provides greater design freedom), so tends to be reserved for the most demanding applications. It can be found in semi-structural parts, such as front ends and under-the-bonnet, which would previously have been fabricated from more expensive engineering thermoplastics or steel.

GFRP, utilizing continuous or very long glass fibre, is produced with a PP matrix. The design considerations for these materials are more closely associated with conventional composites (see Unsaturated Polyester, page 228, Epoxy Resin, page 232, and CFRP, page 236) than molded plastics.

Two different types of PP foam are utilized: EPP (the same as packaging) and structural foam injection molding (SFIM). EPP is molded into thick-walled parts for insulation and impact protection, such as bumpers, side panels, footrests and other interior fittings. It is used as a core material too, such as laminated between layers of SrPP composite, for exceptional strength-to-weight and stiffness.

By contrast, SFIM is based on injection molding with the addition of a foaming agent. As the molten polymer is injected, the foaming agent is activated and causes an expansion of the PP within the mold. Density is controlled by the amount of plastic used (higher loading reduces the space the foam can fill). As well as the processing advantages (less material, improved flow, reduced pressure and so on), foamed parts provide an improved balance of stiffness and impact strength. GF and other additives are incorporated to improve specific properties.

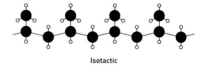

**Isotactic**

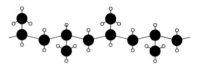

**Syndiotactic**

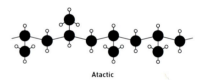

**Atactic**

**Polymer structure**
The properties of PP depend on the orientation and arrangement of the monomers within the polymer. PP forms one of three basic chain structures: isotactic, syndiotactic or atactic. PP made up of stereoregular isotactic or syndiotactic chains twists into neat helices, which crystallize to form a rigid plastic and provide PP with many of its desirable properties. By contrast, the random nature of atactic chains means the material does not crystallize (it remains amorphous) and so yields a rubber-like plastic.

**Motocross fairing**
These side panels – belonging to the Kawasaki KX 450F motocross motorcycle – are injection molded from white PP. The lightweight fairing protects the rider from the exhaust. The gloss outer finish helps to avoid picking up dirt from the track or rub-off from the rider's trousers. ABS is used for similar applications. It provides a superior finish, but is far less durable, and so used mainly for street bikes, not off-road types. GFRP is used for racing fairings (see image, page 228).

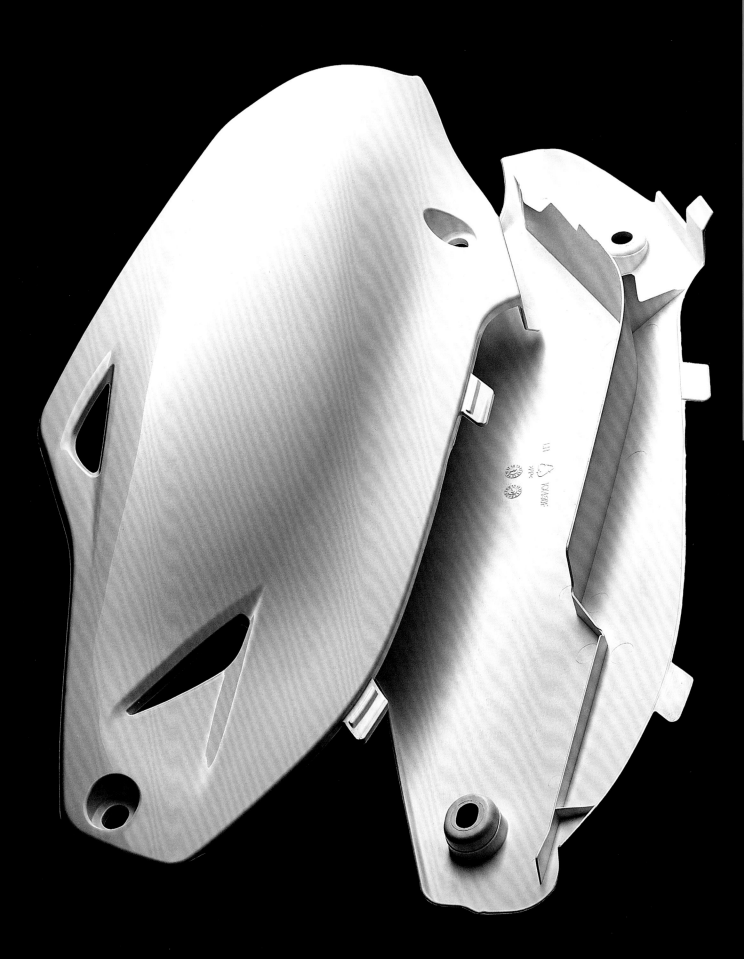

# Polyethylene (PE)

**Also known as**
Also referred to as: polythene, poly
UHMWPE fibre trademark names: Dyneema,
Spectra, Cuben
HDPE nonwoven trademark name: Tyvek

A family of thermoplastics that offer a broad spectrum of properties, PE is utilized in every conceivable plastic end use, from shopping bags to ballistic protection. Naturally translucent with a hazy appearance, it is available in a range of colours. It is tough, resilient and waterproof. Commodity types are inexpensive and have very desirable processing characteristics.

| Types | Typical Applications | Sustainability |
|---|---|---|
| • PE: low-density (LDPE); ultra-low-density (ULDPE); linear low-density (LLDPE); high-density (HDPE); and ultra-high-molecular-weight (UHMWPE) | • Packaging<br>• Protective clothing<br>• Technical textiles<br>• Consumer products and furniture | • Commodity types are widely used<br>• Recycling rates depend on application; LDPE has ID code #4, HDPE #2<br>• High embodied energy |

| Properties | Competing Materials | Costs |
|---|---|---|
| • High impact strength and abrasion resistance<br>• Low density<br>• Translucent | • PP, EVA, PVC and PET<br>• High-performance fibres such as PET, PA, aramid and carbon | • PE is inexpensive<br>• UHMWPE is more expensive and difficult to process, so is typically applied in standard formats |

108

## INTRODUCTION

Polyethylene (PE) is similar to polypropylene (PP) (page 98) in many respects. They are both consumed in huge quantities for many of the same applications. One of the key differences is that manipulation of PE's polymer structure produces plastics with the same basic characteristics, but covering a very broad spectrum of mechanical limits. For example, through modifications in the polymerization process, the length of the polymer chain is increased by several orders of magnitude. This results in a material with far superior strength-to-weight, twice that of standard aramid (page 242). The same characteristics that make PE advantageous for packaging – high tear and puncture resistance – are dramatically increased, making ultra-high-molecular-weight PE (UHMWPE) suitable for the most demanding anti-ballistic situations.

PE materials are semi-crystalline (see page 166) and have excellent resistance to chemicals, wear and fatigue. Like PP, they will float in water. This is as useful in application as for recycling end-of-life. While they have higher impact resistance than PP, they have a lower service temperature, and comparable grades – low-density PE (LDPE) and high-density PE (HDPE) – are not as strong.

It is naturally translucent owing to its crystallinity. The surface feels waxy as a result of its low coefficient of friction. This

**Squeeze bottle**
Designed by Arian Brekveld for Royal VKB. The flexible translucent part is blow molded in heavy-gauge LDPE and the top black part is injection-molded ABS. The bottle is used to prepare and serve dressings and other garnishes. The elasticity of LDPE means it can be squeezed repeatedly without cracking, while its waxy surface prevents ingredients from sticking to the surface inside and out, making the container easier to keep clean and hygienic.

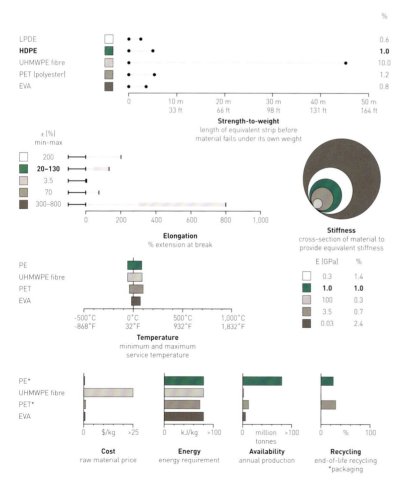

reduces the likelihood of things sticking to it, which is advantageous for some end uses (hygienic) but presents challenges in others (printing and coating).

## COMMERCIAL TYPES AND USES

In comparison with PP it has a simpler polymer structure, the simplest of all commercial plastics, which is either branched or linear. Branched PE is the easiest and least expensive to produce and includes LDPE and ultra-low-density PE (ULDPE). They have a high number of short- and long-chain branches, which prevents the polymer chains packing into a tight crystal structure. This results in low tensile strength, high ductility, good clarity and desirable molding properties. They are utilized mainly in packaging, such as carrier bags, wrapping and semi-rigid containers. And they can be found in durable products, such as toys. ULDPE offers greater low temperature flexibility and flex crack resistance, but it is not so easy to process.

Copolymerizing ethylene with short-chain alpha-olefins results in short branches, resulting in linear low-density PE (LLDPE). Owing to more efficient polymer packing it has slightly higher density, tensile strength and puncture resistance than LDPE and ULDPE. It is mainly used in thin films because of its high toughness and clarity. Other examples include injection-molded tubs and blow-molded containers.

HDPE is a homopolymer produced from ethylene, but using a different catalyst. The result is a linear polymer structure (low degree of branching), which yields higher crystallinity and thus improved strength and stiffness. It is considered a general-purpose plastic, used to make blow-molded bottles, extruded pipes and injection-molded consumer products.

UHMWPE covers a range of grades with a linear structure and very long polymer chains. They are also referred to as high-performance PE (HPPE). Even though the van der Waals bonds (weak molecular-level electrostatic attraction) acting between the polymer chains are not very strong, increasing chain length multiplies the number of overlaps

(density is only slightly higher than HDPE). As a result, it has exceptional strength-to-weight, impact resistance and toughness.

As a low-cost building block in the chemistry of plastics, ethylene is copolymerized with various monomers to create plastics for a range of specialized end uses. For example, ethylene vinyl acetate (EVA) (page 118) is a flexible and tough plastic used in packaging film and foam for shoes and sports products; and acid copolymers and ionomers (page 130) based on ethylene are used in place of crystal glass (page 518) in decorative packaging as well as providing tough, abrasion-resistant films for packaging and sports products.

## SUSTAINABILITY

Plastics have relatively high embodied energy. Where they provide a lightweight solution, such as in the case of packaging, they can offset the energy that goes into production with savings made throughout their lifetime. Reusing and recycling helps to reduce this further still. However, owing to the large number of different formats – bottles, film, wrapping and so on – and composites involving PE, recycling rates remain below 30% globally. This is far lower than estimates suggest for steel and aluminium.

Even so, PE is so widely used that different grades have their own resin identification code number: LDPE is 4 and HDPE is 2. Industrial scrap is straightforward to recycle and is commonly used in products of equal or higher value. Consumer waste must be separated so that it can be reused. The advantage of PE, along with PP, is that it can be separated through flotation, a straightforward and cost-effective process.

It is feasible to produce PE from ethanol sugarcane, as opposed to petroleum. With care, the use of renewable raw material helps to reduce harmful emissions, as well as the destruction associated with mining and refining petroleum products. However, ethanol production from sugarcane can have some detrimental effects, including pollution and deforestation. Developed by Brazilian petrochemical company Braskem, bio-derived PE offers a direct

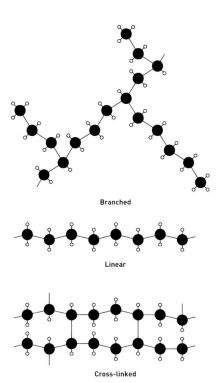

**Branched**

**Linear**

**Cross-linked**

**Polymer structure**
The simplest of the synthesized polymer structures, branched and linear chains consist of repeating ethylene units. Linear chains pack more efficiently and so produce a denser PE with greater crystallinity. LDPE has a branched structure and so remains lightweight and flexible. By contrast, the linear structure of HDPE exhibits higher tensile strength and rigidity. Increasing the length of the chains greatly enhances these mechanical properties: UHMWPE has superior strength-to-weight and toughness. The mechanical properties

of PE are improved by cross-linking the polymer chains. Known as XLPE (or PEX), the thermoplastic is transformed into a thermoset (physically cross-linked) with the addition of a catalyst (peroxide). The weak hydrogen bonds between the polymer chains are replaced with strong carbon–carbon bonds at intervals. These hold the chains tightly together. Compared to conventional HDPE, XLPE has higher molecular weight and thus improved tensile strength and resistance to impact and environmental stress cracking.

**Laminated UHMWPE textile** Designed by Hyperlite Mountain Gear, the drawstring bag is produced using high-strength UHMWPE fibre laminated between thin films of PET. Originally created for racing sails, it is

ideal for outdoor gear thanks to its superior strength-to-weight. Known under the trademark name Cuben Fiber, the UHMWPE is plasma treated to reduce creep (a problem with UHMWPE fibres in performance applications).

## PACKAGING

**Low cost**
PE is the most widely produced and one of the least expensive plastics.

**Lightweight**
Similar to PP, it has low density. This helps to produce ultralight packaging and aids the separation of PE from mixed waste streams.

**Barrier**
While PE has excellent water and chemical resistance, it provides only a fairly good barrier. Owing to its density, HDPE is better than LDPE. They are co-extruded, coated or laminated to improve barrier properties.

**Non-toxic**
Unlike some packaging plastics, including certain grades of PC and PVC, PE is considered non-toxic and safe for food contact.

**Puncture resistance**
It has very good elongation, which provides excellent resistance to puncturing and tearing. LDPE is superior to HDPE in this respect.

**Versatile**
PE is available in virtually all formats, including fibre, film, sheet and molding. LDPE and HDPE have excellent flow characteristics and are suitable for rotation, injection and blow molding.

**Low temperature**
It has excellent low-temperature toughness. Its low melting point is ideal for heat-seal applications and reduces the energy required in production. However, it also means PE is not suitable for applications that require temperature resistance above 80°C (176°F).

alternative to commodity types – such as LDPE, LLDPE and HDPE – and can be recycled through the same channels. It is expensive and is less widely available.

PE provides an alternative to polyvinyl chloride (PVC) (page 122), which is still used in consumer products despite being widely considered to be one of the most harmful plastics.

### PE IN PACKAGING

PE came to prominence in 1946, when it went on sale in the form of airtight Tupperware containers. It was not immediately successful; consumers were wary of this new type of packaging. Sold through so-called Tupperware parties, molded PE containers soon gained popularity in postwar American households as a lightweight and reliable means of containing food. Tupperware is now recognized as one of the most notable products in the history of plastic packaging. Since then, PE has been adopted for virtually every type of end use, from film to fabric and bottles to bags. Its low density combined with its impact resistance means that it is unsurpassed in many applications, providing a low-cost alternative to polyethylene terephthalate (PET, polyester) (page 152).

PE is used in a variety of blow-molded containers, from milk cartons to large-capacity drums. LDPE is selected for applications that require high flexibility and toughness; LLDPE is used in bottles and containers that require superior impact strength and puncture resistance;

HDPE is specified where higher tensile strength and stiffness are required. HDPE has higher chemical resistance, which is useful for packaging certain aggressive foods, medical and industrial products.

Choice of film is determined by the requirements of the application, which include mechanical properties, barrier properties and appearance. LDPE and ULDPE are utilized for their elasticity, for example in stretch-wrap. The increased rigidity and strength of HDPE is utilized in packaging that needs to retain its shape. HDPE films are available in thinner gauges than LDPE types.

Barrier properties depend on density and gauge (thickness). Certain foods require the high-barrier properties of multilayered HDPE. For example, dry

**Extrusion blow molding (EBM)**

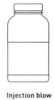

**Injection blow molding (IBM)**

**Blow molding** EBM is the most common plastic blow-molding technique. It is versatile, low-cost and suitable for a wide variety of shapes. Containers are molded with integral handles and multilayered construction. With IBM,

the difference is that the top of the container is injection molded. This allows for more complex and precise details in the neck and mouth. It requires two sets of tooling (one for injection and one for extrusion), making set-up more expensive.

foods, such as cereals, require a good moisture barrier, and certain meats require minimum oxygen exposure. Where an aroma barrier is required a layer of polyamide (PA, nylon) (page 164) is included, and where greater puncture and tear resistance are required, a layer of LDPE or ULDPE is included. LDPE and ULDPE provide a less effective gas barrier and this quality is utilized for certain meats (where exposure to oxygen is necessary to retain freshness).

PE fibres are utilized in packaging in much the same way as PP: woven sacks and knitted nets. Spun-bonded HDPE from DuPont, referred to by its trademark name Tyvek, is breathable, water-resistant and lightweight. Combining the advantages of paper, film and textile, it is utilized in packaging for medical, food and electronics applications. UHMWPE offers many advantages for textile applications. Its exceptionally high strength-to-weight and tear resistance is utilized in high-performance and high-value packaging.

PE films and textiles are corona treated (the surface is modified through exposure to high-voltage, high-frequency electrical discharge) to make them suitable for printing. All conventional techniques can be used. In addition, the base colour of PE can be opaque, tinted or translucent.

### PE IN PRODUCTS, FURNITURE AND LIGHTING

While it is considered a commodity plastic and one of the least expensive, PE offers some exceptional qualities and is unrivalled in some cases. As for packaging applications, PE provides a tough, flexible and water-resistant barrier. Similar to PP, it has a characteristic hazy appearance as a result of its crystallinity. Higher-density or more highly oriented – and thus higher-crystallinity – grades are more opaque.

**Air-filled packaging** An elegant and simple solution to provide cushioning during transportation, air-filled PE film is inexpensive and lightweight. Its high puncture and tear resistance ensure that the cushions maintain their integrity

throughout the journey. More than 99% of the product is made up of air, meaning that prior to inflation and when deflated it takes up only a fraction of the space. This is advantageous for storage, as well as end-of-life.

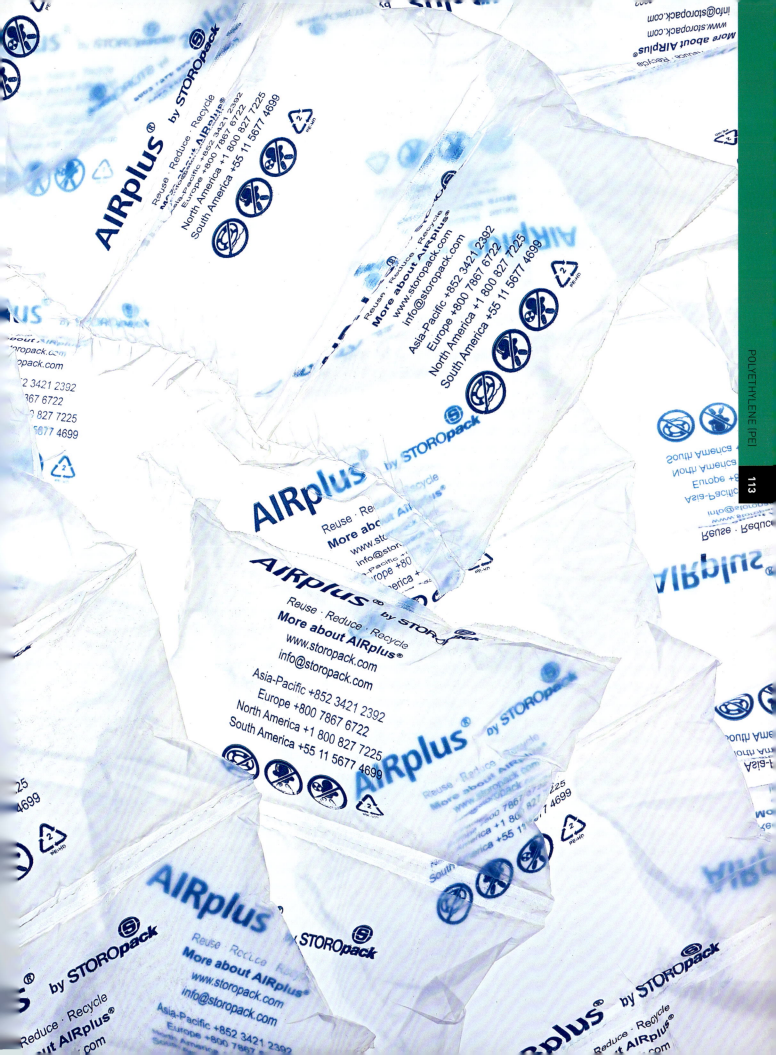

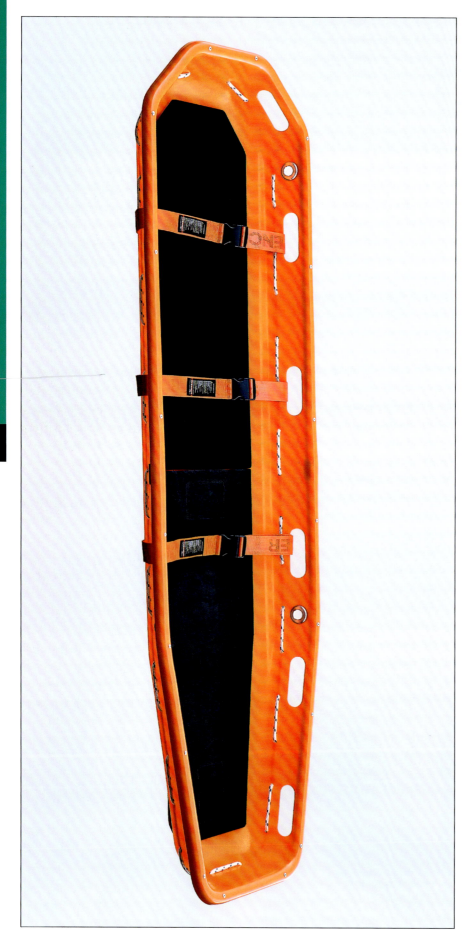

Applications range from domestic lighting to sea defences, and cutting boards to protective equipment. Its unique combination of properties has transformed peoples' lives. For example, lightweight armour, such as helmets and anti-ballistic vests, are produced from HDPE and UHMWPE. Its exceptionally high tear resistance absorbs impact far better than an equivalent weight of alternative material. UHMWPE has been used in hip and knee replacements for decades: it provides a reliable and long-lasting sliding surface within the joint.

Injection and rotation molding are the most commonly used processes for three-dimensional products. High volumes are produced with injection molding. This technique offers many advantages, including the ability to produce complex shapes, co-inject additional materials and incorporate design features and fixtures into a single molding.

Rotation molding is used for lower volumes of hollow parts. While it does offer some of the advantages of injection molding, it is restricted by the lack of pressure and control over wall thickness. However, significant material innovation has opened up opportunities for design. Powders have been created with improved flow characteristics, allowing for more complex and intricate surface details to be reproduced. It is also possible to incorporate foams within the wall thickness by mixing plastics that melt at slightly different temperatures. In other words, the material can be built up in layers, each one having slightly different characteristics, depending on how readily they melt and coalesce.

Blow molding is capable of producing large thin-walled parts with a similar geometry to rotation molding, but is restricted by the relatively high volumes required to justify the tooling costs.

Owing to the extreme molecular weight of UHMWPE, it is challenging

**Lightweight basket stretcher** HDPE is a tough all-rounder, capable of withstanding being carried, dropped and dragged through hard-to-reach places. An ideal material for basket stretchers used in rescue, it provides lightweight full-body support, floats on water and is x-ray compatible.

## PRODUCTS, FURNITURE AND LIGHTING

**Low cost**
The raw material is inexpensive and has desirable molding properties, which results in low total cost.

**Lightweight**
Its low density means that a product with thick walls, such as for enhanced durability, remains relatively lightweight. This is particularly helpful in applications where bulky parts were previously made from steel or wood.

**Durable colour**
Colour is typically applied to the base resin, as opposed to painting or coating the finished part. This results in durable colour that cannot be scratched or worn away. However, PE is degraded by ultraviolet.

**Non-toxic**
It is considered safe for food contact and is even suitable for use in medical implants.

**Rotation-molded lighting** The Jack Light was created by British designer Tom Dixon and launched in 1994. Rotation molded from PE, the uniform hollow shell provides uniform diffusion (any internal features would be silhouetted by the backlighting). It is tough and the colour runs throughout, so scuffs and dents make no difference to the quality of the light.

**Opposite**
**Lightweight nonwoven jacket** Produced from Tyvek, the DuPont trademark name for spun-bonded HDPE textile, the Post Industrial Folk Wear Jacket by Mau weighs less than 225 g (0.5 lb). Tyvek is a high-performance material typically used for industrial products, medical packaging and protective apparel. Unlike conventional woven or knitted fashion textiles, nonwovens are isotropic (non-directional) with a smooth, paper-like surface. They are manufactured in a variety of densities; selection depends on the requirements of the application. In the case of outerwear, nonwoven HDPE provides a soft, printable, tear-resistant, windproof and water-resistant barrier.

**Right**
**Artificial grass** Produced from PE, PP or a mixture of the two, the strips of extruded plastic film are textured and profiled to mimic the texture of grass. Manufactured by TigerTurf, the green PE strips are tufted onto a woven PE backing layer. The length of tuft is determined by the requirements of the application. It can last several years, even under the most demanding playing conditions. Once it has become too worn, it is recycled.

to manufacture directly into finished products. Its very high crystallinity means it becomes rubbery when heated and will not flow like LDPE and HDPE. This restricts the manufacturing to sintering methods, such as ram extrusion and compression molding. Therefore, it is typically applied in standard formats, such as fibre, sheet and rod. Textiles are knitted, woven or spun bonded (nonwoven); ropes are braided; and three-dimensional parts are machined from solid.

## PE IN TECHNICAL TEXTILES AND FASHION

PE fibres are woven, knitted, spun bonded and tufted for a range of technical and fashion items. Used mainly for low-cost industrial and packaging applications, PE is supplied in a variety of forms. PE textiles feature in a range of consumer products, from tear-resistant waterproof city maps to lightweight anoraks.

Heavy-duty HDPE fabric is woven in long lengths and seamless tubes. Lightweight and highly tear-resistant, the brightly coloured textile has become

### TECHNICAL TEXTILES AND FASHION

**Low cost**
PE is inexpensive, and properties range from elastic to high-strength, depending on the grade selected.

**Versatile**
As a thermoplastic, it is produced as film, fibre and nonwoven. It is suitable for thermoforming and provides a reliable welded seal.

**Barrier**
It is resistant to most solvents, acids and alkalis. In addition, it is unaffected by moisture and floats on water.

**Tough**
It is resilient and flexible, and has excellent abrasion resistance.

a familiar feature in all environments, from building sites (tarpaulin) to beaches (windbreak). Woven HDPE laminated with LDPE provides a waterproof lining for ponds and water storage.

PE rope and netting are used in a variety of end uses, including fishing, sports and safety. In such cases it is interchangeable with PP, PET and PA. The advantage of PE is that it is cost-effective, floats and does not absorb water (PA is hydroscopic and loses 10–20% of its strength when wet), and UHMWPE has exceptional strength-to-weight and abrasion resistance.

UHMWPE fibre is commonly referred to by its trademark names: Dyneema and Spectra. These fibres are used alongside carbon fibre (page 236) and aramid (page 242) in the most demanding applications, such as racing sails and bulletproof helmets. Compared to these high-performance fibres, UHMWPE offers greater flexibility and resilience: it is less prone to breaking when flexed. However, it has a significantly lower melting point, which limits applications somewhat.

While LDPE and HDPE are available in a range of colours, UHMWPE is mainly used in its natural state – white. It is available in a range of colours, which have typically been developed for technical reasons, such as identification of medical items, or to improve the visibility of fishing line.

# Ethylene Vinyl Acetate (EVA)

**Also known as**
Common trademark names: Elvax, Ultrathene, Nipoflex, Ateva

**EVA combines ethylene with vinyl acetate to produce a flexible, tough copolymer. It is an excellent barrier to liquids, gases and chemicals. This combination of qualities is utilized in packaging, shoes, sports and industrial products. It is inexpensive and provides a plasticizer-free alternative to polyvinyl chloride (PVC) in food and medical applications.**

| Types | Typical Applications | Sustainability |
|---|---|---|
| • Ethylene vinyl acetate (EVA)<br>• Ethylene vinyl alcohol (EVOH) | • Packaging and toys<br>• Apparel and sports<br>• Medical | • Provides an alternative to PVC<br>• Recyclable and identified by code #7, 'other' |

| Properties | Competing Materials | Costs |
|---|---|---|
| • Flexible and tough<br>• Transparent and glossy<br>• Good colourability | • Natural rubber<br>• LDPE, PVC, TPE, PU<br>• Synthetic rubber | • A little more expensive then LDPE and PVC<br>• Inexpensive to process |

118

## INTRODUCTION

Ethylene vinyl acetate (EVA) is a random copolymer made up of 10–30% vinyl acetate (VA). The VA monomer is incorporated more or less randomly in the polyethylene (PE) (page 108) chain. Lower levels of VA result in a higher degree of PE crystallinity. At around 10% VA, EVA has similar flexibility to plasticized polyvinyl chloride (PVC) (page 122).

Reducing the PE crystallinity, by increasing the VA content, increases elasticity (hardness ranges from 70 Shore A to 45 Shore D). It also lowers the softening and melting point of the polymer. Reducing the energy needed helps make production more cost-efficient. Above around 45% VA content, EVA is completely amorphous (see page 106): there is insufficient distance between the comonomer units in the PE chain to form any crystallinity. Amorphous plastics are more permeable to gases and liquids.

## COMMERCIAL TYPES AND USES

EVA is used in packaging films, bags and extrusion coating. Compared to PE, EVA film has higher elasticity and a lower melting point, qualities particularly useful in packaging applications. EVA provides an alternative to PVC in food packaging. It is biocompatible and used in medical applications such as tubing, devices, medical bags and packaging. It is used in similar applications to thermoplastic elastomers (TPE) (page 194) and is competitively priced.

Foamed EVA is softer and more resilient than PE, with greater recovery

**Plastic raincoat** This translucent raincoat is produced from EVA film. The hems are welded and the jacket may be trimmed to the correct length. It provides a reliable waterproof that is often taken as a precaution; it is inexpensive, compact and lightweight.

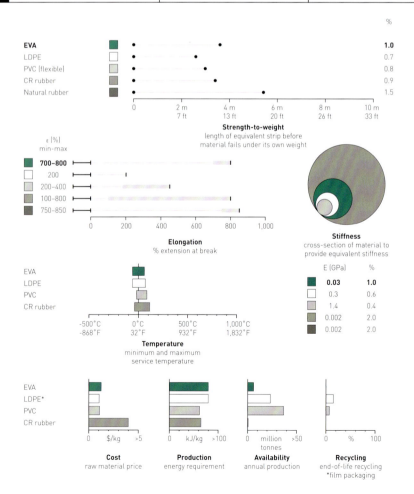

EVA / LDPE / PVC (flexible) / CR rubber / Natural rubber

| | % |
|---|---|
| EVA | 1.0 |
| LDPE | 0.7 |
| PVC (flexible) | 0.8 |
| CR rubber | 0.9 |
| Natural rubber | 1.5 |

0 / 2 m 7 ft / 4 m 13 ft / 6 m 20 ft / 8 m 26 ft / 10 m 33 ft

**Strength-to-weight**
length of equivalent strip before material fails under its own weight

ε (%) min-max

| | |
|---|---|
| 700–800 | |
| 200 | |
| 200–400 | |
| 100–800 | |
| 750–850 | |

0 / 200 / 400 / 600 / 800 / 1,000

**Elongation**
% extension at break

**Stiffness**
cross-section of material to provide equivalent stiffness

| | E (GPa) | % |
|---|---|---|
| | 0.03 | 1.0 |
| | 0.3 | 0.6 |
| | 1.4 | 0.4 |
| | 0.002 | 2.0 |
| | 0.002 | 2.0 |

EVA / LDPE / PVC / CR rubber

-500°C -868°F / 0°C 32°F / 500°C 932°F / 1,000°C 1,832°F

**Temperature**
minimum and maximum service temperature

EVA / LDPE* / PVC / CR rubber

0 / $/kg / >5    0 / kJ/kg / >100    0 / million tonnes / >50    0 / % / 100

**Cost**
raw material price

**Production**
energy requirement

**Availability**
annual production

**Recycling**
end-of-life recycling
*film packaging

characteristics. It is semi-rigid and ranges in density from 30 to 400 kg/m³ (1.9–25 lb/ft³). Closed-cell foam is impervious to liquids and gases. It is used for a range of applications. In sheet form, EVA foam is used in gaskets (automotive and industrial), floor mats (such as for exercise and play areas), packaging, protective cases, toys, costumes and carpet underlay. It is thermoformed into semi-rigid parts, which provide a protective layer in bags and packaging. The surface is typically covered with fabric, such as polyethylene terephthalate (PET, polyester) (page 152), to protect it from wear and abrasion.

EVA foam is molded in three-dimensional shapes. The density is controlled during the molding cycle and is adjusted according to the requirements of the application. It is formed into shoes, insoles, packaging, padding (body

protection) and buoyancy aids (closed-cell foam does not absorb water). In such applications it comes into direct competition with TPE and, in some cases, polyurethane resin (PU) (page 202).

Ethylene vinyl alcohol (EVOH) is formed through the controlled hydrolysis of EVA. This transformation results in a polymer with superior gas barrier properties. However, it is water soluble and tricky to process. It is mostly utilized in multi-layered film and blow-molded packaging to enhance barrier capacity. As with EVA, the exact properties depend on the proportion of the two monomers.

## SUSTAINABILITY

It is comparable with PE in many respects. However, it is not as widely used and so much less likely to be recycled; it is identified by code #7, 'other'.

**Above**
**Frosted-film carrier bag**
The vinyl content of EVA film provides it with a unique rubber-like tactility that sets it apart from PP and PE. This promotional carrier bag was designed by MadeThought for Established & Sons and produced by

Progress Packaging. It is fabricated from frosted EVA to give a translucent quality and the graphics are screen printed on the surface. Screen printing is ideally suited to block colours, such as this logo. It is inexpensive and straightforward to set up. Image courtesy of Progress Packaging.

**Opposite**
**Molded-foam one-piece shoe** Its flexibility, impact strength and low-temperature durability are utilized in molded trainer soles. In this case, the entire shoe is molded from EVA. Building on the success of Crocs EVA shoes, the Puma RS 100

Injex was launched in Japan in 2009. The one-piece shoe comprises two colours, which were molded separately, one on top of the other. A low-cost imitation of the classic RS 100, the slip-on EVA shoe is complete with faux stitching and lace holes.

# Polyvinyl Chloride (PVC)

**Also known as**
Also referred to as: vinyl, plastisol
PVC leather also referred to as: pleather

**PVC is one the most widely used thermoplastics and is often referred to simply as vinyl. It is compounded with a variety of ingredients to tailor its physical properties to the requirements of a wide range of situations. This versatility has helped to maintain PVC's popularity, even after concerns have been raised about the toxicity of some of its ingredients.**

| Types | Typical Applications | Sustainability |
|---|---|---|
| • uPVC (unplasticized)<br>• PVC (plasticized) | • Construction<br>• Fashion and textiles<br>• Packaging | • Moderate levels of embodied energy<br>• Recycling rates depend on application; it is identified by code #3 |
| **Properties** | **Competing Materials** | **Costs** |
| • Rigid to flexible, depending on the plasticizer content<br>• Good resistance to oil and chemicals | • PP, PE, PET<br>• EVA, TPU, TPE, PU, synthetic rubber and natural rubber<br>• Aluminium, timber and steel | • Low material costs<br>• Low manufacturing costs |

122

## INTRODUCTION

Polyvinyl chloride (PVC) is an amorphous plastic (see page 166). Its unique character comes from the inclusion of chlorine atoms in the polymer structure. Although it has an amorphous morphology, PVC is durable and resistant to oils and chemicals, and has fire-retardant properties.

It is naturally transparent, and thin films have good clarity; it is available in a range of vivid colours. However, many of the additives used are non-compatible with the PVC itself, which causes it to become translucent or opaque.

PVC is viscous when molten and therefore impractical for large injection moldings. However, it is well suited to complex extrusions (window frames) and blown film (packaging). It is possible to manufacture PVC with a high-gloss finish.

## COMMERCIAL TYPES AND USES

PVC is either combined with plasticizers to make it flexible, or left unplasticized (uPVC or PVC-U) and so stiff and rigid. The amount of plasticizer determines mechanical properties, including tensile and impact strength. The majority of plasticizers are compounds added to PVC that facilitate movement within the polymer structure. Unlike copolymers, plasticizers are not chemically bonded into the polymer chain. Consequently the chemical is free to move through the plastic and, over time, to migrate to the surface. The plasticizer is lost to the atmosphere and surroundings,

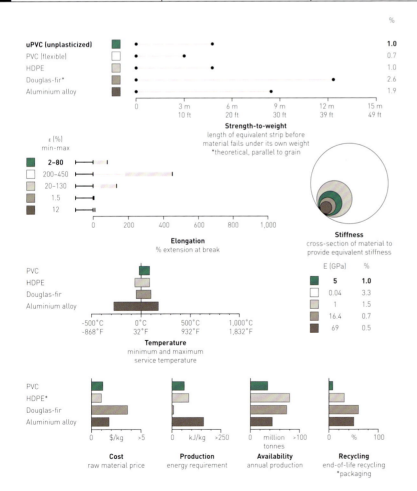

**PVC-clad shopper** Bao Bao Lucent bag by Issey Miyake is made up of triangular plates of PVC clad onto a PET underlayer. The structure and arrangement give the bag an origami-like quality; it folds around the mass of its contents. PVC has a glossy finish and takes vivid colour. These qualities emphasize the faceted design; light is picked up and reflected in several directions.

through evaporation and abrasion, causing the PVC to become embrittled.

Rigid uPVC is used in a variety of applications, from construction to packaging. The pliable, rubber-like quality of flexible PVC is utilized in quite different situations, from faux leather to chemical-resistant gloves.

A range of additives is combined with PVC during compounding to enhance processability, elasticity, impact resistance and fire retardancy. In addition, PVC is alloyed with other high-performance plastics to compensate for its shortcomings. It has good compatibility with a wide range of plastics and

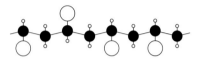

**Polymer structure** PVC has a linear polymer structure like PP (see page 106), but with the addition of relatively large chlorine atoms. The inclusion of chlorine, which is randomly distributed, makes it difficult for the chains to pack together in an orderly fashion. As a result, PVC is amorphous, with only small areas of crystallinity.

However, unlike other amorphous plastics, PVC tends to be quite stiff and brittle. This is because the chlorine atoms facilitate relatively strong bonds between the polymer chains. Including plasticizer reduces the effectiveness of these bonds and so facilitates movement between the polymers. This results in a more flexible plastic.

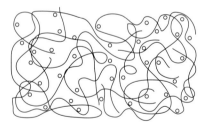

**Plasticized PVC** Plasticizers work by disrupting the strength of the chlorine–carbon bonds (the method depends on the chemical). In doing so, they increase the flexibility and softness of the plastic. Distributed throughout the amorphous structure, ingredients not bound into the polymer chain

are free to migrate to the surface. The evaporation of these chemicals gives PVC its distinctive 'new' smell. Phthalate-based plasticizers are potentially harmful and are small enough to be diffusible when exposed to heat or abrasion, which raises health as well as environmental concerns.

so is available in many different configurations; the performance may be tailored to the specific requirements of each application. For example, impact strength is improved with the addition of acrylonitrile butadiene styrene (ABS) (page 138), polyethylene (PE) (page 108) or ethylene vinyl acetate (EVA) (page 118).

## SUSTAINABILITY

PVC is inexpensive considering its strength and endurance. Its use in pipework and guttering has helped to improve quality of life, by ensuring a safe and reliable infrastructure. It competes with a spectrum of materials – aluminium (page 42), solid timber (see Douglas-Fir, page 314) and steel (page 28), as well as other plastics – as a result of its versatility. Wood is environmentally superior in many respects, whereas the use of metals poses its own challenges.

The embodied energy of PVC is relatively low compared to other plastics, because around half of its molecular weight is derived from salt. The remainder is derived from hydrocarbon feedstock, such as oil or sugar crops.

However, a key ingredient, vinyl chloride (VC) monomer, is highly flammable and carcinogenic. While almost all of the VC monomer is polymerized in the production of PVC, it is possible that a small amount remains unpolymerized and so can migrate from the plastic into food or the surroundings.

A host of other ingredients are mixed with PVC during compounding to improve the efficiency of production and make it suitable for a range of applications. Some of these ingredients are subject to restrictions in many countries. For example, stabilizers used in the production of uPVC, which stop the plastic yellowing, may include tin, lead and cadmium; and the plasticizer used in flexible PVC may contain phthalates (esters of phthalic acid, which are known to be harmful to people and the environment). Non-toxic stabilizers (such as calcium-zinc) and non-phthalate plasticizers are available for sensitive applications, such as toys, packaging and medical devices.

PVC is readily recycled and is identified by code #3. The diversity of use poses a challenge end-of-life, because it is not always straightforward to distinguish PVC from other plastics. It is an inexpensive plastic, which means recycling has to be very efficient to be economically worthwhile. Plastic waste is incinerated for energy recovery if it is not efficient to recycle. The problem with this is that PVC may produce dioxins when incinerated. This is not such a problem in modern incineration plants, where combustion is tightly controlled. Elsewhere, this remains a major concern.

### PVC IN PRODUCTS AND INDUSTRIAL

PVC is one of the most widely used plastics. Applications range from unglamorous industrial parts to iconic toys. This success is partly due to the range of physical properties that can be achieved at relatively low cost. The other key attribute of PVC is that it is compatible with a broad spectrum of manufacturing processes.

Dip molding and rotation molding are used to shape hollow items in a single piece. Dip-molded products have an open-ended profile, so the tool can be removed. Examples include bellows and gloves. By contrast, rotation molding produces completely sealed parts, without any openings, suitable for buoyancy, cushioning and inflatables. With these processes, the wall thickness is constant throughout; it is adjusted to suit the application along with the flexibility of the PVC.

Alternatively, sheets of PVC are welded and inflated, such as in the production of buoyancy aids, bathing pools and blow-up mattresses. PVC is polar – as are thermoplastic polyurethane (TPU) (see Thermoplastic Elastomer, page 194), EVA, polyethylene terephthalate (PET, polyester) (page 152) and polyamide (PA, nylon) (page 164) – and so compatible with radio-frequency (RF) welding. It is also referred to as dielectric or high-frequency (HF) welding. This is a cost-effective welding technique utilized in products, packaging and architecture. As well as running in straight lines, the weld may follow a curvilinear profile.

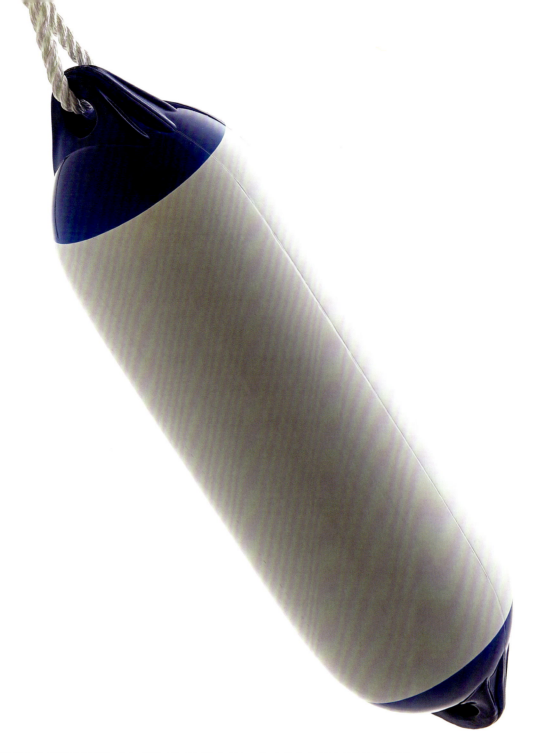

## PRODUCTS AND INDUSTRIAL

### Versatility
Ranging from rubbery to rigid, PVC is suitable for a range of end uses. On top of this, it is inexpensive and compatible with a range of low-volume manufacturing processes, including dip and rotation molding.

### Low cost
PVC is considerably less expensive than its competitors, in particular high-performance elastomers such as silicone (page 212), PU, fluoropolymer (page 190) and synthetic rubber (page 216).

### Colourability
As an amorphous thermoplastic, PVC may be manufactured in a broad spectrum of vivid colours, from transparent to opaque.

### Durability
PVC epitomizes the longevity of plastics: it has a very long service life and its resistance to weathering and chemicals means it may remain in service for decades without maintenance.

### Air-filled fender
Produced by rotation molding, the watertight fender provides cushioning between boat hulls and pontoons. Liquid PVC is poured into the mold, which is rotated as it is heated and cured, ensuring an even wall thickness throughout. The ends are coloured by dip coating. Where further rigidity and strength are required in the eyelet, two types of PVC are combined. It is flattened, and the air expelled, so as to take up less space during storage. As soon as the pressure is released, it bounces back to its inflated state. Additional air may be pumped in to increase cushioning.

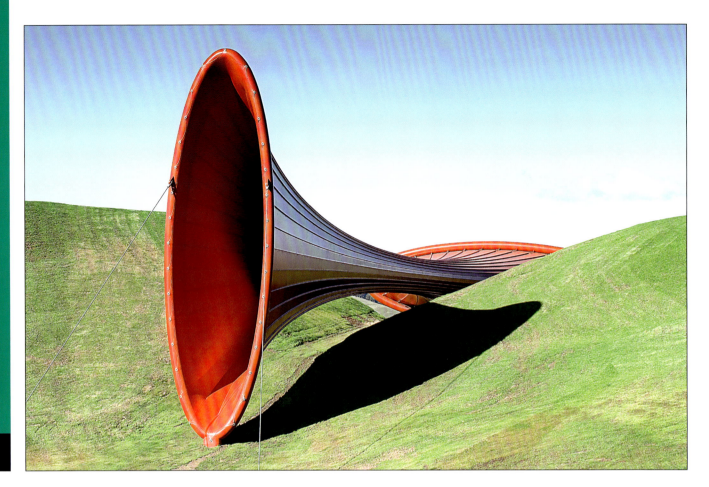

## PVC IN ARCHITECTURE AND CONSTRUCTION

PVC is the most widely applied plastic in building and construction, largely thanks to its use in infrastructure and fittings. Likewise, construction accounts for the majority of PVC consumption. This relationship has evolved over decades, fuelled by the versatility of this relatively inexpensive material.

It is used as an alternative to traditional materials, including glass, wood, metal and rubber. While in some situations and applications this is cost-driven, in others PVC offers important performance advantages. It is strong and low-density, which provides weight savings; it is durable and resistant to weathering, chemicals, impacts and abrasion; and it is relatively easy to install and modify on-site.

The major areas of application for PVC include rigid extrusions (pipes, windows and flooring, for example) and flexible textiles (such as flooring, inflatables and tensile structures). The viscosity of PVC when molten allows for complex extrusions to be made. In other words, simple water pipes and waste pipes, as well as intricate window

**PVC tensile structure**
Created by Anish Kapoor (2009), 'Dismemberment, Site 1' was fabricated and installed by Structureflex. It is located at Gibbs Farm, a 400-hectare (990-acre) sculpture park on the Kaipara Harbour, New Zealand. The steel ellipses weigh 43 tonnes each. The PVC textile is held under tension along monofilament cables, transitioning from a horizontal ellipse to a circle mid-span, through to a vertical ellipse at the other end. Covering 4,300 m² (46,300 ft²), the welded textile construction weighs a mere 5.9 tonnes. PVC was selected because it is able to withstand storms and sunshine, and will retain its bright red appearance for many years. Photo courtesy of Structurflex.

frames with embedded functionality, are equally straightforward and cost-effective to produce.

PVC is applied as a coating onto fabrics, such as PET or PA. Alternatively, it is used as a film without any fibre reinforcement. It is top-coated with acrylic or polyvinylidene fluoride (PVDF) to ensure a lifespan of at least 15 years in normal outdoor conditions. In locations that are exposed to very high levels of

## ARCHITECTURE AND CONSTRUCTION

**Cost-effective**
As a result of its low cost and low density, PVC provides cost–performance advantages compared to pricier materials, such as aluminium and hardwood.

**Durability**
PVC can last 35 years or more in outdoor and underground applications with minimal maintenance. It has good resistance to chemicals, but is vulnerable to temperature extremes.

**Versatile**
Available in a range of shapes and formats, from textiles to extruded profiles, PVC provides an ideal solution in many situations. It can be cut and shaped on-site and is straightforward to weld and join.

**Fire resistance**
PVC burns when exposed to fire, but will self-extinguish and heat production is comparatively low. When PVC burns it emits toxic substances including carbon dioxide ($CO_2$), dioxins and hydrochloric acid.

ultraviolet, PVC can be expected to last only 10 to 15 years. It may be coated with titanium dioxide ($TiO_2$), which provides self-cleaning functionality. This helps to keep the surface brighter and cleaner for longer (the same coating is used on glass).

As a thermoplastic, PVC is suitable for welding or adhesive bonding. Panels are typically fabricated off-site with all the necessary fixings and sleeves to ensure a straightforward installation. The joins are strong and hermetic, which means that PVC structures are secure and weather-tight. They may also be inflated or filled with water.

Alternatives to PVC construction textiles include polyurethane (PU) (page 202) and fluoropolymers (page 190). These plastics offer many advantages, but can be much more expensive.

## PVC IN PACKAGING AND PROMOTION

Rigid uPVC film is clear, glossy and stiff. It has very good gas barrier properties, superior to polypropylene (PP) (page 98) and PE, and excellent resistance to chemicals and oils. It is slightly more permeable to water vapour, which helps to reduce the buildup of condensation in food packaging. Flexible PVC film is used as stretch wrap. However, in recent years it has been largely replaced by LLDPE (see PE).

uPVC has excellent thermoforming characteristics. It is shaped into trays, inserts, clamshells and blister packs (with aluminium lidding). Coated PP provides an alternative to PVC in such applications. It has lower water vapour permeability, which is advantageous in most cases, but is trickier to thermoform as a result of its semi-crystalline structure.

**Fluorescent PVC** NEON by Victionary, released September 2013, features a PVC softcover. The book focuses on new fluorescent graphics, and PVC provides the ideal synthetic cover material. Widely used in bookbinding and stationery, it is flexible and durable, takes colour very well, and can have print applied directly on the surface.

## PACKAGING AND PROMOTION

Colour
Naturally transparent, it is available in a wide range of tints, colours and finishes. The edge glow effect is emphasized with fluorescent dyes.

Low cost
The aesthetic and tactile quality of PVC – high-gloss to soft-touch – sets it apart from conventional materials, and yet it remains inexpensive.

Tactility
The rubber-like quality of PVC is desirable in some situations, such as in padded, gel-filled or flexible items.

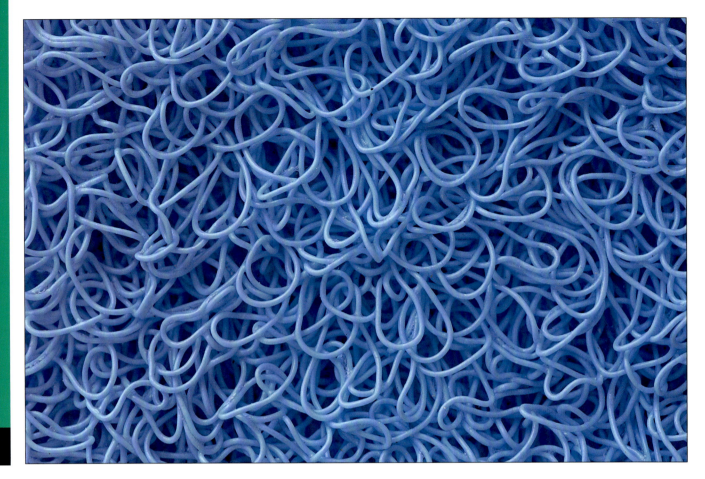

PVC is also used in blow-molded drinks containers. However, as with film, PVC is gradually being phased out of food and medical packaging. Bottles and trays are more often produced from PET and in some cases PP and PE. These materials have become more widely accepted, in particular in food applications.

The flexible lettering used to decorate vans, windows and exhibition walls is cut from thin sheets of PVC. Thickness ranges from 0.8 to 0.08 mm (0.03–0.003 in) for this type of application, and the finish is either matt or gloss. Intricate and multi-coloured designs may be printed onto white or clear PVC, as opposed to cutting out and registering many individual colour films.

RF welding is used to produce hermetically sealed film packaging (EVA offers an alternative to PVC in these applications, but is a little more expensive). Because it creates a watertight seal, items may be gel-filled or inflated. As well as being used for purely functional packaging (blood storage bags), this property is utilized for

decorative applications (book covers); it creates a unique aesthetic and tactility.

Welding is combined with embossing and cutting, which offers greater flexibility for design without adding cost. For example, the welding tool may be engraved, or graphics embossed to give a decorative appearance and relief profile. Tear-seal welding creates a sealed package with the excess removed in a single step. A cutting edge is incorporated adjacent to the welding tool, which compresses the material and allows for it to be separated. As well as determining the perimeter, tear-seal welding is used to create cutouts within the material.

## PVC IN FASHION AND TEXTILES

From inflatable craft to fetish wear, PVC has become synonymous with colourful, low-cost, rubbery textiles. Whether applied as a coating or as a standalone extruded film, the breadth of applications illustrates the versatility of PVC.

PVC-coated textile is a composite that combines the strength and dimensional stability of fibres with the elasticity and

**Loop pile** This hard-wearing PVC floor covering is produced from filaments bonded together directly after extrusion (while they are still molten), in a process also known as silk spurting. The pile is looped in such a way as to trap the maximum amount of dirt and debris when walked on. The size of the loops depends on the speed of the process.

surface resistance of PVC. Fabrics such as PET and PA provide strength in-line with the fibres. PA is more expensive and so tends to be reserved for applications that require higher strength and flexibility, such as inflatables. Otherwise, PET is sufficient and provides a solution fit for industrial textiles through apparel.

PVC was the first synthetic leather, providing an inexpensive alternative to the real thing. In comparison, PVC tends to feel hotter on the skin, stickier, and is not breathable. Known as 'pleather', it is available in a variety of colours with a calendered surface or embossed texture to mimic all of the common leathers (see Cowhide, page 444, Sheepskin, page 452, and Pigskin, page 456) as well as exotic types (page 462). These textiles

**Glossy and colourful**
PVC is transparent and takes colour very well; it is available in a very broad colour range including bright, dark, fluorescent and pastel.

**Tactile**
The flexibility of PVC ranges from stiff to rubber-like, depending on the level of plasticizer. PVC-coated fabrics are stronger and stiffer than standalone film; the exact properties depend on the selected material and coating thickness.

**Cost-effective**
PVC is significantly less expensive than the textiles it imitates, such as oilcloth, leather and latex. Compared to polyurethane (PU), a high-performance synthetic coating used in similar applications, PVC is around half the price.

are used in apparel, footwear, electronics (headphones), luggage, sporting goods, upholstery and car interiors. It has since been superseded by PU-coated fabric, which provides a more realistic and pleasant tactility.

The surface of pleather does not wear in the same way as natural leather and it will crack and eventually start to delaminate. The more stress the PVC is subjected too, the more quickly the composite will break down. The cheapest products are made without textile backing – PVC film is bonded directly onto foam or other substrate – and so will fail more quickly than those on a sturdy textile backing.

Oilcloth is a waterproof textile similar to waxed cotton that was traditionally made from linen with a linseed oil-based coating. PVC-coated cotton provides a cost-effective and versatile alternative. Patterns and decoration are screen-printed, giving an almost unlimited choice of colours and designs. It provides a very practical and inexpensive solution for covers, tablecloths, aprons and bags.

**Waders** Waterproof apparel is typically constructed from PVC-coated PET. For applications that require a high degree of stretch and recovery, PVC is combined with an elastomeric textile, such as TPU (elastane). The seams are stitched and welded to keep the water out. The compression-molded boots are welded to the legs. The least expensive examples utilize PVC. PU boots are used in combination with PVC legs where higher performance is required – it is lighter and longer-lasting, and remains more flexible in cold water.

# Acid Copolymers and Ionomers

**Also known as**
Trademark names: Surlyn, Nucrel, Primacor

Utilized in diverse applications, from film to golf ball covers, these thermoplastics posses a unique set of properties. Those based on polyethylene (PE) are made up of three-quarters or more ethylene monomer, and so share many of the same basic properties. They are differentiated by improved toughness and adhesive bond strength, as well as having superior transparency.

| Types | Typical Applications | Sustainability |
|---|---|---|
| • Acid copolymers based on ethylene: acrylic acid (EAA), methacrylic acid (EMAA), ethyl acrylate (EEA), methyl acrylate (EMA); and ionomer | • Food and packaging films<br>• Sports products<br>• Automotive | • Recyclable and identified by code #7, 'other'<br>• Not collected from mixed waste streams |

| Properties | Competing Materials | Costs |
|---|---|---|
| • Excellent heat sealing<br>• High toughness<br>• Very good resistance to chemicals and abrasion | • TPU and PU<br>• PE and PP<br>• Lead glass | • It is manufactured in small quantities and quite expensive, comparable with PC |

130

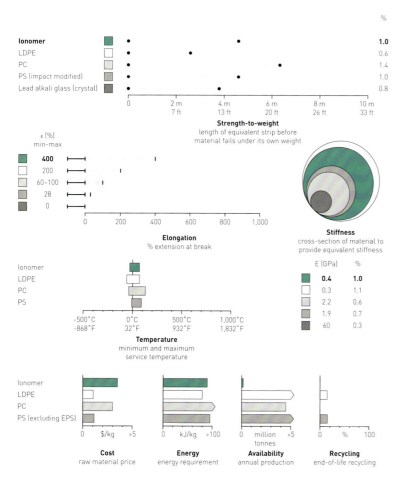

## INTRODUCTION

This family of thermoplastics is based on copolymers of polyethylene (PE) (page 108) and acid. The covalent acidic bonds distributed among the ethylene monomer enhance physical properties compared to PE such as toughness and adhesive bond strength.

Through a process of neutralization, the acid protons are exchanged with metal ions, and ionomers are created. They are characterized by polar ionic clusters (a form of cross-link, see page 110) among the PE. The cross-links are reversible, so while they stiffen, toughen and improve the chemical resistance of acid copolymers, they do not compromise thermoplastic moldability. The strength-to-weight of ionomer is almost twice that of low-density PE (LDPE).

Another type of ionomer is formed from a fluoropolymer copolymer (page 190). Commonly referred to by its trademark name Nafion, it has excellent thermal and chemical properties. As a result, it is utilized in fuel cell membranes.

Acid copolymers and ionomers feature self-healing behaviour. While this has potential to extend products' lifetimes, the property has only recently become the topic of research.

## COMMERCIAL TYPES AND USES

Acid copolymers are typically based on PE, but may be formed from polystyrene (PS) (page 132) and polyurethane (PU) (page 202). They are up to one-third acid content. The amount of comonomer affects the crystallinity (see page 166) – increasing acid content reduces crystallinity. Ionomers are produced by acid neutralization with the addition of zinc, sodium, lithium or other metal salts. Plastics with the potential for ionic properties include PE acid copolymers and fluoropolymer copolymers.

Acid copolymers are mainly applied as film in laminated or blow-molded packaging. They are used in place of PE when improved adhesion, transparency and barrier integrity are required. Packaging lines utilizing acid copolymer films operate at higher speeds, because they have a lower melting point than LDPE. Typical products include pouches and sachets based on either paper or foil.

The high toughness and improved wear resistance of ionomers is utilized in sports products, such as the outer cover of golf balls, bowling balls, crash helmets and ski boots.

They have very good optical clarity and barrier properties and so, like acid copolymers, they are utilized in multi-layered packaging films where colour and graphics are important. Their high elongation is used in stretch packaging and they are thermoformed into clamshell and blister packs.

Ionomer is used in place of crystal glass (page 518) for premium cosmetics and perfume packaging. Combined with polycarbonate (PC) (page 144), ionomer brings about a range of design possibilities. It is molded into complex shapes and its glass-like transparency is enhanced with gloss, frosted or faceted finishes. It pigments very well to produce rich and deep colour saturation. Alternatively, graphics are incorporated and overmolded to eliminate coatings and provide a seamless finish.

It is utilized in caps, jars and inner containers (both rigid and flexible). It remains unaffected by the contents owing to its high chemical resistance. On the outside, its high wear resistance keeps the packaging looking new for longer.

## SUSTAINABILITY

These thermoplastics are produced in relatively small quantities. While they

**Transparent ionomer packaging** Utilizing DuPont Surlyn, the Kenzo Flower In The Air perfume cap incorporates a printed poppy corolla visible from all sides. Through a process of overmolding, the graphic is encapsulated between two layers of highly transparent ionomer – objects appear suspended in the plastic. As well as printed film, DuPont has demonstrated overmolding delicate textiles including lace.

share many of the same characteristics as PE, and are fully recyclable, they are not typically collected and reprocessed.

They are frequently used as an adhesive layer, barrier layer or other part of a multi-material construction. This has many benefits, such as reducing the weight of packaging while helping to maximize the shelf life of food and drink. However, they are impractical, if not impossible, to separate from the metal or paper-based substrate, which renders the whole assembly non-recyclable.

# Polystyrene (PS)

**PS is colourless, hard and brittle. It has excellent light transmission and is available in a range of saturated colours, from tinted to opaque. Impact-resistant grades are modified with rubber to improve ductility and are thus translucent. PS is low-cost and applied rigid or foamed in large quantities to packaging, products and construction.**

| Types | Typical Applications | Sustainability |
|---|---|---|
| • PS: general purpose (GPPS or, simply, PS) and high-impact (HIPS)<br>• Foamed PS: expanded (EPS) and extruded (XPS) | • Packaging<br>• Consumer products and protective clothing<br>• Insulation and flotation | • Widely recycled and identified by code #6<br>• EPS has additional processing steps and its low density presents some recycling challenges |
| **Properties** | **Competing Materials** | **Costs** |
| • Typically hard and brittle; exact mechanical properties depend on grade<br>• Odourless and non-toxic<br>• Poor chemical and weathering resistance | • SAN and ABS<br>• PP, PE and PET<br>• PC and PMMA<br>• Starch-based plastic | • Low material cost and straightforward to manufacture |

132

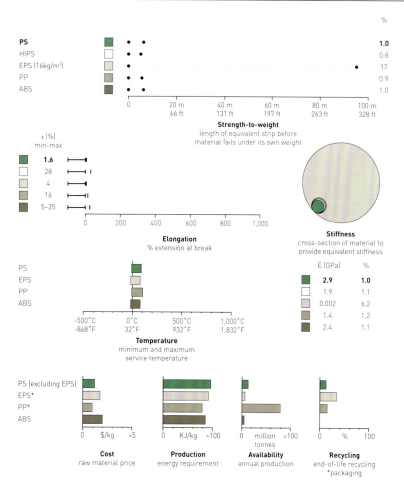

## INTRODUCTION

Even though it has many shortcomings, polystyrene (PS) is cheap and consumed in vast quantities. General-purpose grades are hard, with low tensile strength and ductility, which results in a very brittle material. It is amorphous (see page 166), owing to its atactic polymer structure (see page 106), and so vulnerable to chemicals and weathering. Numerous grades have been developed by modifying the base polymer to overcome these limitations.

With regard to applications in consumer products and automotive design, closely related styrene acrylonitrile (SAN) (page 136) and acrylonitrile butadiene styrene (ABS) (page 138) are superior to PS in many ways. Of course, they are more expensive and have drawbacks of their own, but they provide a stronger and tougher alternative while maintaining the desirable moldability and colourability of PS.

## COMMERCIAL TYPES AND USES

General-purpose PS is predominantly used for low-value items, owing to its relatively low durability. Packaging accounts for the majority: pots, cups and trays are produced with injection molding and thermoforming. The low melting point and high flow of PS make it possible to produce thin-walled parts at high speed and with good dimensional accuracy, although in many cases PS has been substituted with polypropylene (PP) (page 98), polyethylene (PE) (page 108) and polyethylene terephthalate (PET, polyester) (page 152). These plastics offer superior mechanical performance in thin-walled packaging.

A semi-crystalline (see page 166) grade is manufactured under the trade name Xarec. Typically reinforced with glass fibre (GF), semi-crystalline PS has desirable molding properties and dimensional

stability when compared to other GF structural resins. It is highly resistant to hydrolysis and most acids and alkalis; and it has superior dielectric strength to GF polybutylene terephthalate (PBT) (see page 154) and polyamide (PA, nylon) (page 164). It is used to make small electrical components, such as connectors, housings and mobile phone antennas.

**Water pitcher** The excellent light transmission and gloss surface finish results in highly saturated colours. PS degrades when exposed to ultraviolet light, a drawback compounded by its already fragile nature. Therefore, it is typically used for items that are not intended to last long, such as partyware and promotional items. Durable alternatives, such as PC and SAN, are more expensive – around three times for PC and twice for SAN – and so are reserved for items that are designed to last, or intended to be 'unbreakable' (in comparison to glass).

A tougher version of PS, known as high-impact PS (HIPS), is produced with up to 15% polybutadiene included during polymerization. The rubber content enhances the ductility, which increases impact strength at the expense of tensile strength (by around one-third). It is translucent, but takes colour very well.

HIPS is utilized a great deal for the high-quality surface that can be achieved with injection molding. Fine surface details (logos and instructions) reproduce very well, which avoids the necessity of printing graphics and other expensive secondary processes. Examples include single-use items, such as razors, stationery, disposable tableware and promotional giveaways; toys and games (including the iconic Airfix models); and laboratory equipment.

While it is not consumed in the largest quantities by weight, expanded PS (EPS) makes up the majority of packaging by volume. Only 5% or so of an EPS box is PS, the rest is air. The closed-cell structure provides restraint and cushioning. The typical densities are 16, 32 and 48 kg/m³ (1, 2, and 3 lb/ft³). Compressive strength, tensile strength and thermal insulation all increase with density.

Where the items are enclosed, such as food boxes, EPS provides very good thermal insulation thanks to the trapped air cells.

Loose-fill EPS packaging has largely been replaced by inflated PE cushioning (see image, page 113) or loose fill produced from biobased plastic (see Starch Plastic, page 260). Unlike EPS, PE cushioning is simply punctured after use and thereby takes up significantly less space in recycling, and biobased plastics pellets do not contribute to landfill if they are properly composted.

Mold tools are only moderately expensive, so in most cases EPS is molded to the exact requirements of the part it is protecting. All of the surface details are precisely reproduced; quality is determined by density. The surface has poor resistance to abrasion and puncturing. Where this presents a problem, such as in the protection of electronics and appliances, EPS is contained within a card (page 268)

**Pre-expanded PS bead**

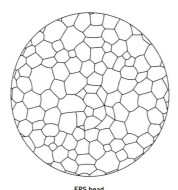

**EPS bead**

**Closed-cell structure**
The process involves a blowing agent (usually pentane), which is added to the PS during polymerization. This causes the small beads of PS to expand to several times their size, forming closed-cell EPS. Very thin sections of PS hold the bead together; its delicate structure is supported by up to 98% air, which is trapped within. The beads are placed into a mold. With steam and pressure they further expand and fuse together to form a rigid cellular structure.

box. Additional layers of foam, such as polyurethane resin (PU) (page 202), are incorporated for improved shock and vibration damping.

Sheet EPS is suitable for thermoforming. Examples include clamshell packaging and trays, such as for takeaway foods. PS is moisture-resistant and EPS has a closed-cell structure, so packaging is unaffected by short-term exposure to liquids.

EPS is used a great deal in construction, primarily for thermal and acoustic insulation. Typically supplied in sheet form, it is molded where necessary (such as for modular construction projects) and applied as large-volume blocks.

Outside these two areas of application, which account for the majority of EPS, it is used for buoyancy (such as in surfboards and floats), for protective clothing (helmets), as a core layer in composite panels and even as geofoam (such as reducing settlement below embankments and for insulation).

PS is foamed during extrusion (XPS) to produce long lengths of closed-cell foam. The difference between EPS and XPS is that the latter is foamed directly in the

extrusion process. This results in a slightly different product, distinguished by colour coding, such as blue, pink and green. While EPS is available in compressive strengths of 0.1 to 0.4 MPa (10–60 psi), XPS is available in higher densities with compressive strength of up to around 0.7 MPa (100 psi). Higher values are particular useful for construction applications.

## SUSTAINABILITY

PS is fully recyclable and marked with the resin identification code #6. It is used for many products outside packaging that are not instantly recognizable as PS (or marked with the resin identification code) and so the vast majority is not recycled but instead contributes to landfill.

EPS, on the other hand, is readily identifiable, but unfortunately contains only a very small amount of PS. It is very impractical to transport EPS to recycling. Compacting systems have been put in place to make it more efficient to transport to where it can be reprocessed into PS. Recycled material is used to make new products, such as packaging (including EPS), stationery, plant pots and coat hangers.

EPS is lightweight and so reduces the energy required for transportation. However, it is not always the most efficient, owing to the bulk of material required. Where a few large items are being shipped, such as appliances, EPS is practical and takes up relatively little space. For smaller items – up to around the size and weight of a laptop – thermoformed trays are more practical. Reducing bulk helps maximize the number of products that can pack in a container.

**Foam packaging** EPS packaging is used to protect the contents from crushing, vibration and thermal fluctuations. It is rigid and so holds everything securely in place during transit; bumpy roads put significant load on packaging of heavy goods. The high bulk and low density of EPS – qualities that lend themselves to protective packaging – pose a challenge end-of-life. While its size makes it impractical to collect and transport, its low density means there is very little reward when reprocessed.

# Styrene Acrylonitrile (SAN) and Acrylic Styrene Acrylonitrile (ASA)

**Also known as**
Trademark name: Luran

**This is a transparent plastic with high resistance to thermal shock and good chemical resistance. It is less expensive and easier to process than high-performance transparent plastics, such as PC and PMMA. As a result, it is utilized in the production of kitchen, laboratory, medical and personal hygiene products and packaging that will not be exposed to such high stresses.**

| Types | Typical Applications | Sustainability |
|---|---|---|
| • SAN<br>• ASA (SAN impact-modified with acrylic ester rubber) | • Packaging<br>• Laboratory, medical and hygiene equipment<br>• Kitchenware | • Recyclable and identified by code #7, 'other'<br>• Not collected from mixed waste |

| Properties | Competing Materials | Costs |
|---|---|---|
| • Transparent (90%)<br>• Stiff and brittle<br>• High thermal resistance | • PS<br>• PMMA<br>• PC | • Almost twice the cost of PS, but relatively easy to process |

136

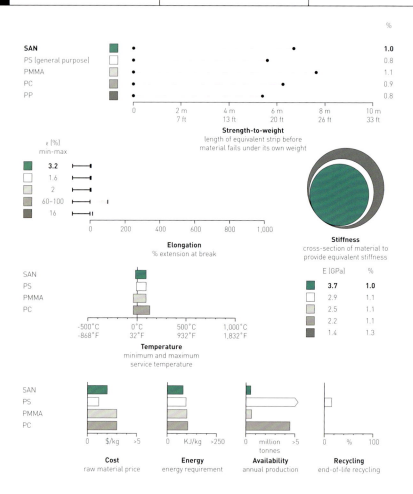

## INTRODUCTION

In terms of mechanical performance, styrene acrylonitrile (SAN) falls between polystyrene (PS) (page 132) and polymethyl methacrylate (PMMA) (page 174). All three are transparent. SAN is tougher than PS (it has roughly twice the elongation); it has high resistance to chemicals, acids and so on; and it is relatively easy to process with a brilliant surface.

## COMMERCIAL TYPES AND USES

SAN is tasteless and non-toxic, and does not contain phthalates or bisphenol A (BPA), ingredients that are considered harmful and are subject to restrictions in many countries. Therefore it is suitable for applications that require contact with food, drink or personal hygiene products.

Bathroom products, such as toothbrushes and cosmetic packaging, make use of its superior surface qualities. It is equally well suited to parts of kitchen appliances, such as mixing bowls (food processors), which must be able to safely withstand hot food as well as dishwashing. Its high resistance to chemicals, including acids, alkalis and oils, mean it is also utilized in laboratory and medical equipment.

It has been used to make furniture too, such as the one-piece seat and back of the Slim chair (Roberto Foschia, 2007). The streamlined design makes use of the colourability and brilliant finish combined with ease of molding.

SAN has very high dimensional stability and its transparency gives excellent depth of colour. Compared to glass (page 508), SAN is much lighter and less expensive. It is formed into a range of complex shapes by injection molding, which allows greater design freedom than glass-forming processes. It is also compatible with extrusion. However, it will not last as long as glass and is prone to fading, or yellowing, after molding and over time.

ABS (page 138) consists of SAN with the addition of butadiene rubber (BR) (page 216). This combination results in a material with the rigidity, hardness and resistance of SAN with superior impact strength. Roughly the same price, ABS is produced in much higher quantities and utilized in a broad range of products.

SAN forms the precursor to acrylic styrene acrylonitrile (ASA). During polymerization an elastomer is introduced to produce a material with similar properties to ABS, but with improved resistance to weathering. It is used in outdoor and automotive applications. The durability of ASA means that colour lasts well, even after prolonged exposure. By contrast, the butadiene content in ABS makes it susceptible to attack by ultraviolet light, heat and chemicals, which over time will lead to discoloration and embrittlement.

ASA eliminates the need for painting in automotive parts. It is used to make grills, rear-view mirrors, trim and caps with a bright, coloured, glossy surface. It is suitable for molding and so used alone, or applied as an overmolding or multi-shot molding to provide a protective transparent (or tinted) top layer. In this way it is commonly used in conjunction with less resistant plastics, such as polyvinyl chloride (PVC) (page 122) and ABS, as well as non-plastic materials such as metal and wood.

## SUSTAINABILITY

The advantage of these styrenics is that they have exceptional resistance to weathering. Used alone, or as a protective layer, they maintain their appearance and the majority of their mechanical properties long-term. This helps to extend the useful life of parts.

Like most thermoplastics, they are fully recyclable. Waste generated in the factory can be fed back into the production line, within limits. They are identified as #7, 'other', which means they are difficult to collect from mixed waste streams.

They contain acrylonitrile monomer (see Polyacrylonitrile, page 180), which on its own is polluting and poisonous.

**Transparent water bottle** 'My Water Bottle' from Danish design brand Stelton is a reusable container that makes use of the transparency and cleanliness of SAN. The molded ABS lid unscrews in two stages to reveal a small and a wide neck. This allows the container to be used as a bottle or a cup, and makes it easier to clean. The open profile is also a manufacturing feature: it allows the SAN to be injection molded with precise wall thickness and internal surfaces. Incorporating a neck profile would mean blow molding the container (because of the undercut), which presents a whole other set of design challenges.

# Acrylonitrile Butadiene Styrene (ABS)

**Also known as**
Trademark names: Cycolac, Novodur, Terluran, Absolac
ABS/PC blend trademark names include: Bayblend, Terez, Cycoloy

**ABS owes its excellent surface finish and superior impact strength to a combination of styrene acrylonitrile (SAN) with butadiene rubber (BR). Produced as an amorphous blend, it is available for blow and injection molding. It is the material of choice for colourful consumer products and toys; visual quality is enhanced with eye-catching additives. It is also suitable for metal plating.**

| Types | Typical Applications | Sustainability |
|---|---|---|
| • ABS<br>• Blends: ABS/PA, ABS/PC and ABS/PVC | • Consumer products<br>• Telecommunications<br>• Automotive<br>• Toys | • Recyclable and identified by code #7, 'other', or 'ABS'<br>• Not typically collected from mixed waste streams |

| Properties | Competing Materials | Costs |
|---|---|---|
| • Tough and ductile<br>• Excellent colour range with superior aesthetics | • PC and PA<br>• SAN and ASA<br>• PP and PE | • Low unit price<br>• Low manufacturing cost |

**138**

## INTRODUCTION

Styrene acrylonitrile (SAN) (page 136) has been in commercial use since the 1940s. It has a good balance of rigidity, hardness and heat resistance. While it is an improvement on its predecessor polystyrene (PS) (page 132), SAN is limited by relatively low toughness. The inclusion of butadiene rubber (BR) (page 216) in the SAN block copolymer results in a terpolymer with reduced strength-to-weight but vastly improved toughness: acrylonitrile butadiene styrene, or ABS.

First commercialized in the 1950s, ABS brought about a design revolution in consumer products. The material combines high-gloss colourability with durability. As a result it has become one of the most popular engineering plastics. Utilized in the manufacture of consumer product enclosures, appliance housing, toys and automotive parts, ABS is a very familiar material. Over the years it has been employed to produce numerous iconic products, including Lego bricks (since the 1960s), the Stelton vacuum jug and the Braun ET66 calculator, to name just a few.

Polycarbonate (PC) (page 144) and polyamide (PA, nylon) (page 164) tend to be used for more demanding applications: they have superior strength-to-weight, thermal properties and toughness. The advantage of ABS is that it is around one-third cheaper, although this depends

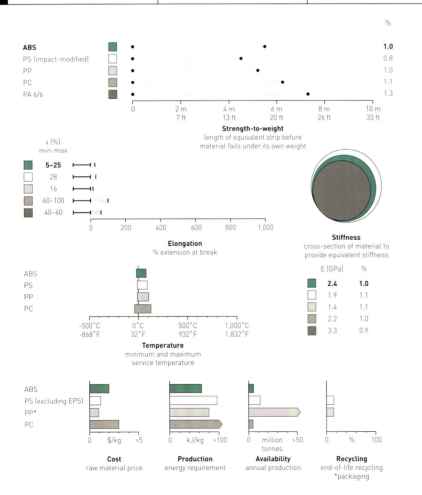

**Strength-to-weight**
length of equivalent strip before material fails under its own weight

| | | % |
|---|---|---|
| ABS | | 1.0 |
| PS (impact-modified) | | 0.8 |
| PP | | 1.0 |
| PC | | 1.1 |
| PA 6/6 | | 1.3 |

ε (%)
min-max

| | | |
|---|---|---|
| | 5–25 | |
| | 28 | |
| | 16 | |
| | 60–100 | |
| | 40–60 | |

**Elongation**
% extension at break

**Stiffness**
cross-section of material to provide equivalent stiffness

| | E (GPa) | % |
|---|---|---|
| | 2.4 | 1.0 |
| | 1.9 | 1.1 |
| | 1.4 | 1.1 |
| | 2.2 | 1.0 |
| | 3.3 | 0.9 |

**Temperature**
minimum and maximum service temperature

| Cost | Production | Availability | Recycling |
|---|---|---|---|
| raw material price | energy requirement | annual production | end-of-life recycling |
| | | | *packaging |

**ABS vacuum jug** The EM77 vacuum jug is one of Danish design brand Stelton's best-selling products of all time. Designed by Erik Magnussen in 1977, the jug is relaunched each spring with a renewed colour and finish. The use of ABS ensures a high-quality glossy appearance, with rich and saturated colour, such as the 'copper brown' shown here. Alternatively, the ABS is coated with rubberized paint to enhance tactility and create a dry, powdery-looking finish.

**Low cost**
ABS is used to manufacture high-quality and durable products for around two-thirds the price of PC or PA equivalent.

**Toughness**
The butadiene rubber content provides the elasticity to spring back from minor knocks and drops. Coatings and blends are used to improve surface toughness, because ABS is not so hard and thus is vulnerable to scratching and wear and tear.

**Visual quality**
The styrene content ensures an excellent surface finish. The mold is reproduced accurately and so all types of in-mold finish are achievable, from high gloss to matt to textured.

**Colourability**
Transparent grades provide superior colourability. The visual aesthetics of ABS are further enhanced with effects pigments, such as incorporating shimmering metal flake.

on the grade, because high-performance grades of PC and PA can work out several times more expensive.

## COMMERCIAL TYPES AND USES

ABS and the various blends are commercially available as injection-molding grades and extrusion grades. They are used unreinforced or with the addition of glass fibre (GF) or mineral fill for added strength and stiffness. Using reinforcement reduces thermal expansion and improves dimensional stability, which is particularly useful in automotive structural parts.

Molded into large and complex parts it is often coated, covered or metal-plated for improved durability and aesthetics. When blended with PA (ABS/PA) or PC (ABS/PC) the surface is more durable and so may be left uncoated. ABS/PA has an excellent matt finish and the material provides improved acoustic damping properties. ABS/PA combines the benefits of both of these materials: excellent impact strength at high and low temperatures, reduced shrinkage compared to conventional PA, high-quality colour and matt surface finish, and chemical resistance.

ABS/PC offers a lower-cost alternative to PC. The ABS contributes processing efficiency and chemical stress resistance and the PC improves dimensional stability, impact resistance and temperature resistance compared to general-purpose ABS. It is used for structural parts that require stiffness, impact strength and high-temperature resistance somewhere in the region between PC and ABS. It offers very good surface properties and so is utilized in parts that require good colour and aesthetics, such as portable

electronic housing, automotive interior parts, safety helmets and computer cases. Fire retardancy may be obtained either by the inclusion of fire-retardant additives or by blending with polyvinyl chloride (PVC) (page 122).

Intense colour is produced with fluorescent dyes. Opacity ranges from tinted to solid colour. The resistance to ultraviolet light and weathering of ABS is inferior to that of acrylic styrene acrylonitrile (ASA) (page 136). Colour will fade more quickly, especially bright and saturated hues. When used outdoors, such as on automotive exterior parts, a coating is required to protect the surface from fading as well as wear and tear.

## SUSTAINABILITY

ABS is fully recyclable. Identified by code #7, 'other', or simply 'ABS', it is not easily separated from mixed waste streams. However, industrial scrap, such as produced during injection molding, is commonly collected and reprocessed along with virgin material. This helps to keep material costs down.

The widespread use of ABS in diverse applications has led to the development of a huge number of different grades and blends with varying levels of reinforcement and colour. To maintain high quality and consistent material, different types should not be mixed during recycling. This is less of a problem in parts where appearance and structure are not of critical importance.

ABS has relatively low embodied energy for a structural plastic; other popular engineering materials, such as PC and PA, consume significantly more energy in manufacture. This contributes to the difference in price of the raw

materials: ABS is around two-thirds the price of PC or PA. However, like all synthetics, manufacturing from crude oil means the source is non-renewable. Also, it contains acrylonitrile monomer (see Polyacrylonitrile, page 180), which on its own is polluting and poisonous. Lego announced that it would try to find a sustainable alternative to ABS by 2030. The company uses several thousand tonnes of the material each year. The challenge is to find a material that is equally safe and survives as long when chewed, trampled and left outside.

## ABS IN PRODUCTS, FURNITURE AND LIGHTING

ABS is used in a range of inexpensive and durable mass-produced products. Its impact resistance and toughness are utilized in parts for telecommunications, appliances, automotive, luggage and sports. In addition to its advantageous mechanical properties, transparent grades of ABS have excellent colourability. Along with conventional pigments and dye systems, many different types of additive are incorporated to enhance the visual effect.

Metal-effect pigments add sparkle and pearlescent colour to plastic. Opacity and coverage depends on the loading, or proportion, which is typically less than 5% by weight. A low concentration of large flakes is used to create a glitter effect, and higher loading with fine particles results in an opaque metallic colour. Used in conjunction with colourant, metal-effect pigments add a layer of depth and intrigue to plastic parts.

**ABS fan housing** The Italian designer Marco Zanuso created the Arianti Fan for Vortice in 1973. The design of the fan exploits many beneficial properties of ABS. It is produced with a high-gloss and saturated colour finish; and the fins require very good flow characteristics during molding to ensure adequate strength and quality. Along with the other influential Italian-based designers of the time – including Ettore Sottsass, Mario Bellini, Gae Aulenti and Richard Sapper – Zanuso was a pioneer of modern plastic products. He is attributed with the first one-piece molded plastic chair (Child's Chair Model No. 4999, manufactured by Kartell, Italy), which he designed in collaboration with Sapper in 1964.

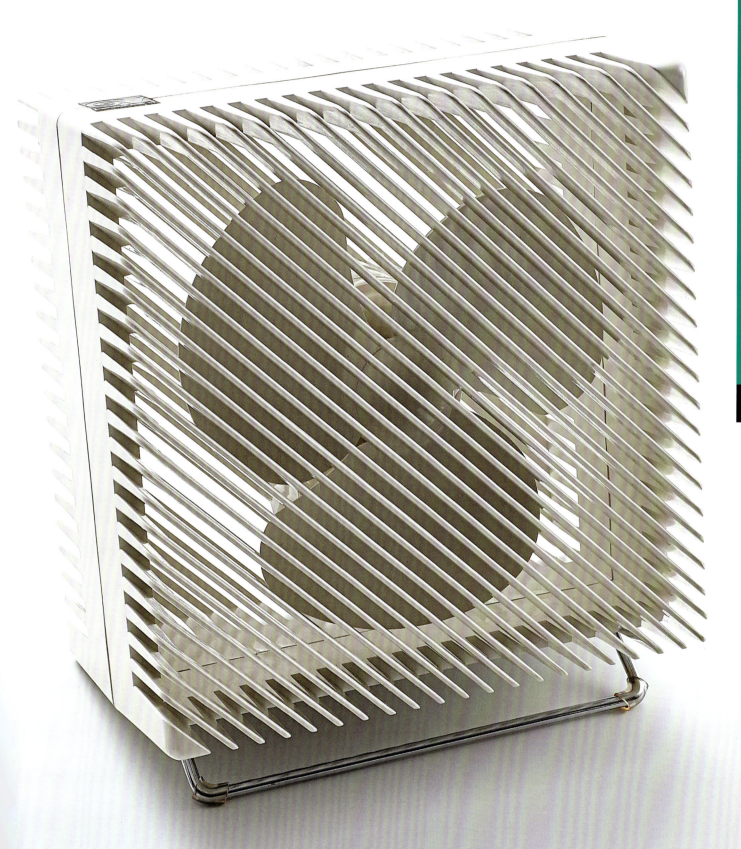

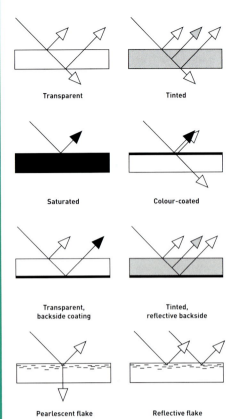

**Transparent**

**Tinted**

**Saturated**

**Colour-coated**

**Transparent, backside coating**

**Tinted, reflective backside**

**Pearlescent flake**

**Reflective flake**

**Pigments and coatings** Optical clarity in transparent plastics depends on light transmission (typically over 85%), reflections (specular or transmissive) and haze (such as from impurities). Introducing a dye or pigment in quantities that are below the saturation point will result in colour tint. Translucency is determined by the amount of colour-absorbing pigmentation. Over around 85% saturation the plastic appears opaque. Quality of colour depends on wall thickness; thinner parts will need higher quantities of pigment to reduce show-through. Applying a coloured coating has the same effect. Coating thickness affects colour saturation, because a thinner (or less saturated) coating will allow more light to pass through. Applying a tinted top coat can enhance visual quality by complementing the colour beneath (for example, a tinted top coat is applied over a reflective flake pigment to add colour). Backside coatings combine the visual qualities of transparent plastic with saturated colour to create visual depth. A reflective coating increases contrast and visibly brightens tinted colour. While the metallic surface of reflective flake reflects almost all of the light, the layered structure of pearlescent flake splits the light and allows some to pass through. This creates a shimmering, iridescent visual quality.

The quality and effect depend on the type of material used. For example, aluminium is silvery (or coloured), bright and reflective. Its relatively low density means that equal coverage can be achieved with much less of the material by weight compared to heavier metals, such as copper and gold. Mica flake is sometimes used as an alternative to metal. The various flake pigments are not compatible with all types of plastic.

Spherical metal particles produce a pinpoint reflection regardless of orientation. Bright flake pigments, on the other hand, will reflect differently depending on their shape and angle. Their orientation will be determined by how the plastic fills the mold. Therefore potential defects, such as change of flow, eddying and convergence of melt fronts, are highlighted. To avoid this, the design of parts incorporating flake pigment tends to avoid complex geometries that might disrupt the flow of the molten plastic, such as holes, ribs and variation in wall thickness. Albeit very challenging, all of this can be overcome if the aesthetic objective is established at the outset.

ABS is polar (like PA, PC and PVC): its molecule has a positive and a negative pole (dipole). Polarity affects the attractive forces between the polymer chains (solubility) and thus permeability; polar plastics are generally more permeable than non-polar ones. Polar plastics are also vulnerable to loss of strength, in particular impact strength, when high concentrations of flake pigment are used. The extent to which the additive reduces strength (tensile and elongation) also depends on the size of flake: smaller particles tend to have a greater impact.

Several types of coating are used in conjunction with ABS. Spray coatings are used to apply colour (or gloss transparency) and enhance durability. Metal coatings produce a cost-effective and versatile alternative to solid metal. As a polar plastic, it is particularly well suited (as are PA and PC), because a strong bond is formed between coating and substrate. Even so, the thin metal layer is relatively easily worn away and therefore should be avoided in high-wear applications and products destined for a long life.

Recently, a new area of application has emerged in the development of additive manufacturing (rapid prototyping or 3D printing) techniques. Fused deposition modelling (FDM), also known as fused filament modelling (FFF), was invented in 1988. It is distinguished by the use of a continuous filament of thermoplastic, typically ABS. Three-dimensional models are split into layers and printed slice-by-slice with a 0.2 mm (0.008 in) diameter filament of plastic extruded from a heated nozzle.

ABS is an engineering material that has an achievable softening point for this type of low-cost desktop additive manufacturing. It is heated up to 230°C (446°F) in the printer nozzle, which causes it to soften sufficiently to lay down and bond to the proceeding layer. Polylactic acid (PLA) (page 262) is used as an alternative for this type of printing. It is generally considered easier to print with because it has a lower melting point and does not require extraction (ABS gives off harmful fumes when heated). It is biobased and so does not have the longevity of ABS; it is a little more expensive and less ductile. High-impact polystyrene (HIPS) (see page 134) is cheaper still, but has inferior mechanical properties. PC, PA and thermoplastic polyurethane (TPU) (see Thermoplastic Elastomer, page 194) are also compatible with certain printers, but are not as commonly used because of their high price point.

**Ski and snowboard safety helmet** The Receptor Backcountry ski helmet made by Swedish company POC features impressive material technologies. It is constructed with a double outer shell: glossy ABS/PC on the outside coupled with a thin layer of PC/PTFE on the inside. This allows for a fully ventilated helmet without sacrificing safety. Referred to as MIPS (multidirectional impact protection system), the two shells are designed to rotate separately during a crash to lessen the effect of oblique impacts on the brain. A layer of aramid (page 242) is incorporated to improve overall stiffness and enhance penetration resistance. The inner shell is in-molded with an expanded polypropylene (EPP) (see Polypropylene, page 98) liner to provide protection against impacts. Altogether, this creates one of the most reliable high-performance safety helmets on the market.

# Polycarbonate (PC)

**Also known as**
Trademark names: Lexan, Xantar, Makrolon

An amorphous engineering thermoplastic used for demanding applications, PC has exceptional toughness, clarity and thermal stability. A number of grades and blends have been developed to overcome the various challenges of different end uses, such as with improved toughness, weathering resistance, reinforcement and flame-retardant properties.

| Types | Typical Applications | Sustainability |
|---|---|---|
| • PC<br>• Blends: PC/ABS, PC/ASA, PC/PET and PC/PBT | • Transportation and aerospace<br>• Consumer products and appliances<br>• Medical<br>• Packaging | • Readily recyclable but not widely collected<br>• It contains harmful chemicals subject to restrictions, such as bisphenol A (BPA) |
| **Properties** | **Competing Materials** | **Costs** |
| • Rigid and tough<br>• Transparent<br>• Good dimensional stability | • ABS, PA and PET<br>• SAN, ASA and PMMA<br>• Aluminium, magnesium and steel<br>• Soda-lime and borosilicate glass | • Moderate to high material costs<br>• Low to moderate manufacturing costs |

144

## INTRODUCTION

Commercial production of polycarbonate (PC) began in 1960. It has since become one of the most significant engineering polymers. While its physical properties are utilized in a range of engineering applications, its desirable aesthetic qualities have had a significant impact on the look and feel of consumer products and automobiles.

Polyamide (PA, nylon) (page 164) is a high-strength engineering plastic used in similar applications to PC; it has superior mechanical properties and tends to be a little more expensive. PC outperforms PA in terms of impact strength, colourability and dimensional stability. Although amorphous PA exhibits excellent colourability and improved dimensional stability, it is even more expensive.

Even so, PC is not cheap: a standard grade is around one-third more expensive than acrylonitrile butadiene styrene (ABS) (page 138) and almost twice the price of aluminium (page 42) for the same weight. Tailored grades, such as used for high-performance optical applications, are several times more expensive.

ABS, or even polypropylene (PP) (page 98), provides a low-cost alternative in applications that do not require the enhanced strength, heat resistance and dimensional stability of PC. For example, while the lens of a headlight assembly is

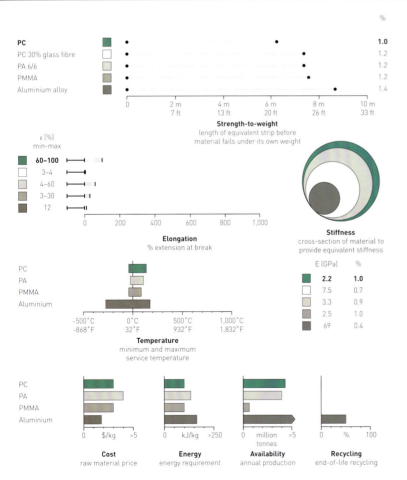

**High-gloss PC housing**
The Plus Minus Zero humidifier, created by Japanese industrial designer Naoto Fukasawa, is wrapped within a high-gloss PC shell. It provides a protective and decorative cocoon. Placed on the floor, the humidifier must be easy to clean and able to withstand knocks. Mimicking a drop of water, its lustrous appearance demonstrates the very high surface quality that can be achieved with injection-molded PC. The design reflects Fukasawa's drive to create emotionally stimulating objects, not just interesting shapes.

most likely PC, the housing that joins it to the structure of the vehicle could well be fabricated from PP.

Polymethyl methacrylate (PMMA, acrylic) (page 174) has superior light transmission and surface hardness. Similar to PC, it is utilized in furniture, lighting and packaging. While its strength-to-weight and stiffness are comparable with PC, it has lower elongation. In other words, it is not as tough and will break more readily than PC on impact.

## COMMERCIAL TYPES AND USES

PC is consumed in significant quantities, exceeding PA by weight, and its use is expanding. It is used alone as a homopolymer, or blended to combine the benefits of two or more resins. It is an amorphous thermoplastic with a linear polymer structure and high molecular weight (long polymer chains). The attraction between the chains, as a result of the phenyl and methyl groups, provides PC with many of its benefits. It is transparent and has high impact resistance and good strength-to-weight.

It is used for diverse applications, including CDs and DVDs, lenses (automotive and interior), product housings and transparent packaging. The base resin is modified to optimize its behaviour for a range of manufacturing processes, including injection molding, blow molding, rotation molding and extrusion. And additives are used to enhance specific properties, such as where flame retardancy, extreme temperature performance or resistance to ultraviolet are required.

Glass fibre (GF) and other reinforcements improve strength, stiffness and dimensional stability at the expense of ductility (impact strength). Reinforcement is used for the structure and framework of products. It helps to improve strength-to-weight and reduce the quantity of material required. An added benefit of GF is that it helps maintain mechanical properties at elevated temperatures.

PC is blended to increase options for material selection. Blends are also referred to as alloys. Unlike copolymers (such as

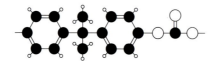

**Phenyl and methyl groups**

**Polymer structure**
PC is a linear polymer consisting of repeating phenyl groups and methyl side-groups. Attraction between the phenyl groups (aromatic rings) holds the polymer chains together. The forces at work affect the physical properties of PC in several ways:

reducing the mobility of the chains increases dimensional stability and heat resistance (but results in lower melt flow); preventing a crystalline structure forming creates a transparent plastic; and it takes more energy to separate the chains, which provides toughness.

styrene acrylonitrile, SAN, page 136) and terpolymers (such as ABS), blends retain the unique properties of each material. In doing so, the best parts of each are retained. For example, PC is blended with polyester – polyethylene terephthalate (PET, polyester) or polybutylene terephthalate (PBT) (page 152) – to create a plastic with better chemical resistance than PC and higher impact strength than PET or PBT. The properties of the blend are tailored to the needs of an application through adjustments in the proportion of each. Examples include car bumpers and power-tool housing. It is typically applied in thick sections, because it has high viscosity when molten.

PC/ABS and PC/ASA (see SAN) combine the mechanical benefits of PC with the molding and cost advantages of ABS and ASA. These blends have lower viscosity when heated and so are better suited to molding thin-walled complex parts. They are used for applications that require higher impact strength and heat resistance than ABS or ASA but require costs below that of PC. They retain the excellent colourability and surface quality of the individual resins. They are popular materials used in consumer products, automotive parts and railway cabins.

## SUSTAINABILITY

As a high-performance engineering plastic, PC contributes to many good causes. It has helped to reduce the weight of transportation (glass replacement), improve safety in dangerous situations

(high-strength helmets and goggles) and improve medical equipment. However, it does have its drawbacks. The majority of PC is produced from bisphenol A (BPA) monomer. BPA is a fundamental part of PC, providing many of its advantageous properties. It has been at the centre of numerous studies, because it poses a risk to people and the environment (it is an endocrine disruptor and oestrogen-mimicker). The concern is that small amounts of the chemicals present in food packaging materials migrate into the contents.

The US Food and Drug Administration (FDA) and the European Food Safety Authority (EFSA) consider BPA to be safe at current levels occurring in foods. In other words, they currently approve the use of PC in food containers and packaging (BPA is found in the epoxy-based coatings used to line the inside of metal cans as well as PC). While the majority of research focuses on food contact, the underlying science can be applied to medical equipment.

Whether it is safe or not, public opinion resulted in a shift away from PC in applications where a 'safer' alternative existed. In 2008–09, BPA was banned from being used in children's food products in European Union countries, and the FDA followed suit in 2012 (although the ban was amended after the use of BPA was largely abandoned).

PC is readily recyclable, but is rarely collected and reprocessed. It has the recycling code #7, 'other', which makes it virtually impossible to identify unless marked with 'PC'. As an engineering material, it is used in a variety of different guises and blends, combined with various

**Glass-fibre-reinforced housing** The housing of this Makita cordless drill is molded PC with 15% glass fibre (GF). Similar to the phone cover (page 148), it is produced by dual-shot molding, whereby the thermoplastic elastomer (TPE) grip is added with a second molding cycle. The GF reinforcement enhances tensile strength, stiffness and dimensional stability. While these are essential properties for such a demanding application, they come at the expense of impact strength and surface quality. Therefore, the housing is molded with a relatively thick wall section to ensure durability. The smooth surface reveals the visual impact of incorporating GF.

additives and reinforcement. Therefore, recycled material from mixed sources is unlikely to be of sufficiently high quality to be used in similar applications to virgin PC.

## PC IN PRODUCTS, FURNITURE AND LIGHTING

The Apple iMac G3, designed by Jonathan Ive and launched in 1998, brought PC to the attention of a wider audience. The design of the iMac's translucent PC housing – originally available only in 'Bondi Blue' and white – was dramatically different from competitors' models of the time. Since then, a plethora of consumer products have utilized PC including phones, tablets, laptops, screens, power tools and kitchen equipment.

Housing, light shades, diffusers and even entire chairs are produced with injection molding. In addition to colour effects produced with pigments and dyes (see ABS), a variety of visual effects are created with molding techniques. Multishot injection molding combines two (dual-shot) or more materials in a single, seamless product. Materials with contrasting colour, opacity and flexibility are molded in sequence. The range of options depends on compatibility. It is not limited to PC; a wide range of plastics is fabricated in this way for decorative and technical purposes. In what is known as 'depth effect', colour (pigment) and graphics (film or transfer) are encapsulated within a transparent or translucent shell to create intriguing visual effects.

A very high-quality finish can be achieved, from polished to matt, because

**Dual-shot injection-molded PC phone cover**
The interchangeable back cover of the Nokia Lumia 620 combines two layers of PC. Each layer is injected separately, one directly onto the other. The two materials form an impenetrable join that cannot be undone. Being translucent, the colours work together, showing through and intensifying one another. While this effect is possible in all types of transparent or translucent plastic, PC provides superior impact resistance and durability overall, essential for products that are likely to be dropped a few times. At the same time, the elasticity of PC allows for the cover to be prised off and replaced without damage.

**Impact strength**
The combined ductility, elongation and strength of PC provide exceptional impact strength in structural applications. Unlike more brittle materials, it rebounds on impact, bending and deflecting to accommodate the load.

**Surface and colour**
The surface of PC is not particularly durable, but combined with texture or coating it is capable of withstanding daily wear and tear. It is transparent and readily coloured, from pastel to fluorescent.

**Moldability**
The melt flow of PC varies according to the grade and through blending with ABS. It shrinks very little and so a very good molded surface finish can be achieved, from gloss to matt.

**Food contact**
Even though bisphenol A (BPA) – a harmful chemical – is used as a fundamental ingredient in the production of PC, it is considered safe for food contact by the FDA and EFSA. It should be noted that many food contact plastics contain potentially harmful ingredients.

PC shrinks very little and so remains an exact copy of the inside of the mold. The surface is not particularly hard, and gloss finishes develop a craze of fine scratches with use. Clear or coloured hard coats are used to prevent scratching. For example, polyurethane (PU) (page 202) coating is several times harder than PC and so provides better resistance to scratching and abrasion.

Reinforcement and additives inadvertently affect visual quality in some cases. For example, glass fibre (GF) produces a fibrous texture on the surface of molded parts. Of course, the proportion of GF will affect this. Likewise, additives and blends can affect transparency and colourability. There are processes available – adaptations to conventional injection molding such as rapid heat cycle (RHCM) – that allow for superior surface finish while using GF. However, part geometry is somewhat restricted and the results are not guaranteed; a lot still depends on part design. Where this is not desirable, a coating or texture is applied.

While applying a texture is much more cost-effective (no added cost during molding), it does not protect the surface to the same extent as a coating. For example, owing to its amorphous structure, PC is vulnerable to chemicals. As a result, it is avoided in applications where there is a risk of exposure to oil, grease or solvents. For structural parts, PC/PBT may provide the necessary chemical resistance. Alternatively, a coating is applied to protect the surface.

While translucent PC provides furniture, lighting and packaging with decorative and functional appeal, it has become irreplaceable in medical

equipment. Where glass (page 508) was used in the past to provide transparency, PC now dominates. And its combination of lightness and toughness helps to improve the agility of medical professionals in life-saving situations. Importantly, it exhibits very good retention of properties when sterilized using the most common methods. This ensures a long shelf life for non-disposable equipment.

Single layer      Dual-shot

Coating (inside)      Coating (outside)

**Depth effect** The transparency of PC (up to 90% light transmission) is used to create intriguing visual effects. Conventional injection molding produces a single layer of material. Making this translucent, as opposed to opaque, will only partially conceal the inner workings of the product. This is used for decorative effect, such as the Apple iMac G3. It is also used for functional purposes, such as to mask the discolouration caused by sterilization of medical equipment. Dual-shot creates two layers of plastic and is trickier to design for. Where they overlap the wall thickness is doubled. With contrasting colour, texture and opacity, a rich visual quality is achieved. In addition, graphics and colour may be encapsulated between the layers (in-mold decoration or ink transfer). Gradients are produced with graphics (dot pattern) by gradually reducing the wall thickness (within reason). Coatings are applied inside and out. Colour coating on the inside, underneath a transparent or translucent molding, produces a similar effect to dual-shot. However, all of the molding features (ribs and gates for example) will be revealed. The level of transparency and frosting of external coatings will have an impact on visual depth effect.

**Impact strength**
Its exceptionally high impact strength combined with moldability enables smooth profiles and design freedom in protective parts.

**Transparency**
Panoramic roofs and light lenses made from PC are around half the weight of glass. Its transparency permits a broad colour range, from tinted indicator lenses to jet-black bodywork. UV-stabilized grades demonstrate long-term colourfastness.

**Versatility**
Many different grades of PC have been developed, each with superior performance in particular areas, such as high heat resistance, flame retardancy and moldability. Blends further expand material selection opportunities.

**Part integration**
PC and its blends enable multiple parts to be produced in a single molding. This helps to improve quality while reducing weight.

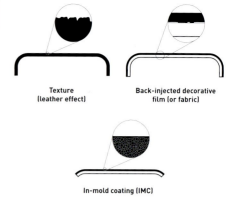

Texture
(leather effect)

Back-injected decorative
film (or fabric)

In-mold coating (IMC)

Like PET, it is blow molded into hollow containers, such as bottles and jars. PC is more than twice the price of PET and four times as expensive than polyethylene (PE) (page 108) and therefore tends to be utilized only where superior impact strength is required. As a result of its durability, PC is used for returnable and reusable packaging.

### PC IN AUTOMOTIVE AND AEROSPACE

PC is used throughout vehicle design, from exterior bumpers and glazing to dashboards and interior cladding. It is also used for similar applications in trucks, buses and trains. Perhaps the most impressive application is the use of PC alongside the highest-performing structural materials – titanium alloy (page 58), carbon-fibre-reinforced plastic (CFRP) (page 236), aluminium and steel (page 28) – in aerospace. For example, it is laminated and formed into lightweight high-strength canopies that make ejection safer and more reliable (see image, page 63).

Performance enhancements developed within the automotive and transportation industries – the largest consumers of molded PC overall – rapidly spread to other end uses.

PC/ABS blends provide an excellent balance of properties for interior parts. They exhibit adequate toughness, stiffness and resistance with improved moldability. The reduced viscosity during molding means that very fine surface details are more faithfully reproduced. This creates the opportunity for a range of tactile qualities to be achieved, without coating, such as leather effect and surface grain.

PC/ASA blends are suitable for interior and exterior parts. ASA has very good resistance to weathering and thus eliminates the need for painting. With injection molding, multiple parts are incorporated in a single molding, such as the front grill and trim.

PC/PET and PC/PBT have very good resistance to chemicals, solvents, lubricants and cleaning agents. They are used for exterior body parts, such as bumpers, air guides, mudguards and spoilers. Indeed, it is feasible to produce the entire exterior of a car using PC and its blends. For example, the panoramic roof, exterior panels and lenses on the Smart Forfour are all PC. The makers claim that this gives a 40% weight reduction compared to conventional materials, such as steel and glass. Such savings have a huge impact on fuel economy, braking distance and overall handling.

Inherently coloured plastics, whereby the colour comes from pigmentation of the resin, are more cost-effective than coatings (typically less than half the price). Unlike coated plastic, damage does not affect the colour, because there is no difference in colour however deep the scratch. But in some cases coatings provide significant benefits. For example, lenses are coated to improve UV-stability, and glazing (such as panoramic roofs) is coated to enhance abrasion resistance. Plasma-generated coatings provide wear resistance similar to that of glass.

**In-molded decoration and effects** A range of decorative in-mold effects is possible with injection molding. They provide a unique tactile or visual quality and eliminate the need for coating. PC/ABS and PC/ASA blends have improved moldablity compared to PC. With these blends, surface textures applied to the mold, such as grain, leather effect and soft touch, are reproduced exactly. A surprising array of material qualities is reproducible. Back-injecting a film allows for a wide range of graphics and print to be incorporated. Decoration is applied to transparent high-strength film, such as PC or PET. It is formed to the shape of the mold, inserted, and plastic is injected from the backside, thus pushing the film to the front and locking the graphics within. Fabric and wood veneer are integrated into plastic moldings using a similar technique. In-mold coating (IMC) combines injection molding with reaction injection molding (RIM). Once the base layer has been molded, a second layer of coating-like resin with low viscosity – RIM PU – is injected over the top. This provides all of the advantages of coating, without all the costly finishing steps. In addition, it brings the advantages of PU: from transparency to colour; thick to thin; and solid to foam. However, geometry is somewhat limited by the process. In an alternative approach, coating is applied 'in-mold' by spraying the inside surface of the tool prior to injecting plastic.

**Light assembly** The lens of this Suzuki GSX-R motorcycle front headlight is molded from high-heat PC. This modified PC provides the necessary high-temperature resistance, impact strength and light transmission. Compared to a glass lens, PC is around half the weight and provides greater design freedom.

# Polyethylene Terephthalate (PET), Polyester

**Also known as**
Acronyms and abbreviations: PES, PEL, PETE, BOPET, poly
Trademark names: Mylar, Melinex, Hostaphan, Dacron, Terylene, Trevira, Corterra, Sorona, Radyarn, Ultradur, Crastin, Rynite

These high-strength engineering plastics have an enviable balance of thermal, mechanical and chemical properties. They are extremely versatile and are available in virtually all formats. Applications range from low-cost commodity items through metal replacement. As a result of its widespread use in disposable packaging, PET is one of the most commonly recycled plastics.

| Types | Typical Applications | Sustainability |
|---|---|---|
| • PET and PET modified with glycol (PETG) <br>• Polytrimethylene terephthalate (PTT) and polybutylene terephthalate (PBT) <br>• Biaxial-oriented polyester (BOPET) film | • Automotive <br>• Textiles <br>• Furniture <br>• Packaging | • Recyclable and identifies by code #1 or 'PET' <br>• PET is one of the most widely recycled plastics |
| **Properties** | **Competing Materials** | **Costs** |
| • Good chemical resistance and thermal properties <br>• Whereas PET has higher tensile strength; PTT and PBT have higher elastic recovery | • PP, PE, PA, PLA, PHA and PHB <br>• Natural, synthetic and animal fibres <br>• Soda-lime glass <br>• Aluminium and steel | • PET is low-cost <br>• Other types are more expensive |

152

## INTRODUCTION

There are two types of polyester: saturated and unsaturated (page 228). These saturated polyesters are thermoplastic – they do not form cross-links between the polymer chains and so can be molded and reprocessed through melting. Biobased thermoplastic polyesters include polylactic acid (PLA) (page 262), and polyhydroxyalkanoates (PHA and PHB) (see PLA).

Patented in 1941, polyethylene terephthalate (PET) has become one of the most widely used thermoplastics and dominant in consumer and industrial products alike. It is the most important thermoplastic polyester and the benchmark against which the others are compared. Its success is due to a combination of performance, adaptability and, most importantly, cost. PET is resistant to most chemicals and has high tensile strength and good thermal properties. Its low cost has led to widespread use, which has been accompanied by high rates of recycling (although comparatively low compared to metals), in particular bottles used for drinks, household products and cosmetics.

**Knitted running shoes**
Nike revolutionized trainers with the development of Flyknit. Before its launch in 2012, uppers were manufactured from leather, mesh, weave or laminate. This lightweight alternative utilizes high-strength polyester fibre. The yarns are knitted with an openwork structure to eliminate material (and weight) where it is not needed. Purported to have taken four years of intensive development, the knitted shoe upper is engineered to provide optimum support, flexibility and breathability. Compared to the company's previous leading running shoe (Zoom Streak 3), the Flyknit is 19% lighter overall. In addition to the technical benefits, the Flyknit unlocked the fashion potential of knitting in shoe construction, including the opportunities of shape, pattern and colour.

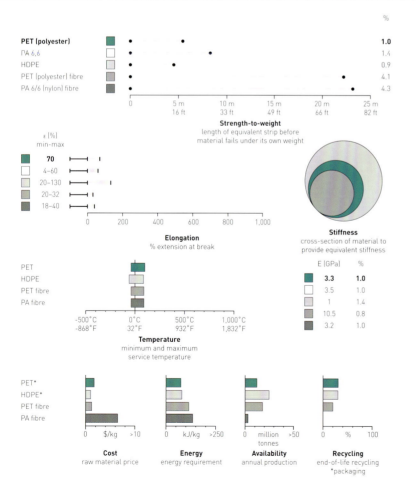

Although most PET includes recycled content, some products make more of it with a recycled PET (rPET) label.

## COMMERCIAL TYPES AND USES

Modifying PET with glycol (PETG) reduces brittleness and premature ageing. Polytrimethylene terephthalate (PTT) and polybutylene terephthalate (PBT) have small differences in their mechanical properties, in particular greater elasticity, but otherwise are similar to PET.

Polyester film is lightweight and high-strength. Stretching during manufacture optimizes the mechanical properties by improving crystallization. PET made in this way is known as biaxial-oriented (BOPET). As a result of its high performance and increased unit price due to the orientation step, it is often considered a speciality film. Even so, it has found use across a spectrum of applications including metallized films (packaging and fancy yarn), vacuum packaging, printed electronics (flexible displays and circuits) and laminated high-performance sails.

Polyester fibre dominates textiles, from apparel through to technical items. It is produced as solid, hollow, textured and filament, and ranges from micro to large denier. Like film, the fibre is stretched (drawn) during manufacture to increase strength and stability. It is by far the least expensive of the apparel fibres, but more expensive than PE and PP for industrial and geotextile applications.

Polyester is synonymous with high-quality blow-molded plastics bottles. Its lightness and impact resistance have led to it replacing glass (page 508) in many cases for packaging water, beverages and cosmetics, among other liquids. The reduction in size and weight saves cost and energy associated with transportation. It prevents breakages too, which can be both messy and dangerous.

Injection-molded polyester is used for engineering applications, such as automotive under-the-bonnet parts, furniture and safety products. It is used unreinforced, or combined with glass-fibre or mineral fill to improve tensile strength and stiffness. Polyester is converted into a thermoplastic elastomer

## TEXTILES

**Low cost**
It is around twice the price of PP, but less than half the price of PA for the same weight.

**Ease of dyeing**
Similar to PA and acrylic, polyester can be dyed at any stage of production, which helps to reduce cost and maximize flexibility.

**Stiffness**
It has very good shape retention. As a result of its high stiffness, the fibre properties will start to break down with repeated bending.

**High strength**
The drawn fibre has four times the strength-to-weight of molded polyester. Among the fibres, it is stronger than PP but slightly less strong than PA.

**Fibre profile**
The cross-section is tailored during spinning depending on the required function. It is produced as solid, hollow, textured and filament, and ranges from micro to large denier. Incorporating a profile that encourages capillary action (to draw moisture away from the body) creates moisture-wicking functionality.

(TPC) (page 194) by combining the rigid plastic with a soft, flexible matrix.

## SUSTAINABILITY

Its widespread use in bottles makes it recognizable and so easier to separate from mixed waste streams. In many parts of the world, including the USA and the EU, PET bottles have separate disposal. This further improves overall efficiency.

While it is not uncommon for PET packaging to be recycled and converted into new textiles, it is much more challenging to reuse plastic from textiles and molded products. This is mainly the result of not being able to quickly and efficiently distinguish one type of plastic from another. To make things harder, multiple plastics are often combined, making it impossible to separate them effectively.

Polyester does not contain bisphenol A (BPA), phthalates or dioxins.

## PET IN TEXTILES

Polyester is a versatile fibre used to make all manner of textiles, from commodity applications to high-performance products. Whether manufactured from virgin material or recycled plastic, it has high strength, good resilience, good temperature resistance and a naturally glossy surface.

PET is the most common type of polyester fibre and is often referred to by trademark names, such as Dacron and Terylene. PTT is a more recent development (even though it has been known for as long, large-scale production has taken time to realize). As a fibre it has improved softness (comparable with PA) and resilience. Trademark names

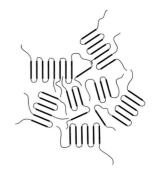

**Semi-crystalline**

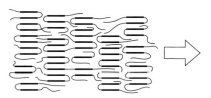

**Oriented crystal arrangement**

**Drawing** The polymer structure of semi-crystalline plastics – PET, PA, PP and PE for example – is characterized by a mixture of highly ordered crystalline regions held together by amorphous (less ordered) regions. Drawing out the polymer – as fibre or film – causes the polymer chains to become oriented. This alignment induces further crystallization and so produces a material with improved tensile strength, stiffness and hardness in the direction of orientation. The crystals form in bands, joined by the amorphous regions (it is these regions that are prone to pilling). In uniaxially drawn materials the stiffness perpendicular to the direction of draw is reduced. This is not a problem for fibres, but would be for films. Therefore, films are drawn biaxially.

include Sorona (partially biobased) and Corterra. PBT fibre, known by trademark names such as Radyarn, feels softer (lower stiffness) and dyes more brilliantly than PET. PBT and PTT have much better elastic recovery (up to 50%), which improves shape retention, in particular for body-hugging garments. They are used for sportswear, underwear and molded textiles (such as car interiors).

PET has a desirable balance of properties for its price. Its lustrous finish produces vivid colour and is utilized in silk imitation fabrics. This same quality can give it a recognizable sheen, something associated with low-cost garments. It has a reputation as a cheap and uncomfortable fabric in apparel. However, as a result of fibre developments (PTT and PBT) and the expanding use of ultrasoft microfibres (PET), polyester is regaining popularity and market share.

Polyester is hydrophobic (repels

water) and so unaffected by water. This is advantageous for sportswear and outdoor clothing and means that it will remain dry to the touch when used as a facing layer over an inner absorbent medium that becomes saturated. When used next to the skin it can feel clammy in warm weather. It is blended with natural fibre, such as wool (page 426), to overcome this. Examples include thermoregulating and moisture-wicking fabrics such as Coolmax and Thermocool.

Polyester fibre is dyed at any stage of production, from raw material to finished article. Items manufactured on equipment that has a lengthy set-up process, such as weaving and warp knitting, can therefore be dyed at a later stage. This avoids having to re-thread machines for each colour and provides the option to choose colours last-minute.

Polyester is dyed a broad variety of colours, ranging from black to fluorescent.

**Laminated PET composite sails** Designed and manufactured by OneSails GBR (East), these sails combine the low-stretch performance of PET film with the exceptional tensile strength of carbon fibre. The sail maximizes strength while minimizing weight. Carbon fibre (or other high-strength reinforcement) is laid along predetermined lines of stress. The sails are built in panels to create the optimum 'flying shape', and adhesive bonded along the seams. Adhesive bonding is lighter than stitching and results in a smoother surface. Photo courtesy of OneSails GBR (East).

It is suitable for several dye systems, including disperse dyeing. This is a technique that is used to produce textiles in solid colour. It is also the principle behind transfer printing. Disperse dyes have the ability to sublimate from one medium to another without becoming liquid (straight from solid to gas). In operation, heat and pressure cause printed colour to transfer from paper

to polyester fabric, making this a clean and efficient process.

Printing onto transfer paper is more straightforward and less expensive than printing directly onto polyester. It is suitable for low volumes and mass production. A large number of printed transfers may be held in stock (paper takes up less space than fabric) to reduce turnaround time.

Its cost-competitive performance has led to a plethora of interior applications, such as mattresses, curtains, carpet and upholstery. It does not have the drape, handle and softness of natural fibres such as cotton (page 410) and linen (see Flax, page 400), nor the abrasion resistance or wool or PA. Therefore, it tends to be avoided in high-wear applications. Otherwise, it will have to be replaced more frequently than these more expensive alternatives. PTT has improved resilience and so is preferable to PET for high-wear applications.

High-strength polyester film is used in many industries. It has very good tensile strength and dimensional stability. While thin films are transparent (and highly reflective when metallized), thicker films are available in a range of translucent and opaque colours. Surface finish ranges from glossy to textured. More expensive than polyvinyl chloride (PVC) (page 122) and polyethylene (PE) (page 108), polyester films tend to be reserved for the more demanding applications.

Polyester film has very little stretch and so is impractical for most types of apparel. Films suitable for this type of application – such as laminated breathable fabric, waterproof outerwear and lightweight footwear – include

polytetrafluoroethylene (PTFE) (page 190), thermoplastic polyurethane (TPU) (see Thermoplastic Elastomer, page 194) and ethylene vinyl acetate (EVA) (page 118).

## POLYESTER IN PACKAGING

Polyester is utilized in a broad range of packaging. The most significant include flexible pouches, blow-molded containers and thermoformed packs.

The use of high-strength film (BOPET) crosses over with technical textiles: even though the requirements may be quite different, the materials are

the same. It is more expensive than commodity films such PP, PE and PVC. The advantage of BOPET is that it has excellent strength and dimensional stability (even at elevated temperatures) combined with barrier properties superior to commodity types.

The packaging of certain items, and to extend shelf life, requires functional coatings. For example, polyvinylidene chloride (PVdC) coating is utilized in flexible packaging, such as for biscuits and pastries, and acrylic coating is used for flexible packaging that contains food or cosmetics. It is also possible to incorporate a thin aluminium coating, or foil (see page 45), on PET. The metallized layer is encapsulated within the structure of the film by lamination or coating. While this combination provides many functional benefits – improved barrier against light, liquids and gases, and shielding against electrostatic interference – it can also be used for aesthetic purposes.

Printed film is used in a variety of applications, from stand-up pouches to vacuum packs and product labels. In addition to its widespread use in packaging, printed film is used to decorate laminated glass panels, to provide anti-glare and anti-reflection performance to electronic displays,

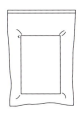

**Vacuum packaging**

**Stand-up pouch**

**Thermoforming**

**Blow molding**

**Knitted polyester fleece**
The Vik hooded sweater by 66°NORTH utilizes Polartec Power Stretch. A blend of materials is used in this lightweight fleece. Polyester (53%) provides excellent insulation: its fineness and shape retention help trap a layer of air. The PA (37%) is comfortable next to the skin and wicks moisture away, transferring it to the outside surface, where it readily evaporates. Its body-hugging fit is enhanced with spandex (9%). The finished fabric is coated to improve water resistance. Synthetic fleece – more practical than wool in many cases – is very popular for outdoor gear, in particular hiking and climbing.

**Film packaging** Film thickness ranges from 10 to 250 microns. Multifunctional films are produced by co-extrusion or coating. By changing the material properties on either side, a range of options becomes available, such as the ability to form a peel-seal in combination with printed film. Tubes and panels of film are bonded or welded to form self-supporting pouches. This combines the functional and cost benefits of film with the design and marketing opportunities of upright packaging. Needless to say, this approach to packaging is gaining popularity.

**Thin-walled rigid packaging** With thermoforming (also called vacuum forming), parts are shaped onto a single-sided mold using vacuum pressure. Parts have an open profile, usually with a flange that is trimmed to size. It is a low-cost process suited to single-use applications. The low pressure limits the level of detail that can be achieved. Blow molding (see also PE), on the other hand, uses an enclosed mold. An extruded tube (or injection-molded parison) is inserted and inflated to fill the cavity. This yields hollow shapes with an even wall thickness. Screw caps and other features are incorporated in a single material, so the molds are expensive.

and for medical films (x-ray). PET film is treated to improve compatibility with high-speed print processes, including screen printing, offset lithography and flexography. For low volumes digital printing is used. The colour and transparency (or metallization) of the film will determine the visual quality that can be achieved.

Corona discharge treatment improves the surface energy (bonding strength) of polyester (and other plastics). A high-voltage, high-frequency electrical discharge is emitted in close proximity to the part causing the molecular bonds on the surface of the plastic to be severed. This allows strong chemical bonds to form with subsequent finishes such as inks, paints and adhesive.

Packaging is sealed with heat- and pressure-sensitive adhesive. The choice of adhesive layer determines whether it is permanent or peel-seal. Where this could affect the taste and aroma of the food, welding is preferred. Both techniques are capable of producing a hermetic seal compatible with vacuum packaging.

Blow-molded polyester containers are strong and light. As with fibre and film, the strength of the plastic is optimized through stretching (orientation) during production. Referred to as injection stretch blow molding (ISBM), this technique is utilized in the production of bottles for domestic, industrial and medical use. Rapid cooling does not give the crystal structure time to form, resulting in water-clear plastic. Colour is added for functional (extending shelf life) and aesthetic purposes.

Predominantly based on PET, a range of additives is used to enhance specific properties. For example, polyester is toughened to create sufficient heat resistance to be used for hot foods such as for takeaways and ready meals.

Like glass and aluminium, PET containers are hygienic and resistant to attack by microorganisms, and will not biodegrade. With careful design and material selection they are even capable of withstanding pasteurization. While PET itself does not react with food or drink, sensitive ingredients are not typically stored in it, because its barrier properties

## PRODUCTS, FURNITURE AND LIGHTING

**Low cost**
PET is a cost-effective engineering plastic and around half the price of PA and PC.

**High strength**
Often reinforced with glass fibre for optimum stiffness and strength-to-weight, it competes alongside PA as well as aluminium alloy for lightweight structural parts.

**Vibrant colour range**
Whether textile, film or molded product, polyester has excellent colourability. It is available in a range of colours. Alternatively, it is produced white and dyed or printed with colour at a later stage.

**Dielectric strength**
It is a good insulator and has dimensional stability. These properties are critical for connectors and printed electronics.

**Chemical resistance**
It has good resistance to many chemicals, including alcohols, fats, oils, fuels and brake fluid.

**Recyclability**
Where possible, using low-grade recycled material reduces cost. Up to 25% recycled content does not affect mechanical properties. Compatible PET products are in theory recyclable along with packaging.

are insufficient to keep oxygen out and carbon dioxide in. To overcome this, such things as tomato ketchup, fruit juice and carbonated drinks are packaged in multilayered PET containers (up to nine layers in some cases). This can work out high-cost, because the barrier layer (such as PA nanocomposite) incorporated during blow molding is expensive. This is why PET beer bottles are restricted to situations where glass would be unsafe and are not more widespread. This will surely change over time with developments in less expensive multilayer constructions, or monolayer PET with in-built (or coated) barrier properties.

Packaging may be produced with a mix of materials and it is not uncommon to see up to 20% recycled content. However, recycling is only possible with compatible polyesters, coatings and co-extruded layers. In other words, not all polyester packaging is recyclable.

### PET IN PRODUCTS, FURNITURE AND LIGHTING

PET textile is used throughout the interior, such as in carpets, curtains and upholstery. Its relatively low wear resistance and vulnerability to pilling mean that it is avoided in high-traffic applications. PTT (triexta) has emerged as an alternative to PET for demanding interior (and automotive) applications. For example, Sorona is a relatively new PTT from DuPont that contains 37% renewable, plant-based ingredients. While it has similar softness, stain resistance, vibrant colour range and colourfastness to PET, it is more resistant to wear and abrasion. It is more expensive, of course,

but this is justified in many applications by its improved durability.

Outdoor applications include lightweight tents, backpacks and ropes. PET fabrics compete with high-performance types such as PA and ultra-high-molecular-weight polyethylene (UHMWPE) (see PE). Although it has lower strength-to-weight, it is considered a good all-round material. Performance coatings maintain the fabric's breathability and enhance specific properties. For example, fabrics are metallized with aluminium to create a highly reflective (light and radiant heat) fabric, while PVC, PU and acrylic coatings improve the material's ability to withstand abrasion and weathering. PET is not used for climbing equipment owing to its relatively low elongation under load (ability to absorb energy in case of a fall) compared to PA.

Polyester textiles are shaped with heat and pressure into three-dimensional structures. This technique is used to form a range of products, from sound absorption panels to furniture to backpacks. It is equally suited to delicate products and to sturdy items lined with EVA foam. A similar technique is used to form pleated items, made famous by designers such as Issey Miyake (Pleats Please collection).

**Aluminized PET packaging** Ingredients that are sensitive to oxygen, such as this TieGuan Yin green tea, require additional protection. Metallizing combines the superior barrier performance of aluminium with the strength and versatility of PET film. Meanwhile, its reflective finish (up to 95%) provides a bright metallic backdrop for the printed graphics.

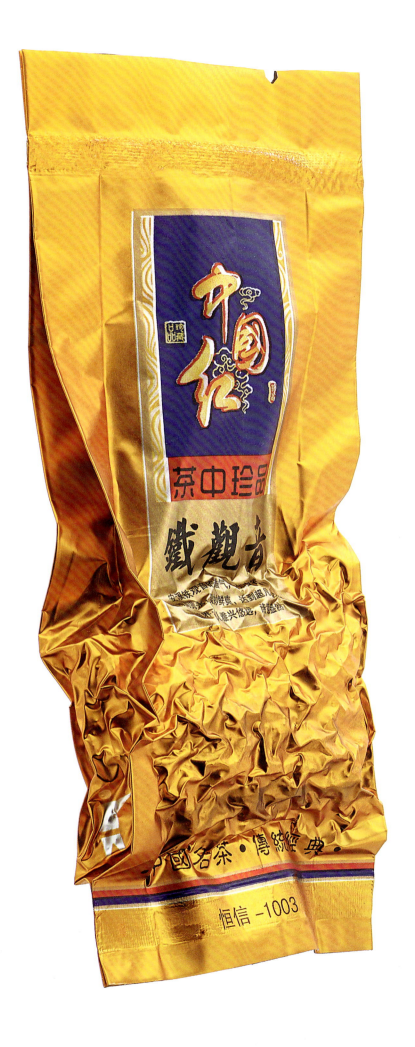

中國紅

茶中珍品

鐵觀音

安溪鐵觀音香氣馥郁，
滋味醇厚，妙鮮爽，送到超凡，
香入雅興悠遠，苦盡甘來

中國名茶 · 傳統經典

恒信 –1003

Injection-molded PET and PBT combine performance with ease of processing and are applied to a range of industrial and engineering parts. Their inherent resistance to weathering and low water absorption are utilized in outdoor products such as photovoltaic panels, gunstocks and automotive parts (windscreen wipers, enclosures and door handles). The improved electrical insulation performance of PBT is utilized in connector blocks and terminals. Like its cousin PET, it is used in the production of large, complex furniture. While it has sufficient tensile strength to be used for the structure, the high flow rate (during molding) allows long thin cross-sections to be molded with relative ease. The

**Above**
**PET mesh upholstery**
The lightweight structure of the Highframe chair, by Italian designer Alberto Meda for Alias in 1992, consists of extruded aluminium elliptical tube joined with die-cast aluminium components. The seat and back are made from PVC-coated

woven PET mesh. As it is held taut by the aluminium structure, the high strength and stiffness of PET fibre ensures that the fabric maintains its shape to provide uniform and consistent support. The PVC coating ensures a durable and weather-resistant finish. Photo courtesy of Alberto Meda.

**Opposite**
**PET acoustic panels**
Alberto Meda and Francesco Meda created the Flap acoustic tile concept for Caimi Brevetti, Italy. Launched in 2013, this novel solution combines the sound absorption of a PET nonwoven with the air space trapped behind. The density of the inner core is optimized for sound absorption and the face fabric tailored for a clean, formal

appearance. They are both constructed from PET and so can be collectively recycled. The light and stiff tile is mounted onto the wall or ceiling and can be adjusted in situ to change the look and sound of the surrounding space. The polygonal design avoids long straight lines and helps to visually break up large areas of panelling. Photo courtesy of Caimi Brevetti.

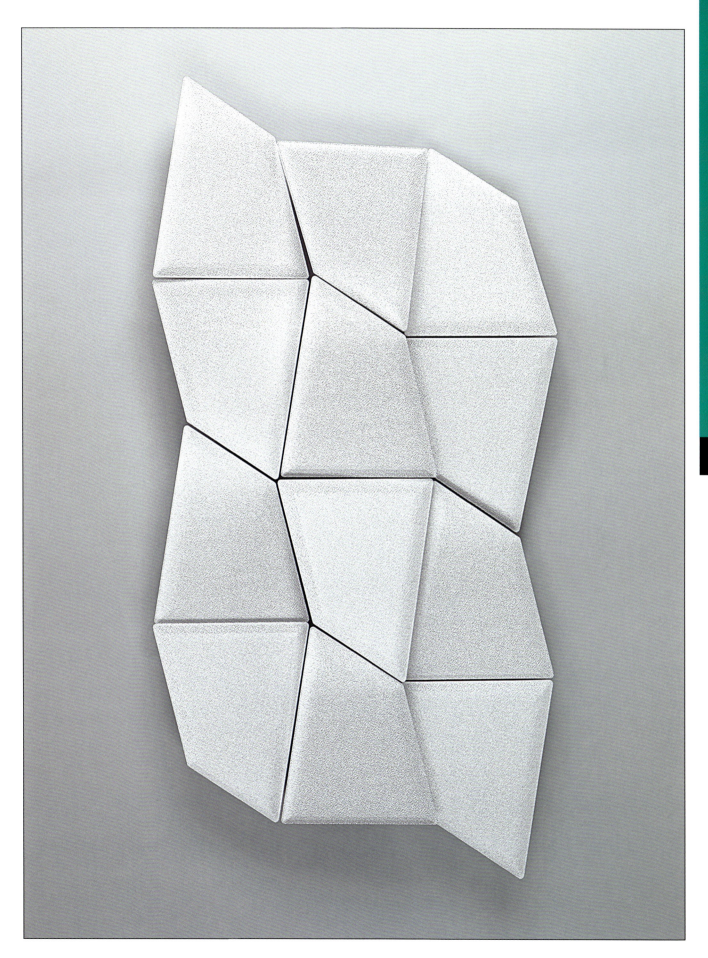

freedom this provides designers has been exploited in products from one-piece chairs to power-tool housing to sports products.

These plastics are used unreinforced for parts that require very high flow rate and superior surface quality. With fibre reinforcement it is more challenging to produce a 'class A' (high-quality, blemish-free) surface, though not impossible. Incorporating up to 50% glass fibre improves mechanical strength and dimensional stability significantly. Grades suitable for food contact (cleanliness and resistance to chemicals) are used in molded packaging, cookware and medical products.

An added advantage of molded polyester is that it is compatible with transfer printing. Ink is sublimated from transfer paper onto the polyester part. With a combination of thermo-forming and prolonged heat and pressure, three-dimensional surfaces are printed. Printing the image onto paper, rather than the surface of the product, creates the opportunity for reproducing intricate

high-resolution images that have previously only been possible on flat materials. The same technique is used as a low-cost alternative to printing directly onto lengths of textile.

BOPET makes an ideal substrate for printed flexible electronics thanks to its low elongation under load. BOPET does not stretch when flexed, which helps to keep circuitry intact. In addition, it has excellent dielectric strength (insulation properties), thermal stability and cut-through resistance. Currently it is utilized in rigid displays (such as to provide antiglare or antireflection properties to the front layer), flexible displays and printed electronics (conductive inks, such as based on copper or silver, are deposited onto the surface).

The flexibility and lightness of BOPET-based electronics presents many opportunities for the fast-growing wearables sector. There are two methods of application: the printed film is permanently set in shape (such as curved display) or allowed to bend in

**Electronic paper FES Watch** The FES Watch from Sony's Fashion Entertainments project is a revolutionary new watch that employs electronic paper for the face and strap. Wearers can select a pattern of their choice to be displayed from 24 different options. An ultra-low-power display technology that utilizes reflected light (as opposed to backlit), electronic paper is based on a flexible polyester (PET) film substrate. The image is created by repositioning particles of different colours within the electronic paper. The different colours, such as black and white, are charged positive and negative respectively. Within each pixel the direction of current determines whether white or black is visible, and thus an image is formed. Photo courtesy of Sony.

application (such as flexible display). While the formed method has been realized in several commercial consumer electronic products, the latter is much more challenging. The stiffness, strength and thermal properties of BOPET make it an ideal substrate for printed electronics. However, these same properties mean that it is not the most ergonomic and comfortable material to wear.

Where body contact is not the primary concern, transparent BOPET printed electronics offer new design possibilities. Thin and flexible displays, transistors, batteries and circuitry are integrated to provide a range of functionality. This low-cost approach to electronics has been adopted in the automotive, consumer electronics, aerospace and packaging industries.

**One-piece PBT cantilever chair** While a one-piece plastic chair is nothing new, the Myto chair pushes injection molding to its limits. The chair is the result of a unique collaboration between BASF (plastic supplier), Plank (manufacturer and distributor) and KGID (Konstantin Grcic Industrial Design). BASF manufactures PBT under the trademark name Ultradur for automotive applications and was looking for ways to break into new markets. KGID was commissioned to take on that challenge and design a chair to be launched at the Salone Internazionale del Mobile 2008, Milan. Through an iterative process of design, a new form of cantilever chair was born. Alongside the design development, engineers tweaked the material properties to provide the optimum balance of tensile strength and mold flow rate. The result is a complex one-piece molding, with thicker sections at the base where the chair needs full strength complemented by thinner sections where flexibility is required. Photo courtesy of Plank.

# Polyamide (PA), Nylon

**Also known as**
Resin trademark names: Grilamid, Zytel, Akulon, Tecamid, Tecast, Ultramid, Rilsan, Ecopaxx, Vestamid
Fibre trademark names: Anso, Antron, Cordura, Enka, Enkalon, Grilon, Meryl, Novadyn, Stanylenka, Tactel, Trilene, Ultron, Zeftron

Consumed in only modest quantities, PA is perhaps the most well-known engineering plastic as a result of decades of successful marketing. Famously applied in hosiery as a low-cost alternative to silk in 1939, it was the first truly synthetic fibre. Nowadays, it can be found in a broad spectrum of end uses, from additive manufacturing to lightweight sportswear.

| Types | Typical Applications | Sustainability |
|---|---|---|
| • PA: 6, 12, 4/6, 6/6, 6/10, 10/10 and 6/12<br>• Polyphthalamide (PPA) | • Textiles and fashion<br>• Automotive and industrial<br>• Products and furniture<br>• Packaging | • Relatively high embodied energy<br>• Challenging to recycle owing to the range of types and mix of ingredients |

| Properties | Competing Materials | Costs |
|---|---|---|
| • Tough, but notch-sensitive<br>• Good thermal and chemical resistance<br>• Hydroscopic (absorbs water) | • Aluminium alloy, cast iron and steel<br>• PP, PC, PET, PBT and POM<br>• Fibres: aramid, PET, viscose, rayon, silk, cotton and linen | • Moderate to high material costs<br>• Moderate manufacturing costs |

164

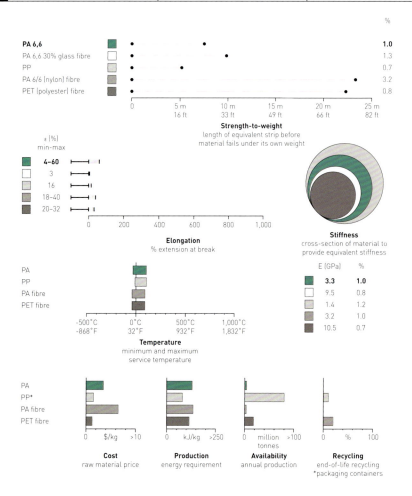

## INTRODUCTION

Polyamide (PA) is available as a high-performance fibre and versatile engineering plastic. It is commonly referred to as 'nylon', a name invented by DuPont. Today, several large chemical companies manufacture PA under various trademark names, but nylon has prevailed and remains in everyday use.

PA fibre revolutionized the fashion and textile industry. It provided a low-cost alternative to relatively expensive textiles including silk (page 420), cotton (page 410) and linen (see Flax, page 400). Compared to its competitors of the time – notably viscose and cellulose acetate (page 252) – PA offered superior colourability, strength and elasticity. First launched in toothbrushes and then hosiery, it quickly spread throughout fashion, as well as industrial and military uses. Over time, polypropylene (PP) (page 98) and polyethylene terephthalate (PET, polyester) (page 152) emerged as less costly alternatives and so diminished PA's dominance. It remains an important fibre in technical textiles, fashion and footwear.

Molded, machined and cast PA is utilized for mechanical and structural applications. As with other engineering plastics, its mechanical properties set it against structural metals, such as aluminium (page 42) and steel (page 28). It is available as powder, used for additive manufacturing. So it is used not only in mass production but also for one-offs and low-volume production.

## COMMERCIAL TYPES AND USES

The exact properties depend on the formulation. PA is typified by a polymer structure of carbon atoms held together by amide groups. In the case of aramid (page 242), a close relative, the polymer is made up of benzene rings held together by amide groups. PA is formed in two

ways, using either a single monomer or with two monomers.

There are several types of PA. The numerical nomenclature is a result of the process: one number (e.g. 6 or 12) indicates the carbon atoms of a single monomer, while a double number (e.g. 6/6 or 6/12) indicates that two monomers were used and the atom count of each. For example, polyamide 6/6 is produced by the reaction of adipic acid (a 6-carbon

dibasic acid) and hexamethylene diamine (a 6-carbon aliphatic diamine).

The proportion of carbon atoms determines the unique characteristics of each type. As the number of carbon atoms rises, the capacity to absorb moisture is reduced. This results in improved dimensional stability and electrical properties, but lower ductility, heat resistance and strength. Higher numbers are typically more expensive.

**Lightweight outerwear**
Synthetic textiles have seen major development since hosiery was first knitted from PA 6/6. The shell of this Uniqlo hooded parka is woven from finely spun PA filaments (similar items are produced using PET; the two fibres are virtually interchangeable in

some cases). Tightly woven to provide a water-repellent finish, the smooth yarn yields a shiny textile. Its superior elasticity and wear resistance enable an ultralight shell that can be collapsed down to a very small package; the absolute minimum material is used to eliminate bulk.

**Amorphous**

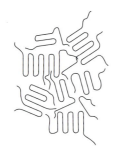

**Semi-crystalline**

**Polymer morphology**
The difference between amorphous and semi-crystalline polymer structures is the order, or lack thereof. Amorphous plastics include PS, ABS, SAN, PMMA, PVC, PC and certain types of PA. As a result of their random structure they are transparent, dimensionally stable with low shrinkage (so less likely to warp post-molding) and do not have a sharp melting point (they gradually soften when heated). Semi-crystalline

plastics, on the other hand, form areas of more densely packed and orderly polymer on cooling (the degree of order depends on the type of plastic, additives and process). Examples include PP, PE, POM, PET, PBT, PEEK and the majority of PAs. These plastics tend to be translucent or opaque (the crystalline areas scatter light), strong, tough, hard, wear-resistant (providing a sliding surface in some cases) and more resistant to chemicals.

**Aliphatic**

**Aromatic**

**Polymer chain structure** Aliphatic polymers consist of straight or branched chains. Examples include PP, PE, PS and certain types of polyester (e.g. PLA, PHA and PHB) and PA. The atoms are joined by single, double or triple bonds. Introducing aromatic content into the polymer backbone has several advantages. Consisting of closed rings of atoms, aromatic polymers are more stable and resistant to heat and chemicals. Plastics have various proportions of aromatic structure

and can be either amorphous, such as PC, or semi-crystalline, such as PET and PPA. The benefits are increased, to a point, by raising the proportion of aromatic content. Aramid and liquid crystal polymer (LCP) have a very high proportion of aromatic content, which provides some exceptional properties. The aromatic structure ensures that the monomers join together into much longer unbroken chains (increased molecular weight), with highly oriented crystal structure.

PA 6 and 6/6 are the most popular thanks to their balance of strength, stiffness and toughness. While they are interchangeable in many respects, PA 6/6 is marginally stronger, stiffer and lighter; PA 6 has slightly higher water absorption, ductility (impact strength and resilience) and ease of processing.

PA is semi-crystalline or amorphous depending on the ingredients. Semi-crystalline PA is tough with good resistance to heat, chemicals and weathering. It is limited somewhat by its affinity for water, which can have an affect on dimensional stability. It is modified to produce flame-retardant, tough and super-tough versions. Naturally white to off-white, depending on the type, it is available in a range of muted colours through black. As well as textiles, it is used for a variety of applications including under-the-bonnet automotive parts (metal replacement), housings (from power tools to handheld electronics), consumer products, cookware and furniture

Amorphous PA is created with certain monomers. It is transparent with impressive light transmission, 94% at 2 mm (0.08 in) wall thickness, which is equivalent to polymethyl methacrylate (PMMA) (page 174). And it is lighter than polycarbonate (PC) (page 144), its closest rival (amorphous PA has lower density than semi-crystalline types). However, it tends to be a little expensive. It is used for applications that demand a combination of transparency (colourability), flexural strength and resistance to chemicals. Examples include lightweight spectacle frames, sports gear, packaging containers (a 'BPA-free' alternative to PC for baby bottles), housings and industrial parts.

PA film is utilized in a variety of applications including flexible food packaging, construction, medical and aviation. It has very good strength, impact resistance, heat resistance and flexibility combined with excellent gas barrier properties. As with PET and PP, biaxially oriented PA (BOPA) provides high stiffness, puncture resistance, barrier properties and transparency.

Its semi-crystalline structure provides excellent resistance to oxygen, flavours

and aroma. These properties help to maintain foods for longer. Used in vacuum packaging and thermoformed shells, it is coextruded with polyethylene (PE) (page 108) and PP, among others, to take advantage of their combined properties.

Polyphthalamide (PPA) is a semi-crystalline semi-aromatic PA. Its partially aromatic structure provides higher heat resistance and lower water absorption. Combined with outstanding chemical resistance, PPA bridges the gap between PA and higher-performance plastics such as PEEK (page 188) and PTFE (see Fluoropolymer, page 190). It is applied in molded parts and fibres for particularly demanding applications, in particular automotive and aerospace parts.

## SUSTAINABILITY

PA is challenging to recycle and categorized by resin identification code #7, 'other'. Along with the various chemistries that need to be separated, PA is often combined with reinforcement, fillers, additives and pigments. Therefore, even though some industrial scrap is reprocessed, it is not commonly recycled.

PA has relatively high embodied energy as a result of production. While the majority is manufactured from oil-derived monomers, new grades have emerged that are produced from natural, renewable ingredients. Conventional ingredients are replaced with monomers derived from castor oil. The proportion ranges from 20% to 100%, depending on the application requirements.

Produced in relatively low quantities, they tend to be more costly than oil-derived equivalents. Examples include Rislan (PA 11), Pebax (polyether block amide, see TPE), Ultramid Balance (PA 6/10), Zytel RS (PA 10/10) and EcoPaXX (PA

**Overmolded GF-reinforced PA handle**
The Fiskars hatchet's handle is injection-molded glass-fibre-(GF-) reinforced PA and features a soft grip overmolded with thermoplastic elastomer (TPE) (page 194). The combination of flexural strength,

lightness and toughness provided by GFPA maximizes usability while reducing the likelihood of breakage. The forged steel blade is insert-molded into the handle. A very strong join is formed, enhanced by the shrinkage of the PA during molding.

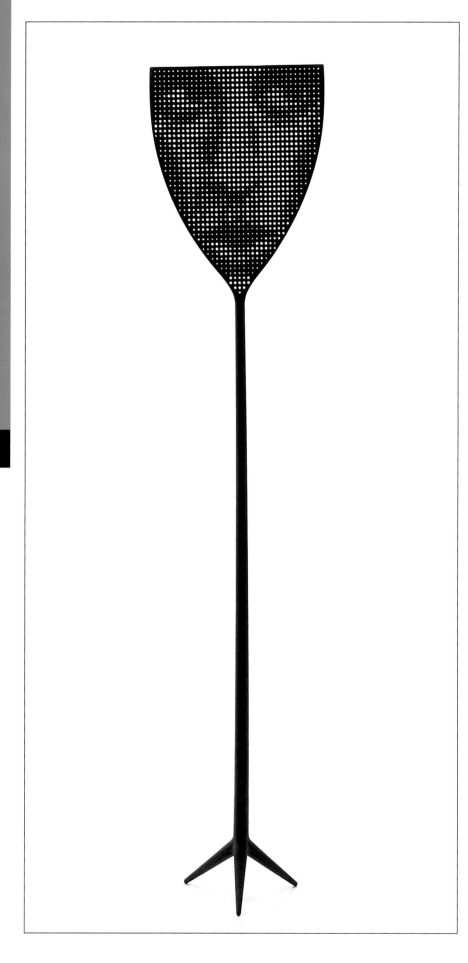

4/10). Each has its own characteristics, depending on the ingredients. Their mechanical properties cover a range of applications from structural automotive parts to transparent packaging film.

## PA IN PRODUCTS, FURNITURE AND LIGHTING

A high-performance thermoplastic with a desirable balance of properties, it is often the first choice for metal replacement applications. From mechanical automotive parts to guitar strings, PA is preferable to metal across an array of end uses.

It is moderately expensive – almost twice the cost of PET and polyoxymethylene (POM, acetal) (page 184), and comparable with PC – and so readily replaced by less expensive plastics once it has proved that they can perform as well as their metal predecessors. As a result, new applications are continually being explored to maintain sales. Today, PA is utilized in products ranging from transparent eyewear to high-temperature cooking utensils and from power tools to one-piece molded furniture.

The diversity of uses demonstrates the versatility of PA. As well as textiles, it is used in molded parts, extruded sections, cast blocks, precision-machined items and additive-manufactured prototypes.

PA is compatible with several mass-production techniques including injection and blow molding. Rotation molding is utilized in the production of low to medium volumes of hollow parts.

There are many reasons for specifying PA in molded parts. It has excellent flexural and fatigue strength and so is used for structural and parts that will be subjected to intermittent loads. It is tough with high elongation and so suitable for use with 'interference fits'. And similar to PP, it is suitable for 'snap fits'. PA's low coefficient of friction is

**Injection-molded fly swatter** Dr Skud from Alessi, designed by Philippe Starck, was first manufactured in 1998. It demonstrates the impressive toughness and flexural strength of PA, and over time, the injection-molded structure will reveal PA's poor dimensional stability. The long stand gradually bends under the weight of the head, giving the face a more quizzical look.

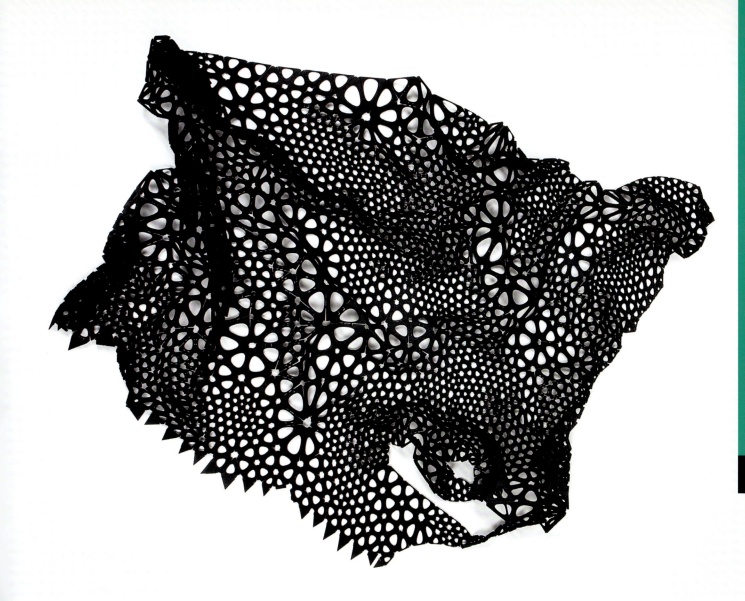

used in bearing and wear applications. Lubricants are added to the base resin to improve its sliding properties. In this respect, it outperforms general-purpose engineering plastics such as POM, PET and ultra-high-molecular-weight polyethylene (UHMWPE) (see PE), and is far less expensive than high-performance types, such as PTFE and PEEK.

Reinforcing molded or extruded PA with glass fibre (GF) leads to significant increases in strength, stiffness and heat deflection temperature. However, it can result in higher anisotropy (different physical properties widthwise to lengthwise), which affects mold shrinkage and ultimately results in higher distortion. This has to be taken into account in the design of the part to avoid it becoming a problem. In the case of PA

6/6, GF does not reduce impact strength, unlike most other plastics, which is an advantage for demanding applications.

Similar to POM and PEEK, it is used as feedstock for machining and is available in cast blocks (PA 6 and 12) or extruded sections (typically PA 6, 6/6, 12 and 4/6). While casting allows for the production of larger blocks, extrusion is less expensive. In addition, molded parts sometimes require machining, such as where areas of very thin wall section are required or for holes and details impractical to mold. In all cases, it is straightforward to achieve a high-quality finish.

Casting is generally used to produce semi-finished parts, such as rods, tubes and sheets. It allows for the production of parts with very thick sections free from voids and with higher crystallinity

**Additive-manufactured structure** Created by Nervous System in 2014, the Kinematics Dress is selective laser-sintered (SLS) PA. The designers, Jessica Rosenkrantz and Jesse Louis-Rosenberg, mix data from body scans with an intricate structure of thousands of triangular panels interconnected by hinges. Produced in a single, articulating piece, it is carefully folded in CAD to make it small enough to fit on the printer bed. Photo courtesy of Nervous System.

(enhanced strength and stiffness) than molded or extruded material. They are tailored to the needs of applications with additives (oils, lubricants and heat stabilizers). In addition, it allows near-net-shape parts to be created, reducing subsequent machining time and waste.

Even though it machines well and parts are manufactured to very accurate dimensions, PA has poor dimensional

## PRODUCTS, FURNITURE AND LIGHTING

**Strength-to-weight**
PA is 40% stronger than PET for the same weight, and PA with 30% GF is stronger and more flexible than high-strength aluminium alloy.

**Tough**
It is tougher than PET and its mechanical properties allow it to be used in structural parts as well as bearing and long-term wear applications.

**Resilience**
PA will deform under load, but returns to its original shape more readily than comparable plastics (see also TPE).

**Low friction coefficient**
The surface feels slippery and is considered 'self-lubricating'. In other words, it does not usually require oils or grease when used for moving parts. The same quality helps the surface to slide over other parts and so deflect wear and abrasion.

**Cost**
While for many end uses it is considered expensive, in some applications PA competes with even more expensive plastics such as PTFE and PEEK, among others.

stability and swells as it absorbs water. Therefore, it is avoided in parts where dimensional accuracy is critical. Moisture absorption has a negative affect on mechanical properties too, including tensile strength, compressive strength, hardness and friction coefficient. The rate of moisture absorption depends on the type; for example, PA 6/12 absorbs around 25% less than PA 6/6 and this is further reduced with additives.

PA powder provides the raw material for additive manufacturing. Compatible with selective laser sintering (SLS), it is used for functional prototypes suitable for working situations. Grades reinforced with GF or carbon fibre (CF) offer superior mechanical properties.

### PA IN AUTOMOTIVE AND AEROSPACE
In recent decades, the use of engineering thermoplastics in automotive and aerospace applications has grown significantly. In pursuit of lighter and more fuel-efficient transportation, lower-performance metal parts are replaced with PA and other engineering thermoplastics. There are countless examples of mechanical and structural PA parts, such as in cooling, electrical and fuel systems.

Adding mineral fill or GF reinforcement to plastic improves strength and stiffness particularly as the temperature is increased beyond the polymer's glass transition temperature (Tg), where the amorphous region becomes pliable. PA reinforced with around one-third GF has proved suitably enduring for demanding applications that were traditionally metal, such as engine covers, air intake

manifolds and radiator tanks. The trend continues, because as well as maintaining or even boosting performance, switching to PA reduces cost and saves as much as 30–50% weight.

Long GF results in parts with higher strength-to-weight, because the same strength can be achieved with fewer fibres. However, they are far more challenging to process, because the fibres are degraded during molding.

As with similar plastics, adaptations to the injection-molding process allow for the production of hollow and foamed parts. Gas-assisted injection molding is used to produce hollow parts, such as PA door handles. A bubble of air is injected during molding, which helps reduce defects and maximize strength in complex geometries. And another technique, known as MuCell, creates foam during molding. This is used to great advantage: it reduces weight,

### AUTOMOTIVE AND AEROSPACE

**Thermal stability**
While PA 6 and PA 6/6 have reasonable heat resistance (110°C [230°F] and 130°C [266°F] respectively), PA 4/6 can tolerate up to around 140°C.

**Chemical resistance**
PA 6 and PA 6/6 have excellent resistance to a broad spectrum of chemicals (but limited resistance to acids), and PPA performs even better as a result of its semi-aromatic structure.

**Moldability**
Semi-crystalline PA has high fluidity when molten, making it efficient to mold and suitable for thin-walled parts. With injection molding, multiple functions may be integrated into a single part, which minimizes cost and the potential for assembly errors.

**Versatility**
As well as molded and extruded parts, PA is utilized as fibre for automotive interiors.

cycle time and the potential for warpage in large parts.

PA 4/6 has higher crystallinity and so has a higher melting point than PA 6 or PA 6/6. However, it is more expensive, which limits application to some extent. PPA has a semi-aromatic structure. This has several benefits: PPA has greater dimensional stability and overall resistance as a result of a higher Tg, higher melting point and significantly reduced absorption (moisture and chemicals) in comparison to PA. Like PA 4/6, it carries a higher price tag than the more common types. It is used in place of metals – cast iron (page 22) and aluminium alloy for example – in increasingly demanding applications, further helping to reduce the weight and improve the performance of transportation.

A transparent semi-aromatic PA has recently emerged, named Novadyn, which is blended to enhance the performance of PA 6 and 6/6. It is targeted at transparent applications where the chemical resistance of PC is insufficient.

PA fibre's outstanding tenacity, elasticity, dye-fastness and high melting point are utilized throughout automobile interiors. Lightweight airbag fabric, woven from PA 6/6, is able to withstand the impulsive loads, mechanical stress and elevated temperatures involved in deployment. Upholstery and carpeting produced from PA endures heavy traffic, spills and abrasion, providing long-lasting quality. A wide range of colours

**Lightweight, crash-resistant PA composite**
Until recently, high-performance fibre-reinforced composites were considered too expensive and impractical for mass production owing to the lengthy cycle time. Through collaboration, Audi AG, Bond-Laminates, the Institute for Composite Materials, Jacob Plastics, Lanxess, and KraussMaffei developed a short-cycle mass-production technique. In operation, a sheet of fibre-reinforced plastic is thermoformed into the shape of the mold and then back-injected with PA in a fully automated process. Known under various names – including SpriForm and FiberForm – this innovation enables the use of high-performance composites in a wider array of automotive parts than was previously possible. This door impact bar test part for the Audi A4 consists of several layers of woven glass fibre in a PA matrix.

and textures is possible, with finishes including bright, semi-dull and dull.

As one of the largest consumers of PA, the automotive industry has explored the potential of reusing the material. Even though many different types exist, and it is often combined with additives, waste PA provides a valuable feedstock for new products. It is surely only a matter of time before the large manufacturers adopt successful recycling practices.

## PA IN FASHION AND TEXTILES
Although widely recognized – promoted under trademark names such as Cordura and Trilene – PA accounts for only a very small percentage of fibres used in fashion and textiles. It has some very desirable properties, but is limited to some extent by the high price. Therefore, as well as pure-PA high-performance textiles, it is utilized in blends to take advantage of the performance at lower price points.

**Lightweight, hard-wearing footwear**
The majority of US Army combat wear is produced with Cordura, including these desert boots. Referred to as 'ballistic fabric', woven PA provides all-round durability, with exceptional abrasion resistance and tear strength. Colour is added during spinning (solution-dyed) or once the fabric has been constructed. The surface can be printed too, such as with camouflage.

## FASHION AND TEXTILES

**Hard-wearing**
It has excellent resistance to surface wear and abrasion, properties utilized in high-traffic applications.

**Elasticity**
It has very high elastic recovery: PA is able to return to its original shape after greater elongation (20–40%) than other high-performance fibres, except elastomers (see TPE, page 194) and rubber (page 216).

**Strength-to-weight**
As a result of drawing during manufacture, and the fibre's mechanical characteristics, PA fibre is more than 300% stronger than molded PA for the same weight. It outperforms PET and PP, but is less than half the strength of UHMWPE for the same weight. When wet, PA loses 10–20% of its strength.

The most common PA blends for apparel applications include cotton and viscose. A good cost–performance balance is achieved with around one-third PA content. It is blended with wool (page 426) to enhance strength, resilience and wear resistance. Used in apparel and carpet, PA accepts acid dyes, as do animal fibres, maximizing flexibility in production.

Fabric constructions have evolved to take advantage of the exceptional properties of PA. For example, ripstop is a woven fabric consisting of slightly larger warp and weft yarns at intervals to stop tearing. Between the bolstered yarns, the fabric is as light as technically possible. It is utilized for large areas of textile that have to withstand significant mechanical loads, such as racing sails, parachutes and hot air balloons.

PA is used in applications where tactility and appearance, as well as mechanical properties, are considered important. While the majority of fibres are produced with a simple round cross-section, varying the shape and contents of the fibre yields sophisticated effects not possible with round fibres. Combined with material selection, textile properties may be tailored to meet the most demanding requirements.

The cross-section of fibres is adjusted during spinning. The outside shape may be regular or irregular, and ranges from dull to glossy. Fibres may be hollow, or with voids, to improve insulation or aid moisture wicking.

In addition, multiple types of PA, as well as other polymers, may be combined in a single fibre. These developments expand the opportunities for visual, as well as functional, design opportunities. For example, combining a coloured core with a translucent sheath produces iridescent colour. Combining a core (such as PA 6/6) with a sheath that has a lower melting point (such as PA 6) enables the fibres to be formed and bonded without affecting ultimate strength.

Thin metal coatings are applied for decorative and functional purposes by plating or vacuum deposition. A variety of base materials is used for applications from conductive textiles to bespoke jewelry. The quality and colour depends on the technique and materials used.

Conductive fabrics, sometimes referred to as smart textiles, are used for technical applications such as electromagnetic interference (EMI) shielding, heat shielding (survival suits and firefighter uniforms, see page 47), radar reflection, antimicrobial (shoes and medical), wearable electronics and flexible heater elements (seats, blankets, pocket linings and gloves). Metal-coated fabrics are also used for decorative applications, such as fancy yarn.

**Round**

**Trilobal**

**Core and sheath**

**Bilateral**

**Ribbon**

**Triangular**

**Segmented ribbon**

**Hollow segmented pie**

**Hollow**

**Multi-channel**

**Islands in-the-sea**

**Radial (after separation)**

**Synthetic fibre cross-section** The cross-section of synthetic fibre affects many properties, including performance, bulk, appearance and tactility. The simplest and most common spun profile is rod-like with a round cross-section. Having learned from nature – cotton, wool and silk have distinct cross-sections that contribute to their unique character – a range of cross-sections has emerged to broaden the appeal of synthetics. Trilobal fibres reflect a lot of light and so appear bright and lustrous. The three-pronged profile adds bulk to a fabric without weight, aids wicking (utilized in sportswear) and provides soil-hiding capacity (useful in carpets). Fibres of this type come in many different designs. Ribbon has a flat oval profile, similar to silk, that reflect lots of light and so appears to sparkle and shimmer when combined with appropriate plastic (such as PA or cellulose acetate). Triangular fibre has a similar lustrous appearance with larger cross-sectional area. Hollow and multi-channel fibres enhance wicking and insulating properties, similar to wool.

**Bicomponent fibre cross-section**
Bicomponent fibres combine the properties of two or more polymers: they are co-extruded and spun together in various configurations. This allows for complex functions that would not be possible with a single polymer. Core-and-sheath fibres consist of a functional inner material (colour, conductive, cooling or high tenacity, for example) surrounded by a decorative or protective outer layer. Bilateral fibres mimic the structure of wool: they are flat until exposed to heat treatment, whereby one side shrinks more quickly than the other and so causes the fibre to crimp. Many different configurations exist with different functions placed side by side. Bicomponent spinning allows for the production of very fine fibre elements, because the delicate strands are protected within a larger matrix. Separating the fine fibres after spinning yields microfibres. This is done mechanically, or by dissolving one component altogether. Microfibre fabrics are very soft and drape well. They are utilized for decorative as well as technical applications.

# Polymethyl Methacrylate (PMMA), Acrylic

Often compared to glass, PMMA is much easier to form and fabricate and so provides far greater design freedom. It is available in a range of colours, from tinted to opaque. Frequently used in combination with lighting, it has very high light transmission, which results in glowing colour. It is strong and hard, but a little brittle.

| Types | Typical Applications | Sustainability |
|---|---|---|
| • PMMA | • Products, furniture and lighting<br>• Packaging and point-of-sale<br>• Glazing and interiors<br>• Jewelry and accessories | • Moderate embodied energy<br>• Recyclable, identified by code #7, 'other'<br>• Impractical to separate from mixed waste |

| Properties | Competing Materials | Costs |
|---|---|---|
| • Scratch-resistant<br>• High strength and stiffness<br>• Transparent and resistant to weathering | • SAN, PC and PS<br>• Soda-lime glass, crystal glass | • Moderate material costs, although PMMA composite is more expensive<br>• Low manufacturing costs |

174

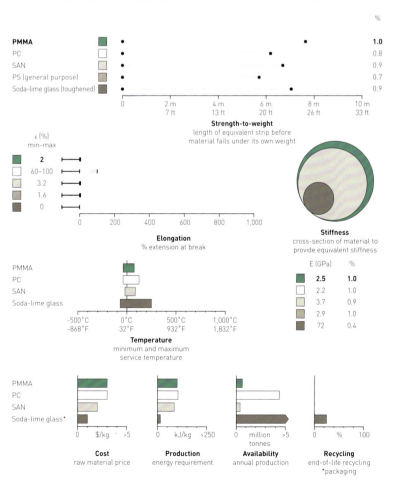

## INTRODUCTION

Similar to polycarbonate (PC) (page 144) and polystyrene (PS) (page 132), polymethyl methacrylate (PMMA) is an amorphous thermoplastic (see page 166). As a result of the chaotically arranged polymer chains, all three are transparent with good dimensional stability and low shrinkage. Their mechanical properties set them apart from one another: PMMA has excellent strength-to-weight, high stiffness and good surface hardness; PC has far higher impact resistance owing to its combination of elongation and stiffness; and PS is less strong but stiffer and so much more brittle. While PMMA and PC are around the same price, depending on the grade, PS is half the price for the same weight.

PMMA is often likened to glass: available in transparent sheets, it is suitable for many of the same end uses. Compared to plain soda-lime glass (page 508), PMMA has far higher strength-to-weight. Glass that has been tempered (toughened) – as will be the case in any load-bearing application – has much higher tensile strength and is more closely matched to PMMA.

PMMA has greater resistance to impact than glass, and when it fails, PMMA cracks and forms large blunt splinters. Glass on the other hand, will shatter. This is desirable in some cases, such as automotive glazing, although in many applications greater impact resistance is preferable. Of course, if impact resistance is the critical property, PC outperforms both of these materials.

The optical quality of PMMA does not decrease as rapidly as glass with increased thickness. Therefore, applications that require substantial load-bearing sections of transparent material – aquariums, underwater vessels and aircraft windows – are typically PMMA.

## COMMERCIAL TYPES AND USES

PMMA is compatible with all thermoplastic forming techniques, but because of the types of application it is predominantly shaped by injection molding and extrusion.

Similar to polyamide (PA, nylon) (page 164), the monomer – methyl methacrylate (MMA) – may be cast into blocks. Cast PMMA is more expensive than extruded sheet, but offers many advantages. It has far superior surface quality and optical properties (up to 92% light transmission); it is resistant to a higher service temperature (around 10°C [50°F] more than extruded PMMA); and has better chemical resistance.

Sheets of cast PMMA are made in two

**Injection-molded tinted PMMA** The lustrous transparency of PMMA is unlike any other plastic. Combined with colour, the high-gloss surface gives the illusion of crystal glass (page 518) in a product that would be impractical in such as material. The Kartell Shanghai Vase, by Mario Bellini, stands nearly half a metre (20 in) tall and yet is light and portable. Injection molded from PMMA, it is available in a range of colours, including vacuum-metallized versions.

ways: in blocks between sheets of glass, or as continuous sheet between two polished stainless-steel bands. Owing to the low volumes, it is possible to make bespoke production runs, such as a particular colour and depth of surface texture. As a result of the casting process, it has far higher molecular weight (chain length) than extruded PMMA, which makes it stiffer and easier to cut and fabricate. Unlike other thermoplastics, it is hard enough to be polished.

PMMA is combined with reinforcement and additives to enhance specific properties. PMMA is not conventionally used for high-strength-fibre-reinforced composites (see Unsaturated Polyester, page 228). Instead, PMMA is combined with mineral – primarily aluminium trihydrate, derived from bauxite – to produce a composite with unique aesthetic properties. Perhaps the best-known example is Corian, manufactured by DuPont. As a result of the combination

of plastic and mineral, this combines a luxurious stone-like surface with many of the desirable properties of PMMA – it can be thermoformed, machined and adhesive bonded. It is utilized in worktops, interiors, cladding and furniture.

Other monomers such as methyl acrylate and acrylonitrile can be joined with MMA to form different types of acrylic plastic. Changing the proportion of these monomers in the copolymer affects elasticity and other properties.

POLYMETHYL METHACRYLATE (PMMA), ACRYLIC

## PRODUCTS, FURNITURE AND LIGHTING

**Transparency**
At up to 92% light transmission, PMMA has equivalent transparency to glass and is superior to all other thermoplastics (PC is around 89%).

**Optical effects**
There is an unrivalled range of standard sheet materials to choose from, including different colours, tints, light diffusion and other optical effects. PMMA's resistance to ultraviolet ensures that optical quality is maintained long-term.

**Surface hardness**
PMMA has the highest surface hardness of the thermoplastics. Coatings are used to further improve resistance to scratching and wear. Even so, it cannot compete with glass in terms of surface durability.

**Cast transparent table**
Designed by Oki Sato, founder of Japanese design studio Nendo, the Transparent Table was created for Milan Design Week 2011. The top is produced from planks of PMMA that have been cast from wood with a pronounced grain. The result is a faithful reproduction of the surface quality of wood, including bevelled edges, in grey-tinted plastic. Photo by Masayuki Hayashi.

**Weathering resistance**
Its high resistance to ultraviolet means it maintains its colour and finish long-term, even when used outdoors.

**Strength-to-weight**
It is around twice the strength of glass for the same weight. Tempering improves the strength of glass, but it is still heavier than PMMA for the same strength.

**Transparency**
PMMA has very high light transmission and is roughly equivalent to high-quality glass. In thick sections PMMA has superior optical quality.

**Colour**
PMMA is available in a vast range of standard colours and finishes.

## SUSTAINABILITY

PMMA is reasonably inert and does not pose any health risks as long as there is no residual monomer; MMA is allergenic. It is tasteless and certain grades are suitable for food contact.

PMMA is readily recyclable. Scrap from reliable sources, such as production facilities, can be ground and converted back into pellets suitable for molding and extrusion. Identified by code #7, 'other', it is not easily separated from mixed waste streams and so is rarely recycled end-of-life.

Chemical recycling reduces PMMA to its original monomer of MMA. In a process known as depolymerization, PMMA is heated to over 500°C (932°F) in contact with molten lead, which causes the polymer chains to break down. While this yields high-purity MMA, the use of lead has negative environmental impacts. Alternative techniques are being explored to try to overcome the reliance on lead.

## PMMA IN PRODUCTS, FURNITURE AND LIGHTING

PMMA's transparency and high-quality surface are utilized in items ranging from mobile phone screens to large pieces of cast furniture and injection-molded lighting. It has high strength-to-weight and is resistant to most regular chemicals. Its only major drawback is that it is a little brittle – a result of its high stiffness combined with low elongation.

High-end and large-format phones and tablets feature aluminosilicate glass (page 522) screens. Compared to regular glass (soda-lime), this has far superior strength and stiffness. PMMA is utilized in low-end consumer products to give the illusion of glass at a fraction of the price. While they may look similar at first glance, the higher aesthetic qualities

of glass – crisp surface reflections and stiffness – quickly become apparent when the screen is in use.

A key benefit of transparent plastic, compared to glass, is that it can be injection molded. Of the thermoplastics, PC and PMMA are the highest-performing structural, transparent types. The difference between them is that whereas PC has far higher impact resistance, PMMA has superior light transmission and scratch resistance. The types of application each has come to dominate illustrate these differences: PC is used to make visors, riot shields, reusable containers, front headlights and power-tool housing; and PMMA is used to make lenses, light guides, tail lights, signage and point-of-sale displays. While they are both commonly injection molded, PMMA is also frequently applied in sheet form.

Similar to other transparent materials, the edges of PMMA sheet parts glow brighter than their surroundings. This phenomenon, known as 'edge glow' or 'lit edge', is the result of light passing through the surface and refracting internally until it meets a cut edge. The same effect can be seen in scored lines (such as made by laser cutting) and is amplified through the use of fluorescent pigments. This property is utilized in signage (so the light source can be concealed), plastic optical fibre, promotional items, eye-catching packaging and point-of-sale.

A very high gloss finish can be achieved with PMMA. This is emphasized with vacuum metallizing, which adds a highly reflective aluminium coating to the surface of the plastic. Utilized in reflectors and lampshades, it is either protected on the backside of the plastic, or applied to the outside surface to give the illusion of solid metal.

## PMMA IN ARCHITECTURE AND CONSTRUCTION

PMMA is used in place of glass in floors, walls, ceilings, roofs and cladding. It is used throughout interiors as furniture, lighting, signage and interactive displays. It offers many advantages compared to glass, as previously described, presenting architects with greater design freedom as well as providing benefits in application.

Frei Otto and Gunther Behnisch utilized PMMA to dramatic effect in the tensile canopy that sweeps over the Munich Olympic Stadium. Covering a large area, lightweight PMMA ensured that weight was kept to a minimum. This helped to conserve material and allowed for greater spans to be achieved. Completed in 1972, the transparent canopy remains in use to this day.

Relatively easy to process, PMMA sheet is suitable for thermoforming, laser cutting and machining. With these processes a wide range of shapes is producible at relatively low cost (an added benefit of laser cutting is that it yields a high-gloss edge finish). Glass, on the other hand, is much more challenging to produce in three-dimensional forms.

Sheets are available in a very wide range of thickness and standard colours, from transparent to opaque and fluorescent to pastel. The transparency and quality of diffusion depends on additives and surface treatments. It is laminated with film (and other sheets) to create depth or colour shift and encapsulate textile or other intriguing effects. When cast, objects may be trapped within to create floating layers or diffusing effects.

**CNC-machined transparent façade**
The Reiss headquarters in London features a five-storey PMMA façade. During the day, sunlight is refracted in the panel profile. At night, LED strips beneath each panel illuminate the PMMA, creating a dramatically different appearance. The façade was originally conceived as cast glass with fabric draped behind, but the architects at Squire and Partners, who designed the building, realized the limitations of this approach and sought PMMA as the alternative. Cast in very large sheets that are machined to produce a linear pattern with varying thickness, the translucent material offers a shielded glimpse of light and movement within.

# Polyacrylonitrile (PAN), Acrylic Fibre

**Also known as**
Common trademark names: Dralon, Dolan, Dolanit, Kanekalon, Kanecaron

The majority of PAN is applied in acrylic and modacrylic fibre. The exact properties depend on the ingredients. It provides a versatile apparel fibre that is used alone or to supplement wool and cotton. Its high resistance to ultraviolet and weathering is utilized in a range of exterior applications, from convertible automobile roofs to yacht upholstery.

| Types | Typical Applications | Sustainability |
|-------|---------------------|----------------|
| • PAN<br>• Fibres: acrylic and modacrylic<br>• Structural plastics: SAN and ABS | • Knitwear and faux fur (pile fabric)<br>• Interior and exterior textiles<br>• Industrial items | • Production uses more energy than commonly used fibres such as PET and PP<br>• Not easy to recycle |

| Properties | Competing Materials | Costs |
|------------|---------------------|-------|
| • From soft to stiff, depending on the ingredients<br>• Weather-resistant, chemical-resistant and slow to burn | • Wool and cotton<br>• Viscose and CA<br>• PET, PA and PP fibre | • Not as cheap as PET and PP, but still relatively low-cost compared to natural fibres |

180

## INTRODUCTION

This section focuses on the use of polyacrylonitrile (PAN) in acrylic and modacrylic fibres, and as a precursor in the production of carbon fibre (page 236). For its use in structural plastic, see styrene acrylonitrile (SAN) (page 136) and acrylonitrile butadiene styrene (ABS) (page 138).

It is not as strong as polyethylene terephthalate (PET, polyester) (page 152), polyamide (PA, nylon) (page 164) or polypropylene (PP) (page 98), and loses around 15% of its strength when wet. Even though PAN is thermoplastic, it does not melt when heated. Instead, heat causes the fibre to break down and foam, a quality used in intumescent paints and seals. This heat sensitivity means that PAN-based apparel must be washed and ironed at relatively low temperatures to ensure the fibre does not lose its desirable properties. While acrylic is readily flammable, modacrylic is flame-retardant and so used in protective clothing and contract interior fabrics.

PAN has a highly crystalline structure (see page 166). As a result, the fibres are used in applications that demand high resistance to chemicals and weathering. It has very good resistance to most acids and alkalis, comparable with PP. And it has excellent weather resistance; its light-fastness is superior to all other common textile fibres.

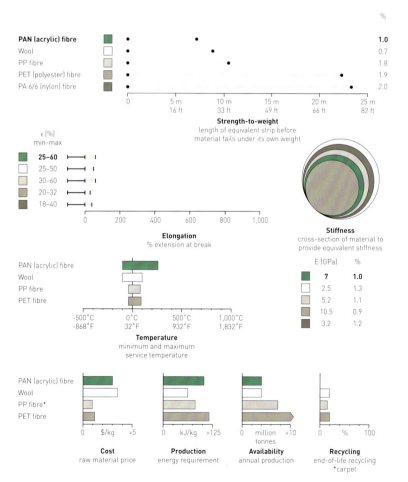

**Acrylic-blend knitwear**
This cable-knit jumper from Topshop is made up of two-thirds acrylic. This helps to keep the retail price as low as possible, a key requirement for high-street brands. Even though it is mostly synthetic fibre, it has the feel and appearance of wool. It will not irritate the wearer's skin and is generally easier to care for than wool. It is also lighter than wool, which means chunky knitted items do not become too heavy and cumbersome.

**PAN linear polymer**

**Stabilized**

**Cyclization**

**Carbonization**

**Carbon fibre production** Most carbon fibre is produced using PAN as the precursor. The process is part chemical, part mechanical. First, the PAN is drawn out and stabilized by heating in atmosphere to around 200–300°C (392–572°F). This makes the bonds in the linear polymer rearrange and become more thermally stable. Next, it is heated to 700–1,200°C (1,292–2,192°F) (without oxygen), which causes most of the non-carbon atoms to be expelled. The remaining carbon atoms form tightly bonded crystals that are aligned parallel to the long axis of the fibre. Roasting at high temperature causes the remaining nitrogen to be expelled and adjacent chains to join side by side and form planes of carbon atoms in a hexagonal lattice.

In the case of soft textiles, such as apparel and interior items, it offers a lower-cost alternative to wool (page 426) and cotton (page 410). It is often blended with these natural fibres to take advantage of the benefits of both. It is soft and light by comparison, which adds bulk and increases insulation. As a synthetic, it is not prone to damage by moths or mildew. It is utilized in knitwear, such as jumpers, jackets and socks. It has very high wicking capacity (moisture is drawn away from the wearer and rapidly transported to the surface of the fabric, where it evaporates), a property used in sportswear and socks.

## COMMERCIAL TYPES AND USES

PAN homopolymer fibre is reasonably stiff, strong and resistant. It is extremely difficult to dye and so combined with monomers that increase dyeability. As a copolymer, it is compatible with a range of dyeing techniques, at any stage from raw polymer to fibre. It is particularly well suited to bright colours. Because of its excellent ultraviolet resistance, colours are longer-lasting than with most other dyed fibres. Solution-dyed colour (colour is added to the monomer prior to spinning) is the most durable; the colour is consistent throughout the cross-section of the fibre.

Acrylic fibre contains at least 85% acrylonitrile (AN); the properties of the fibre are tailored to the requirements of the application. It is a virtually pure homopolymer, and its weather resistance is utilized for the most demanding outdoor applications, such as car roofs, marine textiles and tensile structures. It has superior weathering resistance and light-fastness compared to similarly priced synthetics. It retains its mechanical properties, colour and flexibility far longer than lower-cost alternatives, such as PET and PP. Durability, flexibility and resilience are enhanced through the addition of a range of monomers.

Short fibres are applied as flock, such as to decorate packaging and promotional items. The fibres are bonded to paper (page 268), board and textile – standing on end – to produce a velvet-like surface. Its lustrous surface is combined with vivid colour. Depending on the length and diameter of fibre, it can provide a soft, smooth texture, or a rigid, durable finish.

Modacrylic fibre contains additional ingredients, such as vinyl chloride, and only 35–85% AN. As a result of the added ingredients, modacrylic fibre is flame-retardant with enhanced elastic recovery. These qualities come at the expense of resilience and abrasion resistance; modacrylic is prone to pilling and matting.

The lower softening point of modacrylic fibres allows them to be stretched, embossed and molded more readily than acrylic. As an industrial fibre, modacrylic is utilized in paint rollers, filters and as reinforcement.

## SUSTAINABILITY

PAN, acrylic and modacrylic fibre is produced by solvent spinning. In the process of dry spinning, the PAN and copolymers are suspended in a solvent and pumped through the spinneret. The solvents evaporate as the filaments pass from the spinneret into the air. Alternatively, the fibres are produced with wet spinning, where the filaments are drawn from the spinneret through a chemical or solvent bath. This makes it easier to control and reclaim the chemicals used in production. Modacrylic fibre is produced only using dry spinning.

The spinning technique determines the cross-section of the fibre, and thus affects its properties. The dog-bone shape produced by dry spinning promotes flexibility (softness) and a lustrous surface. By contrast, the round and bean-shaped profiles produced by wet spinning result in a stiffer, more resilient fibre.

After spinning, both types of fibre pass through the same treatments, such as drawing (see PET), crimping and drying. In the production of acrylic fibre, roughly the same amount of water is consumed as in the production of wool.

AN, the key ingredient in acrylic and modacrylic fibres, and one of the most important industrial chemicals, is polluting and poisonous. It is an extremely hazardous material to work with and very volatile, producing flammable and toxic air concentrations at room temperature. On top of this, PAN uses more energy in production than PP, although it is roughly equivalent to PET. It is much more challenging to recycle than other common thermoplastic fibres, because it cannot be remelted. Of course, waste from production can be directly recycled, but end-of-life waste fabric is rarely, if ever, recycled.

**Faux fur jacket** Its fineness and high elastic recovery yields light and dense pile that can be woven and knitted to resemble fur (page 466) and hair (such as for fashion wigs and toys). The fibres may be produced with controlled heat-shrinkage properties. When fibres of different shrinkage capacity are mixed in the surface of pile fabric, the application of heat causes them to take on different lengths and shapes. Thus the fur takes on a more realistic appearance. Sophisticated colour effects are created with various spraying and dyeing techniques.

# Polyoxymethylene (POM), Acetal

**Also known as**
Other common names: polyacetal
Trademark names: Delrin, Ultraform, Hostaform, Celcon

**This high-strength and low-cost engineering material is used for demanding applications that require precision and durability. There are many examples of POM replacing metals in engineering parts. The surface has a very low coefficient of friction, which makes it feel slippery and is why it is used in gears, bearings and zips. This same property makes it hard to paint or adhesive bond.**

184

| Types | Typical Applications | Sustainability |
|---|---|---|
| • POM-C (copolymer)<br>• POM-H (homopolymer) | • Automotive<br>• Gears, bearings and zips<br>• Telecommunications and appliances | • Recyclable and identifies by code #7, 'other', or 'POM'<br>• Not collected from mixed waste streams<br>• Off-gases during molding |
| Properties | Competing Materials | Costs |
| • High-strength<br>• Dimensional stability<br>• Low coefficient of friction and resistance to wear | • PA, PET and PP<br>• PTFE<br>• Steel and aluminium alloy | • Low material cost<br>• Low manufacturing costs |

## INTRODUCTION

Since it was first commercialized by DuPont in 1960, polyoxymethylene (POM) has evolved to fulfil a range of quite specialized functions. It is distinguished by a combination of strength and low friction. These properties lend POM to parts that are exposed to long-term wear and abrasion and must maintain mechanical performance. Mechanisms and components that make use of this include gears, bearings, rollers, bushes, zips, conveyor belts, medical products (such as delivery devices), car door handles, electronics (shavers and mobile phones) and pumps.

Low-friction plastics help to reduce maintenance and extend the life of products. Compared to metal parts, such as a car door check (to restrict opening distance), there are obvious maintenance and cleanliness advantages of using such plastics. For example, they eliminate the need for lubrication, and promote quieter and more efficient movement in sliding parts. Compared to polyamide (PA, nylon) (page 164) and polytetrafluoroethylene (PTFE) (page 190), two other low-friction plastics, POM is much less expensive. These plastics have other advantages, though, where POM cannot compete: PTFE has exceptional temperature properties and PA is a lot stronger for the same weight with equal stiffness.

## COMMERCIAL TYPES AND USES

There are two main types of POM, copolymer (two monomers) and homopolymer (single monomer), identified by letters C and H respectively. They are both manufactured primarily from formaldehyde (see page 224), although the processes are different. The properties can vary by around 10% and in many cases they are interchangeable.

POM-C has higher temperature

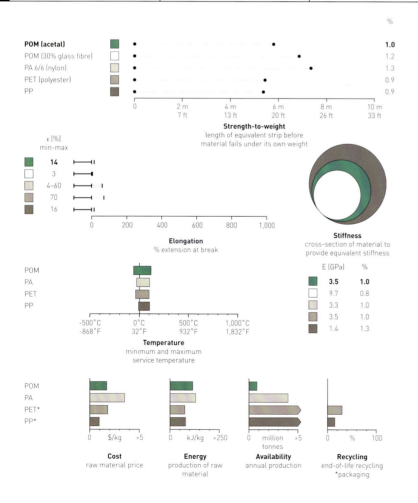

| | % |
|---|---|
| POM (acetal) | 1.0 |
| POM (30% glass fibre) | 1.2 |
| PA 6/6 (nylon) | 1.3 |
| PET (polyester) | 0.9 |
| PP | 0.9 |

**Strength-to-weight**
length of equivalent strip before material fails under its own weight

ε [%]
min-max

| | |
|---|---|
| 14 | |
| 3 | |
| 4–60 | |
| 70 | |
| 16 | |

**Elongation**
% extension at break

**Stiffness**
cross-section of material to provide equivalent stiffness

| | E [GPa] | % |
|---|---|---|
| POM | 3.5 | 1.0 |
| PA | 9.7 | 0.8 |
| PET | 3.3 | 1.0 |
| PP | 3.5 | 1.0 |
| | 1.4 | 1.3 |

**Temperature**
minimum and maximum service temperature

**Cost**
raw material price

**Energy**
production of raw material

**Availability**
annual production

**Recycling**
end-of-life recycling
*packaging

resistance than POM-H as a result of the junctions in the polymer chains, which act to slow the thermal degradation process. Without these joins in the polymer chains, the molecular structure breaks down rapidly (known as unzipping) as a result of equal bond strength. However, the melting point of POM-C is around 10°C (50°F) lower than that of POM-H and as a result it will deflect at a lower temperature threshold.

POM-H has higher crystallinity, which produces higher tensile strength, stiffness and creep resistance (gradual change over time under load) compared to POM-C. It also has significantly better impact resistance. Therefore, it is used in thinner sections than POM-C. These differences mean that parts designed to withstand long-term exposure to abrasion and elevated temperatures tend to be fabricated from POM-C, whereas

**Speaker grille** POM is used throughout car interiors in parts that need to be colour-matched (without spray coating) and accurately molded. It is tough and resistant to scratching, ideal for locations where it may get knocked and abraded. The speaker grille is molded in one piece with snap fits integrated for assembly. Thanks to its high flow rate, POM fills evenly across thin sections. Precise hexagonal ribs are incorporated across the back of parts to aid molding and increase overall stiffness while ensuring optimal sound quality.

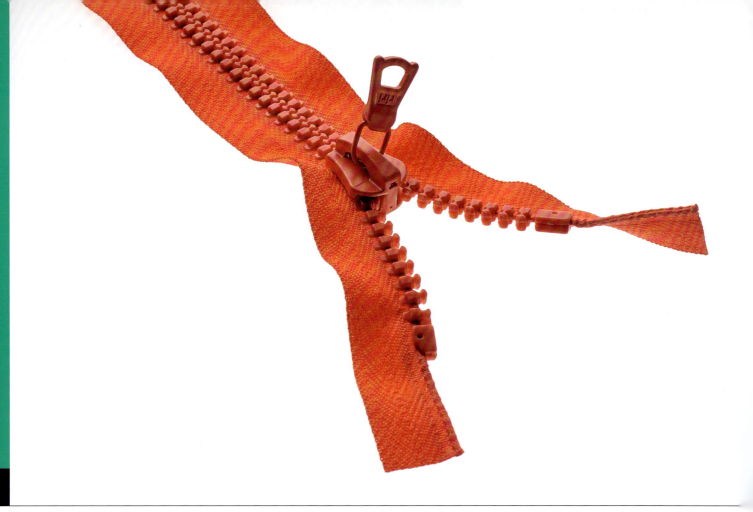

POM-H is preferred for its short-term mechanical properties.

In addition to unreinforced and glass-filled grades it is available with several modifications including toughened (higher molecular weight), increased wear resistance (low friction) and ultraviolet-stabilized. Each of these changes has trade-offs. For example, increasing toughness increases viscosity, which makes thin mold sections harder to fill.

## SUSTAINABILITY
Like other thermoplastics, POM is fully recyclable. It is not manufactured in sufficient quantities to warrant separation from mixed waste streams and so post-consumer waste is not typically recycled. Industrial scrap, such as produced during molding and machining, is more commonly recycled.

POM converts into a gaseous product through decomposition when heated for a prolonged time. The gaseous product is formaldehyde, meaning that extraction is required to protect anyone in the vicinity. POM has the potential

### AUTOMOTIVE

**Low cost**
It is a very cost-effective material for engineering applications. Compared to a painted metal part, an equivalent injection-molded POM part works out around one-third cheaper.

**Toughness**
It has a good balance of strength and elongation, comparable with PP and PA, resulting in a tough plastic suitable for demanding functional and aesthetic applications.

**Wear resistance**
The low-friction surface is durable and resistant to abrasion.

to decompose entirely, which can lead to dangerous pressure build-up in the injection-molding machine. Therefore, high temperatures must be avoided, as should cycle delays.

Toughened POM has the potential to release low levels of isocyanates during molding. These are known to cause severe irritation to eyes and gastrointestinal and respiratory tracts. Repeated exposure can lead to sensitization in some individuals,

**Injection-molded POM zip fastener** The colourful teeth of molded zips – injected directly onto the polyethylene terephthalate (PET, polyester) (page 152) tape – are made with POM. Their durability is utilized in all types of garment construction from medium- to heavyweight. POM's low-friction surface makes it easier to open and close the teeth, minimizing the energy required while reducing wear and abrasion. Using molded plastic teeth means that all types of colour are theoretically possible, including metallic, saturated, fluorescent and phosphorescent (glow in the dark). While it is not usually possible to specify the colour, this freedom means there are many standard options available. The colour of the teeth is matched to the tape or contrasting.

making them subject to severe asthma attacks if they are exposed again.

## POM IN AUTOMOTIVE
POM is found throughout car interiors and under the bonnet, in particular uncoated mechanical parts. Applications include closures, handles and vents. It is possible to colour-match with POM, but the range that can be achieved is limited by the off-white base colour. Dark colours

and tones, such as commonly used for automotive parts, are readily achievable.

Parts that demand a tough and wear-resistant plastic, such as around the door and footwell, are commonly made from POM. Owing to its high crystallinity, POM is vulnerable to shrinkage, especially when reinforced with glass fibre. Therefore, large covers tend to be manufactured from amorphous plastics such as ABS/PC (page 138) or PP instead. For parts that require light resistance a blend of PBT and ASA would be better.

Materials that include styrene – ABS/PC and PBT/ASA – have superior appearance. The styrene helps reproduce the surface of the mold more accurately than with POM. Therefore, a higher-quality finish is possible, from gloss to matt.

While POM is tough, its high crystallinity makes it notch-sensitive (relatively brittle) and so sharp corners and protrusions tend to be avoided.

## POM IN PRODUCTS, FURNITURE AND LIGHTING

The use of POM in lighters, such as the colourful Bic, as well as injection-molded zips makes it quite familiar. These products make use of two distinct properties: chemical resistance and low friction respectively.

The colour range of these products provides a good indication of what can be achieved with POM. It is crystalline and only available in opaque colour. As well as conventional pigments, a range of metallic effects can be achieved (see page 140). Producing parts with colour and effects built in to the resin reduces secondary operations. Removing painting and preparation is less expensive and reduces overall environmental impact.

## PRODUCTS, FURNITURE AND LIGHTING

**Low friction**
The slippery surface, similar to PA, reduces friction between moving parts. This helps to reduce the energy required while minimizing wear and abrasion through traction.

**High strength**
It is comparable with PET in many ways: they are both crystalline, have equivalent strength-to-weight and stiffness, and cost about the same.

**Chemical resistance**
It has excellent resistance to a broad range of chemicals including alcohols, ketones, detergents, fuel and oil.

**Machinability**
Similar to PA, POM machines very well with conventional cutting equipment. It is available in several standard sizes of extruded rod, tube, strip and sheet.

**Waterproof CNC-machined case** The excellent machinability of POM is utilized in military equipment, such as this waterproof carry case. A solid rod of coloured POM is turned on a lathe – using the same techniques as for metal turning – to produce the finished part. There is no injection molding involved in this case. Extruded POM is available in a very limited colour range. If the volumes justify it, then bespoke colour is possible.

# Polyetheretherketone (PEEK)

**Also known as**
Trademark names: Victrex, Vestakeep, Tecapeek, Zyex

**These expensive plastics are used as an alternative to lightweight metals in demanding aerospace and medical applications; their mechanical properties are enhanced with fibre reinforcement. They are resistant to high temperature, which makes them tricky to process. Nevertheless, they are compatible with injection molding, additive manufacturing, machining and spinning.**

| Types | Typical Applications | Sustainability |
|-------|---------------------|----------------|
| • Polyaryletherketone (PAEK)<br>• PEEK<br>• Polyetherketone (PEK) | • Automotive and aerospace<br>• Medical<br>• Electrical | • Its extreme properties make it an energy-intensive material to manufacture and fabricate<br>• Impractical to recycle |

| Properties | Competing Materials | Costs |
|------------|--------------------|----|
| • High-strength, tough and hard-wearing<br>• High-temperature and good chemical resistance | • Aluminium and steel<br>• PTFE and PA<br>• Fibre-reinforced epoxy and polyester | • IVery high material cost and expensive to manufacture |

## INTRODUCTION

Some of the highest-performing thermoplastics, they are capable of withstanding prolonged exposure to temperatures up to 250°C (482°F) or more. They also have excellent resistance to chemicals and abrasion, and low water absorption, and they emit little smoke or toxic fumes when exposed to fire.

They are expensive and available in relatively small quantities, resulting in high price: polyetheretherketone (PEEK) is more than 20 times the cost of polyamide (PA, nylon) (page 164) and 40 times more expensive than aluminium (page 42) for the same weight.

They are semi-aromatic, semi-crystalline thermoplastics, with phenyl groups (see Polycarbonate, page 144) linked by oxygen bridges (ether and carbonyl – that is, ketone). The exact properties depend on the ratio of ketone to ether groups. As a result, various configurations exist, stretching to polyetherketonetherketoneketone (PEKEKK).

They are utilized in parts that were previously fabricated from metal – as metal replacement – as well as parts conceived to take advantage of their unique properties. Compared to metal casting and fabrication, plastic injection molding offers far greater design freedom. Where the volumes justify the expensive mold costs, it creates the opportunity for greater part integration and reduced wall thickness. Savings accumulate over the lifetime of the part: these plastics are lighter (improving fuel efficiency) with exceptional endurance (longer lasting without maintenance).

Low volumes are produced with machining and additive manufacturing. Machining has many advantages compared to injection molding, even in mass production. For example, it

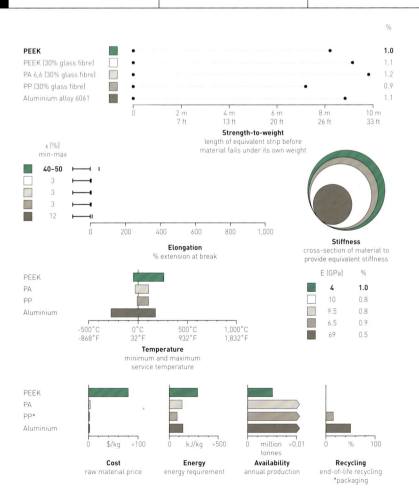

| | | % |
|---|---|---|
| PEEK | | 1.0 |
| PEEK (30% glass fibre) | | 1.1 |
| PA 6,6 (30% glass fibre) | | 1.2 |
| PP (30% glass fibre) | | 0.9 |
| Aluminium alloy 6061 | | 1.1 |

**Strength-to-weight**
length of equivalent strip before material fails under its own weight

ε (%) min-max

| | |
|---|---|
| 40–50 | |
| 3 | |
| 3 | |
| 3 | |
| 12 | |

**Elongation**
% extension at break

**Stiffness**
cross-section of material to provide equivalent stiffness

| | E (GPa) | % |
|---|---------|---|
| | 4 | 1.0 |
| | 10 | 0.8 |
| | 9.5 | 0.8 |
| | 6.5 | 0.9 |
| | 69 | 0.5 |

PEEK / PA / PP / Aluminium

**Temperature**
minimum and maximum service temperature

PEEK / PA / PP* / Aluminium

**Cost**
raw material price

**Energy**
energy requirement

**Availability**
annual production

**Recycling**
end-of-life recycling
*packaging

is capable of producing parts with varying wall thickness, undercuts and complex details that are not practical with injection molding. Additive manufacturing is not so widely used, but developments continue to emerge. Powder and filament are suitable for selective laser sintering (SLS) and fused deposition modelling (FDM) respectively.

A key advantage of additive manufacturing over machining is that with careful planning much less material is wasted, which is a major benefit considering the high price of these plastics. However, it should be noted that SLS powder is significantly more valuable than machining feedstock, so waste from this process is much more of a consideration than in machining. Process selection will depend on the number of parts (multiple parts can be nested on an SLS bed) and geometry (simple shapes are cost-effective to machine).

## COMMERCIAL TYPES AND USES

PEEK is the most well-known and important member of the polyaryletherketone (PAEK) group. It has very good mechanical properties and chemical resistance, maintained up to 260°C (500°F). And its excellent sliding properties (low surface friction) eliminate the need for lubricants in moving parts such as gears and bearings. It is naturally beige and sometimes used black. It can be coloured, but rarely is.

Unreinforced PEEK is roughly equivalent to high-performance aluminium alloy in terms of strength-to-weight, but is more flexible with higher elongation. Reinforced PEEK is considerably stiffer and stronger. Combined with continuous carbon-fibre (CF) (page 236) reinforcement, PEEK offers the same strength and stiffness as stainless steel at only around one-third of the weight.

As a spun fibre, PEEK is suitable for braiding, weaving and knitting – similar to so-called super fibres, including meta-aramid (page 242), PA and ultra-high-molecular-weight polyethylene (UHMWPE) (see Polyethylene, page 108). While PEEK fibre is outperformed in terms of strength and resilience, its thermal

and chemical endurance is unrivalled. It is used mainly for industrial applications, but is suitable for the same end uses as molded PEEK.

PAEK, PEK, PEKEKK and other family members offer many of the same advantages with slight differences. For example, PAEK emits the least toxic fumes when burned and polyetherketone (PEK) has higher temperature resistance (30°C [86°F] more than standard PEEK).

Like PEEK, PAEK is biocompatible and is utilized for surgical implants. It is non-cytotoxic and the foreign body response is similar to that found for UHMWPE. One of the principal benefits is that when reinforced with CF, it more closely matches the elastic modulus of bone (the femur in particular) than other materials.

Where bespoke bone repairs are required, data produced from computer tomography (CT) scanning is used to fabricate the exact shape of plastic required. Parts are manufactured to fit the exact dimensions of the patient. Plastic implants are compatible with X-ray, CT and magnetic resonance imaging (MRI) techniques, which allows the healing site to be closely monitored.

They are used in the housing and structure of medical equipment too. They are resistant to sterilization and remain dimensionally stable in hot water, steam and most solvents and chemicals.

## SUSTAINABILITY

While they are readily recyclable, only production waste is typically reprocessed (the high cost helps to minimize waste). It is not practical to collect material end-of-life and separate for recycling.

The high embodied energy, as a result of raw material production, is offset in part by the savings made throughout the lifetime of a relatively lighter product. For example, in aerospace and automotive applications, increasing fuel efficiency outweighs the cost.

**Carbon-fibre-reinforced PEEK** Conventionally made from steel, these Aven tweezers are injection-molded PEEK with 30% carbon fibre. They are electrostatic discharge- (ESD-) safe and offer an alternative to PTFE-tipped tweezers intended for handling delicate components in cleaning, chemical, and assembly procedures.

# Fluoropolymer

**Also known as**
Trademark names: Teflon, Tecaflon, Gore-Tex,
Tefzel, Fluon, Polyflon, Norton, Xylan
Fibre trademark names: Teflon, Tenara, Dyneon
ETFE cladding trademark names: Texlon

**This family of thermoplastics exhibits some exceptional properties, in particular their superior resistance to chemicals, heat and weathering. They are very expensive and so applied in the lowest volumes possible, such as coating, film and fibre. Known mainly by their trademark names, such as Teflon and Gore-Tex, they have become household names as a result of sustained marketing.**

| Types | Typical Applications | Sustainability |
|---|---|---|
| • Polytetrafluoroethylene (PTFE)<br>• Ethylene tetrafluoroethylene (ETFE)<br>• Perfluoroalkoxy (PFA)<br>• Fluorinated ethylene propylene (FEP) | • Roofs, canopies and temporary structures<br>• Apparel and technical textiles<br>• Cookware and packaging | • High embodied energy<br>• Perfluorooctanoic acid (PFOA) is used in production and is known to be harmful to people and animals |
| **Properties** | **Competing Materials** | **Costs** |
| • High chemical, heat and weather resistance<br>• Low coefficient of friction<br>• Flexible with high elongation | • Silicone, PU, PVC, TPE, PA and PE<br>• PBO, aramid and carbon fibres<br>• Technical ceramics | • Very high material cost<br>• PTFE has very high production costs; melt-processable types are less expensive to fabricate |

**190**

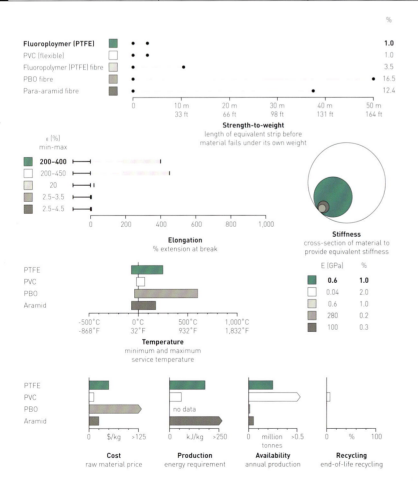

## INTRODUCTION

Fluoropolymers are so called because they contain fluorine in the chemical structure. The carbon–fluorine bonds are stable, unreactive and one of the strongest chemical bonds. As a family, they have very good resistance to chemicals, heat and weathering. They have very low surface energy and a low coefficient of friction, so nothing much will stick to the surface.

Their unique combination of properties is utilized for demanding applications in architecture, agriculture, automotive, industry, packaging and cookware. But they are very expensive and can be challenging to fabricate, which limits their use somewhat. Where heat resistance and chemical endurance is not critical, much less expensive thermoplastics that have similar characteristics – such as polyamide (PA, nylon) (page 164), polyethylene (PE) (page 108) and polyvinyl chloride (PVC) (page 122) – are used.

## COMMERCIAL TYPES AND USES

Polytetrafluoroethylene (PTFE) was the first to be discovered – by scientists at DuPont in 1938 – and remains the most

**Non-stick fluoropolymer coating**
While PTFE (as well as other types of fluoropolymer) coating is primarily used for industrial purposes, its exceptional 'non-stick' and 'self-lubricating' properties have proved indispensable in a range of consumer applications, including this 2002 redesign of the iconic Allex scissors by Hayashi Cutlery. PTFE is applied in powder form along with colour and other enhancements. The powder is applied dry, such as with electrostatic coating, or suspended in liquid and spray-coated (the liquid evaporates to leave a dry powder on the surface). The part is sintered to homogenize and bond the PTFE to the substrate, resulting in a durable and impenetrable coating. The high temperatures involved limit compatible materials.

popular. Similar to PE, it has a linear polymer structure. The difference is that in a fluoropolymer some or all of the hydrogen atoms are replaced with fluorine. As a result of their unique composition, the polymer chains form a very closely packed crystalline structure (see page 166); fluoropolymers are the highest-density plastic.

PTFE has some exceptional properties: it is resistant to most chemicals and is capable of operating in environments up to 250°C (482°F) or more without significant loss of chemical resistance (although mechanical properties become significantly degraded after around 200°C [392°F]).

Of course, these advantages do not come without drawbacks. As well as being very expensive, PTFE is very difficult to fabricate, and has low tensile strength and poor resistance to abrasion.

It is not compatible with conventional thermoplastic forming processes – injection molding, blow molding and so on – owing to its very high melting point and crystallinity. It is shaped (or applied as coating) in powder form and sintered to form a homogenous plastic. Tubes and profiles with continuous cross-section are paste-extruded (very fine PTFE powder is mixed with lubricant and pressed through a die); films are paste-extruded or skived (peeled on a lathe) from a compression-molded rod and sintered; simple parts are compression molded and sintered; and complex parts and thin-walled hollow containers are isostatic molded (a rubber mold is filled with powder and exerted to high pressure; the resulting part is sintered).

It is applied as a 'self-lubricating' bearing or sliding surface in automotive and aerospace, 'non-stick' coating on metal and glass, cable coating, implantable medical devices and high-strength fibre. PTFE is known under many different trademark names, including Teflon, Texolon, Polyflon, Fluon and Tecaflon.

It is naturally white but can be coloured with pigments. As with other engineering plastics, it is reinforced with glass fibre (GF) (page 522) and carbon

fibre (CF) (page 236) to improve strength, stiffness and resistance to heat.

Rapidly stretching PTFE creates a microporous material even stronger than conventional PTFE. Known as expanded PTFE (ePTFE), it has some unique properties. The size of the pores and nature of the material mean that vapour is free to pass through without allowing liquid to penetrate. Developed by Bob Gore in 1969, the material was first used for industrial applications, such as joint sealant. Nowadays it is applied in thin films that provide 'breathability' in high-performance garments and packaging. It is commonly referred to as Gore-Tex, W. L. Gore & Associates' trademark name for the material, although several competitors have emerged since the original patents expired who have their own trademark names.

An alternative approach to breathability is achieved with the use of films that exhibit high moisture vapour transmission rate (MVTR), such as films extruded from thermoplastic polyamide elastomer (TPA) (see Thermoplastic Elastomer, page 194).

PTFE fibre is either spun or extruded. The properties of the spun fibre – produced with a cellulose matrix that is subsequently removed and the PTFE sintered – are comparable with generic PTFE. Paste-extruded fibre (ePTFE), on the other hand, has higher tensile strength (two to three times) coupled with lower shrinkage. While they are mainly used for industrial applications (rope, filtration and gaskets, for example), their resistance to heat, chemicals and weathering makes them useful in architectural and marine awnings. ePTFE is also used for dental floss. Naturally brown through white, the fibres are produced in a range of colours. They are typically referred to by their trademark names: for example, Teflon fibre is matrix spun, and Tenara and Dyneon are paste extruded.

Attempts to modify and improve on the basic properties of PTFE led to the copolymerization of tetrafluoroethylene (TFE) with a range of monomers. As a result, there now exist many variations. Most are used for very specialized

industrial applications, such as cable sheathing and barrier films.

Ethylene tetrafluoroethylene (ETFE) consists of alternating ethylene and TFE units in the polymer chain. It was discovered much later than PTFE and first commercialized by DuPont in 1973. As a result of the copolymerization, ETFE can be processed with conventional thermoplastic forming techniques, such as injection molding, blow molding and extrusion. It is tough, lighter than PTFE, impact-resistant, abrasion-resistant and tear-resistant, and can tolerate temperatures ranging from -100°C to -150°C (-148°F to -238°F). It is not quite as resistant to chemicals as PTFE, but still very durable.

Perfluoroalkoxy (PFA) and fluorinated ethylene propylene (FEP) are melt-processible, the same as ETFE. While PFA is almost interchangeable with PTFE in application, it is considerably more expensive. FEP is less expensive, but has lower chemical resistance and melting point. It is used for industrial applications where temperature resistance is critical.

### SUSTAINABILITY
Fluoropolymers are a hazardous group of materials to make, owing to the chemicals required. Perfluorooctanoic acid (PFOA), also known as C8, is used in the polymerization of trafluoroethylene (TFE). It is known to be harmful to people and has been associated with increased incidence of cancer. While it may be undetectable in the finished material (it is removed and recovered for reuse during the final steps of fluoropolymer production), the use of such harmful ingredients in the raw material production cannot be ignored.

As with other thermoplastics, fluoropolymers can be recycled at the end of their useful life. The process is much more straightforward for the melt-processible types, including ETFE, PFA and FEP. Scrap produced in manufacturing can be directly reused. However, owing to the nature of applications and low volumes, fluoropolymers are rarely recycled end-of-life, if at all.

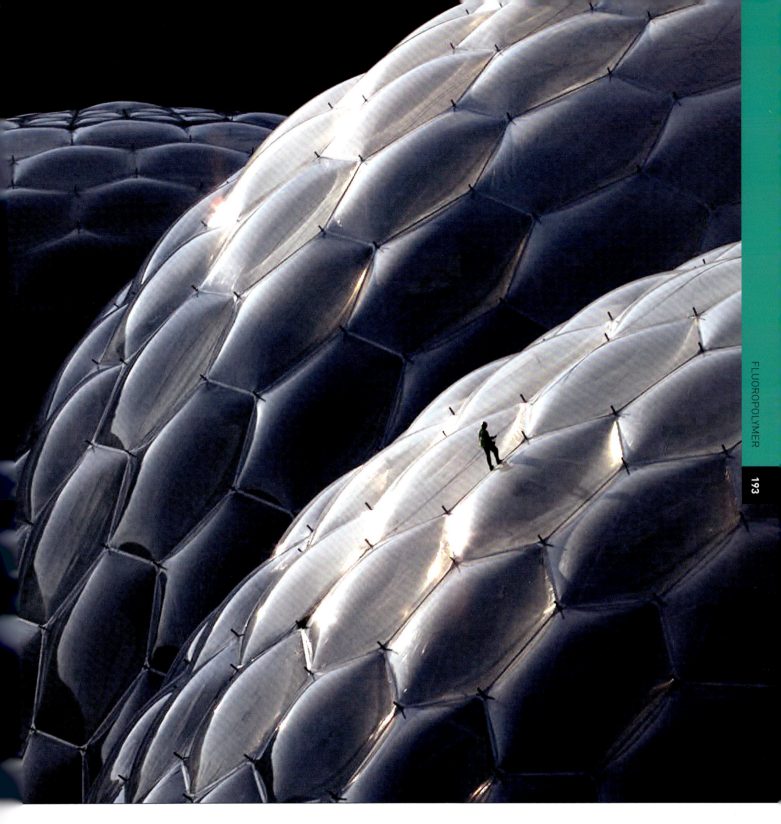

**Ultralight ETFE cladding** ETFE film (or foil) is lightweight, transparent and very durable. Originally used as an inert coating, agricultural film (greenhouses) and to cover leisure centre swimming pools and zoological gardens, it first demonstrated its value to modern architecture in the Eden Project, Cornwall, UK (2001). Designed by Grimshaw Architects, the bubble-like biomes were inspired by the geodesic system made famous by American architect and inventor Richard Buckminster Fuller. It is the largest self-supporting transparent building envelope in the world. Constructed by Vector Foiltec – the company that invented ETFE cladding technology and today produces it under the trademark Texlon – each biome is clad with hundreds of bespoke panels. Each one consists of layers of ETFE, welded around the perimeter to trap a layer of insulating air within. The ETFE is unaffected by ultraviolet, wind and rain. It can even tolerate abrasion from flying grit and sand. The low coefficient of friction ensures that dirt and dust do not stick to the surface; this helps to maintain the very high light transmission (up to 95%). Since this successful project, ETFE panelling has gone on to be used in many other buildings, ranging from private dwellings to grand Olympic stadiums. Photo courtesy of Vector Foiltec.

# Thermoplastic Elastomer (TPE)

TPEs are a group of rubber-like plastics compatible with melt-forming techniques, in particular injection molding and recycling processes. They can be stretched several times their length and when the load is released will rebound to their original shape. They are widely utilized in toys, footwear and sports products, as well as apparel and footwear.

| Types | Typical Applications | Sustainability |
|---|---|---|
| • Block copolymers: styrenics (TPS); copolyester (TPC); urethane (TPU); and polyamide (TPA)<br>• Polyolefin blend (TPO) and alloy (TPV) | • Textiles, footwear and sports products<br>• Consumer products and furniture<br>• Industrial and automotive | • Recyclable and identified by code #7, 'other'<br>• Not collected from mixed waste streams |

| Properties | Competing Materials | Costs |
|---|---|---|
| • Elasticity and modulus depends on type<br>• Melt-processible<br>• Moderate strength and surface resistance | • Natural rubber<br>• PU, silicone and synthetic rubber<br>• PE, EVA, ionomer and PVC | • Moderate material costs<br>• Low manufacturing costs |

194

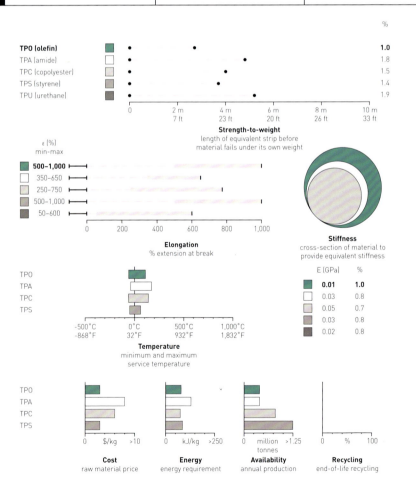

## INTRODUCTION

This group of plastics, collectively known as thermoplastic elastomers (TPE) bridges the gap between plastics and rubbers. Hence they are also sometimes referred to as thermoplastic rubbers (TPR). Unlike thermosetting elastomers (see Polyurethane, page 202, Silicone, page 212, and Synthetic Rubber, page 216), TPEs do not form chemical cross-links and so are compatible with injection molding, blow molding, thermoforming and other melt-forming processes. The combination of rubber-like properties with the processing efficiency of plastics presents many opportunities for design.

This family of elastomers is made up of two distinct groups: block copolymers (see page 196); and polyolefin blends and alloys. The properties of each depend on the base polymers and proportion

**Wearable technology housing** The Nike+ Fuelband activity tracker was launched in 2012. It is encapsulated – all except for the batteries, catch and USB connector – within a TPE shell. A flexible circuit board is mounted onto an injection-molded PP chassis. The whole assembly – including circuit board, processor, sensors, antenna, USB connector and LED lights, but excluding the batteries – is reinserted into the mold and overmolded with TPE in a two-stage process (inside then outside). This approach to construction is particularly challenging, because if anything goes wrong in the final overmolding stage, then the whole assembly (including labour, components and materials) is wasted.

**Amorphous block copolymer** Consisting of two or more monomers separated into long sections of the polymer backbone chain (blocks), the individual types form distinct groups separate from each other. For example, TPS polymer chains are constructed from styrene end-blocks and butadiene mid-blocks. In their solid state, the thermoplastic end-blocks bond together (to form physical cross-links) and the elastomeric mid-groups provide high elongation. When heated, the bonds between the styrene blocks are weakened, which allows the polymer to flow.

**Semi-crystalline block copolymer** In the case of TPU, the diisocyanate and polyol (long-chain diol) react to form soft segments while the diisocyanate and short-chain diol form rigid segments. Thus, each TPU polymer chain consists of random alternating soft and rigid segments. On cooling, the chains organize into distinct areas, with the hard parts forming highly organized clusters that act as physical cross-links (providing toughness and physical performance). The soft parts form an amorphous and flexible structure (providing elasticity). The overall properties depend on the length and proportion of soft and rigid blocks, which is determined by the starting ingredients. TPC has a similar semi-crystalline structure. It contains hard segments of polyester – such as polybutylene terephthalate (PBT) (Polyethylene Terephthalate, page 152) – with soft segments that are either polyether (TPC-ET), polyester (TPC-ES) or a combination of the two (TPC-EE). TPA consists of soft segments of polyether with a rigid block of PA. The type of PA has a bearing on the physical properties. The same morphology can be achieved with a single type of plastic by combining two types of polymer structure (such as atactic and isotactic, see page 106). For example, in the case of elastomeric polypropylene (PP), isotactic blocks form into highly crystalline groups joined by rubbery areas of amorphous atactic parts; this has a similar effect to joining thermoplastic and elastomeric blocks.

of elastomeric content. A wide range of hardness (flexibility) is possible, from gel-like to semi-rigid. Measured on the Shore durometer scale, TPE range from 0 Shore A (very soft) through 85 Shore D (rigid).

## COMMERCIAL TYPES AND USES

In the case of styrene-based elastomers (TPS), flexibility is provided by the addition of butadiene in the styrene chain. As a result of its linear structure – styrene-butadiene-styrene – it is also abbreviated as SBS. Produced in relatively large quantities, they are cost-effective compared to the other block polymers. TPSs are used in footwear, sports products, toys, adhesives and gaskets. They are vulnerable to ultraviolet and high temperatures. These properties are enhanced through hydrogenation, whereby the mid-block becomes ethylene-butylene (SEBS). Hardness ranges from 0 Shore A through 65 Shore D.

Thermoplastic copolyester elastomer (TPC) offers clarity, toughness and flexibility combined with resistance to heat and chemicals. It has excellent processibility compared to other TPEs, but is relatively expensive. Hardness ranges from 35 to 85 Shore D. Flexible grades are used in medical and pharmaceutical packaging and tubing; semi-rigid grades are used in structural parts in automotive, furniture and sports products.

Thermoplastic polyurethane (TPU) consists of the same classes of raw materials as thermosetting PU (page 202). The principal difference is that TPU does not form chemical cross-links. Consequently, they can be heated, melted and formed with conventional injection molding and extrusion.

The hardness of TPU ranges from around 70 Shore A to 75 Shore D. With the exception of elasticity, all of the mechanical and physical properties improve as rigidity is increased. TPU has high wear and abrasion resistance, good tensile strength and low-temperature flexibility. Depending on the grade and additives used, it may be transparent, coloured, paintable, biocompatible and flame-retardant. The versatility of the chemistry means TPU is suitable for a range of situations, such as footwear,

textiles, laminates, medical equipment, sports goods, wire and cable jacketing (as an alternative to PVC, see page 122) and conveyor belts.

There are two main types of TPU: polyether and polyester. Although similar in many ways, polyether TPU has higher resistance to hydrolysis (preferred for wet environments), better low-temperature flexibility and is lighter. Polyester TPU has superior resistance to abrasion and is less affected by oils and chemicals.

TPSiV elastomer is a hybrid of TPU and cross-linked silicone (page 212) produced by Dow Corning. It combines the benefits of TPU with the softness and resistance to ultraviolet and chemicals of silicone. It is available in hardness ranging from Shore A 50 to 80 and owes its unique tactility to the silicone content. It takes colour well and exhibits excellent light-fastness. Its many desirable properties are used in wearable technology, handheld electronics and home appliances.

There are several grades of thermoplastic polyamide elastomer (TPA). The principal type consists of soft polyether held together by rigid blocks of polyamide (PA, nylon) (page 164), also known as polyether block amide (PEBA). TPAs offer the widest range of properties (mechanical and chemical) among the TPEs. They are low-density with good strength-to-weight (comparable with TPU) and excellent fatigue resistance, combined with good resistance to chemicals and large operating-temperature window. Hardness ranges from 70 Shore A to 70 Shore D. Their mechanical properties are suitable for a range of sports equipment (footwear, outer soles and ski boots), textiles and medical products. They tend to be more expensive than other TPEs.

Similar to fluoropolymer (page 190), films extruded from TPA are waterproof and breathable. The difference is that TPA is not microporous; breathability

**Children's bath toys** The colourful and rubber-like Flexibath toys are injection-molded TPE. It is considered a safe material; they do not contain any harmful ingredients. In fact, several TPEs are suitable for sensitive food contact applications, such as eating utensils for babies.

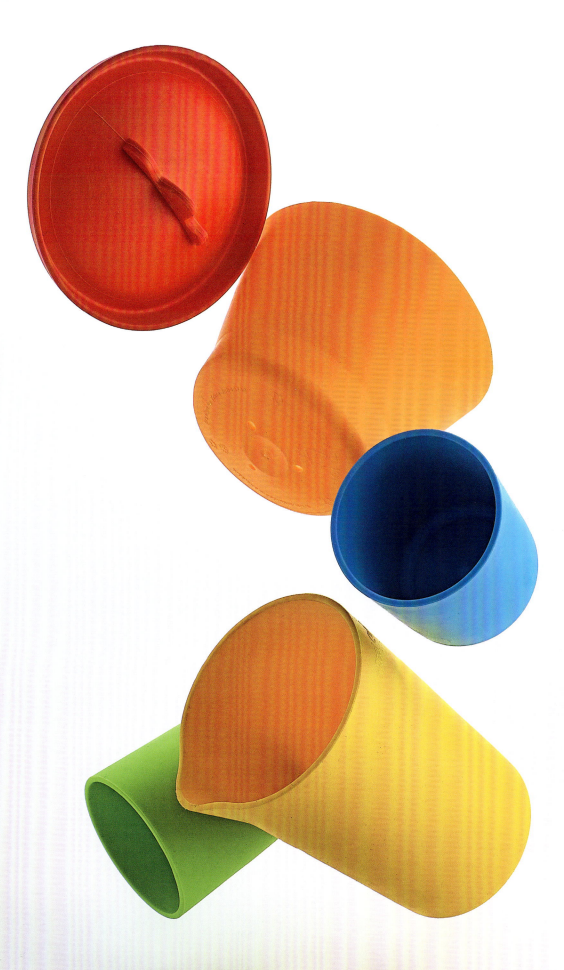

# PRODUCTS AND FURNITURE

### Versatile
TPEs are commonly formed with injection molding, blow molding and extrusion, as well as other melt-processing techniques. A wide range of geometries and scales is possible, providing greater design freedom than with thermoset elastomers.

### Flexible
A broad range of hardness is possible, from ultrasoft gel to structural plastic. As a result, TPEs fulfil a wide variety of functions, from impact-absorbing shoe soles to flexible ergonomic seat backs.

### Colourful
The range of possibilities depends on the ingredients; the highest-quality saturated colour is achieved with transparent grades, such as TPO and TPS.

**Opposite**
**Alpine ski boot** Since their introduction, TPEs have contributed to lighter-weight and more comfortable, durable and secure ski boot designs. They are constructed with a hinged overlap between the upper and lower parts to allow the wearer easy access, and material selection for each part depends on performance requirements. The shell (lower) and cuff (upper) of the Rossignol Alltrack Pro 130 are injection-molded TPU (polyether type). The level of flexibility is carefully controlled to ensure that loads are transferred efficiently from the skier to the ski edge, thus maximizing control. TPU provides very good low-temperature

flexibility and impact strength (absorbing shocks and protecting the skier in case of a fall), and resistance to weathering, scratching and abrasion. As well as ski boots, this tough and lightweight material is utilized in the construction of inline skates, ice hockey boots, hiking and climbing boots and sports shoe soles. TPO and TPA are utilized in similar situations. TPO is the least expensive and is used in more economical products. TPA, on the other hand, provides superior low-temperature flexibility, resistance to weathering, energy loss factor (most efficient springback of all TPEs) and resistance to flex fatigue. It is also the most expensive.

**Right**
**Flex back task chair**
The Generation by Knoll, 2009, makes innovative use of TPC and PBT. Created by Formway Design of New Zealand, the chair responds elastically to the user's sitting position. The flex back net is molded from TPC over a figure-8 structure to provide multidirectional

movement. The flex back net is constructed from Hytrel RS, a DuPont TPC that contains renewably sourced ingredients. Hytrel RS grades have lower environmental impact than the petrochemical-based materials they replace, without compromising performance. Photo courtesy of Knoll, Inc.

is the result of the film's high moisture vapour transmission rate (MVTR). They are utilized in construction, packaging and sports apparel.

Thermoplastic polyolefins (TPO) are blends of polypropylene (PP) (page 98), un-cross-linked ethylene propylene terpolymer rubber (EPDM) (see Synthetic Rubber, page 216) and polyethylene (PE) (page 108). Hardness ranges from 30 Shore A to 50 Shore D. They have excellent impact resistance and good chemical resistance, properties utilized in impact protection (such as car bumpers).

Thermoplastic vulcanizates (TPV) combine PP with a cross-linked elastomer, such as EPDM, acrylonitrile-butadiene rubber (HNBR) or natural rubber.

Compared to TPO, it has higher chemical resistance and heat resistance (up to 120°C [-184°F]) . It is used in automotive under-the-bonnet applications.

## SUSTAINABILITY
TPEs are melt-processible and so readily recycled. While it is unlikely they will be collected from mixed waste streams, scrap from production can be reprocessed directly. This offers many advantages compared to thermoset elastomers.

TPC and TPA may contain renewably sourced biobased ingredients. As with their parent polymers (see PET, page 152, and PA, page 164), there are potential benefits to this, as well as drawbacks to watch out for.

Some of the ingredients are more harmful than others. For example, diisocyanate used in the production of TPU is toxic and must be handled carefully during production.

## TPE IN PRODUCTS AND FURNITURE

The combination of premium aesthetics, moldability and elasticity sets TPEs apart. They are utilized for their overt tactility, as well as technical parts hidden from view, from small overmoldings to large pieces of furniture.

TPE is overmolded onto substrates to provide a soft-touch finish, improved grip, waterproofing, flexibility and seamless integration of design features (flexible buttons and closures). Material selection depends on the technical and aesthetic requirements, because, for example, TPEs have varying compatibility. Polymers with a similar chemical nature – for example, TPS with styrene-based plastics such as polystyrene (PS) (page 132), acrylonitrile butadiene styrene (ABS) (page 138) and styrene acrylonitrile (SAN) (page 136) – ensure high compatibility and thus a reliable bond. In some cases, TPEs are compatible with polymers outside their chemical group – so certain grades of TPS are compatible with PA, PP and PE.

The range of design opportunities possible with overmolding is beautifully demonstrated in existing products. Leading examples include wearable electronics, such as Nike+ Fuelband (TPE), Jawbone Up (TPU) and Mi Band (TPSiV), to name just three; tool housing (see image, page 147) and handles (see image, page 167); toys (tyres, balls and surfaces); sports products; children's eating utensils; kitchen utensils (handles and lids); medical equipment; and personal care (toothbrushes, shavers, curlers and so on).

As well as being utilized in tactile products, TPEs are engineering plastics that fulfil a range of performance criteria suitable for demanding end uses. From automotive parts to diving fins to ski boots, TPEs provide reliable flexibility. The amount of give is determined by a combination of material selection, geometry and wall thickness. In thick sections, the plastic will be quite stiff and is sturdy enough for fixing points. Thinner

sections exploit the high elongation and rebound, providing superior conformability and impact resistance.

Constructed from TPC fabric stretched over a PET frame, the Aeron chair by Herman Miller revolutionized ergonomic task chair design. The molded frame incorporated grooves and screw holes to attach the fabric panels, so no drilling or other assembly was required. Since then, several new configurations have emerged. While they may look different, they all rely on the inherent flexibility and durability of TPE to provide just the right balance of support and movement.

## TPE IN FASHION AND TEXTILES

TPU is the most widely used of the TPEs in fashion and textiles. It is applied for its high stretch and recovery as fibre and film. Along with other TPEs, it is utilized in molded products, ranging from wearable electronics housing to shoe soles.

TPE fibre is better known as elastane or spandex. Typically produced from TPU, it may also be based on TPC or TPA. Used in close-fitting sportswear, it is combined with non-elastic fibres that offer a desirable tactility and finish. Up to around 40% TPE yields a high-stretch fabric useful for body-hugging garments, such as swimwear, undergarments and leggings. It is used in compression garments for both sport and medical applications.

The most effective way to combine

such contrasting properties, while maintaining the highest-quality fabric, is to mix the materials in a single filament (see PA). Known as bicomponent, multicomponent or multifilament, these composite filaments are produced by mixing two or more materials during spinning. Thus the elasticity of TPE may be combined with high-strength PA.

Non-synthetic fibres, such as cotton (page 410), are combined with TPE during subsequent spinning phases. The non-synthetic fibre is wrapped around the elastomeric one, which provides a desirable finish while maintaining elasticity. Known as core-spun, or covered, this technique is used to bring stretch and recovery to otherwise stiff woven garments, such as skinny jeans, while increasing the stretch and recovery of knitted constructions.

High-quality faux leather is produced with nonwoven TPU. Unlike coated or laminated types, which are produced with TPU film, PVC film or PU, nonwoven TPU is breathable as a result of the entangled fibres. It is lightweight, long-lasting and such an effective fake that it can be hard to distinguish from genuine split leather. Applications range from garments and footwear to molded phone covers and sports products.

TPU film is applied onto textiles to provide a waterproof, durable and colourful finish. The advantages are similar to PU coating and PVC laminating in many respects. TPU types are utilized in a wide range of applications, from advertising banners to medical products to high-performance outerwear. A major advantage of TPU over PU is that it is compatible with welding. This is useful for producing high-strength watertight seams (inflatables and waterproofs) as well as laminated textiles.

**Composite trainer** The Nike Air Max 90 has been through several material and finish iterations since it was launched. This model features a laminated upper, consisting of coloured layers of TPU bonded onto a knitted mesh and synthetic base layer. Known as Hyperfuse, the three-layered construction almost eliminates stitching while providing a durable and breathable upper.

# Polyurethane (PU)

**Also known as**
Also abbreviated as: PUR, PUL
Trademark names: Baydur
Foam trademark names: Betafoam, Sweepex, Pottscorer, Padiflex, Bulpren, Filtren, Lamiflex
Textile trademark names: Porelle, Ultraleather, Brisa, Cora, Promessa, Osmo, Mesathane

**PU is a thermosetting plastic: as it cures, permanent cross-links form between polymer chains, resulting in a very durable and resilient material. It is exceptionally versatile and by adjusting the blend of ingredients, without changing the basic chemistry, a wide range of properties is achievable. PU is available as rigid plastic, elastomer and low- to high-density foam.**

| Types | Typical Applications | Sustainability |
|---|---|---|
| • MDI/polyol, TDI/polyol, or a combination of the two | • Upholstery and insulation<br>• Sports products<br>• Apparel and industrial textiles<br>• Prototyping and low-volume production | • Cannot be directly recycled but various options exist, such as grinding and reuse or particle bonding<br>• An efficient feedstock for incineration |

| Properties | Competing Materials | Costs |
|---|---|---|
| • Durable and resistant to flexural fatigue, abrasion and tearing<br>• Becomes embrittled with prolonged exposure to ultraviolet | • Expanded PP (EPP), expanded PE (EPE) and EVA foam<br>• PVC, TPE, natural rubber, synthetic rubber and silicone | • Low material cost<br>• Low to moderate production costs |

202

## INTRODUCTION

Invented in the 1930s, polyurethane (PU) now exists in many different types. Through adjustments in the ingredients and additives, PU has proved successful in diverse applications, from upholstery and insulation to shoe soles and composite textiles.

Polyurethane is either thermoplastic (TPU) (see TPE, page 194), or thermoset (PU). The difference is that thermoset PU forms physical cross-links between the polymer chains while TPU does not. Once cured, these links are permanent and cannot be undone with heat. As a result, PU is more durable and resilient than TPU, but is not melt-processible.

As well as competing head-on with its thermoplastic counterpart in apparel and technical textiles, flexible PU crosses over in application with polyvinyl chloride (PVC) (page 122), silicone (page 212) and synthetic rubbers (page 216), as well as with natural rubber (page 248). PU offers strength and durability at low density. Another advantage is that – unlike PVC – its elasticity comes from

**Memory foam** Memory foam (also called viscoelastic, temper or slow-recovery foam) is popular in mattresses, earplugs and upholstery. It is widely used in hospitals, where it helps to prevent pressure sores in patients who stay in bed for prolonged periods of time. It is a type of open-cell foam characterized by slow recovery after deformation, with a density range of 30–100 kg/m³ (1.9–6.2 lb/ft³). Its firmness, support and recovery rate are affected by temperature (lower temperatures cause the foam to become stiffer). Even body temperature can affect how the foam behaves (making it softer). Therefore, it is not so suitable for parts where ambient temperature cannot be controlled, such as in automotive, backpacks and outdoor sports products. Manufactured using conventional equipment, its relatively high price is the result of challenges associated with its viscoelasticity (production is slower).

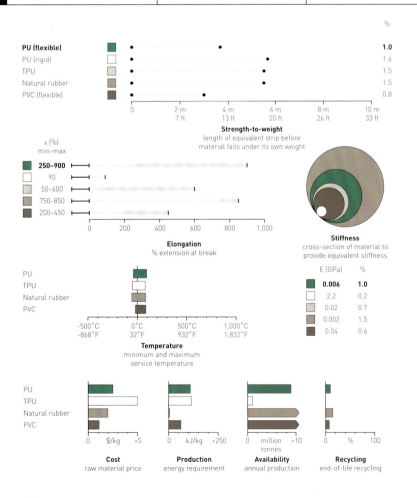

| | | % |
|---|---|---|
| PU (flexible) | | 1.0 |
| PU (rigid) | | 1.6 |
| TPU | | 1.5 |
| Natural rubber | | 1.5 |
| PVC (flexible) | | 0.8 |

**Strength-to-weight**
length of equivalent strip before material fails under its own weight

ε (%) min-max

| | |
|---|---|
| 250–900 | |
| 90 | |
| 50–600 | |
| 750–850 | |
| 200–450 | |

**Elongation**
% extension at break

**Stiffness**
cross-section of material to provide equivalent stiffness

| | E (GPa) | % |
|---|---|---|
| | 0.006 | 1.0 |
| | 2.2 | 0.2 |
| | 0.02 | 0.7 |
| | 0.002 | 1.5 |
| | 0.04 | 0.6 |

PU
TPU
Natural rubber
PVC

**Temperature**
minimum and maximum service temperature

PU
TPU
Natural rubber
PVC

**Cost**
raw material price

**Production**
energy requirement

**Availability**
annual production

**Recycling**
end-of-life recycling

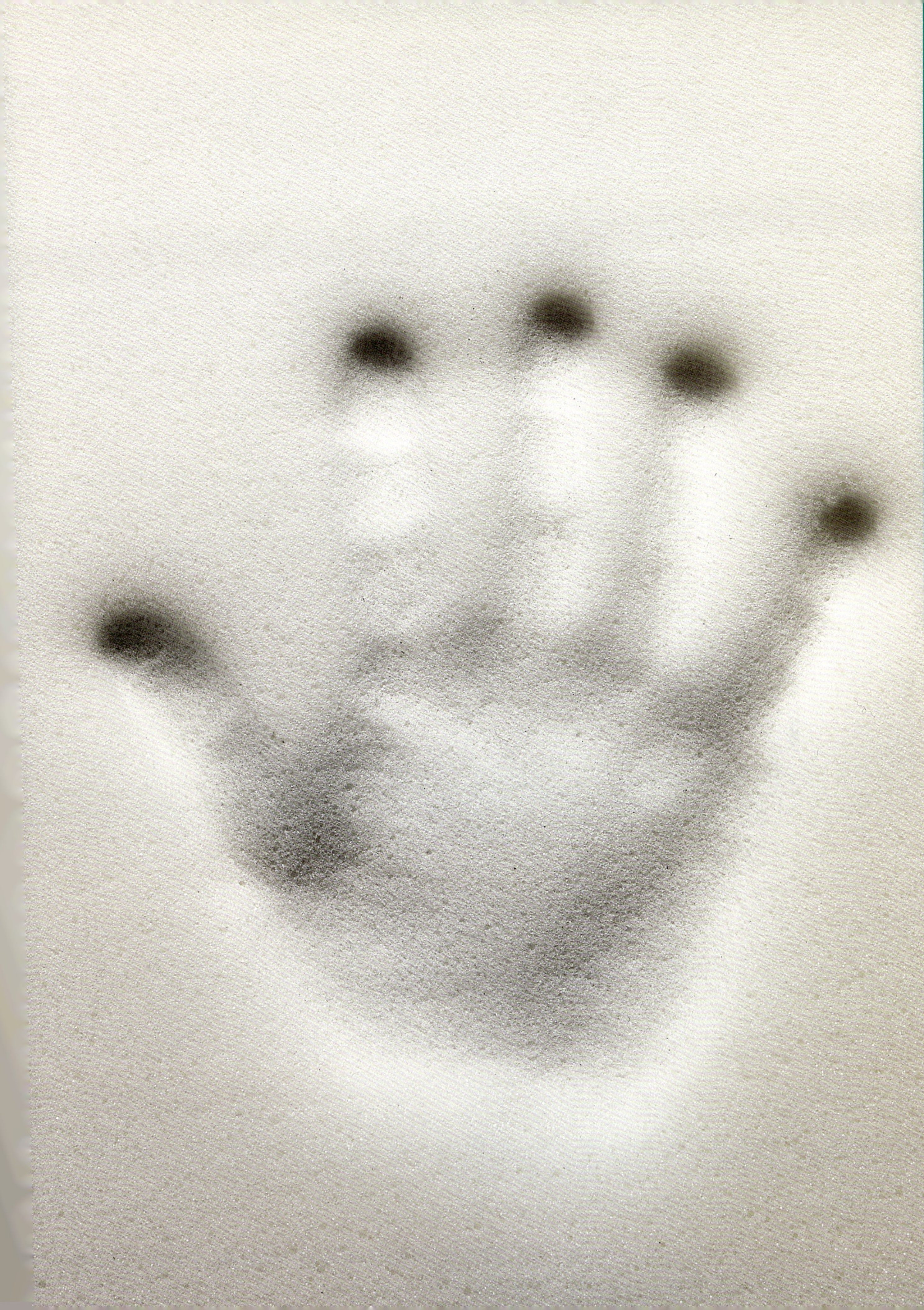

the blend of ingredients and not from the addition of plasticizers.

As a material used in model making, prototyping and low-volume production, PU competes with castable grades of polyamide (PA, nylon) (page 164), epoxy (page 232) and silicone. What sets PU apart is its versatility and low price point.

## COMMERCIAL TYPES AND USES

PU is not the result of polymerizing a monomer. Instead, it is born from the reaction of diisocyanates with polyol (long alcoxyether chains). Unlike thermoplastics – which are first produced as granules or sheet and subsequently manufactured into products – PU is polymerized in the shape of the final product.

The type and blend of diisocyanate and polyol determines the properties of the final polymer, such as rigidity or flexibility. The diisocyanates used include methylene diphenyl diisocyanate (MDI), toluene diisocyanate (TDI), or a combination of the two. While MDI is generally used to make rigid parts, TDI is mainly used in the production of low-density flexible foams.

Foam density is determined by the quantity of the blowing agent, which is mixed with the raw ingredients during manufacture. Chemical types are mixed into the raw ingredients and are triggered by reaction with isocyanate or thermal decomposition. They react to give off gas, such as nitrogen ($N_2$) or carbon dioxide ($CO_2$), and thus cause the material to foam. Or $CO_2$ or $N_2$ may be applied directly to the liquid ingredients as physical blowing agents. Dense foams are typically formed with chemical blowing agents, and physical blowing agents are used to produce lower-density foam. The density can be adjusted from 20 kg/m³ to over 400 kg/m³ (1.25–25 lb/ft³) and the proportion of air can be less than half or more than 95%. For comparison, solid PU has a mass of 1,250 kg/m³ (78 lb/ft³).

As a result of the versatility of PU's basic chemistry, it is suitable for a diversity of end uses. Around a quarter is used as rigid foam (such as for building insulation, model making and pattern making), a third goes into flexible foam (upholstery and mattresses, for example), 10% is molded foam (automotive parts,

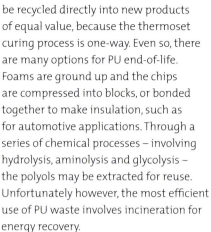

**Relaxed**              **Stretched**

**Cross-links**
Thermosetting plastics have permanent cross-links that hold the chains together tightly (see page 110). Elastomers, such as synthetic rubber and PU, have few cross-links and the other bonds between the chains are weak, which allows them to slide over one another when stretched. As the elastomer is stretched, the polymer chains become more oriented, producing semi-crystalline-like regions. Rigid thermosets, such as epoxy and polyester, have a high number of cross-links, preventing the chains from moving so freely.

upholstery and sports products) and the rest is applied as coating (apparel and industrial textiles), adhesive or other products.

## SUSTAINABILITY

PU foam is highly insulating: in less than a year the energy saved by a building's PU insulation is greater than the energy consumed in its production. As well as buildings, its thermal insulation capacity is utilized in refrigeration and transportation.

The isocyanates that are off-gassed during the reaction are harmful and known to cause asthma. The MDI system produces fewer isocyanates than the TDI method. In the past, blowing agents have been a cause for concern. Starting in the EU and the USA, chlorofluorocarbon (CFC) was phased out of foam production during the 1990s, while the use of hydrofluorocarbons (HCFC), which were considered somewhat less destructive to the ozone layer, has been banned from the majority of foam production since the 2000s.

PU is relatively straightforward to collect and separate, because it tends to be used in large blocks. PU cannot

be recycled directly into new products of equal value, because the thermoset curing process is one-way. Even so, there are many options for PU end-of-life. Foams are ground up and the chips are compressed into blocks, or bonded together to make insulation, such as for automotive applications. Through a series of chemical processes – involving hydrolysis, aminolysis and glycolysis – the polyols may be extracted for reuse. Unfortunately however, the most efficient use of PU waste involves incineration for energy recovery.

## PU IN PRODUCTS, FURNITURE AND LIGHTING

Three-dimensional parts are molded directly from the raw ingredients. The chemicals are combined in a mold cavity, where they react to form the finished part. Known as reaction injection molding (RIM), this technique is utilized in the production of furniture, lighting, sports products and automotive parts. Unlike injection molding, which is used in the mass production of millions of identical parts, RIM tends to be used for low volumes, up to tens of thousands.

RIM is used to produce parts similar to injection molding. Indeed, it is often used to make prototypes of parts that will be injection molded in the long term because the tooling costs are considerably cheaper while the unit costs are much higher. Details such as snap fits, threaded inserts and vents can be molded into the part with minimal cost implications.

For prototypes and very low volumes, RIM molds can be produced by CNC machining blocks of rigid PU tooling

**Synthetic leather**
PU leather provides a cost-effective alternative to natural leather for high-wear and demanding applications. Also referred to as leatherette, it is produced by coating PU onto a suitable textile. The surface is embossed with grain pattern so that it looks and feels more like the genuine article. Commonly used in bicycle seats, footwear, sports products and upholstery, PU leather is easier to maintain and more consistent than natural material. PU-coated fabric is not the only type of synthetic leather; alternatives include PVC coating, TPU laminate and needle-punched TPU fibres (see TPE).

resin. This technique is relatively inexpensive and is a very rapid way of producing a functional prototype suitable for application and testing.

RIM is used to produce items such as housings for medical devices, vending machines, appliances and fridges, as well as automotive bumpers, bodywork and interior panels. For high-strength and more demanding applications, the resin can be reinforced with glass fibres (GF) or mica, for example. This is known as reinforced reaction injection molding (RRIM).

The majority of foam is produced in giant blocks, known as slabstock, which are cut to size (such as for insulation). The process is limited to lengths of 60 m (197 ft); any larger than this and the blocks would be very difficult to handle. For shorter production runs and longer lengths, round blocks (called logs) are molded and sheet foam is peeled from the outside like veneer (page 290).

PU foam is soft and yet provides a high level of support. It is durable with excellent shape retention; even after prolonged deformation it will bounce back to its molded shape. The foam cell structure is either open or closed. Open-cell foams tend to be softer and are upholstered or covered. Closed-cell foams are self-skinning and used to produce low-cost furniture without a fabric cover.

PU foam is used extensively in upholstery; it is the most commonly used cushioning material. The shapes of chairs, sofas and similar items are produced

**Opposite**
**Machined coffee table** Designed by Nendo for Arketipo, 2009, the Moya low table consists of a PU base topped with glass. Cut from a single block of foam, the seamless concave surface beneath the glass gives the illusion of infinity. Without shadows or edges, there is no sense of depth. Photo by Masayuki Hayashi.

**Right**
**Molded floor lamp** Carrara was designed by Alfredo Häberli in 2001, and is produced by Luceplan, Italy. Molded from fire-retardant PU, the seamless lamp is painted satin white or glossy black. This results in an elegant and unobtrusive lamp, which stands 1.85 m (6 ft) tall and appears as if sculpted from a solid block of material. Photo courtesy of Luceplan.

**Versatile**
The versatility of PU is unrivalled: it provides designers with the capability to produce the same quality in a one-off as in a mass-production item. From foam to rigid panels, this creates many opportunities to experiment, as well as to realize design ideas.

**Compatibility**
Not only is PU applied as an adhesive and coating onto a whole host of substrates, but it also may be used as a core in composite laminates.

**Lightweight**
Foamed plastics are lightweight, buoyant and insulating. The ability to precisely adjust, or specify, PU foam density ensures the most efficient product.

from sheets of foam assembled together. High volumes may be produced from molded foam, whereby the finished shape is achieved in a single step. Known as cold-cure foam molding, it differs from RIM only by the inclusion of a blowing agent.

Overmolding provides the opportunity to incorporate a metal structure (for self-supporting parts, such as sofa armrests), electronics (for sensors and under-seat heating) or fabric cover (eliminating the need for a separate upholstering step). Complex multifunctional parts are produced by molding an insert, which is assembled with all the necessary components, followed by overmolding with a seamless foam skin.

As well as furniture, cold-cure foam molding is utilized for car interiors, sound insulation, aircraft seating, padding (backpacks and protective clothing), fitness products (weights and trainers) and shoe soles. Foam selection depends on the application and design. For example, seat padding is typically around 50–60 kg/m³ (3–3.75 lb/ft³), sound insulation is around twice that, and self-skinning foam is up to 400 kg/m³ (25 lb/ft³). As well as density, the firmness (elasticity), compression modulus (in most cases, higher density equals higher modulus), flex fatigue and resilience may all be independently considered.

The first PU surfboard blank was produced in the 1950s. Rigid foam is shaped by hand, or with CNC machining, and fibre-reinforced plastic (FRP) (page 236) is applied to the surface, resulting in a very strong laminated structure. The same technique is used to produce sculpture, furniture and props for theatre and film.

## PU IN AUTOMOTIVE AND AEROSPACE

Molded PU is utilized throughout the interior and exterior of vehicles. Large and complex parts are molded in a single step with the desired finish. One of the advantages of PU is that it is molded from a liquid, which means it reproduces fine surface texture very well. This quality is used in interior panels, such as to imitate the quality of leather (see Cowhide, page 444) or produce a soft-touch finish. Exterior applications require a coating to protect the PU from ultraviolet.

PU is applied as a spray-coat, providing colour and protecting surfaces from wear and abrasion. Using a combination of PU processing and injection molding, the coating may be applied directly in the mold. Known as in-mold coating (IMC) (or clear coat molding), it is compatible with a range of materials, including molded plastic and wood veneer. The outside surface finish is governed by the tool texture, which may be gloss or matt. So,

even if molding over an irregularly shaped veneer, the surface will be smooth. Not only does this process reduce steps and increase efficiency, but it also enables highly controllable and consistent finishes to be applied exactly the same each time (see also Polycarbonate, page 144).

Using the same approach, soft and leather-like finishes may be created on the surface of molded plastics. Soft PU is over-molded onto an existing part – typically injection-molded polycarbonate (PC) – with a highly textured finish. The surface quality is similar to PU-coated textile.

Foams are used in automobiles in a variety of ways, including seating, bumpers, acoustic panels and hermetic seals. Selection depends on the application. The properties are tweaked according to type of use. For example, the foam used in off-road vehicle seating formulated to dampen vibrations will feel different from that used to provide a smooth ride in a luxury vehicle. The foam used in aircraft must meet stringent aviation combustion requirements.

The foam and cover of an upholstered seat may be combined in a single molding process. A synthetic fabric, such as PU-coated or PVC-coated textile, is placed into a mold and drawn onto the surface by a strong vacuum. Once in place, foam is injected behind to fill the cavity and hold the textile in shape.

Rigid PU foam is utilized as the core in high-strength composite constructions.

## AUTOMOTIVE AND AEROSPACE

**Versatile**
A huge range of properties is possible, which means that PU is suitable for a diversity of applications. Reducing the number of different materials used in a vehicle helps to improve the efficiency of recycling.

**Low-volume**
Set-up for low-volume production is inexpensive and turnaround is relatively swift. This creates many opportunities for design.

**Resistant**
PU is inherently resistant to mold and mildew. Antimicrobial compounds are added to ensure a long service life in outdoor and marine applications.

**Surface quality**
Even though PU molding is a low-pressure process, the liquid resin reproduces fine surface textures and details very well. Parts are spray-painted to enhance the surface, achieve the desired colour and provide resistance to ultraviolet.

**Composite fuel cell**
High-performance composite fabrics are utilized in a range of demanding applications, from the transportation of flammable liquids to high-strength pneumatic bellows. This novel fuel cell, custom-produced by ATL for a GTE endurance racing car, consists of a proprietary formulation of PU reinforced with high-tenacity PA. The combination of materials yields a rugged and safe fuel cell that exceeds FIA (Fédération International de l'Automobile) standards and offers performance gains through weight saving and fuel system optimization. The choice of elastomer matrix depends on the application; alternatives to PU include fluoropolymer (page 190), nitrile rubber and polychloroprene (see Synthetic Rubber, page 216), and PVC. Likewise, for applications that require even greater weight saving or flexibility, the PA reinforcement is replaced with aramid (page 242).

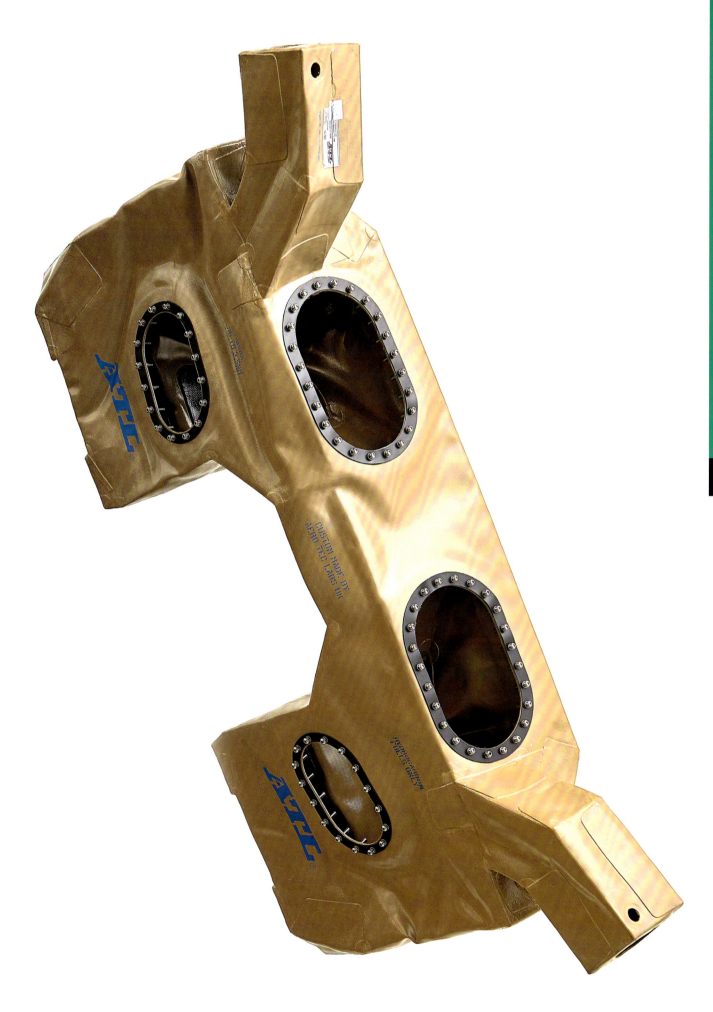

The performance of sheet materials – veneer, plywood and FRP, for example – is greatly enhanced when a foam core is sandwiched between two sheets, because the stiffness is increased without adding significant weight.

PU is compatible with polyester- (page 152) and epoxy- (page 232) based composites. Sheets are laminated with FRP and cut to size (a similar technique is used to produce insulated panels for construction). Spars and other flat structural members are made in this way.

Alternatively, shaped foam (formed by molding or milling) is clad with a FRP skin. Similar to how surfboards are made, this approach allows for the greatest design freedom. It is used to produce aerodynamic parts, such as roofs, spoilers and winglets (upturned wingtips on aircraft). The reverse is also possible: a hollow molded part may be foam-filled to enhance stiffness and reduce vibration.

There are many other types of plastic foam, such as expanded polystyrene (EPS) (page 132), expanded polypropylene (EPP) (page 98) and expanded polyethylene (EPE) (page 108). These thermoplastic materials provide an alternative to PU foam in some cases: EPS is also utilized in packaging; and EPP and EPE provide an alternative for engineering applications and technical products (the foam is semi-rigid to rigid with good impact-absorption properties), such as for sports and leisure. The principal advantage of PU is that it has highly controllable physical characteristics, which provide a range of possible performance capabilities.

The use of foam in automotive applications has helped to increase the proportion that is collected and recycled, because the industry must adopt increasingly stringent recycling practices to keep up with regulations

**Peppermint 'vinyl' skirt** PVC and PU are both applied as coating onto woven fabric, typically polyethylene terephthalate (PET, polyester) (page 152). While PVC tends to be stiffer and heavier with a high-gloss shine, PU-coating is more elastic with a silky finish. They may be combined to take advantage of the benefits of both. This skirt was sold as 'vinyl', but is constructed from PU-coated PET.

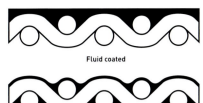

**Fluid coated**

**Impregnated**

**Film/membrane laminated**

**Cross-section through coated textiles**
Coatings are applied to enhance the visual and functional properties of textiles. The end result depends on the technique and mix of materials. Liquids, pastes and foams are applied to one side of the fabric using a process known as direct coating. The coating is spread over the surface by a doctor blade. The thickness is adjusted by changing the height of the blade. Liquids are impregnated into fabric by dip coating. This is a straightforward technique, whereby the fabric is suspended in the coating bath for a set period of time. The rate of absorption depends on the fibre properties. Alternatively, a thin film or membrane is applied by lamination. This technique allows for materials not suitable for liquid application (such as microporous films) to be used. With heat and pressure, the film conforms to the surface of the textile. Once coated, a range of additional finishing techniques may be utilized, such as calendering and embossing.

and legislation. PU foam is collected, separated and shredded. The small foam chunks are adhesive-bonded together to make rebond, which is used for acoustic insulation (including in automotive applications) and as carpet underlay. Alternatively, finely ground particles of waste foam are put back into automotive components as inexpensive filler.

## PU IN FASHION AND TEXTILES

PU is applied as coating, membrane and foam for a range of fashion and technical textile end uses. It is often compared to PVC, TPU and ePTFE (see Fluoropolymer, page 190). These thermoplastics are used in similar applications, but each has its specialism: PVC is the least expensive; TPU is very similar to PU, but can be processed using thermoplastic techniques; and ePTFE offers superior chemical and heat resistance, making it suitable for medical and other demanding applications.

Low cost
PU is around half the price of TPU. It is twice the price of PVC, but has higher strength-to-weight so less material is required for equivalent performance.

Appearance
It is available in a wide range of vivid colours, from saturated to fluorescent. Unlike TPU, PU cannot be dyed. Therefore, colour must be added in solution, prior to application. Compared to PVC, embossed PU offers a much more realistic-looking leather imitation.

Durable
PU is strong, lightweight and more durable than natural rubber and leather. It has superior strength, elongation and recovery compared to PVC.

Waterproof and breathable
Microporous PU is hydrophobic, breathable, durable and suitable for high-flex applications.

PU coating provides a waterproof barrier on textiles. As well as apparel, it is suitable for technical textiles. Examples include pneumatic bellows, inflatable kayaks, industrial fabric, tents and tensile structures (such as canopies and marquees).

Unlike PVC, it can be breathable. There are two different ways this is achieved: either it breathes by absorbing and dissipating vapour (sweat) through the diffusion of water molecules through the polymer structure, or it is microporous and so allows vapour to pass through, while repelling water.

The thickness of non-porous films affects water vapour transfer rate: the thinner the membrane, the faster vapour passes through. Thin films utilized in garments are lightweight, flexible and highly breathable. Thicker coatings are suitable for gloves, hats and other items that require more substantial waterproofing (though at the expense of breathability).

Microporous PU works on the same principal as ePTFE: vapour passes through in gas phase. Therefore, it is much more effective (less likely to become clammy and uncomfortable in use) and longer-lasting. While it is more expensive than non-porous types, it is significantly less expensive (and more durable) than ePTFE. It is used in high-quality apparel, sportswear and tents.

# Polysiloxane, Silicone

Silicone is a tough and resilient high-performance material. It is resistant to abrasion, water, chemicals and heat. It provides good grip with low surface friction, making it practical and easy to clean. These qualities are used in three-dimensional parts, coatings and adhesives. A relatively expensive plastic, silicone serves applications from cooking utensils to medical equipment.

| Types | Typical Applications | Sustainability |
|---|---|---|
| • High-temperature vulcanizing (HTV)<br>• Room-temperature vulcanizing (RTV)<br>• Liquid silicone rubber (LSR)<br>• Thermoplastic vulcanizate (TPV) | • Cookware<br>• Automotive and industrial parts<br>• Molds and model making | • Impractical to recycle<br>• High embodied energy |

| Properties | Competing Materials | Costs |
|---|---|---|
| • Low surface energy<br>• High flexibility<br>• Low- to high-temperature resistance | • PU, synthetic rubber and natural rubber<br>• TPE and EVA | • High material cost<br>• High manufacturing cost |

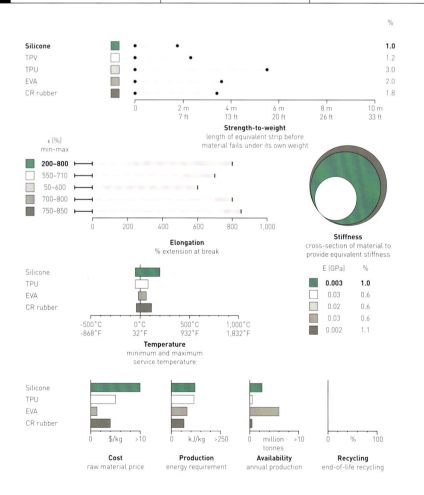

## INTRODUCTION

Developed in the 1940s, silicones come in many forms, including fluid, rubber, gel and resin. This provides a great deal of flexibility in application. As well as the molding compounds, adhesives and coatings that designers are concerned with, silicones can be found in applications ranging from shampoo to waste-water treatment.

They are stable across a wide temperature range – no degradation occurs between -50 and 200°C (-58–392°F), and special formulations are capable of -90 to 300°C (-130–572°F) – and inherently resistant to bacteria. Silicones have low levels of volatile organic compounds (VOCs), which makes them suitable for food preparation and packaging, and medical applications.

Silicone is considered hypoallergenic and safe for use in baby products. Examples include sippy cups, spoons and bottle teats. It has good tear strength, and so can tolerate chewing and pulling. It can withstand repeated high-temperature sterilization without showing any deterioration. The same properties are useful for medical applications, such as respiratory tubing and intravenous infusion lines. It is used in prosthetics too, both to mimic the look and feel of skin and to provide cushioning and comfort.

## COMMERCIAL TYPES AND USES

Silicone is classed as a semi-organic material thanks to the inclusion of silicon. Its polysiloxane backbone consists of alternating silicon and oxygen (inorganic) surrounded by methyl groups (the organic part). The silicon–oxygen bonds are very strong and account for many of silicone's desirable properties.

Silicone is produced from the reaction of silicon with methyl chloride and a suitable catalyst (such as copper oxide).

Its chemical structure allows for them to be produced in a number of variations, from short chain fluids to long chain elastomers.

Silicone requires vulcanization (toughening by curing) to become a thermosetting elastomer. Whatever the method of curing, the result is the same: permanent cross-links are formed between the polymer chains.

Resins are classified according to the curing method and temperature. High-temperature vulcanizing (HTV) silicone is supplied as a molding compound and cured at high temperature, typically

during molding or extrusion. Applications span automotive, appliance and consumer products.

Liquid silicone rubber (LSR) is supplied as a two-component compound vulcanized by addition curing. The liquid is mixed and pumped into the mold, where it cures. This provides many processing advantages, such as being able to produce complex thin-walled geometries. They are utilized in range of products from automotive parts to cookware and swimming masks.

Room-temperature vulcanizing (RTV) silicone is also supplied as a two-

**Baking mold** The low- and high-temperature resistance of silicone, combined with its pliability and non-stick surface, make it an ideal material for a variety of kitchenware, from ice cube trays and oven mitts to utensils and baking molds. Indeed, silicone is one of the few plastics that can tolerate going straight from freezer to oven and back again. It can be produced in a range of vivid colours, from translucent to opaque.

**Mechanicial**

**Chemical and/or electrostatic**

**Absorption**

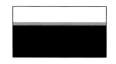

**Diffusion**

**Mechanisms of adhesion** Adhesion describes the process of dissimilar materials clinging to one another. The forces at work are generally a mix of mechanical, chemical and electrostatic interaction. Mechanical bonding is formed by liquid adhesive filling surface voids and then hardening. This relies on the substrate surface being rough, with many peaks and cavities for the adhesive to penetrate. Chemical bonding involves the formation of covalent, ionic or hydrogen bonds across the interface. Only certain adhesives form chemical bonds (including silicone). This mechanism does not rely on phsyical interlocking and surface roughness. Physical absorption relies on intimate contact between the adhesive and the substrate. Bond strength is determined by weak molecular-level forces. How much of the surface is covered by the adhesive (a process known as wetting) depends on the relative surface energy. Low-energy polymers easily wet high-energy substrates, such as glass and metal. Substrates with low surface energy – such as fluoropolymer, PE, PP and silicone – are not easily wet by other materials. This is useful for non-stick applications, such as in cookware and medical. In diffusive adhesion, the molecules of two materials are mixed. For example, welding thermoplastic causes the joint interface to coalesce. As it cools, a strong diffused join is formed. This method relies on using compatible polymers that have sufficiently mobile polymer chains (when heated).

component resin. When mixed, the polymer forms cross-links and hardens. A modified version of RTV silicone is cured using ultraviolet. They are utilized in mold making and prototyping, as well as in the production of consumer electronics, appliances and machinery.

Silicone that is intended to cure on-site in sealing materials and adhesives has a slightly different composition. All of the ingredients are mixed in a single component and cross-linking occurs on contact with moisture in the atmosphere. The smell given off by these silicones is residual cross-linker, such as acetic acid.

Silicone resin is applied as adhesive and coating. It is very effective in both cases, because it has low surface energy (and so spreads very thinly over surfaces) and forms chemical bonds with the substrate. Compatible with most materials, silicone adheres equally well to rough and smooth surfaces. Once cured, the low surface energy prevents other materials from bonding to its surface.

As an adhesive, it is utilized in automotive, aerospace, construction and consumer products. It is applied as coating onto textiles, as well as to provide a waterproof barrier on a range of surfaces, from delicate printed circuit boards (PCBs) to masonry. The bond energy is high, which helps to minimize ageing; in some cases ageing is virtually nonexistent.

The properties of silicone, as a coating, are effectively transferred onto the substrate. It provides excellent resistance to water and weathering and can be used to produce an airtight finish. Durability is determined by material selection. Rigid silicone provides resistance to scratching and chemicals. Elastomeric coatings, by contrast, are not so resistant to chemicals, in particular strong acids.

It is non-conductive and an excellent electrical insulator. This quality is utilized in technical applications, such as self-lubricating electrical connectors (automotive and aerospace). Indeed, entire products may be coated, such as medical implants, to form a permanent, impenetrable and protective skin.

Cross-linked silicone is combined with thermoplastic polyurethane (TPU) (see TPE, page 196) to take advantage of its beneficial properties in injection molded products. Thermoplastic silicone-urethane – one such material is TPSiV, a patented thermoplastic vulcanizate (TPV) from Multibase, a Dow Corning company – combines the low surface energy, unique tactility, heat resistance and chemical resistance of silicone, with the lower cost (TPU is at least half the price of silicone), colourability and relatively higher tensile strength of TPU (even though silicone has high elongation, it has rather low tensile strength, a major drawback). There are several grades available: as

tensile strength and tear strength are increased, flexibility and elongation at break are reduced. Hardness ranges from Shore A 50 to 80.

As well as injection molding and overmolding, TPSiV is compatible with post-fabrication operations, such as thermoforming, welding and heat sealing. This combination is used in sensitive applications, spanning medical products and wearable electronics.

## SUSTAINABILITY

Silicone is not an oil derivative like most conventional plastics. And while production requires the use of significant energy, its unique properties help to increase the efficiency, durability and productivity of various products. A report commissioned by the Global Silicones Council concluded that using silicone (as well as the closely related siloxane and silane) products reduces carbon dioxide equivalent emissions by a factor of nine. In other words, for every kilogram of emissions associated with the production of silicones, 9 kilos of emissions are saved through their use. While these results are very generalized and refer mainly to technical applications – antifoaming agents, paint additives, lubricants and glass-fibre (GF) coating for composites – it is clear that enhancements offered by silicone make a significant contribution to offsetting the impact of their production.

Most types of silicone are impractical to recover and recycle; they are used in small parts and can be difficult to distinguish from other elastomers. As a thermoset they form permanent cross-links. By contrast, TPSiV can be remolded several times without significant loss of quality. This makes it much more possible to reuse scrap and other reliable sources of waste directly in new products.

**Bathroom radio** The Lexon Tykho radio was designed by Marc Berthier, 1997. The electronics are encapsulated in an acrylonitrile butadiene styrene (ABS) (page 138) case covered in a two-part silicone housing. The buttons and speaker cone are seamlessly integrated into the front half, forming a splashproof barrier suitable for bathroom use. The radio frequency is adjusted by rotating the antenna.

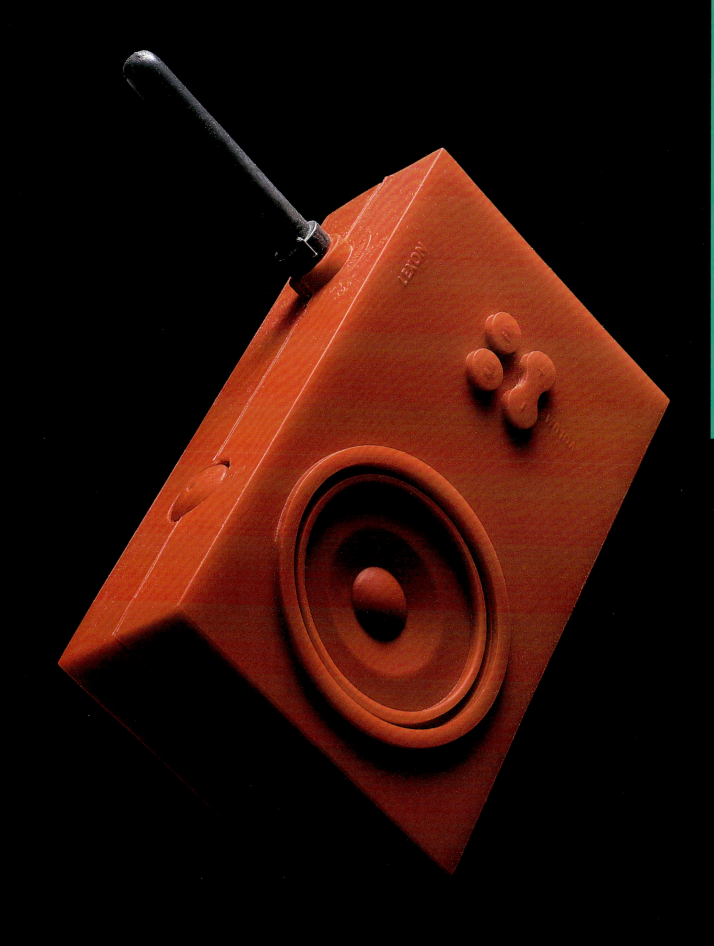

# Synthetic Rubber

**Also known as**
SBR: Buna-S, Duradene, Neolite
BR: Diene
CR: neoprene (formerly DuPrene)
NBR: Buna-N
IR: Natsyn

**This group of thermosetting elastomers provides an alternative to natural rubber. They are applied for their superior resistance to chemicals, weathering and heat. Used mainly in automotive and transportation, in particular tyres, they are also found in construction, sports and fashion items. Covering a range of elasticity, the exact properties depend on the type of rubber.**

| Types | Typical Applications | Sustainability |
|---|---|---|
| • SBR, BR and NBR (butadiene)<br>• IIR and IR (isoprene)<br>• CR (chloroprene)<br>• EPR and EPDM (ethylene) | • Gaskets and seals<br>• Automotive and tyres<br>• Footwear, fashion and textiles<br>• Sports products | • Impractical to recycle<br>• Moderate embodied energy |

| Properties | Competing Materials | Costs |
|---|---|---|
| • Superior resistance to heat, weathering and chemicals<br>• From rigid to flexible with good rebound properties | • TPE, EVA, PVC and fluoropolymer<br>• PU and silicone<br>• Natural rubber and latex | • Moderate to high cost (although typically less than natural rubber), depending on the type and grade<br>• Moderate manufacturing costs |

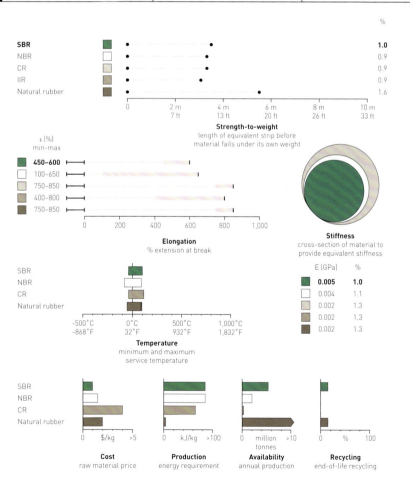

## INTRODUCTION

The drop in natural rubber (page 248) production and availability during World War I and II triggered an acceleration in the commercial realization of synthetic rubbers. The first to emerge were the families of polybutadiene rubber (BR), styrene butadiene rubber (SBR) and polychloroprene rubber (CR). BR and SBR were developed for use in tyres and, to this day, this application accounts for the majority of their use. CR has a more balanced combination of properties that make it the most multi-purpose rubber.

From the 1930s onwards, these rubbers saw significant development, and several others emerged based on similar chemistry. They are polymers that are cross-linked through vulcanization (curing). Most require the addition of carbon black and other fillers to achieve the final properties. Like natural rubber, they are supplied in latex form, bales of crumb or flake, all of which require further compounding and curing prior to manufacture into useful articles.

The synthetic rubbers described here are interchangeable with silicone (page 212) and polyurethane (PU) (page 202) in certain situations. These may also be considered synthetic rubber, but offer unique advantages as a result of their chemistry. Thermoplastic elastomers (TPE) (page 194), as well as the other elastomeric thermoplastic materials – polyvinyl chloride (PVC) (page 122), ethylene vinyl acetate (EVA) (page 118)

**Compression-molded air supply** Complex three-dimensional rubber parts are produced in a single piece with compression molding. This air intake is fabricated from nitrile rubber (NBR). Similar parts are manufactured from natural rubber and ethylene propylene diene (EPDM). Material selection depends on the specifics of the application.

and fluoropolymer (page 190) – are also used in similar applications. The main difference is thermoplastics do not develop any cross-links between the polymer chains. As a result, they can be melted, and exhibit inferior resistance to weathering and chemicals compared to synthetic rubber. Fluoropolymer is an exception, but is so much more expensive that its application is limited.

## COMMERCIAL TYPES AND USES

BR has excellent resistance to abrasion and good elasticity, and remains flexible at low temperatures. Developed in the 1920s, it was not produced on a large scale commercially until the 1960s. It is mainly used in the treads and sidewalls of tyres, providing good crack resistance and low rolling resistance (good fuel efficiency). Hardness ranges from 40 to 90 Shore A. It is also used as the core in golf balls. It has a low glass transition temperature (around -90°C [-130°F]), or Tg. This is the point at which the amorphous regions in the polymer structure become mobile. While this ensures many of its desirable properties, it also means BR provides poor traction in cold, damp conditions. As a result of this and its poor processing properties, it is most often blended with SBR or natural rubber. It is also copolymerized with polystyrene (PS) (page 132) to increase toughness (see Acrylonitrile Butadiene Styrene, page 138).

One of the first truly synthetic rubbers, SBR has become the most widely consumed. A copolymer of butadiene and styrene, it is found in two principal types based on different manufacturing: solution (S-SBR) and emulsion (E-SBR). S-SBR has superior mechanical properties. It is applied mainly in car and light truck tyres (treads and carcasses) for their excellent resistance to abrasion and impact. Other applications include shoe soles, conveyor belts, hoses, flooring, gaskets and toys. Hardness ranges from 30 to 95 Shore A. Compared to natural rubber, it has low resilience and low tear strength, particularly as temperature is increased. As a result, SBR is used for less demanding situations.

Isobutylene isoprene rubber (IIR), also known as butyl rubber, exhibits low permeability to gases, high resistance to weathering and chemicals, and good resistance to abrasion, with hardness around 40 to 90 Shore A. These properties are used in tyre linings (or inner tubes) and other speciality applications. It is also a good electrical insulator, with high-temperature resistance.

CR is widely known as neoprene (formerly trademarked by DuPont as DuPrene). The success of CR is due to its unique balance of mechanical strength and resistance to weathering, chemicals, fuels and oils. It is modified through copolymerization and blending. It can be relatively soft compared to the others (hardness ranges from 20 to 95 Shore A), but is prone to stiffening over time. It is relatively expensive and used in technical applications, such as conveyor belts, hoses and gaskets. It is also popular in fashion and textiles, providing a waterproof barrier in wet- and drysuits.

Acrylonitrile butadiene rubber (NBR), also known as nitrile rubber, is used mainly for its resistance to oil, chemicals and fuels across a wide temperature range. The proportion of acrylonitrile to butadiene is adjusted to produce a range of elastomers with varied resistance and temperature properties. Hardness ranges from 40 to 95 Shore A. Raising the acrylonitrile content increases oil and solvent resistance, tensile strength and resistance to abrasion at the expense of resilience and low-temperature flexibility. The general-purpose grades provide a cost-effective solution in most situations. Several variations exist for demanding applications. For example, hydrogenated NBR (HNBR) has significantly higher heat resistance; and adding carboxylic acid groups to the polymer backbone (XNBR) results in an elastomer with increased strength and resistance to abrasion.

Ethylene propylene diene (EPDM) and ethylene propylene rubber (EPR) are high-performance elastomers based on the same chemical building blocks as polyethylene (PE) (page 108) and polypropylene (PP) (page 98). The difference between EPDM and EPR is that the former is a terpolymer and the latter a copolymer. The ethylene and propylene monomers combine to form a stable polymer with good resistance to weathering and chemicals. Inclusion of diene in the formation of EPDM terpolymer increases compressive strength and stiffness. These rubbers are durable, with good stability at low and high temperatures and excellent resistance to weathering. Carbon black is added to enhance strength, elasticity and resistance to ultraviolet. White EPDM is available for applications where heat gain is a concern (titanium dioxide is added to reflect the sun's rays) and virgin EPDM is available in a range of muted colours. It is mainly utilized for automotive (seals) and construction (roofs, seals and flashing) applications.

Polyisoprene rubber (IR) is similar to natural rubber in many respects; they have the same basic chemical formula. Both exhibit good tear strength, tensile strength and compressive strength. It was not until the 1960s that a synthetic version exhibiting suitable properties was realized. Developed by Goodyear, IR continues to be utilized in high-performance tyres, as well as in gaskets and footwear. Its consistency and purity (natural rubber contains impurities that can cause allergic reactions) make it suitable for medical items, such as gloves, condoms, tubing and needle shields.

## SUSTAINABILITY

The production techniques vary according to the base polymer. Owing to the cross-linked structure, these materials are more challenging to recycle than thermoplastics. Recycled material is less expensive than virgin. There are three main methods used: devulcanization, reclaim and crumb.

Scrap made up of a single type of rubber may be devulcanized. In other words, the sulphur cross-links are broken down to reveal the original polymer.

**Extruded inner tube**
Butyl rubber (IIR) exhibits good resistance to abrasion, tearing and flexing. These qualities combined with its exceptional resistance to gas permeability make it an important material for inner tubes. Produced as a continuous tube, it is cut to length and welded to produce a cylindrical inner tube. Once complete, the tube is vulcanized to take it to full strength.

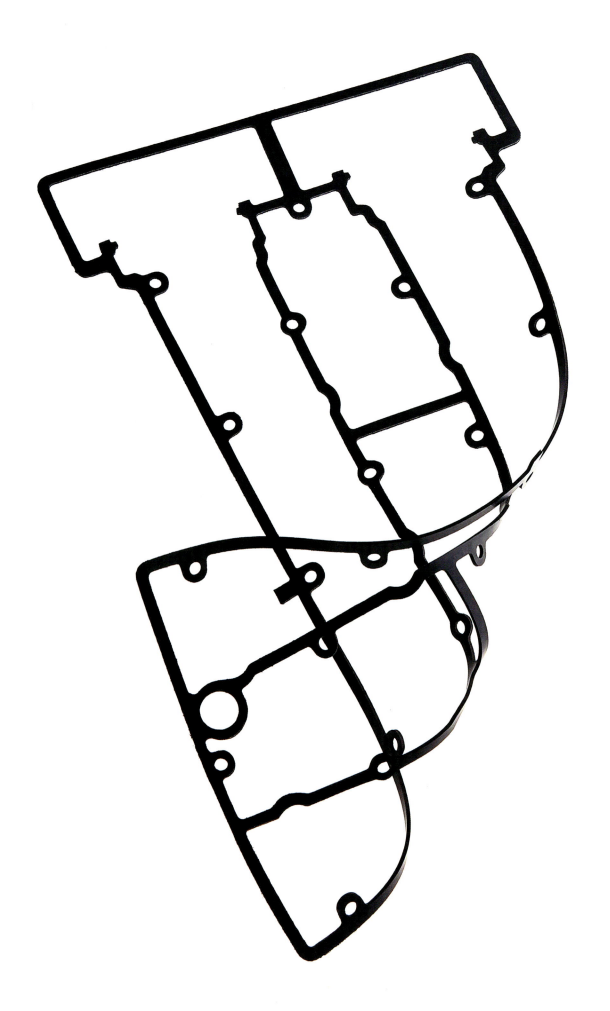

Reclaim refers to waste that has been rendered fit for reuse by a series of thermal and chemical processes. While it is possible to remove the majority of foreign material that has been mixed in with the rubber – plastic and metal reinforcement – it is not always feasible to separate the fillers, additives and different types of polymers. Therefore, it is a lower-grade material.

Material unsuitable for either of these methods, such as waste tyres, is ground up to make crumb. Used as filler in new rubber products, it is inexpensive and so helps to reduce overall cost. It is added to other materials too, such as to increase resilience or impact absorption properties. Waste that is not recyclable is incinerated or disposed.

Non-petroleum sources have been explored in an attempt to produce renewable synthetic rubber. For example, limestone is used as a feedstock for CR. While it does not use oil, it is mined and a great deal of heat is required, meaning the environmental benefit is negligible.

## SYNTHETIC RUBBER IN AUTOMOTIVE AND TRANSPORTATION

The automotive industry, and transportation generally, consumes the majority of synthetic rubber. These materials are utilized in many forms, but their largest area of application is in tyres.

Modern tyres are a complex construction with all of the necessary functions built into the tyre wall, removing the need for an inner tube. The inner airtight layer is predominantly IIR, followed by layers of fibre-reinforced (typically polyethylene terephthalate, page 152) and steel wire-reinforced SBR and BR and a steel wire-reinforced bead, surrounded with composite rubber tread. The formulation of rubber depends on the end use (such as hot or cold climates) and where in the tyre you look. As the need for heat resistance increases, so does the proportion of natural rubber: car tyres are around three-quarters synthetic, truck tyres around one-quarter, and aircraft tyres are produced with up to 100% natural rubber.

Inner tubes are still used for bicycles, scooters and other small-tyre vehicles. In cycling, IIR competes with latex (natural rubber). Butyl offers good value for money, but latex can be used thinner. This results in a lighter tyre (a saving of around 10g [0.02 lb] per tube) with higher flexibility (improved ride). It is more permeable, however, and requires inflating frequently.

The majority of synthetic rubber parts use a similar approach to production: they are compounded, formed and joined prior to vulcanizing. This provides a good deal of design freedom. The uncured resin is easily shaped (such as with extrusion and compression molding) and can be heat welded like thermoplastics. Once vulcanized, the form is set and cannot be undone with heat alone.

## SYNTHETIC RUBBER IN FASHION AND TECHNICAL TEXTILES

Such is the usefulness of synthetic rubber that it can be found in fashion items as well as technical textiles. The same basic materials and processes are applied in both. Sheets of material used to construct three-dimensional items – from apparel to inflatables – are typically rubber-coated textile. Similar to PU, PVC and TPE, rubber coating provides a durable, waterproof barrier. The added benefits of rubber are that it has superior resistance to liquids (oils, chemicals and fuels), weathering and heat.

Wetsuits and survival suits are produced from sheets of CR cut and fabricated like regular cloth. Wetsuits work by holding a thin layer of water next to the skin, which is warmed by the body. Drysuits, on the other hand, are produced from thicker CR (5–7 mm [0.2–0.3 in]), to keep the wearer completely dry. Produced with a closed-cell structure, they trap gas within the tiny pockets to provide insulation and buoyancy. While this is practical in shallow water, the cell structure cannot stand up to the pressure of deep water. To prepare for this, CR is crushed with heat and pressure prior to use. This effectively collapses the cell structure, reducing a sheet from, say, 7 mm to 4 mm (0.3 in to 0.16 in).

A layer of jersey (knit) is applied to the outside surface; it provides colour and

**Profiled gasket**
Synthetic rubber has 'shape memory'. In other words, when load is applied it will deform, but will continually try to return to its original shape. This property is utilized in seals and gaskets. All types of synthetic rubber are suitable; choice comes down to the application. This automotive engine example uses nitrile rubber (NBR), which offers excellent resistance to oils and fuels, even at elevated temperature.

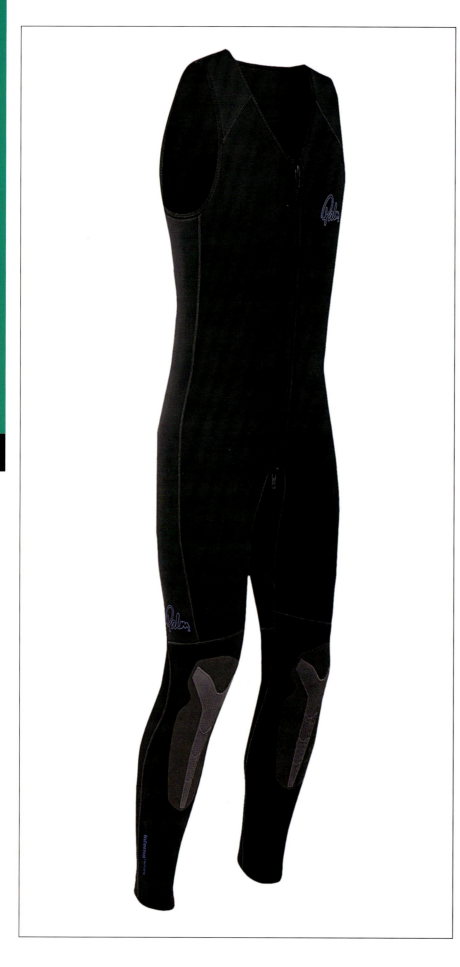

reduces scuffing. The CR may be printed onto directly, but the surface will not be so durable. On the inside, a knitted liner enhances comfort and freedom of movement. PET and TPU (elastane) are typically used to provide a mix of support and stretch. All of the seams are stitched and taped (adhesive bonded) to ensure water-tightness. The elasticity of CR maximizes performance by ensuring that garments fit snugly.

The alternative to CR is a so-called membrane drysuit. These are produced from a laminate of various materials, but typically include a rubber (CR or IIR) layer to keep the water out. They are lightweight and keep the wearer dry, but lack the insulation offered by foam.

Dip molding is used to produce gloves and seals (cuffs and neck). It is a low-cost process suitable for all types of synthetic (mainly CR and silicone), as well as natural rubber. The outside surface tends to be glossy, while the inside surface will be an exact replica of the mold. Therefore, parts are often turned inside out after molding to reveal the more precise inner surface in application.

Unlike dip molding, compression molding is capable of producing parts with thick and thin wall sections. Rubber shoe soles are produced in this way. It is possible to combine multiple colours too, such as in rubber logos and badges. This is achieved with multiple pressing stages; each colour is made separately and then combined in a final molding.

**Left**
**Thermal long john**
Produced by Palm Equipment, this highly insulating under-layer is constructed with 5 mm (0.2 in) thick foamed CR. The seams are glued and blind stitched, and the knees are heavily reinforced, to ensure a tough companion for cold-water rafting and other demanding water sports. Photo courtesy of Palm Equipment.

**Opposite**
**Wetsuit boot** The Zhik Soft Sole dinghy boot is fabricated from 4 mm (0.16 in) thick foamed CR. The topside is textured to aid hiking (leaning over the edge of the boat to counteract its heeling) and the inside is laminated with jersey knit for comfort. The laces run up the side so as not to get in the way during hiking. The layered CR upper and flexible rubber sole are adhesive bonded.

# Formaldehyde-Based: Melamine (MF), Phenolic (PF) and Urea (UF)

**Also known as**
MF trademark names: Melmac, Ultraplas
PF trademark names: Bakelite, Novotext, Tufnol, Oasis
UF trademark names: Formica, Beetle

**Based on formaldehyde, these are among the oldest synthetic plastics. Utilized alone, or providing the matrix in a diversity of composites, melamine, phenolic and urea remain some of the most significant thermosetting plastics. Their durability, insulation properties and high resistance to heat and chemicals are utilized in demanding applications.**

| Types | Typical Applications | Sustainability |
|---|---|---|
| • Melamine-formaldehyde (MF)<br>• Phenol-formaldehyde (PF)<br>• Urea-formaldehyde (UF) | • Electrical housings, plugs and sockets<br>• Cookware and utensils<br>• Adhesive and foam | • They are impractical to recycle and have moderate embodied energy<br>• Exposure to formaldehyde can cause adverse health effects |

| Properties | Competing Materials | Costs |
|---|---|---|
| • High heat resistance and chemical resistance<br>• Hard and durable surface | • PA, PET and POM<br>• Epoxy and UP<br>• Earthenware, stoneware and porcelain | • Raw materials are moderately expensive<br>• Production is high-cost |

## INTRODUCTION

These thermosetting plastics are formed into three-dimensional parts with heat and pressure. During the curing process, a complex network of cross-links forms, which provides the materials with some very desirable properties, including resistance to weathering and chemicals, dimensional stability at high temperature and good electrical insulation.

They are the result of condensation polymerization with formaldehyde and melamine, phenol or urea. Epitomized by Bakelite, formaldehyde condensation resins were the first truly moldable synthetic plastics. Patented in the early 1900s, Bakelite was originally conceived as a low-cost alternative to shellac. Development was slow at first and it was not until the original patent expired in the 1920s, stimulating competition, that the full potential of phenol-formaldehyde (PF) was unlocked through research and development. Several companies began developing the material and for the first time, mass-produced plastic products became widespread.

## COMMERCIAL TYPES AND USES

Bakelite was originally available only in dark colours, in particular brown and black. This was mainly done to hide the fillers (such as powdered wood) used to give Bakelite its strength. When the patents expired, new formulations were created that did not require the fillers and so a range of colours emerged.

PF is utilized in laminated plastics. Layers of paper, glass fibre (GF) or cotton (page 410) are combined with resin,

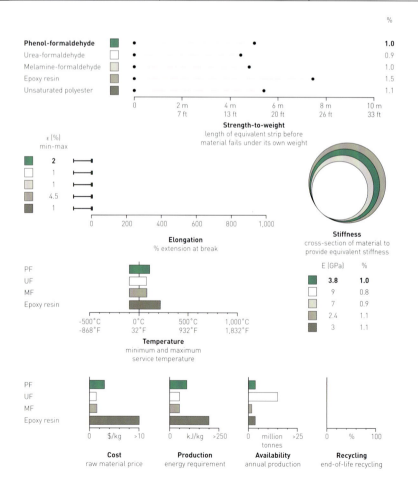

**Kitchen utensils** The Krenit salad set, created by Danish materials engineer and designer Herbert Krenchel, first went into production in 1953. Today, Normann Copenhagen manufactures it in MF in a range of colours, from white through blue, red, grey and black.

pressed and heated to form a strong, rigid sheet material. Predominantly used for electrical insulation, it is not as tough as similar fibre-reinforced plastics (FRP) and so avoided in load-bearing and high-stress applications. But it is very economical and so widely used in less demanding electrical insulation situations that require a dimensionally stable, rigid and resistant material.

Patented in 1924, UF is naturally white – an immediate advantage over PF. It exhibits excellent colour retention, with good electrical properties and temperature resistance. It is the most widely used of the formaldehyde trio, primarily in wood products such as particleboard, medium-density fibreboard (MDF) and plywood. Other types of wood-based panel are produced with PF.

Melamine formaldehyde (MF) was not utilized until much later; it began to emerge in consumer goods around the 1930s and 1940s. Compared to UF, MF has superior surface properties. Its higher resistance to water and staining mean it is suitable for use in cooking and dining. And like the others, it is used as a surfacing material and laminate. Indeed, more than half of all MF goes into laminates, such as Formica.

Such was its early success that ceramic dinnerware manufacturers became worried about its long-term potential. MF plates, bowls and cups were molded with a coloured exterior and white interior, mimicking glazed ceramic (see Clay, page 480). The quality of these two materials is quite different, and with time MF's limitations became apparent. Although it does not break so easily when dropped, it is prone to chipping and the surface is vulnerable to scratching and staining.

High volumes are produced with injection molding. Only certain types are compatible and the process is severely limited compared to injection molding thermoplastics. Owing to their brittleness, it is not recommended to have any sharp features. Thin cross-sections are best avoided, because the material is very viscous and so does not flow well through confined spaces. The minimum wall thickness that can be achieved in most applications is around 2 mm (0.08 in),

although in some cases it will be possible to go thinner. As with thermoplastics, the overall wall thickness should not vary too much to avoid the part warping as a result of differential cooling.

Many thermoset parts are assembled with screws. Threads are formed in three ways: molded with threaded core, which is removed after molding; threaded insert (typically metal) is overmolded; or the thread is cut into the molded plastic part.

Compression molding is the oldest and simplest method of producing parts from these materials. The molds typically consist of only two parts: the cavity and the press side. It is inexpensive to set up and preferred for low to medium volumes, as well as being utilized for mass production. However, it is more labour-intensive than injection molding and so the unit price will be higher.

With this technique, multiple colours may be incorporated in a single piece. Each colour is molded in sequence, one on top of the other. So for example, two-tone tableware (cups, bowls and plates) is produced by compression molding the outside shape and then molding the lining directly inside. The mold half that shapes the inside profile is swapped between the first and second press to allow for the extra wall thickness.

Decoration is applied to these thermosets in-mold using a two-stage process. The resin is molded and partially cured. At this point, a decal with the desired print is placed on top of the part and the mold is clamped shut and the curing cycle completed. The print layer is encapsulated beneath a thin layer of clear resin and as the molding cycle completes it is permanently bonded to the surface of the part, encapsulating the graphics beneath.

Alternatively, decoration is applied after forming by dye sublimation (see Polyethylene Terephthalate, page 152). This process offers a great deal of flexibility and is suitable for molded products and laminates alike. However, owing to the inks used, it is not considered safe for eating utensils.

The simple split mold limits the geometries that can be achieved with compression molding. As a result, transfer

molding was developed. Bridging the gap between compression and injection, this technique allows for more complex parts than are possible with simple compression and the set-up costs remain lower than for injection molding.

These resins are applied as foam in a diversity of applications, from wet floral foam (for holding flowers in position and providing a supply of water) to building insulation. However, as a result of the potential for formaldehyde to be off-gassed during the lifetime of the product, it is no longer used in applications where air quality may be affected.

## SUSTAINABILITY

Formaldehyde can cause irritation of the eyes, skin and throat. High levels of exposure may cause some types of cancer (it has been shown to cause cancer in animals). Utilized in the production of these plastics, formaldehyde is off-gassed from the surface during their lifetime. The amount of vapour given off can increase with heat.

MF is used in eating utensils, as well as the handles of pots, pans and other kitchen equipment. The US Food and Drug Administration (FDA) and the European Food Safety Authority (EFSA) consider it safe for use in the manufacture of these items. However, even though it has high-temperature resistance (it is dishwasher safe), it is not recommended to heat or serve hot acidic food in MF because of the increased risk of melamine-formaldehyde migrating out of the plastic.

Formaldehyde is used in many applications where off-gassing may be a concern. Large-scale application in buildings – insulation foam and wood products, for example – can result in severely depleted air quality. As a result, it has been superseded in these situations by safer alternatives, such as polyurethane (PU) (page 202).

**Laminated birch plywood tray** This press-molded birch plywood tray by Silk & Burg features an MF surface. Half of all MF goes into the production of laminates. It provides a hard, durable and hygienic outer layer suitable for a range of situations. The print is applied by dye sublimation, resulting in vibrant colour.

# Unsaturated Polyester (UP) Resin

**Also known as**
UP molding compound (PMC): sheet molding compound (SMC) and bulk molding compound (BMC), which is also known as dough molding compound (DMC)
Bio-derived UP: Envirez

By far the most widely applied thermoset in composite laminating, UP resin is combined with high-strength fibres in the production of vessels, buildings and furniture. Composites utilizing UP are low-cost and provide equivalent strength-to-weight to engineering thermoplastics. They are easy to use and compatible with a range of fabrication techniques.

| Types | Typical Applications | Sustainability |
|---|---|---|
| • Room temperature curing: orthophthalic and isophthalic<br>• Polyester molding compounds (PMC) | • Furniture and interiors<br>• Automotive and marine<br>• Construction | • Impractical to recycle<br>• Off-gases volatile organic compounds (VOC) |

| Properties | Competing Materials | Costs |
|---|---|---|
| • Moderate mechanical properties<br>• High cure shrinkage<br>• Isophthalic types have superior water resistance | • Epoxy, PF, UF and MF<br>• PA, PET, PBT, POM, PEEK<br>• Steel and aluminium alloy | • Low material cost<br>• Moderate to high manufacturing cost |

## INTRODUCTION

Unsaturated polyester resin (UP) is a hard and brittle thermosetting plastic. It is used alone for small castings, mixed with a variety of fillers, or combined with high-strength-fibre reinforcement in the production of composite laminates. These are inexpensive and versatile materials compatible with a range of manufacturing techniques, from one-off to mass production.

Unlike epoxy (page 232) and formaldehyde-based resins (page 224), UP forms side-by-side cross-links, which makes them prone to brittleness. Epoxy and formaldehyde-based resins form complex three-dimensional cross-linked structures, which are far more durable.

Polyesters are produced through the reaction of certain alcohols and acids. Such is the diversity of starting ingredients that a wide variety of polyester exists. Thermosetting types, first patented in the 1930s, differ from thermoplastic polyester (see Polyethylene Terephthalate, page 152, and Polylactic Acid, page 262). They are unsaturated with double bonds between the carbon atoms. The cross-linking means they will not melt when heated.

**Fibre-reinforced-plastic (FRP) race fairing**
Production fairings are typically acrylonitrile butadiene styrene (ABS) (page 138) or polypropylene (PP) (page 98). Manufactured by hand, FRP fairings are more expensive than injection-molded thermoplastic. However, they are preferred on the track, because they are lighter and more durable, and can be readily repaired. A gel coat is applied to the mold prior to laminating. Layers of GF-reinforced UP are bonded directly to it so that when demolded, the gel coat provides a smooth outer surface. This combination provides the most cost-effective composite fairing. Superior strength-to-weight is achieved with aramid fibre (page 242) or carbon-fibre- (page 236) reinforced epoxy. But these materials are much more expensive.

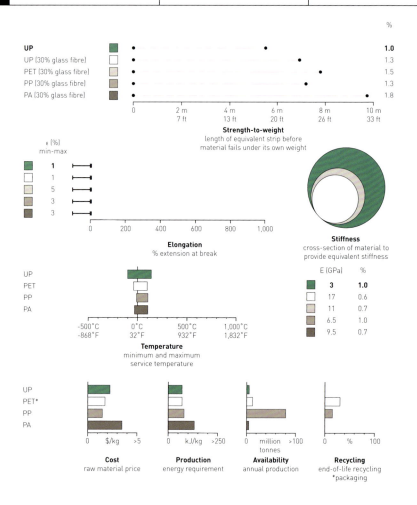

Strength-to-weight
length of equivalent strip before material fails under its own weight

| | | % |
|---|---|---|
| UP | | 1.0 |
| UP (30% glass fibre) | | 1.3 |
| PET (30% glass fibre) | | 1.5 |
| PP (30% glass fibre) | | 1.3 |
| PA (30% glass fibre) | | 1.8 |

ε (%) min-max

| | |
|---|---|
| | 1 |
| | 1 |
| | 5 |
| | 3 |
| | 3 |

Elongation
% extension at break

Stiffness
cross-section of material to provide equivalent stiffness

| E (GPa) | % |
|---|---|
| 3 | 1.0 |
| 17 | 0.6 |
| 11 | 0.7 |
| 6.5 | 1.0 |
| 9.5 | 0.7 |

Temperature
minimum and maximum service temperature

**Cost**
raw material price

**Production**
energy requirement

**Availability**
annual production

**Recycling**
end-of-life recycling
*packaging

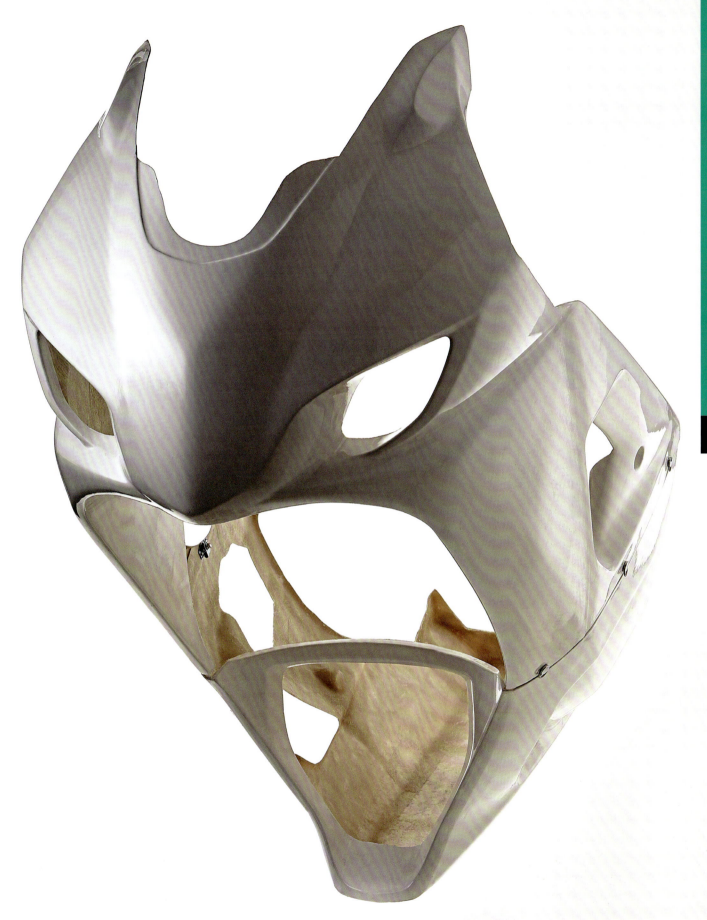

## COMMERCIAL TYPES AND USES

Liquid UP is typically supplied in solution along with up to 50% styrene monomer. The styrene allows the cross-linked polymer structure to form without any by-products (i.e. a copolymer of polyester and styrene). The curing process is inevitable and as a result, UP has a limited storage life (an inhibitor is often added to slow the process). The rate of reaction is too slow to be practical for manufacture, so a catalyst is added to promote polymerization. The catalyst (typically an organic peroxide such as methyl ethyl ketone peroxide, or MEKP) does not take part in the chemical reaction, but merely activates the process.

Carried out at room temperature, the process is exothermic (generates heat) and can reach temperatures well in excess of 100°C (212°F). This depends on the amount of catalyst used and part thickness. Filler materials are included to impart specific properties (such as flame retardance), reduce the amount of UP used (to reduce cost) and facilitate the molding process (reducing exothermic heating in thick sections, for example).

The most common partnership is with glass-fibre (GF) (page 522) reinforcement. Owing to the low-cost nature of the material, it is often used with chop strand mat (CSM) as opposed to woven GF. CSM consists of long strands of GF laid randomly on top of one another, held in place by a binder. While UP on its own is quite brittle with only moderate strength, UP reinforced with CSM is stiff and one-third lighter for the same strength. The use of continuous GF greatly improves mechanical properties: a composite consisting of 70% GF roving is around two and a half times stronger than one consisting of 30% CSM. The strength gain achieved with CSM is typically enough for the sort of situations UP is useful for. Using continuous fibres is significantly more expensive, both in terms of raw materials and production.

The strength-to-weight of UP reinforced with CSM is comparable with thermoplastics mixed with a comparable percentage of GF, including polyethylene terephthalate (PET, polyester) (page 152) and polypropylene (PP) (page 98).

Polyamide (PA, nylon) (page 164) matrix is stronger, as is polyetheretherketone (PEEK) (page 188). However, these materials are more expensive, the latter significantly so.

Material selection is not always driven by cost of raw material. Such is the simplicity of the curing and laminating process that UP does not require any expensive equipment or machinery. These composites are equally well suited to being laid up by hand or to fully automated production (such as resin transfer molding or resin infusion). This presents many opportunities for design that are quite different from those of thermoplastics. For example, there is no size limit for UP composite structures, especially those made using manual techniques. As a result, they are utilized in the production of many items that would not be practical in thermoplastics. Examples include the hulls and decks of dinghies, yachts and workboats; building façades and roofing systems; furniture and interiors; and sculpture.

UP shrinks between 5 and 10% during curing. This causes fibre reinforcement and other fillers to 'print through' and create a visible texture on the surface. Gel coats are used to minimize the visual impact. They are applied to the mold prior to laminating or molding and ensure a clean surface free from defects. They enhance surface durability too, improving resistance to wear and water absorption.

Polyester molding compounds (PMC) are a more recent development. First applied in the 1960s, they have seen significant development. There are two principal types: sheet molding compound (SMC) and bulk molding compound (BMC), which is also known as dough molding compound (DMC). They consist of a pre-mix of resin with chopped GF. The difference is that whereas SMC is used to produce sheet components with a more or less constant wall thickness, BMC (or DMC) is used to produce three-dimensional parts. SMC produced with continuous fibres will yield higher-strength parts.

The advantage of PMCs is that they are suitable for compression molding. With the application of heat and pressure, the resin and fibres flow to fill a mold cavity. This results in much shorter cycle times than composite laminating, in the region of two to five minutes. The low cost of this approach to achieving high-strength parts means PMCs compete with steel (page 28) and aluminium alloy (page 42) in some cases. Suitable for mass production, they are utilized in a range of situations including electrical and telecommunication parts, automotive parts, furniture and even parts for the construction sector (doors and roofs).

As with composite laminates, PMCs have faced stiff competition from injection-molded thermoplastic composites in recent years. While injection-molded parts may be structurally inferior, as a result of the reduced length of the fibre reinforcement, the process offers many advantages. It is typically less expensive (faster cycle times), capable of producing more complex parts with thinner wall sections, and compatible with a wider range of materials. It also results in less waste.

## SUSTAINABILITY

The main environmental impacts arise as a result of the mix of materials. They are impractical to recycle owing to their chemical structure, which is cross-linked. This means that any scrap produced in manufacture must be disposed of.

Another problem with UP is that curing produces volatile organic compound (VOC) emissions. Styrene-free and ultra-low-VOC resins exist, but their mechanical properties are typically inferior to conventional grades; they tend to be more brittle.

Similar to epoxy, certain ingredients may be swapped for renewably sourced biobased chemicals, by-products of other processes, or recycled materials. This helps to reduce the environmental impact of the raw material by lowering carbon dioxide emissions and reducing dependence on crude oil. The first commercial example, known by the trademark name Envirez, was utilized in SMC body panels for John Deere tractors. Since its introduction in 2002, many new grades have been developed, with biobased content ranging up to 22%.

**Molded FRP chair** First produced in 1950 by Herman Miller, this chair by American designer Charles Eames utilizes GF-reinforced UP. Following experimentation with laminated plywood (see Engineered Timber, page 296) and pressed steel, Eames produced a series using molded FRP. A preform of CSM is laid into the mold and soaked with resin. With heat and pressure the resin is cured. When it was realized in the late 1980s that these materials have negative environmental impacts, production at Herman Miller ceased. An alternative was released in 2001, injection molded from GF-reinforced polypropylene (PP). However, the visual, tactile and mechanical properties of these two approaches are quite different. Herman Miller has since developed a more sustainable technique for producing the FRP shell with long fibres, honouring the Eames original design without the negative aspects of conventional UP. As before, a long GF preform is soaked with resin and compression molded, resulting in the same surface variation and striation that helped make the original such an iconic and collectible design.

# Polyepoxide, Epoxy Resin

**Also known as**
Bio-derived epoxy trademark name: Super Sap

A thermosetting resin with good all-round mechanical properties, epoxy is used in adhesives, coatings and castings. One of the most important areas of application is to provide the matrix in carbon-fibre-reinforced plastic (CFRP). These composites' superior strength-to-weight and resistance to degradation has transformed entire industries, including aerospace, automotive and marine.

| Types | Typical Applications | Sustainability |
|---|---|---|
| • Room-temperature curing<br>• High-temperature curing | • Automotive, aerospace and marine<br>• Floors and worktops<br>• Coatings and adhesives | • Impractical to recycle<br>• High embodied energy |

| Properties | Competing Materials | Costs |
|---|---|---|
| • Excellent adhesion and good mechanical properties<br>• Good resistance to heat and chemicals<br>• Poor resistance to ultraviolet | • UP, PF, UF and MF<br>• PA, PET, PBT, POM, PEEK, PMMA<br>• Titanium, magnesium and aluminium alloys | • Moderate to high material cost<br>• High manufacturing cost |

232

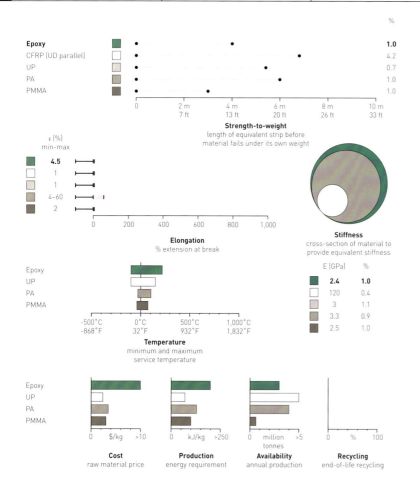

## INTRODUCTION

Epoxy differs from unsaturated polyester (UP) (page 228) resin in that a hardener (typically an amine) rather than a catalyst cures the resin. In other words, both materials take part in the chemical reaction to form the polymer. This contributes to the formation of a complex three-dimensional cross-linked structure. The reaction is irreversible and no by-products are formed.

The epoxy family is diverse, including adhesives, coatings, casting resins and laminating resins. On top of this, there are many different types of hardener. By combining the appropriate resin and hardener the properties can be tailored.

Epoxy has high adhesive strength and its surface energy is low enough to ensure very good coverage over most materials (see Polyurethane, page 202). Combined with low shrinkage, which ensures that the join area is not disturbed during curing, this ensures that a strong bond is formed. This quality is very important to epoxy's success: it is, in most cases, used in combination with other materials.

## COMMERCIAL TYPES AND USES

Epoxies are either one-part or two-part. Single-component types, also known as 'dry' or semi-solid epoxy resin (SsEP), are cured with heat: the hardener is pre-mixed with the epoxy and the two react when the temperature is sufficiently high. As a result of their chemistry they have very good heat resistance and can operate in environments up to 220°C (428°F).

**Cast resin tabletop**
Designed by Japanese architect Jo Nagasaka as a prototype for Established & Sons, 'Iro' was exhibited at London Design Festival, 2013. Brightly coloured resin encapsulates planks of Douglas-fir. The subtle wood grain is suspended beneath a polished and practical surface. Photo by Peter Guenzel; courtesy of Schemata Architects.

Such pre-mixed epoxies are used in the production of fibre-reinforced plastic (FRP). Known as prepreg, epoxy resin is impregnated into the fibre reinforcement in preparation for composite laminating. This approach ensures that the correct proportion of resin is used in combination with the fibres. This is essential to achieve the desired mechanical properties. While it is most commonly used in combination with carbon fibre (CF) (page 236), several other types are suitable, including glass (GF) (page 522) and aramid (page 242).

As an FRP matrix, epoxy competes directly with other thermoset resins, in particular UP. UP is significantly less expensive – between $1.5 and $3 per kilogram compared to around $5–20 per kilogram – and consumed in larger quantities in more industries. Epoxy offers higher thermal and mechanical properties, higher water resistance, flexible curing time and lower shrinkage.

Its low shrinkage is critical to its success. Not only does it ensure the highest bond strength and dimensional stability, it minimizes 'print-through' (fibres becoming visible on the surface).

CF-reinforced epoxy composites are used alongside and in direct competition with lightweight metal alloys – aluminium (page 42), magnesium (page 54) and titanium (page 58) – in the production of aircraft, racing cars and high-performance yachts. In mass-production situations, epoxies are limited, because they are expensive, a drawback compounded by slow production rates and the fact that the waste cannot be recycled.

Where epoxies have demonstrated the potential of plastics to replace metals, thermoplastics now show promise. Depending on the requirements of the application, various thermoplastics are used in place of thermosets, including polyamide (PA, nylon) (page 164), polyetheretherketone (PEEK) (page 188) and polypropylene (PP) (page 98). Each has its benefits and drawbacks in comparison with epoxy, but one advantage they all share as thermoplastics is that they can be formed with just heat and pressure. There is none of the mess associated with curing, volatile organic compounds (VOCs), storage issues or handling concerns. This presents many opportunities, in particular for mass production.

Room-temperature curing epoxy exists as a two-part system, whereby the hardener and epoxy are supplied separately. A slight drawback of this approach, also known as 'wet' or liquid epoxy resin (LER), is that if the chemicals are not used in exactly the correct ratio, one will be left over, which affects the final mechanical properties. As a result of the different chemistry, they have superior chemical resistance, but lower heat resistance, up to around 140°C (284°F).

The absence of heat for curing presents many opportunities for design and manufacture. The mixed resin may be poured, painted or cast before it hardens. The rate of reaction, known as 'pot life', determines how long the resin can be manipulated. The length of time depends on the type of hardener used and can range from a few seconds to several years. A long curing times reduces the likelihood of cracking in large parts.

Two-part resins are used in adhesives, coatings (water pipes, packaging, electronics, vehicles, marine, construction and interiors) and castings (model making, sculpture, furniture and jewelry). Objects are encapsulated within resin for technical reasons, as well as for decorative appeal. Furniture designers and artists have encapsulated all sorts of objects in clear and tinted resin. But in the case of electronics, an epoxy coating provides an insulating watertight jacket.

Polymethyl methacrylate (PMMA, acrylic) (page 174) and polyurethane (PU) (page 202) may be cast into similar objects and are less expensive. PMMA and epoxy have more or less equivalent mechanical properties, the difference being that epoxy is thermoset and so exhibits superior resistance. PMMA is hard enough to be polished and has superior clarity (up to 92% light transmission) and resistance to ultraviolet compared to epoxy. These properties yield very high surface quality. PU, on the other hand, is much more elastic (higher flexibility and elongation) and so is better for absorbing impacts. It has higher resistance to wear than epoxy, superior clarity and does not degrade as quickly in ultraviolet (although it too will eventually become yellow).

Both epoxy and PU are used as floor coverings. Each has its place, but on the whole, epoxy is preferred for situations that require high hardness and compressive strength, such as warehouses and distribution centres. PU is more elastic, with better grip, and so utilized in car parks and walkways.

## SUSTAINABILITY

While epoxy has contributed to lighter and more fuel-efficient transportation, it has many drawbacks. First, it is thermoset, which means it is impractical to recycle. Second, it has high embodied energy. And third, some of its ingredients are harmful to people and the environment, in particular bisphenol A (BPA) monomer (see also Polycarbonate, page 144). BPA is a key ingredient of epoxy resin, alongside epichlorohydrin (ECH). It is estimated that around 85% of all epoxy is derived from reacting these two ingredients.

Such is the negative impact of epoxies that alternatives are continually being sought. Once such material, Super Sap by Entropy Resins, uses biobased and renewable ingredients. Their raw materials are co-products or waste products of other industrial processes, and 37% is biobased. As a result, they claim that production of their materials produces half of the greenhouse gas emissions of conventional petroleum-based epoxy. So far, they have developed resin systems and viscosities suitable for laminating, resin infusion, compression molding and casting.

**Experiments in resin** This series of experimental materials, created by Ansel Thompson, demonstrates the artistic potential of epoxy resin. Top: brightly coloured sheets of epoxy are cut into strips and laid within a white epoxy matrix to create an undulating linear pattern. Middle: clear casting resin is combined with strips of anodized aluminium. The ripples cast shadows through the material, creating a unique visual quality depending on the angle of view. Bottom: aluminium foam is filled with resin and polished. Each cell takes on a different shade of grey, depending on the shape of foam behind.

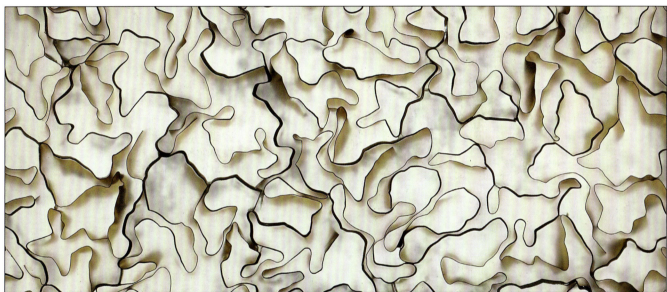

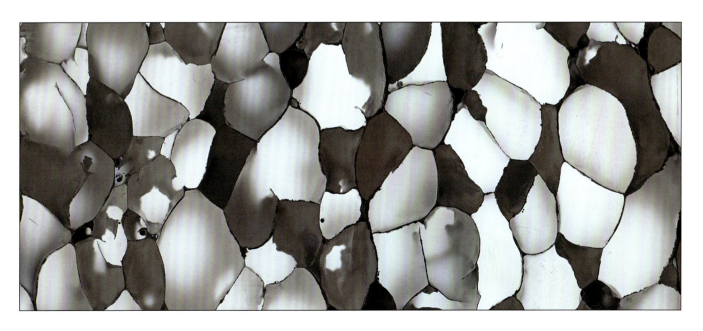

# Carbon-Fibre-Reinforced Plastic (CFRP)

Fibres consisting of very strong crystalline carbon filaments are used to strengthen plastic and concrete. The fibres are short and randomly mixed in, or continuous and oriented according to the anticipated loads. Carbon fibre is compatible with thermoplastic and thermoset matrices; material selection depends on the application. The ultimate properties depend on the material mix.

| Types | Typical Applications | Sustainability |
|---|---|---|
| • CF: ultra-high-modulus (UHM); high-modulus (HM); intermediate-modulus; high-tensile (HT); and super-high-tensile (SHT) | • Automotive and aerospace<br>• Sports and military<br>• Construction | • Composites are impractical to recycle, although the high value of carbon fibre presents a significant incentive |

| Properties | Competing Materials | Costs |
|---|---|---|
| • High strength-to-weight<br>• Stiff and brittle<br>• High resistance to heat and chemicals<br>• Conductive | • PBO, aramid and UHMWPE fibre<br>• Glass and steel fibre<br>• Aluminium, magnesium and titanium alloys | • Material costs are high, but have been steadily decreasing thanks to increased demand<br>• Moderate to high manufacturing costs |

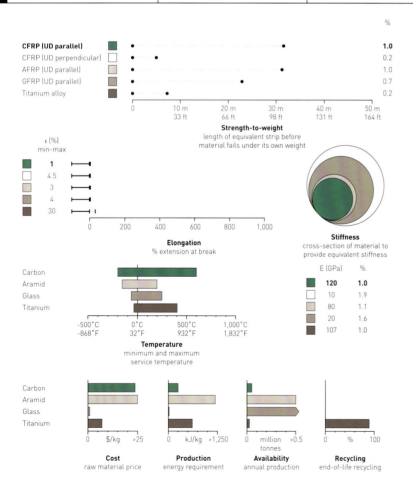

## INTRODUCTION

Commercially available since the 1960s, carbon fibre (CF) has some exceptional properties. Made up of carbon crystals, it is available only in black; and it is not the strongest of the so-called super fibres – ultra-high-molecular-weight polyethylene (UHMWPE) (see Polyethylene, page 108) and polyphenylene benzobisthiazole (PBO) (page 246) have higher strength-to-weight. CF is unique for its combination of strength, stiffness and stability as well as its resistance to weathering, chemicals and high temperatures.

CF is the product of oxidizing polyacrylonitrile (PAN), or acrylic fibre (page 180). Tightly bonded carbon crystals form in-line with fibre orientation. CF contains at least 90% carbon. Fibres with higher concentrations of carbon (upwards of 99%) are referred to as graphite. There are other types of polymer precursor, such as viscose (page 252), but PAN is by far the most common. The quality and performance of CF are highly dependent on the consistency and crystallinity of the precursor.

Until recently, CF was very expensive because of the high cost of production. Increased demand, in particular from automotive and aerospace, has led to a reduction in price over the years; it is now a fraction of the price it was only a decade ago. This price drop combined with developments in mass-production manufacturing techniques, has led to the adoption of CFRP in numerous high-end consumer products.

## COMMERCIAL TYPES AND USES

While there are many different types of CF, from low to high modulus (an indication of stiffness) and increasing in tensile strength, there are many different configurations of CFRP possible, including off-the-shelf and bespoke patterns. This presents numerous opportunities for design.

Based on the properties of CF, it can be categorized as follows (ultimate tensile strength given in GPa): ultra-high-modulus (UHM) (>2.25); high-modulus (HM) (1.52.5); intermediate-modulus (IM) (4.5); high-tensile (HT) (3.3); and super-high-tensile (SHT) (>4.5). It is further categorized according to heat treatment. Ranging from around 1,000°C to 2,000°C (1,832–3,632°F), higher treatment temperatures result in higher strength and stiffness.

Fibre-reinforced plastic (FRP) – regardless of whether it is CFRP, aramid-fibre-reinforced plastic (AFRP) (page 242), glass-fibre-reinforced plastic (GFRP) (see Unsaturated Polyester, page 228) or another type of fibre altogether – is categorized according to the combination of materials and orientation of the fibres.

FRPs are produced with thermoplastic and thermoset resin. The main difference between these two matrices is that thermoplastics can be formed through heating and melting, and thermosets cannot because the polymer chains form permanent cross-links. As a result, different manufacturing processes are required for each: whereas thermoplastics are melt-processible (injection molding and thermoforming, for example), thermosets are laid up and cured in a one-way reaction (such as compression molding and prepreg lamination).

As well as the design opportunities and constraints of these different approaches, the two groups of materials have distinct properties. Thermoplastics cover a broad performance spectrum, including low-cost and resilient polypropylene (PP) (page 98), strong

**Composite football boot** The Nike Mercurial football boot sole plate consists of CF-reinforced thermoplastic polyurethane (TPU) (see TPE, page 194). The plate is overmolded with TPE and bonded to the shoe upper like a conventional boot. The stiffness of CF combined with the elasticity of TPU is said to improve acceleration. The perceived benefits justify a high price tag and this has not gone unnoticed: as well as football boots, CF-reinforced TPU has appeared in cycling shoes, ski boots, trainers (and even laptops and mobile phones).

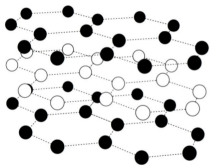

**Carbon fibre crystal structure** Through prolonged heat treatment, the hydrogen and nitrogen are expelled from PAN, to leave behind planes of carbon atoms in a hexagonal lattice structure (see also PAN, page 180). Only weak forces act between the planes, which allows them to slide over one another (this makes graphite brittle and is why a pencil leaves a mark). The planes are oriented along the length of the fibre, entangled with one another (carbon fibres's exceptional strength comes from this interlocking). Prolonging the heat treatment results in the formation of almost pure graphite.

and tough polyamide (PA, nylon) (page 164) and exceptionally resistant fluoropolymers (page 190). The formation of physical cross-links in the structure of thermosets results in a plastic with greater resistance to heat and chemicals. Their tensile strength is not so great – see epoxy (page 232) and unsaturated polyester (UP) (page 228), for example – but they tend to be harder and more durable than thermoplastics.

CF is most commonly paired with epoxy, because together they provide exceptional strength and durability. This combination is compatible with a range of manufacturing processes, including prepreg lamination (panels for racing cars and aerospace), compression molding (high-volume production parts for automotive and sports products) and filament winding (cylindrical parts for automotive and industry).

Combining CF with thermoplastics expands the range of geometry opportunities. CF is compatible with all forms of thermoplastics, including injection-molded parts (sports and

**Composite bicycle frame** The goal for the Colnago C60 was to make a more efficient bicycle design, with no sacrifice in strength or reliability and causing less rider fatigue. A mix of cylindrical and star-shaped tubes is used. The various cross-sections help to reduce weight, because increasing volume allows for thinner wall sections than is possible with alloy tube.

The CF-reinforced parts of the frame – profiled head tube, oversized down tube, asymmetric seat tube, bottom bracket lug and forks – are formed individually and assembled together. Hollow parts are molded using inflatable bellows to ensure a consistent internal profile. The finished frame is painted, concealing the CFRP beneath. Photo courtesy of Colnago.

automotive parts), sheet parts (yachts, racing cars, aerospace) and film laminations (construction, racing sails).

Akin to graphite, CF is highly conductive. This is advantageous in some cases and problematic in others. As well as the benefits associated with conductivity in certain end uses (anti-static shielding, for example), it presents a significant challenge when used in combination with metals owing to the risk of galvanic corrosion. This occurs when conductive materials with contrasting nobility come into contact in the presence of an electrolyte. The more active material acts as the anode and is thus corroded. Lightweight alloys, including aluminium (page 42) and magnesium (page 54), are prone to severe galvanic corrosion when used in combination with CFRP. Therefore, they must be insulated from one another. By contrast, titanium alloy (page 58) and CFRP do not corrode one another – a significant advantage in weight-critical applications, in particular in aerospace.

## SUSTAINABILITY

The process is complex and energy-intensive: carbonization is carried out in a controlled atmosphere in excess of 2,600°C (4,712°F) for a number of hours. Higher temperatures yield higher quality and higher strength of fibre. As with similar high-performance materials, the potential weight savings associated with CFRP help to offset the large amount of energy that goes into producing it.

Composites are challenging to recycle. However, thanks to growing demand and the high price of CF, recycling initiatives are under way that aim to reverse this trend. While melting or burning can remove thermoplastic matrix, thermosetting plastic (the most commonly used matrix) must be dissolved.

Research has demonstrated that press-molded composites, comprising 50% recovered CF and 50% thermoplastic, offer half the tensile strength and 90% of the tensile modulus of an equivalent composite based on virgin materials. Even so, owing to the inherent challenges, a reliable source of recycled CF is still some way off.

**Composite surfboard fin** Produced by Californian surfboard brand Futures Fins, this design comprises a mix of materials for ultimate ride performance. The shape, foil and flexibility are all carefully considered in fin construction, as they collectively contribute to the board's performance. This example consists of both CFRP and GFRP; and the honeycomb structure is a nonwoven polyethylene terephthalate (PET, polyester) (page 152) core material (also known by its trademark name Lantor Soric). Using a process known as resin infusion (a development on resin transfer molding), the CF and GF are assembled around the nonwoven core, placed into a closed mold and epoxy is drawn in under vacuum. The honeycomb cells of the core are separated by canals, through which the resin can flow. Once cured, this creates a plastic honeycomb, adding strength while minimizing weight (the honeycomb has very low resin uptake and saves around one-third of the weight compared to solid laminate).

**Unidirectional**

**Plain**

**Twill**

**Satin**

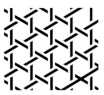

**Triaxial**

**Bespoke**

CF, as with other high-strength filaments, is strongest in tension. Therefore, fibre arrangement is a critical factor in the overall strength-to-weight of CFRP parts. Unidirectional fabrics are constructed with yarns running in parallel to align all of the yarns' strength. They are typically applied in layers, oriented according to the precalculated stress. Woven fabrics, on the other hand, are typically standard configurations. They consist of warp yarns (running lengthwise in the direction of the loom) and weft yarns, also called filling yarns (running widthwise). Plain weave is the simplest of all (also called 0-90 and biaxial). Each warp goes over and under the adjacent wefts, and vice versa, known as a 1/1 weave.

The face and back are identical. Using the same pattern, but weaving groups of two or more warps with the same number of wefts, produces a basket weave. There are fewer interlacings, making these fabrics more pliable. In twill weave, each warp or weft floats across two or more weft or warp yarns, or 2/1. Satin weaves have at least four floats for every overlap, or 4/1. Triaxial weave is made with two warps and one weft. The yarns are interlaced at 60 degrees to create a fabric with greater dimensional stability. It is light and strong and typically uses only half the number of yarns as a plain weave. Alternatively, yarns are laid down in a bespoke configuration to maximize strength and minimize the amount of material required.

**Strength-to-weight**
Compared to conventional monolithic engineering materials, CFRP offers exceptional weight savings. However, strength is highly dependent on fibre orientation: perpendicular strength is only around 20% of longitudinal strength.

**Stiffness**
CFRP has higher rigidity than other fibre-reinforced plastics and high-performance metal alloys, but is less stiff than steel and certain copper alloys.

**Durability**
CFRP is very durable and resistant to fatigue, which means that these parts will not wear out as quickly as metal alternatives.

**Corrosion resistance**
Combined with epoxy, or other suitable thermoset, CF offers exceptional resistance to corrosion. However, polymers are vulnerable to moisture ingress.

**Conductive**
The high conductivity of CF is useful for certain applications, such as providing anti-static shielding. However, it causes galvanic corrosion when in contact with certain metals, in particular aluminium and magnesium.

## CFRP IN AUTOMOTIVE AND AEROSPACE

Through developments in production and engineering, CF is becoming widespread in automotive and aerospace. In the past, its high price tag limited applications to low-volume high-value parts. Through economies of scale, the price has come down to the point at which CFRP is suitable for use in mass-production applications. Once commercialized, innovation in these sectors quickly becomes available elsewhere, such as has been witnessed in the consumer goods, sports, recreation and construction of recent years.

Utilizing CFRP reduces the weight of aircraft by around 20% compared to conventional aluminium alloys, which reduces fuel consumption. There are now numerous significant applications in aerospace, including the Airbus A350's fuselage (four-skin panel sections assembled onto frames) and wings, and the Boeing 787's airframe and primary structure. CFRP is used wherever tension loads are prevalent, and avoided in parts that will be subjected to compression. The opposite is true for aluminium, titanium and steel. As a result, more than half of these aircraft are FRP, around 20% aluminium and 15% titanium.

Vehicles and vessels see similar benefits to aircraft: compared to steel and aluminium CFRP saves around 50% and 30% weight respectively. Racing cars and yachts have, for a long time, been primarily constructed from CF-reinforced epoxy. A major consideration for mass-production transportation is the safety of passengers in a crash. A limitation of

CFRP is its brittleness; whereas metal deforms on impact, CFRP shatters. Racing drivers are protected by a super-strong monocoque structure, constructed from thick sections of CF. The same approach has been adopted for production cars, albeit pared down to make it cost-effective. For example, in the case of the BMW i3 electric car, the CFRP inner body (partial monocoque) is mounted onto an aluminium chassis (supporting running gear, suspension and chassis) and the outer body is constructed from plastic panels.

As a result of its crystal structure, CF is anisotropic and is strongest along its length. The bonds between the crystal planes are relatively weak, making CF brittle and prone to failure when bent. Thus, fibre orientation is critical to maximizing strength-to-weight. A huge range of fibre configurations exists, from standard weave patterns to technical fabrics created solely for composite lamination.

Each configuration has its benefits. Unidirectional fabrics provide a great deal of control, because each layer can be oriented differently, from anywhere between 0 and 90 degrees. Biaxial woven fabrics are oriented at 0 and 90 degrees. Plain weave provides a balanced appearance: the front and back look identical. The high number of overlaps gives a high level of crimp, which results in relatively low mechanical properties compared to other weave styles (spreading out the fibres to produce low-profile tape reduces crimp). Twill fabrics provide higher drape, because there are fewer interlacings between warp and weft. Satin weave allows the fibre to be woven in the closest proximity. Essentially an extension of twill weave, satin weaves are flat and have a high degree of drape. However, because of the low number of interlacings, they can be tricky to work with, because the fibres readily slip out of alignment.

Fabrics are cut into patterns, similar to garment making, and draped around three-dimensional profiles. Joins are staggered wherever possible in order to reduce the potential weaknesses. They are typically applied as prepreg, by which the resin is pre-impregnated into the fibre reinforcement. This technique ensures the correct proportion of resin, which is critical to ensure predictable and optimum properties.

Braiding and filament winding are used to construct seamless tubular structures. The difference between these two is that while braiding creates a weave pattern, filament winding overlaps the fibres. The latter approach is much more versatile, because fibre orientation can be modified with each layer, maximizing strength-to-weight. It is, of course, more time-consuming, so braiding is preferred for high-volume applications.

The most advanced composite arrangement is achieved with bespoke fibre placement. According to CAD data, fibres are laid-down along predetermined lines of stress. They are placed by a computer-guided head and held in place through lamination. While this is the most complex and time-consuming, the weight savings and thus competitive advantage justify the cost in applications such as racing sails (see Aramid, page 242), Formula One and spacecraft.

**Composite door module** Manufactured by Prodrive for an Aston Martin GT3 competition car, this door module is produced from CF prepreg. The panels are cut and laid into the mold by hand (to ensure consistency the mold is accompanied by a detailed instruction manual). Once prepared, the mold and CF prepreg are placed into a sealed bag and a vacuum is applied. This is placed into an autoclave, in which the temperature and pressure are raised to cure the resin matrix.

# Aromatic Polyamide, Aramid

**Also known as**
P-aramid trademark names: Kevlar, Twaron, Technora
M-aramid trademark names: Nomex, Conex

Invented around 50 years ago, aramid fibre is utilized in high-performance protective clothing, sports equipment and lightweight composite laminates. Better known as Kevlar and Twaron, its trademark names, aramid fibre is strong and stiff with excellent cut and heat resistance. It is naturally bright golden yellow and also available in black.

| Types | Typical Applications | Sustainability |
|---|---|---|
| • Para-aramid (p-aramid)<br>• Meta-aramid (m-aramid) | • Automotive, aerospace and industrial textiles<br>• Protective clothing<br>• Racing and sports products | • Very energy-intensive to produce<br>• Impractical to recycle |
| **Properties** | **Competing Materials** | **Costs** |
| • High strength and stiffness, with low creep<br>• High resistance to heat and abrasion<br>• Poor resistance to ultraviolet | • Glass, carbon, PBO and UHMWPE<br>• PA and PPA | • High material cost<br>• High manufacturing cost |

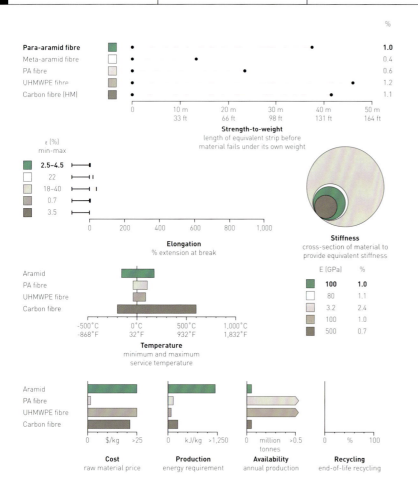

## INTRODUCTION

Aramid includes a range of high-performance synthetic fibres. While some types are renowned for their resistance to penetration, others are prized for their inherent heat resistance and flame-retardant properties.

Used alone, or in combination with other so-called super fibres – carbon (CF) (page 236), glass (GF) (page 522), fluoropolymer (page 190) and ultra-high-molecular-weight polyethylene (UHMWPE) (see Polyethylene, page 108) – aramid offers a unique set of properties. Compared to CF it is less brittle and has greater resistance to fatigue (it does not lose strength through repeated flexing); it has higher strength-to-weight than GF; it is far less expensive than fluoropolymer; and it has low creep (resistance to deformation under load) and high heat resistance compared to UHMWPE. However, it is vulnerable to ultraviolet and does not tolerate compressive forces.

The difference between aramid and polyamide (PA, nylon) (page 164) is that aramid has an aromatic structure (polymer backbone consists of closed rings of atoms) and PA is aliphatic (linear or branched polymer chains). Aramid has a high proportion of aromatic content, which provides it with high dimensional stability and heat resistance. Its strength is due to the rigid rod-like molecular structure, which forms a highly oriented crystalline polymer.

## COMMERCIAL TYPES AND USES

The two principal types are meta-aramid (m-aramid) and para-aramid (p-aramid). DuPont developed m-aramid in the 1960s and continues to produce it under the trademark name Nomex. Similar in appearance to PA, m-aramid is made up of poly meta-phenylene isophthalamide (MPIA). It is not as strong as PA or

p-aramid (the polymer structure does not align as efficiently during spinning), but has superior heat resistance and dimensional stability. At the point at which PA fibre melts – around 250°C (482°F) – m-aramid retains two-thirds of its strength; it does not break down fully until around 370°C (698°F). It has good low-temperature properties too and does not show embrittlement until around -160°C (-256°F).

It is used in applications that require high-temperature stability and flame resistance, such as in aircraft, racing cars and protective apparel. As well as being applied directly in fibre form (woven, knitted and braided textiles), it is utilized in fireproof nonwovens, such as in the production of honeycomb core composite panels. Where high strength is required, m-aramid is reinforced with p-aramid.

Introduced commercially by DuPont in the early 1970s, p-aramid presented a breakthrough in high-strength fibres.

**Motorcycle jeans**
Aramid is perhaps best known for its use in protective apparel. As well as the obvious – bulletproof vests and heat-resistant gloves – it can be found concealed in more everyday attire. These motorcycle jeans, manufactured by Hood Jeans, feature a woven p-aramid lining that extends down to the shins. The superior cut and abrasion resistance of p-aramid provides the wearer with enhanced protection in the event of a tumble down the tarmac.

Hailed as the strongest fibre for its weight, it has since been surpassed by other so-called super fibres, including UHMWPE and polyphenylene benzobisthiazole (PBO) (page 246). These fibres are used alone, or combined for ultimate strength and durability.

It is commonly referred to by its trademark names, most notably Kevlar and Twaron. Technora is a black-coloured aramid (solution-dyed) produced by Teijin.

Made up of poly-paraphenylene terephthalamide (PPTA), p-aramid fibre is produced using the dry-jet wet-spinning technique. The polymer is dissolved in concentrated sulphuric acid solvent and extruded through a spinneret. The spinneret is placed a short distance above the coagulation bath so the fresh fibres pass through air prior to solvent. The liquid crystal domains orient and align in the direction of flow. The crystal alignment is further refined with heat treatment, which yields fibres with a tensile modulus two or more times greater and half the elongation.

It is available in a variety of textile formats, including filament, staple (short lengths), roving (bundle of parallel filaments), spun yarn, textured yarn and nonwoven. Fibres and yarns are compatible with conventional weaving, knitting and braiding techniques. End uses include high-strength rope and cord (parachutes and rescue ropes), protective clothing (bulletproof vests, cut-resistant gloves and extreme sportswear), speaker cones and industrial fabrics.

P-aramid textiles are utilized in laminated composites. As fibre reinforcement, a significant advantage of p-aramid, compared to PBO and carbon, is that it is less brittle and has higher resistance to fatigue. Therefore, it performs equally well in flexible and rigid composites. Examples of flexible end uses include sailcloth (in combination with polyethylene terephthalate [PET, polyester, page 152] film), tyres (combined with synthetic rubber, page 216) and inflatables (with polyurethane [PU], page 202, or synthetic rubber). Rigid (and semi-rigid) composites include panels for automotive and aerospace; molded racing boat hulls, propellers (aircraft and wind turbines),

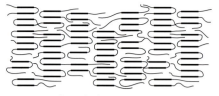

**Conventional oriented polymer**

**Liquid crystal polymer (LCP)**

**Polymer structure** The aromatic rings (see page 166) ensure that the monomers join together into straight, unbroken chains. There is very little amorphous region and the polymer chains pack into a neat and highly oriented crystal structure, even without drawing. This results in a fibre with significantly higher tenacity, stiffness and chemical resistance. Its highly oriented structure, a phenomenon referred to as liquid crystal, contrasts with the random arrangement of conventional oriented polymer structure (consisting of entangled amorphous and crystalline regions). The structure of aramid is anisotropic and so gives much higher strength and modulus along the length of the fibre. Repeated bending and compression causes kink bands and fibrillation (separation of the rod-like structure) to occur.

lightweight construction (cantilevered roofs); sports products; consumer electronics (it is non-conductive and so suitable for phone and tablet back covers); and rigid ballistic protection (helmets and vehicle protection).

In addition to prefabricated textiles for composites, a range of advanced fibre-placement technologies has been developed to make the most of super fibres' exceptional properties (see also Carbon-Fibre-Reinforced Plastic, page 236). Alternatively, filaments are cut into short lengths (staples) and injection molded with thermoplastic. Aramid has higher strength-to-weight than glass fibre (GF) and performs very well in fatigue. However, it is significantly more expensive and because its compressive properties are poor it is limited to tension-dominated end uses.

Similar to PBO, which also has a liquid crystal polymer (LCP) structure, bending and compression cause the rod-like molecular structure to come apart (fibrillate) and develop kink bands, which reduces tensile strength. In the

case of composite laminations, the extent to which the fibres can bend is limited. However, because knot and loop strength is only around one-third of tensile strength, end terminations for rope and cable are of concern. With the correct end fittings the full strength of aramid is maintained in tensile applications.

The same characteristics that make aramid weak in buckling provide exceptional toughness. During failure, the kinks and micro-fibrillation absorb a great deal of energy. This ability to absorb energy is what makes aramid useful for ballistic protection.

## SUSTAINABILITY

Aramid is an energy-intensive material to produce: per unit weight it has relatively high embodied energy compared to other synthetic fibres. At the end of its useful life it is impractical to recycle, especially if it is in composite form. Aramid is mainly used in safety-critical applications, wherein the materials must be reliable and predictable. Therefore, only new material is used.

Used in ballistic protection, aramid boasts life-saving qualities. And as with other high-performance materials, it has contributed to lighter-weight transportation, which goes some way towards offsetting the high embodied energy.

**Fibre-reinforced racing sail laminate** In the construction of lightweight racing sails, p-aramid is used alongside other super fibres, including carbon (the black fibres in this construction) and UHMWPE. They are all very strong and are selected for their complementary properties: p-aramid fibre has excellent energy absorption and resistance to abrasion; carbon fibre is stiff with exceptional tensile modulus; and UHMWPE has higher strength-to-weight than p-aramid coupled with high resilience (less prone to breaking when flexed). Rovings are sandwiched between films of PET. They are laid along predetermined lines of stress to minimize the amount of fibre and thus keep weight to the absolute minimum.

# Polyphenylene Benzobisthiazole (PBO)

**This so-called super fibre exhibits the highest strength and stiffness of any polymer; it outperforms steel, aramid and carbon. It is expensive and utilized in the highest-performance applications. Examples include racing boat rigging, bow strings and tethers for aerospace and Formula One. It is available in a range of standard colours, including gold, brown and black.**

| Types | Typical Applications | Sustainability |
|---|---|---|
| • PBO fibre: as spun (AS) and high modulus (HM) | • Protective clothing<br>• Sports<br>• Rope and rigging | • Not practical to recycle<br>• Production is energy-intensive |

| Properties | Competing Materials | Costs |
|---|---|---|
| • Very high strength and stiffness<br>• Poor resistance to abrasion, ultraviolet and moisture | • Fibres including ePTFE, LCP, UHMWPE, aramid, carbon and glass | • Very expensive, but not quite as high as PTFE fibre |

246

## INTRODUCTION

Often compared to para-aramid (page 242), another so-called super fibre, polyphenylene benzobisthiazole (PBO) exhibits superior strength and stiffness. It has almost zero creep (non-recoverable stretch after prolonged load) and very low elongation (it stretches only around 3%).

## COMMERCIAL TYPES AND USES

PBO is an aromatic (see page 166) heterocyclic rigid-rod polymer consisting of oxazole rings. This structure is even more rigid than that of aramid and is even more challenging to manufacture. It has been commercialized by only one company, Toyobo (Japan), under the trademark name Zylon.

Two types of fibre are available: as spun (AS), which is subsequently heat-treated (500–700°C [932–1,292°F]) to form high modulus (HM). The key differences are that HM fibre has significantly higher tensile modulus, lower elongation at break and lower moisture regain (0.6%, versus 2% for AS fibre).

PBO has poor resistance to abrasion, ultraviolet and moisture. When exposed to the elements, moisture and ultraviolet cause breakages to occur in the aromatic ring structure (as a result of hydrolysis), which significantly decreases the strength and reliability of the fibre. As a result, it is not recommended for use outdoors without adequate protection. This flaw was tragically exposed by PBO police body armour failing to prevent a bullet from penetrating (the officer survived, but sustained severe injuries).

Protection is applied in different ways, depending on the application requirements. For example, braided rope is wrapped with a synthetic jacket, and woven or nonwoven textiles are laminated between synthetic films.

PBO decomposes at high temperature

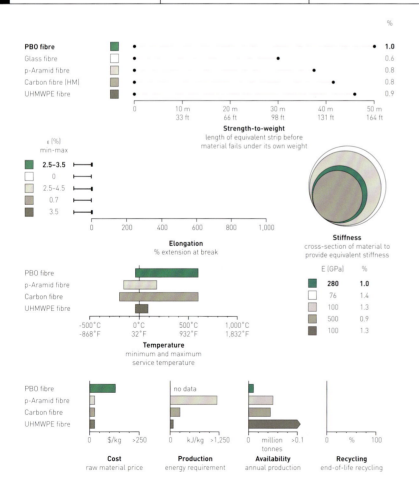

– degradation does not begin until around 650°C (1,202°F) – without melting. It exhibits excellent flame resistance and is affected by very few solvents thanks to the rigid molecular backbone. As a result of its unique properties, PBO is utilized in some very demanding applications, including protective clothing, sports products (such as bow strings and bicycle tyres) and as reinforcement in composites.

Braided PBO rope and cable are used for racing yacht rigging and tethers (industrial, aerospace and racing cars). Securing the rope presents a challenge, because tying a knot reduces the strength of PBO by around one-third (bending causes kink bands and fibrillation to occur). Strength is further reduced if the knot is subjected to cyclic loads. While splicing offers a reasonable solution, it is more reliable to apply end fittings or terminations. With the correct fittings, PBO offers weight savings of up to 65% compared to steel wire or rod.

## SUSTAINABILITY

Production is energy-intensive and so embodied energy (no data available) will be higher than commodity fibres.

Similar to aramid, it is converted from raw material into fibre by solvent spinning, specifically dry-jet wet spinning (a variant of wet spinning). In this method, polymerization is carried out in phosphoric acid solvent. The polymer solution is extruded above the coagulation bath, and so passes through atmosphere before entering the bath. The air gap prevents the formation of micro voids, which negatively affect PBO fibre properties.

Dry-jet wet spinning uses harmful chemicals. Even so, the advantage of this method is that in liquid form chemicals are more easily controlled and may even be reclaimed or recycled.

**Plaited rope jacket**
This 24-plait jacket is braided with two parallel PBO yarn and encapsulates a UHMWPE core. Developed for racing yachts, PBO rope offers exceptional strength and delivers smooth and accurate control on winches, even under extreme loads. It can be used unprotected in applications where longevity is not an issue.

# Natural Rubber and Latex

**Natural rubber latex is present in many species of plant, but the majority is derived from the Pará rubber tree of the Amazon basin. It has been used to waterproof clothing and shelter for more than a millennium. Since its chemistry was unlocked it has faced stiff competition from synthetic alternatives, but nevertheless remains a widely used and commercially important engineering material.**

| Types | Typical Applications | Sustainability |
|---|---|---|
| • Latex: high or low ammonia<br>• Sheet rubber: pale crepe, air-dried sheet (ADS) and ribbed smoked sheet (RSS)<br>• Technically specified rubber (TSR) | • Tyres, tubes and seals<br>• Waterproof textiles<br>• Upholstery and cushioning | • Low embodied energy<br>• Some people are allergic to the proteins in latex<br>• Can be fair trade and certified |

| Properties | Competing Materials | Costs |
|---|---|---|
| • Superior resilience<br>• Tough and elastic<br>• High tear strength | • Synthetic rubber, PU and silicone<br>• TPE, PVC and EVA | • Low to moderate raw material costs<br>• Moderate production costs |

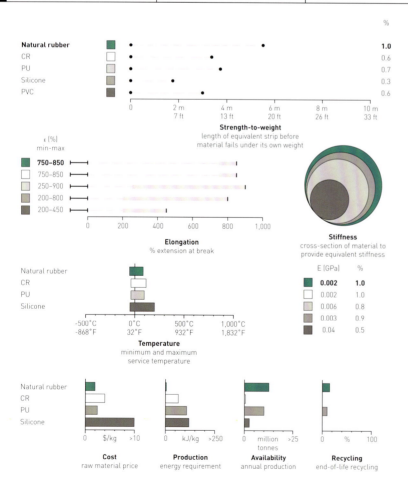

## INTRODUCTION

Although Scottish surgeon James Syme invented rubberized fabric, it was Charles Macintosh who patented a method fit for the high street in 1823. Soon after, in 1839, Charles Goodyear learned that the addition of heat and sulphur alters the consistency of rubber, later to be known as the vulcanization process. His discovery revolutionized the rubber industry.

The use of rubber in pneumatic tyres greatly increased demand for the raw material. Produced from the sap of the Pará rubber tree, it had a limited production area of the tropical regions of South America, Africa and Asia. When supplies were cut off during World War I and II, the development of synthetic alternatives was accelerated.

Today, there are many different types of synthetic rubber (page 216), which are widely available and of reliable composition. One was even developed using the same polymer backbone, polyisoprene. Even so, natural rubber remains an important material for critical applications, because it has very high resilience, tensile strength, elongation, abrasion resistance, tear strength and fatigue resistance. Hardness ranges from Shore A 30 to 90. While there is no single direct replacement

**Rubber-bonded cotton jacket** Created by Hancock, this jacket is constructed from a layer of vulcanized rubber sandwiched between two layers of cotton. To ensure the jacket is watertight, all of the seams are bonded with rubber glue. Made by hand, these jackets involve a great deal of craftsmanship in their production. Thomas Hancock, the English inventor instrumental in the development of the original Mackintosh coat in the 1820s, was the historical inspiration behind this new British brand, co-founded in 2012 to produce modern macs based on the original elegant solution. Photo courtesy of Hancock.

that competes equally in all areas, individual properties have been improved on with synthetic rubbers.

## COMMERCIAL TYPES AND USES

The term 'latex' describes any polymer in a water-based liquid state. In other words, it is not restricted to natural rubber. Natural rubber latex is the white sap derived from the rubber tree, or other suitable plant. It is refined and processed to make it suitable for use in dip molding or coating. Or, it is further processed and dried to make rubber.

There are several types of rubber raw material. When tapped from the tree, ammonia is added to preserve it. Concentrated latex is sap that has been centrifuged to around 60% dry rubber content (DRC). There are two main types: high ammonia (HA) and low ammonia (LA). The difference is 0.6–0.8% versus 0.2–0.3% ammonia respectively. HA is the most common type and is used as the starting material for dip molding. Products include gloves, balloons and condoms. LA latex is used in situations where air quality could be affected.

Prior to application, the latex concentrate is compounded with additives, including vulcanizing agents (sulphur, activator and accelerator), stabilizer pigments and fillers. It is applied using a range of processes, including dip molding, casting, foaming and spraying. Pre-vulcanized latex is the most straightforward to use and simply requires drying after application. Vulcanizing latex is less expensive, but requires heating post-forming to activate the cross-linking agents.

Pale crepe rubber is completely white. It is produced from latex that has been thoroughly washed and coagulated with sodium hydrogen sulphite. It is milled as thin (around 1 mm [0.04 in]) and thick (3–5 mm [0.1–0.2 in]) sheets. Thicker sheets, such as sole crepe (15 mm [0.6 in]), consist of many layers laminated together. In addition to the high-quality pale crepe, there are several other types produced from rubber scrap.

Ribbed smoked sheet (RSS) is made directly from latex that has been treated and coagulated with formic acid or acetic acid. It is air dried and smoked in ovens to vulcanize. It is lower quality than pale crepe, with a higher proportion of contaminates. Air-dried sheet (ADS) is produced in smoke-free rooms, which results in an unvulcanized and more transparent material.

Technically specified rubber (TSR), also known as block rubber, is graded according to precise parameters defined by ISO and according to country of origin. Examples include Standard Malaysian Rubber (SMR) (previously known as Hevea crumb) and Standard Indonesian Rubber (SIR). Produced from latex and dry rubber, the ingredients are carefully controlled to ensure desirable properties. It has become the most widely traded form of raw rubber. Its consistency makes it suitable for more technically demanding applications, such as tyres and gaskets. Indeed, aviation tyres contain a high proportion of natural rubber, as do tractor and truck tyres.

Skim rubber is produced as a by-product of latex concentrate. It has low DRC, around 5%, and is processed in much the same way as RSS.

Raw rubber is masticated (shredded) and compounded (mixed and combined with fillers) in preparation for use. It is formed into the desired shape, such as with extrusion, molding and calendering. At this stage, the polyisoprene chains are held together by weak chemical bonds, which allows them to be pressed into shape. Through exposure to heat and sulphur (vulcanization), usually with activators and accelerators, permanent physical cross-links are formed that hold the material in shape (see Polyurethane, page 202). This is what makes rubber a useful material: it will always try to spring back to its original shape when deformed.

Natural rubber is frequently blended with other rubbers to achieve desirable properties, ideally at a lower price. For example, in the case of automobile tyres, natural rubber is mixed with polybutadiene rubber (BR) and styrene butadiene rubber (SBR).

Compression molding is the simplest way to make rubber products and is often the most economical. With heat and pressure, rubber is forced into the mold cavity and vulcanization occurs after a set period of time. Bridging the gap between compression and injection, transfer molding is used for more complex parts. A slug of rubber is forced into a close mold cavity under pressure. Injection molding is limited by the high cost of the molds. Utilized for high volumes of parts, faster cycle times lead to lower unit price.

## SUSTAINABILITY

The majority of the raw material is tapped from the Pará rubber tree (*Hevea brasiliensis*). Many other species of plant produce latex and, in recent years, new types of rubber have emerged from alternative sources. For example, Yulex produces certified rubber from the sap of the guayule plant (*Parthenium argentatum*). Its processes are sustainable and the raw materials are renewable, making this a very exciting development. In its pursuit of sustainability, Patagonia has combined Yulex guayule rubber with polychloroprene rubber (CR) in its wetsuits. It has made this proprietary rubber available to the rest of the surf industry in an attempt to get volumes up and prices down and reduce overall environmental impact compared to using pure CR.

Rubber is a thermoset material and it is not possible to recycle it directly. Instead, waste material is shredded. The recycled material, known as 'crumb', is used as a filler material for shock-absorbing floors (such as for playgrounds), insulation, asphalt and aggregate.

Some people are allergic to the proteins in latex and in the most extreme cases the reaction can be life-threatening. For applications that require contact with people or food, a modified grade is used, which has lower levels of protein and so is less likely to cause an allergic reaction.

**Marbled balloon**
Mass-produced latex balloons are dip molded in translucent or opaque colour. Once molded, a range of patterns and graphics may be applied to the surface. Marbled patterns that cover the entire surface are reproduced with water transfer printing. A layer of ink is floated on the print bath. It may be printed or hand-poured. As the balloons are dipped, ink is transferred to the surface of the latex.

# Cellulose Acetate (CA) and Viscose

**Also known as**

CA: Biocetta, Natureflex, Cellulon, Vegemat, Tenite, Uvex, Excelon, Spartech
CA film: acetate, Cellophane, Rayophane
CA fibre: Acele, Avisco, Celanese, Chromspun, Estron
Viscose fibre: rayon, modal, lyocell
Lyocell fibre trademark name: Tencel

**Cellulose forms the basis for a range of materials, from richly coloured plastics to soft textile fibres. It is derived from many different types of raw material including wood, bamboo and cotton. The conventional extraction techniques are complex and unsustainable. New methods have been developed that are non-polluting and recycle chemicals in a virtual closed-loop process.**

| Types | Typical Applications | Sustainability |
|---|---|---|
| • Cellulose acetate (CA), CA butyrate (CAB) and CA propionate (CAP)<br>• CA fibre: acetate and triacetate<br>• Viscose, modal and lyocell | • Spectacle frames and accessories<br>• Apparel and home textiles<br>• Technical textiles for health and well-being | • Renewable raw materials<br>• Moderate to high embodied energy<br>• Recyclable and biodegradable end-of-life |

| Properties | Competing Materials | Costs |
|---|---|---|
| • Plastic: high gloss, high toughness and good chemical resistance<br>• Fibre: low strength, highly absorbent, soft and comfortable with good drape | • Plastics including: PA, PET, PP<br>• Fibres including: PP, PET, cotton, silk, wool<br>• Aluminium and titanium in eyewear | • Moderate to high raw material costs<br>• Typically low manufacturing costs; but handmade CA is high-cost |

252

## INTRODUCTION

Cellulose has been used in the production of plastics for more than a century. These are semi-synthetic materials; they are derived from natural and potentially renewable sources, but require the addition of chemicals to form a usable material. Cellulose acetate (CA) is the most common and is often referred to simply as acetate. Its use in high-quality spectacle frames, because it feels comfortable natural to the skin, makes it a very familiar material to many.

CA film is relatively expensive and applications are somewhat limited as a result of its low strength. In many cases it has been superseded by lower-cost and more reliable synthetics, such as polypropylene (PP) (page 98) and polyethylene terephthalate (PET, polyester) (page 152).

Cellulose-based fibres, produced from regenerated cellulose, were originally developed as an alternative to relatively expensive natural fibres, such as cotton (page 410), silk (page 420) and wool (page 426). As such, they are often produced as a replacement, mimicking the visual qualities of these materials, or blended with them to reduce the overall cost of the fabric. As a result of developments in the quality of low-cost synthetics, such as PP, PET and polyamide (PA, nylon) (page 164) in recent decades, regenerated cellulose fibres have themselves faced stiff competition.

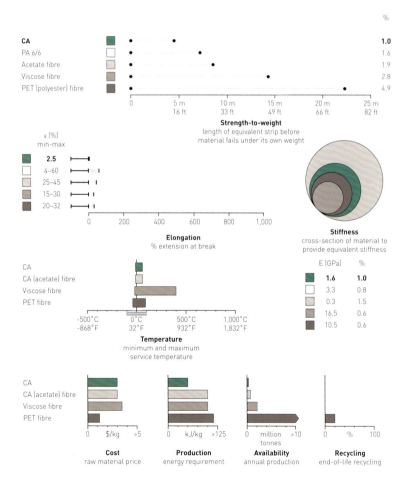

**CA**, **PA 6/6**, **Acetate fibre**, **Viscose fibre**, **PET (polyester) fibre**

| | % |
|---|---|
| CA | 1.0 |
| PA 6/6 | 1.6 |
| Acetate fibre | 1.9 |
| Viscose fibre | 2.8 |
| PET (polyester) fibre | 4.9 |

**Strength-to-weight**
length of equivalent strip before material fails under its own weight

ε (%) min-max

| | |
|---|---|
| | 2.5 |
| | 4–60 |
| | 25–45 |
| | 15–30 |
| | 20–32 |

**Elongation**
% extension at break

**Stiffness**
cross-section of material to provide equivalent stiffness

| | E (GPa) | % |
|---|---|---|
| | 1.6 | 1.0 |
| | 3.3 | 0.8 |
| | 0.3 | 1.5 |
| | 16.5 | 0.6 |
| | 10.5 | 0.6 |

CA, CA (acetate) fibre, Viscose fibre, PET fibre

**Temperature**
minimum and maximum service temperature

CA, CA (acetate) fibre, Viscose fibre, PET fibre

**Cost** raw material price — $/kg >5

**Production** energy requirement — kJ/kg >125

**Availability** annual production — million tonnes >10

**Recycling** end-of-life recycling — % 100

**Monochrome spectacles** Handmade by Larke, these frames are cut and crafted from solid sheets of CA. This design was created in collaboration with Darkroom, London. The pattern is inherent to the plastic and so runs uninterrupted around the frame. Such is the ease with which new patterns are created that each season brings entirely new colour configurations.

## COMMERCIAL TYPES AND USES

Cellulose is obtained from many types of raw material – such as wood, cotton and bamboo – with varying concentrations of the natural polymer. Like starch (see Starch Plastic, page 260, and Polylactic Acid, page 262), cellulose is a polysaccharide made up of repeating glucose molecules. Through a process of esterification, CA is extracted from the raw materials using acetic acid. The exact chemicals used depend on the starting material.

CA is combined with butyrate (CAB) and propionate (CAP) to enhance specific properties. They are characterized by high toughness, high clarity and good surface properties. These qualities are utilized in spectacle frames and tool handles alike. CAB has lower moisture absorption, higher impact strength (higher elongation) and higher temperature resistance than CA. By comparison, CAP is utilized for its superior chemical resistance. Applications include drug delivery and surgical instruments.

They contain around 70% plant-based components. They are combined with plasticizer (see Polyvinyl Chloride, page 122) and various additives to make them suitable for a range of situations. Similar to petroleum-derived thermoplastics, CA, CAB and CAP are compounded and extruded as pellets suitable for a range of manufacturing processes. Applications include handles, toys and stationery. Thin films are used in packaging and sheets are thermoformed into containers.

CA film is often referred to as Cellophane. While this is a trademark name owned by Innovia Films, it is used as a generic reference for transparent films in some regions. The regenerated cellulose is plasticized with glycols and water to reduce brittleness and improve transparency. Having been in use for decades, it is perhaps most familiar in its applications as confectionery wrapping and the transparent window in envelopes. It is also used to package fresh cheese, cigars and tampons. It provides a durable

**Above**
**Mazzucchelli cellulose acetate** The highest-quality spectacle frames are cut from block-pressed CA sheet. The various colours are placed by hand before pressing, so each frame will be unique. This close-up image of a small sample measuring no more than 30 mm (1.2 in) demonstrates the craftsmanship involved. The pattern is gradually built up over many stages: each colour combination is the result of a separate block that has been pressed, cut and reassembled in such a way that a desirable pattern is achieved. Combined with the physical properties of cellulose acetate, this gives a special quality that cannot be reproduced in any other material.

**Opposite**
**Transparent racing fuel filter** The toughness, transparency and chemical resistance of CA are utilized in racing fuel filters. The housing of the Moose Racing filter is molded CA, ultrasonic welded to form a hermetic unit. The filter element is made of PA.

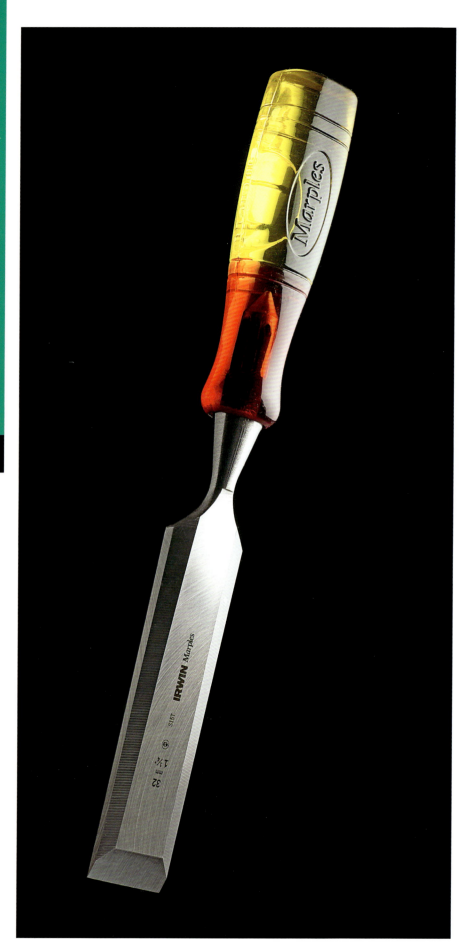

backing for transparent adhesive tape, or Sellotape – hence the name.

It has high permeability to moisture and very low permeability to gases. Coatings provide the barrier and sealing properties necessary for many applications. Unfortunately, these prevent CA film from being compostable.

Cellulose is converted into fibres by various techniques. While there are several different sources of cellulose, it is the production technique rather than the raw material that defines the fibre's properties.

Acetate is typically produced from wood pulp-derived cellulose by dry spinning. The extracted polymer is dissolved in acetone to produce a viscous solution suitable for spinning. The solution is pumped through the spinneret into warm air and the acetone evaporates from the filaments. This technique produces large amounts of volatile organic compounds (VOCs).

The difference between acetate and triacetate is the number of cellulose hydroxyl groups: triacetate is more completely acetylated (more than 92% is converted into acetyl groups). As a result of its slightly different chemical structure it has higher heat resistance and wet strength.

Acetate fibres are used to make fabrics worn close to the skin, such as nightwear, dresses and linings. They are often blended with cotton and wool to provide added shape retention. They can be produced to exact requirements, are safe for skin contact and are highly absorbent. This makes them useful for technical applications, such as filters, diapers and face wipes.

Viscose is wet spun. In this process cellulose is chemically extracted from wood pulp and mixed with sodium

**High-impact chisel** CAB has been utilized in tool handles for more than 50 years. It provides a good balance of toughness, hardness and strength, combined with a warm, smooth finish. Guaranteed shatterproof, even with repeated hammer blows, it makes an ideal chisel handle. This is the original Irwin Marples design featuring a two-tone handle. They have since been redesigned, but continue to utilize CAB. The blade is forged and tempered from chromium-vanadium steel (page 28).

hydroxide (caustic soda). After a suitable length of time, which can be up to 50 hours, to allow the material to mature, carbon disulphide is introduced to form sodium cellulose xanthate. This produces a yellow crumb-like substance, which is dissolved in sodium hydroxide and further ripened into a viscous solution, which is forced through spinnerets. The high shear (lateral strain), caused by the combination of high viscosity and high pressure through the spinneret, results in alignment of the molecular structure lengthways. The filaments are drawn into a bath of dilute sulphuric acid, which decomposes the xanthate and regenerates the cellulose into a solid fibre.

High wet modulus (HWM) viscose has improved tenacity. By altering the chemical process, the structure of the fibre is improved. When at the cellulose xanthate stage, sodium hydroxide is introduced and the filament is stretched several hundred percent as it is squeezed through the spinneret. This maximizes the crystallinity and chain length in the finished fibre, resulting in a stronger material with reduced fibrillation.

Viscose is used mainly for its aesthetic and absorbent properties in applications ranging from fashion to home textiles. Its lustrous surface and natural sheen are utilized in embroidery threads. Technical applications include wipes, filters and medical bandages.

Modal fibre is a modified version of HWM viscose. It has improved properties – strength and dimensional stability – as a result of adjustments to the manufacturing process and a higher degree of polymerization. It is highly absorbent and so continues to feel dry even if it has soaked up a lot of water. Combined with softness, this quality makes it particularly well suited to intimate apparel.

Lyocell is a more recent development and commercial production began in 1992. The process was developed as an alternative to conventional viscose, with

**Film packaging** CA film is a speciality product. Recently it has been superseded by PP and polyethylene (PE) (page 108) in many situations; they are less expensive and provide greater versatility. Even so, CA film remains in use; it has unique properties that set it apart from these lower-cost alternatives. For example, the breathability of the film is essential for certain packaging situations, such as mold-ripened cheeses. The film is perforated in applications where greater airflow is required.

the aim of reducing the environmental impact. Viscose production creates many by-products, such as sulphur, metal salts (copper and zinc) and ammonia, which are potentially harmful to people and the environment if not properly managed.

Lyocell overcomes this by using much less harmful chemicals in a virtual closed-loop process. Production begins with the wood pulp, which is dissolved in a solution of N-methylmorpholine-N-oxide (a form of amine oxide known as NMMO) with water. The resulting dope is squeezed through spinnerets to form filaments with good molecular alignment. The filaments are then fed into diluted NMMO solution to set the fibre structure in place. The fibres are washed and wound and the NMMO solution is recovered and reused.

The modified wet-spinning process produces a fibre without any by-products. The filament has a rounded profile and a smoother longitudinal appearance than viscose. The physical properties are more comparable with cotton in many respects. Applications include apparel (in particular baby clothes) and facial wipes.

## SUSTAINABILITY

Extracting and refining cellulose for use in plastics and fibres requires a great deal of energy. So while they may be from renewable sources, the total environmental impact is equivalent to conventional plastics.

There has been continual development to try to reduce the negative impacts. For example, lyocell is significantly better than conventional viscose. Another notable example is M49® CA, manufactured by Mazzucchelli, which uses a plasticizer derived from biomass (as opposed to petroleum) and is free from phthalates.

Bamboo (page 386) is a fast-growing and renewable source of material used to produce viscose and lyocell, as well as natural plant fibre. The natural staple fibre, as well as fibres produced with the lyocell method, may be sustainable. However, the majority of bamboo fibre is viscose and therefore the yarn and fabric will have the same environmental impacts of all other types of material produced with the same method.

Similar to starch-based plastics, cellulose-based plastics offer several options end-of-life. They may be recycled, although this is generally unlikely. Certain types are biodegradable. They are utilized in packaging and envelopes (windows) for example, which are suitable for composting.

## CELLULOSE IN PRODUCTS AND ACCESSORIES

CA is commonly used to make spectacle frames, jewelry and other fashion accessories. The original tortoiseshell

### PRODUCTS AND ACCESSORIES

**Gloss**
These plastics have a high-gloss surface and feel warm to the touch, which helps them feel natural next to the skin. The surface is described as self-shining, because it is soft and so dents and rebounds as opposed to scratching.

**Colour**
CA is coloured with a range of pigments and effects, including translucent colour, opaque colour, and metallic and pearlescent effects. The clarity (up to 90%) of CA ensures high-quality colour.

**Impact strength**
These materials are inherently tough and can withstand heavy impact. Their elasticity depends on the proportion of plasticizer.

mimic, it is relatively inexpensive, easy to work, comfortable, flexible and available in an almost infinite array of colours and patterns. Coloured patterns are produced with a mix of handcraft and machine. Pieces of coloured CA are carefully arranged in molds and pressed into blocks. The colour runs throughout, and as sheets are sliced from the top each layer reveals a unique pattern.

In an effort to produce the same beautiful colourways at reduced price, the Italian company Mazzucchelli has devised many innovative ways to co-extrude multicoloured sheets. This creates a material with the pattern running along the length of plastic.

Relatively modern synthetic plastics, such as PA and polycarbonate (PC) (page 144), offer many advantages over CA in similar products. They are tough, transparent (high-quality colour) and highly resilient. However, patterns are not possible with injection molding. Instead, they have to be applied by secondary process, such as printing or spraying. So while these materials may offer superior mechanical properties, the aesthetics are quite different and the finish will not be as durable.

## CELLULOSE IN FASHION AND TEXTILES

Fibres produced from regenerated cellulose are often compared to high-quality natural fibres, such as cotton, silk and wool. The advantage of semi-synthetics is that while they are derived from natural, renewable materials, their properties are highly controllable.

### FASHION AND TEXTILES

**Softness**
These fibres have good body and drape, and they feel comfortable next to the skin.

**Absorbency**
The fibres are highly absorbent and so continue to feel dry even after having soaked up water. This quality is utilized in items ranging from intimate apparel to diaper liners.

**Colour**
The fibres have a lustrous surface and can be dyed or produced in a wide range of durable colours.

They are uniform and can be modified in many ways that are impossible or impractical for natural fibres. For example, when the fibre is being processed and still in solution, it may be coloured (known as solution-dyed) and modified with additives to produce much higher-quality results than can be achieved once the filament has been spun. In addition, the diameter, length, shape and composition (see page 173) may be changed during production.

Fibres dyed in solution have excellent colourfastness, whereas yarn-dyed fabric is prone to fading over time and with exposure to the elements. Fibres with low surface energy, such as lyocell, or smoother surface profile, such as HWM viscose, are more difficult to treat and dye. While it is possible to create the same range of colour as viscose, it will be more expensive and the colour may not be as long-lasting.

**Lyocell dress** This H&M kimono is produced from 100% lyocell. When using wood obtained from sustainably managed forests and producing the fibre in a closed-loop production process, recovering the majority of chemicals used, this material has lower environmental impacts than viscose. For example, Tencel is produced from the pulp of trees from sustainably managed forests certified by the Forest Stewardship Council (FSC). Raw materials that yield a high percentage of cellulose, such as eucalyptus trees, reduce waste and further improve sustainability. Once converted into yarn it uses the same chemical processes, such as dyeing, to convert it into the finished goods.

# Starch Plastic

**Starch is obtained from plants, such as potatoes, maize, wheat and rice, among others. Each species has a unique starch granule. It is applied as is, with only minor modifications, or combined with fillers and biodegradable polymers. Used mainly for single-use items destined for composting, starch plastics offer a low-cost and low-impact alternative to petroleum-derived plastics.**

| Types | Typical Applications | Sustainability |
|---|---|---|
| • Starch-based plastic<br>• Thermoplastic starch (TPS) | • Disposable items (diapers, cutlery and so on)<br>• Packaging | • Depends on source of biomass<br>• Fully biodegradable |

| Properties | Competing Materials | Costs |
|---|---|---|
| • Low tensile strength<br>• Good impact properties<br>• Sensitive to humidity | • PS, EPS, PP, PE, PET<br>• PLA, PHA, PHB<br>• Paper | • Low to moderate raw material costs<br>• Low manufacturing costs |

260

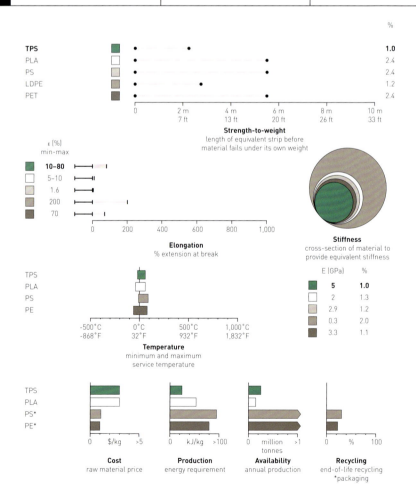

## INTRODUCTION

Production of bio-derived plastics is increasing and new types are continually being developed. Two principal categories have emerged: compostable plastics and standard plastics based on renewable resources. The first includes materials such as plastics derived from starch or cellulose (page 252). Their properties can be similar to petroleum-derived plastics but they require around one-third less energy to produce. The second group includes many conventional plastics, such as polyethylene (PE) (page 108) based on bio-ethanol, polyamide (PA, nylon) (page 164) from castor oil, and polyethylene terephthalate (PET, polyester) (page 152) based on bio-propanediol.

A further distinction is made between compostable and biodegradable. The difference is that 'compostable' means that they fulfil US and EU standards (ASTM 6400 and EN 13432 respectively) for degrading in composting conditions (more than 90% must be converted into carbon dioxide [$CO_2$], water and biomass within 90 days), whereas 'biodegradable' simply means the material can be broken down into $CO_2$, water and biomass by microorganisms within a reasonable length of time.

## COMMERCIAL TYPES AND USES

Starch is a polysaccharide made up of a number of sugar molecules bonded together (glucose). It contains a mix of linear and branched polymers, which form a partially crystalline structure (see page 166). In its native form, starch will not melt; it decomposes before the crystalline melting point is reached.

Starch-based plastic does not require extensive processing. By contrast, polylactic acid (PLA) (page 262) and polyhydroxyalkanoates (PHA) (see PLA) are produced by bacterial fermentation followed by polymerization. This makes them expensive.

The crystalline structure of starch is broken down with thermo-mechanical action. Through a process of gelatinization, starch granules absorb plasticizer (such as water), which reduces the strength of the intermolecular bonds. The resulting material can be melt-processed using conventional plastic equipment, such as injection molding, extrusion and thermoforming. It is used in a range of packaging and single-use items, including compostable loose-fill packaging (peanuts), thermoformed trays and blown film (bags and wrapping).

Starch contains hydroxyl groups (oxygen–hydrogen units), which are hydrophilic. This means that starch is vulnerable to humidity and therefore unsuitable for many applications. It has poor mechanical properties and is prone to ageing after molding. To produce a more useful material, while maintaining biodegradability, it is blended with PLA and PHA.

## SUSTAINABILITY

While biobased plastics tend to have lower embodied energy than their oil-based counterparts, they do not necessarily have low environmental impact overall. There are many factors to take into account, from raw material production through performance in application. As with conventional plastics, the full impacts can be assessed only by carrying out a thorough life-cycle analysis (LCA). The source of biomass is critical, because the impact of growing the crops may outweigh the benefits, such as deforestation, genetic modification (GM), petroleum-powered machinery, displacing local food production and increasing food prices.

**Compostable cutlery**
Compostable plastics are beneficial in several situations. Where recycling is impractical or uneconomical, biodegradation avoids items becoming debris and polluting the land or sea. A good example is takeaway food. Disposed food, packaging and utensils are unlikely to be separated and will likely end up in landfill. If starch-based plastics are used for all the non-food items, then a homogenous waste is created that is suitable for composting.

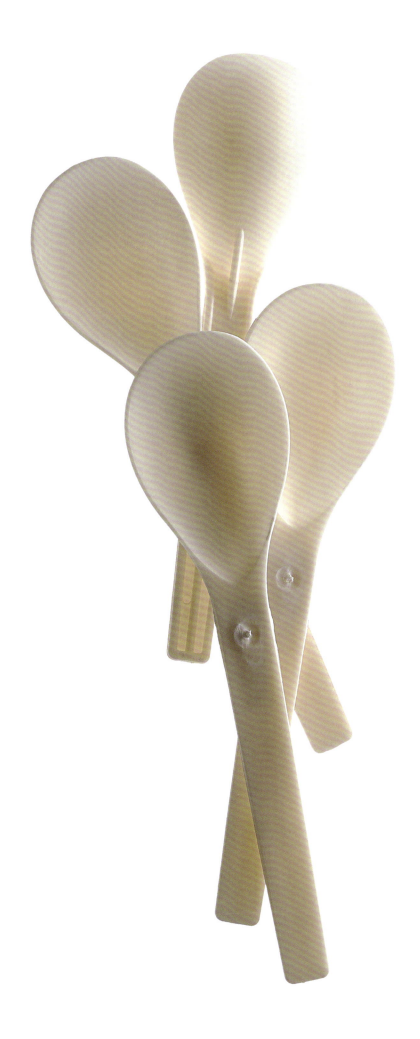

# Polylactic Acid (PLA)

**PLA is a bioplastic that can be extruded, injection molded and drawn as fibre much like conventional thermoplastics. It is derived from natural lactic acid that is harvested from the starch present in potatoes, maize, wheat and rice, among other plants. It is used in packaging and other potentially compostable items, including diapers and plant pots.**

| Types | Typical Applications | Sustainability |
|---|---|---|
| • Polylactic acid (PLA)<br>• Polyhydroxyalkanoate (PHA) and polyhydroxybutyrate (PHB) | • Packaging<br>• Textiles<br>• Stationery | • Wholly biobased<br>• Compostable or recyclable end-of-life |
| **Properties** | **Competing Materials** | **Costs** |
| • Excellent gloss, transparency and clarity<br>• Brittle, but can be toughened | • TPS<br>• PE, PP, PET, PS, EVA | • Moderate raw material price<br>• Slightly more expensive to manufacture than commodity thermoplastics |

262

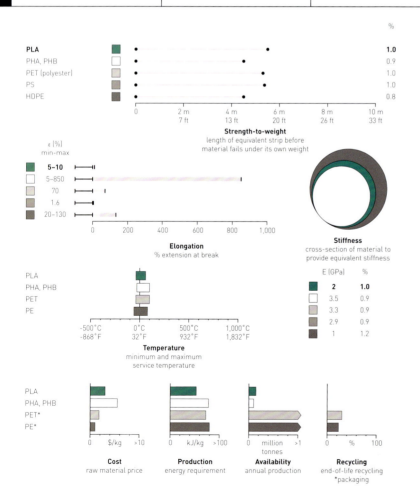

### INTRODUCTION

Polylactic acid (PLA) is the only commercially significant bioplastic wholly derived from renewable sources. Production is a little more expensive than for petroleum-derived plastics and as a result, PLA costs around two or three times as much as its non-bio-derived competitors.

Properties range from stiff and rigid to flexible, depending on the exact ingredients. Already used to make bottles, packaging film, toys, cutlery, stationery, composites and consumer electronic parts, it is being explored for many more applications as the demand for natural, renewable materials increases.

Starch provides the raw material, dextrose, which is processed by fermentation to yield lactic acid. The lactic acid molecule consists of rings of lactide. Through a process of polymerization, the rings are opened up and joined to make long chains. Just like conventional polymers, the basic resin is pelletized in readiness for production.

Like PLA, polyhydroxyalkanoates (PHA) are produced via the bacterial fermentation of sugar. Depending on the production method, a range of monomers can be produced. Microorganisms feed on the sugars and multiply. When a sufficient quantity has been produced the nutrient content is modified (such as limiting oxygen or nitrogen) and excess carbon is added, causing the bacteria to synthesize

**Bioplastic drinking cup**
Several types of PLA are certified for food contact. It has excellent gloss, transparency and clarity. These qualities are essential for food packaging that must look clean and not obstruct the view of the contents. In addition, it has very good aroma barrier properties. While this does not affect drinking cups, it is advantageous in trays and containers that sit on the shelf for a long period of time.

PHA. Following biosynthesis, the cell walls of the bacteria are broken down and the monomer is extracted and purified, ready for polymerization. From the range of different monomers many different properties can be achieved.

The most widely studied is polyhydroxybutyrate (PHB), which has similar properties to polypropylene (PP) (page 98). However, it is significantly more expensive – about four times so, taking into account the density – and this has limited production and application. So far, there are only a handful of commercial examples: the two main trademark names are Mirel and Sogreen. Rather than being used alone, they are often blended with PLA or TPS to broaden the range of possible applications.

All of these examples – PLA, PHA and PHB – are forms of thermoplastic polyester (see also Polyethylene Terephthalate [PET, polyester], page 152). They are degraded by microbes, which cause enzymatic hydrolysis of the ester linkage. In other words, they are fully biodegradable in microbial active environments.

## COMMERCIAL TYPES AND USES

PLA is compatible with thermoplastic processing equipment. Grades have been developed for packaging applications, to compete with polyethylene (PE) (page 108), PP, polystyrene (PS) (page 132) and PET. It has excellent stiffness and transparency, qualities utilized in thermoformed trays, blow-molded bottles and blown film.

It is also suitable for injection molding. It is used for similar applications to PS, such as disposable razors, stationery, and reusable packaging and eating utensils (cups, plates, cutlery and so on).

As a textile fibre, PLA offers many advantages. It is comfortable as a result of its high wicking properties and moisture management, and it is easy-care. Produced with a round profile, it has a smooth appearance. Its processing characteristics are more or less equivalent to those of PET. It is suitable for a range of uses, including apparel, home textiles (bedding, rugs and upholstery) and nonwovens (diapers, cloths and packaging).

PLA filament is compatible with additive manufacturing (rapid prototyping). In a process known as fused deposition modelling (FDM), or fused filament modelling (FFF), the filament is melted and deposited layer by layer to build complex three-dimensional structures. It provides an alternative

**Bioplastic granules**
PLA plastic granules look just like conventional thermoplastic. The raw polymer is extruded in long lengths and cut into pellets ready for further processing.

to acrylonitrile butadiene styrene (ABS) (page 138). Even though it is more expensive, it does not require extraction (ABS gives off harmful fumes when melted), which is a major advantage in the sort of environments where these desktop printers are being utilized. In addition, it has a slightly lower melting point and is less prone to warp post-built.

It is available in a range of bold and pearlescent (see page 142) colours, and the demand for PLA in FDM applications has fuelled the development of new, eye-catching grades. Metallized PLA is produced using various copper alloy (page 66) powders. The result is a heavier, denser model that can be polished. A wood-filled grade is available made using a range of raw ingredients, including bamboo (page 386) and poplar (page 330), among others. PLA has been modified to produce a toughened grade (higher impact strength) and flexible PLA (similar to thermoplastic elastomer [TPE], page 194).

## SUSTAINABILITY

Similar to thermoplastic starch (TPS) (page 260), the use of natural renewable materials helps minimize the overall environmental impact. However, the production of PLA requires higher energy input, consuming more fossil fuels. NatureWorks claims that its material, Ingeo, results in 75% lower carbon dioxide ($CO_2$) emissions than traditional materials like PS and PET.

As with all bio-derived plastics, the source of biomass is critical to ensure a sustainable material (see TPS). While the majority of the raw material used for PLA is derived from maize, many other plants yield suitable sugary starters. In the future and with developments in the production process, it is expected that a wider range of agricultural by-products will become available.

Bioplastics have more end-of-life options available than any petroleum-derived plastics. PLA may be recycled, composted, incinerated or converted back into lactic acid.

Much like conventional thermoplastics, scrap from production can be directly recycled without significant loss of quality. Recycling post-consumer waste is more challenging at present, because PLA is identified by code #7, 'other', and so mixed with other plastics. It is impractical to separate these plastics in sufficient quantities to produce recycled PLA from end-of-life material.

PLA is compostable. Technically, this means that it fulfils US and EU standards (ASTM 6400 and EN 13432 respectively), which require that more than 90% must be converted into $CO_2$, water and biomass within 90 days under controlled conditions. Unfortunately, this does not mean that it will break down in domestic composting situations.

**Bioplastic tea bag** Tea bags are typically woven polyamide (PA, nylon) (page 164) or nonwoven polypropylene (PP). To produce a more sustainable product, some tea makers have switched to woven PLA filament. While these bags are not necessarily 'home compostable', as some advertising implies, they have lower overall environmental impact than those made from conventional thermoplastics.

# WOOD

# 3

# Wood Pulp, Paper and Board

Paper is an age-old material now produced on a huge scale at terrific speed. It has been utilized for thousands of years and its versatility ensures that it remains the material of choice for many applications. On its own it can be quite delicate, a quality used in packaging and lightweight structures. Or it can be formed into strong, dense board.

| Types | Typical Applications | Sustainability | |
|---|---|---|---|
| • Pulp: softwood, hardwood, plant and leaf<br>• Paper and board: single layer, multilayer, coated, uncoated or laminated | • Printed media and packaging<br>• Decorations and lighting<br>• Model making and pattern making | • Raw materials may be sourced from certified forests | • Chemicals and water consumed in production<br>• Widely collected and recycled |
| **Properties** | **Competing Materials** | **Costs** | |
| • Consistency depends on production method<br>• Smooth to coarse<br>• Low tear strength | • PP, PE and PET film, nonwoven laminate and sheer<br>• Woven cotton, hemp and jute<br>• EPS, EPP and EPE | • Commodity types are inexpensive<br>• Specialist types can be very expensive | |

268

## INTRODUCTION

The methods used to make paper by hand have changed very little since the Han Dynasty in China (206 BCE–220 CE). Fibrous material is pulped with water to release the cellulose fibres and drained through a mesh. Once dry, the natural binders contained within the fibres, released by beating, hold the randomly oriented structure together. Paper was used to make writing materials and money; production expanded, and with the development of printing, paper became an essential part of our everyday lives.

Since knowledge about papermaking spread from China across Asia, the Middle East and Europe there has been constant progress in raw materials and production. Modern industrialized paper production, based on wood fibre, produces sheets with precise dimensions and uniform properties at several hundred metres per minute.

Fresh forest fibres are used in the production of pulp, paper and board. Many types of wood are used for pulp, such as spruce and pine (page 304) and birch (page 334). Spruce and pine produce long fibres, whereas birch provides excellent optical properties. The mulberry tree provides one of the oldest fibres used in papermaking, and continues to be used in parts of Asia for high-quality paper.

Some plant fibres, such as hemp (page 406), flax (page 400) and cotton (page 410), may also be incorporated to improve

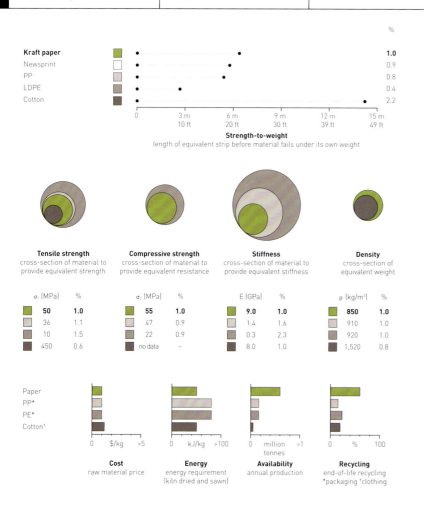

**Kraft paper** | 1.0
Newsprint | 0.9
PP | 0.8
LDPE | 0.4
Cotton | 2.2

**Strength-to-weight**
length of equivalent strip before material fails under its own weight

| | 0 | 3 m<br>10 ft | 6 m<br>20 ft | 9 m<br>30 ft | 12 m<br>39 ft | 15 m<br>49 ft |
|---|---|---|---|---|---|---|

**Tensile strength**
cross-section of material to provide equivalent strength

| $\sigma_t$ (MPa) | % |
|---|---|
| **50** | **1.0** |
| 36 | 1.1 |
| 10 | 1.5 |
| 450 | 0.6 |

**Compressive strength**
cross-section of material to provide equivalent resistance

| $\sigma_c$ (MPa) | % |
|---|---|
| **55** | **1.0** |
| 47 | 0.9 |
| 22 | 0.9 |
| no data | – |

**Stiffness**
cross-section of material to provide equivalent stiffness

| E (GPa) | % |
|---|---|
| **9.0** | **1.0** |
| 1.4 | 1.6 |
| 0.3 | 2.3 |
| 8.0 | 1.0 |

**Density**
cross-section of equivalent weight

| $\rho$ (kg/m³) | % |
|---|---|
| **850** | **1.0** |
| 910 | 1.0 |
| 920 | 1.0 |
| 1,520 | 0.8 |

Paper
PP*
PE*
Cotton†

**Cost**
raw material price
0 — $/kg — >5

**Energy**
energy requirement (kiln dried and sawn)
0 — kJ/kg — >100

**Availability**
annual production
0 — million tonnes — >1

**Recycling**
end-of-life recycling
0 — % — 100
*packaging †clothing

**Die-cut vase** Created in 2010 by Japanese firm Torafu Architects, the Airvase exploits many of the unique properties of paper. The sheet is thin and easily perforated, making it cost-effective in production. Manipulated by hand, its balance of stiffness and lightness ensures that the structure stays upright, bouncing back to shape. Each side is a different colour, so the appearance changes depending on the angle of view.

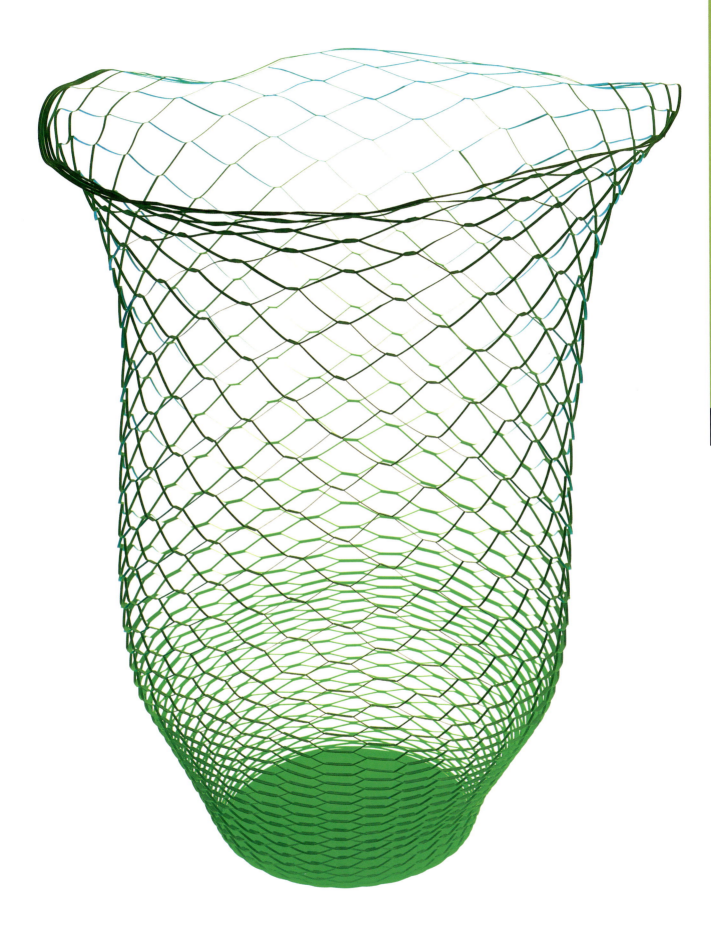

# TYPES OF PAPER AND BOARD

### MACHINE FINISHED
General-purpose paper and board that is typically smooth on both sides. Paper over 150 g/m² is also called paperboard.

**Newsprint paper, 40–50 g/m²** The least expensive paper that can tolerate high-speed printing processes, it is an uncoated mix of mechanical pulp and recovered paper. Printing on such lightweight stock is quite specialized and so print lines are often dedicated.

**Bank and bond paper, 50–120 g/m²** A crisp, tough, high-quality writing paper used for letterheads, home and office printing and other stationery. Paper up to 63 g/m² is classified as bank and over that is bond.

**Book paper, 60–90 g/m²** Used in the production of textbooks (not illustrated books) it consists of mechanical pulp with a little chemical pulp for strength.

**Magazine and printing paper, 80–260 g/m²** Also uncoated, but made up of mostly chemical pulp (also known as wood-free) and so less prone to yellow over time.

**Art board, over 300 g/m²** Heavy uncoated stock used for book covers. Identified as 1-ply, 2-ply and so on.

### SPECIALIST COATED
A range of coatings has been developed to fulfil the requirements of niche applications.

**Chromo, 75–130 g/m²** Waterproofed on one side, which is useful for labels, wrapping and posters. So called because it was originally produced for the chromolithography process. Also available as board.

**Carbonless paper, 40–240 g/m²** Also known as no carbon required (NCR) and chemical paper, it is coated to obtain duplicates without the need to use carbon paper. A microencapsulated colourless dye is coated onto the surface. Writing or printing pressure breaks the capsules and releases the dye, which reacts with a coating on the adjacent sheet to produce visible colour. The coated may be applied to the front (CF), back (CB) or both sides (CFB).

**Impregnated** Paper is utilized in a range of industrial applications, such as building materials, roofing and filters. It is impregnated with resin – such as epoxy (page 232) or phenolic (page 224) – in the production of high-performance sheet materials.

### SANITARY AND HOUSEHOLD
Chemicals are added to achieve certain desired qualities in the end product, such as wet strength adhesive (for paper towels) or silicone (non-stick surfaces on baking paper).

**Facial tissue, 14–18 g/m²** Facial tissues and paper handkerchiefs are soft, absorbent, disposable papers for use on the face. They contain a high proportion of virgin pulp, but may contain some recycled content. They are combined with softener, lotion and perfume.

**Tissue, 14–50 g/m²** These are highly absorbent papers used in toilet paper, kitchen towel, napkins and so on. They are often produced from multiple plies (the minimum ply weight is 7 g/m²), which increases the surface area and thus absorption capacity.

**Bakery paper, 30–90 g/m²** The two main types are parchment and greaseproof (bakery release) paper. Both are designed to have a non-stick surface suitable for baking and packaging. Parchment is produced by passing paper through sulphuric acid, to gelatinize the surface. Greaseproof paper is coated with silicone.

### MACHINE COATED
Paper coated in-line with a layer of mineral – such as china clay (kaolin) – on the surface to improve smoothness, gloss and print quality. White paper typically has a high loading of optical brightener, which absorbs ultraviolet and emits it in the visible spectrum, to make it look brighter. Titanium dioxide is added to improve opacity and reduce show-through.

**Lightweight coated paper, up to 45 g/m²** A thin paper that can be as little as 40 g/m². It is used in high-volume magazines, brochures and catalogues.

**Bible paper, 40–75 g/m²** Also known as lightweight coated (LWC), this is a high-quality, lightweight book paper. It is the same weight as newsprint, acid-free (so longer-lasting) and suitable for printing large tomes, such as dictionaries and encyclopaedias.

**Art paper, 75–130 g/m²** A very high-quality paper used for a range of colour printing, from home/office to magazines. Also referred to as medium-weight coated (MWC) and heavyweight coated (HWC).

**Cast coated (CC) paper, 80–400 g/m²** This paper provides the highest level of gloss and is used for high-quality colour printing, for example labels and cartons.

### MATT
Used as high-quality printed media, the textured surface prevents light from being reflected and so reduces glare.

**Antique, 70–90 g/m²** Paper that comes straight from the machine without any finishing. It is the roughest surface that can be printed in-line (although much rougher paper may be printed with manual and low-volume techniques, such as screen printing).

**Cartridge, 70–220 g/m²** A bulky white paper used for artwork and stationery, similar in appearance to antique.

**Silk, 90–300 g/m²** Smooth, but without reflections. It is used for high quality product brochures, for example, because it combines high readability with high-quality print reproduction.

### FOLDING BOXBOARD
Also known as cartonboard, it may be coated or uncoated and is typically constructed from multiple layers of pulp. As well as speeding up the process, multilayer forming allows for different types of fibre to be combined in a single sheet. So for example, low-cost middle layers of mechanical and recovered pulp may be sandwiched between layers of high-quality chemical pulp. The outside surface is typically coated white and the inside is off-white. If it is white on both sides then it is also referred to as white-backed. It may be laminated with plastic film, aluminium foil or greaseproof paper, among other materials.

**Solid bleached board (SBB), 200–500 g/m²** A high-quality folding boxboard made from chemical pulp that is strong, smooth and medium density. It exhibits excellent embossing and printing characteristics. It is used to package high-value items including foods, cosmetics, pharmaceuticals and confectionery.

**Solid unbleached board (SUB), 200–500 g/m²** Its high tear strength is utilized in packaging for cereals, frozen foods, chilled food and in carrier cartons.

### CALENDERED
Also referred to as glazed, this paper has a high-lustre surface. Paper is passed between highly polished rollers, and through a combination of heat, pressure and friction is compressed to a smooth finish. In the case of coated paper, a high-gloss finish is achievable.

**Uncoated calendered, 40–75 g/m²** A range of cost-effective papers suited to newspaper supplements, catalogues and advertising material.

**Supercalendered (SC), 50–60 g/m²** Containing a large proportion of mineral filler, the paper is heavily calendered to produce a very smooth and glossy surface. It is used in magazines.

**Lightweight coated (LWC), 50–75 g/m²** This is a low-cost paper used in magazines. It contains a mix of chemical and mechanical pulp and is calendered to a glossy finish.

**Glassine, 50–90 g/m²** A glossy translucent paper that is resistant to water, air and grease. It forms the basis for greaseproof paper.

### GENERAL PACKAGING
A range of paper and board used for protection and promotion.

**Tissue paper, 20–50 g/m²** A lightweight packaging material utilized in domestic and industrial situations. Wrinkled tissue is called crêpe.

**One-side coated paper, 50–100 g/m²** A range of papers coated on one side, with a gloss or embossed finish. They are used for labels, wrappers and flexible packaging. It is treated on the backside to avoid curling.

**Coloured paper, 80–300 g/m²** Also called cover paper, this is uncoated stock used for covers, packaging and stationery.

**Kraft, 70–300 g/m²** A strong paper made up of long unbleached chemically extracted fibres. The higher strength is the result of the chemical pulping process. Adhesive is incorporated to improve wet strength. Known as wet-strength kraft, it retains around 25% of its tensile strength when saturated. It is utilized as an outer ply to provide water resistance. As with other paper types, it may be bleached, coated and waxed.

**Laminated paper** Coated or uncoated paper laminated with aluminium foil or extruded polyethylene (PE) (page 108) film.

**Corrugate** Consists of flat outer sheets sandwiching a fluted paper core. Ranging from micro-flute to triple-walled corrugate, it provides higher stiffness-to-weight that solid board. It is available in a range of thicknesses and configurations produced from any combination of virgin and recovered fibre, and may be bleached or unbleached.

**White-lined chipboard (WLC), 160–190 g/m²** A recycled pulp base is covered with a high-quality white-coated surface layer. It is used to make low-cost carton packaging, such as shoeboxes, electronics and other non-food items.

**Greyboard, over 250 g/m²** A low-cost solid board produced from recovered material. While it is principally used to provide the stiffness in hardback book covers, its surface may be exposed to lend an industrial aesthetic in promotional material.

durability and resistance to tearing. In fact, before paper production was industrialized, most of the fibres came from recycled plant fibre-based textiles, called 'rags'. Leaf fibres – in particular abaca and sisal (page 394) – are used in the production of specialist high-quality papers. Some man-made fibres may also be added, such as polyethylene terephthalate (PET, polyester) (page 152), viscose (page 252) and glass fibre (GF) (page 522).

## COMMERCIAL TYPES AND USES

Industrialized papermaking involves pressing moist fibres together, which are dried to form sheets ranging from ultra-lightweight tissue to stiff packaging board. It is made with virgin wood pulp, recycled fibrous materials, plant fibres, or a combination of these to provide specific mechanical, visual and tactile properties.

Wood fibres are extracted by mechanical means, chemical processing, or by chemi-thermomechanical pulping (CTMP). Mechanical grinding converts around 95% of the raw material into pulp. The fibres are extracted by pressing the logs against a rough-surfaced, rotating stone. This produces stiff, short, airy fibres that are less dense than chemical or CTMP. High yield means that mechanical

**Folding hand fan**
Thought to have originated in Japan between the 6th and the 9th century, after the import of paper production from China, the folding hand fan relies on paper's impressive ability to tolerate repeated folding and yet remain stiff. Rapidly evolving from status symbols into decorative objects, the folding fan became popular in Europe in the 17th century. This colourful design comes from HAY, Denmark.

pulp is generally the lowest cost. The high lignin content of mechanical pulp means that the paper will turn yellow over time. Therefore it is used to make newsprint and similar products, but is not suitable for long-lasting products, such as books.

**Printed wrapper** The premium quality of paper wrapping is hard to beat. Folded around its contents, the paper has creases that prevent the wrapper coming undone accidentally. This panettone from Italian baker G. Cova & C is wrapped in beautifully decorated paper. It is stiff with a smooth surface, which readily accepts high-quality print. The two principal printing techniques used in packaging are offset lithography and flexography, referred to as 'offset' and 'flexo'. Both are capable of very high-quality colour reproduction. Selection depends on the application, because while offset tends to be sharper, flexo is less expensive to set up and so is suitable for lower volumes.

and molded pulp can be made from 100% recovered paper.

The look (including colour), feel and performance of recycled pulp can be virtually indistinguishable from virgin pulp. However, heavily contaminated waste requires substantial reprocessing to make bright white paper. The use of recovered paper is not always the preferred option if, for example, superior lightness and stiffness are required.

The quality of paper is defined according to grammage ($g/m^2$), thickness (microns), bulk (relationship between $g/m^2$ and microns), roughness (or smoothness), absorbency and opacity. Selection depends on aesthetic requirements as well as technical considerations for production. As a result of the huge diversity of paper types available, a range of standard configurations has evolved (see page 270).

## SUSTAINABILITY

Sourced correctly, paper is renewable, and at the end of its useful life it is biodegradable. This gives it a sustainability advantage over alternative single-use materials, such as nonwoven polypropylene (PP) (page 98) and polyethylene (PE) (page 108). However, the same impermanence limits the range of applications.

Industrial papermaking consumes large quantities of water, bleach, dyes and other chemicals. By contrast, handmade paper produced with local and renewable materials has little if any negative impact on the environment. In many cases, papermaking provides small communities with a vital source of income.

In the chemical pulping process, the fibres are extracted by dissolving the lignin with chemicals and heat. This reduces the pulp to around 50% of the wood raw material, and significantly reduces the lignin content. Fibres of chemical pulp are flexible and produce a strong network with a large number of strong bonds. Therefore, they are used in high-quality papers and the outside surfaces of packaging board. The majority of this type of production uses the kraft method. Fibres are extracted and the lignin chemically dissolved by mixing wood fibres with a solution of caustic soda and sodium sulphide, and cooking them inside a digester. It provides the building block for many types of high-strength paper, including printing paper, tissue, filters and even Japanese washi (see page 276).

CTMP is made from wood chips that have been chemically and thermally softened, then ground in disk refiners. The fibres are more flexible and more durable than ground wood pulp, and have higher density.

During production, the pulp is transferred between meshes and conveyors, which are travelling at speed and align the fibres in the direction of travel. Therefore, paper is usually stiffer in the 'machine direction' (MD) and more easily creased across its width (CD).

Most pulp products can be manufactured from recovered paper. There are several categories of pulp-based recovered materials, such as corrugated, mixed, magazines, office waste, newspaper, high-grade, and pulp substitutes (such as waste from a sawmill).

Compared to recycled pulp, virgin pulp is lighter, stiffer and of a known composition. These characteristics make it preferable for applications that demand high performance and clean composition. During recycling, the length of the wood fibres is slightly reduced each time. Therefore, many paper-based products are manufactured using a mix of recycled pulp with virgin material. Even so, many products, such as tissue, newspapers, magazines, corrugated containers

## PACKAGING

### Folding endurance
Paper can be folded repeatedly without tearing. The total number of folds it can tolerate before it fails depends on the direction of the grain: folding endurance is higher across the grain (CD).

### Tensile strength
Ultimate strength depends on fibre type, length and orientation. Paper is stronger in machine direction (MD) than cross direction (CD), because the fibres orient lengthwise during production.

### Low cost
Produced in vast quantities, paper is a cost-effective packaging material available in an unrivalled range of formats. Set-up costs for molded pulp limit the process to high-volume production.

### Printability
The printing industry evolved around the qualities of paper. While very high-quality results can be achieved at a reasonable price, the search for maximum efficiency continues to drive development of new products and configurations.

**Folded carton** Boxes and cartons, such as this organic food packaging produced by English company Alexir Packaging, are cut and constructed in a continuous high-speed process. First of all, the high-quality board is printed. Die cutting is used to punch out the shape and indent the fold lines. The profiled parts are fed into a folding and gluing line. Each of the folds is made in a carefully worked-out sequence: first the horizontal folds are formed and glued in place; then the vertical folds are made, and the parts are pressed flat and stacked. They are kept flat for shipping and assembled only when they are ready to be used in the shop.

Virgin wood pulp must be from sustainably managed forests (see Veneer, page 290) to ensure minimum environmental impact. There is virtually no waste in paper and board production. All of the materials are converted into other raw materials or used as biofuel. At the end of their life, pulp products can be recycled.

Paper products offer the widest possible range of end-of-life options. Even though paper is biodegradable it is typically more effective to recycle, because this reduces water and air pollution, reduces materials going to landfill, requires less energy than virgin pulp production and reduces the consumption of raw materials. Even so, paper-based materials account for around one-third of the waste produced in the EU and the USA, by weight, which is more than any other material.

Mixed materials are much more difficult, and in some cases impossible, to recycle. For example, paper-based drinks cartons (long-life products) are laminated with around 20% plastic and 5% aluminium, making them impossible to recycle by conventional means.

## WOOD PULP, PAPER AND BOARD IN PACKAGING
Paper has good stiffness and will hold a crease. And as with plastic and metal, folding makes it stronger. Origami has exploited this quality for centuries, and the same principles are utilized in packaging and other engineered structures. The difference between paper

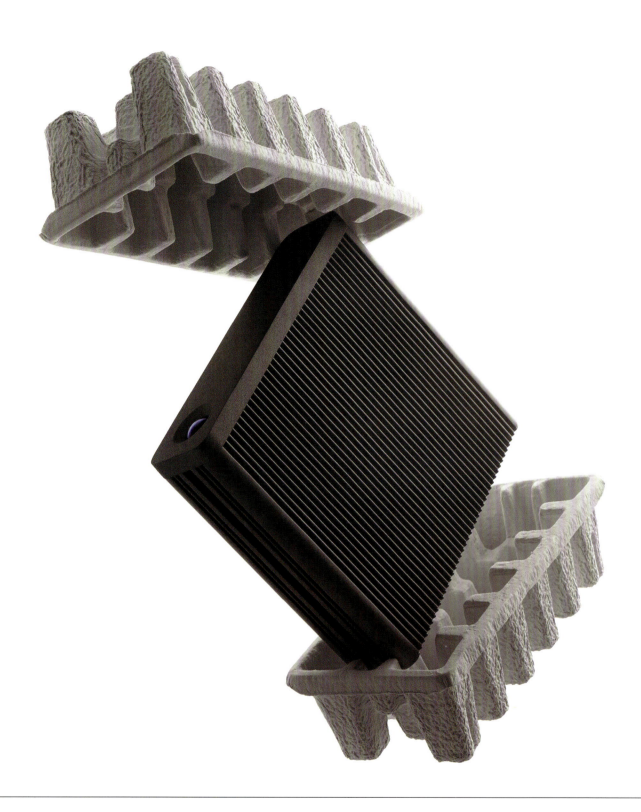

**Above**

**Molded pulp** Molded pulp is a terrific form of packaging: unit cost is low and at the end of its useful life, it can be recycled along with other paper packaging materials. It is naturally grey or brown, depending on the ingredients. Typically, brown pulp is made up of kraft paper and grey pulp is composed of recycled newsprint. Additives are used to improve specific properties, such as making the pulp waterproof or resistant to oil. These molded trays protect LaCie's extruded aluminium hard drive. They locate it within the box, keeping it clear of the walls and so protecting it from impact during shipping.

**Opposite**

**PaperFoam packaging** PaperFoam was developed by the young Dutch company of the same name as an alternative to conventional pulp, as well as EPS. It consists of 70% potato starch, 15% wood pulp and a few proprietary ingredients. It is mixed with food colouring and a little water. The water causes the starch to foam when molded, resulting in a stiff, lightweight part. Unlike pulp production, which is messy and requires a great deal of water, PaperFoam is injection-molded. It may be expensive to set up (as is molded pulp), but it presents many opportunities for designers. It is clean, rapid and precise. For lower volumes, compression molding may be used.

**Above and opposite Three-dimensional washi** These two projects are by Nendo, a Japanese company founded by Oki Sato in 2002. They both use a type of traditional Japanese paper called washi. Paper company Taniguchi Aoya Washi produces the Bi-color Washi lampshade (above). The company is the only producer of three-dimensional washi in Japan. Like molded pulp, the fibres (mainly from the mulberry tree) are mixed with water and collected on the surface of a screen where they dry. The colour is dyed in two steps while the shades are being shaped. While the inside is a bright white that does not interfere with the colour of the lamp, the exterior may be decorated with a bright or dark colour. The second project (opposite) is manufactured by Ozu-washi for Ikazaki Shachu. Named cs007, it uses washi from the Aichi Prefecture, which has been renowned for its paper since the Heian Period (794–1185). The recipe includes the mitsumata plant (Oriental paper bush) and sumi (a black ink used in calligraphy). The paper is made flat and then pressed into the shape of a plate. Photo of Bi-color Washi lampshade by Akihiro Yoshida; photo of cs007 by Hiroshi Iwasaki.

and most other stiff materials is that it can be repeatedly folded without tearing. Known as folding endurance, this allows for packaging to be designed with flaps and closures that would not be practical in most other sheet materials. PP is one of the few plastics to exhibit the same property, in which case it is referred to as a living hinge.

A huge range of finishes exists. Paper is laminated with metallized PET to produce an optical mirror-finished material, known as mirror board, or mirriboard. A range of effects is achievable, including coloured-tinted and holographic. The surface of paper is flocked to produce a decorative and luxurious feel. Paper is coated with adhesive – all over or just selected areas – and coloured flock powder is applied. The surface is suitable for printing, embossing (pressure is applied to form an indent, known as deboss, or a raised surface profile, known as emboss) and foil blocking. Laminated or coated sheets can be processed like conventional paper, such as with printing (although not all inks will stick).

By its very nature, paper is susceptible to water absorption. And when wet, it loses tear strength. Nonetheless, tissue constructions have been developed that have very good tear strength, and paper laminated with plastic forms the base material for cartons used to package liquids.

Over the years many alternatives to wood-based paper have emerged. Nonwovens are made up of fibres (natural and synthetic) bonded together, not unlike paper. Nonwoven synthetic materials, such as DuPont Tyvek, are lightweight, resistant to tearing and unaffected by water. Manufactured from high-density polyethylene (HDPE) (see PE) fibres, its exceptional durability is utilized in a range of packaging and printed media.

Sheet plastics, known as synthetic paper, provide an alternative in some situations. Various plastics – but mainly PP, PE and PET – have been used instead of paper-based products in cartons and boxes as well as many non-packaging items (see polymer banknote, page 105). Lightweight woven textiles, such as

gauze and mesh are soft and not stiff like paper, but they may be used in place of lightweight tissues, such as for packaging, where high tear strength is required.

Molded paper pulp packaging transfers the benefits of paper into three-dimensional structures. Waste from the paper industry is shredded, mixed with water, pulped and molded. It can be reused or recycled and is completely biodegradable end-of-life. The smoothness of the molding is improved by wet pressing or hot pressing during the drying cycle. With such techniques logos and fine text can be embossed into the molding. Here, paper competes with synthetic foams, such as expanded polystyrene (EPS) (page 132), expanded polypropylene (EPP) (see PP) and expanded polyethylene (EPE) (see PE).

## WOOD PULP, PAPER AND BOARD IN PRODUCTS AND FURNITURE

Paper is manipulated in a number of ways. It is folded with permanent creases, molded with steam and pressure, cut into yarn, scored, twisted, torn, embroidered, embossed and printed. Meanwhile, new techniques are emerging that are transforming paper and its potential, such as printable electronics (circuitry and antennas, for example) and thermochromatic additives (change colour according to temperature).

Paper is converted into structural panels in a number of different ways. Sheets are rolled, folded and laminated to make sandwich panels similar to metal (see Titanium, page 58). Strips of

paper are adhesive bonded and formed into a honeycomb structure. Applied as the core in fibre-reinforced plastic (FRP) constructions, paper honeycomb is lightweight and provides good energy absorption properties. It is utilized in car doors as well as building materials (doors and panels).

As a manual process, handmade paper provides scope for experimentation. Indeed, paper is considered an art form in many cultures and skilled makers are highly regarded. Design starts with the choice of ingredients and method of processing. Virtually any type of fibrous material may be incorporated, as long as the base ingredients are derived from enough cellulose-based fibres to provide binding resins. In the past, recycled textile was often used. Termed rag, textiles were shredded and added to paper to improve strength and resilience. Nowadays, the proportion of materials other than wood fibre is a good indicator of quality; higher-quality papers tend to incorporate a higher percentage of non-wood fibres.

Petals, leaves and flowers may be incorporated for decorative effect. They are typically picked fresh on the day to maintain their colour, or alternatively they may be dried and pressed. Using the same principle, virtually any type of thin and flexible material may be incorporated. Some fibres are purely decorative, while others improve strength and other important properties. They are laid down randomly, in simple patterns or complex configurations. To secure them in the paper structure, they are either mixed in with the fibres or placed between layers of thin tissue. They can be more prominent on one side than the other, depending on where in the lay-up they are placed.

**Flat-pack speaker** This Muji cardboard speaker mixes packaging production with electronics. Die-cut from lightweight board, the fold lines are scored in the same process just like a conventional carton. Perhaps the ultimate low-cost electronics, it is shipped flat and assembled by the consumer.

CAUTION
Do not leave in a hot place in the car near the heater, for long time.
Do not use them with a sound distorted for a long time. Speakers may overheat and cause fire.
This product is not waterproof. Please be careful not to soak into water, or get it wet.

ATTENTION

CAUTION
Do not leave this product in the car near the heater, for a long time.
Do not use them with a sound distorted for a long time. Speakers may overheat and cause fire.
This product is not waterproof. Please be careful not to soak into water, or get it wet.

ATTENTION

# Bark

**Bark includes all the tissue on a tree outside of the woody stem. From cork to mulberry, its properties can be attributed to the protective role each type plays on the tree trunk. It is antibacterial and antifungal with excellent water-shedding properties. Traditionally associated with indigenous handicraft, bark has recently shown great potential for modern design.**

| Types | Typical Applications | Sustainability |
|---|---|---|
| • Stripped bark<br>• Bark cloth | • Packaging<br>• Textiles<br>• Furniture | • Bark may be sourced renewably and the income supports local communities in many cases |

| Properties | Competing Materials | Costs |
|---|---|---|
| • Impervious to water and breathable<br>• Antimicrobial and antifungal<br>• Strong but brittle | • Paper, veneer and leather<br>• Cotton, hemp and jute<br>• Synthetic fabric: PP, PET and PA | • Low to moderate for commodity types (e.g. birch and palm)<br>• Moderate to high for those that require more handwork (e.g. paper mulberry) |

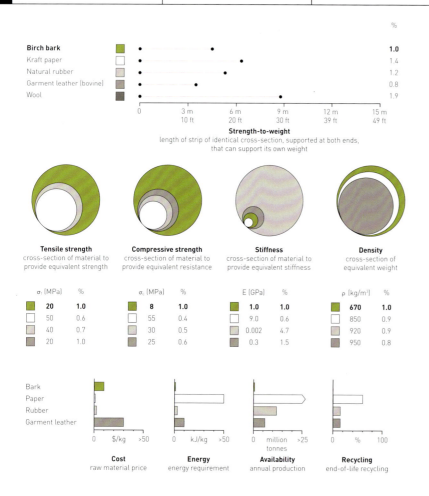

Strength-to-weight
length of strip of identical cross-section, supported at both ends, that can support its own weight

|  | % |
|---|---|
| Birch bark | 1.0 |
| Kraft paper | 1.4 |
| Natural rubber | 1.2 |
| Garment leather (bovine) | 0.8 |
| Wool | 1.9 |

**Tensile strength**
cross-section of material to provide equivalent strength

**Compressive strength**
cross-section of material to provide equivalent resistance

**Stiffness**
cross-section of material to provide equivalent stiffness

**Density**
cross-section of equivalent weight

| $\sigma_t$ (MPa) | % | $\sigma_c$ (MPa) | % | E (GPa) | % | $\rho$ (kg/m³) | % |
|---|---|---|---|---|---|---|---|
| 20 | 1.0 | 8 | 1.0 | 1.0 | 1.0 | 670 | 1.0 |
| 50 | 0.6 | 55 | 0.4 | 9.0 | 0.6 | 850 | 0.9 |
| 40 | 0.7 | 30 | 0.5 | 0.002 | 4.7 | 920 | 0.9 |
| 20 | 1.0 | 25 | 0.6 | 0.3 | 1.5 | 950 | 0.8 |

Bark
Paper
Rubber
Garment leather

**Cost**
raw material price

**Energy**
energy requirement

**Availability**
annual production

**Recycling**
end-of-life recycling

## INTRODUCTION

Bark has been harvested since prehistoric times to make writing material, apparel, storage, canoes and shelter. As a result of the high level of skill required to harvest bark and the few people capable of doing it, these can be quite expensive materials. To this day it is worked using traditional techniques, which have changed very little over the generations.

The qualities and character vary according to the type of tree and method of extraction. The outside and inside will have different properties. The inside surface will be softer, unless it is the inner bark, in which case the two surfaces will be similar (but removing this inner layer is fatal to most species of tree). It is used in its natural colour, which varies according to the type of tree and time of year when it was harvested. If decorated then it is typically dyed using natural ingredients, in keeping with tradition.

'Lenticels' cover the surface of bark. Functioning as pores, they provide a pathway for oxygen and carbon dioxide to travel between the internal woody tissue and the atmosphere. Otherwise, bark is impervious to water and gases. In the case of birch (Betulaceae family) (page 334), and some other species, the lenticels are visible as distinctive linear markings on the surface.

Either side may be exposed in application. The inside surface will be smooth and uniform. These are useful properties for the inner surface of food

**Cherry bark tea caddy**
Known as kabazaiku, craftwork involving cherry bark has existed in Japan for centuries. It is left natural or polished (pictured) to reveal the rich colour and highlight the linear markings (lenticels, similar to birch). In the case of tea storage, cherry bark provides ideal conditions. While it is impervious to moisture and so maintains the correct humidity, the lenticels allow the contents to breathe.

containers, for example. The outside surface is typically more undulating and decorative.

Bark is made up of much the same material as wood – cellulose, hemicellulose, lignin and so on – but in different proportions. It typically contains less cellulose and hemicellulose and a higher proportion of fats, waxes and essential oils. These provide the bark with its healing and protective antibacterial and antifungal properties. Their benefits have been exploited in medicine and remedies for millennia. Likewise, when applied to packaging, these ingredients protect the contents in the same way that bark protects the tree.

Certain species of tree yield a bark that can be beaten into a paper-like textile, a much more resilient material that can be flexed without breaking. Dating back thousands of years, these materials were likely the precursor to paper. Moisture and beating release resins from within the bark that provide the binding material. Examples include tapa cloth from the paper mulberry tree (*Broussonetia papyrifera*), cedar bark cloth (from coniferous trees, Cupressaceae family, see Cypress Family, page 318; not cedars) and Ugandan bark cloth from the mutuba tree (*Ficus natalensis*).

## COMMERCIAL TYPES AND USES
The mix of bark and its use depends on geographical location and how the indigenous people have traditionally exploited its many properties.

There are many different types of birch, which grow across North America,

Asia and Europe. It is a very versatile tree and over the years every part has found application in useful items. The bark is typically harvested in the early summer months and has a distinctive shimmering white outer. People living within each region where the tree grows evolved slightly different ways of using the bark. For example, in North America sheets of bark are stitched together and used to make containers and canoes, whereas in northern Europe and Siberia, the bark is cut into strips and woven to make baskets, shoes and packaging.

Bark is not a very durable material. Woven shoes will wear through in a couple of weeks or so. Products that are not flexed and abraded can last much longer. It is resistant to decay and can last decades outdoors or submerged in water. Birch bark was used in traditional Finnish fishing nets.

The paper mulberry is cultivated across Asia and the Pacific. Fibres from its inner bark are highly prized for making paper, such as Japanese washi (see also page 276), Thai saa and Chinese xuan. In the Pacific region, an alternative technique developed. Strips of the inner bark are beaten together to make a soft and flexible material suitable for writing and drawing on, as well as items of clothing. Known as tapa cloth, it is used to make sarongs, scarves and hats. It was once the main source of clothing on the Pacific islands of Fiji, Tonga and Tahiti. Nowadays it is reserved for ceremonial occasions.

In Uganda, the inner bark of the mutuba tree is used to make a similar textile. Harvested during the wet season,

**Bark upholstery**
Taburet is a stool designed by Anastasiya Koshcheeva, 2015. Strips of birch bark are sewn together and held taut over a welded steel (page 28) frame. By mixing traditional Siberian handcraft techniques with modern materials and processes, Anastasiya has brought this age-old material into the contemporary design space. Photo by Crispy Point Agency.

it is beaten with wooden mallets to make it softer and more pliable. Naturally terracotta in colour, it can be bleached to off-white and dyed black – white or black cloth being so highly prized that it is the attire of kings and chiefs. Almost wiped out by low-cost mass-produced cotton (page 410), the cloth is now produced by just a few craftspeople.

These materials are also being explored as potential fibre reinforcement

**Birch bark canoe** Birch bark canoes were an integral part of native North American culture in many areas. The skills required to build them were handed down through generations; nowadays few people have the knowhow to build one. This example was designed and built by Steve Cayard, Maine, 2010, to reflect the Wabanaki tradition. The process starts with stripping long lengths of bark. Unlike wood and canvas canoes, the structure is built from the outside in, starting with the bark and finishing with the ribs and planking. First, the bark is laid out and sewn up with spruce (page 304) roots. It is formed into an envelope around a framework of northern white-cedar gunwales (see Cypress and Cedar) and rock maple (page 330) thwarts. The bark is used inside out, giving a smooth tan outer surface. It is lashed together with spruce roots and the inside lined with pre-bent ribs. In the ribbing process, boiling water is poured over the bark to make it pliable. It is gradually forced into the shape of the canoe and all the slackness removed. The seams are gummed with pine rosin and lard. Photo by Steve Cayard.

**Stripping bark** The part of the bark that is harvested depends on the species. In most cases, it is the outer bark that is stripped. The inner bark, which is sandwiched between the outer bark and woody core, is left uncut, because damaging it can be fatal for the tree. How it is removed depends on the species and how it will be used. For example, long strips used for weaving may be removed as long spirals around the circumference, or cut lengthwise. Once the bark is cut it is stored flat, or rolled against its natural curve. Each piece will have a different appearance depending on the thickness, diameter of the trunk, size of the lenticels, branch scars, colour and texture. Strength depends on the type and method of production, but all barks are stronger along the length of the fibres. Paper (page 268) has far superior mechanical properties. Even though the two materials are made up of much the same ingredients, paper is refined to remove the variability and weakness of the original material.

in composites. One such example is Barktex, a Ugandan–German venture. Modern developments that combine bark fibre with natural or synthetic resin are reminiscent of traditional bark canoes. Development is not as widespread as natural-fibre reinforcement (see Hemp, page 406, and Jute, page 404), mainly owing to limited availability of materials. With the correct mix of materials, bark has the potential to create lightweight and high-strength materials with interesting visual and tactile properties unlike any other composite.

On the west coast of North America, the native peoples used coniferous tree (Cupressaceae family) bark to make cedar cloth. It too was used in clothing. The bark was also woven into jewelry, baskets, hats and shelter.

Palm trees (Arecaceae family) are native to the tropics, but they can be found across Europe and North America. The bark is stripped and used to make items of waterproof clothing, such as capes and hats. It has a very fibrous texture, which is utilized in bushcraft to make strong cordage.

## SUSTAINABILITY

Harvesting bark can be as sustainable and renewable as softwood (see Pine, page 304) if done mindfully. It can be taken from certain trees without causing irreparable damage, if only the outer bark is removed and the inner bark – which transports water and nutrients up the tree – remains intact. However, it is generally best to take bark from trees that have recently been, or will soon be, felled.

# Cork

The unique properties of cork are the result of its chemistry and three-dimensional closed-cell structure. It comes from the bark of the evergreen cork oak (*Quercus suber*), which grows across the western Mediterranean and North Africa. It is harvested from the trunk approximately every ten years, which is the time it takes for the bark to regrow.

| Types | Typical Applications | Sustainability |
|---|---|---|
| • Unprocessed<br>• Granules<br>• Compound agglomerate, rubberized or bonded | • Packaging<br>• Insulation<br>• Furniture | • Low embodied energy<br>• Renewable and available from certified forests |
| **Properties** | **Competing Materials** | **Costs** |
| • Impervious to water and gases<br>• Good insulator<br>• Resists spreading laterally when pressed | • Plastic foams, such as EVA, PE, PP and PU<br>• Rubber and leather | • Low to moderate material cost and manufacturing cost |

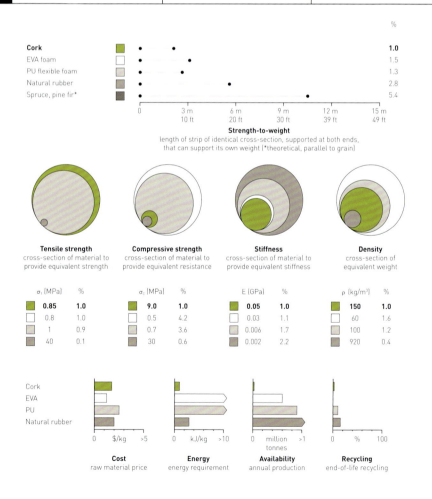

| | % |
|---|---|
| Cork | 1.0 |
| EVA foam | 1.5 |
| PU flexible foam | 1.3 |
| Natural rubber | 2.8 |
| Spruce, pine fir* | 5.4 |

0    3 m / 10 ft    6 m / 20 ft    9 m / 30 ft    12 m / 39 ft    15 m / 49 ft

**Strength-to-weight**
length of strip of identical cross-section, supported at both ends, that can support its own weight (*theoretical, parallel to grain)

**Tensile strength**
cross-section of material to provide equivalent strength

**Compressive strength**
cross-section of material to provide equivalent resistance

**Stiffness**
cross-section of material to provide equivalent stiffness

**Density**
cross-section of equivalent weight

| $\sigma_t$ (MPa) | % | $\sigma_c$ (MPa) | % | E (GPa) | % | $\rho$ (kg/m³) | % |
|---|---|---|---|---|---|---|---|
| 0.85 | 1.0 | 9.0 | 1.0 | 0.05 | 1.0 | 150 | 1.0 |
| 0.8 | 1.0 | 0.5 | 4.2 | 0.03 | 1.1 | 60 | 1.6 |
| 1 | 0.9 | 0.7 | 3.6 | 0.006 | 1.7 | 100 | 1.2 |
| 40 | 0.1 | 30 | 0.6 | 0.002 | 2.2 | 920 | 0.4 |

Cork
EVA
PU
Natural rubber

0    $/kg    >5        0    kJ/kg    >10        0    million tonnes    >1        0    %    100

**Cost**
raw material price

**Energy**
energy requirement

**Availability**
annual production

**Recycling**
end-of-life recycling

## INTRODUCTION

Used to seal wine bottles since the 17th century, cork remains an important industrial and domestic material. It is made up of around one-half suberin. This inert waxy substance is impermeable to water and provides cork with its antimicrobial and antifungal properties (gases and water are transferred between the atmosphere and the woody core via so-called 'lenticular channels'). Combined with its high compressibility and flexibility, this makes cork the ideal natural material for sealing bottles.

Like wood, cork contains lignin, polysaccharides (cellulose and hemicellulose), waxes and tannins. They both contain around the same proportion of lignin. This hard natural polymer provides rigidity. Around 25% of cork is cellulose and hemicellulose. This is far less than wood, which contains around 50% cellulose alone. Cellulose is a strong semi-crystalline polymer (see page 166), which prevents the cells from collapse. Aligned with the direction of growth, these natural polymers provide strength parallel to the grain.

Cork has a honeycomb-like cell structure. The columns of cells are oriented around the growth rings, which are stacked facing outward (radial). As a result, cork is anisotropic: it has roughly equivalent properties in all directions perpendicular to radial, which are different from its properties parallel to radial. For comparison, the cell structure of wood runs lengthwise (axial). The variability in density (approx. 120–240 kg/m³ [7.5–15 lb/ft³]), ingredients and cell size results in a material whose properties are near impossible to accurately predict.

Owing to its structure, cork has a Poisson's ratio close to zero – this means that it exhibits very little lateral expansion when compressed. This is why corks are relatively easy to insert into and remove from the necks of wine bottles. Natural rubber (page 248), with a Poisson's ratio of 0.5, would expand laterally when compressed, preventing it from being inserted.

The closed-cell structure and woody nature of cork makes it an efficient thermal insulator. Likewise, cork provides good soundproofing. The low density and high porosity means sound transmission is poor; sound waves are absorbed and converted into thermal energy.

Since the turn of the century, the price of unprocessed cork has fallen by nearly 50%. This is largely due to competition from synthetic alternatives, in particular ethylene vinyl acetate (EVA) (page 118) and polyurethane (PU) (page 202). Compared to these, cork has a limited range of variation in properties; it is inevitably bound to natural growth patterns.

## COMMERCIAL TYPES AND USES

More than three-quarters of the world's cork comes from the western Mediterranean (Portugal, Spain and parts of France). The vast majority goes into the production of bottle stoppers. As a result, the quality of the raw material is judged based on its suitability for this purpose.

The first bark is removed when the tree is around 250 mm (10 in) in diameter, or around 20 years old. It is highly irregular and not suitable for stoppers. Instead, virgin bark and often the second stripping (harvested after another 9–12 years) are used to make agglomerate (blocks).

To make agglomerate, cork scraps (including those from stopper production) are broken into small pieces and compressed in an autoclave (high-pressure heating chamber) at around 300°C (572°F). The high temperature causes the suberin (and other binders present in the cork) to become plastic

**Fishing float** Cork's low density makes it very buoyant, a property that has been utilized in fishing floats for millennia. It contains a high proportion of waxy suberin, which prevents it from soaking up any water; and the natural resins make it resistant to decay, so it can last many decades. This example was handmade by Ian Lewis, one of the few float makers left in the UK.

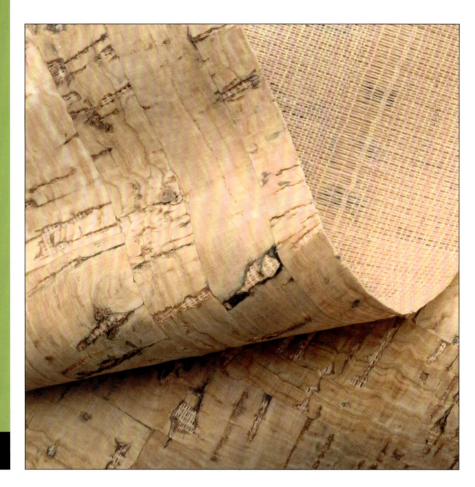

This causes the gas trapped within the cells – which make up around 60% of the material by volume – to expand and create a more uniform cell structure. Therefore, most mechanical properties for cork are assessed post-boiling.

and the high pressure forces the particles to swell and bond together. Known as expanded cork, the resulting material is naturally dark (almost black) and used in construction for sound and thermal insulation and vibration damping.

This form of agglomerate is a wholly natural material, but has significantly lower strength than prime cork. Binding the particles with plastic (such as PU or synthetic rubber, page 216) yields a much stronger and more resilient material. By varying the packing density and synthetic binder a variety of properties can be achieved, from flexible to rigid. Selection depends on the requirements of the application. Known as compound agglomerated, rubberized or bonded cork, it is used to make products ranging from high-performance gaskets and flooring (linoleum, for example) to toys and shoe soles. It is also used to make stoppers for wine that will be consumed within six months of bottling.

Three-dimensional items are compression molded into the final shape, or cut from solid block. Particle size ranges from fine powder up to around 12 mm (0.5 in). Micro-agglomerated cork is made up of particles between 0.5 and 2 mm (0.02 to 0.08 in) and around 3% binder (by volume). The small particle size yields a consistent quality and smooth surface finish. The least expensive material is produced from lower-quality and large pieces of cork.

Cork from the third harvest is suitable for stopper production. It is graded according to quality, which is determined by the colour, thickness and defects. The best bits of the bark are punched out to make stoppers, which equates to around one-third of total production. They are cut in-line with the direction of growth of the tree, so the lenticular channels (passageways for gas and water) run across the width of the cork.

There exists a wide range of standard profiles, from parallel-sided wine bottle stoppers to capped corks. As a natural and variable material, the stoppers must pass a series of inspections to ensure they are fit for purpose.

Cork is prepared for use by boiling.

## SUSTAINABILITY

Cork is renewable, sustainable and available from certified forests. Once a tree is old enough, the bark is peeled every ten years or so. The average cork oak yields 40–60 kg (88–132 lb) of bark. Harvesting cork remains a manual and highly skilled process. Removing the outer bark does not damage these trees permanently and they may continue yielding cork for 200 years. The practice has existed for so long that complementary agriculture has evolved to utilize the spoils from the oak, such as rearing black Iberian pigs (fed exclusively on acorns) for *pata negra* ham. The cork oak is considered so important to biodiversity that in Portugal it is illegal to cut down the tree, dead or alive.

At the end of the product's useful life cork can be recycled or composted. Every year around 12 billion cork stoppers are consumed. Recycling schemes were recently set up to take back the cork. Examples include Green Cork in Portugal, Ecobouchon in France, Etico in Italy and Recork in the USA. If using rubberized cork, the waste is likely disposed in landfill.

# Veneer

Wood is cut in thin slices, either across the width of the log, or from around the circumference, to produce patterned sheets of veneer. The unique colour and figuring of each piece are determined by the species, method of production and growth rings. Both softwoods and hardwoods are eligible; figured grain caused by branches and disease is the most sought after.

| Types | Typical Applications | Sustainability |
|---|---|---|
| • Sliced<br>• Peeled<br>• Laminated | • Furniture<br>• Interiors<br>• Automotive<br>• Musical instruments | • Depends on the type of wood and distance travelled<br>• Specifying veneer reduces the consumption of exotic hardwood |
| **Properties** | **Competing Materials** | **Costs** |
| • Unique visual qualities<br>• Anisotropic like solid timber<br>• Mechanical properties depend on species and production | • Solid timber<br>• Cellulose acetate<br>• Phenolic and melamine | • Peeled veneers are low-cost<br>• Sliced veneers are moderate- to high-cost<br>• Figured grain is the most expensive |

290

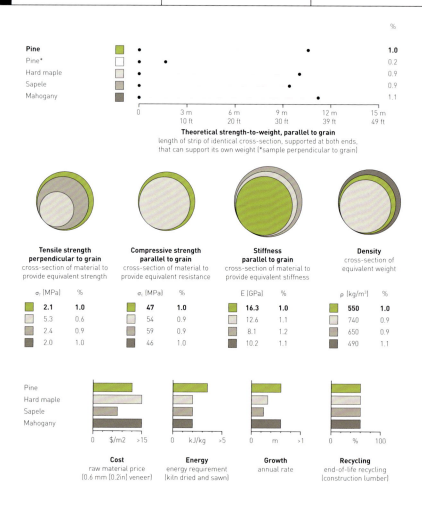

**Theoretical strength-to-weight, parallel to grain**
length of strip of identical cross-section, supported at both ends, that can support its own weight (*sample perpendicular to grain)

| | | % |
|---|---|---|
| Pine | | 1.0 |
| Pine* | | 0.2 |
| Hard maple | | 0.9 |
| Sapele | | 0.9 |
| Mahogany | | 1.1 |

| 0 | 3 m<br>10 ft | 6 m<br>20 ft | 9 m<br>30 ft | 12 m<br>39 ft | 15 m<br>49 ft |
|---|---|---|---|---|---|

**Tensile strength perpendicular to grain**
cross-section of material to provide equivalent strength

| $\sigma_t$ (MPa) | % |
|---|---|
| 2.1 | 1.0 |
| 5.3 | 0.6 |
| 2.4 | 0.9 |
| 2.0 | 1.0 |

**Compressive strength parallel to grain**
cross-section of material to provide equivalent resistance

| $\sigma_c$ (MPa) | % |
|---|---|
| 47 | 1.0 |
| 54 | 0.9 |
| 59 | 0.9 |
| 46 | 1.0 |

**Stiffness parallel to grain**
cross-section of material to provide equivalent stiffness

| E (GPa) | % |
|---|---|
| 16.3 | 1.0 |
| 12.6 | 1.1 |
| 8.1 | 1.2 |
| 10.2 | 1.1 |

**Density**
cross-section of equivalent weight

| $\rho$ (kg/m³) | % |
|---|---|
| 550 | 1.0 |
| 740 | 0.9 |
| 650 | 0.9 |
| 490 | 1.1 |

| | Pine<br>Hard maple<br>Sapele<br>Mahogany |
|---|---|

**Cost**
raw material price
[0.6 mm (0.2in) veneer]
0 — $/m2 — >15

**Energy**
energy requirement
(kiln dried and sawn)
0 — kJ/kg — >5

**Growth**
annual rate
0 — m — >1

**Recycling**
end-of-life recycling
(construction lumber)
0 — % — 100

## INTRODUCTION

Veneer has two main purposes: it provides a decorative surfacing material for furniture and interiors; or multiple layers are laminated into high-strength engineered timber (page 296), which is used mainly in construction and furniture making.

Wood is a natural composite. It is made up of xylem tissue, a fibrous material consisting mostly of elongated, rigid-walled cells that provide trees with an upward flow of water and mechanical support. Annual growth rings develop as a consequence of seasonal change and can be used to tell the age of the tree. Early in the growing season tree growth is rapid and the wood is typically lighter in colour, because the cells are larger. Darker rings indicate slower growth from later in the growing season. Some trees grow fast, tall and straight; others are slower-growing with interlocking grain (see page 368). The annual rings are intersected with rays, which are structures radiating from the centre of the tree to transport food and waste laterally. The combination of rings and rays produces patterns and flecks of colour that are exposed when the tree is sliced to make veneer.

As a result of all these variables, veneers from different species and locations will have particular visual qualities. As a natural, edible and biodegradable material, wood is prone to attack by insects, animals, decay and disease. Qualities that may be considered defects in some applications, such as distortion of the growth rings caused by

**Wooden textile**
Created by Elisa Strozyk for Gestalten in Berlin, triangular pieces of dyed veneer are arranged and bonded on a flexible textile backing, used to decorate interiors. The behaviour of the fabric depends on the geometry and size of each tile. Photo courtesy of Elisa Strozyk.

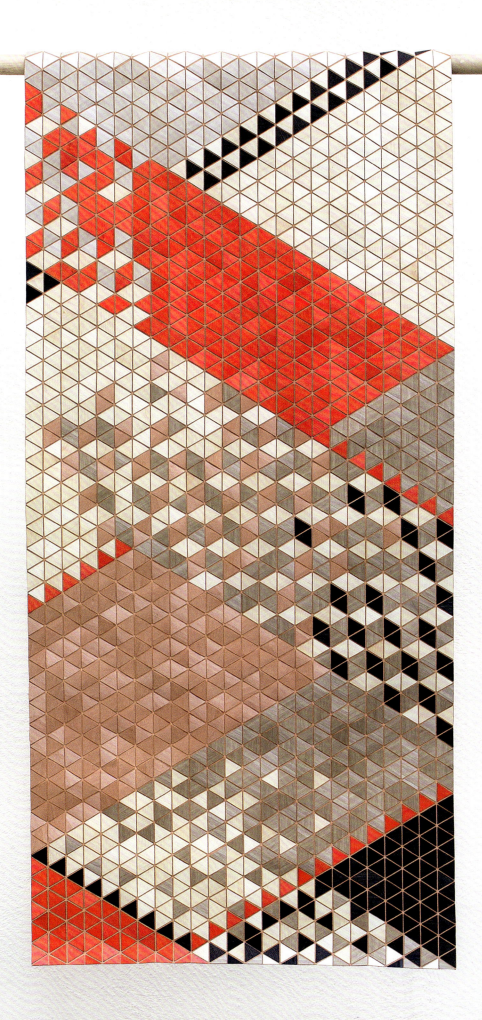

**European ash** A light-coloured hardwood used for decorative purposes and in the production of strong and resilient plywood (page 354).

**French beech** Quarter-cut veneer has a distinctive silvery fleck (rays). It is dense and hard with a tightly packed grain, and is used in furniture (page 338).

**Scandinavian birch** Commonly applied in furniture and interiors, as veneer and plywood, birch has a light colour and uniform texture (page 334).

**Bird's eye, sugar maple** Figured maples are rare and expensive hardwoods that have naturally figured grain pattern (page 330).

**Lebanese cedar** A light softwood related to pine, cedar produces natural oils that repel insects and protect it against decay.

**Sweet cherry** An expensive hardwood with a straight and uniform grain, cherry is prized for its lustrous colour and finish (page 360).

**Spanish sweet chestnut** A lightweight and durable hardwood, chestnut has excellent resistance to decay (page 346).

**Ebony** An exotic hardwood prized for its dark colour and superior surface hardness. Many species are now endangered (page 374).

**Mahogany** Genuine mahogany is an exotic hardwood prized for its lustrous surface quality and durability. Many types are endangered (page 372).

**Burr, Canadian oak** Figured oaks are very rare and expensive.

**Bog oak** The wood has been stained dark brown by the tannins found in the bogs where it grows.

**Padauk** A very dense and stable wood, padauk is utilized for its decorative colour.

**Scandinavian pine** This common softwood is harvested for a range of applications. It stains and paints to an excellent finish (page 304).

**Rosewood** A richly coloured, dense hardwood with a sweet smell, rosewood is expensive and popular in musical instruments and furniture (page 374).

**Sapele** An alternative to mahogany, sapele produces hard-wearing and decorative veneer; it is known for its rich colour and figured grain (page 372).

**Black walnut** This is a dense, strong and heavy wood. Walnut is a highly valued hardwood with a straight grain (page 348).

**Wengé** A dark chocolate-coloured exotic hardwood, wengé has a very hard surface. It is now critically endangered (page 374).

**European yew** Thought to be one of the most ancient trees, yew grows with a straight grain and few knots.

branches and disease (figured grain), are highly prized for wood veneers.

## COMMERCIAL TYPES AND USES

Both softwoods and hardwoods are converted into veneers. Softwoods are coniferous and typically evergreen trees and include spruce and pine (page 304), and cedar (see Cypress Family, page 318). Hardwoods are typically deciduous and broad-leaved trees. They range from commonly used types, such as oak (page 336), birch (page 334) and maple (page 330), to more exotic and expensive types such as rosewood (see Exotics, page 374), teak (page 370) and mahogany (page 372). In addition to the diversity of rich and beautiful colours, they may also grow with highly figured grain patterns. These can be rare and desirable, depending on the pattern and colouring, and greatly increase the cost of the veneer.

Wood veneers are cut from all types of tree. Decorative types are sliced around 0.6 mm (0.02 in) thick, while structural veneer is peeled and ranges from 1 to 5 mm (0.04 to 0.2 in). Exotic and rare hardwoods are typically produced much thinner, and range from 0.1 to 1.5 mm (0.004 to 0.06 in) thick, backed with a nonwoven to avoid splitting.

The size and appearance of veneer is affected by the slicing technique. Rotary-peeled veneers can be very large, because the veneer is cut continuously from around the circumference of the log. Sliced veneers are cut in strips from one face of the log, so the size is determined by the width of the tree.

If the area to be covered is larger than the veneer, separate pieces are laid side by side. The visual impact of the grain pattern will depend on the arrangement. The two most common configurations are 'bookmatch' and 'slipmatch'. Choice depends on the degree of figure (grain) and colour together with the desired effect.

Veneers may be used on their own or laminated to form high-strength and lightweight structures. For example, wood veneers are laminated together with strong adhesive to make load-bearing engineered timber. Cutting wood into strips, or veneers, and bonding it back

together greatly improves its strength and resistance to shrinking, twisting and warping. For structural applications, the wood should be free from defects, such as knots, to ensure an even grain.

Bending veneers during laminating further increases the strength. Three-dimensional laminated parts are used to make furniture, for example. The most flexible timbers include birch, beech (page 338), ash (page 354), oak and walnut (page 348). Combined with other woodworking techniques, laminating offers designers a great deal of creative freedom (see Engineered Timber, page 296).

Many of the processes used to shape, profile and finish paper and leather can be applied to thin veneer, such as die cutting, laser cutting, embossing and printing techniques. For secondary processes such as these, the qualities of wood must be taken into account, because most processes are not set up to accommodate the natural dimensional variation of wood.

## SUSTAINABILITY

Whether applied as a decorative surface layer, or as the entire structure, veneer is just one ingredient in a composite construction. Compared to solid lumber, this leads to an increase in the total embodied energy, which depends on the sum of all ingredients used. For example, adhesive is required to join the veneers to substrates and one another; this is typically formaldehyde-based (page 224).

The sustainability of the wood depends on the source and species. Several types of commonly used veneer, such as birch, are readily available from well-managed forests. Certification schemes, such as the Programme for the Endorsement of Forest Certification (PEFC) and the Forestry Stewardship Council (FSC), verify the flow of wood from forest to factory and end use, which is essential to ensure that the timber comes from sustainable sources. Only around 7% of forests are covered by forest certification globally – even though around half of Europe's forests and 40% of North America's are certified. Using wood originating from certified sources or covered by wood origin tracing systems helps to

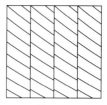
**Slipmatch**

**Bookmatch**

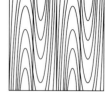
**Reverse slipmatch**

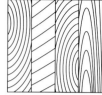
**Random matched**

**Veneer arrangement**
If the surface area is larger than a single piece of veneer, they are laid side by side as either 'bookmatched' or 'slipmatched' depending on the wood grain. Slipmatching means taking sliced veneers from a log and placing them side by side. This type of arrangement is most common in quarter-cut veneers. Reversing alternate veneers produces

a wavy pattern in crown-cut veneer and herringbone pattern in quarter-cut veneer. In bookmatching, facing pieces of veneer mirror one another, like the pages of a book, to create a symmetrical and repeating pattern. Of course, the individual sheets can be arranged in any number of different ways, including mismatch, or completely randomly.

avoid using wood originating from controversial sources (such as countries where deforestation takes place).

Slow-growing and rare woods, including several species of exotic hardwood, are more challenging to source sustainably. Applying these woods as veneer to a fast-growing and renewable timber substrate, as opposed to using solid timber, reduces their consumption.

**Laminated maple chair**
Designed by Frank Gehry in 1990, the Cross Check arm chair is manufactured by Knoll. An original approach to bentwood furniture, the family of chairs was the result of several years of experimentation by Gehry. Hard white maple veneer is cut into 50 mm (2 in) wide strips and laminated to 6- to 9-ply thickness.

The grain runs along the length in each layer – taking advantage of the anisotropic properties of wood – to maximize strength and spring tension. Bonded with urea adhesive (page 224), the composite is both structural and flexible, allowing a reassuring amount of movement. Photo courtesy of Knoll.

# Engineered Timber

**Also known as**
Also referred to as: ply, wood composite, laminated timber, wood panel
Trademark names: Kerto, Trus Joist, Timberstrand, Microllam, Parallam, GP Lam, Fiberstrong, Masonite

These wood-based composites extend the maximum cross-sectional size and length that can be achieved with sawn timber. Engineers and designers have exploited their potential in projects ranging from flatpack furniture to multi-storey buildings. A diversity of standard formats exists, manufactured to precise specifications, to fulfil specific requirements.

| Types | Typical Applications | Sustainability |
|---|---|---|
| • Panel<br>• Lumber<br>• Wood-plastic composite (WPC) | • Products and furniture<br>• Construction<br>• Transportation | • Low embodied energy<br>• Extends the number of species that can be used in engineering situations<br>• Available from certified forests |

| Properties | Competing Materials | Costs |
|---|---|---|
| • High strength-to-weight, but depends on the species and method of production<br>• Consistent and reliable | • Aluminium and steel<br>• PVC<br>• Pine, spruce, Douglas-fir, larch, and cypress (such as western red-cedar) | • Low to moderate for commodity types (e.g. birch and palm)<br>• Moderate to high for those that require more handwork (e.g. paper mulberry) |

## INTRODUCTION

Timber offers many advantages in construction: it is widely available and renewable and has impressive strength-to-weight. However, sawn lumber is limited by its natural variation, anisotropy (it is much less strong perpendicular to the grain), and the maximum cross-section and length that can be achieved. To overcome these drawbacks, wood is cut into smaller pieces, or veneer (page 290), and joined back together with high-strength adhesive (see Phenolic, page 224, and Polyurethane, page 202). This provides two significant advantages over sawn lumber. First, it spreads the defects (eliminating the major ones) to produce a more homogenous and reliable construction material. Second, their size is limited by transportation and handling, rather than by a tree's natural growth, which creates opportunities for longer spans and uninterrupted surfaces.

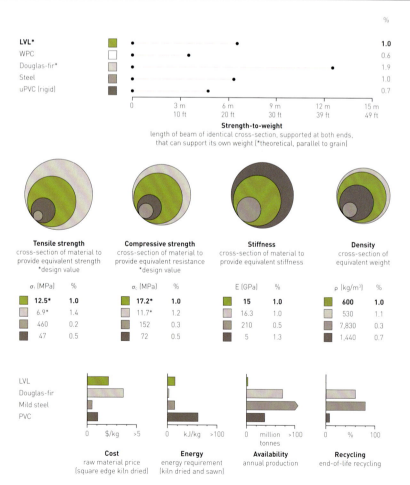

**LVL*** 1.0
WPC 0.6
Douglas-fir* 1.9
Steel 1.0
uPVC (rigid) 0.7

%

0   3 m / 10 ft   6 m / 20 ft   9 m / 30 ft   12 m / 39 ft   15 m / 49 ft

**Strength-to-weight**
length of beam of identical cross-section, supported at both ends, that can support its own weight (*theoretical, parallel to grain)

**Tensile strength**
cross-section of material to provide equivalent strength
*design value

| σ_t (MPa) | % |
|---|---|
| 12.5* | 1.0 |
| 6.9* | 1.4 |
| 460 | 0.2 |
| 47 | 0.5 |

**Compressive strength**
cross-section of material to provide equivalent resistance
*design value

| σ_c (MPa) | % |
|---|---|
| 17.2* | 1.0 |
| 11.7* | 1.2 |
| 152 | 0.3 |
| 72 | 0.5 |

**Stiffness**
cross-section of material to provide equivalent stiffness

| E (GPa) | % |
|---|---|
| 15 | 1.0 |
| 16.3 | 1.0 |
| 210 | 0.5 |
| 5 | 1.3 |

**Density**
cross-section of equivalent weight

| ρ (kg/m³) | % |
|---|---|
| 600 | 1.0 |
| 530 | 1.1 |
| 7,830 | 0.3 |
| 1,440 | 0.7 |

LVL
Douglas-fir
Mild steel
PVC

0   $/kg   >5

**Cost**
raw material price
(square edge kiln dried)

0   kJ/kg   >100

**Energy**
energy requirement
(kiln dried and sawn)

0   million tonnes   >100

**Availability**
annual production

0   %   100

**Recycling**
end-of-life recycling

**Plywood** A huge range of standard configurations exists. Clockwise from top: birch sandwich with sound-insulating core (used in the transport industry for sound insulation, in particular the floors or trains and buses), birch with plastic-coated tan-coloured fibreboard (reusable formwork), silver thermoplastic-coated birch (very durable panels that are weather- and crack-resistant, suitable for demanding indoor and outdoor applications), phenolic film-overlaid birch plywood (provides a smooth and durable surface suitable for formwork and as a maintenance-free sheathing panel for transportation and agriculture), debossed resin-coated birch (used in flooring: a wire pattern is impressed into the surface for durability and anti-slip protection), beech (high-quality hardwood panel suitable for interior use), and spruce (lightweight general-purpose plywood). The two in the middle are diamond debossed resin-coated birch (durable flooring material) and a three-layer panel consisting of 4 mm (0.16 in) thick heat-treated ash outer layers and birch core (another high-quality hardwood panel suitable for interior use).

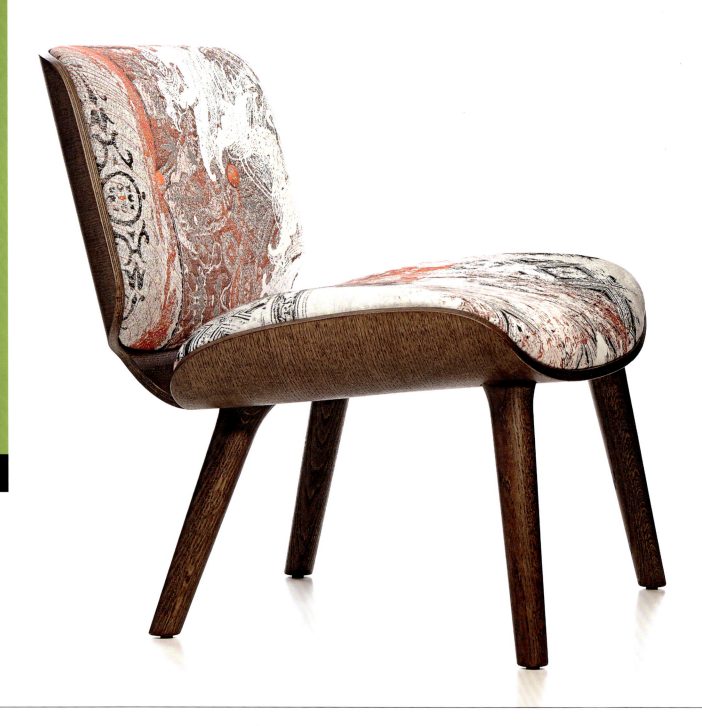

Engineered timber ranges from finger jointing to reconstituted boards. A variety of standard types is available, which vary according to the manufacturer; each offers a unique combination of technical and aesthetic performance. It is possible to create one's own configuration based on project requirements. The number, thickness and orientation of the layers, as well as the species, may all be adjusted.

## COMMERCIAL TYPES AND USES
Wood-based composites are broadly divided into structural products (panels and lumber), non-structural (panels) and wood-plastic composite (WPC).

Panels consist of layers of veneer or compressed reconstituted wood, bonded with high-strength adhesive. Plywood is made up of laminated veneers (plies) and categorized as structural (stress-rated) or non-bearing. Panels are covered by product standards, depending on country of origin or import, that cover the durability of the veneer and the moisture resistance of the adhesive. Low emissions standards have been established for panels that are destined for interior use.

**Oak veneer lounge chair**  Dutch designer Marcel Wanders created the Nut lounge chair for Moooi, 2013. Produced from oak-veneered plywood, with solid oak legs, this version is stained cinnamon. The veneers are pressed and laminated to produce a strong, rigid shell. Photo courtesy of Moooi.

Produced in a range of standard sizes from 1220 x 2440 mm (48 x 96 in) to 1525 x 3660 mm (60 x 144 in), thickness ranges from around 4 mm to 50 mm (0.16 to 2 in), depending on the species. Many standard configurations exist.

Softwood plywood is typically

spruce or pine (page 304). It has good strength-to-weight and is used for structural applications where mechanical functionality is more important than visual properties. It is also known as shuttering ply, because it is commonly used as such, providing a temporary structure (known as formwork) to hold concrete in shape while it sets. They are graded according to surface finish, including non-sanded, plugged (knots plugged and sanded), sanded and knot-free.

Hardwood plywood tends to be used for its appearance, although some species are suitable for structural applications. Birch (page 334) plywood is a high-quality panel with excellent physical and mechanical properties. It is heavier than softwood types (750 kg/m³ [47 lb/ft³] compared to only 500 kg/m³ [31 lb/ft³] for spruce) and more expensive. It is used for high-quality furniture, shop fitting and interiors. Industrial applications include dies (for die cutting) and engineering patterns (casting).

Poplar (page 324) plywood is lightweight with similar mechanical properties to spruce (although it does not have the same impressive resistance to decay). It is used in applications where weight is critical, such as transportation (vehicles and trailers), furniture, doors, boats and packaging.

To take advantage of the flexibility of birch and poplar, thin plywood (typically 3-ply) may be laminated with the grain running in the same direction throughout. This allows for much tighter bends to be formed than panels with cross-grain. The grain may be specified to run the length of the board, or across its width.

Surface quality is graded (best to worst) A, B, C and D. Quality ranges from a blemish-free face suitable for high-quality painting to non-sanded. Backside quality is determined as (best to worst) 1, 2, 3 and 4. Where both sides are faced with high-quality veneer, the plywood is graded AA, AB and so on. Thus, AA or A1 is the highest quality and used where both sides will be visible in application. A4 and B4 have one good side and so are useful where one side will be hidden.

Exterior-grade plywood is produced using durable veneer laminated with an adhesive that has high resistance to moisture. It is also referred to as water and boil proof (WBP). Marine plywood is engineered for used in high-humidity environments and is fully structural. The most durable types use woods that have high resistance to decay, such as tropical species (also called tropical plywood). They are suitable for boat building and decking.

Reconstituted wood panels include oriented strand board (OSB), fibreboard and particleboard.

OSB, also known as sterling board, is produced from strands of wood cut from small diameter logs. This makes for a much more cost-effective product. The strands are aligned and assembled in layers (three to five), mimicking the perpendicular grain of plywood. They are mixed with water-resistant adhesive and bonded together with heat and pressure. It is suitable for structural applications and is often used as the web in I-joists as well as providing the structural base layer in roofs, walls and floors. One of the drawbacks of this approach is that the edges are vulnerable to water absorption and swell when wet. And increasing the amount of adhesive and bonding surface area, compared to plywood, increases the likelihood of creep.

Waferboard is produced from the same ingredients as OSB, and belongs to the same set of materials collectively referred to as flakeboard. The principal difference with waferboard is that the strands are not aligned. As a result, it is less expensive, but has inferior mechanical properties. It is used in the production of low-cost furniture laminated with a decorative face veneer.

There exists a number of different particleboard and fibreboard composites. They are manufactured from a mix of wood particles, hot-pressed with high-strength adhesive.

Particleboard, also known as chipboard, is an inexpensive wood panel widely used in construction and furniture making. It is high-density and has a uniform consistency, but is not very strong in tension. It is often found in kitchens,

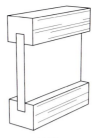

**I-joist**

**Finger joint**

**Structural lumber**
I-joists are designed to resist flexural and axial loads. The flanges (top and bottom) are produced from softwood or LVL; the grain runs lengthwise. The web is generally made from OSB, fibreboard or plywood. Finger-jointing is the

simplest means of producing continuous lengths of timber (such as used in the production of glulam and CLT). Planks are cut into small pieces (lamellas) free from major defects, which are glued together with their grain aligned lengthwise.

**Cross-grain**

**Parallel-grain**

**Laminated veneer**
These structural timbers are produced by bonding together multiple veneers (plies) under high pressure. Large flat panels, such as plywood, are produced with an odd or even number of plies depending on requirements. The

veneers are oriented so the grain runs perpendicular in each layer. LVL is laminated with all the grain running longitudinally to maximize strength-to-weight (lengthwise). In some cases, cross-grain plies are incorporated to improve stability.

**Laminated veneer**

**Bentwood**

**Forming** The minimum bend radius is determined by the thickness of the individual veneer, so many thin sheets may be stacked up and bent very tightly. Thanks to wood's

anisotropic properties, it bends more easily perpendicular to the grain. Solid wood is steamed so it can be bent (see page 357), but the minimum radius will still be larger than for laminated veneer.

**Injection-molded WPC**
This storage pot from Rig-Tig by Stelton features an injection-molded acrylonitrile butadiene styrene (ABS) (page 138) base and WPC lid. Plastic filled with wood flour can be injection molded using conventional equipment; the design opportunities are much the same as for plastic without filler. The only real difference is that the plastic composite takes on wood-like colour and mottled appearance. Of course, the colour and consistency depend on the filler and may be adjusted to fit the application.

(HDF). These are versatile materials with excellent machinability. The smooth surface and consistent structure make fibreboard an ideal material for cutting and painting to an exceptionally high-quality finish. MDF is utilized in non-load-bearing applications in furniture making, interiors, panelling, shelving, storage, acoustic enclosures (speakers), packaging and countless other situations. At over 800 kg/m³ (50 lb/ft³), HDF is heavier and more stable than MDF (around 450–800 kg/m³ [28–50 lb/ft³]). It is used as an alternative to hardboard in flooring and cabinetmaking.

Wood-composite lumber is produced in long lengths, up to 25 m (82 ft), manufactured as a continuous billet. The limit is set by transportation and handling restrictions. Like structural panel products, they are stress-rated and produced from softwood, hardwood or a mixture of the two. At equivalent weight, the design value can be more than twice that of structural sawn softwood lumber, such as spruce, Douglas-fir and larch.

The strongest of these are produced from lengths of timber of veneer bonded together using high-strength adhesive. Glued laminated timber (glulam) consists of three or more layers of finger-jointed lamellas (short pieces of lumber) glued together with the grain aligned lengthwise. The thickness of the lamellas depends on the application: ranging up to 45 mm (1.8 in), thinner sections can be bent to smaller radii. The same approach is used to produce lightweight structural panels. In this case, it is known as cross-laminated timber (CLT, crosslam or Xlam).

Laminated veneer lumber (LVL) is constructed like plywood: layers of veneer are bonded with adhesive; the direction

bathrooms and offices; the surface is covered with decorative veneer or melamine (page 224).

Hardboard is also commonly referred to by the trademark name Masonite, after its inventor, William H. Mason. Tempered hardboard is produced with the addition of water-resistant oil (originally linseed oil). After baking, this yields a more stable and durable product. The surface finish depends on the method of production. In the wet process, wood chips are converted into fibres and aligned over a screen, where they dry to form a stiff board (bonded by the natural resins in the wood). Hot pressing produces a gloss finish on both sides. As with paper (page 268), the quality of the panel depends on the type and length of wood fibre.

In the case of fibreboard, synthetic adhesive is used to bind the particles together, which yields a stronger product with a superior surface finish. It is classed as medium-density (MDF) or high-density of grain depends on the application. The natural variation of wood, such as strength-reducing defects, is dispersed throughout the product. As a result, these lumber products have higher-strength values. They are used throughout construction in load-bearing applications, such as columns, beams and joists. Produced from 3 mm (0.12 in) veneers, LVL is available in configurations up to 75 mm (3 in) thick.

Strand-based lumber – parallel strand lumber (PSL) and laminated strand lumber (LSL) – is not as strong, but it is less expensive. Like OSB, it is produced from smaller logs. The wood is cut into strands, coated with adhesive, aligned and bonded together with heat and pressure. While the strands used in LSL are up to around 300 mm (12 in) long, those used in PSL can be up to 3 m (10 ft) long. As a result, PSL is stronger and suitable for applications similar to LVL.

Wood–plastic composite (WPC) combines wood powder (flour) with thermoplastic such as polypropylene (PP) (page 98), polyethylene (PE) (page 108) or polyvinyl chloride (PVC) (page 122). This results in a material that mixes some wood-like characteristics with the ability to be molded like plastic. The properties depend on the choice of plastic and proportion of wood additive (up to 55%). Often used in decking, WPC is said to offer a low-maintenance and dimensionally stable product suitable for exterior use. While PP, PE and PVC are suitable for use outdoors, the wood flour is prone to water absorption. On top of this, unlike 100% plastic or solid lumber, WPC is not so straightforward end-of-life.

## SUSTAINABILITY

As with lumber and veneer, all the wood should be from certified forests. An advantage of engineered timber is that it can be produced from the by-products of lumber production. Additionally, it can be produced from non-structural species, such as poplar, and so reduces the burden on lumber-yielding trees.

The increased reliability and consistency of engineered timber means that it can span longer distances in construction and thus reduce materials

## PRODUCTS AND FURNITURE

**Strength-to-weight**
The improved consistency, reliability and strength of laminated timber versus sawn lumber present many opportunities for designers. Thinner and lighter structures are possible, without forfeiting the highly desirable aesthetic and tactile qualities of wood.

**Versatility**
The majority of wooden furniture produced today relies on engineered timber in one form or another. From dense fibreboard to injection-molded WPC, these composites can be produced in virtually all formats, from panels to lumber to three-dimensional moldings.

**Cost**
The raw materials are less expensive by volume than structural metals, such as steel and aluminium. In addition, they can be processed using conventional woodworking equipment.

overall. It is estimated that a two-storey timber frame house that uses wood in the floors and windows too, saves 8 tonnes of carbon dioxide compared to an equivalent masonry house.

The veneers are laminated using phenol formaldehyde (PF) (page 224) adhesive. Formaldehyde is a widely used industrial chemical, such as for glues, paints and textiles. Products that use it must conform to international formaldehyde emissions limits to reduce the negative impact on indoor air quality. Urea formaldehyde (UF) glued products have slightly higher emissions but they still fulfil the requirements of the most demanding European standards relating to formaldehyde emissions and content.

Hardboard is produced without the addition of synthetic adhesive. While this means it has lower embodied energy (similar to paper) and lower environmental impact overall, it is not as strong as those products manufactured with synthetic adhesive.

## ENGINEERED TIMBER IN PRODUCTS AND FURNITURE

Such is the versatility and importance of engineered timber that applications stretch from low-cost shop fitting to iconic designs by the likes of Charles and Ray Eames, Alvar Aalto, Walter Gropius and Marcel Breuer. Offering low-cost utility through high-quality, high-strength laminated veneer, the design opportunities are vast but depend on the adhesive and method of production.

**Extruded plastic lumber** Long lengths of WPC are extruded from a mix of wood flour and PVC or PE. Similar to sawn-wood decking, it is available in a range of standard sizes. As an extrusion, it is possible to produce all manner of profiles, from thin-walled cylinders through to heavy-duty box sections.

Plywood was the earliest form of engineered timber and was commercially available at the turn of the 20th century. Soon after, designers began utilizing laminated veneer in products and furniture. Less expensive and easier to process than aluminium (page 42) and steel (page 28), laminated wood provided designers with the opportunity to experiment with lightweight structures. Its importance continues today, fuelled by its use in contemporary designs and numerous technological breakthroughs.

**LVL** This sample comes from Metsä Wood and goes by the trademark name Kerto. It is strong, stable and reliable. It is produced from 3 mm (0.12 in) thick rotary-cut softwood veneer bonded to form a continuous billet. The billet is cut to length and sawn into beam, plank or panel sizes. Metsä Wood produces three standard types: Kerto-S, Q and T. Kerto-S is engineered for long spans; the grain runs longitudinally. Kerto-Q, pictured here, is a stable panel product. One-fifth of the plies are glued crosswise to improve lateral bending strength and stiffness. Kerto-T, the lightest, is ideal for load-bearing and non-bearing structures, such as stud walls. It is the same as Kerto-S, but made from lighter veneer.

Engineered timber is available in a range of standard grades. It is applied as is, or finished with paint, lacquer or laminate. Through a combination of painting and polishing, a very high-quality, high-gloss finish can be achieved. Indeed, some of the most expensive interiors are no more than an MDF base coated with multiple layers of highly polished lacquer.

A range of sheet materials is applied to plywood, particleboard and MDF. A phenolic finish is useful for applications that require a durable, colourful surface. It can be found indoors and out (although the colour will change over time with exposure to ultraviolet) in both domestic and industrial situations. Decorative-veneered panels are used to give the appearance of solid high-value timber at a fraction of the price. Common finishes include ash, beech, cherry, maple, oak, sapele and walnut. The visual quality depends on the species and method of production (see Veneer).

Wood will only bend willingly in one direction (across the grain); multi-direction bending would require the wood to stretch beyond its elastic limit. However, three-dimensional veneer lamination – originally developed and patented by Reholz, now owned by Danzer – allows for much greater curvature to be achieved. Ultra-thin plies are reinforced with thread, which prevents them from splitting, and formed with heat and pressure. Several species can be formed in this way including beech, oak and cherry.

WPC offers a completely different tactility, something between wood and plastic. The majority is produced using conventional synthetic plastics, such as

PP and PVC. While the use of wood flour reduces the use of plastic, WPC cannot be recycled and will deteriorate more rapidly than pure plastic. Bioplastic offers an alternative matrix. Examples include starch plastic (page 260) and polylactic acid (PLA) (page 262). The embodied energy for these plastics is lower than conventional types, and at the end of their useful life the items may be compostable.

### ENGINEERED TIMBER IN ARCHITECTURE AND CONSTRUCTION
Engineered timber has become an indispensable material in construction. Ranging from temporary structures to

## ARCHITECTURE AND CONSTRUCTION

**Strength-to-weight**
The design values for engineered timber are higher than for sawn lumber. In addition, their properties are consistent throughout, which means they can span greater distances.

**Low impact**
Timber is a natural, renewable and sustainable building material. It uses significantly less energy to grow, extract, manufacture, transport, install, use, maintain and dispose of than other construction methods. Engineered timber can replace structural concrete, masonry and steel.

**Cost**
Engineered timber is rapid to install on-site and does not require any special equipment to cut, join and modify. The production of prefabricated panels, such as floor cassettes, is centralized to keep costs to a minimum. Once on-site, a timber frame building can be erected at the rate of one floor per day. Even so, a CLT floor can be up to twice the price of a prestressed concrete equivalent.

**Precision**
Very high tolerances are achieved through prefabrication of modular construction components.

multi-storey buildings, it is applied for both its technical and its decorative merits. Not only is it utilized in the fabric of buildings, it has become an essential part of the construction process, such as providing scaffolding and shuttering (formwork) for concrete.

Engineered timber can provide a finished surface as soon as it is installed. All of the features and openings may be produced at the factory prior to getting on-site. This ensures computer-guided precision. In the same way as sawn lumber, it can be fixed, modified and shaped using conventional tools and equipment when on-site.

CLT is gaining momentum as a lightweight structural material. By joining small pieces of wood to make large panels, the natural variation and defects are minimized. It can be produced to virtually any size up to around 3 x 24 m (10 x 79 ft) and 400 mm (15.75 in) thick (three to seven layers), although a panel of this size will be very challenging to transport. Its versatility allows architects to create uninterrupted monolithic surfaces (structural spans up to 8 m [26 ft] have so far been achieved). The appearance depends on the species; it is typically manufactured from spruce, but may be any of the softwoods.

**Curved whitewood glulam superstructure**

The Living Planet Centre, headquarters of the WWF-UK, was designed by Hopkins Architects (2013). The new building sits on a concrete podium, whose perimeter is planted with shrubs, trees and flowers. The 80 m (262 ft) long curved timber gridshell spans 37.5 m (123 ft), providing a vast flexible-use interior space. Constructed from spruce, glulam provides a lightweight and cost-effective solution. The arches are fabricated from several layers of spruce, finger-jointed to make long lengths. Adhesive is applied as they are layered up. While the adhesive is still wet, the arched profile is formed and the strips clamped together. Once cured, the edges and faces are sanded to a smooth finish (see also Larch, page 310, and Spruce, Pine and Fir). Photo by Airey Spaces.

# Spruce, Pine and Fir

**Also known as**
Generically referred to as: whitewood (W), redwood (R), spruce-pine-fir (SPF)

This family of coniferous trees includes several commercially important species that share similar characteristics. They are fast-growing and utilized mainly in construction and pulp production. The resins in the wood do not provide adequate protection when exposed to conditions favourable to decay, so the timber must be impregnated or preserved if used outdoors.

| Types | Typical Applications | Sustainability |
|---|---|---|
| • Pine: eastern white, western white, sugar, southern yellow and Scots<br>• Spruce: Sitka and Norway<br>• Fir: balsam and alpine | • Construction and engineered timber<br>• Furniture and interiors<br>• Musical instruments | • Available from certified forests<br>• Broad global distribution |

| Properties | Competing Materials | Costs |
|---|---|---|
| • High fibre strength<br>• Low density and easy workability<br>• Clean white to off-white colour that weathers to a light grey | • Larch, Douglas-fir, cypress (such as western red-cedar), engineered timber<br>• Steel, concrete<br>• PVC | • Competitively priced<br>• Straightforward to process |

## INTRODUCTION

These are popular softwoods consumed in large quantity around the world. Quality ranges from inexpensive sawn lumber scattered with knots through to highly prized quarter-sawn planks suitable for musical instruments.

The timber has a straight grain and uniform texture. It has a light colour, ranging from white to reddish-pink, depending on the species. When exposed to the elements, it becomes progressively darker. Often though, they are concealed beneath a layer of paint.

They are vulnerable to decay and so are primarily used indoors. Applications range from non-structural elements – such as furniture, partition walls and so on – through timber frame construction. They are used extensively in engineered timber (page 296) and pulpwood (see Paper, page 268).

Lumber is graded by two methods: visual grading and machine stress rating. Visual grading is carried out once the lumber has been sawn. Experienced graders sort each piece based on visual characteristics known to affect lumber

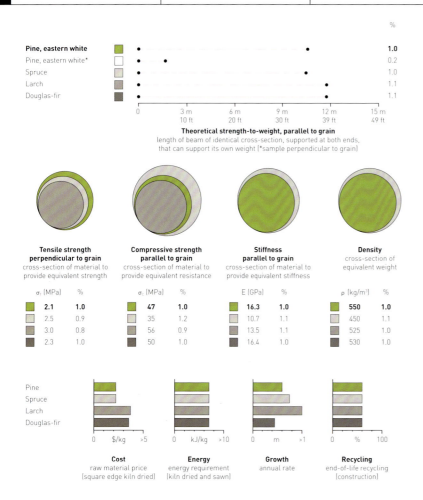

Pine, eastern white — 1.0
Pine, eastern white* — 0.2
Spruce — 1.0
Larch — 1.1
Douglas-fir — 1.1

**Theoretical strength-to-weight, parallel to grain**
length of beam of identical cross-section, supported at both ends, that can support its own weight (*sample perpendicular to grain)

| **Tensile strength perpendicular to grain** cross-section of material to provide equivalent strength | | **Compressive strength parallel to grain** cross-section of material to provide equivalent resistance | | **Stiffness parallel to grain** cross-section of material to provide equivalent stiffness | | **Density** cross-section of equivalent weight | |
|---|---|---|---|---|---|---|---|
| $\sigma_t$ (MPa) | % | $\sigma_c$ (MPa) | % | E (GPa) | % | $\rho$ (kg/m³) | % |
| 2.1 | 1.0 | 47 | 1.0 | 16.3 | 1.0 | 550 | 1.0 |
| 2.5 | 0.9 | 35 | 1.2 | 10.7 | 1.1 | 450 | 1.1 |
| 3.0 | 0.8 | 56 | 0.9 | 13.5 | 1.1 | 525 | 1.0 |
| 2.3 | 1.0 | 50 | 1.0 | 16.4 | 1.0 | 530 | 1.0 |

Pine
Spruce
Larch
Douglas-fir

| **Cost** raw material price (square edge kiln dried) | **Energy** energy requirement (kiln dried and sawn) | **Growth** annual rate | **Recycling** end-of-life recycling (construction) |
|---|---|---|---|
| 0  $/kg  >5 | 0  kJ/kg  >10 | 0  m  >1 | 0  %  100 |

**Violin front and back**
Traditionally, the highest-quality stringed instruments are produced with a quarter-sawn solid spruce soundboard. Sound waves generated by playing an instrument pass through the wood along the grain; spruce is thought to produce the richest tones. The tree is felled in the winter months, when it is said to be 'sleeping'. This ensures the lowest oil and water content, because the tree is at its least active. It is sawn and left to air-dry for ten years or more. When ready, it is hand-carved to make the soundboard. The wood is 'tuned' throughout the process; by tapping on the surface an experienced maker can hear where material needs to be removed. The sound quality only improves with age, because as the wood dries out it becomes stiffer and thus more responsive to the musical vibrations. In this example, the back is produced from maple (page 330).

strength, such as knots, checks, shakes, splits and slope of grain. While this has proved reliable, machine rating reduces the likelihood of variability. This is particularly advantageous for demanding structural situations where physical properties must be accurately determined. Machine stress-rated (MSR) lumber has been mechanically tested (non-destructive) using standardized equipment to determine physical properties such as bending strength, modulus of elasticity (E) and tensile strength. It is also subject to visual grade limits on known defects. Recently, a similar product called machine-evaluated lumber (MEL) has become available.

## COMMERCIAL TYPES AND USES

As sawn construction lumber, species with similar properties are grouped under generic names, which depend on the country of origin. For example, in the USA and Canada several moderate-strength species are grouped under the banner spruce-pine-fir (SPF); and in Europe pine is referred to as redwood (ER) and spruce as whitewood (EW).

SPF is further divided into eastern and western species. The former include black spruce (*Picea mariana*), red spruce (*P. rubens*), white spruce (*P. glauca*), jack pine (*P. banksiana*) and balsam fir (*Abies balsamea*). Western species include white spruce, Engelmann spruce (*P. engelmanni*), Lodgepole pine (*P. contorta*) and alpine fir (*A. lasiocarpa*). This division is the result of the effect climate has on the quality of timber. Eastern SPF tends to grow more slowly and so yields higher-strength timber. Western SPF, on the other hand, grows larger.

Pine lumber has a distinctive resinous odour. It ranges from light brown heartwood to white sapwood, with conspicuous growth rings. It has moderate strength and good machining properties. It is used mainly in light structural work and as pulp.

Commercially, they are designated as soft or hard. Soft pines – such as the eastern white (*Pinus strobus*), western white (*P. monticola*) and sugar (*P. lambertiana*) – yield a light-coloured timber with a uniform texture and subtle growth pattern. Compared to the hard pines, the timber has low strength and poor resistance to impact. The wood is uniform and processes very well, which makes it useful in window frames, doors and furniture, as well as light construction work.

Hard pines are heavier and more durable. They include several species, which are generically referred to as 'yellow' or 'red' as a result of their colouration. The exact properties depend on the climate and growing conditions. For example, southern yellow pines such as the longleaf (*P. palustris*) and shortleaf (*P. echinata*) yield a durable timber comparable with Douglas-fir in some respects. It is moderately heavy and hard, which makes it suitable for interior joinery, such as stairs, shelving and furniture. It is also applied in construction and as engineered timber. Yellow pines from faster growing areas will have only moderate strength and bridge the gap between the soft pines and slower-grown varieties.

Red pine includes Scots pine (*P. sylvestris*) and Norway pine (*P. resinosa*). They are distinguished by reddish-brown heartwood. Scots pine has enormous distribution throughout the northern hemisphere. As a result, the quality depends on the climate where it was grown; slower-grown timber will be stronger and harder. Norway pine has moderate strength and impact resistance, and good machining properties. It is used principally in construction, packaging and pulp.

Spruces produce a very light-coloured timber (although Sitka is slightly darker), with little contrast between heartwood and sapwood. It has almost no odour. They have moderate strength and good stiffness. They are used in light construction work, engineered timber and as pulp for papermaking. The wood has a uniform, knot-free appearance and shrinks very little after seasoning. This produces a timber with superior acoustic properties. As a result, spruce is utilized in soundboards for musical instruments, such as piano, cello and violin.

The two most significant species are Sitka (*P. sitchensis*) and Norway (*P. abies*). They have a fine, even texture with a consistent straight grain. While construction lumber is inexpensive, old-growth timber that is free from knots and suitable for musical instruments is very highly prized.

The firs (not including Douglas-fir, page 314, a high-strength wood suitable for construction) yield a pale timber usually covered with knots. It is lightweight (385 kg/m³ [24 lb/ft³]), with relatively low strength, stiffness and resistance to impact. It is used as pulpwood and for light structures.

## SUSTAINABILITY

These timbers make up the majority of all softwood production. They have minimal impact on the environment. In fact, the energy used in production – harvest, process and transport – may be less than is stored in the wood by photosynthesis during its lifetime. Each 1 m³ (35 ft³) of tree growth absorbs approximately 0.9 tonnes of carbon dioxide. Therefore, replacing materials such as concrete (page 496) or steel (page 18) with wood can significantly reduce carbon dioxide emissions.

Pine, spruce and fir are available from renewable sources. It takes around three years for a young stand to become well established and the trees will be at least 60 years old before they are cut down. During this time they will be 'thinned' at least twice. The thinnings are used as biofuel or pulp, or left to rot on the land.

**Spruce glulam and steel hybrid structure**
The Moor Market, located just outside the city centre of Sheffield, England, was completed in 2013. Designed by Leslie Jones Architects, the covered market features a curved gridshell structure produced from spruce glued laminated lumber (glulam) (see page 300). Spruce is the primary material used to make glulam and provides a cost-effective and practical solution. Off-site prefabrication allows for the delivery to site of structural work and internal panels as they are required. Photo by Hufton+Crow.

# Hemlock

Hemlock is similar to pine, but with fewer knots; it is a little stronger and more expensive. It grows across North America, and is utilized mainly in construction, joinery and plywood. It is reddish-brown with a distinctive growth pattern thanks to the visually contrasting growth rings. The grain is relatively straight and it can be planed and polished to a fine finish.

| Types | Typical Applications | Sustainability |
|---|---|---|
| • Hemlock: eastern, or Canadian; and western, or Pacific | • Structural lumber and engineered timber<br>• Interior joinery<br>• Furniture and packaging | • Available from certified forests<br>• Limited to North America |

| Properties | Competing Materials | Costs |
|---|---|---|
| • Straight-grained, knot-free timber<br>• Moderately hard and strong<br>• Only slightly resistant to decay, but very easy to treat | • Spruce, pine, fir, Douglas-fir and larch<br>• Oak, mahogany and sapele | • Moderate and around 25% more expensive than pine<br>• Equivalent manufacturing costs |

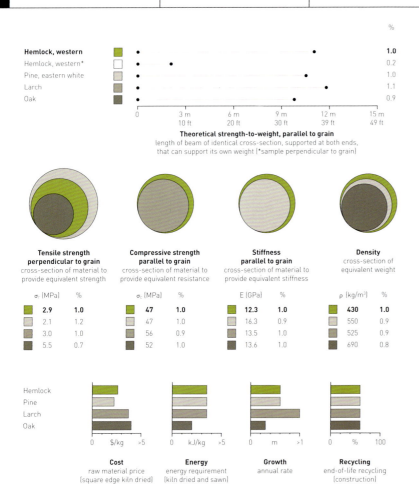

## INTRODUCTION

Slow-grown hemlock (*Tsuga* genus) yields a very high-quality and tough timber. It can grow more slowly than its closest rivals, pine, spruce and fir (page 304), because it can endure shady conditions, although in favourable conditions it grows just as fast. Hemlock is self-pruning, resulting in a tall, branch-free trunk. In dense stands the majority of the stem may be clear, which yields knot-free, high-quality lumber.

However, it is prone to radial shake (separation of the rings), which significantly reduces structural strength. As a result, it does not have such a good reputation as pine, spruce and fir for structural lumber. This flaw, as with other structural defects, is easily spotted in logs before sawing and so is unlikely to make it through to lumber stage.

The heartwood is typically light reddish-brown, a similar colour to beech (page 338). The sapwood may be slightly lighter in colour, but is otherwise indistinguishable. Similar to Douglas-fir (contrary to what the name suggests, it is not a true fir, see page 314), the growth rings are highly visible as a result of the difference in colour between spring and summer growth.

## COMMERCIAL TYPES AND USES

There are two main commercial species of hemlock cultivated in Canada and the USA: eastern (*T. canadensis*), also known as Canadian, and western (*T. heterophylla*), also known as Pacific. There are slight differences in the lumber, which are mainly due to the difference in growing conditions. The western hemlock grows largest and represents a valuable surviving source of large, clear timber. It yields harder and stronger (15–20%) timber, with a straighter grain and lower resin content.

In order to simplify design and marketing the lumber is often mixed with other species of the same region. For example, a North American coastal mix of western hemlock and Amabilis fir or grand fir is marked as HEM-FIR; and eastern hemlock is combined with tamarack (North American larch, page 310) and graded as HEM-TAM.

Once dry, the wood is very stable. It has a relatively straight grain, which means that it machines well and a fine split-free finish can be achieved. Its strength is somewhere between that of pine and Douglas-fir. As a result, it is used interchangeably with these timbers, providing a cost-effective alternative to the latter. Examples include timber frame construction, joinery and millwork (doors, windows and moldings).

Its strength and receptiveness to preservative make it useful for exterior applications too, such as bridges and piling. And it can be treated effectively with fire-retardant, which is useful for public buildings and interior applications.

It is used in log home construction. Its high tannin content protects it from insect attack. The bark used to be more valuable than the timber, providing a rich source of tannic acid for the leather and fur tanning industry. The wood becomes harder as it dries, and so cutting and drilling is preferably done while the timber is still green (wet).

## SUSTAINABILITY

Hemlock makes up a large proportion of the North American forests. Unfortunately, the eastern hemlock is currently threatened by the hemlock woolly adelgid pest, which was accidentally introduced into North America from Asia around the middle of the 20th century. The trees decline and typically perish within five to ten years of infestation.

It is available from certified sources. Major commercial cultivation is limited to the USA and Canada. Industrial-scale harvesting of western hemlock (as well as of western red-cedar, see Cypress Family, page 318) from ancient forests can threaten what remains of these unique habitats.

**Turned winder newel post** Hemlock is commonly used for internal joinery, such as this part taken from a kite winder flight of stairs. It has adequate mechanical properties for light structures; delivering good bending strength, shear strength and stiffness. It machines very well, glues easily and has good nail- and screw-holding capabilities. Typically supplied unfinished, it yields a high-quality painted or stained finish.

# Larch

A member of the pine family (Pinaceae), larch is valued for its strength and durability. It has good all-round properties suitable for construction and cladding, making it one of the most economically significant softwoods. The resinous timber protects itself from rotting, even in damp conditions. The heartwood is a yellowish- to reddish-brown, turning to silvery-grey over time.

| Types | Typical Applications | Sustainability |
|---|---|---|
| • Western, eastern (tamarack and American), Siberian, European and Japanese | • Construction<br>• Furniture<br>• Boat building | • Widely available from certified sources<br>• Quick-drying<br>• Kiln drying yields more stable boards but is not essential for cladding |

| Properties | Competing Materials | Costs |
|---|---|---|
| • Resistant to decay (moderate to high depending on type)<br>• Good strength-to-weight | • Pine and Douglas-fir<br>• Cypress (such as western red-cedar)<br>• Oak | • Low to moderate depending on whether it is local or imported |

310

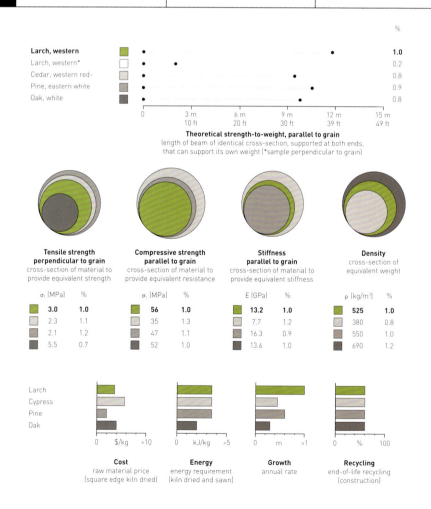

|  | % |
|---|---|
| Larch, western | 1.0 |
| Larch, western* | 0.2 |
| Cedar, western red- | 0.8 |
| Pine, eastern white | 0.9 |
| Oak, white | 0.8 |

**Theoretical strength-to-weight, parallel to grain**
length of beam of identical cross-section, supported at both ends,
that can support its own weight (*sample perpendicular to grain)

**Tensile strength perpendicular to grain**
cross-section of material to provide equivalent strength

| $\sigma_t$ (MPa) | % |
|---|---|
| 3.0 | 1.0 |
| 2.3 | 1.1 |
| 2.1 | 1.2 |
| 5.5 | 0.7 |

**Compressive strength parallel to grain**
cross-section of material to provide equivalent resistance

| $\sigma_c$ (MPa) | % |
|---|---|
| 56 | 1.0 |
| 35 | 1.3 |
| 47 | 1.1 |
| 52 | 1.0 |

**Stiffness parallel to grain**
cross-section of material to provide equivalent stiffness

| E (GPa) | % |
|---|---|
| 13.2 | 1.0 |
| 7.7 | 1.2 |
| 16.3 | 0.9 |
| 13.6 | 1.0 |

**Density**
cross-section of equivalent weight

| $\rho$ (kg/m³) | % |
|---|---|
| 525 | 1.0 |
| 380 | 0.8 |
| 550 | 1.0 |
| 690 | 1.2 |

Larch
Cypress
Pine
Oak

**Cost**
raw material price (square edge kiln dried)

**Energy**
energy requirement (kiln dried and sawn)

**Growth**
annual rate

**Recycling**
end-of-life recycling (construction)

## INTRODUCTION

Larch (*Larix* genus) provides a reasonably cost-effective material for cladding as well as structural work. It has quite a distinctive grain pattern thanks to pronounced growing seasons and is typically covered with lots of small knots, making it easy to spot on buildings.

The highest-quality timber is reserved for furniture making and boat building. Larch is around one-third heavier than western red-cedar (see Cypress Family, page 318) for the same cross-section. While this means it is not as well suited to lightweight boats, its high resistance to denting and abrasion make it a useful material for hardy hulls, decking and other similarly demanding applications.

The wood is quick-drying, but prone to considerable movement – much more so than other members of the pine family. Kiln-drying techniques produce a more stable timber. Even so, it is not recommended to interlock boards, such as with tongue-and-groove joints or hidden fixings. Planks tend to be feathered and overlapped instead.

Larch is relatively brittle. It is rarely used in bentwood applications, although a small amount of curvature is feasible, and it is pre-holed to avoid splitting when joining with nails or screws.

## COMMERCIAL TYPES AND USES

Larch is a deciduous conifer and sheds its leaves in the autumn. Several species are

**Larch folding chair** The Profile Chair was designed by Canadian studio Knauf and Brown, 2012. Pivoting around a single axis, similar to the famous Plia (1967) by Giancarlo Piretti, this modern interpretation of the folding chair combines powder-coated steel with solid larch. The wood is used in the parts a person comes into contact with – seat and back – while steel provides the structure. The pivoting mechanism is stripped down to just a few components. Photo by Knauf and Brown.

**Opposite**
**Curved glulam arches**
The Winter Garden in Sheffield, England, was designed by architects Pringle Richards Sharratt and completed in 2002. The giant glass-clad structure consists of 21 parabolic arches spanning a 70 x 22 m (230 x 72 ft) space. The central section rises up 22 m (72 ft) to allow the trees to grow into maturity. Larch glulam provides a lightweight and elegant solution; the structure weighs only two-thirds of an equivalent steel version and three-quarters less than concrete would. Constructed from untreated larch, the arches will weather to silvery-grey. Photo by Peter Mackinven.

**Right**
**Untreated larch cladding** The Summer House in Southern Burgenland, Austria, was created by Judith Benzer of 24gramm Architektur and completed in 2009. The shape was inspired by the 'Kellerstöckel' (winemaker's cellars), that are typical of this region of Austria. Clad entirely with untreated larch, the outward-facing surfaces have gradually turned silvery-grey. Photo by Martin Weiss.

| Unweathered | 6 months | 10 years |

**Weathering cycle of untreated larch**
Normally used outdoors, untreated larch turns silvery-grey over time and with exposure to the elements. If this is not desirable, stain or paint is used. However, the high resin content makes treatment difficult. The sapwood is not as durable as the heartwood and so requires a protective coating if destined for application outdoors.

useful as timber, and while they are native to certain parts of the world, most grow happily throughout America, Europe, Russia and Asia. Common types include eastern (*L. laricina*) (also known as tamarack and American), western (*L. occidentalis*), Siberian (*L. sibirica*) (also called Russian), European (*L. decidua*) and Japanese (*L. kaempferi*).

Eastern larch is the most prolific through North America and grows to around 20 m (65 ft). Western and European larch grow taller, to around 30 m (100 ft), yielding longer boards. In warmer climates, such as the UK, larch grows more quickly and yields a less strong and dense timber with more knots. Slow-grown larch, such as from Siberia, produces a dense and strong timber that is far superior to pine and spruce (page 304), and cypress and cedar. The knots are less pronounced and the high resin content provides excellent durability.

Larch is available in a range of formats including lumber, particleboard and structural glued laminated lumber (glulam) (see page 300). Thanks to its higher strength and durability, Siberian and slow-grown larch is preferred for structural applications, including glulam. Veneer is produced from straight-grained and knot-free larch. It is often smoked (fumed) or stained, making use of the pronounced grain, to take on the appearance of more expensive dark-colour wood such as walnut (page 348) or wengé (see Exotics, page 374).

From humble cabins to fortresses, larch has been used in construction for millennia. Considering its durability, larch provides a reasonably cost-effective structural and cladding material. It is typically less expensive than oak and western red-cedar, but this depends on location and availability.

## SUSTAINABILITY

Larch is widely available from certified and well-managed forests. Compared to other softwoods it is relatively fast-growing. High-quality larch that has a clear grain and is relatively knot-free is likely to be more than 100 years old. Forestry works on the principal of harvesting every 50 years or so. Therefore, even though more larch is grown each year than felled, applications that demand very high-quality timber, such as boat building, are likely depleting old larch stocks.

It is majority heartwood – the sapwood converts into heartwood quickly in this species – and this is the most durable part of the tree. Ultimately, durability depends on the species and speed of growth; slow-grown larch can be expected to last for a century or more in construction without any treatment. There are countless examples of long-standing log cabins local to sources of durable timber. However, in temperate and warmer climates sawn untreated wood may not last more than 25 years.

# Douglas-fir

**Douglas-fir is a high-performance timber that rivals steel; it is stiff and strong for its weight with similar mechanical properties to larch. It is one of the best-known commercial timbers and used in a broad spectrum of applications, from decorative floors and windows to structural lumber. It is moderately resistant to decay and will survive outdoors for a few years if left untreated.**

| Types | Typical Applications | Sustainability |
|---|---|---|
| • North American (coastal or interior) and European | • Construction and engineered timber<br>• Furniture and interiors<br>• Pulp | • Available from certified forests<br>• Cultivated across northern hemisphere |

| Properties | Competing Materials | Costs |
|---|---|---|
| • Straight-grained<br>• High strength- and stiffness-to-weight<br>• Yellowish- to reddish-brown heartwood with creamy white sapwood | • Larch, cypress (such as western red-cedar), hemlock, pine and spruce<br>• Oak and iroko | • Moderate raw material cost<br>• Good working properties |

## INTRODUCTION

Douglas-fir (*Pseudotsuga menziesii*) is an evergreen coniferous tree in the family Pinaceae. It is comparable with larch (page 310) – they are often graded together as Douglas-fir–larch (D Fir-L or DF-L) – and used in many of the same situations as pine (page 304), cypress (such as western red-cedar) (page 318) and hemlock (page 308). Contrary to what the name suggests, it is not a true fir (*Abies* genus) (page 304) and for this reason is often written as 'Douglas-fir'. It is named after David Douglas, a Scottish botanist who documented the tree in the Pacific Northwest. The species name refers to Archibald Menzies, who identified the tree years earlier on Vancouver Island.

The branch-free trunk of tall trees (particularly from North American coastal forests) yields a high-quality knot-free timber available in long lengths. There is a vast difference between this and the wide-ringed core-wood of juvenile trees. Compared to other softwoods, it is stiff, with a good balance of tensile and compressive strength; it sits alongside larch as the strongest of the softwoods. While they share many of the same properties, Douglas-fir is less resinous, which means it is suitable for exposed interior structural woodwork, but not as durable as larch when used outdoors.

It has a distinctive appearance: heartwood colour ranges from yellowish- to reddish-brown, with a creamy white sapwood. The wood has a pronounced grain as a result of the contrast between the springwood and summerwood, which is particularly visible when sawn to expose the vertical grain (known as plain-sawn). It gradually becomes darker over time and with exposure to daylight, eventually turning grey. It has good finishing properties and holds paints, varnishes and stains very well.

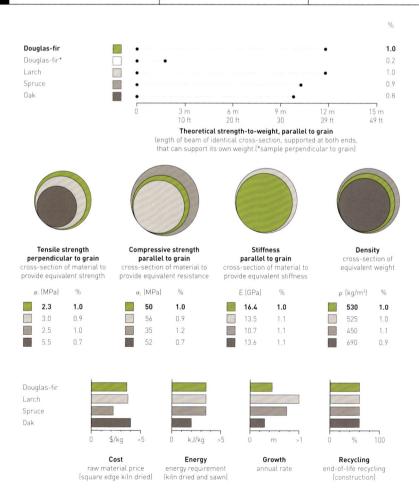

| | | % |
|---|---|---|
| Douglas-fir | | 1.0 |
| Douglas-fir* | | 0.2 |
| Larch | | 1.0 |
| Spruce | | 0.9 |
| Oak | | 0.8 |

| 0 | 3 m<br>10 ft | 6 m<br>20 ft | 9 m<br>30 | 12 m<br>39 ft | 15 m<br>49 ft |

**Theoretical strength-to-weight, parallel to grain**
length of beam of identical cross-section, supported at both ends, that can support its own weight (*sample perpendicular to grain)

| Tensile strength perpendicular to grain | | Compressive strength parallel to grain | | Stiffness parallel to grain | | Density | |
|---|---|---|---|---|---|---|---|
| cross-section of material to provide equivalent strength | | cross-section of material to provide equivalent resistance | | cross-section of material to provide equivalent stiffness | | cross-section of equivalent weight | |
| σ_t (MPa) | % | σ_c (MPa) | % | E (GPa) | % | ρ (kg/m³) | % |
| 2.3 | 1.0 | 50 | 1.0 | 16.4 | 1.0 | 530 | 1.0 |
| 3.0 | 0.9 | 56 | 0.9 | 13.5 | 1.1 | 525 | 1.0 |
| 2.5 | 1.0 | 35 | 1.2 | 10.7 | 1.1 | 450 | 1.1 |
| 5.5 | 0.7 | 52 | 0.7 | 13.6 | 1.1 | 690 | 0.9 |

Douglas-fir
Larch
Spruce
Oak

| 0 | $/kg | >5 | 0 | kJ/kg | >5 | 0 | m | >1 | 0 | % | 100 |

| **Cost** | **Energy** | **Growth** | **Recycling** |
|---|---|---|---|
| raw material price (square edge kiln dried) | energy requirement (kiln dried and sawn) | annual rate | end-of-life recycling (construction) |

## COMMERCIAL TYPES AND USES

Douglas-fir grows throughout the USA, Canada, the UK, France, New Zealand and Australia. Where the timber was grown affects its properties. For example, there are two North American varieties: coastal and interior. Trees from coastal forests tend to grow much faster and so are larger, with a lighter colour, coarse grain and large knots. By contrast, timber from interior forests (also known as Rocky Mountain Douglas-fir) tends to be smaller, with a finer, tighter grain. European Douglas-fir tends to be similar to North American interior-grown trees.

Douglas-fir is available in many grades, from high-quality knot-free structural lumber to common timber. Similar to larch, pine and cypress, it is adhesive bonded to form lightweight engineered timber (page 296).

It is used to make sleepers, pilings, railway ties and similar hard-wearing outdoor structures. It is widely used in industrial situations too, such as tanks and containers. In terms of durability outdoors, it is rated alongside pine, spruce and hemlock; it has an average lifespan of five to ten years outdoors untreated. For situations that require a higher level of

**Truss roof structure**
The atrium roof of Central City Shopping Centre, in Surrey, British Columbia, Canada, covers 3,400 m² (37,000 ft²) of entrance space. Designed by Bing Thom Architects and structurally engineered by Fast + Epp, the complex curving geometry is supported by a 2.1 m (7 ft) deep tetrahedral space truss with a central kingpost and cable

support. The round timbers are Douglas-fir peeler cores (what is left of a log once it has been rotary peeled, see Veneer, page 290). Relatively inexpensive by-products of the plywood industry, the heartwood cores provide a strong bar that contributes towards a lightweight and efficient roof structure. Photo by Fast + Epp.

**Wood, steel and glass** Douglas-fir has a beautiful natural appearance. This visitor pavilion at the Palace of Versailles, Paris, designed by Explorations Architecture, combines a wooden brise-soleil (sun baffle) with a structure of steel (page 28) and glass (page 508). Inspired by the dense rows of torii gates leading to the Fushimi Inari Taisha shrine, Japan, the pavilion was constructed in 2008 and provides a temporary main entrance to the palace. The Douglas-fir slats reduce the effects of the sun's glare and provide a warm colour backdrop. Photo by Michel Denance.

durability, it is treated with preservative. This extends its useful life outdoors to 30 years or more.

It is relatively easy to work, has good surface durability (as a result of its high density) and dimensional stability. Its high fibre strength provides excellent nail-holding capability. These properties are utilized in joinery, cabinetmaking and frames for windows and doors. Its high surface durability and resistance to cracking make it suitable for flooring; it is one of the few types of softwood capable of maintaining its appearance and remaining level under extreme wear.

It has relatively long fibres (around 4 mm [0.16 in]), which are strong and utilized in pulp and hardboard. Owing to its colour, it is not generally suitable for white paper and board.

## SUSTAINABILITY

Douglas-fir is one of the few species available in large sizes from managed and certified forests. Applying timber in long uninterrupted spans helps to reduce overall material consumption; here Douglas-fir provides a cost-effective solution. Alternatively, lumber is cut into smaller pieces and reassembled as engineered timber, which makes the most of its strength-to-weight. Long-span beams are utilized in bridges and stadiums, and in load-carrying horizontal frameworks for residential, commercial and industrial structures.

**Weatherproof cladding** A range of standard cladding profiles exists, which vary from one manufacturer to another. Thickness ranges from 6 mm (0.24 in) for feather-edge up to 22 mm (0.9 in) for tongue and groove. Sawn lumber is passed by a spindle cutter to produce a continuous profile up to any length. The depth, texture and orientation (horizontal, vertical or diagnal) may all be specified by the designer, which offers flexibility even with standard shapes. Bespoke profiles are produced by redesigning the shape of the cutter. Selection depends on budget (species, thickness, machining and overlap), aesthetics and required durability.

**Weathered wood cladding** Another project by Explorations Architecture, this sports centre in the French commune of Arpajon, near Paris, is clad with strips of Douglas-fir. The heartwood becomes greyer over time, which helps it to blend into the surrounding parkland. Photo by Michel Denance.

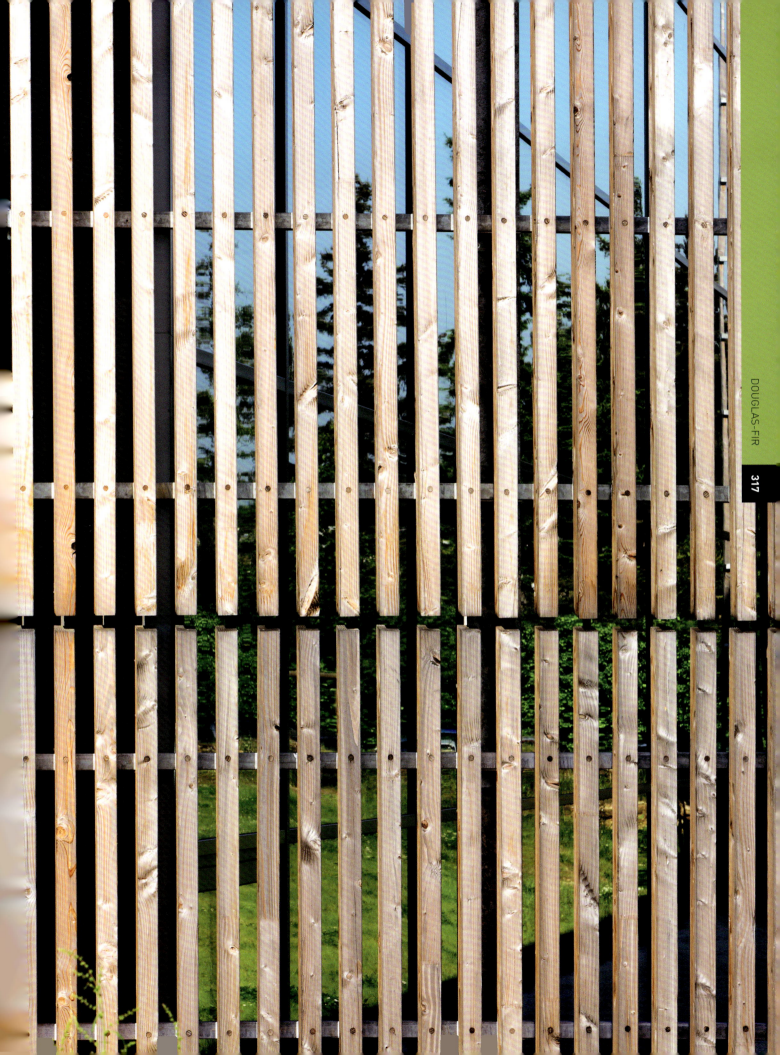

# Cypress Family

Wood from this coniferous family is utilized for its aromatic as well as its mechanical properties. Found throughout the world, the species depends on location. The heartwood has a natural resistance to decay, superior to that of any softwood. It is used in diverse applications, from boatbuilding to table tennis bats. Some are highly sought after for ceremonial buildings.

| Types | Typical Applications | Sustainability |
|---|---|---|
| • Cedars (such as western red-) <br> • Cypress (such as Nootka and bald) <br> • Redwood <br> • Chinese-fir | • Construction and outdoors <br> • Boats and canoes <br> • Pencils | • While some are harvested for timber, others are considered endangered owing to over-exploitation <br> • The dust can be a powerful sensitizer |
| **Properties** | **Competing Materials** | **Costs** |
| • Lightweight and low-density <br> • Resistant to decay (durability) <br> • Aromatic | • Pine, spruce, larch and Douglas-fir <br> • Oak and iroko | • Low to high depending on species and grading <br> • Low density means it is more expensive per unit weight than per unit length |

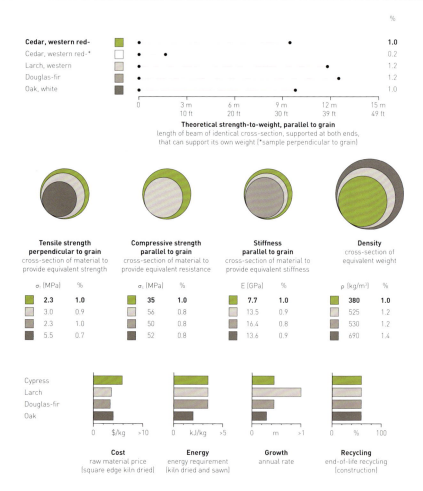

Cedar, western red-
Cedar, western red-*
Larch, western
Douglas-fir
Oak, white

| | % |
|---|---|
| | 1.0 |
| | 0.2 |
| | 1.2 |
| | 1.2 |
| | 1.0 |

0   3 m / 10 ft   6 m / 20 ft   9 m / 30 ft   12 m / 39 ft   15 m / 49 ft

**Theoretical strength-to-weight, parallel to grain**
length of beam of identical cross-section, supported at both ends, that can support its own weight (*sample perpendicular to grain)

| **Tensile strength perpendicular to grain** <br> cross-section of material to provide equivalent strength | | **Compressive strength parallel to grain** <br> cross-section of material to provide equivalent resistance | | **Stiffness parallel to grain** <br> cross-section of material to provide equivalent stiffness | | **Density** <br> cross-section of equivalent weight | |
|---|---|---|---|---|---|---|---|
| $\sigma_t$ (MPa) | % | $\sigma_c$ (MPa) | % | E (GPa) | % | $\rho$ (kg/m³) | % |
| 2.3 | 1.0 | 35 | 1.0 | 7.7 | 1.0 | 380 | 1.0 |
| 3.0 | 0.9 | 56 | 0.8 | 13.5 | 0.9 | 525 | 1.2 |
| 2.3 | 1.0 | 50 | 0.8 | 16.4 | 0.8 | 530 | 1.2 |
| 5.5 | 0.7 | 52 | 0.8 | 13.6 | 0.9 | 690 | 1.4 |

Cypress
Larch
Douglas-fir
Oak

| 0   $/kg   >10 | 0   kJ/kg   >5 | 0   m   >1 | 0   %   100 |
|---|---|---|---|

**Cost** <br> raw material price (square edge kiln dried) | **Energy** <br> energy requirement (kiln dried and sawn) | **Growth** <br> annual rate | **Recycling** <br> end-of-life recycling (construction)

## INTRODUCTION

Even though they are not directly related, many species in the cypress family (Cupressaceae) are named after cedar (*Cedrus*) because they have a similar aroma and durability. True cedar, namely cedar of Lebanon (*C. libani*), is a member of the pine family (Pinaceae) (page 304). They are differentiated by means of a hyphen, such as western red-cedar.

The mechanical properties of the timber vary. On the whole it is not particularly strong, but it is very light. Its low density makes it easy to work to a fine finish with hand tools and machines, but it is prone to denting and scratching. The wood is relatively straight-grained and unblemished. Its clean and pleasant appearance is highly prized for its aesthetic as well as for its mechanical benefits.

The Native American tribes of North America have exploited the timber's lightness and water resistance for generations to make boats and canoes, for example. In Japan, these same properties are used in the construction of bathrooms, tubs and buckets. While some species will bend well to conform to a curvaceous profile, the lightness of others makes them prone to splitting. Therefore, various construction techniques have evolved so that the beneficial properties of these woods may be utilized in the broadest range of applications.

Like cedar, these woods have a distinctive smell (and taste). It is recognizable in pencils, mothproof clothes hangers and shoe trees. The aroma comes from oil naturally present in the wood – darker-coloured woods smell stronger. In mothproofing it works by repelling insects and in shoe trees it is said to combat odour. The oil is extracted and consumed as a fragrance in perfume, aromatherapy and natural insect repellents.

## COMMERCIAL TYPES AND USES

There are many species in the cypress family that yield valuable timber for products, furniture and construction. These mostly evergreen conifers are found throughout the world, stretching from the north to southern climates.

Western red-cedar (*Thuja plicata*) grows up to 60 m (195 ft) tall and is found throughout the western United States and Canada. It is closely associated with American Indians, to whom this tree is important for many purposes. The Quinault, Cowlitz and Skokomish tribes, to name a few, value every part of the tree, from the bark to the timber to the leaves. It is used in medicine, clothing, home building, basketry and canoes.

While it is not particularly strong, it is light and extremely resistant to decay. It is commercially important in construction, inside and out, as well as used in decking, furniture and roof shingles. From heartwood to sapwood, unweathered timber ranges from dark brown to off-white.

**Hinoki bathing bucket**
Japanese cypress has an immaculate straight grain, light uniform coloration and pleasant aroma. These qualities make it a desirable material for bathing products, including tubs and buckets, as well as entire bathrooms. Cutting and shaping yields a smooth surface, which is easy to keep clean. This watertight bucket is produced in the same way as a cask, using a technique known as coopering. There are no adhesives, nails or screws holding the staves (vertical planks) and base together. Instead, the staves are precisely tapered and bevelled, and copper (page 66) hoops are placed around them. Driven down tightly, the hoops hold the staves together.

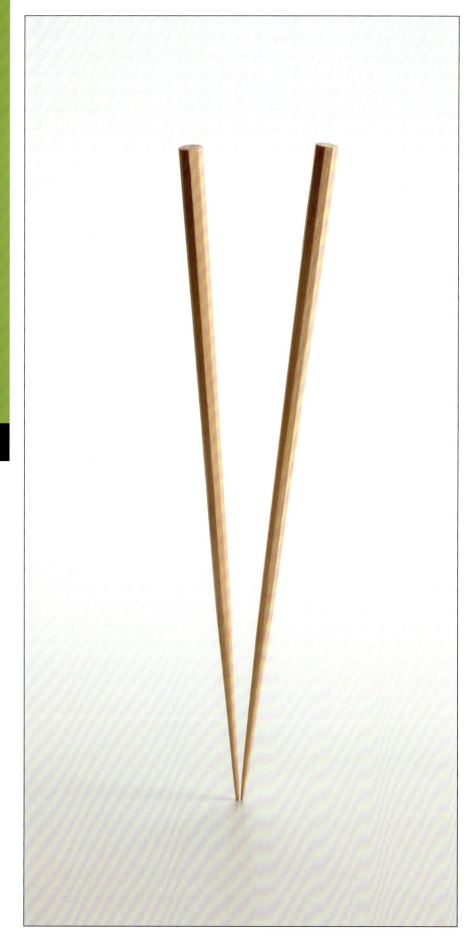

Eastern white-cedar (*Thuja occidentalis*), also known as northern white, is one of the lightest structural timbers and ideally suited to boatbuilding. Like western red, it continues to be used by American Indians, such as the Micmacs and Ojibwe, to produce the structure of bark canoes, roof shingles and baskets. It has excellent resistance to water and repels beetles and termites. Unweathered colour ranges from pale brown to off-white. It grows up to around 20 m (65 ft) tall.

Eastern red-cedar (*Juniperus virginiana*) is also known as red, pencil or aromatic cedar. It is a slow-growing tree from southern and eastern North America reaching heights of up to 15 m (50 ft). Originally used to make pencils, it has mostly been replaced by the less expensive incense-cedar (*Calocedrus decurrens*). Unweathered, it has a pinkish to yellowish to purple-red colour and is very resistant to decay. Its highly aromatic nature works well as an insect repellent and so it is utilized in hangers and wardrobe linings.

Incense-cedar is also known as white-cedar. It is lightweight, soft and not as strong as eastern red, but an improvement on western red. Combined with a straight grain, this means that the timber is relatively easy to cut and finish with a very smooth surface. It is used to make pencils because it sharpens to a fine finish and is resistant to splintering (good for working and chewing). It has very good resistance to decay and so is used outdoors (shingles and posts) as well as in basketry. It is native to western North America and grows up to around 45 m (148 ft) tall.

**Japanese disposable chopsticks** Hinoki and sugi are used to make a range of eating utensils, including platters, cutting boards and chopsticks. The wood is soft and light, which makes it easy to cut with a very smooth profile. Hinoki is thought to have been used to make some of the earliest Japanese chopsticks, with examples dating back to the 7th century. The discarded wood remained intact as a result of its superior durability. Interestingly, many of the discoveries were made around ancient temples constructed of the same wood.

Port Orford-cedar (*Chamaecyparis lawsoniana*) is also known as Oregon-cedar and Lawson's cypress. As its name suggests, it is native to western North America. It grows up to 50 m (164 ft) tall and the raw timber is light yellow to off-white with a densely packed straight grain. Its uniform visual quality is combined with moderate strength and durability, making it a desirable timber for high-quality toys, boxes and construction (Japanese shrines and temples). Its use originally stretched from shipbuilding to arrow shafts to guitar soundboards, and as a result it has been greatly overexploited. It is now in limited supply and consequently very expensive.

Japanese-cedar (*Cryptomeria japonica*) and Japanese cypress (*Chamaecyparis obtusa*) are better known as sugi and hinoki, respectively, in their native Japan. These are important timbers in Asia and widely cultivated in China and Thailand, as well as Japan. Sugi can reach 70 m (230 ft) or more in height. The raw timber has a reddish-pink colour and is used in construction and furniture making. Similar to Port Orford-cedar, hinoki appears light and uniform, with a straight grain. It grows more slowly than sugi and to half the height. Cut to conceal the knots, it is used in furniture, bathroom products and sake cups.

Nootka cypress (*Cupressus nootkatensis* and *Chamaecyparis nootkatensis*) is also known as yellow cypress, yellow-cedar and Alaska-cedar, among other names. Native to western North America, it is also found throughout Europe and grows up to 40 m (130 ft) tall. The light-yellow to off-white timber has a very straight and uniform grain unsurpassed in furniture construction. The surface is hard and durable and polishes to a high sheen. It is extremely durable in the ground and resistant to decay. It is one of the strongest in its family (around one-third stronger than western red). Its beneficial properties are utilized by American Indians, in particular the Nuu-chah-nulth, or Nootka (from where the tree derives its name), in the construction of boats and canoes, as well as for carvings and musical instruments.

Redwood (*Sequoia sempervirens*) was logged virtually to extinction. Considered one of the tallest trees, it grows to a staggering 100 m (330 ft) or more. Its size, lightness and softness combined with resistance to decay made it a very cost-effective timber for high-volume applications such as building, roof shingles, telegraph poles and railway sleepers among others. Redwood lumber now comes from managed plantations around California, and across Europe and New Zealand. The unweathered wood is yellow to very dark brown, is close-grained and polishes well. Not to be confused with red-coloured tropical timbers (page 374) or Scots pine (*Pinus sylvestris*), which is often referred to as redwood to differentiate it from whitewood.

Bald cypress (*Taxodium distichum*) is also known as swamp cypress or simply cypress. Native to southeastern North America, it grows up to 40 m (130 ft) tall. Unlike other cypress trees, this is a deciduous conifer that drops its needle-like leaves each winter. It is not particularly fast-growing and so not as widely available as some of the other species. It produces a very durable wood with high resistance to shrinking and warping. The wood does not impart substances that affect flavour and so is turned into water containers and barrels, for example. It has excellent resistance to insects and water, which are useful properties for outdoor construction and roof shingles. The roots form into winding shapes (knees), which are harvested and carved into furniture and ornaments.

Chinese-fir (*Cunninghamia lanceolata*), also known as Chinese-cedar, although it is neither a fir nor a cedar, is one of the most valuable sources of timber for construction and furniture in Asia. It is closely related to *C. konishii*, which is now considered endangered because of overexploitation. Native to southern China (where it is known as shanmu), Taiwan and Vietnam, it grows to heights of 50 m (165 ft) or more. The wood is pale yellow to off-white with reddish hues. It is very durable with decay resistance comparable to its cousin western red. Therefore, it is used for many of the same applications, including boatbuilding, construction, decking and furniture making.

Unweathered    6 months    10 years

**Weathering cycle of untreated western red** The various cypress and cedars yield light-pink to reddish-brown heartwood and light off-white sapwood. The colour difference can be difficult to distinguish in some cases, in particular those species that have very narrow sapwood. The heartwood contains oils that repel water coupled with fungicidal and anti-bacterial properties. This imparts a distinctive aroma. The more durable species may be left outdoors untreated and submerged in water. The finest knot-free timber with tightly packed growth rings is reserved for the most visually demanding applications. The colour depends on the species and from where in the trunk the timber was derived. Over time, the wood will turn silvery-grey. There are countless examples of ancient buildings and furniture that have survived to this day, in particular in Japan where sugi (Japanese-cedar) and hinoki (Japanese cypress) enjoy celebrity status.

## SUSTAINABILITY

The usefulness of several of these species has led to severe depletion in the wild. For example, the Mulanje cypress (*Widdringtonia whytei*) from South Africa, Ciprés de las Guaitecas (*Pilgerodendron uviferum*) from South America, certain Chinese-firs and wild redwood are all labelled as threatened on the IUCN (International Union for Conservation of Nature) Red List.

Many of these timbers can be sourced from well-managed forests, in particular the eastern red-cedar, incense-cedar, Nootka cypress, bald cypress, eastern white-cedar and western red-cedar. While members of the cypress family are found throughout the world, certain species are restricted to relatively small geographic areas. Therefore, when specifying a particular type of timber, care should be taken to ensure it does not have to travel further than necessary.

The natural defence that these timbers have to decay and insects can in some cases affect people. The dust produced by cutting and working the wood of certain species acts as a severe irritant and can lead to respiratory problems as well as other health issues.

## ARCHITECTURE AND CONSTRUCTION

**Lightweight**
It is low-density: almost one-third lighter than Douglas-fir and half the weight of oak. This means that while it is not particularly strong, it has very good strength-to-weight and so is very practical as cladding.

**Softness**
It is relatively straightforward to cut and work to a fine finish. Its low density contributes to its relatively high insulation value.

**Sustainable**
Several species are available from PEFC- and FSC-certified forests. Grown throughout the world, the timber is likely to be available from local sources.

**Durability**
The heartwood has superior resistance to decay and the oil in certain species repels insects. It provides a long-term solution – there are many examples of ancient buildings that prove its endurance. Where necessary, sapwood is treated with preservative.

### CYPRESS FAMILY IN ARCHITECTURE AND CONSTRUCTION

While these timbers are used in a variety of applications, their long-established and varied role in construction warrants further discussion. It competes with several other species of softwood, including varieties of larch (page 310) and pine. It competes with hardwoods too, in particular oak (page 342) and iroko (page 366).

Planks are cut into profiles – there are countless standard shapes, or bespoke designs are made – for window frames, louvres, decking, fencing and cladding (overlapping slats are used in strip boat construction also). It is much less stiff than other timbers used for similar applications, but has superior resistance

to decay. Therefore, it is mainly reserved for outward-facing surfaces. The timber is graded according to its visual quality.

Throughout the world it is used as roofing and siding material. Known as shingles, small neat tapered tiles are overlapped to provide protection from sun, rain and snow. They are known as shakes when produced from split timber. Being susceptible to fire and relatively expensive, they are not as common today as they have been in the past.

The ability of certain species to resist warping and cracking with changes in humidity is very important during production, as well as in use, especially because they are often manufactured in one climate and shipped to another. Planks are often shipped green (not dried)

**Western red-cedar shiplap** The curved profile of the London Olympic Velodrome, designed by Hopkins Architects and completed in 2011, is fabricated from overlapping strips of western red-cedar. The prefabricated panels span approximately 8 m (26 ft) between the steel (page 28) trusses. A smooth curve is maintained by dividing each panel into four parts. Strips of aluminium (page 42) conceal the end grain and provide a visually clean division between each facet. Louvre panels, fabricated from a different profile, provide ventilation. A coating of oil helps to preserve the colour of the wood and enhance its natural durability. Photo courtesy of Hopkins Architects.

**Western red-cedar interior** The National Assembly for Wales (also known as the Senedd) building was designed by Richard Rogers Partnership and completed in 2005. The main funnel (known as the Oriel) and ceiling are clad with western red-cedar. Employing a bespoke assembly system, each panel consists of several strips held in place by concealed fixings. To accommodate the varying radius of the shape, each panel has a trapezoidal profile. The gently undulating tones of wood contribute to the interior's warm ambience.

when used for outdoor applications. They are dried (naturally or using a kiln) to reduce their moisture content and improve stability where necessary.

# Poplar, Aspen and Cottonwood

These utilitarian hardwoods are available from certified forests across the northern hemisphere. The timber compares favourably with pine and spruce, as well as some low-density hardwoods. It is resistant to splitting and has no taste or odour when dry, which makes it useful in veneer and food packaging. Aspen is the principal timber used to make matches.

| Types | Typical Applications | Sustainability |
|---|---|---|
| • Poplar: white, black and balsam<br>• Aspen: bigtooth, European and quaking<br>• Cottonwood: black and eastern | • Packaging, trunks and boxes<br>• Engineered timber<br>• Matches | • Available from certified forests<br>• Wide distribution and often intermingled with softwoods, such as spruce, pine and fir |

| Properties | Competing Materials | Costs |
|---|---|---|
| • Lightweight and relatively soft<br>• Colour ranges from greyish- to reddish-brown heartwood to off-white sapwood<br>• Poplar is tasteless and odourless when dry | • Spruce, pine and fir<br>• Engineered timber<br>• Oak, beech and birch | • Inexpensive hardwood<br>• Low manufacturing costs |

324

## INTRODUCTION

By volume, these are some one of the least expensive hardwoods. Their strength is comparable to pine and spruce (page 304). However, they are rarely used as lumber and are more often converted into veneer (page 290), plywood (page 296) or pulp (page 268). This is because of several factors: even though fast-growing, poplar and aspen do not grow very large and so do not provide a reliable source of adequately sized lumber; the timber often has unsound knots, which weakens the overall structure; it is not durable; and it has poor nail- and screw-holding capabilities.

They do convert into veneer very well and resist splitting. This is perhaps best demonstrated by their use in matches (in particular aspen). Veneers are cut into strips, impregnated, coated and covered with a fire-making head. Not only do the sticks need to tolerate the rigours of mass production, but they must also be able to safely withstand striking.

## COMMERCIAL TYPES AND USES

Confusingly, in North America poplar timber comes from two genera: *Populus*

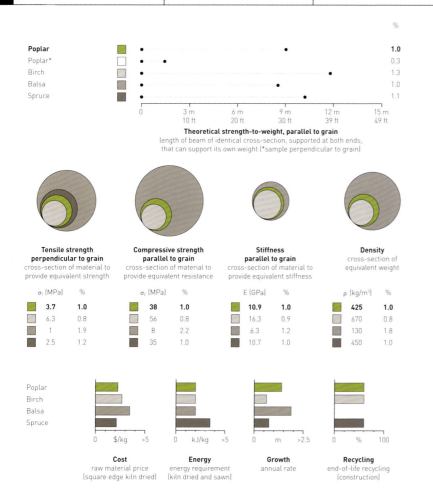

| | | % |
|---|---|---|
| Poplar | | 1.0 |
| Poplar* | | 0.3 |
| Birch | | 1.3 |
| Balsa | | 1.0 |
| Spruce | | 1.1 |

**Theoretical strength-to-weight, parallel to grain**
length of beam of identical cross-section, supported at both ends, that can support its own weight (*sample perpendicular to grain)

**Tensile strength perpendicular to grain**
cross-section of material to provide equivalent strength

| $\sigma_t$ (MPa) | % |
|---|---|
| 3.7 | 1.0 |
| 6.3 | 0.8 |
| 1 | 1.9 |
| 2.5 | 1.2 |

**Compressive strength parallel to grain**
cross-section of material to provide equivalent resistance

| $\sigma_c$ (MPa) | % |
|---|---|
| 38 | 1.0 |
| 56 | 0.8 |
| 8 | 2.2 |
| 35 | 1.0 |

**Stiffness parallel to grain**
cross-section of material to provide equivalent stiffness

| E (GPa) | % |
|---|---|
| 10.9 | 1.0 |
| 16.3 | 0.9 |
| 6.3 | 1.2 |
| 10.7 | 1.0 |

**Density**
cross-section of equivalent weight

| $\rho$ (kg/m³) | % |
|---|---|
| 425 | 1.0 |
| 670 | 0.8 |
| 130 | 1.8 |
| 450 | 1.0 |

Poplar
Birch
Balsa
Spruce

**Cost**
raw material price
(square edge kiln dried)

**Energy**
energy requirement
(kiln dried and sawn)

**Growth**
annual rate

**Recycling**
end-of-life recycling
(construction)

**Dutch *klompen***
Farmers, fishermen, gardeners and craft workers wear clogs to protect their feet while they work. They provide a low-cost alternative to leather boots. They have done so for generations; the exact date of the first wooden shoes will never be known (old clogs often ended up as firewood), but a pair was discovered in Amsterdam that dated back to around 1250. Decorations originally evolved as a way to distinguish ownership. Exquisite carved and painted clogs were worn at weddings and displayed in the house afterwards. Today, they are officially accredited as safety shoes with the European CE mark. They are traditionally carved from poplar, but are also produced from willow (from the same family, Salicaceae) (page 328). A lighter version designed for dancing in is produced from ash (page 354).

**Left**
**Cheese packaging**
Poplar has several
qualities that make
it suitable for food
packaging: as a
veneer it is resistant
to splitting; when
dry it has no taste or
odour; it is lightweight
and economical. This
style of poplar box
provides cheese with a
traditional appearance.
This quality has not
gone unnoticed and
similar packaging
has been used for
cosmetics, chocolate
and various other
items to give them
a 'handcrafted' look.

**Opposite**
**Veneer-covered wing**
These wing halves, each
measuring 50 cm (20
in) long, come from
the Bobolink-DL model
glider. An expanded
polystyrene (EPS) (page
132) core is sandwiched
between two layers of
black poplar veneer.
The leading edge and
wing tip are finished
with solid wood to
ensure the optimum
aerodynamics. It is
a very lightweight
method of construction;
the structure weighs
a mere 90 g (0.2 lb).

Blockboard

Veneer core

**Low-density plywood**
Poplar, aspen and
cottonwood are
commonly used to
make plywood. The
advantage of using
these timbers, as
opposed to other
hardwoods, is their
relatively low mass.
Similar to softwoods,
they are utilized in a
number of different
formats (see page 299),
including laminated
veneer lumber (LVL)
and oriented-strand
board (OSB). Blockboard
consists of a core of
strips, cut from poplar
or similar low-density
wood. This provides a
cost-effective solution
for applications that
require very light, thick
boards. Alternatively,
layers of veneer are
built up to the desired
thickness. Low-density,
low-cost boards
are produced with
relatively thick veneer.
Plywood of this type is
used in the production
of trailers, doors, boats,
furniture and toys.
Where a high-quality
finish is required, a low-
density poplar core, or
other suitable timber,
may be sandwiched
between decorative
veneer, medium-density
fibreboard (MDF) or
melamine (page 224)
for example.

and *Liriodendron*. Tulipwood (*L. tulipifera*)
is also known as yellow-poplar, tulip-
poplar or simply poplar. Colour ranges
from creamy white to olive-green, which
helps to differentiate the timber from
*Populus*. It is one of the largest hardwood
trees in North America and yields high-
quality lumber and veneer.

The principal commercial species of
poplar are white (*P. alba*) (also known
as American aspen), black (*P. nigra*) and
balsam (*P. balsamifera*).

When dry, poplar does not have any
odour or taste. These qualities mean that
it is a useful packaging material. It is
used to make boxes, cartons and cheese
packaging. It can be bent into moderately
tight curves when dry. However, it is not
suitable for steam bending (see page 357),
because it has relatively short fibres.

There are three main species of aspen:
bigtooth (*P. grandidentata*), European
(*P. tremula*) and quaking (*P. tremuloides*).
The woods are virtually indistinguishable
from one another.

Cottonwood varieties include black
(*P. trichocarpa*) and eastern (*P. deltoides*)

(also known as American cottonwood
and eastern poplar). They are capable of
producing large amounts of clear lumber
and veneer.

All these hardwoods are lightweight
with moderate compressive strength.
They are often concealed within doors,
furniture and trunks (luggage), providing
an inexpensive core material. Similar to
spruce, solid poplar is suitable for use in
soundboards in stringed instruments.
It has similar resonance. However, it is
not as aesthetically appealing and so is
typically dyed or laminated and hidden
behind a layer of decoration. Cut into
veneers, they are utilized in engineered
timber (page 296) and laminated flooring.

## SUSTAINABILITY
They grow across the northern
hemisphere and are readily available
in many continents. They are relatively
fast-growing – so much so that they are
considered a potential biofuel crop – and
provide a renewable source of timber for
many light-structure applications.

The properties of these timbers, as
well as other non-durable woods, are
improved with heat treatment. Raising
the temperature of the wood to between
160 and 260°C (320–500°F) in a controlled
atmosphere affects the chemical
composition of the wood, resulting in a
darker, more dimensionally stable, durable
and weather-resistant material.

# Willow

**Also known as**
Also referred to as: sallow, osier
As a weaving material, also known as: wicker

While its combination of lightness and shock resistance is utilized in sports equipment, certain species' twigs provide valuable basket-making materials, thanks to their flexibility and speed of growth. It is a common tree in the deciduous forests of North America, Europe and Asia, but in limited availability. It is used to make furniture, sports equipment, crates and baskets.

| Types | Typical Applications | Sustainability |
|---|---|---|
| • Willow includes many species, commercial examples include: black, white, crack and almond | • Sports equipment, in particular cricket bats<br>• Baskets and crates<br>• Furniture and joinery | • Availability depends on location; for example black willow is popular in the USA and white willow is more common in Europe and Asia |
| **Properties** | **Competing Materials** | **Costs** |
| • Low density<br>• Interlocking grain<br>• Moderate shock resistance | • Hickory and poplar<br>• Bamboo, jute and sisal<br>• PP, PE and similar synthetics used in basketry | • Low-cost raw material, although the finest grades used in professional crickets bats can be very expensive |

## INTRODUCTION

Willow (*Salix* genus) has been used since ancient times to make useful objects. Early examples of woven willow include baskets, traps, shelter and fences. The distinctive appearance of certain species and its powerful healing properties have led to its becoming an icon in some cultures. The ancient Egyptians used willow bark as a remedy for aches and pains, and we now know this quality can be attributed to salicylic acid (a key ingredient of aspirin).

Willow lumber ranges from pale reddish- to greyish-brown heartwood to off-white sapwood. Willow rods are available in a range of colours: brown rods have been dried and used with their bark intact; buff willow has been boiled for several hours and the bark removed; and white willow is peeled without boiling.

Certain species have a somewhat interlocked grain (see page 368), which prevents the wood from splitting easily but can also make it tricky to work with.

## COMMERCIAL TYPES AND USES

There are many different species, ranging from ground-hugging shrubs to large broad-leaved trees. Poplar, aspen and cottonwood (page 324) belong to the same family, Salicaceae.

Black willow (*Salix nigra*) is also called the American or swamp willow, and is the most important commercial species in North America. It is harvested for lumber and the timber is used in joinery, furniture making, crates and veneer.

A variety of white willow (*S. alba*), which grows in UK, is the principal timber used in the production of the highest-quality cricket bat blades. It is very carefully graded and processed to provide just the right mix of lightness, strength and rebound. Willow has been used in the production of bats for centuries,

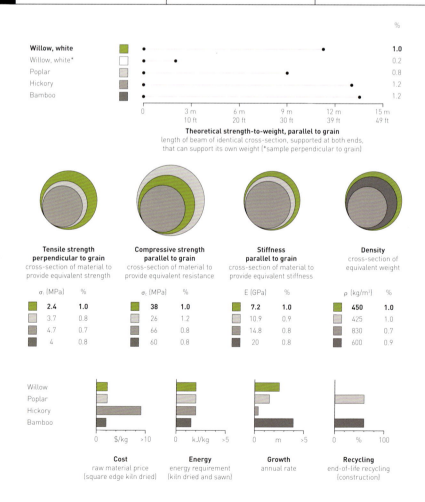

%
| | | | |
|---|---|---|---|
| Willow, white | | | 1.0 |
| Willow, white* | | | 0.2 |
| Poplar | | | 0.8 |
| Hickory | | | 1.2 |
| Bamboo | | | 1.2 |

0 · 3 m / 10 ft · 6 m / 20 ft · 9 m / 30 ft · 12 m / 39 ft · 15 m / 49 ft

**Theoretical strength-to-weight, parallel to grain**
length of beam of identical cross-section, supported at both ends, that can support its own weight (*sample perpendicular to grain)

| Tensile strength perpendicular to grain<br>cross-section of material to provide equivalent strength | | Compressive strength parallel to grain<br>cross-section of material to provide equivalent resistance | | Stiffness parallel to grain<br>cross-section of material to provide equivalent stiffness | | Density<br>cross-section of equivalent weight | |
|---|---|---|---|---|---|---|---|
| σ, (MPa) | % | σ, (MPa) | % | E (GPa) | % | ρ (kg/m³) | % |
| 2.4 | 1.0 | 38 | 1.0 | 7.2 | 1.0 | 450 | 1.0 |
| 3.7 | 0.8 | 26 | 1.2 | 10.9 | 0.9 | 425 | 1.0 |
| 4.7 | 0.7 | 66 | 0.8 | 14.8 | 0.8 | 830 | 0.7 |
| 4 | 0.8 | 60 | 0.8 | 20 | 0.8 | 600 | 0.9 |

| | Cost | Energy | Growth | Recycling |
|---|---|---|---|---|
| Willow | | | | |
| Poplar | | | | |
| Hickory | | | | |
| Bamboo | | | | |

0 · $/kg · >10 · · · 0 · kJ/kg · >5 · · · 0 · m · >5 · · · 0 · % · 100

**Cost**
raw material price (square edge kiln dried)

**Energy**
energy requirement (kiln dried and sawn)

**Growth**
annual rate

**Recycling**
end-of-life recycling (construction)

and continues to be the material of choice, because it offers a good balance of properties. Several alternatives have been explored, but have either proved unworthy or have been banned by the governing body, the Marylebone Cricket Club (MCC). Examples include aluminium (page 28), bamboo (used in the handle, page 386), poplar and laminated willow (the layer of adhesive reduces flexibility and so makes the bat more efficient).

Certain species of willow are suitable for basket making, such as the white, the osier varieties (*S. viminalis* and *S. purpurea*) and the almond (*S. trianda*). Also referred to as basket willows, these and related species send up new twigs in spring that grow quickly. In one season, a rod (withy) can reach up to 2.4 m (8 ft). Indeed, it grows so fast and efficiently that it is utilized as a biofuel. New willow beds take around three years to mature

**Wicker gondola** Wicker baskets woven with willow withies have been used for centuries to carry, package, store and bury. While they are utilitarian by nature, basket weaving is considered an art form.

and with careful management they may be productive coppices for up to 30 years.

The same type of withies used in basketry form the precursor to the charcoal used by artists, in filtration and as propellant in pyrotechnics, for example.

## SUSTAINABILITY
Throughout its natural range, willow provides a sustainable and fast-growing renewable source of timber and wicker. Withies can be harvested every few years, while lumber trees take decades to mature.

The rods used here have been peeled without boiling to retain a light colour. Rods of varying thickness are used; selection depends on the flexibility that is required for each part of the structure.

**Vertical rib**

**Radial rib**

**Plain-weave** The warp (vertical stakes or radiating spokes) and weft (horizontal strands) are placed at right angles, alternately passing over and under one another, to produce a checked pattern (see diagram, page 240). Of course, any weave can be followed, but plain-weaves are the most straightforward and so least time-consuming. Using rigid warp ribs and flexible weft strands produces the familiar willow basket texture. Changing the angle and pattern of the ribs allows for circular, oval and three-dimensional shapes to be produced. This is useful for the base, lid or entire basket.

# Maple

While hard maple is tough and shock-resistant, it is prized for its beautiful white colour. In very rare cases, the grain becomes distorted and produces desirable patterns, such as bird's-eye and quilted. These are sliced into veneer and command a high price. The tree is also famous for its sap, which is converted into sweet and flavoursome maple syrup.

| Types | Typical Applications | Sustainability |
|---|---|---|
| • Hard maple: sugar and black<br>• Soft maple: bigleaf, red and silver | • Musical instruments<br>• Baseball bats, gun stocks and tool handles<br>• Furniture, workbenches, butcher blocks and flooring | • Widespread throughout North America, Europe, Africa and Asia<br>• Available from certified forests<br>• Considered a respiratory sensitizer |
| **Properties** | **Competing Materials** | **Costs** |
| • Hard maple has excellent resistance to shock and wear<br>• Highly figured grain pattern in rare cases<br>• Not durable to decay, vulnerable to insects | • Birch, poplar, sycamore, beech, oak, walnut and ash<br>• Spruce | • Moderately priced timber and relatively straightforward to work<br>• Figured pieces, such as bird's-eye, will be much more expensive |

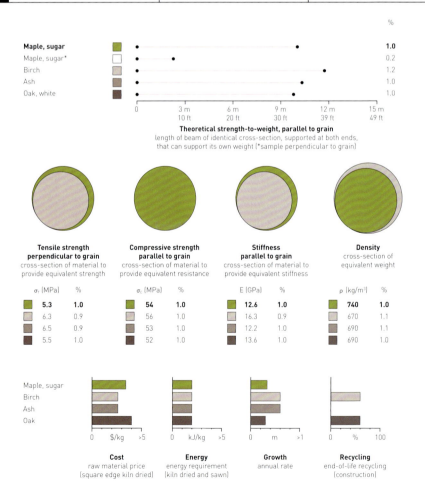

| | % |
|---|---|
| Maple, sugar | 1.0 |
| Maple, sugar* | 0.2 |
| Birch | 1.2 |
| Ash | 1.0 |
| Oak, white | 1.0 |

**Theoretical strength-to-weight, parallel to grain**
length of beam of identical cross-section, supported at both ends, that can support its own weight (*sample perpendicular to grain)

**Tensile strength perpendicular to grain**
cross-section of material to provide equivalent strength

| $\sigma_t$ (MPa) | % |
|---|---|
| 5.3 | 1.0 |
| 6.3 | 0.9 |
| 6.5 | 0.9 |
| 5.5 | 1.0 |

**Compressive strength parallel to grain**
cross-section of material to provide equivalent resistance

| $\sigma_c$ (MPa) | % |
|---|---|
| 54 | 1.0 |
| 56 | 1.0 |
| 53 | 1.0 |
| 52 | 1.0 |

**Stiffness parallel to grain**
cross-section of material to provide equivalent stiffness

| E (GPa) | % |
|---|---|
| 12.6 | 1.0 |
| 16.3 | 0.9 |
| 12.2 | 1.0 |
| 13.6 | 1.0 |

**Density**
cross-section of equivalent weight

| $\rho$ (kg/m³) | % |
|---|---|
| 740 | 1.0 |
| 670 | 1.1 |
| 690 | 1.1 |
| 690 | 1.0 |

| | |
|---|---|
| Maple, sugar | |
| Birch | |
| Ash | |
| Oak | |

**Cost**
raw material price (square edge kiln dried)

**Energy**
energy requirement (kiln dried and sawn)

**Growth**
annual rate

**Recycling**
end-of-life recycling (construction)

## INTRODUCTION

Maple (*Acer* genus) is considered a symbol of strength and endurance. It is an important tree, especially in Canada, where the leaf of the sugar maple (*A. saccharum*) adorns the national flag. A valuable commercial timber, it is used in a broad spectrum of applications, from dance floors to musical instruments.

The heartwood is creamy white to dark reddish-brown, depending on the growing conditions. The sapwood can be almost white; it is the sapwood that tends to be used, as opposed to the heartwood as is the case with most other timbers. The highest-quality lumber is graded according to whiteness, which limits availability somewhat. Number 1 indicates 100% sapwood and number 2 indicates that all faces are sapwood, except for up to 50% of the backside. The same colour selection guidelines are used to grade other sapwood-yielding hardwoods, such as ash (page 354) and birch (page 334).

## COMMERCIAL TYPES & USES

Maples are referred to as either 'hard' or 'soft'.

Hard maple includes sugar, also known as rock, and black (*A. nigrum*). Sugar maple yields the strongest and hardest timber. Black is very similar and so they tend to be grouped together commercially. Highly figured grain patterns – such as bird's-eye, curly and quilted – most commonly occur in the hard maples. They are rare and expensive and so tend to be applied as veneer (page 290).

Hard maple has very good shock resistance, wear resistance and surface hardness. These properties are utilized in a range of applications – it is an important commercial timber – including flooring (from gymnasiums to bowling alleys), furniture, sports equipment (in

particular baseball bats and snooker cues), butcher blocks (end-grain chopping boards), tools and utensils.

It is one of the principal woods used in the construction of musical instruments, such as the backs, sides (ribs) and necks of violins, cellos and similar instruments. It is considered to have good tonal qualities – Stradivari and Guarneri, the old masters of violin making, selected maple for the back and the tradition has continued to this day (see image, page 305). The most prominent feature of maple is its figured grain. Applied to the back of instruments,

flame and curl are popular, because they produce an interesting optical effect that shifts from dark to light depending on the angle of view. Drums are also made of maple, as well as birch.

It is relatively easy to work, but tends to dull cutting tools quickly as a result of its hardness.

As a result of the widespread application of hard maple, it comes into comparison with several other hardwoods. Similar to ash, it has a good balance of properties for use in sports equipment, including baseball bats and

**Compact and lightweight stool**
Colour Stool was created by Dutch design partners Scholten & Baijings for the Japanese furniture maker Karimoku New Standard, 2011. Its design makes reference to the traditional way of sitting in Japan, which is popular because it takes up very little room. Maple is prized for its lightness of colour

and dense, smooth surface. Everything is produced to the highest standards of Japanese craftsmanship: the seat is carved by computer-guided machine and is thicker in the middle to ensure sturdiness; the legs vanish into the seat, the joint concealed in a recess; and a crisp linear pattern is created by spray painting the colour and sanding excess away. Photo by Scholten & Baijings.

### Baseball bat

Wooden baseball bats are typically made of maple, ash or birch, with ash being the most popular. Bamboo (page 386) and composite constructions have also been explored, but are not legal in all leagues. Material selection comes down to individual preference. The high density of sugar maple results in a heavy bat, which is preferred by professionals, because its balance of hardness and stiffness allows players to exert a great deal of force on the ball. This example is the Marucci AP5 Pro Model, handcrafted from top-quality sugar maple. The barrel has been rubbed with bone to increase surface hardness. The physical properties of ash are comparable to maple in many ways, but it is not as hard, so the ball will not bounce from the surface with the same vigour. This 'softness' provides surface flexibility, creating a 'sweet spot' that is also referred to as the springboard effect: on impact the wood compresses and rebounds. Birch is lighter and stiffer, which is more forgiving to mis-hits and so popular for beginners and those new to wooden bats.

snooker cues. The two are also suitable for steam bending, a useful quality in items ranging from furniture to sleds. Like beech (page 338), oak (page 342) and walnut (page 348), maple is used in high-quality joinery, furniture and interiors. What sets maple apart from all these woods, other than its density, is its beautiful white colour. One wood that has a similar appearance is birch. Indeed, these two are used in many of the same situations, from furniture to musical instruments. Maple, however, is considerably harder-wearing.

As its name suggests, sugar maple produces the sweetest and most flavoursome syrup; its sap has the highest sugar content of the *Acer* genus.

Other species of maple are considered soft. This is relative and only in comparison to hard maples; they tend to be less strong (20%), hard (25%), heavy (20%) and so on. They grow faster than hard maple, which explains the difference in properties. The principal species in this category are red (*A. rubrum*), silver (*A. saccharinum*) and bigleaf (*A. macrophyllum*). The red and silver grow in similar locations and tend not to be segregated commercially even though the timber may look quite different.

Soft maples are inferior to hard maples in many ways, but perform adequately for many of the same situations, including furniture, musical instruments and interiors. Like hard maple, they have good steam bending properties. They are less expensive and so also utilized in lower-grade items, such as crates and pallets.

### SUSTAINABILITY

Maple is available from certified forests and is considered one of the most sustainable sources of hardwood. Selecting 'hard' or 'soft', as opposed to individual trees, increases the likelihood of using local timber, because not all species grow everywhere.

Like oak, hard maple is considered a slow-growing tree. In other words, it takes a relatively long time for the tree to reach a suitable size for harvesting. However, one of the advantages of hard maple is its hard-wearing surface; it will outlast most other woods in demanding applications, such as flooring and butcher blocks.

*Cryptostroma corticale* is a species of fungus that grows abundantly under the bark of maple trees. It is thought to be responsible for the defect known as spalting, a marblized effect that is prized by wood carvers. Loggers and sawmill workers who are repeatedly exposed to its spores can become hypersensitized and suffer fever, fatigue and coughing as a result.

Trees are tapped for their sap to make maple syrup. If conservative tapping guidelines are followed, the tree will remain healthy and productive for generations. Maple yields less sugar than cane for the same area. This is inevitable since maple trees make up part of a diverse forest ecosystem and are not planted as a monocrop like sugar cane. Owing to the relatively low sugar content of maple sap (around 2%), it takes 44 litres (46 US quarts) of sap to produce just 1 litre (just over 1 US quart) of syrup. Heat is required to boil down the sap; if this is generated using renewable biofuel, then the process will be more or less carbon neutral.

**Pub table** Aberrant Architecture created this table for *Wallpaper** magazine's 'Handmade' exhibition, 2012. Named Devil Amongst the Tailors, after a tabletop skittles pub game, their design combines American maple and cherry (page 360). Two versions were created, the other one featuring an American ash top and black walnut base. The metalwork, including the foot rail, handles and locks, is silver patinated brass (page 66). The table was produced in collaboration with the American Hardwood Export Council (AHEC) and hand-crafted by Benchmark, UK, using traditional joinery techniques. The table features a lid that when raised, reveals a private workstation and when closed, can be used to play bar skittles. Photo by Angus Thomas.

# Birch

Birch is a truly all-purpose tree: the timber is strong and versatile; the fibres are good for pulp; the bark is used in the construction of lightweight canoes; the wood is burned in smokers to flavour food; the sap is tapped and used in food, drink and syrup; the leaves are used in tea and cosmetics; and the twigs are used in saunas to provide a relaxing aroma.

| Types | Typical Applications | Sustainability |
|---|---|---|
| • Birch: yellow, silver and paper, among others | • Furniture, products, toys and utensils<br>• Engineered timber, paper and pulp<br>• Toothpicks and single-use cutlery | • Widely cultivated throughout the northern hemisphere and available from certified forests<br>• Can be a sensitizer |

| Properties | Competing Materials | Costs |
|---|---|---|
| • Fine-grained with a satin-like sheen<br>• High strength-to-weight and quite hard<br>• Poor resistance to decay and susceptible to insect attack | • Maple, poplar, beech, alder and hornbeam<br>• Spruce, pine and fir | • Low to moderate raw material cost<br>• Good processing properties |

334

## INTRODUCTION

Like the tree, birch (*Betula* genus) timber is versatile and used in many formats, from lumber to veneer (page 290), and plywood (see Engineered Timber, page 296) to paper (page 268).

The lack of visual contrast between the growth rings gives birch a plain appearance. This aesthetic 'cleanliness' means birch can be used to cover large areas without becoming too overbearing.

The tone depends on the species. Typically, the sapwood ranges from white to pale yellow, and the heartwood is light to golden brown. As with maple (page 330), it is the sapwood that is primarily used. It is reasonably straight-grained, but in some cases is slightly wavy, with a uniform and fine texture.

The aesthetic attributes of birch combined with the strength and versatility of plywood, means that, over the years, this combination has featured in many iconic designs, including Arne Jacobsen's Series 7 chair (1955), Charles and Ray Eames's DCW side chair (1946) and Alvar Aalto's Stool 60 (1933) (see image, page 337).

As well as individual pieces of furniture, birch plywood is used to clad entire interiors. Typified by the exposed end-grain (revealing the laminated construction), birch plywood is utilized in the construction of partition walls, stairwells, cupboards and fitted kitchens. One of the many advantages of using flat sheets of plywood for furniture and

**Flexible veneer packaging** Used as gift packaging for fine Chinese tea, birch veneer provides a flexible lid that wraps around the curved profile. A whole range of woods can be applied in this way, including walnut, sapele, red oak, maple, cherry and beech. The same concept is used to package wine, food and other luxury items (see poplar packaging, page 326).

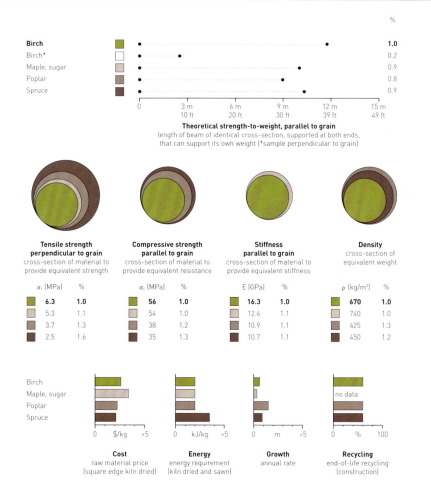

| | | % |
|---|---|---|
| Birch | | 1.0 |
| Birch* | | 0.2 |
| Maple, sugar | | 0.9 |
| Poplar | | 0.8 |
| Spruce | | 0.9 |

**Theoretical strength-to-weight, parallel to grain**
length of beam of identical cross-section, supported at both ends, that can support its own weight (*sample perpendicular to grain)

| Tensile strength perpendicular to grain | | Compressive strength parallel to grain | | Stiffness parallel to grain | | Density | |
|---|---|---|---|---|---|---|---|
| cross-section of material to provide equivalent strength | | cross-section of material to provide equivalent resistance | | cross-section of material to provide equivalent stiffness | | cross-section of equivalent weight | |
| σ_t (MPa) | % | σ_c (MPa) | % | E (GPa) | % | ρ (kg/m³) | % |
| 6.3 | 1.0 | 56 | 1.0 | 16.3 | 1.0 | 670 | 1.0 |
| 5.3 | 1.1 | 54 | 1.0 | 12.6 | 1.1 | 740 | 1.0 |
| 3.7 | 1.3 | 38 | 1.2 | 10.9 | 1.1 | 425 | 1.3 |
| 2.5 | 1.6 | 35 | 1.3 | 10.7 | 1.1 | 450 | 1.2 |

Birch
Maple, sugar
Poplar
Spruce

| Cost | Energy | Growth | Recycling |
|---|---|---|---|
| raw material price (square edge kiln dried) | energy requirement (kiln dried and sawn) | annual rate | end-of-life recycling (construction) |

interiors is that it is quick and efficient to cut to size using a computer-guided router. The parts of the design are worked out in CAD – including joints and other details that can be cut in the same operation – and transferred to 2D. Waste and cost are minimized by carefully nesting the parts on the sheet (typically 1,220 x 2,440 mm [48 x 88 in]). The process is highly repeatable. In other words, once a design (or technique) has proved successful, it may be recreated exactly using the CAD data, anywhere in the world. Manufacturing items close to where they are needed saves the cost and time associated with transportation.

## COMMERCIAL TYPES AND USES

There are many species of birch and several of the names are used somewhat interchangeably. The two principal commercial species in North America are yellow birch (*B. alleghaniensis*) and paper birch (*B. papyrifera*). Yellow is also known as American yellow, hard and curly; and white is also referred to as American white, canoe and silver. Paper birch is not as strong or hard as yellow birch. Silver birch (*B. pendula*), also known as white birch, grows across Europe, Russia and Asia.

Birch is often differentiated commercially according to its country or region of origin. For example, it is labelled as Baltic, European or American. While the wood may come from the same species, there are sometimes differences in grading. This results in varying standards and areas becoming known for certain qualities, as well as shortfalls.

It has very good working properties and a fine finish can be achieved relatively easily. As a result, it is useful for many different areas of application, including toys, utensils, packaging, joinery and even single-use cutlery and toothpicks.

It is applied extensively as veneer, both for decorative purposes and as plywood. The appearance of veneer depends on the method of production. It is similar, in many ways, to maple and sycamore. Rotary-peeled veneers, such as used to make plywood, are very plain with an arching grain pattern that may be barely visible. More expensive veneers are sliced

across the grain to make the most of the colour variation. In some instances the wood has a rippled, almost three-dimensional appearance known as flame. The effect is emphasized by the natural sheen of the cut surface.

Birch plywood has many advantageous properties: it is strong for its weight; aesthetically pleasing (almost white and relatively knot-free); cost-competitive compared to similar hardwood products; and sustainable. It has been explored in all manner of applications, from bicycle frames to flatpack furniture, and from interiors to aircraft. It is available with a range of finishes, including veneer-covered, fibreboard-covered, phenolic-coated and thermoplastic-coated (see image, page 297). Each has its merits and drawbacks; selection depends on the application requirements.

Birch bark is a material unto itself (page 280). It has been used for generations to make practical items ranging from packaging to canoes. People living in the regions where the trees grow have each evolved their own unique ways of utilizing the material.

Birch pulp is produced from forest thinnings (trees removed from forests to improve the growth of those remaining) and waste generated during plywood production. It is used in papermaking for its superior surface and optical properties.

## SUSTAINABILITY

Birch is considered a sustainable and renewable timber. It is available from certified forests throughout the northern hemisphere. However, care must be taken when sourcing the timber, because illegal logging is widespread in regions from where it is derived, including Russia, Estonia and Latvia.

In the forests that yield certified wood, more trees are planted than are felled to ensure a plentiful supply of timber for the future. Care is taken to preserve deadwood and retention trees for biodiversity during harvesting and to protect the wildlife. Regulations govern which parts of the forest should be left untouched to safeguard nature, such as along streams, banks and where rare species have been discovered.

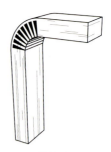

Widthwise                    Lengthwise

**Kerfing** This technique provides an alternative to laminated veneer (see page 299) and steam bending (see page 357) for producing bent wooden lumber. As well as birch, other suitable woods include beech, oak, elm, ash, willow, maple, hickory, larch, iroko and poplar; it depends on their flexibility and resistance to splitting. It is also suitable for engineered timber; some standard panels exist that are pre-cut to allow for bending. The wood is cut, reducing its thickness and thus allowing tighter bends to be formed. In the case of widthwise cutting, the thickness of the cut (kerf) allows the wood to be shaped around a former. It removes the material that would otherwise need to be compressed for the shape to be achieved. Gaps remain where the material has been removed, which

can be filled, covered over, or left exposed. To maintain the curved profile, a sheet is laminated to the inside surface. A much neater way to produce the same profile, as in the case of the Aalto stool (opposite), is to make the cuts lengthwise. This converts the solid wood into a laminated veneer-like structure. In other words, the cut area can be bent like veneer, but remains attached to solid wood. The cuts finish at different heights to avoid the area becoming weakened. Thin strips, the same thickness as the kerf, are adhesive-bonded within the cuts. Clamped around a former, the adhesive cures to form a permanent and very strong bentwood structure. This latter approach is only really suitable for use when the bend is near the end of the piece.

**Lightweight stacking stool** Created by Alvar Aalto and presented for the first time in 1933, Stool 60 is still produced by Finnish furniture company Artek to this day. The design of the birch legs provides strength, stability and stackability. Using a technique that was revolutionary for the time, a solid piece of birch is sawn lengthwise in-line

with the grain. Thin pieces of plywood are adhesive-bonded in the gap left by the blade (kerf). Heating or steaming the wood allows the bend to be formed and it is clamped around a mold while the adhesive cures. The end result is a seemingly effortless design that is one of the most recognizable pieces of Scandinavian modernism.

# Beech

Beech is an all-round, moderately priced and commonly used hardwood. Native to Europe, North America and Asia, it is in high demand and readily available. The heartwood ranges from pale cream to light reddish-brown and quarter-sawn lumber has a silvery fleck (rays). While it is not particularly resistant to decay, it is hard-wearing with good working properties.

| Types | Typical Applications | Sustainability |
|---|---|---|
| • Beech: European and American | • Toys, tools, musical instruments and cooking utensils<br>• Furniture, flooring and interiors<br>• Pulp and cellulose | • Readily available in its native Europe, Asia and North America<br>• Available from certified forests |
| **Properties** | **Competing Materials** | **Costs** |
| • Flexible and suitable for steam bending<br>• Reasonably hard-wearing<br>• Straight grain and uniform texture | • Oak, chestnut, birch, mahogany, cherry, ash, hornbeam and maple | • Moderately priced raw material with good working properties<br>• A little tricky to season owing to checking and distortion |

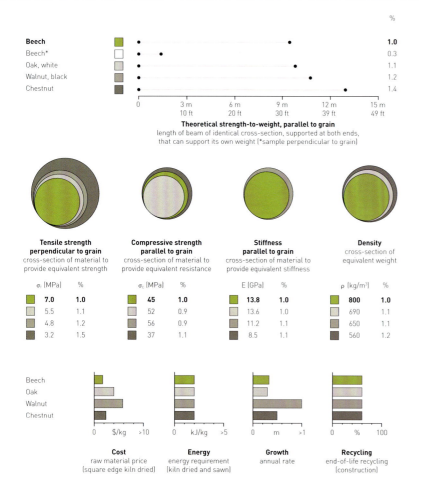

|  |  | % |
|---|---|---|
| Beech | | 1.0 |
| Beech* | | 0.3 |
| Oak, white | | 1.1 |
| Walnut, black | | 1.2 |
| Chestnut | | 1.4 |

0 | 3 m / 10 ft | 6 m / 20 ft | 9 m / 30 ft | 12 m / 39 ft | 15 m / 49 ft

**Theoretical strength-to-weight, parallel to grain**
length of beam of identical cross-section, supported at both ends, that can support its own weight (*sample perpendicular to grain)

**Tensile strength perpendicular to grain**
cross-section of material to provide equivalent strength

| $\sigma_t$ [MPa] | % |
|---|---|
| 7.0 | 1.0 |
| 5.5 | 1.1 |
| 4.8 | 1.2 |
| 3.2 | 1.5 |

**Compressive strength parallel to grain**
cross-section of material to provide equivalent resistance

| $\sigma_c$ [MPa] | % |
|---|---|
| 45 | 1.0 |
| 52 | 0.9 |
| 56 | 0.9 |
| 37 | 1.1 |

**Stiffness parallel to grain**
cross-section of material to provide equivalent stiffness

| E [GPa] | % |
|---|---|
| 13.8 | 1.0 |
| 13.6 | 1.0 |
| 11.2 | 1.1 |
| 8.5 | 1.1 |

**Density**
cross-section of equivalent weight

| $\rho$ [kg/m³] | % |
|---|---|
| 800 | 1.0 |
| 690 | 1.1 |
| 650 | 1.1 |
| 560 | 1.2 |

Beech / Oak / Walnut / Chestnut

0 | $/kg | >10

**Cost**
raw material price
(square edge kiln dried)

0 | kJ/kg | >5

**Energy**
energy requirement
(kiln dried and sawn)

0 | m | >1

**Growth**
annual rate

0 | % | 100

**Recycling**
end-of-life recycling
(construction)

## INTRODUCTION

Beech (*Fagus* genus) has become familiar in many different situations thanks to its many desirable qualities and excellent workability. It can be found in everyday items ranging from toys to utensils and flooring to furniture. It is straight-grained and, like ash (page 354), it is flexible enough to be suitable for steam bending.

It is dense and hard with a tightly packed grain. The timber has very good machining properties; it cuts and polishes very well, resulting in a smooth and splinter-free surface. It is hard-wearing with good resistance to abrasion. It takes surface treatments and preservative treatments very well, which helps to compensate for its low durability when exposed to the elements. When dry, the wood has no taste or odour.

It is quite porous and prone to moisture absorption. As a result, it is liable to cupping and bowing in application. In most situations this is not a problem, but where flatness is important for functionality – such as worktops and chopping boards – the distortion may become a hindrance.

It has similar strength to birch (page 334) and oak (page 342), but owing to its short fibre length and low elasticity, it is not so suitable for structural applications.

## COMMERCIAL TYPES AND USES

Beech trees grow very large, up to heights of 30 m (98 ft) or more, and yield large, high-quality lumber. It is also available as round, veneer (page 290) and plywood

**Spinning top** Turned from solid beech, the spinning top by Danish design brand HAY is cleverly constructed to include a free-spinning ring. Beech polishes well and the wood has no taste or odour – these qualities are why it is common in kitchen utensils too. It is hard, heavy, and tough enough to tolerate being chewed and dropped.

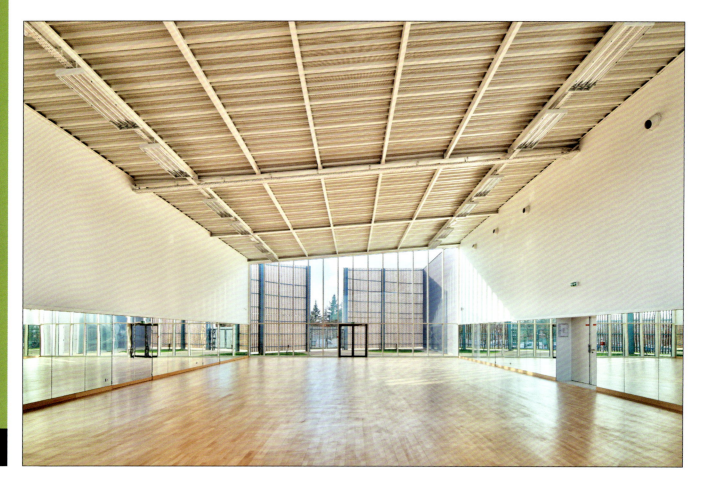

(see Engineered Timber, page 296).

While there are many different species, the two principal commercial types are European (*F. sylvatica*) and American (*F. grandifolia*). They are known by many other names, depending on their country of origin, such as English beech, Japanese beech, Danish beech and so on. American beech tends to be darker and less consistent; and production of high-grade lumber is somewhat more limited than in Europe.

Beech is often steamed, which improves its properties by equalizing the moisture content and killing any possible pests. This results in a more stable timber less prone to distortion in use (steaming relieves drying stresses). The high temperature causes the beech to change colour and become a darker pinkish-red. The colour is uniform and remains unchanged over time (beech that has not been treated has greater colour variation and will become grey over time). Veneer is often steamed for these reasons. By contrast, boards may be only 'lightly steamed' to take advantage of the treatment while maintaining a lighter, more desirable colour.

Beech is found throughout the home, workshop and factory. Its properties are utilized in toys, tools, pulleys, cooking utensils, food containers and musical instruments. It is used extensively in furniture making, including the iconic steam-bent Thonet No. 14 chair (today known as the No. 214). From the overall structure to dowel-reinforced joints that hold everything together, it is used for chairs, workbenches, tables and lighting.

## SUSTAINABILITY

Beech is available from certified forests throughout the northern hemisphere. European beech is widely available; it is one of the most common hardwoods and makes up more than half of Europe's hardwood forests. While most of the world has seen a decrease in hardwood forest size as a result of industrial harvesting, Europe has experienced a significant increase in standing timber as a result of management practices and planting programmes.

**Above**
**Dance studio floor**
This dance studio is located in a sports centre in the French commune of Arpajon, near Paris, designed by Explorations Architecture (for a view of the outside, see weathered wood cladding, page 317).

Beech was chosen for the floor because it can withstand the heavy use and high impact of sports activities. It provides a lighter – and more spacious – appearance than oak, another popular dance studio flooring. Photo by Michel Denance.

**Opposite**
**Carved furniture**
Designed by Japanese industrial designer Naoto Fukasawa for Maruni Wood Industry (2008), the Hiroshima armchair is available in beech (pictured), oak and walnut. It is a beautiful example of what can be achieved by mixing traditional skills with modern machining. The appearance of the wood, including colour and grain, is carefully selected to ensure harmony in the finished

piece. The upper and lower parts of the backrest (excluding the arms) are cut from the same piece of lumber. And while the back is cut from cross-grain wood, the arms are cut from straight-grained wood. They are roughly shaped, pegged and glued and then finished using CNC machining. The chair is assembled and the joins are worked over by hand. Finally it is coated with a urethane varnish to protect the surface. Photo by Yoneo Kawabe.

# Oak

Oak is the most important hardwood of the northern hemisphere. There are many species, broadly divided into two groups: red and white. This botanical differentiation helps to select the most appropriate material for any given situation: white oak is heavy, dense, waterproof and durable, red oak is lighter, less expensive and has superior working properties.

| Types | Typical Applications | Sustainability |
|---|---|---|
| • White: eastern, bur, overlap, post, Garry, swamp, Chinquapin, among others<br>• Red: northern, southern, scarlet, willow, among others | • Timber frame construction<br>• Furniture, joinery, interiors and flooring<br>• Toys, products, tools and utensils | • Available from certified sources<br>• Most abundant and widespread hardwood in the northern hemisphere<br>• Can be a sensitizer |
| **Properties** | **Competing Materials** | **Costs** |
| • Hard, heavy and strong<br>• White oak is very durable and non-porous<br>• Red oak has superior working properties and cuts smoothly | • Chestnut, hickory, maple<br>• Larch, cypress (such as western red-cedar) and Douglas-fir<br>• Steel and concrete | • Moderate material cost<br>• Straightforward to process |

342

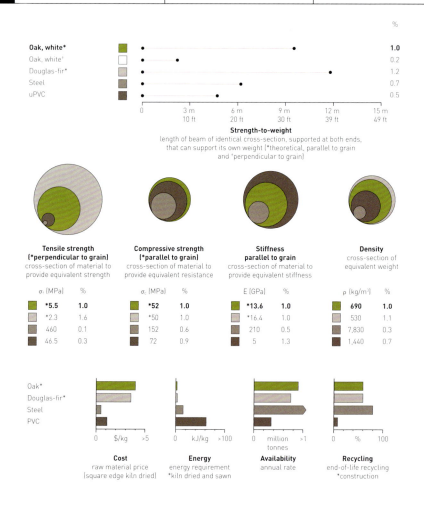

| | % |
|---|---|
| Oak, white* | 1.0 |
| Oak, white† | 0.2 |
| Douglas-fir* | 1.2 |
| Steel | 0.7 |
| uPVC | 0.5 |

0 | 3 m / 10 ft | 6 m / 20 ft | 9 m / 30 ft | 12 m / 39 ft | 15 m / 49 ft

**Strength-to-weight**
length of beam of identical cross-section, supported at both ends, that can support its own weight (*theoretical, parallel to grain and †perpendicular to grain)

| Tensile strength (*perpendicular to grain) cross-section of material to provide equivalent strength | | Compressive strength (*parallel to grain) cross-section of material to provide equivalent resistance | | Stiffness parallel to grain cross-section of material to provide equivalent stiffness | | Density cross-section of equivalent weight | |
|---|---|---|---|---|---|---|---|
| σ_t (MPa) | % | σ_c (MPa) | % | E (GPa) | % | ρ (kg/m³) | % |
| *5.5 | 1.0 | *52 | 1.0 | *13.6 | 1.0 | 690 | 1.0 |
| *2.3 | 1.6 | *50 | 1.0 | *16.4 | 1.0 | 530 | 1.1 |
| 460 | 0.1 | 152 | 0.6 | 210 | 0.5 | 7,830 | 0.3 |
| 46.5 | 0.3 | 72 | 0.9 | 5 | 1.3 | 1,440 | 0.7 |

| | |
|---|---|
| Oak* | |
| Douglas-fir* | |
| Steel | |
| PVC | |

| Cost raw material price (square edge kiln dried) | Energy energy requirement *kiln dried and sawn | Availability annual rate | Recycling end-of-life recycling *construction |
|---|---|---|---|
| 0   $/kg   >5 | 0   kJ/kg   >100 | 0   million tonnes   >1 | 0   %   100 |

## INTRODUCTION

Oak (*Quercus* genus) is an impressive timber with great versatility. It provides the benchmark that all other northern hemisphere timbers are compared to. Applications stretch from contemporary utilitarian objects to treasured antiques. As testament to its enduring popularity, in applications where it has been replaced by more modern materials, its appearance is mimicked with decorative laminate.

Oak is applied as lumber and veneer (page 290); it lends itself well to both and in rare cases the grain is highly figured. The heartwood is typically light brown and may have a greenish, pinkish or yellowish tinge. The sapwood can be nearly white, but is not always clearly demarcated from the heartwood.

Oak contains a lot of tannin. The highest concentration is found in the bark and this is why it has long been used in the preservation of leather (page 444). It helps make the timber resistant to decay, but also contributes to some of oak's downsides. The high tannin content means that oak is a sensitizer to some; it can cause skin, eye and respiratory irritation. And like chestnut (page 346), its acidity is harmful to metals, in particular iron (page 22). Over time black stains will develop around steel (page 28) nails and screws. Therefore, galvanized (see Zinc, page 78) or copper (page 66) fixings are recommended, because these metals are less susceptible to the corrosive influence of acetic acid. The same phenomenon is responsible for bog oak (see page 293), which turns black as a result of being buried in peat for many years.

Oak is well suited to steam bending and veneer lamination. Similar to hickory (page 352), it can be shaped around tight curves quite successfully. However, oak has a large coefficient of drying shrinkage, which means it is liable to split, check

(form cracks in the surface or end) and honeycomb. Once dry, there is very little movement.

## COMMERCIAL TYPES AND USES

It accounts for the majority of the Fagaceae family. Other members of the family include beech (page 338) and chestnut.

Oaks have evolved into two distinct groups: white and red. Being from the same genus, the two groups share many qualities and their grain and colour does not always make them easy to differentiate. There are many species in each group and they are rarely separated commercially; oak is sold as either 'white' or 'red'. The exact species depends on where the timber has come from.

White oaks are so called because the principal timber-yielding tree was the eastern white oak (*Q. alba*). Since a single species cannot keep up with demand, several other species that have similar properties are sold alongside. Examples include bur (*Q. macrocarpa*), European (*Q. robur*), overcup (*Q. lyrata*), post (*Q. stellata*), Garry (*Q. garryana*), swamp white (*Q. bicolor*), Chinquapin (*Q. muehlenbergii*), swamp chestnut (*Q. michauxii*) and chestnut (*Q. prinus*).

Similarly, red oaks are named after the principal species, which includes the northern red oak (*Q. rubra*) and southern red oak (*Q. falcata*). Other species sold alongside include scarlet (*Q. coccinea*), willow (*Q. phellos*), water (*Q. nigra*), black (*Q. velutina*) and pin (*Q. palustris*), among others. While some types have a distinctive pinkish colour, others look similar to white oak.

While there are clear differences in the performance of the timber from each group, there can be wide variation

**Veneered packaging**
This modern interpretation of a Dutch butte (travel case) by Dutch designers Scholten & Baijings for Established & Sons, 2010, is constructed from oak veneer. The interior has been coated with fluorescent paint and the black illustrations, which are inkjet printed on the surface prior to forming, tell the story of the life of a tuna. It is coated with clear lacquer to protect the surface from ultraviolet. Photo courtesy of Scholten & Baijings.

between the species, especially in the case of red oaks. This is because the properties are determined by a combination of factors including type, soil, climate, processing and so on. Variation is inevitable in such a widely cultivated and applied timber. Therefore, care must be taken when specifying oak to ensure these differences do not cause distortions or aesthetic dilemmas in application.

White oaks grow more slowly than reds and so tend to be heavier (750 versus

**White oak**

**Red oak**

### Grain and rays in oak

It is the combination of rings and rays that determines the pattern on the surface of the sawn timber. White oak species tend to grow more slowly, which means they have a more tightly packed grain. The rays, which radiate out from the centre of the tree to transport food and waste laterally, are shorter in red oak. They produce long flecks in white oak that can be quite decorative. They are lighter than the surrounding timber –

it is also known as silvery oak – and so staining will tend to exaggerate their appearance. This is not the case for red oaks, because the flecks are darker, so relatively dark stains can be used. These samples are quarter-sawn, which means they have been cut in a pattern radiating from the centre. They would look quite different if plain-sawn (cut parallel to centre): the grain would be wider with characterful swirls and the rays less visible.

690 kg/m³ [47 vs 43 lb/ft³] for red oak) with a tightly packed grain. The timber is renowned for its combination of strength, density and resistance to wear.

Red oaks perform well and are suitable for many of the same situations. They are often used in construction and so sold in larger volumes, which means they are often less expensive. Being softer than white oak means they are easier to work. They are utilized in furniture, joinery, cabinetmaking and interiors. Both types are popular flooring materials: oak makes up around three-quarters of hardwood flooring in North America and two-thirds in Europe.

Red oaks have large, thick-walled pores. By contrast, the pores in white oaks tend to be clogged with tyloses. These are bulging outgrowths that form a foam-like structure within the pores that blocks water movement. This helps to make it more durable (resistant to decay) than red oak and is why it is utilized in applications that demand long-term durability, such as wine barrels and other types of cooperage, boats and cladding.

**Solid wood table**
Created by French designer Jean Prouvé in 1941 and today produced by Vitra, the Table Solvay is manufactured from solid oak (pictured) or walnut (page 348). While oak may be heavy, it is long-lasting and will comfortably endure everyday use. It has proved to be a very suitable timber for all manner of furniture, from farm tables to office desks and from laminated chairs (see image, page 298) to fine cabinetwork. Photo courtesy of Vitra.

### SUSTAINABILITY

Even though it is slow-growing, oak is available in large quantities and remains the most abundant hardwood genus in the northern hemisphere (in North America alone oak accounts for around one-third of hardwood forests). Red oaks grow more abundantly than the white species; they are more readily available as large boards with uniform grain.

As a long-lasting and durable timber, white oak is commonly available reclaimed. The majority of new growth oak comes from North America, Europe and Australia. Trees are felled when they reach 25 or 30 years old. It is a widely available timber, so care must be taken to

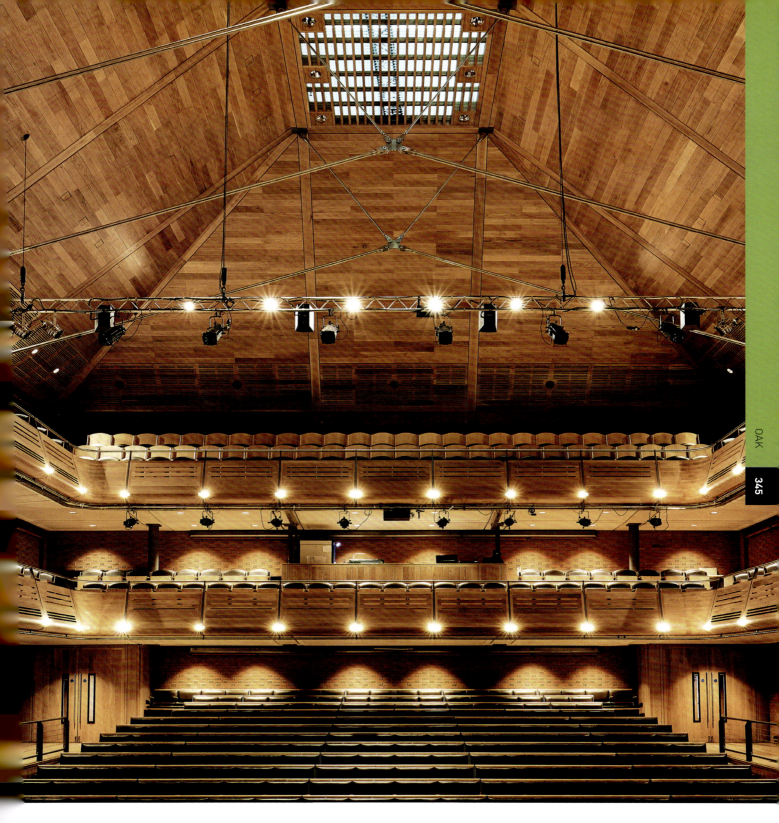

ensure that it is harvested from certified forests. Caution is advised regarding oak originating from Poland, Russia and Ukraine, owing to evidence of the destruction of ancient forests as well as illegal logging.

As a result of its widespread application, oak comes into competition with a host of other types of material.

Compared to plastic, for example (see Polyvinyl Chloride, page 122), oak provides a sustainable and renewable material that can be safely recycled, composted or incinerated. The impact of production is limited to forestry, transportation and sawmills; this contrasts dramatically with the energy- and chemical-intensive processes of plastic production.

**Wood-lined interior**
Performing arts venue The Apex in Bury St Edmunds, England, features a striking oak-lined 500-seat auditorium designed by Hopkins Architects (2010). The oak has stood up well to the rigours of countless live events. On both floor and roof, 18 mm (0.7 in) thick oak is fixed to plywood backing to optimize the acoustics. For the seating a mix of solid and veneer was required. American white oak was selected for its consistency of colour and grain.

# Chestnut

Chestnut is a handsome, durable timber. It can survive untreated outdoors for many decades. Indeed, a great deal of chestnut used today is reclaimed from old timber frame structures. Riddled with wormholes, it matures to a rich golden-brown colour as a result of the high tannin content. Sweet chestnut is also well known for its edible seeds.

| Types | Typical Applications | Sustainability |
|---|---|---|
| • Chestnut: American, sweet, Japanese and Chinese | • Interior and exterior joinery, and furniture<br>• Products<br>• Cladding and flooring | • Very limited supply in North America, but remains common across Europe, parts of Asia and Africa<br>• American chestnut tends to be reclaimed |

| Properties | Competing Materials | Costs |
|---|---|---|
| • Excellent resistance to decay, although prone to insect attack<br>• Difficult to treat owing to tannin content<br>• Moderate density and splits readily | • Oak, ash, iroko, walnut<br>• Cypress (such as western red-cedar) and larch | • Moderate to high cost<br>• Moderate working properties |

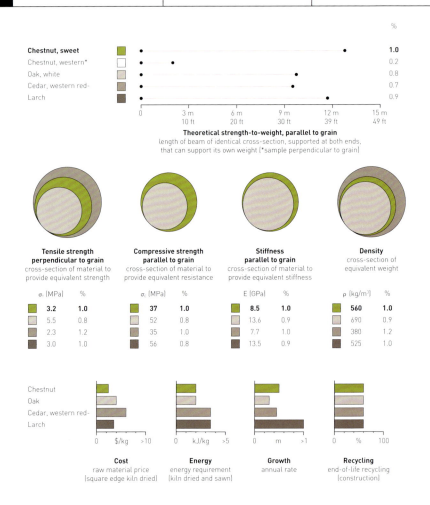

%

| | | |
|---|---|---|
| Chestnut, sweet | | 1.0 |
| Chestnut, western* | | 0.2 |
| Oak, white | | 0.8 |
| Cedar, western red- | | 0.7 |
| Larch | | 0.9 |

0    3 m / 10 ft    6 m / 20 ft    9 m / 30 ft    12 m / 39 ft    15 m / 49 ft

**Theoretical strength-to-weight, parallel to grain**
length of beam of identical cross-section, supported at both ends, that can support its own weight (*sample perpendicular to grain)

**Tensile strength perpendicular to grain**
cross-section of material to provide equivalent strength

**Compressive strength parallel to grain**
cross-section of material to provide equivalent resistance

**Stiffness parallel to grain**
cross-section of material to provide equivalent stiffness

**Density**
cross-section of equivalent weight

| σ_t (MPa) | % | σ_c (MPa) | % | E (GPa) | % | ρ (kg/m³) | % |
|---|---|---|---|---|---|---|---|
| 3.2 | 1.0 | 37 | 1.0 | 8.5 | 1.0 | 560 | 1.0 |
| 5.5 | 0.8 | 52 | 0.8 | 13.6 | 0.9 | 690 | 0.9 |
| 2.3 | 1.2 | 35 | 1.0 | 7.7 | 1.0 | 380 | 1.2 |
| 3.0 | 1.0 | 56 | 0.8 | 13.5 | 0.9 | 525 | 1.0 |

| | Cost | Energy | Growth | Recycling |
|---|---|---|---|---|
| Chestnut | | | | |
| Oak | | | | |
| Cedar, western red- | | | | |
| Larch | | | | |

0   $/kg   >10    0   kJ/kg   >5    0   m   >1    0   %   100

**Cost**
raw material price (square edge kiln dried)

**Energy**
energy requirement (kiln dried and sawn)

**Growth**
annual rate

**Recycling**
end-of-life recycling (construction)

## INTRODUCTION

Chestnut (*Castanea* genus) lumber is moderately soft and light. Colour depends on the species and ranges from whitish-yellow to medium-brown heartwood. The sapwood stands out, because it has a much lighter, pale off-white colour. The heartwood is rich in tannins, which makes it durable in the ground and suitable for use outdoors, requiring no preservatives.

Similar to oak (page 342), its acidity (acetic acid) means it will corrode metals that it is left in contact with, especially when in damp or humid conditions. Metals used in furniture and construction most susceptible to attack – and that should be avoided – include steel (page 28), lead and zinc (page 78). Copper (page 66) is also affected, but to a lesser extent.

While it is not as strong as oak (around 20% less), its low density results in impressive strength-to-weight; its lightness is comparable with some species of poplar (page 324). High-quality, defect-free boards are used in many of the same sorts of applications as oak, including timber frame structures, joinery and furniture.

Dried wood is prone to ring shake, whereby the wood splits along the growth rings. It has a coarse texture and is prone to splitting, which means it does not turn particularly well. Even so, it can be worked by hand to a high-quality finish.

## COMMERCIAL TYPES AND USES

American chestnut (*C. dentata*) was once a common tree in the eastern hardwood forests. It was a popular timber used in a range of utilitarian applications. However, at the turn of the 20th century, the species was almost completely wiped out by chestnut blight fungal infection. As a result, old-growth chestnut is very rare and expensive in the USA.

Today, most American chestnut lumber is reclaimed, or imported from Europe. It is also known as wormy chestnut, so called because it is riddled with insect damage. It tends to come from beams used in timber frame construction, which are de-nailed and sawn into boards. Being quite old, it has a beautiful golden-brown colour. With modern finger-jointing techniques (see page 299), smaller pieces of timber with the major defects removed are reassembled into long lengths of high-quality lumber.

Asiatic chestnuts, such as the Japanese (*C. crenata*) and Chinese (*C. mollissima*) species have inherent resistance to the blight that swept across the USA. They are being planted as timber trees as well as crossbred with the more vulnerable species to try to find a suitable hybrid.

The sweet chestnut (*C. sativa*) is also known by its origin, such as Spanish, European and so on. It is faster-growing than its American cousin and less heavy. In colour and grain, the heartwood can resemble oak, but lacks the silvery ray flecks. Unfortunately, some areas of Europe have suffered losses from blight after it was accidentally introduced to Italy from the USA.

Thanks to its inherent durability, chestnut has historically been used for exterior applications including shingles and shakes (cladding), siding and fencing. It is also available as veneer (page 290). Where it is still common, it can be purchased for a reasonable price and is suitable for use in joinery and furniture.

Certain species are easier to carve than others. For example, while the Japanese produce kitchen utensils and rice bowls from their native species (kuri); the French have traditionally used chestnut for decorative moldings (doors and windows) and furniture.

## SUSTAINABILITY
Similar to willow (page 328) and poplar, chestnut is coppiced in managed plantations. The rods are harvested for use in shingles (cladding), fencing and stakes. Lumber is available from certified sources, although large stock is in short supply in many countries as a result of the impacts of blight.

**Chestnut-clad cabinet**
The Shake cabinet, created by British designer Sebastian Cox and produced by furniture makers Benchmark, comprises a solid ash (page 354) carcass clad with chestnut shakes. Traditionally used as sustainable weatherproofing for roofs and walls, shakes are produced by cleaving (splitting) chestnut along the grain to form thin, light rectangular wooden tiles (also called shingles). They are kept as thin as possible to minimize the amount of material, thus reducing waste and weight. Timbers used in a similar way include oak and western red-cedar (see Cypress Family, page 318). Photo courtesy of Sebastian Cox.

# Walnut

The chocolate-coloured timber of walnut is highly prized for its mechanical properties. It is dense and hard with a tightly packed grain. The wood resists splitting and shocks, qualities utilized in luxury decorative veneer and gunstocks alike. Timber with a highly figured grain, such as burr and crotch, is rare and very expensive.

| Types | Typical Applications | Sustainability |
|---|---|---|
| • Black (American), claro, Persian (also named after its place of origin, such as English or French) and butternut (white) | • Furniture making<br>• Gunstocks<br>• Automotive and marine | • Available from sustainable sources around the world<br>• The dust can be a sensitizer |

| Properties | Competing Materials | Costs |
|---|---|---|
| • Hard and dense wood<br>• Resists shock and splitting<br>• Resistant to decay but susceptible to insects | • Oak<br>• Mahogany<br>• Teak | • Moderate for plain wood and high for figured woods |

348

## INTRODUCTION

Walnut (*Juglans* genus) is an important domestic hardwood in North America, Europe and Asia. Its appearance and mechanical properties place it between the light-coloured hardwoods – including oak (page 342), hickory (page 352) and beech (page 338) – and expensive exotic timbers, such as teak (page 370) and mahogany (page 372).

The heartwood ranges through dark-brown tones, from chocolate to deep purplish-black. A more homogenous colour is produced with steam treatment, although this is not always desirable. Highly figured grain patterns and rich contrasting colours make walnut very desirable to some. The colour is comparable with timbers such as cherry (page 360) and the now very rare genuine mahogany. Solid walnut has some very useful properties. On the whole it is comparable with oak and beech, although its slightly lower density gives it improved strength-to-weight.

It is very often applied as veneer (page 290). This expands the use of walnut into areas where it may otherwise be impractical, or too expensive. Logs are cut along their length (as opposed to around the circumference) to make full use of the colour and grain pattern. The veneer is bonded onto a preformed substrate, or laminated and bent to shape. Applied for its beauty and dark colour, walnut veneer is found in an array of applications, from cabinets to dashboards to tea sets.

## COMMERCIAL TYPES AND USES

Several are cultivated for timber, in particular black (*J. nigra*), claro (*J. hindsii*), Persian (*J. regia*) (native to Iran, but often referred to by its place of origin, such as English or French), Peruvian (*J. neotropica*) and butternut (*J. cinerea*) (also known as white). It is available as lumber and veneer.

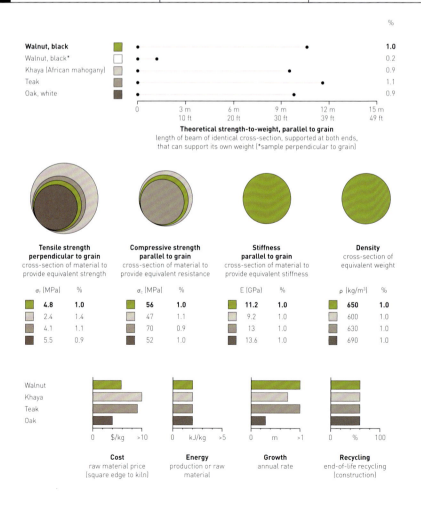

|  |  | % |
|---|---|---|
| Walnut, black | 🟩 | 1.0 |
| Walnut, black* | ⬜ | 0.2 |
| Khaya (African mahogany) | ⬜ | 0.9 |
| Teak | ⬜ | 1.1 |
| Oak, white | ⬛ | 0.9 |

**Theoretical strength-to-weight, parallel to grain**
length of beam of identical cross-section, supported at both ends, that can support its own weight (*sample perpendicular to grain)

| Tensile strength perpendicular to grain | | Compressive strength parallel to grain | | Stiffness parallel to grain | | Density | |
|---|---|---|---|---|---|---|---|
| cross-section of material to provide equivalent strength | | cross-section of material to provide equivalent resistance | | cross-section of material to provide equivalent stiffness | | cross-section of equivalent weight | |
| $\sigma_t$ (MPa) | % | $\sigma_c$ (MPa) | % | E (GPa) | % | $\rho$ (kg/m³) | % |
| 4.8 | 1.0 | 56 | 1.0 | 11.2 | 1.0 | 650 | 1.0 |
| 2.4 | 1.4 | 47 | 1.1 | 9.2 | 1.0 | 600 | 1.0 |
| 4.1 | 1.1 | 70 | 0.9 | 13 | 1.0 | 630 | 1.0 |
| 5.5 | 0.9 | 52 | 1.0 | 13.6 | 1.0 | 690 | 1.0 |

Walnut
Khaya
Teak
Oak

| **Cost**<br>raw material price (square edge to kiln) | **Energy**<br>production or raw material | **Growth**<br>annual rate | **Recycling**<br>end-of-life recycling (construction) |
|---|---|---|---|
| 0  $/kg  >10 | 0  kJ/kg  >5 | 0  m  >1 | 0  %  100 |

Black walnut is native to eastern North America and commonly referred to as American walnut. It is a relatively fast-growing hardwood and reaches heights of 35 m (115 ft) or so. The heartwood has very good resistance to decay, but is susceptible to insect attack. The sapwood is not nearly so durable and is typically a contrasting creamy-white colour. The timber has a coarse grain but is relatively easy to work. Irregular and figured grain makes it trickier to cut and plane smooth. The wood has a natural sheen, which is emphasized with finishing – an excellent polish can be achieved.

The other walnuts are similar in most aspects – the colour differs slightly according to location and type. Black walnut is the most widely available and typically the least expensive of the dark-coloured types. The cost depends to a large extent on the colour, grain pattern and figuring. The butternut, or white walnut, stands out for its lighter colouration and softer wood.

Black and claro are considered to be very durable (resistant to decay). And while European and Peruvian are less so, but still moderately resistant, butternut is the least resistant of all walnuts.

In the USA timber is graded according to the rules set out by the National Hardwood Lumber Association (NHLA). Buyers and sellers worldwide rely on the NHLA to ensure specific levels of quality. The NHLA grades have been altered for this species because of the availability and nature of timber growth. The FAS (first and seconds) grade is used to qualify long clear (defect-free) cuttings (pieces) best suited to high-quality furniture and interiors. Minimum size in general is 150 mm (6 in) wide by 2.4 m (8 ft) long timber consisting of 85% to 100% clear wood. In the case of walnut, the minimum size has been reduced – 127 mm (5 in) wide by 1.8 m (6 ft) long – to encourage more use of the wood.

Associated with high-end modern furniture of the 20th century, solid walnut was employed by influential designers such as Charles and Ray Eames, Hans Wegner and George Nakashima (see image overleaf) among others. It continues to be used in the construction

of new products, often as an alternative to lighter coloured oak and beech.

Solid timber is suitable for handwork, milling and lathe turning. The grain varies considerably, depending on the tree and from where the timber was cut. Open-grained areas are the easiest to cut, but a superior finish is achieved by polishing close-grained areas. Care is taken with the coarse texture, because cutting can tear out fragments from the surface, in

**Urushi box with walnut lid** Produced by husband and wife team Kenichi and Minako Fujii, this box combines urushi lacquer with a walnut lid. Urushi is a traditional Japanese lacquering technique. The resin comes from the urushi tree and is used to make traditional Chinese and Korean, as well as Japanese, lacquerware. After the sap is tapped from the tree it undergoes a period of ageing for three to five years and refined. It is built up in thin layers and polymerizes to form a durable coating. The walnut lid is finished with beeswax.

**Left**
**Walnut straight-backed chair**  The Straight Chair was designed by American architect and furniture maker George Nakashima in 1946 and is manufactured by Knoll. This modern interpretation of the Windsor uses black walnut in the seat, legs and backrest. The spindles are turned from hickory, a close relative of walnut. Because walnut is less dense than dark hardwoods of equal value and moderately strong, it is relatively easy to work. This quality helped Nakashima to transfer his craftsmanship to high-volume production without any loss of quality. Photo courtesy of Knoll.

**Opposite**
**In-molded walnut dashboard**  Modern wood trim and dashboards combine natural materials with mass production. This is technically very challenging, because each piece of veneer is unique and the molding process requires absolute precision. In preparation, the veneer is heated and compression molded onto a backing layer. The stabilized preform is then firmly clamped into one half of the injection molding tool. The mold closes and one or more thermoplastics are injected to fill the cavity. The plastic holds the veneer in place while providing fixing points for the dashboard. It is coated with polyurethane (PU) (page 202) to protect it from wear and tear and the elements. It is often mimicked with printing techniques in modern cars to add decorative value to otherwise plain interiors.

particular with end grain. Therefore, deep cuts along the grain tend to be avoided. Burrs and other figured patterns require filling to ensure a smooth surface.

The visual appeal of veneer is used throughout the interior, from laminated seating to tableware. Decorative veneers are typically very thin and are crown-cut or quarter-cut. While the former produces a rich elliptical pattern with a highly decorative appeal, quarter-cutting results in a more uniform linear grain pattern better suited to laminated bentwood.

The earliest automobiles were constructed from a mixture of solid wood, steel (page 28) and cast iron (page 22). Nowadays, wood is often used to distinguish high-value cars and luxury yachts. It has come to represent the hand craftsmanship and individuality of the past.

Wood is much more expensive than stamped metal or injection-molded plastic and far less practical for the interior of an automobile. However, the colour and tactility connotes warmth, elegance and luxury. One of the challenges of using wood is that it cannot be formed into such complex shapes as metal and plastic without significantly reducing its structural performance. Therefore, the shape of wooden parts is somewhat limited.

Solid timber is machined for a range of applications outside transportation. The problem in vehicle design is that it cannot be guaranteed to perform in a predictable fashion. Where this is not a problem, such as in parts that are not critical for protecting the occupants, solid wood is a viable material option, albeit an expensive one. Veneer is more versatile, because it is applied as a decorative layer onto 'engineered' substrate, such as metal or molded plastic.

## SUSTAINABILITY

Walnut is grown in many countries and so it is often possible to purchase local timber that has been PEFC or FSC certified. Veneers are processed in factories and so not quite as widespread, but are still reasonably available. The timber is harvested from plantations, as well as wild trees.

The dust produced during machining is a sensitizer and can affect eyes and breathing. Adequate ventilation and goggles are typically required for cutting and sanding.

# Hickory and Pecan

These deciduous trees provide some of the hardest, heaviest and strongest timber of the northern hemisphere. They are found through North America, Europe and Asia. Pecan hickories are not quite as hard or dense as true hickories, but nevertheless have many of the same attributes. These timbers can be machined to a fine finish and will hold a sharp edge.

| Types | Typical Applications | Sustainability |
|---|---|---|
| • Hickory: shagbark, shellbark, mockernut and pignut<br>• Pecan hickory: pecan, water, bitternut and nutmeg | • Sports equipment and tool handles<br>• Wooden aircraft<br>• Furniture, joinery and flooring | • Although widely distributed, they are not particularly common outside North America and are very slow-growing<br>• Available from certified forests |

| Properties | Competing Materials | Costs |
|---|---|---|
| • Straight grain<br>• Very heavy<br>• Strong, stiff and hard with excellent impact resistance | • Ash, maple, birch<br>• Bamboo<br>• PA, PET, POM and similar engineering thermoplastics | • Moderate- to high-cost raw material<br>• Their high density and hardness make them hard to process |

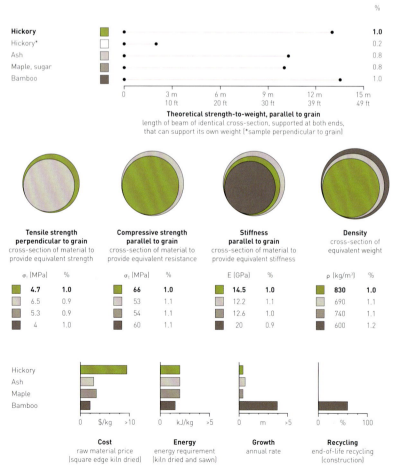

| | % |
|---|---|
| Hickory | 1.0 |
| Hickory* | 0.2 |
| Ash | 0.8 |
| Maple, sugar | 0.8 |
| Bamboo | 1.0 |

**Theoretical strength-to-weight, parallel to grain**
length of beam of identical cross-section, supported at both ends, that can support its own weight (*sample perpendicular to grain)

**Tensile strength perpendicular to grain**
cross-section of material to provide equivalent strength

| σ$_t$ (MPa) | % |
|---|---|
| **4.7** | **1.0** |
| 6.5 | 0.9 |
| 5.3 | 0.9 |
| 4 | 1.0 |

**Compressive strength parallel to grain**
cross-section of material to provide equivalent resistance

| σ$_c$ (MPa) | % |
|---|---|
| **66** | **1.0** |
| 53 | 1.1 |
| 54 | 1.1 |
| 60 | 1.1 |

**Stiffness parallel to grain**
cross-section of material to provide equivalent stiffness

| E (GPa) | % |
|---|---|
| **14.5** | **1.0** |
| 12.2 | 1.1 |
| 12.6 | 1.0 |
| 20 | 0.9 |

**Density**
cross-section of equivalent weight

| ρ (kg/m³) | % |
|---|---|
| **830** | **1.0** |
| 690 | 1.1 |
| 740 | 1.1 |
| 600 | 1.2 |

Hickory
Ash
Maple
Bamboo

**Cost**
raw material price
(square edge kiln dried)

**Energy**
energy requirement
(kiln dried and sawn)

**Growth**
annual rate

**Recycling**
end-of-life recycling
(construction)

## INTRODUCTION

These trees are cultivated for their timber and nuts. Although they grow throughout the northern hemisphere, and a little in the south, availability is somewhat limited outside North America. As a result, they are not well known or much used.

Hickory (*Carya* genus) has an unrivalled combination of strength, stiffness and hardness. In terms of strength-to-weight, it is comparable with bamboo (page 386) and comfortably outperforms steel (page 28). As a result of these impressive physical characteristics, it has historically been an important structural timber. The Deperdussin Monocoque Racer, built by Société Pour les Appareils Deperdussin in 1912, is famous for raising the world speed record for aircraft to 202 km/h (126 mph). In this early example of monocoque construction, hickory was utilized in the structure of the fuselage and wings, skinned with several thin layers of tulipwood in a plywood-like construction. The result was a lightweight, streamlined shape with a virtually clear internal space.

Today, its use in tool handles and sports equipment puts hickory in direct competition with high-performance plastics such as glass-fibre-reinforced polypropylene (GFPP) (page 98) and polyamide (GFPA, nylon) (page 164). While these materials offer flexibility in terms of design and performance, they lack the natural and adaptable quality of wood.

Like ash (page 354), hickory lends itself to steam bending. Straight-grained and knot-free stock can be bent to reasonably tight curves, much smaller than for an equivalent cross-section in ash.

It is vulnerable to decay and should not be left outdoors untreated.

## COMMERCIAL TYPES AND USES

Hickory is often divided into true hickories and pecan hickories. They are the same genus (*Carya*) and belong to the same family as walnut (Juglandaceae). The main differences are that pecan hickories are lighter, softer and less elastic. This is only true within the genus, because they are still heavy and dense compared to other hardwoods. True hickory includes shagbark (*C. ovata*), shellbark (*C. laciniosa*), mockernut (*C. tomentosa*) and pignut (*C. glabra*). Pecan hickory includes pecan (*C. illinoinensis*), water (*C. aquatica*), bitternut (*C. cordiformis*) and nutmeg (*C. myristiciformis*).

The many different species have a similar appearance. The heartwood ranges from pale brown to darker brown and the sapwood is nearly white. The colour contrast between the heartwood and sapwood, as well as throughout these regions (such as 'bird pecks' and mineral streaks), can be visually interesting. True hickory tends to be lighter coloured than pecan hickory, but this depends on growing conditions. The grain is straight and the texture uniform.

It is tricky to work, partly because it is so dense, but can be produced with a fine smooth finish and crisp edge. While the pecan hickories are softer and so easier to carve, they cannot compete with walnut and chestnut (page 346) for ease of working. They shrink less than hickory and so tend to be more stable in application. As a result, they are well suited to joinery and furniture making.

The strength, elasticity and durability of hickory are utilized in wooden sports equipment, such as golf shafts, tennis rackets, baseball bats (see also Maple, page 330) and skis (see also Ash). However, in most modern equipment high-performance plastics and composites have superseded wood.

Its impressive hardness and resistance to wear are utilized in flooring. Hickory is more than a third harder than oak (page 342), a commonly used hardwood flooring. As a result, it performs extremely well, especially in high-traffic areas.

## SUSTAINABILITY

While it is considered a sustainable source of timber, hickory grows slowly and can take many decades to reach a suitable size for harvesting.

**Felling axe handle**
True hickories have a relatively low lignin content. This hard natural polymer contributes to wood's rigidity. Therefore, when dry, hickory has a spring-like elasticity. This provides it with exceptional impact resistance. It is commonly used in axe handles for this reason: when the axe head strikes the wood the handle flexes and so absorbs some of the shock.

# Ash

**Also known as**
Thermally modified ash also known by trademark names: Cambia, Thermowood, Thermo Ash

Ash is a utility hardwood popular for its ease of working, physical properties and pronounced grain. It is strong and flexible for its weight, yielding a timber with impressive toughness and shock resistance. It is available as thermally modified timber as well as compressed wood, which expand the range of applications and make this a truly versatile material.

| Types | Typical Applications | Sustainability |
|---|---|---|
| • Ash: black, white, green, Oregon and European | • Tool handles and furniture<br>• Sports equipment (sleds, rackets, baseball bats and oars, for example)<br>• Flooring | • Widespread across Europe, Asia and North America<br>• Dust can be a sensitizer |
| **Properties** | **Competing Materials** | **Costs** |
| • Tough, elastic and shock-resistant<br>• Not very durable and vulnerable to insect attack<br>• Pronounced grain | • Oak, hickory and maple<br>• Iroko, teak, mahogany and other tropical hardwoods<br>• Engineering plastics such as PA and PET | • Low to moderate raw material cost<br>• Relatively easy to process |

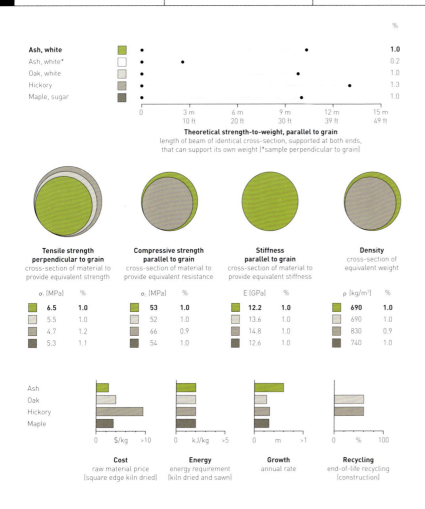

| | % |
|---|---|
| Ash, white | 1.0 |
| Ash, white* | 0.2 |
| Oak, white | 1.0 |
| Hickory | 1.3 |
| Maple, sugar | 1.0 |

**Theoretical strength-to-weight, parallel to grain**
length of beam of identical cross-section, supported at both ends, that can support its own weight (*sample perpendicular to grain)

**Tensile strength perpendicular to grain**
cross-section of material to provide equivalent strength

| $\sigma_t$ (MPa) | % |
|---|---|
| 6.5 | 1.0 |
| 5.5 | 1.0 |
| 4.7 | 1.2 |
| 5.3 | 1.1 |

**Compressive strength parallel to grain**
cross-section of material to provide equivalent resistance

| $\sigma_c$ (MPa) | % |
|---|---|
| 53 | 1.0 |
| 52 | 1.0 |
| 66 | 0.9 |
| 54 | 1.0 |

**Stiffness parallel to grain**
cross-section of material to provide equivalent stiffness

| E (GPa) | % |
|---|---|
| 12.2 | 1.0 |
| 13.6 | 1.0 |
| 14.8 | 1.0 |
| 12.6 | 1.0 |

**Density**
cross-section of equivalent weight

| $\rho$ (kg/m³) | % |
|---|---|
| 690 | 1.0 |
| 690 | 1.0 |
| 830 | 0.9 |
| 740 | 1.0 |

Ash
Oak
Hickory
Maple

**Cost**
raw material price
(square edge kiln dried)
0 $/kg >10

**Energy**
energy requirement
(kiln dried and sawn)
0 kJ/kg >5

**Growth**
annual rate
0 m >1

**Recycling**
end-of-life recycling
(construction)
0 % 100

## INTRODUCTION

The Vikings considered ash (*Fraxinus* genus) to be the king of trees. Indeed, it is often used in similar situations to red oak (page 342), including cabinetry and flooring. Like oak, ash has a straight, open grain and coarse texture. And even though it does not have the same silvery ray flecks, it can be stained to look just like it. Ash has higher strength-to-weight, but is a little softer, which is advantageous for cutting and shaping. The heartwood ranges from light to medium brown, depending on the species, and the sapwood is nearly white. It is the light-coloured sapwood that is generally preferred.

Black ash (*F. nigra*) is utilized in basket making. Its flexibility and durability are unrivalled for this purpose. Within the annual growth, ash forms a porous honeycomb-structured spring wood followed by a dense summer wood. It is the latter that is utilized in basketry. To separate it from the early growth, which forms weak connecting layers, a log is soaked in water and pounded. This crushes the spring wood and allows strips (called splints) of summer wood to be peeled off. This technique has been practised by generations of Native American tribes, in particular the Potawatomi, Penobscot, Abenaki and Algonquin. It is used in combination with materials found nearby, such as birch bark (page 334) and sweetgrass.

## COMMERCIAL TYPES AND USES

Ash lumber is sold in a variety of ways: sometimes according to species or the growing region; and other times differentiated as sapwood or heartwood. This can lead to some confusion, because while white ash (*F. Americana*) and black ash (also known as brown ash) are commercially important, the sapwood

may be sold as 'white ash' and the heartwood as 'brown ash'.

There are several species that are closely related to, and virtually indistinguishable from, white ash. These include green ash (*F. pennsylvanica*), Oregon ash (*F. latifolia*) and European ash (*F. excelsior*). The timber from these trees is generally considered superior: it tends to be heavier (by around 10%), harder and stronger than black ash. This

means that it is generally more desirable and so more expensive. Even so, the quality crosses over and in many cases they may be used interchangeably.

Both are popular in furniture making, for many reasons. It has excellent working properties and machining quality, has good nail- and screw-holding properties, and glues well. It can be carved, sanded and polished to a fine finish. It is used for the carcass, rungs and backrests of

**Bentwood easy chair**
Danish furniture designer Hans Wegner created the Peacock Chair in 1947. It is manufactured by PP Møbler, Denmark, of solid ash with a paper cord seat. Taking inspiration from the classic English Windsor chair, the steam-bent backrest is supported by extravagantly shaped sticks. The flat part of the sticks, which inspired the name of the chair, are located just where the sitter's back rests. This chair was the first of many large, lavish designs that Wegner created. Photo by Jens Mourits Sørensen, courtesy of PP Møbler.

**Traditional sled** This horn-shaped sled, manufactured by Sirch, Germany, is produced from white ash. It has been the timber of choice for sleds for generations, offering just the right balance of lightness, springiness and strength. The runners are steam bent for optimal strength-to-weight and steel strips protect their undersides. The woodwork is double-lacquered to protect it from the elements. Photo courtesy of Sirch.

a range of furniture. Notable examples include slat-back Shaker chairs, Windsor chairs and Hans Wegner's beautiful Peacock Chair (previous page; see also chestnut cabinet, page 347).

White ash is often compared to hickory (page 352) and maple (page 330), which are expensive alternatives. It is not as strong, stiff or hard as hickory. Even so, it has been used in many similar and demanding applications, including light aircraft (Royal Aircraft Factory S.E.5 biplane, 1916), automobiles (original Jaguar XK, 1949) and bicycle frames.

Like maple, ash is utilized in modern sports equipment, in particular baseball bats and snooker cues. It is elastic and a little softer than maple, which offers some performance advantages; indeed, many baseball players prefer it. And the two look very different, because ash has a much more pronounced grain.

Like these two hardwoods, ash competes with high-performance plastics (such as polyamide [PA, nylon], page 164) and lightweight structural metals (such as aluminium, page 42, and magnesium, page 54). It is not as predictable, or mass-producible, as these modern materials. Ash's biggest advantage is that it is a natural, renewable, sustainable material. It is relatively inexpensive, too. The surface polishes to a smooth finish and is improved with everyday use, which contributes to the user-friendliness of bats, handles and furniture.

Ash tends to be limited to indoor application, because it is not sufficiently durable to survive outdoors untreated. Recently, however, it has become available as a thermally modified timber (TMT) (see also plywood samples, page 297). Using a process introduced in the 1990s, originally developed to improve the durability of softwoods, timber is heated to around 200°C (392°F) in a controlled (oxygen-free) atmosphere. This reduces the moisture content to around 5%, which is very low compared to conventional seasoning, and permanently alters the wood's chemical and physical properties.

Treated wood is less able to absorb water and so remains dimensionally stable and is much more durable. Its resistance to decay matches that of teak (page 370), which means that the wood can be used outdoors without any further treatment. It will not react to changes in humidity like untreated timber. This produces superior surface quality and improves the ability of the wood to take on stain or paint finishes. The heating process yields a material less susceptible to insect attack, because the food sources within the wood are destroyed. Therefore, it does not require any chemical treatments and will be longer-lasting.

Another benefit is that TMT has reduced conductivity. This is particularly useful in construction. Treated window frames, doors and cladding, for example,

**Bentwood** The advantage of steam bending and compressed wood (bentwood) is that the grain runs along the entire length. If the bend is made across more than one axis, the timber will be twisted to align the grain. In other words, the grain will remain on the same face along the entire length of timber. This maximizes strength and minimizes the amount of material needed. However, bentwood is not always practical. Suitable quality timber may not be available, or the part may be too large. Steam-bent parts are prone to springback over time and so require fixing along their length where possible. Alternative methods used to form a curved profile include laminating veneer (see page 299), glulam (see page 300), kerfing (see page 336) and combining short lengths with joints. Finger-jointing (see page 299) is often used, and while there are many advantages to this – shorter lengths are more economical; the bends can be tighter than with steam bending; multiple types of wood may be combined; and the cross-section design is not quite so limited – it cuts through the grain and so will not be as efficient or inherently strong as an equivalent steam-bent part.

properties. It is also converted into 'compressed wood', which can be bent cold. After being subjected to extreme thermomechanical compression along their length, ash and several other common hardwoods – oak, cherry maple, beech, elm and hickory – become extremely flexible. They can be bent around tight and multiaxial curves in their green state and then dried to fix the shape. It is referred to as cold-bend, compressed wood or compwood, for example. So far, it has been applied in furniture and architecture.

## SUSTAINABILITY

It is considered a sustainable hardwood and is available from certified forests. TMT is an innovative process that means ash is suitable for outdoor use without the use of chemicals, preservatives or coatings. However, it requires additional energy to produce the material, because a great deal of heat is required.

Ash has very low moisture content when 'green' (freshly cut). At around 45%, it is far 'dryer' than hardwoods like oak, beech and birch, which are around 75%. This means less energy is required to season or thermally modify the timber.

Ash trees are being killed off by a combination of the fungal disease ash dieback and the emerald ash borer. Caused by the fungus *Hymenoscyphus fraxineus*, ash dieback slowly kills the tree starting from the leaves. The larvae of the emerald ash borer feed on the inner bark of the tree, which disrupts its ability to transport water and nutrients, ultimately killing the tree. The species is in decline and the effects of the fungus and the beetle are spreading quickly, and as a result there are serious concerns about the future of the ash population.

can help to improve the thermal stability of a building. This goes some way to offsetting the energy put into the heating process in the first place.

TMT produces a wood with a permanently dark colour that is less prone to change over time and with exposure to ultraviolet. This elevates utility hardwoods, such as ash, to sit alongside more exotic timbers, such as mahogany (page 372) and iroko (page 366). Through multiple cook temperatures a range of colour options within a single species can be achieved without the use of stains. Some other species that can be successfully treated include poplar (page 324), maple, birch (page 334), elm (page 358), oak and hickory.

TMT is often marketed under trademark names, such as Cambia, Thermowood and Thermo Ash. It is suitable for use both indoors and outdoors. Typical applications include garden furniture, cladding, decking and flooring. It can be expected to last 25 years or more outdoors.

Ash has pretty good steam bending

**Spade handle** The wood used in handles is selected for uniformity and straightness of grain. It is split and bent at the top to accommodate the 'YD' handgrip. While the cost and physical properties of ash may not be a match for modern alternatives, such as steel (page 28) and glass-fibre-reinforced plastic (see PA), it remains popular. The unpainted wood absorbs sweat and guarantees a firm grip. In this case, it is combined with a mirror-polished stainless-steel blade.

# Elm

This hardwood was once plentiful, but the tree has been decimated throughout North America and Europe by Dutch elm disease. It is a hardy and durable wood utilized in flooring, furniture and boatbuilding. The grain changes direction each year. Known as interlocked, it helps prevent the wood from splitting, but means it is trickier to work with.

| Types | Typical Applications | Sustainability |
|---|---|---|
| • American, cedar, English, Dutch, rock and wych | • Furniture and tools<br>• Flooring<br>• Boatbuilding | • In short supply owing to the impact of Dutch elm disease<br>• Dust can be a sensitizer |

| Properties | Competing Materials | Costs |
|---|---|---|
| • Interlocked grain<br>• Medium-dense with a coarse texture<br>• Not very stable and prone to warp and check | • Oak, walnut, chestnut, hickory and ash<br>• Larch, cypress (such as western red-cedar) and Douglas-fir<br>• Iroko, mahogany and teak | • Moderate to high for a northern hardwood<br>• Tricky to process owing to interlocked grain; considerable wastage |

## INTRODUCTION

Elm (*Ulmus* genus) is a multi-purpose hardwood that is, in many ways, comparable with cherry (page 360), oak (page 342) and walnut (page 348). It is a popular furniture-making timber in China (referred to as yumu), from antiques to modern design.

The heartwood is light to medium reddish-brown. Depending on the species, the highly distinguished grain can range from an appearance similar to ash (page 354) through to tropical species, such as acacia (page 364). The beautiful figuring present in quarter-sawn boards is due to the interlocked grain (see page 368). However, this same feature causes problems when working with the wood. The slope of the grain switches from year to year – what causes this to happen is unknown and it is not common in hardwoods from temperate forests – and can lead to tear out when cutting and planing.

The interlocked grain provides the wood with good resistance to splitting, which is useful for steam bending and ensures good nail- and screw-holding properties. Similar to hickory (page 352), certain species of elm have good shock absorption. Over the years, this quality has been utilized in tool handles and sports equipment.

## COMMERCIAL TYPES AND USES

There are several species of elm that grow across the temperate regions of the world, From North America to Asia, American (*U. americana*), slippery (*U. rubra*), English (*U. procera*) and wych (*U. glabra*) are some of the largest and most prevalent. These are medium-density with a coarse texture.

Elm species that yield a harder higher-density lumber (720 kg/m3 [45 lb/ft³] as opposed to 570 kg/m3 [35 lb/ft³]), sometimes referred to as 'hard' elms,

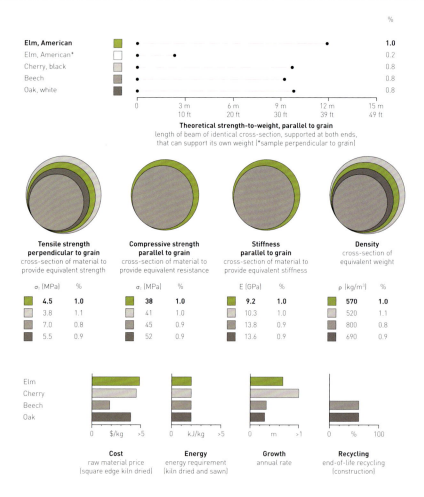

| | | % |
|---|---|---|
| Elm, American | | 1.0 |
| Elm, American* | | 0.2 |
| Cherry, black | | 0.8 |
| Beech | | 0.8 |
| Oak, white | | 0.8 |

**Theoretical strength-to-weight, parallel to grain**
length of beam of identical cross-section, supported at both ends, that can support its own weight (*sample perpendicular to grain)

**Tensile strength perpendicular to grain**
cross-section of material to provide equivalent strength

| $\sigma_t$ [MPa] | % |
|---|---|
| 4.5 | 1.0 |
| 3.8 | 1.1 |
| 7.0 | 0.8 |
| 5.5 | 0.9 |

**Compressive strength parallel to grain**
cross-section of material to provide equivalent resistance

| $\sigma_c$ [MPa] | % |
|---|---|
| 38 | 1.0 |
| 41 | 1.0 |
| 45 | 0.9 |
| 52 | 0.9 |

**Stiffness parallel to grain**
cross-section of material to provide equivalent stiffness

| E [GPa] | % |
|---|---|
| 9.2 | 1.0 |
| 10.3 | 1.0 |
| 13.8 | 0.9 |
| 13.6 | 0.9 |

**Density**
cross-section of equivalent weight

| $\rho$ [kg/m³] | % |
|---|---|
| 570 | 1.0 |
| 520 | 1.1 |
| 800 | 0.8 |
| 690 | 0.9 |

Elm
Cherry
Beech
Oak

**Cost**
raw material price (square edge kiln dried)

**Energy**
energy requirement (kiln dried and sawn)

**Growth**
annual rate

**Recycling**
end-of-life recycling (construction)

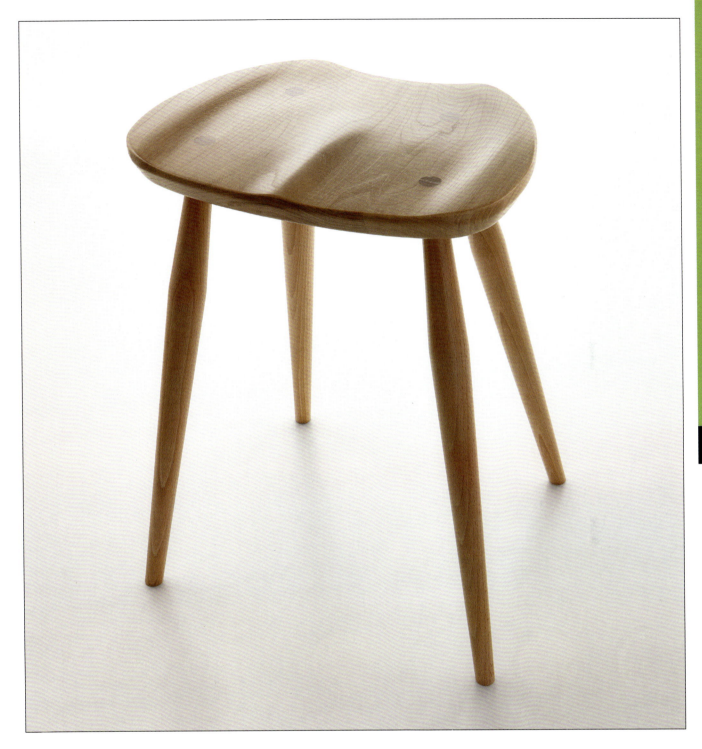

include cedar (*U. crassifolia*) and rock (*U. thomasii*), among others.

The Asiatic elms, such as Chinese (*U. parvifolia*) and Japanese (*U. davidiana* var. *japonica*), have contrasting growth rings, resulting in wave-like patterning in plain-sawn lumber, which is popular in furniture making. Southern Chinese elm, which is a little darker, yields a very dense timber (900 kg/m3 [56 lb/ft³]). It is strong and tough, but very difficult to work.

## SUSTAINABILITY

North American and European elms are rare these days as a result of Dutch elm disease (devastating fungal disease) and so are available in small quantities. The Asiatic elms are more resistant. Healthy trees can live to be very old, but are harvested for lumber at around 50 or 60 years.

Elm dust can be a sensitizer that causes skin and eye irritation.

**Elm and beech stool**
Elm is particularly well suited to seats, tabletops, drawer fronts and other parts of furniture that endure daily wear and tear. This stool from British furniture manufacturer Ercol features a solid elm seat, carved into the familiar saddle shape. The lathe-turned beech (page 338) legs come right through the seat and a wedge is driven into the end grain to reinforce the joint. The founder of the company, Lucian Ercolani, designed this stool in the 1950s, and it has since gone back into production as part of the Originals collection.

# Cherry, Apple and Pear

Cherry is one of the most popular hardwoods in North America. It is relatively easy to work and beautifully figured; it develops a characteristic rich dark orange-amber patina as it ages. Apple, pear and other fruitwoods are typically available only as small pieces of lumber. Their appearance ranges from plain to highly figured and some are quite aromatic.

| Types | Typical Applications | Sustainability |
|---|---|---|
| • Cherry: black (American or wild), sweet (European or wild), plum and apricot<br>• Apple<br>• Pear | • Furniture and cabinetry<br>• Tools and utensils<br>• Instruments, ornaments and tableware | • Available from sustainable forests<br>• Dust can be a sensitizer |

| Properties | Competing Materials | Costs |
|---|---|---|
| • Stable, moderately dense and strong<br>• Straight, uniform grain<br>• Good surface quality | • Walnut, oak and ash<br>• Exotics, iroko, acacia and mahogany | • Moderate to high raw material price |

360

## INTRODUCTION

Cherry (*Prunus* genus) is an important commercial timber throughout North America, Europe and Asia. Similar to oak (page 342) and walnut (page 348), it has many endearing qualities that make it desirable for furniture and cabinetry.

The heartwood is distinctively reddish-brown, and the colour darkens over time as a result of chemical reactions taking place within the wood. The growth patterns produce a highly figured appearance, which give the wood a naturally beautiful character. However, it may contain pith flecks and gum pockets, which can present a challenge for finishing, in particular staining. It is sometimes imitated using less expensive woods, such as poplar (page 324), stained dark red.

Apple (*Malus* genus), pear (*Pyrus* genus), quince (*Cydonia* genus) and the other fruitwoods could be considered 'exotic', since they are available in such small quantities and are relatively pricey. The wood tends to be denser than cherry, except for pear. Their appearance depends on the species and ranges from dramatically green-figured pistachio (*Pistacia* genus) to plain-looking quince, which has a subtle grain pattern.

Some of them – in particular peach (*Prunus persica*) and apricot (*P. armeniaca*) – smell just like their fruit when they are sanded or sawn. This aromatic quality

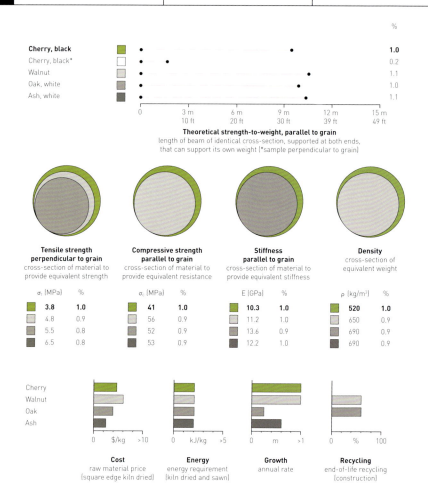

|  |  | % |
|---|---|---|
| Cherry, black | ■ (green) | 1.0 |
| Cherry, black* | □ | 0.2 |
| Walnut | ■ | 1.1 |
| Oak, white | ■ | 1.0 |
| Ash, white | ■ | 1.1 |

0   3 m / 10 ft   6 m / 20 ft   9 m / 30 ft   12 m / 39 ft   15 m / 49 ft

**Theoretical strength-to-weight, parallel to grain**
length of beam of identical cross-section, supported at both ends, that can support its own weight (*sample perpendicular to grain)

| Tensile strength perpendicular to grain<br>cross-section of material to provide equivalent strength | | Compressive strength parallel to grain<br>cross-section of material to provide equivalent resistance | | Stiffness parallel to grain<br>cross-section of material to provide equivalent stiffness | | Density<br>cross-section of equivalent weight | |
|---|---|---|---|---|---|---|---|
| σ_t (MPa) | % | σ_c (MPa) | % | E (GPa) | % | ρ (kg/m³) | % |
| 3.8 | 1.0 | 41 | 1.0 | 10.3 | 1.0 | 520 | 1.0 |
| 4.8 | 0.9 | 56 | 0.9 | 11.2 | 1.0 | 650 | 0.9 |
| 5.5 | 0.8 | 52 | 0.9 | 13.6 | 0.9 | 690 | 0.9 |
| 6.5 | 0.8 | 53 | 0.9 | 12.2 | 1.0 | 690 | 0.9 |

Cherry
Walnut
Oak
Ash

| Cost<br>raw material price (square edge kiln dried) | Energy<br>energy requirement (kiln dried and sawn) | Growth<br>annual rate | Recycling<br>end-of-life recycling (construction) |
|---|---|---|---|
| 0  $/kg  >10 | 0  kJ/kg  >5 | 0  m  >1 | 0  %  100 |

**Swedish block former in cherry**  Cherry wood is used for the molds and formers used to shape molten glass. The wood is saturated with water to stop it cracking when the hot glass comes into contact. The tight and uniform grain of cherry, as well as of pear and apple, holds in the water much better than other woods. The combination of steam and charred wood surface produces a smooth finish on the glass. This block was lathe-turned by Gary Guydosh of Hot Block Tools, Pittsburgh, Pennsylvania.

**Pear wood soprano recorder** Pear wood is traditionally used to make woodwind instruments. Its low density and fine texture result in a warmer tone and quieter sound than heavier alternatives, such as African blackwood, rosewood and ebony (see Exotics, page 374). Maple and sycamore are used to produce similar instruments, as well as the other fruitwoods. They are often impregnated with wax to help stabilize and preserve the wood.

is used in smokers to lend a pleasant flavour to meat.

## COMMERCIAL TYPES AND USES

There are several species of cherry. The principal commercial timber comes from black cherry (*P. Serotina*), which is also known as American or wild cherry. The tree grows to around 25 m (82 ft) and yields large, clear, high-quality boards.

It is softer than oak and walnut, and has a clean, straight grain. This means it is straightforward and satisfying to work and carve. It has moderate bending properties and when applied as veneer may be formed into gentle curves. It is used in a variety of applications – similar to oak and walnut – such as furniture, panelling, handles, molding, interiors (boats and cars) and instruments (guitars, harps and violins, for example).

Cherry is very stable, once dry. This quality is utilized in stamps and molds, for example. It is also useful in furniture. The heartwood is durable and resistant to decay, although this wood is rarely used in applications outdoors. The sapwood is not resistant to decay and is vulnerable to insect attack.

Cherry is typically more expensive than oak or maple, but less than walnut. Sweet cherry (*P. avium*), also called European or wild cherry, is around one-third less expensive than American black cherry. The trees do not grow as tall and so the lumber tends to be smaller. At up to 650 kg/m³ (40 lb/ft³), it is also heavier. It is a good general-purpose joinery timber used for furniture, interiors and flooring.

Plum and apricot are subgenera of *Prunus*. The wood is not normally commercially available, but appears in small carvings, such as knife handles and ornaments. Apricot is used in woodwind and stringed instruments for its acoustics.

There are several species of pear; the prevalent ones being the common pear (*P. communis*) and the Swiss pear (*P. nivalis*). It is strong, and less dense than most other fruitwoods. It has a fine grain and very uniform texture and works very well. The trees barely reach 10 m (33 ft), but yield a very high-quality lumber suitable for carving and veneer. The base colour is an even brown, not too dissimilar from American mahogany. There is a discreet pinkish tinge to the wood, which is often enhanced through heat treatment. Occasionally the wood is figured with dark streaks running the length of the board.

Its stability is utilized in drawing equipment, utensils and combs, for example. It has good acoustic properties, which make it suitable for woodwind and stringed instruments.

Apple starts out quite pale, but turns to a reddish-brown colour similar to cherry. The wood is quite difficult to come by. In Europe, orchards that have passed maturity are cut down and converted into lumber. The trees tend to be fairly small, because they are pruned to keep the fruit within reach of the pickers. Like pear, it is prized for small carvings, as well as for woodwind and stringed instruments.

## SUSTAINABILITY

None of these species is listed as threatened. However, apart from cherry, they are rare and hard to come by. This is not to say they could become vulnerable; the trees are simply more valuable for their fruit than for timber. While they may be available locally for a reasonable price, such as from a felled orchard, imported stock tends to be quite expensive.

**Solid cherry wood chair** Created by Danish furniture designer Hans Wegner, 1952, the Cow Horn Chair is manufactured by PP Møbler, Denmark. Cherry is popular in furniture making, because it is relatively easy to work and is highly decorative. The backrest is produced from two pieces of wood, cut from the same piece to ensure colour and grain uniformity. Instead of hiding the craftsmanship involved in the join, Wegner has highlighted it through the use of contrasting rosewood. Photo by Katja Kejser and Kasper Holst Pedersen, courtesy of PP Møbler.

# Acacia

This thorny tree yields a richly coloured and highly decorative timber. It is native to Australia, but found throughout the tropical and subtropical regions. It is considered a pest and an invasive species in some places. As well as timber, the acacia provides a valuable source of tannin, which is used in leather production. It also yields edible seeds and gum.

| Types | Typical Applications | Sustainability |
|---|---|---|
| • Acacia: koa, wattle, blackwood and salwood | • Boat construction, timber frame houses, flooring and engineered timber<br>• Musical instruments<br>• Products and furniture | • Native to Australia, but also found in Asia, the Pacific Islands, Africa and the Americas<br>• The dust can be a sensitizer |

| Properties | Competing Materials | Costs |
|---|---|---|
| • Moderately durable, but susceptible to insect attack<br>• Highly variable colour<br>• Resistant to preservative | • Walnut, sapele, mahogany, iroko and teak<br>• Douglas fir, cypress and larch | • Low to moderate<br>• Decorative veneer can be very expensive<br>• Excellent processing |

364

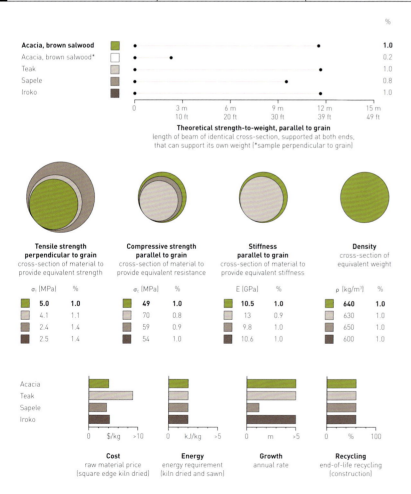

|  | % |
|---|---|
| Acacia, brown salwood | 1.0 |
| Acacia, brown salwood* | 0.2 |
| Teak | 1.0 |
| Sapele | 0.8 |
| Iroko | 1.0 |

| 0 | 3 m<br>10 ft | 6 m<br>20 ft | 9 m<br>30 ft | 12 m<br>39 ft | 15 m<br>49 ft |

**Theoretical strength-to-weight, parallel to grain**
length of beam of identical cross-section, supported at both ends, that can support its own weight (*sample perpendicular to grain)

| Tensile strength perpendicular to grain | | Compressive strength parallel to grain | | Stiffness parallel to grain | | Density | |
|---|---|---|---|---|---|---|---|
| cross-section of material to provide equivalent strength | | cross-section of material to provide equivalent resistance | | cross-section of material to provide equivalent stiffness | | cross-section of equivalent weight | |
| $\sigma_t$ (MPa) | % | $\sigma_c$ (MPa) | % | E (GPa) | % | $\rho$ (kg/m³) | % |
| 5.0 | 1.0 | 49 | 1.0 | 10.5 | 1.0 | 640 | 1.0 |
| 4.1 | 1.1 | 70 | 0.8 | 13 | 0.9 | 630 | 1.0 |
| 2.4 | 1.4 | 59 | 0.9 | 9.8 | 1.0 | 650 | 1.0 |
| 2.5 | 1.4 | 54 | 1.0 | 10.6 | 1.0 | 600 | 1.0 |

Acacia
Teak
Sapele
Iroko

| 0 | $/kg | >10 | 0 | kJ/kg | >5 | 0 | m | >5 | 0 | % | 100 |

| **Cost** | **Energy** | **Growth** | **Recycling** |
|---|---|---|---|
| raw material price (square edge kiln dried) | energy requirement (kiln dried and sawn) | annual rate | end-of-life recycling (construction) |

## INTRODUCTION

Certain species of acacia (*Acacia* genus) yield timber comparable with mahogany (page 372) and walnut (page 348). Growth rings can be rather indistinct in some, with others having great colour variation. Sapwood ranges from straw to grey-white; heartwood is golden or reddish-brown.

It is classed as moderately durable; some species are more resistant to decay and can tolerate damp conditions. However, it generally requires protecting when used outdoors. It is similar weight to mahogany; density increases with age.

## COMMERCIAL TYPES AND USES

There are many hundred species of acacia and only a few are harvested commercially for timber. The many generic names that acacia is known by – such as blackwood and wattle – are used interchangeably between the species.

Brown salwood (*A. mangium*) is a major plantation species in the humid tropical lowlands of Asia, including Indonesia and Malaysia. It is utilized on an industrial scale as lumber and pulp (see Paper, page 268). Timber referred to simply as acacia is most likely derived from this tree. It yields a hard, heavy, tough and strong wood. It is dimensionally stable and suitable for use in outdoor furniture and window frames.

Blackwood (*A. melanoxylon*) is cultivated in temperate countries such as Brazil, Chile, South Africa, New Zealand and parts of Australia. It produces a high-quality timber utilized in furniture making, cabinetry and joinery. It should not be confused with African blackwood, which is a species of rosewood (see Exotics, page 374).

Koa (*A. koa*) is native to Hawaii. It is a desirable timber and relatively expensive (outside the Pacific Islands). It is in short supply and not considered sustainable

in the long term. Therefore, it is mainly applied as veneer. It is considered a good tonewood and is used in the soundboards of musical instruments (see also Maple, page 330, and Spruce, page 304).

## SUSTAINABILITY

It grows vigorously and takes only around 20 years for a stand to be ready for harvest, depending on the intended use. In the past, demand has exceeded supply. This was mainly due to poor management of plantations. Nowadays, the trees are cultivated throughout Asia as well as their native Australia.

The dust can be a sensitizer. Exposure can lead to dermatitis, asthma, and nose and throat irritation.

IKEA sources brown salwood from Indonesia, Vietnam and Malaysia. It is much less expensive than exotic hardwood and more sustainable.

**Handcrafted tray**
Acacia has very good working properties and is suitable for all types of hand and machine work. It is also suitable for steam bending. The wood has a natural lustre, which is emphasized by polishing to a smooth finish. This brown salwood tray has been carved from a plain-sawn plank to make the most of the undulating colours.

# Iroko

**Also known as**
Also referred to as: African teak, African oak
Within Africa, known by various names depending on country of origin: semli, odom, rokko, oroko, bang, mandji, moreira, tule, intule, kambala, mvule

Iroko heartwood starts out yellow and gradually darkens to a rich chocolate-brown. It is very durable and can be used outdoors untreated. As a result, it is commonly used in boatbuilding, garden furniture and decking. It is a massive tree free from branches for much of its trunk and yields large, high-quality lumber.

| Types | Typical Applications | Sustainability |
|---|---|---|
| • Iroko | • Boat and house construction<br>• Furniture, product and musical instruments<br>• Flooring and interiors | • Distributed across central Africa and listed as vulnerable owing to deforestation<br>• Can be a sensitizer |

| Properties | Competing Materials | Costs |
|---|---|---|
| • Very durable and resistant to insect attack<br>• Heartwood darkens over time to rich chocolate colour<br>• Interlocked, irregular grain | • Oak and walnut<br>• Teak, mahogany and sapele<br>• Ash, poplar and other thermally modified timbers | • Moderate for a tropical hardwood<br>• Difficult to process and dulls cutting blades |

366

## INTRODUCTION

Iroko (*Milicia* genus, also known as *Chlorophora* genus) is applied as lumber and veneer for decorative and functional purposes. The bole is straight and clear of branches up until around 25 m (82 ft). The tree canopy can reach twice that height and the trunk 2 m (7 ft) in diameter. These are valuable trees, economically and environmentally. And in some cultures in Africa, the trees are revered as sacred.

It is the heartwood of iroko that is the most durable and desirable. It is protected from decay and insect attack by its natural oils. As a result, it can be used outside untreated. Ranging from pale yellowish-brown to dark chocolate-brown, it is clearly demarcated from the yellowish-white sapwood. It has a medium to coarse texture, but the wood is hard and has good nail- and screw-holding properties.

The timber occasionally contains large deposits of calcium carbonate. Known as 'stone', they take their toll on cutting tools and can cause problems during processing. It has an interlocked and irregular grain, which can cause some tear-out to occur during cutting. Otherwise, the wood machines and carves relatively well.

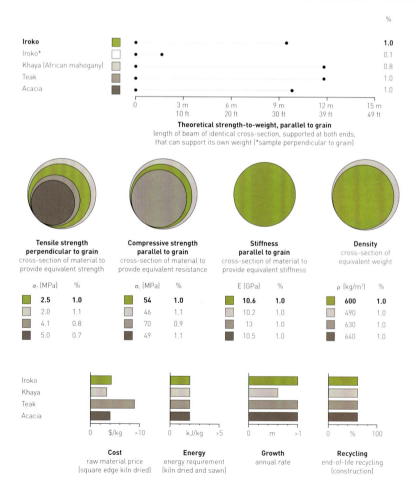

| | | % |
|---|---|---|
| Iroko | | 1.0 |
| Iroko* | | 0.1 |
| Khaya (African mahogany) | | 0.8 |
| Teak | | 1.0 |
| Acacia | | 1.0 |

**Theoretical strength-to-weight, parallel to grain**
length of beam of identical cross-section, supported at both ends, that can support its own weight (*sample perpendicular to grain)

**Tensile strength perpendicular to grain**
cross-section of material to provide equivalent strength

| σ_t (MPa) | % |
|---|---|
| 2.5 | 1.0 |
| 2.0 | 1.1 |
| 4.1 | 0.8 |
| 5.0 | 0.7 |

**Compressive strength parallel to grain**
cross-section of material to provide equivalent resistance

| σ_c (MPa) | % |
|---|---|
| 54 | 1.0 |
| 46 | 1.1 |
| 70 | 0.9 |
| 49 | 1.1 |

**Stiffness parallel to grain**
cross-section of material to provide equivalent stiffness

| E (GPa) | % |
|---|---|
| 10.6 | 1.0 |
| 10.2 | 1.0 |
| 13 | 1.0 |
| 10.5 | 1.0 |

**Density**
cross-section of equivalent weight

| ρ (kg/m³) | % |
|---|---|
| 600 | 1.0 |
| 490 | 1.0 |
| 630 | 1.0 |
| 640 | 1.0 |

Iroko
Khaya
Teak
Acacia

**Cost**
raw material price (square edge kiln dried)
0 $/kg >10

**Energy**
energy requirement (kiln dried and sawn)
0 kJ/kg >5

**Growth**
annual rate
0 m >1

**Recycling**
end-of-life recycling (construction)
0 % 100

**Outdoor furniture**
The original tubular steel frame 'chair with no legs', designed by Dutch architect and furniture designer Mart Stam in 1931, was named the S 43. It continues to be manufactured by Thonet in Germany. In the case of the S 43, Stam combined the steel frame with a molded plywood (see Engineered Timber, page 296) seat and back. Thonet first presented garden chairs using the same design in 1935 under the name B 33 g. Today, it is known as S 40 and produced with FSC-certified iroko. Extremely durable outdoors, protected by its natural oils, iroko can last many years exposed to the elements. Photo courtesy of Thonet.

## COMMERCIAL TYPES AND USES

The wood comes from two species (*M. excelsa* and *M. regia*). There does not appear to be any significant difference between the two. It is prized for its appearance and inherent durability. Applications include garden furniture and decking. It is also utilized in construction, such as for window frames, sills, doors and cladding.

It is often found in countertops, in particular in laboratories and science classrooms. This is because iroko performs very well in continually damp or chemically hazardous situations. And it is hard enough to tolerate everyday use.

Its chemical resistance, in particular its resistance to acids, is the reason why it has been utilized in chemical storage tanks. Nowadays, these are much more likely to be produced from rotation-molded polyethylene (PE) (page 108), polypropylene (PP) (page 98) or similar low-cost synthetic material.

It is used in river and sea constructions, such as jetties, piers, pontoons and locks. Other large-scale construction projects include timber frame houses and bridges. It is applied as solid lumber, or converted into engineered timber (page 296), such as glued laminated timber (glulam). This allows for much greater spans to be achieved. However, engineered timber manufactured from iroko will be significantly more expensive than products manufactured from softwoods, such as the more commonly used spruce, pine and fir (page 304). Also, it is not recommended to use iroko untreated in applications where it will be in continuous contact with the ground.

Iroko is often compared to teak (page 370) and other durable tropical hardwoods. The two are similar in terms of grain structure, density and colour. Teak is very expensive and in short supply owing to variety of trade restrictions. Iroko is not as strong, stiff or durable, but is suitable for many of the same situations and remains affordable (around one-third of the price of teak). In Europe, iroko is steadily gaining popularity. In the USA, it has not been quite so successful; as long as teak is available it remains the material of choice for such things as boatbuilding.

It is also compared to oak (page 342). These two timbers, from opposite sides of the world, do share some similarities. Like iroko, white oak can be used outdoors untreated; iroko is a similar weight (although oak can be a little heavier), responds well to steam bending and costs about the same. As a result, they are used for many of the same applications, such as furniture, countertops and cladding. Oak has a more figured appearance, in particular quarter-sawn white oak, which is covered with silvery ray flecks. The colour of iroko, on the other hand, appears to ripple, an effect that is a result of the alternating spiralled grain. So, even when stained the same colour, they have a quite different appearance.

## SUSTAINABILITY

It is available from certified forests. It grows rapidly and is ready for harvesting after around 50 years.

In the wild it is listed as vulnerable, because it has been extensively logged and the species is in decline. Tropical rainforests are regarded as extremely sensitive ecosystems and it can take decades, or even centuries, to recover from heavy logging activity. Africa contains around 20% of the world's tropical forests. Agricultural practices, logging and development projects are reducing the size of the forests by around 1% annually. In some parts of Africa, only around one-fifth to one-quarter of the forests remain. As a result, these trees have protected status in a number of the countries where they grow. Countless schemes and plantation initiatives have been launched to try to counter the problem.

In addition, the illegal logging of iroko has been linked to conflicts in regions where it grows. Along with other valuable tropical hardwoods, gemstones (page 476) and precious metals, there is evidence that sales help to fund armed groups.

Exposure to the dust may lead to health problems, such as asthma, dermatitis and nettle rash. It is recommended to wear protective breathing equipment when working the timber. In less responsible forestry operations and sawmills, workers may not be adequately protected.

**Interlocked grain**
Many of the tropical hardwoods feature an interlocked grain. Examples include iroko, mahogany (page 372), African mahogany, sapele, bossé, rosewood and padauk (see Exotics, page 374). Some of the northern hardwoods can also have an interlocking grain, such as elm (page 358), sycamore and maple (page 330). This illustration represents a quarter-sawn sample (the cut radiates out from the centre of the log). The long edge faces towards the centre, from where the growth rings originate. New fibres are laid down in a spiral around the axis of the tree (this is different from straight-grained wood, such as ash [page 354], oak and wengé [see Exotics]). Interlocking grain is caused by these spirals periodically changing direction (the reason for this is not known). In other words,

each year the slope of the grain switches from left to right. This results in an interesting optical effect known as ribbon-stripe: the colour shifts from dark to light depending on the angle of view. This is caused by the different angles of the fibres exposed on the surface. It is most noticeable in quarter-sawn boards, because the growth rings are at right angles to the face of the board. This can present some challenges when working with the timber, as the grain is prone to tearing out during planing and similar surface operations. It does not have a significant affect on the strength of the wood. Other grain disturbances – such as figured grain and knots – might, because the strength of wood is greatest along the grain. Therefore, significant deviations mean less of the grain runs in parallel.

**CNC-carved box** This vanity tissue box by Greek contemporary product design studio Greece is for Lovers is CNC-milled from solid iroko. A layer of wax is applied to the surface, which fills the grain and results in a smooth, lustrous finish. Photo by Nikos Alexopoulos.

# Teak

One of the most desirable timbers for boatbuilding and outdoor furniture, teak is both expensive and hard to come by. The golden-brown heartwood is highly resistant to decay and most insects – it is considered one of the most durable timbers. While it is relatively stiff and strong, it is surprisingly easy to work by hand or machine.

| Types | Typical Applications | Sustainability |
|---|---|---|
| • Burmese teak<br>• Non-Burmese teak (plantation teak) | • Boatbuilding<br>• Outdoor furniture<br>• Construction | • Available from certified sources<br>• The dust can be a severe sensitizer |

| Properties | Competing Materials | Costs |
|---|---|---|
| • Strong<br>• Good dimensional stability<br>• Very durable | • Iroko<br>• Sapele<br>• Mahogany | • One of the most expensive timbers |

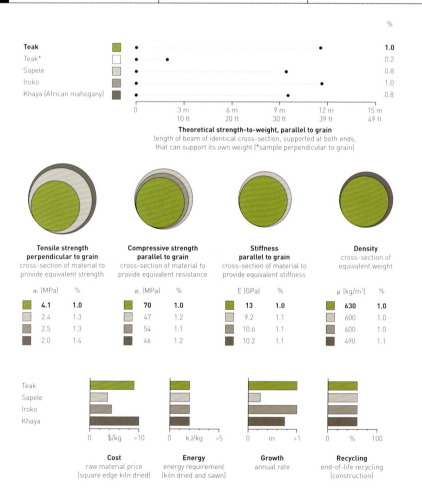

| | % |
|---|---|
| Teak | 1.0 |
| Teak* | 0.2 |
| Sapele | 0.8 |
| Iroko | 1.0 |
| Khaya (African mahogany) | 0.8 |

0 · 3 m / 10 ft · 6 m / 20 ft · 9 m / 30 ft · 12 m / 39 ft · 15 m / 49 ft

**Theoretical strength-to-weight, parallel to grain**
length of beam of identical cross-section, supported at both ends, that can support its own weight (*sample perpendicular to grain)

| Tensile strength<br>perpendicular to grain<br>cross-section of material to<br>provide equivalent strength | | Compressive strength<br>parallel to grain<br>cross-section of material to<br>provide equivalent resistance | | Stiffness<br>parallel to grain<br>cross-section of material to<br>provide equivalent stiffness | | Density<br>cross-section of<br>equivalent weight | |
|---|---|---|---|---|---|---|---|
| $\sigma_t$ (MPa) | % | $\sigma_c$ (MPa) | % | E (GPa) | % | $\rho$ (kg/m³) | % |
| 4.1 | 1.0 | 70 | 1.0 | 13 | 1.0 | 630 | 1.0 |
| 2.4 | 1.3 | 47 | 1.2 | 9.2 | 1.1 | 600 | 1.0 |
| 2.5 | 1.3 | 54 | 1.1 | 10.6 | 1.1 | 600 | 1.0 |
| 2.0 | 1.4 | 46 | 1.2 | 10.2 | 1.1 | 490 | 1.1 |

Teak · Sapele · Iroko · Khaya

| Cost<br>raw material price<br>(square edge kiln dried) | Energy<br>energy requirement<br>(kiln dried and sawn) | Growth<br>annual rate | Recycling<br>end-of-life recycling<br>(construction) |
|---|---|---|---|
| 0 — $/kg — >10 | 0 — kJ/kg — >5 | 0 — m — >1 | 0 — % — 100 |

## INTRODUCTION

Teak (*Tecona* genus) has been used in its native countries – India, Myanmar (Burma) and Thailand – for thousands of years in the construction of high-quality buildings, boats and furniture. Natural oils in the heartwood make it impervious to sun, rain, frost and snow. There are examples of ancient teak structures that have remained intact to this day. When used under cover, teak heartwood has a virtually indefinite lifespan, because it is resistant to most insects too.

Its moderate density and large fibres make it relatively easy to work by hand and machine. However, deposits of silica that build up in the wood through its lifetime can dull cutting blades. It has a straight and tightly packed grain. A high-quality finish can be achieved and it polishes very well. These properties are utilized in precious hand carvings, such as chess pieces and ornaments, as well as turned items.

When used exposed outdoors, without treatment, the heartwood slowly changes from dark golden-brown to silvery-grey. It is expensive and so not used in as large quantities as other weather-resistant timbers (see Cypress Family, page 318, Larch, page 310, and Oak, page 342).

It is very stable and does not warp or crack. Nor does it turn black when in contact with metals. These properties, along with its inherent durability, make it a very desirable material for boat decks and trim. The high price tag means that only the most valuable boats, in particular cruisers and superyachts, can take advantage of teak.

## COMMERCIAL TYPES AND USES

Even though it is relatively fast-growing, it remains very expensive because it is highly desirable and fairly scarce. Teak supply has seen some turbulent times.

Until recently, the majority of teak came from Myanmar. Known as Burmese teak, it is considered superior in every aspect. Supplies were virtually halted when the USA introduced the Burmese Freedom and Democracy Act in 2003, banning the import of Burmese products as a sanction against the country's repressive leadership. Many other parts of the world, including the EU, followed suit.

Following the easing of the ban in 2012 in the EU (and the USA soon after), the Myanmar Ministry of Forestry announced that it would restrict the export of raw teak in 2014 in a bid to increase sales of higher-value finished goods. In the past, prices were kept artificially low by the import of illegally logged timber. Since the EU Timber Regulation (2010) puts the responsibility of a traceable supply chain onto the timber supplier, the trade in illegally harvested timber and timber products has declined. On top of this, overall teak production has been in steady decline (around 15% each year) owing to the restrictions put in place to try to counter deforestation.

As a result, most teak is now sourced from managed plantations, such as in Indonesia, from where a large proportion of global supply is derived. Plantation teak is grown faster than it would grow naturally. This type of cultivation requires fertilizer and irrigation, and could have adverse affects on the quality of timber as well as the local environment. The timber is considered by many to be inferior to old stock Burmese teak.

There are many teak substitutes available at a lower price, albeit still relatively expensive compared to temperate hardwoods. Several include teak in their name even though they are not related, such as Brazilian teak (*Dipteryx* genus), Rhodesian teak (*Baikiaea* genus) and African teak (*Pericopsis* genus). They all have dark-coloured heartwood, but have inferior durability. Iroko (page 366) has similar properties to teak and is often used as a less expensive alternative (sometimes referred to as African teak).

## SUSTAINABILITY

Its long lifespan means that old teak can be just as good as new, if not better.

While it is impossible to understand the full extent of teak recycling, it is likely to be relatively high due to the extremely high cost of the raw material. Teak used in construction is unlikely to be disposed of or burned if there is any way it can be reclaimed and reused. As a result, there are many examples of new furniture made from old teak.

The dust produced during cutting and sanding is a powerful sensitizer and can cause severe reactions. Suitable protective clothing is required to avoid it affecting the eyes, skin and respiratory system.

**Teak monkey**
Created by Danish designer Kay Bojesen in 1951, the monkey is part of a series of wooden animals for Rosendahl. The teak is contrasted with lighter-coloured limba heartwood in the belly, hands, feet and face. Although intended as a children's toy, the high price of teak means it is more likely treasured as an ornament and heirloom than a plaything.

# Mahogany Family

Genuine mahogany is a tropical hardwood that yields huge clear boards with beautiful grain and colour. Threatened in the wild, it is commercially available only from plantation-grown trees. Popular substitutes include khaya (African mahogany) sapele and bossé. Much of the timber comes from plantations and trade is controlled, because many species are threatened in the wild.

| Types | Typical Applications | Sustainability |
|---|---|---|
| • True mahogany: Honduran, Mexican and Cuban<br>• Khaya (African mahogany), sapele, bossé and Spanish-cedar, among others | • Boatbuilding and construction<br>• Products and furniture<br>• Musical instruments | • Very few trees left in the wild; almost all true mahogany comes from plantations<br>• Some related species are sustainable<br>• Can be a sensitizer |
| **Properties** | **Competing Materials** | **Costs** |
| • Not particularly strong, but very stable<br>• Figured grain and natural lustre<br>• Durability ranges from moderate to high | • Walnut, oak, teak, acacia and several of the exotic hardwoods | • Moderate to high, depending on the species and quality<br>• Good working properties |

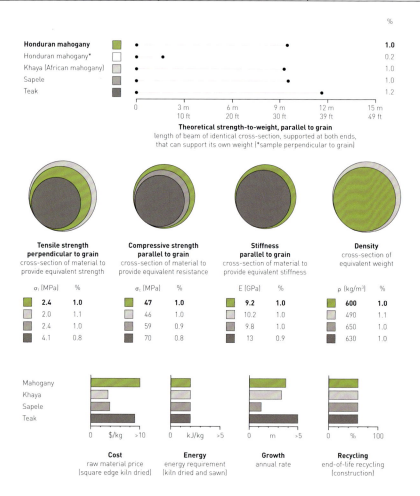

| | % |
|---|---|
| Honduran mahogany | 1.0 |
| Honduran mahogany* | 0.2 |
| Khaya (African mahogany) | 1.0 |
| Sapele | 1.0 |
| Teak | 1.2 |

0   3 m / 10 ft   6 m / 20 ft   9 m / 30 ft   12 m / 39 ft   15 m / 49 ft

**Theoretical strength-to-weight, parallel to grain**
length of beam of identical cross-section, supported at both ends, that can support its own weight (*sample perpendicular to grain)

**Tensile strength perpendicular to grain**
cross-section of material to provide equivalent strength

| $\sigma_t$ (MPa) | % |
|---|---|
| 2.4 | 1.0 |
| 2.0 | 1.1 |
| 2.4 | 1.0 |
| 4.1 | 0.8 |

**Compressive strength parallel to grain**
cross-section of material to provide equivalent resistance

| $\sigma_c$ (MPa) | % |
|---|---|
| 47 | 1.0 |
| 46 | 1.0 |
| 59 | 0.9 |
| 70 | 0.8 |

**Stiffness parallel to grain**
cross-section of material to provide equivalent stiffness

| E (GPa) | % |
|---|---|
| 9.2 | 1.0 |
| 10.2 | 1.0 |
| 9.8 | 1.0 |
| 13 | 0.9 |

**Density**
cross-section of equivalent weight

| $\rho$ (kg/m³) | % |
|---|---|
| 600 | 1.0 |
| 490 | 1.1 |
| 650 | 1.0 |
| 630 | 1.0 |

Mahogany
Khaya
Sapele
Teak

**Cost**
raw material price (square edge kiln dried)
0   $/kg   >10

**Energy**
energy requirement (kiln dried and sawn)
0   kJ/kg   >5

**Growth**
annual rate
0   m   >5

**Recycling**
end-of-life recycling (construction)
0   %   100

## INTRODUCTION

The name 'mahogany' is given to many different types of wood, all of which belong to the Meliaceae family. Being related, they share many properties. However, the term 'true mahogany' is generally reserved for timber derived from trees of the *Swietenia* genus. All of the species in this genus – principally Cuban (*S. mahogani*) and Honduran (*S. macrophylla*), also known as American, Brazilian and so on – are threatened in the wild.

It is not as strong or stiff as teak (page 370). Nor is it as durable against decay; and it is susceptible to insect attack. Even so, it is used for shipbuilding and can be left outdoors untreated for extended periods of time. One of its most impressive qualities is its stability. Shrinkage is only around half that of most other common hardwoods, so it is less prone to warp and check (split in the end or face) as it dries.

Colour ranges from pale brown to rich dark or reddish-brown. Over time, and with exposure to ultraviolet, it will become gradually darker. Its lustrous and highly decorative appearance was utilized by cabinetmakers in the 18th and 19th centuries. Much of the furniture produced in Europe and North America around that time – including the work of Thomas Chippendale, Thomas Hope, Thomas Sheraton, Charles-Honoré Lannuier and Duncan Phyfe – was constructed from mahogany, as well as from walnut (page 348) or oak (page 342).

It has a uniform texture and excellent working properties. It is suitable for all types of hand and machine work, and has moderate steam-bending properties. As well as lumber, it is utilized as veneer (page 290). In rare cases, mahogany comes with highly figured grain, such as fiddleback and curly.

## COMMERCIAL TYPES AND USES

Of the true mahoganies, only the Honduran is commercially available. It is grown in plantations and marketed under several names, such as American, Brazilian and big-leaf mahogany. While it is a genuine mahogany, plantation-grown timber will never be as high quality as large, old trees that have grown slowly.

Piggybacking on the desirability and success of this genus, several related genera – all from the Meliaceae family – are commonly accepted as 'mahogany'. Some of the most popular and significant of these include khaya, also known as African mahogany (*Khaya* genus), sapele (*Entandrophragma* genus), bossé (*Guarea* genus) and Spanish-cedar (*Cedrela* genus). These are fine woods in their own right and are generally interchangeable with true mahogany.

Khaya, sapele and bossé are all native to Africa. Khaya (principally *K. invorensis*) is slightly more brittle than true mahogany, but otherwise a suitable alternative. It is more widely available and less expensive. Sapele (*E. cylindricum*) is larger than the khaya and has slightly higher density, which yields a timber with superior working properties. The timber is known for its rich colour and figured grain. Bossé (principally *G. cedrata* and *G. thompsonii*) is typically only available as decorative veneer. It has a similar appearance to sapele, with golden-brown heartwood. Highly figured pieces are expensive.

These woods tend to have an interlocked or wavy grain, which can make them more difficult to work with than true mahoganies. The grain is prone to tearing when cut. Heartwood ranges from moderately durable to very durable, depending on the species and age of tree.

Spanish-cedar, also known as Brazilian-cedar, is native to South America and the Caribbean. It is not a true cedar (*Cedrus* genus); it is so called because it yields an aromatic wood with a cedar-like scent that is insect-repellent. It is lightweight with moderate durability.

There are several other species marketed as mahogany that are not even closely related. Examples include Philippine mahogany (also known as meranti or lauan, terms that cover a

range of woods from southeast Asia) and Indian mahogany (*Toona* genus).

## SUSTAINABILITY

True mahoganies are moderately fast-growing, taking around 40 to 60 years to reach an economically viable size. They are considered vulnerable in the wild and the trees are protected by international laws.

Some of the extended family members grow at around the same pace, and some much more slowly. Many of them are considered vulnerable or endangered in the wild, in particular Spanish- and Brazilian-cedar, khaya and sapele. Illegal logging is widespread across Africa and South America.

**Laminated guitar sides**
Mahogany is a popular choice for guitar sides and backs; it provides a less expensive alternative to rosewood (see Exotics, page 374). It is denser than cypress (page 318) and spruce (page 304), and provides a warm, soft tone. As a result, they make a great combination. For example, the Gibson J-160E used by John Lennon for much of the Beatles' early work was of mahogany and spruce construction.

Therefore, it is essential to source the timber from well-managed forests, ideally those that are certified.

The dust from some species, in particular sapele and bossé, is a known sensitizer and can cause respiratory, eye and breathing problems.

# Exotics

These are highly sought-after multi-purpose hardwoods. Many of them grow slowly and are relatively scarce, but demand is high and several species are considered threatened or endangered. There is a magnificent range of colours, from pink and purple to jet-black. They are expensive outside their growing range and often only available as small blanks or veneer.

| Types | Typical Applications | Sustainability |
|---|---|---|
| • Ebony (inc. blackwood and wengé), rosewood, padauk, katalox, macacauba, bubinga, pink ivory, ziricote, bocote, greenheart, lacewood and zebrawood | • Construction and boats<br>• Cabinetry and musical instruments<br>• Tool handles and sports equipment | • Many of these species are vulnerable or endangered<br>• Dust can be a sensitizer |

| Properties | Competing Materials | Costs |
|---|---|---|
| • Rich contrasting colours and figured grain<br>• Strong, hard and dense<br>• Decay resistance depends on species | • Teak, mahogany and walnut<br>• Oak, beech, ash, maple and birch<br>• Cypress (such as western red-cedar), larch and Douglas-fir | • Very high raw material cost<br>• Can be challenging to process |

374

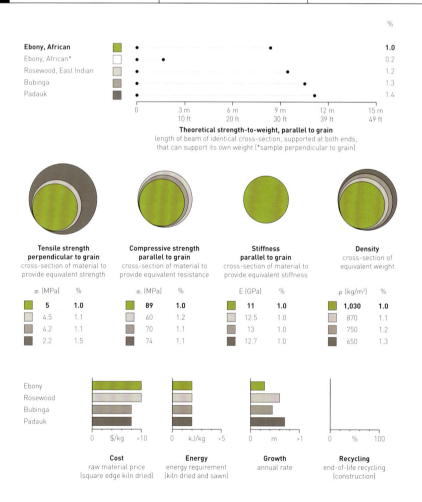

| | % |
|---|---|
| Ebony, African | 1.0 |
| Ebony, African* | 0.2 |
| Rosewood, East Indian | 1.2 |
| Bubinga | 1.3 |
| Padauk | 1.4 |

**Theoretical strength-to-weight, parallel to grain**
length of beam of identical cross-section, supported at both ends,
that can support its own weight (*sample perpendicular to grain)

**Tensile strength perpendicular to grain**
cross-section of material to provide equivalent strength

| σ, (MPa) | % |
|---|---|
| 5 | 1.0 |
| 4.5 | 1.1 |
| 4.2 | 1.1 |
| 2.2 | 1.5 |

**Compressive strength parallel to grain**
cross-section of material to provide equivalent resistance

| σ, (MPa) | % |
|---|---|
| 89 | 1.0 |
| 60 | 1.2 |
| 70 | 1.1 |
| 74 | 1.1 |

**Stiffness parallel to grain**
cross-section of material to provide equivalent stiffness

| E (GPa) | % |
|---|---|
| 11 | 1.0 |
| 12.5 | 1.0 |
| 13 | 1.0 |
| 12.7 | 1.0 |

**Density**
cross-section of equivalent weight

| ρ (kg/m³) | % |
|---|---|
| 1,030 | 1.0 |
| 870 | 1.1 |
| 750 | 1.2 |
| 650 | 1.3 |

Ebony
Rosewood
Bubinga
Padauk

**Cost**
raw material price (square edge kiln dried)

**Energy**
energy requirement (kiln dried and sawn)

**Growth**
annual rate

**Recycling**
end-of-life recycling (construction)

## INTRODUCTION

There are hundreds of exotic tropical hardwoods. A handful of species – in addition to the examples covered elsewhere in this book, including acacia (page 364), iroko (page 366), teak (page 370), mahogany (page 372) and balsa (page 378) – have become familiar throughout the world, defined by a unique set of properties. Over the years, and following the overexploitation of many of these rare woods, the price has risen and they have become very scarce. Some are available in limited quantities; the export of others has been outlawed to give the forests a chance to recover. The Convention on International Trade in Endangered Species of Wild Fauna and Flora (CITES) is an international treaty drawn up in 1973 to protect species against overexploitation. Checking the CITES status helps to ensure the suitability of lumber.

Tropical hardwoods share many of the same traits. Several are very durable and can be used outside untreated. They contain natural oils that repel insects and protect the wood from damp. They are strong, and account for some of the hardest and densest timbers of all. The grain is straight, spiralled or interlocked (see page 368). The latter two produce decorative bands of colour throughout the wood, but can also make it tricky to cut, plane and finish.

## COMMERCIAL TYPES AND USES

They fall into groups according to their physical and aesthetic properties: such as hardness, colour or grain pattern.

There are several species of wood that yield very dark heartwood. African ebony (*Diospyros* genus) stands out for its jet-black appearance and superior surface hardness. It is an exceptionally strong and dense wood (one of the few that will sink) that can be polished to a very smooth finish. It is utilized in tool handles, piano keys and other parts of musical instruments. There are many species in the genus, but only a few yield the desirable black heartwood (in particular *D. crassiflora*). This presents a major problem: supplies are severely depleted as a direct result of exploitation. It is now endangered, in some cases critically. It is a similar case for wengé (*Millettia laurentii*) and African blackwood (*Dalbergia melanoxylon*) is not far behind. These trees yield a similarly dense, hard and dark-coloured wood to ebony.

There are sustainable alternatives to ebony. While they may not be as dense or hard, they can be equally beautiful. Dark-coloured walnut (page 348), for example, is available from certified forests and is considerably less expensive. Another interesting alternative is bog oak (see veneer example, page 293). Turned black through a reaction between its own tannins and the peat bogs where it can be found buried, the wood is expensive and hard to find. However, because the tree is already dead, there is no harm in using the timber.

Rosewood (*Dalbergia* genus) represents another significant group of exotic tropical hardwoods. The timber is prized for its density, hardness and very dark red colour. It is popularly used in guitars and furniture. While genuine rosewood comes only from the *Dalbergia* genus, the term 'rosewood' is applied quite liberally to any number of richly hued tropical timbers. The Brazilian and Madagascan varieties (*D. nigra* and *D. maritima* respectively), as well as African blackwood (*D. melanoxylon*, as mentioned above) and cocobolo (*D. retusa*), among others, are near threatened or endangered as a result of illegal logging.

East Indian rosewood (*D. latifolia*), however, is available as plantation-grown lumber. Kingwood (*D. cearensis*) is very dense and hard. It is not considered

**Ebony handle** Ebony is exceptionally hard and dense. The distinctive black heartwood consists of small pores and a fine even texture. It polishes very well and the finish is improved through use. This species is now classified as endangered.

Pink ivory
(*Berchemia zeyheri*)

African padauk
(*Pterocarpus soyauxii*)

Zebrawood
(*Microberlinia
brazzavillensis*)

Ziricote
(*Cordia dodecandra*)

Bocote
(*Cordia alliodora*)

African ebony
(*Diospyros genus*)

endangered, but is typically only available as small blanks and veneer, because the tree itself is quite small.

Padauk (*Pterocarpus* genus) has striking red-coloured heartwood; with age and exposure to sunlight it turns deep maroon. It is very durable and resistant to wear. It is used in cabinetry, carving, knife handles and billiard tables. It is endangered and typically only available as veneer and small turning blanks.

Katalox (*Swartzia* genus) has rich dark brown, nearly black, heartwood. Like rosewood and ebony it has high density and hardness, which makes it tricky to work. It is very strong, especially in compression. It is not listed as endangered, but is still reasonably expensive for a tropical hardwood.

The heartwood of macacauba (*Platymiscium* genus) varies from dark red

to purplish-brown. It is known by many names, including macawood, granadillo, Amazon rosewood and orange agate. It is a versatile timber used in situations from flooring to musical instruments. It is quite expensive, because it is hard to find and certain species are endangered.

Bubinga (*Guibourtia* genus) features richly coloured heartwood with black streaks. It frequently has highly figured grain, such as flamed and quilted. The trees are huge and yield large strong lumber. It has been known to be used as a less expensive alternative to rosewood.

Pink ivory (*Berchemia zeyheri*) is much lighter-coloured than these rich dark woods. It is exceptionally rare and so very expensive. It is used for small items and typically hand-carved. Examples include handles, chessmen and veneer inlay. It is hard, strong, stiff and very durable.

Ziricote (*C. dodecandra*) is a high-density wood that compares favourably with teak; it features a dark-brown heartwood and clearly demarcated yellowish sapwood. It yields a lustrous finish with a distinctive grain pattern (referred to as 'landscaped'). Closely related bocote (*C. alliodora*) is not quite as strong, but it has excellent finishing properties. It is used in furniture making, cabinetry, boat decking and tool handles. They are both utilized in musical instruments and can be quite expensive. Some members of the genus are endangered.

Greenheart (*Ocotea rodiei*) is so called because it has olive-green heartwood with dark streaks running throughout. It is exceptionally stiff and has been known to split violently. To avoid this, sawmills secure the section of the log that has

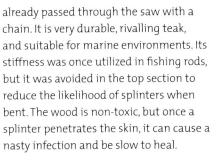

already passed through the saw with a chain. It is very durable, rivalling teak, and suitable for marine environments. Its stiffness was once utilized in fishing rods, but it was avoided in the top section to reduce the likelihood of splinters when bent. The wood is non-toxic, but once a splinter penetrates the skin, it can cause a nasty infection and be slow to heal.

There are sustainable alternatives to these dark-coloured woods that have equally intriguing colour and depth, such as oak (page 342), acacia (page 364) and walnut. Recently, thermally modified timber (TMT), such as ash (page 354) and poplar (page 324), has emerged as an interesting alternative. Once treated, the wood turns a dark chocolate colour; the shade depends on the conditions. It is extremely durable, stable and suitable for use outdoors untreated.

There is a huge diversity of colour and grain pattern. Certain genera have very strong visual character, such as lacewood (*Panopsis* genus), leopardwood (*Roupala* genus) and zebrawood (*Microberlinia* genus). These woods are strong and hard, often with interlocked grain. They are used for small carvings and decorative trim. The patterns are most prominent in quarter-sawn lumber or veneer.

## SUSTAINABILITY

Tropical timber is a valuable commodity. The demand from North America, Asia and Europe for these woods has always outstripped sustainable supply. Using even a small amount of threatened or endangered species contributes to the decline of the rainforests.

One of the main differences between tropical and temperate forests is that

**Rosewood table**
Produced by Arkana circa 1970, this table bases its design on Eero Saarinen's tulip table for Knoll. The top is produced from East India rosewood and the base is die-cast aluminium (page 42) painted white.

the former contain many more species. This biodiversity means that individual species are spread thinly. When a tropical hardwood is in demand, the population is rapidly depleted. By contrast, temperate forests contain higher percentages of single species and can better tolerate industrial harvesting. It is always worth considering which material presents the greatest total benefit for an application.

The dust from many species of tropical hardwood is considered a sensitizer and exposure can lead to health problems. Therefore, it is recommended to wear protective breathing equipment.

# Balsa

**Also known as**
Composite core material trademark names:
Balsaflex, Balsasud, Baltek

Balsa is utilized for its unrivalled low density. It has a porous, sponge-like structure, which once seasoned yields a lumber that is lightweight with good strength-to-weight. It is soft, making it easy to carve and shape. The trees grow tall and fast and are ready to be harvested within five to ten years; the majority now comes from plantations.

| Types | Typical Applications | Sustainability |
|---|---|---|
| • Balsa | • Lightweight core in composite construction (surfboards, wind turbine blades)<br>• Model aeroplanes and toys<br>• Buoyancy | • Available from certified sources<br>• Fast-growing trees<br>• Dust can be a sensitizer |

| Properties | Competing Materials | Costs |
|---|---|---|
| • Density ranges from around 50 to 350 kg/m³ (3–22 lb/ft³) or more<br>• Good strength-to-weight<br>• Straight grain with coarse texture | • Paulownia, poplar, cypress, spruce, pine and fir<br>• Paper, bark and cork<br>• EPS, EPP, EPE and other foamed plastics | • Low per unit volume; high per unit weight<br>• Low-cost to process |

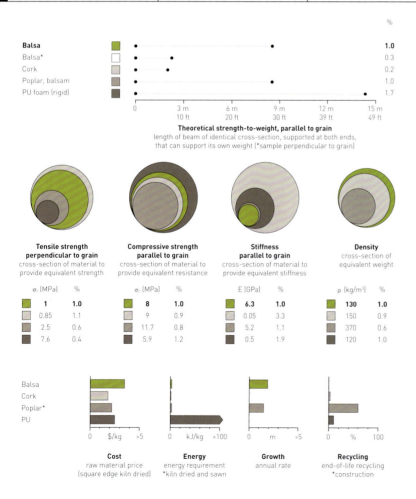

| | % |
|---|---|
| Balsa | 1.0 |
| Balsa* | 0.3 |
| Cork | 0.2 |
| Poplar, balsam | 1.0 |
| PU foam (rigid) | 1.7 |

**Theoretical strength-to-weight, parallel to grain**
length of beam of identical cross-section, supported at both ends, that can support its own weight (*sample perpendicular to grain)

**Tensile strength perpendicular to grain**
cross-section of material to provide equivalent strength

| $\sigma_t$ (MPa) | % |
|---|---|
| 1 | 1.0 |
| 0.85 | 1.1 |
| 2.5 | 0.6 |
| 7.6 | 0.4 |

**Compressive strength parallel to grain**
cross-section of material to provide equivalent resistance

| $\sigma_c$ (MPa) | % |
|---|---|
| 8 | 1.0 |
| 9 | 0.9 |
| 11.7 | 0.8 |
| 5.9 | 1.2 |

**Stiffness parallel to grain**
cross-section of material to provide equivalent stiffness

| E (GPa) | % |
|---|---|
| 6.3 | 1.0 |
| 0.05 | 3.3 |
| 5.2 | 1.1 |
| 0.5 | 1.9 |

**Density**
cross-section of equivalent weight

| $\rho$ (kg/m³) | % |
|---|---|
| 130 | 1.0 |
| 150 | 0.9 |
| 370 | 0.6 |
| 120 | 1.0 |

Balsa
Cork
Poplar*
PU

**Cost**
raw material price (square edge kiln dried)

**Energy**
energy requirement *kiln dried and sawn

**Growth**
annual rate

**Recycling**
end-of-life recycling *construction

## INTRODUCTION

Balsa (*Ochroma pyramidale*) is a tropical tree and so, despite its softness, is classed as a hardwood. It owes its lightness to a microscopic structure of water-filled cells, that when dry become thin-walled pockets of air. It is the sapwood that yields the most useful timber.

## COMMERCIAL TYPES AND USES

Balsa varies considerably in grain and density. Quality is determined by weight. The highest-quality grades, known as 'competition' or 'contest', are classed as ultralight, up to 85 kg/m³ (5 lb/ft³), or light, up to 95 kg/m³ (6 lb/ft³). The most plentiful is medium, which includes light-medium, up to 120 kg/m³ (7.5 lb/ft³), medium, up to 150 kg/m³ (9 lb/ft³), and medium-hard, up to 190 kg/m³ (12 lb/ft³). Above that is classed as hard. As the density increases, so too does the strength, stiffness and hardness.

As with all types of lumber or veneer, the angle it is cut from the log will affect its physical properties. Plain-sawn balsa is known as A-grain. The slice is made parallel to the axis of the tree so the grain runs in long arcs and swirls. It is flexible across its width and prone to warp and cup. This type is ideal for skinning model aircraft, such as around the fuselage or wings. Quarter-sawn sheets are marked C-grain. The cuts radiate out from the centre of the log and so the growth rings are aligned lengthwise in straight lines. It will be stiffer and much more reluctant to bend, even if soaked overnight in water. Randomly sliced wood is known as B-grain.

Balsa is used extensively in model making, in particular for model aircraft. Generally, lighter grades are selected for the parts of the model that will be put under the least stress, such as nose, wingtip and skin. Heavier grades are required for structural parts, such as the fuselage, stringers and wing spars.

Similar to plastic foam – see polyurethane (PU) (page 202), polystyrene (PS) (page 132), polypropylene (PP) (page 98) and polyethylene (PE) (page 108) – balsa is utilized as a core in composite lay-ups. Panels are fabricated from end-grain blocks (so the grain runs perpendicular to the plane of the skins) and provide very good strength- and stiffness-to-weight. The blocks may be mounted onto a flexible backing, allowing the panel to conform to simple curves. One of the downsides of using wood is that it is susceptible to moisture and will rot if not well surrounded with resin. Applications include composite boat hulls, boards, skis and wind turbine blades.

Like cork (page 286), its low density is useful in situations that require buoyancy. Examples range from surfboards to fishing floats and lures.

Balsa is the lightest of all the woods, but is not always the most practical. Alternatives include paulownia (*Paulownia tomentosa*), 280 kg/m³ (17.5 lb/ft³), balsam poplar (page 324), 370 kg/m³ (23 lb/ft³) and western red-cedar (see Cypress Family, page 318), 380 kg/m³ (24 lb/ft³).

## SUSTAINABILITY
Although balsa still grows plentifully in the wild, the majority of timber is derived from plantation-grown trees from Ecuador. It is available from certified sources.

**Hollow balsa surfboard**
Produced by Yana Surf of Lake Oswego, Oregon, this board is constructed from solid balsa skinned with high-strength glass-fibre-reinforced epoxy (GFRP) (page 236). Before PU foam cores became readily available in the 1960s, surfboards were built from wood. However, it was not until the invention of GFRP that entire surfboards could be produced from balsa. Yana Surf starts by gluing together long lengths of 'competition grade' balsa. The board is roughly shaped by hand. It is then cut and chambered (hollowed out to reduce weight). The board is reassembled, the shape is finished, and it is covered with GFRP. The decals are printed on translucent rice paper and embedded in the coating, so they become a structural part of the design. Photo courtesy of Yana Surf.

# PLANT

**4**

# Rattan

Rattan is a fast-growing climbing palm that can comfortably reach up to 100 m (328 ft) in length. The solid-core stem is converted into reed and the bark into cane, both of which are utilized in furniture, basketry and handicrafts. It is found throughout the tropic regions of Asia and Africa, and provides a valuable source of income to many rural communities.

| Types | Typical Applications | Sustainability |
|---|---|---|
| • Most common commercial types include manau and sega | • Basketry, mats and upholstery<br>• Traps and parcels<br>• Construction and shelter | • Derived from tropical forests; the majority is harvested from the wild<br>• Provides a valuable source of income for rural communities |

| Properties | Competing Materials | Costs |
|---|---|---|
| • Long semi-flexible core<br>• Not durable and vulnerable to insect attack<br>• Defects include discoloration and insect pinholes | • Paper<br>• Willow, poplar, bamboo, grass, rush and sedge<br>• Strips of plastic, such as PE, PP and PVC | • Low-cost raw material<br>• Labour-intensive to process |

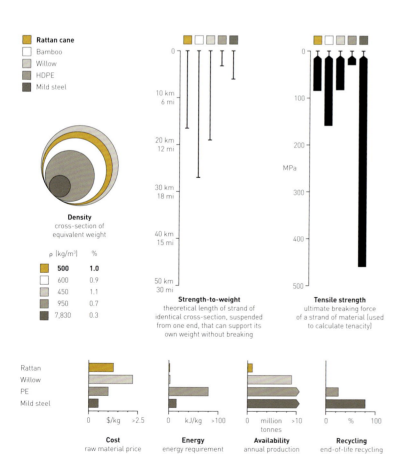

Rattan cane
Bamboo
Willow
HDPE
Mild steel

**Density**
cross-section of equivalent weight

| ρ (kg/m³) | % |
|---|---|
| 500 | 1.0 |
| 600 | 0.9 |
| 450 | 1.1 |
| 950 | 0.7 |
| 7,830 | 0.3 |

**Strength-to-weight**
theoretical length of strand of identical cross-section, suspended from one end, that can support its own weight without breaking

**Tensile strength**
ultimate breaking force of a strand of material (used to calculate tenacity)

**Cost**
raw material price

**Energy**
energy requirement

**Availability**
annual production

**Recycling**
end-of-life recycling

## INTRODUCTION

Cane furniture is defined by the unique qualities of rattan. In Southeast Asia it represents the most important non-wood forest product (NWFP). For a time, the export of raw material was banned in many countries to increase the value of the material and protect wild stocks (theoretically).

As a result of erratic supply and inevitable variability of the raw material a range of alternatives has emerged. In the early 20th century Lloyd Loom furniture was launched in the USA and the UK, using a version in which kraft paper (page 268) was twisted round a metal wire. Promoted as superior to rattan, it remains in production to this day. Several plastics are manufactured to mimic rattan. The most common is polyethylene (PE) (page 108). Primarily used for outdoor furniture, it provides superior weather resistance (although it is vulnerable to ultraviolet) and is resistant to insects and moisture.

Rattan is similar to bamboo (page 386), except the stems are solid. Measuring up to 30 mm (1.2 in) in diameter, with long internodes (distance between the nodes), they can grow to more than 100 m (328 ft) long. Akin to willow (page 328), birch bark (page 280) and other traditional basketry materials, rattan weaving mixes utility with expression. When produced by hand, beautifully complex patterns are possible.

## COMMERCIAL TYPES AND USES

These are climbing vines that belong to the palm family (Palmae or Arecaceae). Rattan is a generic name for several hundred species in the subfamily Calameae. They are spread over 13 genera, but most commercial rattan is derived from only a handful of types. The largest and most popular is *Calamus* genus, in particular manau (*C. manau*) and sega (*C. caesius*). These species yield the familiar

light yellow cane with a lustrous surface. The reed is a uniform off-white with a clean-looking appearance. Bleaching improves whiteness.

Once harvested, rattan is stripped of its spiny sheaths, whips and leaves. Beneath this defensive outer layer lies the peel, or bark. It is separated from the woody core and cut into strips. Known as cane, it is utilized in basketry, upholstery and windings (such as handles). Such is the popularity of woven cane that large sheets are machine-woven according to standard patterns, such as plain, twill, herringbone, star or octagonal.

They are, in some cases, woven to mimic painstaking manual techniques that are rarely practised these days.

Woven cane yields a relatively low-profile surface. It is stronger and harder than the core, with a lustrous surface. Typically left uncoated, it will gradually turn darker over time and with exposure to ultraviolet.

The core is converted into strands, called reed. Nowadays, this is the most commonly used part of the rattan. The diameter (gauge) ranges from around 1 mm (0.04 in) to over 15 mm (0.6 in). Round reed yields a highly textured

**Curved upholstery**
Omi Tahara designed the Wrap sofa for Yamakawa Rattan, a Japanese company whose factory is located in Ciberon, Indonesia, from where the majority of rattan products are derived. The combination of materials produces a light-looking structure with a comfortable suppleness. In total, 1.2 km (0.75 mi) of rattan strands are hand-woven and held taut over a steel framework. Split reed was selected for its light and uniform colour. It is coated with clear lacquer for added protection. Photo by Lorenzo Nencioni.

**Opposite**
**Lightweight basket**
A traditional item from Borneo, this Anjat basket – a version of a backpack – is hand-woven with a mix of plain and dyed cane. The black colour comes from soaking and boiling the rattan fibres with plants and other natural dye-bearing ingredients. The natural-coloured cane is gradually darkening with age. The processes involved are labour-intensive and can take days, depending on the complexity of the design.

**Right**
**Cheese-making basket** Kalathaki, which translates as 'little basket', is a soft sheep's cheese from Limnos, Greece. The distinctive surface patterning comes from the basket in which it is produced. This example is woven from reed rattan around a steam-bent top and bottom. The straight reeds are reinforced with grass that has been twisted and woven to create an interlocked structure.

**Transverse cross-section through rattan**
Rattan is a natural composite and, similar to bamboo, is made up of polysaccharides (cellulose and hemicellulose), lignin and starch, among other ingredients. The outer layer is made up of epidermis and cortex. In some species it is clearly demarcated, while in others it is not so clearly defined. The inner core consists of fibrous sheaths packed around vascular bundles. It is softer and lighter than the smooth outer bark. Density increases with age and is greater towards the outside edge, which improves strength. Thus, the base of the stem will be stronger than the tip. Older stems have a thicker layer of fibre around the outside, which provides superior working properties. During processing, the stem and bark are often separated. The bark is slit into thin strands of cane and the inner core is cut to make reed.

surface when woven. Alternatively, it is sliced into strips and processed into flat, semi-oval, oval or semi-round strands.

A versatile material, it is used in a variety of woven applications, such as upholstery and baskets. In preparation for weaving, it is soaked in water to improve flexibility. It is porous and absorbent, which makes it much more suitable for painting or staining than cane.

Smaller stems (sticks) are derived from the whips or spines or are the stems of young rattans. They are dried in the sun, or smoked with sulphur (to sterilize the wood and improve surface properties). Thicker stems (poles) intended for sturdier applications, such as furniture making, are boiled in oil to increase the long-term durability of the wood.

Many different formats of rattan may be used on the same item. For example, furniture is constructed with steam-bent rattan poles stayed with smaller sticks. It is relatively easy to bend and will conform to curves as little as three times material thickness. Strong and slim strands of cane are wrapped around the joints to hold the structure together. Reed is a uniform colour, which is useful for large areas of woven material, such as upholstery and tabletops.

## SUSTAINABILITY
Rattans are either single-stemmed or multi-stemmed. While the former can only be harvested once, the latter provides a renewable supply of material. Southeast Asian countries are the biggest producers. Here, rattan provides an alternative to logging vulnerable and endangered timber. However, it is also threatened with overexploitation in some regions and wild rattan population is on the decline.

The high starch content means it is vulnerable to insect and fungi attack. Fungi stain the rattan, causing it to discolour. This can happen almost immediately after harvest and render the rattan useless for furniture (owing to reduced strength). To hide the defect, it is stained a dark colour. To prevent infestation from insects, poles are treated with insecticide. Of course, this has environmental consequences.

# Bamboo

Bamboo is exceptionally versatile and provides many valuable materials, from food to construction lumber. It is harvested at various stages of development, depending on the end use. It is fast-growing and provides a valuable economic resource for many small communities. The wood is lightweight and easy to transport, and processing does not require highly skilled labour.

| Types | Typical Applications | Sustainability |
|---|---|---|
| • Principal genera: *Phyllostachys, Dendrocalamus, Bambusa, Oxytenanthera, Chusquea* and *Guadua* | • Construction, furniture, sports equipment and utensils<br>• Pulped to make paper and semi-synthetic fibres (viscose) | • As a wood substitute bamboo reduces the pressure on forests<br>• Valuable resource for small communities<br>• Widespread availability |
| **Properties** | **Competing Materials** | **Costs** |
| • High strength-to-weight<br>• Vulnerable to fungi and insect attack<br>• Pale yellow to almost white wood with a tough outer skin whose colour varies | • All types of wood and rattan<br>• Engineering plastics, steel and concrete<br>• Synthetic and natural fibres | • Low-cost raw material<br>• A large amount of processing is needed, but does not require highly skilled labour |

386

## INTRODUCTION

Since ancient times, the opportunities of bamboo were well known in the Far East. Over the last few decades it has emerged as a valuable, and sometimes superior, alternative to wood throughout the rest of the world. It is exceptionally versatile and, like wood, can be cut down and used as it is, or converted into engineered timber (page 296), veneer (page 290), pulp, paper (page 268), charcoal and even viscose (page 252).

Bamboo is classified as a subdivision (Bambusoideae) of the grass family (Poaceae) (page 392), although as a resource, it is typically discussed with wood products. It forms an integral part of forestry and agriculture across Africa, Asia and Central and South America. There are vast growing stocks and, along with rattan (page 382), it is considered a major non-wood forest product (NWFP).

Bamboo has impressive strength-to-weight parallel to grain. Comparable with hickory (page 352), it outperforms most other woods and offers considerable weight savings compared to concrete (page 496) and steel (page 28).

However, bamboo is a natural material and there is inevitable variation in the mechanical performance. So while the physical properties of steel and concrete are well known and documented, the properties of bamboo depend on many factors, including type, direction of grain, age and height. Importantly, the density, strength and stiffness of bamboo increases with age and the optimum point to harvest is at around five years

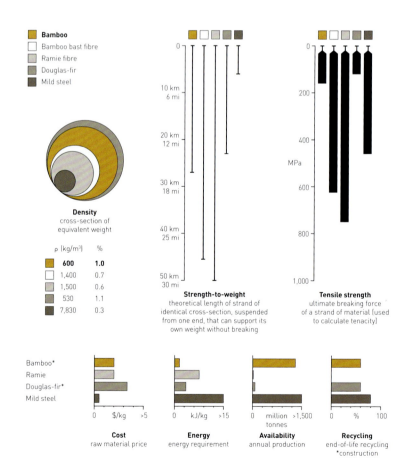

**Bamboo**
□ Bamboo bast fibre
▨ Ramie fibre
▨ Douglas-fir
▨ Mild steel

**Density**
cross-section of
equivalent weight

| ρ (kg/m³) | % |
|---|---|
| **600** | **1.0** |
| 1,400 | 0.7 |
| 1,500 | 0.6 |
| 530 | 1.1 |
| 7,830 | 0.3 |

**Strength-to-weight**
theoretical length of strand of
identical cross-section, suspended
from one end, that can support its
own weight without breaking

10 km / 6 mi
20 km / 12 mi
30 km / 18 mi
40 km / 25 mi
50 km / 30 mi

**Tensile strength**
ultimate breaking force
of a strand of material (used
to calculate tenacity)

MPa

Bamboo*
Ramie
Douglas-fir*
Mild steel

**Cost**
raw material price
0 — $/kg — >5

**Energy**
energy requirement
0 — kJ/kg — >15

**Availability**
annual production
0 — million tonnes — >1,500

**Recycling**
end-of-life recycling
0 — % — 100
*construction

**Kitchen utensil**
Designed by Stig Ahlstrom for Design House Stockholm, Sweden, these tongs double up as chopsticks. Cut from solid bamboo and held together with a stainless steel ring, they are nice and quiet to use and will not damage delicate cooking surfaces.

old. In structural situations, wood and bamboo must be engineered so that the allowable stress is far below the failure stress to allow for these inconsistencies. By contrast, predictable materials, such as steel, concrete and engineered timber, can be designed to perform much closer to their 'known' failure stress.

## COMMERCIAL TYPES AND USES

The species of bamboo and where it originates from are important, because transporting culms (poles) around the world consumes a great deal of energy unnecessarily. Compared to timber, unprocessed culms require considerably more space, making them less practical to handle and store. Of course, this is not the case for chipped or engineered bamboo.

There are nearly 100 genera of bamboo and more than 1,000 species. They are broadly divided into herbaceous bamboos and woody species. Of the several woody bamboos, a few genera stand out. These include *Phyllostachys*, *Bambusa*, *Dendrocalamus*, *Gigantochloa*, *Oxytenanthera*, *Chusquea* and *Guadua*.

*Phyllostachys* is a genus of Asian bamboo that grows to around 30 m (98 ft). It is perhaps the best-known bamboo, and is popularly referred to by its Japanese name 'moso'. It is stiff and strong with a fine grain, which yields a high-quality wood. Its hardness is comparable with red oak (page 342). As a result of these desirable properties, it is used in a range of construction, door frames, flooring, furniture and utensils; most of the bamboo products imported to Europe and North America from China are produced from this genus. The young shoots are edible and provide a valuable

food source. While the majority of these species are very stiff, *P. bambusoides* is flexible enough to be suitable for basketry.

*Bambusa* is a widespread genus that can be found from South America to Australia. It is commonly used to make paper. While certain species are suitable for structural applications, it has a high starch content, which makes it vulnerable to decay. *B. oldhamii*, also known as giant timber, is known for its long olive-green culms. *B. textilis*, or weaver's bamboo, is so called because it offers a choice basketry material that is strong, yet pliable and absent of prominent nodes.

*Dendrocalamus* is another Asian genus that provides timber and edible shoots. Asper (*D. asper*) and Latiflorus (*D. latiflorus*) are good for heavy construction such as houses and bridges. They are also utilized in engineered timber, flooring, furniture and utensils. Black asper (*D. asper f. niger*), also known as Hitam, has a tough black outer layer with lighter bands of colour circling the nodes.

*Gigantochloa atroviolacea*, also known as Java black or tropical black bamboo, yields purplish-black culms. Like the black asper, it is only the outer layer that is dark; the woody core is a tan colour. It is not suitable for structural situations, but is popular for decorative applications, such as musical instruments and furniture.

*Oxytenanthera* is a genus that is distributed across tropical Africa. It grows with a particularly thick-walled culm and can be harvested after only three or four years. *O. abyssinica*, known as lowland or savannah bamboo, is used for a wide range of applications, from construction to basketry. Young stems and seeds are edible and the sap is used to make

beverages. Its efficient growth yields high-quality charcoal, a valuable source of fuel.

*Chusquea* and *Guadua* from Central and South America can grow to be very tall, and yield a high-quality timber. They are becoming more widely available and provide a viable alternative to moso for certain situations. The wood of *Guadua* is very strong with a coarse grain. It is stiffer than moso and provides a superior structural material. However, it is not as hard and so not as suitable for applications vulnerable to denting and scuffing, such as flooring and doorframes.

## SUSTAINABILITY

The majority of bamboo products come from China, where it has been exploited as a practical material since Neolithic times. Millions of people depend economically on bamboo. Its value to individuals and smallholders is unrivalled among the structural materials. It also plays a role in helping to reduce climate change and in carbon sequestration.

As a wood substitute, bamboo reduces the pressure on naturally regenerated

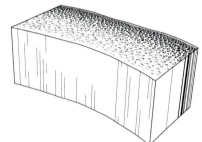

**Transverse cross-section through bamboo culm** Like wood, bamboo is a natural composite made up of polysaccharides (cellulose and hemicellulose) and lignin. Cellulose forms strong linearly oriented fibrils (slender fibres), which have a higher length-to-width ratio than typically found in wood. A lignin-hemicellulose matrix holds them together as hollow prismatic cells. The structure of bamboo is more complex than wood and similar in nature to bone (page 442): the fibres are packed together in honeycomb-like cells, with increasing density towards the outside of the stem, which optimizes flexural strength and rigidity. A tube is far more efficient than a solid rod, because the closer the material is to the centre, the less flexural strength it can provide. This is bamboo's solution for growing very fast but remaining lightweight. The inclusion of nodes, which form bulkheads along the stem, helps to prevent it buckling.

## ARCHITECTURE AND CONSTRUCTION

**High strength-to-weight**
It has impressive strength-to-weight, comfortably outperforming most woods. Parallel to grain, it is in the region of 400–500% stronger than mild steel for the same weight. Of course, steel is stronger per unit volume, but has far higher density.

**Locally available**
Bamboo grows vigorously in tropical climates and it is even possible to cultivate it in temperate regions. Reducing the shipping required helps to maintain low embodied energy. However, the processing is labour-intensive and so it is often cheapest when purchased from China or India even if it is subsequently shipped around the world.

**Low cost**
The raw material costs are low and around half that of popular woods such as oak and Douglas-fir (page 314). However, prices for engineered bamboo can be much higher, often exceeding the cost of these woods.

### Modular construction

The innovative Blooming Bamboo home (BB home), by H&P Architects in Vietnam, is intended to provide affordable, flood-proof housing. Using locally available materials and building know-how, the vernacular design can be erected by the homeowner within a matter of weeks at a cost of US$2,500. Tightly packed rows of bamboo poles are used in the walls, floors and roof (right). The walls and roof are propped open for ventilation (top). The outside is finished according to the local climate and will look different depending on the available materials – poles, bamboo wattle, fibreboard, coconut leaf and so on – in order to help it sit comfortably within its surroundings. Photos courtesy of H&P Architects.

forests. It grows extremely fast and can reach full height within a single year. After that, the stem begins to harden and will improve with age until it begins to decay. Very little energy is required to convert the raw culm into a usable material. If the culm is cut up and processed into engineered timber then it will contain adhesive, which increases the embodied energy and associated negative environmental impacts.

It grows naturally on the forest floor, but an increasing proportion is cultivated

on agricultural land. One of the major advantages of bamboo is that it is suitable for marginal land that cannot support crops. However, it is not immune to overexploitation and some species have become vulnerable or even endangered as a result of intensive harvesting. Additionally, forests are in some cases being cleared to make way for more profitable bamboo plantation, which has a negative impact on biodiversity.

## BAMBOO IN ARCHITECTURE AND CONSTRUCTION

Bamboo is used in a variety of formats in architecture. The culms are cut and used without further processing, such as for scaffolding, bridges and houses. Alternatively, the culm is cut into smaller pieces and converted into engineered timber, also known as structural bamboo products (SBP). Similar to spruce, pine and fir (page 304), it is mixed with high-strength adhesive (see Formaldehyde, page 224) and formed into panels and lumber for a range of applications.

One of the major challenges is the lack of standardization and huge variability in mechanical properties. There are many different species and each matures at a slightly different rate. Add to this the radial density gradient (bamboo is stronger towards the outside of the culm), and it becomes very difficult to predict how bamboo will perform in application.

Bamboo is perishable and will last only two or three years outdoors without suitable treatment. In addition, the starch content provides a food source for insects and makes it vulnerable to fungi. To counter this problem, bamboo is impregnated with preservative.

It is currently being explored as fibre reinforcement for resin, which could then be used to strengthen concrete (page 496). This would offer an alternative to conventional steel reinforcement.

**Steamer basket** This humble cooking utensil has been in use in China for centuries, if not millennia, and has remained virtually unchanged. Even since the development of cooking utensils in a range of modern materials, the bamboo steamer remains omnipresent throughout Asia and has been adopted the world over.

## PRODUCTS, FURNITURE AND LIGHTING

**Versatility**
Bamboo is available in a wide range of formats, from unprocessed culms to engineered timber. This maximizes the range of possible applications, which may be beneficial for both aesthetic and economic reasons.

**High strength**
Bamboo has excellent strength-to-weight in line with grain. This is particularly advantageous for situations where lightness is of greater importance than slenderness.

**Availability**
Grown throughout the world, bamboo is widely available as a low-cost raw material.

Considering its superior strength-to-weight, bamboo has the potential to revolutionize the concrete building sector. Bamboo is not without its drawbacks and work is under way to produce a cost-effective, stable and predictable material suitable for large-scale application.

## BAMBOO IN PRODUCTS, FURNITURE AND LIGHTING

Small products are cut directly from the culm. Larger pieces are produced from long lengths of culm or smaller pieces converted into SBP. In some ways it is similar to working with wood: it is anisotropic and stronger parallel to grain; it is prone to tear-out when cut across the grain; and it shrinks as it dries (more so than most woods). However, that is where the similarities end.

Bamboo is tubular, not solid, and the density varies throughout its thickness, increasing towards the outside edge. Over the years, techniques have evolved to make the most of its inherent strength, as opposed to treating it like solid wood.

The culms may be bent in a number of ways. When green (freshly cut) they can be bent using heat, such as with a blowtorch. To prevent it from breaking, the nodes may be perforated and the internodes filled with sand. This stops the tube collapsing. Bent around a former, the shape is set once they have fully dried.

Once dry, the poles may be bent, but will need to be permanently fixed in place. Alternatively, V-shaped notches are cut from the inside edge about two-thirds of the way through (see also kerfing, page 336). The remaining stem will bend more easily, allowing tight curves to be formed.

Split bamboo is utilized in basket making. The Chinese in particular have a long history with this material and still use it to make a range of practical items, from hats, storage and cooking utensils to fishing traps. Flexible bamboo with long internodes (length of culm between each node) is generally preferred. Its use overlaps with other common basketry materials, such as rattan, willow (page 328) and bark (page 280). As with these materials, the techniques used in bamboo basketry depend on country and region.

As well as the 'rigid' textiles used in basketry, bamboo is converted into 'soft' fibres for use in fashion and technical textiles. Bast fibres are extracted from the culms by separating them from the rigid lignin-hemicellulose matrix. They provide a material similar in nature to hemp (page 406), jute (page 404) and the other bast fibres. It is very difficult to come by as a raw fibre and not particularly cheap.

A much more cost-effective method is to grind up bamboo and use it as the raw material in the production of semi-synthetic fibre, namely viscose and cellulose acetate (page 252). However, in this case, the end result will be no different from fibres produced from other cellulose-yielding feedstock, such as wood and cotton (page 410).

In Indian and China, bamboo provides one of the main raw materials used in the production of paper. An advantage of bamboo is that the fibres have a higher length-to-width ratio than typically found in wood. This provides added strength and flexibility. It can be processed using much the same equipment as wood, so several manufactures have begun using the plant as a raw material alongside conventional raw materials such as spruce and birch (page 334). Also called tree-free or non-wood paper, a broad range of papers can be made from bamboo pulp.

# Grass, Rush and Sedge

**Also known as**
Bulrush: reedmace and cattail
Sedge: bulrush (some species)
Seagrass: Indonesian rush

Ranging from the use of sedge in ancient Egyptian writing materials (papyrus) through to modern Japanese rush floor coverings (tatami); the stems and leaves of these plants provide a valuable raw material for many practical applications. They are woven as they were harvested, or chemically and mechanically processed to extract the individual fibres.

| Types | Typical Applications | Sustainability |
|---|---|---|
| • Grass; seagrass, rush; bulrush; and sedge | • Upholstery, basketry, matting and thatching<br>• Hats and shoes<br>• Shelter and cordage | • Broad distribution<br>• Fast-growing and renewable<br>• Many are available as an agricultural by-product |

| Properties | Competing Materials | Costs |
|---|---|---|
| • High-strength along their length<br>• Variegated colouring<br>• Become brittle over time | • Bamboo, rattan, willow, poplar and bark<br>• Paper<br>• Strips of plastic, such as PE, PP and PVC | • Low-cost raw materials<br>• While some types require very little preparation, others are labour-intensive to convert into workable material |

392

## INTRODUCTION

These monocot flowering plants played an important role in the development of modern civilization. They have provided raw materials in the production of food and beer for millennia, and are of enormous economic significance. The stems and leaves are strong and flexible. As well as being converted into woven goods, the fibrous content is utilized in the manufacture of paper (page 268), particleboard (see Engineering Timber, page 296) and plastic composites.

These are cellulosic materials containing lignin and other resinous substances. The hollow stem is not very strong, but is very light as a result of its tubular construction. Depending on the species, it may be cylindrical, triangular or crescent-shaped. The properties vary along its length, which limits how much of the stem is usable.

Available throughout the temperate and tropical regions of the world, these plants do not need much processing to make them usable, and many can be applied straight from harvest. However, applying them requires skill and experience. They have mostly been superseded by plastics – which have become the go-to low-cost and ubiquitous material that these natural fibres once were – but remain a valuable material for niche applications.

Kraft paper (page 268), twisted to increase strength and bulk, closely resembles rush (family Juncaceae), bulrush (family Typhaceae) or raffia (see Leaf Fibres, page 394). It is sometimes called fibre rush or Danish cord. The colour is uniform and, unlike natural fibre, it will not change over time. Reasonably inexpensive, it is suitable for both manual and machine-weaving techniques and is used in many of the same situations as twisted rushes.

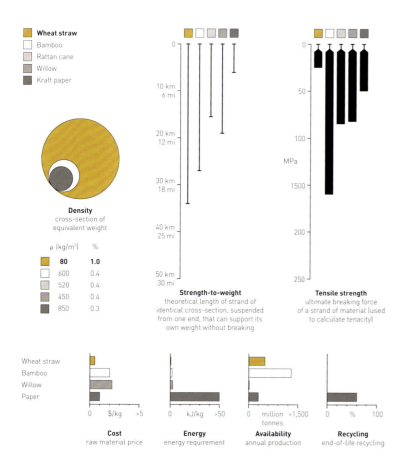

**Wheat straw**
Bamboo
Rattan cane
Willow
Kraft paper

**Density**
cross-section of
equivalent weight

| ρ (kg/m³) | % |
|---|---|
| **80** | **1.0** |
| 600 | 0.4 |
| 520 | 0.4 |
| 450 | 0.4 |
| 850 | 0.3 |

10 km
6 mi

20 km
12 mi

30 km
18 mi

40 km
25 mi

50 km
30 mi

**Strength-to-weight**
theoretical length of strand of
identical cross-section, suspended
from one end, that can support its
own weight without breaking

0

50

100

MPa

1500

200

250

**Tensile strength**
ultimate breaking force
of a strand of material (used
to calculate tenacity)

Wheat straw
Bamboo
Willow
Paper

0    $/kg    >5
**Cost**
raw material price

0    kJ/kg    >50
**Energy**
energy requirement

0    million    >1,500
tonnes
**Availability**
annual production

0    %    100
**Recycling**
end-of-life recycling

## COMMERCIAL TYPES AND USES

The grass family (Poaceae) consists of thousands of species of flowering plants, including the subfamily bamboo (Bambusoideae) (page 386). It is one of the most abundant groups of plants and is widely distributed.

The stems are hollow except for the leaf-bearing nodes, which create bulkheads at regular intervals. Strong fibres run the length of the stem, which help to keep the grass upright as it grows. They are cut and woven green, or dried to make straw. It remains a popular choice for milliners and is sold as straw or sennit (this may also be made from hemp [page 406] or similar fibrous material). Applications range from formal styles (such as the straw boater, known as the can-can in Japan) to practical conical hats (such as worn by farmers throughout Southeast Asia).

Like rattan (page 382) and willow (page 328), they are coiled, plaited, woven and knitted into basket structures. Multiple strands are often twisted together to make them easier to handle and quicker to assemble.

While rush (family Juncaceae), bulrush (family Typhaceae) and sedge (family Cyperaceae) are commonly referred to as grasses, they are in different families. These flowering plants are found in wetlands, although sedge can grow almost anywhere. Seagrass (family Posidoniaceae and Zosteraceae, among others) is in a different order (Alismatales) and is found in salty water.

These plants are applied in much the same way as grass, with techniques evolving around specific species, depending on location and need. For example, seagrasses and rushes are used in woven chair seats and floor coverings.

**Diagonal cross pattern weave** This footstool was created by Catalan designer Guillem Ferrán and is manufactured by Casa Constante, Spain. It is a contemporary design that makes use of techniques that have been practised for generations. Bulrush is twisted into cord and woven in a diagonal cross directly onto the sturdy pine frame. Photo courtesy of Guillem Ferrán.

And the fibrous inner pith of sedge is used to make papyrus paper, evidence of which dates back to the ancient Egyptians.

## SUSTAINABILITY

The stems may be available as agricultural residue. If they are harvested from the wild, care is required to ensure that they are sourced in a sustainable fashion. While many species are perennial and can tolerate being cut – they grow from the base, not the tip – others are not so enduring.

# Leaf Fibres

**Also known as**
Abaca: manila hemp, sinamay
Sisal: New Zealand flax, henequen, yucatan, parasisal
Panama: paja toquilla
Weaving materials generically referred to as: sennit, wicker, straw

These fibres are derived from a handful of tropical plants. Extracting them from leaves is laborious and, as a result, some of the finer types are hard to come by and expensive. Knowledge about these materials resides with skilled artisans in small communities who continue to make traditional items, from the famous panama hat to intricately figured piña garments.

| Types | Typical Applications | Sustainability |
|---|---|---|
| • Piña (pineapple); sisal (and henequen); abaca; and panama | • Fashion fabrics and technical textiles<br>• Upholstery, carpets and matting<br>• Basketry and packaging | • Provide a valuable source of income to rural communities<br>• Pesticides and fertilizers often used<br>• Renewable |

| Properties | Competing Materials | Costs |
|---|---|---|
| • Strong and resilient<br>• Good resistance to tearing<br>• Long fibres ranging from off-white to almost black | • Man-made fibres, such as viscose, acrylic and polyester<br>• Silk, cotton and wool<br>• Grass, rush, sedge and coir | • Low to high raw material cost, depending on the quality and type<br>• Extraction is labour-intensive, making the highest-quality fibres very expensive |

## INTRODUCTION

These are important historical fibres that have been employed by generations of weavers throughout the tropics. In addition to continuing as a principal fibre in traditional items, they are being explored as fibre reinforcement in modern composites.

Similar to bast and cotton (page 410), leaf fibres are cellulosic. Their role in nature is structural: they are strong and stiff as a result of having to keep the plant upright. The fibres used to make yarn consist of multiple individual strands of cellulose wrapped together in bundles. They are stripped from the leaf by hand or machine, cooked and dried to ensure a high-quality and rot-resistant fibre.

## COMMERCIAL TYPES AND USES

Different leaf fibres have surprisingly contrasting properties, which affect the areas of application. The quality depends on the species and method of extraction: manual methods yield superior-quality fibre, but are much more expensive.

Sisal is a succulent plant from the same family (Agavaceae) as that used to make tequila. Many different species yield a hardy fibre – including New Zealand flax (*Phormium tenax*) and henequen (*Agave fourcroydes*) – but the most common commercial crop is *Agave sisalana*. Sisal is the most widely used of leaf fibres, but

**Panama hat** The Montecristi Panama hat, famous for its suppleness, comes from Ecuador. They were brought by merchants to Panama and from there shipped around the world. Their unique quality is the result of careful material selection, painstaking preparation and intricate handwork. The finest hats are produced with fibres that are split to reduce their diameter and thus produce a smoother texture. Weaving takes several days, after which the hat is beaten to make it supple. The final shape, such as the fedora (pictured), is produced by blocking.

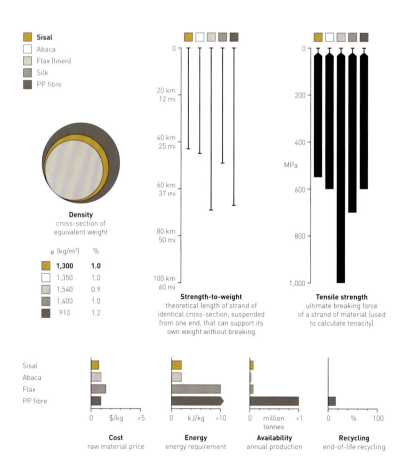

**Legend:**
- Sisal
- Abaca
- Flax (linen)
- Silk
- PP fibre

**Density**
cross-section of equivalent weight

| ρ (kg/m³) | % |
|---|---|
| 1,300 | 1.0 |
| 1,350 | 1.0 |
| 1,540 | 0.9 |
| 1,400 | 1.0 |
| 910 | 1.2 |

**Strength-to-weight**
theoretical length of strand of identical cross-section, suspended from one end, that can support its own weight without breaking

20 km / 12 mi
40 km / 25 mi
60 km / 37 mi
80 km / 50 mi
100 km / 60 mi

**Tensile strength**
ultimate breaking force of a strand of material (used to calculate tenacity)

MPa: 0, 200, 400, 600, 800, 1,000

**Cost**
raw material price
0 — $/kg — >5

**Energy**
energy requirement
0 — kJ/kg — >10

**Availability**
annual production
0 — million tonnes — >1

**Recycling**
end-of-life recycling
0 — % — 100

(Sisal, Abaca, Flax, PP fibre)

still makes up only around 0.1% of natural fibre production.

The Maori were the first to exploit New Zealand flax, to make rope, twine, fishing nets, baskets and outerwear. Even though the plant is known as 'flax' in New Zealand it is nothing like the flax used to make linen (page 400). Mexico remains the only significant commercial source of henequen. *A. sisalana* is also native to Mexico, but is widely cultivated in many other countries.

These are fast-growing plants and harvesting can begin after a couple of years or so. The leaves grow to around 1.5 m (5 ft) long and yield strong fibres typically 0.6–1.2 m (2–4 ft) long. They are variegated off-white to light yellow and used in their natural colour or dyed. It remains productive for around a decade, having produced hundreds of leaves, at which point it flowers and dies.

Sisal is a hardy, utilitarian fibre. Originally, the sharp leaf tip was cut

from the plant with fibre intact and used like a needle and thread. Its long fibres are converted into rope, cord and twine, which are further processed into carpets, matting, baskets and bags. Shorter fibres are utilized in papermaking (page 268). It is resistant to seawater and so suitable for use in marine environments. In many cases, sisal has been replaced with polypropylene (PP) (page 98), which is equally strong, but lighter, more consistent and straightforward to process.

Abaca comes from the plant (*Musa textilis*) of the same name, of the family Musaceae. It is fast-growing: the plant reaches maturity after 18 months to two years and can be harvested every four months or so. The strong fibre is derived from the plant's petioles (leaf sheaths around the stem), as opposed to the flat banana-like leaf canopy. Colour ranges from dark brown to red to off-white, depending on the species and position of the petiole in the stem.

**Nonwoven pineapple fibre** This new textile, known by the trademark name Piñatex, is produced from waste leaves from the pineapple industry. Conceived by Spanish designer and entrepreneur Carmen Hijosa, it is being developed by Ananas Anam, a company she founded to bring the material to market.

After several years of research a strong and breathable fabric was produced. With treatment, the material can closely resemble leather and is available in different thicknesses. These prototypes include a shoe by Camper and designs by SmithMatthias and Carmen Hijosa. Photo courtesy of Ananas Anam.

The majority of fibre, also known as manila hemp (although it is not related to true hemp, page 406), comes from the Philippines. It can be up to 3 m (10 ft) long, depending on the method of extraction, and is strong like sisal. Traditionally, it was used in ship's rigging and strong paper (sometimes known as manila paper). Most still goes into paper production, ranging from bank notes to tea bags.

Piña fibre comes from the leaves of the pineapple plant (*Ananas comosus*), in particular the Red Spanish variety. It was named during the Spanish rule of the Philippines, when the pineapple was introduced there, and hence why both the fibre and the textile are known as piña (Spanish for pineapple). Its quality and surface lustre are comparable with silk (page 420). It is naturally ivory-white and can be dyed a range of colours.

It is very expensive as a result of the laborious processing involved, and only a small number of weavers still work with the material. This limits its use to very high-quality woven fabrics such as used to make decorative items, including tablecloths, handkerchiefs and ceremonial garments (wedding dresses, for example).

The fibre used to produce the very finest panama hats is derived from a palm-like monocot, named the panama hat plant (*Carludovica palmata*). The fibres come from the central leaf spikes, which can be up to 1 m (3.3 ft) long. The plant comes from Ecuador and the hat-making process – from fibre extraction to weaving to blocking – is laborious and exceptionally skilful, which is why the finest hats are so incredibly expensive.

## SUSTAINABILITY

Leaf fibres are very low-impact when used locally – production requires very little energy, especially because so much is done by hand. When exported, they provide a valuable source of income for rural communities. Colour ranges from off-white to almost black, so different colours and patterns are achievable without dye (anyway, several of the fibres

**Piña lace dress** This cocktail dress by Oliver Tolentino makes the most of piña's unique properties; the floral pattern is hand-embroidered and accented with calado embroidery (eyelets), emphasizing the natural lustre and translucent qualities of the fibre. It is worn over a cotton lining. The fashion designer is promoting traditional Filipino materials and techniques through his work; as well as piña he celebrates abaca, jute and silk, among others. Working between Beverly Hills and Manila, he places these materials in a modern context, making gowns and dresses fit for the grandest ceremonies. Photo courtesy of Oliver Tolentino.

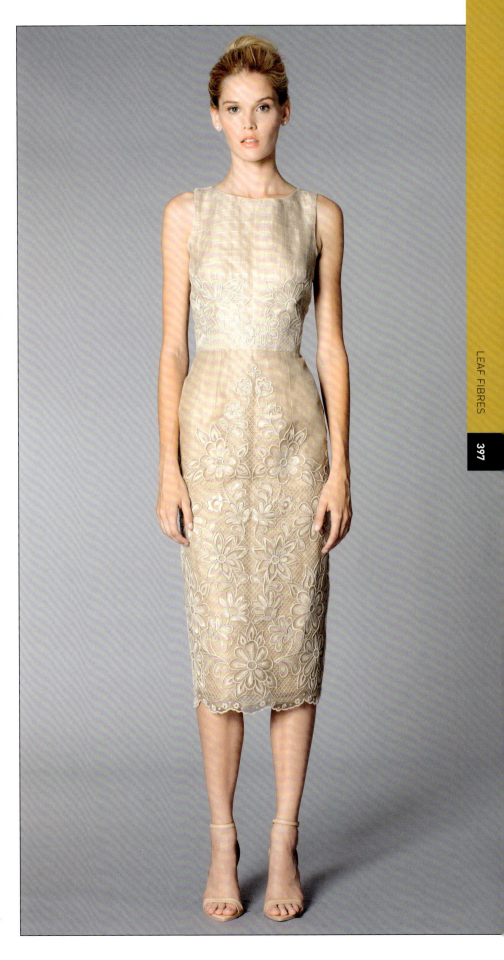

**Shape retention**
Several of these fibres are utilized in hat making, because they tolerate being formed with heat and pressure, and retain their shape and strength.

**Tradition**
Applications and aesthetics have evolved around the unique qualities of these fibres. In some cases, it even matters where and how individual plants were grown. The value of this intimate knowledge helps to sustain their use.

**Low cost**
While the cost does fluctuate considerably, depending on demand, commodity types – sisal and abaca – remain relatively inexpensive. Machine-decorticated fibres will be the least expensive, but will be of inferior quality to those extracted by hand.

**Sustainable**
Leaf fibres are renewable and bring diversity to otherwise monocrop plantations, such as sugarcane. They give smallholders a valuable source of revenue.

do not give satisfactory results when dyed because of their variegated colour).

Sisal is the most common of the leaf fibres and the biggest producers are located in South America and Africa. Plantation-grown crops are productive and inexpensive compared to wild or smallholder-grown leaves. However, there are many environmental problems associated with this, including reduced biodiversity; diseases and pests (leading to an increase in chemical pesticides); and a decline in soil fertility (leading to an increase in chemical fertilizers).

Natural fibres are recyclable and biodegradable at the end of their useful life. While the fibre makes up only a fraction of the leaf, nothing usually goes to waste; the leafy matter is used as fertilizer, feed or biofuel.

## LEAF FIBRES IN FASHION AND TEXTILES

Leaves are a readily available resource and, with manual methods, the long fibres are extracted from the plant intact. Once dry, they are ready for application in everyday items. This gives them an advantage over fibres extracted from the stems of plants (bast), such as hemp and flax, which require retting to break down the tough lignin matrix. Of course, the preparation of high-quality leaf fibres for decorative and ceremonial items takes significantly more work, but this is the case for all fibres, not just those from leaves.

These fibres are utilized by hat makers in a range of styles. They are collectively referred to as 'straw' along with the stems and leaves of grass, rush and sedge (page 392). What sets them apart is their combination of lightness, durability and formability. They remain the material of choice for spring and summer styles, such as the panama and women's formal hats.

Sinamay is a type of woven abaca used in hat blocking. The sheets are pressed with heat into three-dimensional shapes in a single operation. It is one of the few fibres that can be worked in this way while retaining its strength and integrity.

Parasisal, a fine woven fabric produced from sisal fibre, is used in haute couture millinery. It is high-quality and long-lasting and produces a very smooth finish. As with abaca, it can be left soft and flexible, or stiffened and blocked to take on a permanent shape.

Abaca straw hoods are woven in China and the Philippines, and panama and sisal straw comes mainly from South America. They may take days or even weeks to make by hand, depending on the quality and raw materials.

Sisal and abaca are a little stiff and coarse to be suitable for garments. Piña, on the other hand, is a luxurious and lustrous fibre similar to silk. Originating from the Philippines, it is hand-woven

into lightweight fabric that is perfectly suited to the tropical climate. It is sometimes blended with locally available silk and cotton to produce a more delicate fabric. It is traditionally used for intricately decorated fabrics, such as ceremonial brocade and lace.

## LEAF FIBRES IN PRODUCTS, AUTOMOTIVE AND CONSTRUCTION

These tough fibres are used in a range of items, such as baskets, floor covering and shelter. In the tropics, sisal and abaca provide an alternative to grass and sedge. Fibres require more preparation than the stems of these plants, but yield items of superior quality and strength.

As with other natural fibres, they have seen steady decline since man-made alternatives became widely available. However, in recent years, there has been growth in non-traditional markets, fuelled by their combination of strength and sustainability.

Similar to bast fibres, sisal and abaca are being explored as fibre reinforcement for high-performance composites. Potential developments include low-cost reinforced concrete (page 496) and fibre-reinforced plastics composites for automotive application (see Flax). Applications like this help to maintain the value of the raw material and support the local rural communities.

They are already utilized in paper, providing good folding endurance and high tear strength for a cellulose-rich fibre. These properties are employed in speciality papers, such as tea bags, banknotes, filtration and high-quality tape backings. Each year, around 0.07 million tonnes of fibre goes into pulp, providing a very small, but valuable, contribution to global paper production (300 million tonnes).

**Sisal basket** No two traditional African sisal baskets look the same. Farming villages grow, dye and weave their own sisal. While natural dyes produce a quite muted appearance (pictured), very bold colours are possible with acid dyes (water-soluble sodium or ammonium salts).

## PRODUCTS, AUTOMOTIVE AND CONSTRUCTION

**Tenacity**
While they may not be as strong as hemp and flax, they have good strength-to-weight.

**High absorbency and folding endurance**
Sisal and abaca pulp is superior to softwood for use in commodity and speciality papers. Indeed, almost all abaca harvested goes into paper production.

**Low cost**
Sisal and abaca are relatively inexpensive, but the quality is highly variable. Local artisans obtain much of their fibre stock free of charge from the forest.

# Flax, Linen

High-quality flax, more commonly known as linen, is prized for its strength, soft hand and high lustre. None of the rest of the plant is wasted. The woody core is utilized in particleboard and animal bedding or incinerated to reclaim the embodied energy; shorter fibres are converted into pulp for paper and board; and the seeds provide food.

| Types | Typical Applications | Sustainability |
|---|---|---|
| • Long flax fibres: line, sliver, roving and yarn<br>• Short flax fibres: tow and yarn | • Linen, such as bedding and clothing<br>• High-performance composites, such as for sports equipment, furniture, automotive and musical instruments | • Natural and renewable<br>• Few or no pesticides or fertilizer required<br>• Low embodied energy for a high-performance fibre |
| **Properties** | **Competing Materials** | **Costs** |
| • Hardy with high strength-to-weight<br>• Variable quality<br>• Absorbent | • Hemp, ramie, jute, grass and leaf fibre<br>• Carbon, glass and aramid fibre<br>• PP, PET and PA fibre | • Varies considerably depending on quality and market trends<br>• Processing is labour-intensive |

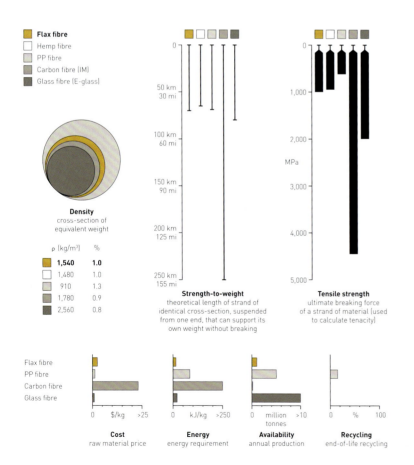

**Flax fibre**
Hemp fibre
PP fibre
Carbon fibre (IM)
Glass fibre (E-glass)

**Density**
cross-section of equivalent weight

| ρ (kg/m³) | % |
|---|---|
| 1,540 | 1.0 |
| 1,480 | 1.0 |
| 910 | 1.3 |
| 1,780 | 0.9 |
| 2,560 | 0.8 |

**Strength-to-weight**
theoretical length of strand of identical cross-section, suspended from one end, that can support its own weight without breaking

**Tensile strength**
ultimate breaking force of a strand of material (used to calculate tenacity)

Flax fibre
PP fibre
Carbon fibre
Glass fibre

**Cost**
raw material price

**Energy**
energy requirement

**Availability**
annual production

**Recycling**
end-of-life recycling

## INTRODUCTION

The fibre is obtained from the stem of the flax plant (*Linum usitatissimum*) of the family Linaceae. Having been cultivated for thousands of years, it is believed to be one of the earliest fibres used to make textile. While evidence dates back to 7,000 BCE, it is known that the ancient Egyptians were producing very fine linen by 4,000 BCE for use in everything from mummy shrouds to ship sails.

Flax thrives in the temperate climate found in Europe and Asia. The strongest and highest-quality fibre has, in recent centuries, mainly come from Ireland, Normandy (France) and Belgium. The biggest competitors are cotton (page 410) and man-made fibres. Cotton is nowhere near as durable or strong, but is far softer and more easily dyed; and is around half the price. Man-made fibres – in particular polypropylene (PP) (page 98) and polyamide (PA, nylon) (page 164) – have come to dominate many of the applications where flax previously thrived.

Testament to the enduring properties of flax, high-quality linen remains a desirable fabric for high-end apparel, bedding, table cloths and interior applications. And because of its low environmental impact and hardy properties, it is continually being explored in new areas of application.

Flax is, along with hemp (page 406) and ramie (page 408), the strongest and stiffest of the plant fibres. The impressive strength-to-weight of these fibres is being

**Linen shirt** This shirt comes from Thomas Ferguson, an Irish company that has been weaving local linen for more than 160 years. The fabric is soft and fine, with a wonderful natural lustre. It is popularly used in bedding, towelling and warm weather apparel, because it has excellent absorption properties: the fibre can gain up to one-fifth of its weight in water without feeling damp.

utilized in high-performance composite materials, which greatly expands their use and potential for the future.

## COMMERCIAL TYPES AND USES

There are two general types of flax grown commercially: one for oilseed and the other for fibre. The seed is a good source of omega-3 fatty acid and other nutrients. Fibres from this plant are too short for linen, but are suitable for use as a raw material in the manufacture of paper (page 268). They may be converted into 'tow' and twisted into yarn using similar equipment to that used for cotton. Known as cottonizing, it is more cost-effective than linen, but of inferior quality.

The raw, 'retted' stems (see below) of the fibre plant are known as straw. The fibres, which are liberated from the stem by crushing, 'scutching' and 'hackling',

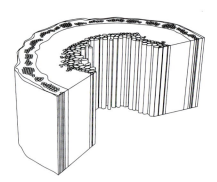

**Transverse cross-section through plant stem** The main stem of bast-fibre-yielding plants, such as flax and hemp, is made up of a lignified core. This is surrounded by a spiralling fibre bundle structure, which is protected beneath a waxy outer layer made up of the epidermis and cuticle. The stem is made up of around one-third fibre, by weight. All these natural fibres consist of long cells with relatively thick cell walls of cellulose and lignin, which make them stiff and strong. The length depends on the height of the plant. To extract them, the stems must be retted over a period of weeks. This process

involves soaking them in water, or lying them in the damp field where they were harvested. This allows microbes to break down the hemicellulose-pectin matrix that surrounds the fibre bundles. This is a lengthy process and alternatives are being explored that employ chemicals or enzymes. However, these have not yet proved to be economically viable for large-scale use. Once retted, the stems are decorticated (mechanically crushed) to reveal the fibres, and waste material is removed by combing. When carried out by hand, these processes are known as scutching and hackling respectively.

**Absorption properties**
It is highly absorbent and can gain up to one-fifth of its weight in water without feeling damp. On top of that, it gets stronger when wet.

**Stiffness**
Linen garments are relatively stiff and so will not cling to the body like those made from cotton or wool. This helps to improve breathability. However, it also means linen is susceptible to creasing.

**Long-lasting**
Flax fibre is hardy and resistant to ultraviolet. Cared for correctly, it will comfortably outlast cotton, wool and silk equivalents.

**Technical performance**
It is one of the highest-performing natural fibres and more than twice the strength of cotton. As a natural fibre reinforcement in polymer matrix composites, flax offers comparable strength-to-weight with E-glass, but is only around one-quarter the strength of carbon.

are gathered in a long bundle known as 'line'. Carding produces a 'sliver', which, if required, is further processed by combing and bleaching. Once the desired quality of fibre is achieved the sliver is converted into a 'roving' (loosely twisted) and spun into yarn.

Used as composite fibre reinforcement, new yarn formations and fabric constructions have emerged to improve performance. Alignment is critical and unidirectional fibres give the greatest performance properties, because they travel the shortest distance between two points. In other words, they do not pass over, under or around one another. The challenge of using flax, as opposed to conventional fibre reinforcement such as carbon (page 236) and glass (page 522), is that it is not continuous and has some natural variation.

## SUSTAINABILITY

Retting involves laying the flax stalks out in the field where they were cut and allowing naturally occurring microorganisms to break down the pectin that bonds the fibres to the stem. In the past, flax was retted in ponds and streams, which polluted the surrounding waterways. More recently developed chemical retting techniques are quicker but also potentially harmful to the fibre and the environment.

These plants grow with little or no added fertilizer, pesticide or herbicide. This is in stark contrast to cotton. They also make up an important part of crop rotation, thanks to their beneficial effects on following crops. It is best to use the fibre untreated if possible, known as 'natural', to avoid the use of bleaching and dyeing chemicals. If not, water-based

systems without heavy metals or other toxic ingredients are available.

## FLAX IN FASHION AND TECHNICAL TEXTILES

The fibre ranges from coarse to fine, depending on the type, source and method of conversion from plant to fibre. The fibre consists of nodes, or slubs (perpendicular dislocations), along its length, which adds some flexibility, but decreases strength. Very fine linen will have long straight fibres, with a consistent diameter and free from visible nodes.

Linen is considered superior to cotton in many respects. However, since the industrialization of cotton spinning in the 18th century, which brought the price down significantly, the use of cotton expanded at the expense of the other natural fibres. The preparation of flax is laborious, which limits the bulk of production to Eastern Europe and China. Raw material price ranges considerably: fine long fibres are approximately ten times the price of low-quality short fibres.

Flax is naturally light brown to dark grey. The tough fibre is whitened in the sun (grass bleaching) or with chemical bleaching. Using chemicals weakens the fibre and so is avoided wherever possible, or it is dyed muted colours to avoid heavy bleaching.

It is utilized as fibre reinforcement for polymer matrix composites. Originally aimed at replacing glass, flax has become the most widely used natural fibre in composites and demand is growing. Examples include interior parts such as reinforced seat backs, door panels and rear passenger decks. Applications outside the automotive industry include wind turbine blades and sports equipment.

Hemp, jute (page 404), ramie and the leaf fibres (page 394) are utilized in similar situations, but to a lesser extent.

Flax-reinforced plastics offer many advantages compared to unreinforced types, including reduced weight and increased vibration dampening. On top of this, flax offers many environmental and worker benefits compared to conventional glass or carbon reinforcement. While natural-fibre-reinforced composites are no more recyclable than conventional types, they have far lower embodied energy and are suitable for incineration (energy recovery) end-of-life. These are the key drivers for their adoption in the automotive industry. And of course, if a biobased or biodegradable resin is used as the matrix, then the composite may be compostable.

They are compatible with all standard composite processing including vacuum bagging, resin transfer molding (RTM), press molding, pultrusion and filament winding. In addition, short flax fibre is suitable as an additive for extruded and injection-molded thermoplastics.

As a natural fibre, flax has some limitations. The properties are variable. While most of this is equalized during the preparation and spinning of the yarn, there will inevitably be some inconsistency in physical and mechanical attributes. Its high moisture absorption properties mean that it must be sealed in with resin, especially if the part is to be used outdoors. Also, it is vulnerable to degradation at around 200°C (392°F) and so not suitable for parts that will be exposed to high temperatures.

**Bio-fibre-reinforced composite** The Clara compact concert ukulele from Blackbird Guitars is constructed from Ekoa, a flax-fibre-reinforced bio-epoxy (page 232). Built in San Francisco, the parts are fabricated in much the same way as if they were glass-fibre- or carbon-fibre-reinforced plastic. Sheets of unidirectional (UD) flax are impregnated with high-strength bio-epoxy. They are cut and draped over a mold. With heat and pressure, the resin consolidates, resulting in a strong, lightweight part. The soundboard is tuned for optimal rigidity and density without bracing, combining the tone of wood with the lightness and durability of composite. Photo courtesy of Blackbird Guitars.

# Jute and Kenaf

Jute yields a hardy and inexpensive fibre traditionally used to produce hessian, gunny and burlap. Used in geotextiles, carpets, webbing and other industrial fabrics, it is the most widely consumed bast fibre and second only to cotton among the vegetable fibres. Kenaf yields a fibre with similar characteristics and is utilized in many of the same situations.

| Types | Typical Applications | Sustainability |
|---|---|---|
| • Jute: white and tossa<br>• Kenaf | • Sacking and industrial fabrics<br>• Geotextiles<br>• Upholstery and carpet backing | • Little or no pesticide or fertilizer required<br>• Very low embodied energy |

| Properties | Competing Materials | Costs |
|---|---|---|
| • Coarse and tough<br>• Stiff and brittle with low resilience<br>• Lose around 10% of their strength when wet | • Hemp, flax and leaf fibres<br>• Man-made fibres such as PP, PET and PA | • Low-cost, but depends on weather conditions and yield<br>• Labour-intensive to process |

404

## INTRODUCTION

India and Bangladesh have for centuries been the biggest producers of these fibres. As with most plant fibres, they have been superseded in traditional applications by man-made alternatives. In the case of jute and kenaf, the primary competitor is polypropylene (PP) (page 98), which is now used to make synthetic hessian and burlap. It is produced as a brown-coloured staple fibre so that when converted into sacks and ropes, such as used to package coffee and other luxury goods, it mimics the rustic appearance of jute.

Jute and kenaf are more brittle and generally considered inferior to other plant fibres. This is because they contain a higher proportion of lignin (hard resinous substance also found in wood). Jute and kenaf contain around 10% and 20% respectively, whereas flax (page 400) contains only around 2%, and ramie (page 408) and cotton (page 410) do not contain any at all. What the high lignin content does offer is stiffness and low elongation. While this presents challenges in weaving operations, they are useful properties for creating dimensionally stable composites.

Jute is sometimes referred to as the golden fibre, although the colour varies from reddish-brown to pale yellow. As a low-cost industrial material it is mainly used in its natural state, but is compatible with several of the principal dyeing techniques. Bleaching damages the fibre and so is generally avoided. Kenaf is lighter-coloured, from off-white to yellow.

## COMMERCIAL TYPES AND USES

Jute is obtained from two species of *Corchorus*: white jute (*C. capsularis*) and tossa jute (*C. olitorius*). Tossa is produced in the largest quantities and provides a stronger and smoother fibre.

It is anti-static, provides good sound insulation and has low thermal

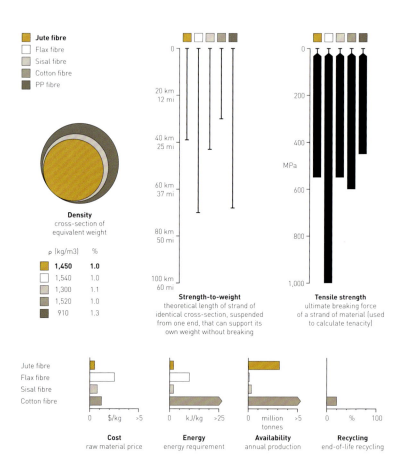

Jute fibre
Flax fibre
Sisal fibre
Cotton fibre
PP fibre

**Density**
cross-section of
equivalent weight

| ρ (kg/m3) | % |
|---|---|
| 1,450 | 1.0 |
| 1,540 | 1.0 |
| 1,300 | 1.1 |
| 1,520 | 1.0 |
| 910 | 1.3 |

20 km
12 mi

40 km
25 mi

60 km
37 mi

80 km
50 mi

100 km
60 mi

**Strength-to-weight**
theoretical length of strand of
identical cross-section, suspended
from one end, that can support its
own weight without breaking

MPa

200

400

600

800

1,000

**Tensile strength**
ultimate breaking force
of a strand of material (used
to calculate tenacity)

Jute fibre
Flax fibre
Sisal fibre
Cotton fibre

0   $/kg   >5

**Cost**
raw material price

0   kJ/kg   >25

**Energy**
energy requirement

0   million   >5
    tonnes

**Availability**
annual production

0   %   100

**Recycling**
end-of-life recycling

conductivity. Along with its stiffness, low elongation and low base cost, these properties are utilized in carpet backing, linoleum reinforcement, shoe soles and upholstery underlining. It is blended with cotton, as well as synthetics, to produce softer fabrics that take advantage of its strength and bulk.

Jute is vulnerable to degradation by microbes, fungi and ultraviolet. Its highly biodegradable nature is useful for products not intended to last long, such as single-use packaging and geotextiles for land restoration.

Kenaf (*Hibiscus cannabinus*) comes from the same family (Malvaceae) and is used in many of the same situations. Like flax, it is utilized as reinforcement in polymer matrix composites for automotive application. In 2012, Ford introduced kenaf in the interior door bolster (panel) of the Escape model. It was combined with PP matrix in a 50–50 mix. Not only did its inclusion reduce the amount of plastic, it also cut the weight of the door by 25%, improving fuel economy.

Kenaf is an alternative to softwood fibres in the production of pulp and paper (page 268). It yields more fibre than wood for the same land area and requires less energy to convert into pulp, because it is lower-density and contains less lignin.

## SUSTAINABILITY

Like other bast-fibre-yielding plants, jute is a rain-fed crop that has little need for fertilizer or pesticides. However, like flax it requires retting (see page 402), which must be carefully controlled to avoid pollution. Kenaf has high yield and its relatively light colouring means it requires less bleaching than equivalent fibres.

**Utility shoe** Espadrilles feature a braided jute (or hemp) sole. The name derives from esparto, a type of grass (page 392) that was once used in the sole. Originally crafted in Catalonia and the surrounding Pyrenees, they were worn by dancers, priests and infantrymen alike. A long length of braided fibre coiled in a spiralling pattern forms the sole. Strong cord is passed through the coiled jute, from one side to the other, and pulled tight to compact the fibres, and the cotton canvas upper is sewn on top. While they are still made by hand in parts of Spain, the majority are mass-produced elsewhere.

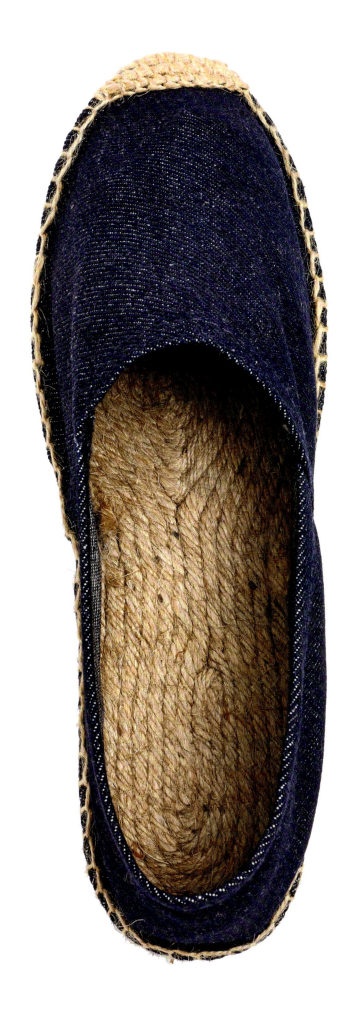

# Hemp

**Industrial hemp is a fast-growing plant that yields hardy fibres from its stem. It has inherent antimicrobial properties, which means it is resistant to mold and mildew. It is also endowed with natural resistance to degradation by heat, ultraviolet and salty water. Considered by some to be the ultimate natural fibre, hemp has featured in textiles for millennia.**

| Types | Typical Applications | Sustainability |
|---|---|---|
| • Long hemp fibres: line, sliver, roving and yarn<br>• Short hemp fibres: tow and yarn | • Paper and pulp<br>• Apparel<br>• Rope and twine | • Natural and renewable<br>• Few or no pesticides or fertilizer required<br>• Low embodied energy for a high-performance fibre |

| Properties | Competing Materials | Costs |
|---|---|---|
| • Good strength-to-weight and high aspect ratio<br>• A little stiffer and coarser than flax<br>• Antimicrobial | • Flax, ramie, jute, grass and leaf fibre<br>• Carbon, glass and aramid fibre<br>• PP, PET and PA fibre | • Varies considerably depending on quality and market trends; yarn for weaving is expensive<br>• Processing is labour-intensive |

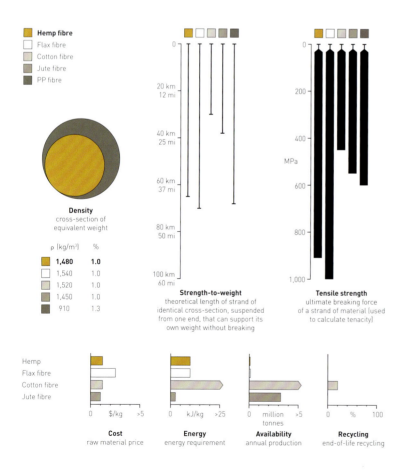

**Legend:**
- Hemp fibre
- Flax fibre
- Cotton fibre
- Jute fibre
- PP fibre

**Density**
cross-section of equivalent weight

| ρ (kg/m³) | % |
|---|---|
| 1,480 | 1.0 |
| 1,540 | 1.0 |
| 1,520 | 1.0 |
| 1,450 | 1.0 |
| 910 | 1.3 |

**Strength-to-weight**
theoretical length of strand of identical cross-section, suspended from one end, that can support its own weight without breaking

**Tensile strength**
ultimate breaking force of a strand of material (used to calculate tenacity)

Hemp
Flax fibre
Cotton fibre
Jute fibre

**Cost**
raw material price

**Energy**
energy requirement

**Availability**
annual production

**Recycling**
end-of-life recycling

## INTRODUCTION

Hemp is a variety of *Cannabis sativa* of the family Cannabaceae. Its close association with marijuana is its major drawback. Even though the plants cultivated for fibre do not contain enough of the psychoactive cannabinoid tetrahydrocannabinol (THC) to be useful for medicine or as a recreational drug, production is heavily regulated and banned in many places. As a consequence, industrial hemp is commercially grown in only a handful of countries; the largest producers are Europe and China.

Hemp originated in China and spread to Europe around the time of the Vikings (8th–11th centuries). Once widely cultivated, it was considered a very important crop. It was used in cordage: rope and canvas were originally produced from it. Hemp fabric is often compared to linen (see Flax, page 400). The main difference is that hemp contains a higher proportion of lignin, which means it is a little stiffer and coarser. Colour ranges from off-white to brown or green. It is typically used in its natural state, because bleaching weakens the fibre.

In addition to textiles, hemp is utilized as fibre-reinforcement for polymer matrix composites. In this field, it is in competition with flax, jute and kenaf (page 404) and leaf fibres (page 394). Henry Ford explored its potential for automotive body parts in the 1940s. He combined hemp with other natural fibres in a plastic matrix. It was said to be lighter with greater resistance to impact than steel models of the time. Evidently, this development did nothing to unsettle the dominance of steel (page 28): it remains the most commonly used material for this application, and long-fibre-reinforced plastic composites are almost exclusively limited to the racetrack. However, recent developments in materials and

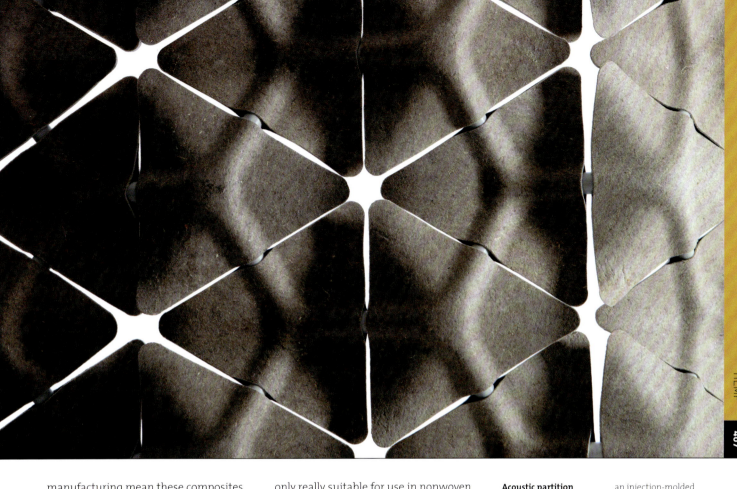

manufacturing mean these composites have become affordable for use in mass-production cars (see also GFRP in UP Resin, page 228, and CFRP, page 236).

Some time after Ford's hemp experiments, production of the fibre was outlawed in the USA (although small-scale cultivation has since been allowed in some states under strict regulation), as a consequence of its association with THC, and declined dramatically elsewhere from 1960s onwards owing to competition from cotton (page 410) and man-made fibres. Since the 1990s, as interest in sustainability has grown, production of hemp has witnessed a small resurgence.

## COMMERCIAL TYPES AND USES

Industrial hemp with a very low THC content (<0.3%) has been legalized in the UK, Germany, Austria, Switzerland, Canada and Australia. These countries account for around one-third of global production; the rest comes from China.

The majority of hemp fibre produced in Europe contains a mix of long and short fibres. Known as 'total fibre line', it is only really suitable for use in nonwoven textiles (such as insulation for automotive and construction). This is in stark contrast to flax, which is processed into long, fine yarn suitable for high-value textiles. This is reflected in the raw material price.

Fashion fabrics, geotextiles (mulch fleeces) and fibre reinforcement make up a very small proportion of total consumption; the majority goes into paper production. Hemp pulp is more expensive than wood pulp, which limits use to speciality papers that require its superior strength.

## SUSTAINABILITY

Hemp is cultivated and processed with similar techniques to flax. It can have a more positive impact on the environment, because it yields much more fibre for the same area – around twice as much – and can be grown without chemicals.

When assessing total environmental impacts it is important to consider whether it was grown using organic methods or intensive farming practices. It grows very quickly and establishes a

**Acoustic partition system** The Scale modular system consists of large triangular panels pressed from recycled hemp fibre. It was designed by Benjamin Hubert, of London design agency Layer, for Woven Image, a textile design company based in Australia. The panels attach to an injection-molded acrylonitrile butadiene styrene (ABS) (page 138) framework, mounted on aluminium (page 42) baseplates. The concept was developed over a period of three years, resulting in an elegant system that is straightforward to assemble and thus truly adaptable. Photo courtesy of Layer.

canopy that prevents weeds growing. This helps to avoid the use of fertilizer and herbicide. In addition, it has good resistance to most pests, so it can be grown without the use of pesticides. Textiles grown without the use of chemicals and finished with no chemical bleaching or dyeing are sustainable and can be safely composted end-of-life, returning the nutrients back to the soil.

As with flax, nothing goes to waste. While most hemp is grown for its fibre, the seeds are a source of food and the hurds (stalks) are used for animal bedding.

# Ramie

Ramie yields a long and light-coloured fibre that can be bleached to a bright white. It is highly absorbent, so comfortable to wear in hot weather, and naturally resistant to microbes and mildew. It is mainly used in the countries where it grows, as exported fibre tends to be expensive owing to the labour-intensive production processes.

| Types | Typical Applications | Sustainability |
|---|---|---|
| • Ramie: white (China grass) and green (rhea)<br>• Nettle | • Apparel<br>• Interior textiles<br>• Pulp and paper | • It can be harvested several times per year for up to 20 years<br>• Fibres are extracted using chemicals |

| Properties | Competing Materials | Costs |
|---|---|---|
| • Light colour and high affinity for dyes<br>• Resistant to microbes, mildew and ultraviolet<br>• High absorbency | • Flax, hemp and cotton<br>• Man-made fibres, in particular viscose and polyester | • Moderate to high raw material costs<br>• Labour-intensive to process into fibre |

## INTRODUCTION

Ramie (*Boehmeria nivea*), also known as China grass, belongs to the Urticaceae family. It yields a strong bast fibre with a silk-like lustre. The colour is naturally off-white and it can be bleached to a clean white, providing a good base for dyeing bright colour.

It has existed in Far Eastern textiles for millennia and its fineness is particularly popular in Japan, where it is known as jofu. It is more complex to produce than linen (see Flax, page 400) owing to the high proportion of gums and pectins that surrounds the fibres. In addition to the various mechanical processes involved in decortication, chemicals are required for de-gumming. The whole process is time-consuming and labour-intensive. As a result, it tends to be expensive.

Once processed, the fibre contains a high proportion of cellulose. Its highly crystalline (see page 166) structure means that the fibre has low elasticity, elongation and abrasion resistance. This presents some challenges in production, such as making it difficult to weave and impractical to knit. Like cotton (page 410), it is treated or blended to enhance wrinkle resistance and durability. Even so, care is required, because the fibres are prone to cracking and breaking when bent repeatedly.

## COMMERCIAL TYPES AND USES

China is the largest cultivator and consumer of ramie (the Chinese refer to is as tschou-ma). It is produced to a much lesser extent in Africa, South America and India. Green ramie (*B. nivea* var. *tenacissima*), also known as rhea, is thought to have originally come from the Malay Peninsula and is better suited to tropical climates.

The fibre is strong and becomes around 25% stronger when wet. Similar to

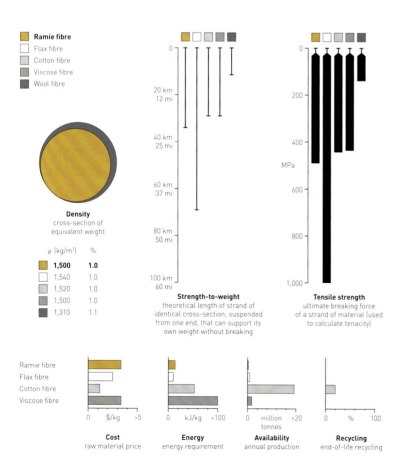

Ramie fibre
Flax fibre
Cotton fibre
Viscose fibre
Wool fibre

**Density**
cross-section of equivalent weight

| ρ (kg/m³) | % |
|---|---|
| 1,500 | 1.0 |
| 1,540 | 1.0 |
| 1,520 | 1.0 |
| 1,500 | 1.0 |
| 1,310 | 1.1 |

**Strength-to-weight**
theoretical length of strand of identical cross-section, suspended from one end, that can support its own weight without breaking

**Tensile strength**
ultimate breaking force of a strand of material (used to calculate tenacity)

Ramie fibre
Flax fibre
Cotton fibre
Viscose fibre

**Cost**
raw material price

**Energy**
energy requirement

**Availability**
annual production

**Recycling**
end-of-life recycling

linen, ramie is absorbent and this means it is comfortable to wear, especially in warm weather. It is woven into fabrics suitable for shirts, suits and trousers.

Ramie is often blended with other fibres to impart some of its desirable properties. Increasing elasticity allows ramie to be used in knitted applications, such as sweaters and dresses. It is combined with wool (page 426) to make it lighter and reduce shrinkage, and with cotton to increase strength and lustre.

European nettle (*Urtica dioica*) is similar to ramie; it comes from the same family and is being re-explored as a renewable fibre for apparel and technical textiles. This successful perennial grows throughout temperate regions of North America, Europe and Asia. It grows without the need for herbicides and pesticides, and is a perennial, so does not need to be grown from seed. As a textile fibre, however, it is cultivated in very low quantities.

## SUSTAINABILITY

Ramie is very fast-growing and highly productive, which can lead to rapid deterioration in soil nutrients and thus require the use of fertilizer. It is harvested

**Terry bath mitt** This bath scrubber makes good use of many of ramie's beneficial properties. The fibre is highly absorbent, more so than most other vegetable fibre, as a result of its porous cellulose structure. It is resistant to microbes and mold, and is unaffected by damp. On top of this, it is stiff and strong (stronger when wet), keeps its shape and does not shrink after washing.

several times per year and the root may be productive for up to 20 years. It is more susceptible to disease than other bast fibre plants and so is more likely to be sprayed with chemicals, but may still be grown in a sustainable manner.

# Cotton

**Also known as**
Trademark names include: Supima, Natural Blend
(indicating 60% or more cotton)

**The soft fibres that form a cotton boll, which aids the dispersal of the seeds in the wind, provide an unrivalled combination of suppleness and strength. They are economical to extract and efficient to process, making them the ideal high-volume fibre. Organic farming provides an alternative to the chemical-heavy industry that has evolved around this unique material.**

| Types | Typical Applications | Sustainability |
|---|---|---|
| • Extra-long staple (ELS) cotton: Egyptian giza, American pima and Sea Island<br>• Upland cotton<br>• Asiatic cotton | • Apparel<br>• Interior fabrics<br>• Packaging | • Organic production eliminates the use of GM, as well as the vast quantities of pesticide and fertilizer associated with industrial cotton production |

| Properties | Competing Materials | Costs |
|---|---|---|
| • Soft and breathable<br>• Dyes very well<br>• Low resiliency | • Flax, hemp and ramie<br>• Silk and wool<br>• Man-made fibres, such as viscose and polyester | • Low to moderate raw material costs<br>• Efficient to process |

410

## INTRODUCTION

This high-quality and versatile fibre has been utilized in textiles since prehistoric times. It is derived from the boll (seedpod) of the cotton plant (*Gossypium* genus). Unlike bast fibres, whose role is to keep the plant upright, it is non-structural, resulting in a soft and supple fibre.

Cotton production scaled up dramatically following the invention of the mechanized sawtooth gin in 1793. The hand-operated roller gin (or churka gin) had been used for centuries to process long-staple cotton fibres. While it is practical to process long-staple fibres in this way, 1 kg (roughly 2 lb) of short-staple cotton takes a day to process by hand. By contrast, the motorized sawtooth gin operates at high speed and can produce tonnes of fibre per hour.

Unlike most other plant fibres, worldwide production of cotton continues to grow. It too, has faced stiff competition from man-made fibres, in particular polyethylene terephthalate (PET, polyester) (page 152). So, while it has seen dips in demand, it has remained competitive thanks to its low cost – as a result of continual developments in cultivation and production – and its unique combination of properties.

Nowadays, cotton cultivated in the USA, Australia and Israel is harvested by machine. The remainder, which accounts for approximately two-thirds of total production, is mostly picked by hand. Hand-picked cotton is superior quality, but is only economically feasible in regions where the wages are low, such as in central and southern Asia.

## COMMERCIAL TYPES AND USES

Cotton is graded according to length, uniformity, colour (whiteness), fineness (diameter), strength and contamination. Quality varies according to where it

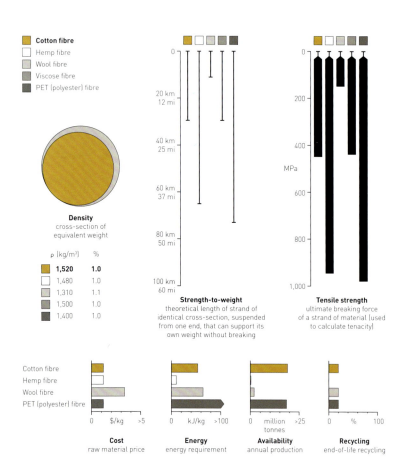

Cotton fibre
Hemp fibre
Wool fibre
Viscose fibre
PET (polyester) fibre

**Density**
cross-section of
equivalent weight

| ρ (kg/m³) | % |
|---|---|
| 1,520 | 1.0 |
| 1,480 | 1.0 |
| 1,310 | 1.1 |
| 1,500 | 1.0 |
| 1,400 | 1.0 |

**Strength-to-weight**
theoretical length of strand of
identical cross-section, suspended
from one end, that can support its
own weight without breaking

**Tensile strength**
ultimate breaking force
of a strand of material (used
to calculate tenacity)

**Cost**
raw material price

**Energy**
energy requirement

**Availability**
annual production

**Recycling**
end-of-life recycling

was grown, as a result of differences in climate, cultivation and soil.

There are three principal groups of commercial cotton: extra-long staple, or ELS (*G. barbadense*); upland cotton (*G. hirsutum*), which yields a medium to long staple; and the short-staple Asiatic varieties (*G. herbaceum* and *G. arboreum*).

With a fibre length of more than 28 mm (1 in), ELS produces the highest-quality fabrics. There are several varieties, including American pima, Egyptian giza, Sudanese barakat and Indian suvin.

Pima cotton is named after the American Indian Pima people and was previously known as American-Egyptian. Now, it is cultivated in the United States, Australia, Israel and Peru, among other countries. Pima is also referred to by the trade name Supima, after the association

**Colourful baby romper**
Cotton and wool (page 426) are commonly used in baby clothing and sleepwear. The advantage of cotton is that it is soft, smooth, hypoallergenic (unlikely to cause an allergic reaction) and much easier to care for. Wool, on the other hand, offers superior insulation, elasticity and resiliency.

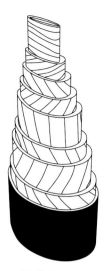

Spiralling fibrillar structure in
mature cotton fibre

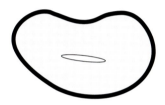

Transverse cross-section
through mature cotton fibre

**Cotton fibre structure**
Cotton fibre (lint) grows as a unicellular strand from the seed boll. The mature fibre, which is almost pure cellulose, is constructed of several layers: the lumen (hollow canal up the middle) and cuticle (outer waxy layer), are separated by spiralling fibrils (small strands of cellulose) in concentric layers that run at alternate angles. Cotton cellulose has a higher degree of polymerization and crystallinity (see page 166) than wood cellulose. This results in a fibre with higher strength. Having not been put under any load during its lifetime, the fibre tends to be quite soft and supple. The tubular structure accounts for its absorption capacity. As it takes on water it swells; changing from bean-shape to round in cross-section. When used in densely woven fabric, the swelling closes the gaps to create a waterproof and windproof barrier. So, without any coating or laminating, some cotton fabrics are weatherproof.

**Ventile** Densely woven cotton, known by the trademark name Ventile, is naturally weatherproof. Water absorption causes the fibres to swell, thus closing up the gaps in the weave so that it sheds subsequent water. It is made from the finest ELS and so more expensive than waxed cotton. Originally created for British pilots in WW2, who needed a fabric that was breathable when dry and waterproof when wet, the majority now comes from a Swiss mill. This is the Nigel Cabourn M43 Flight Jacket. Photo courtesy of Nigel Cabourn.

that promotes this luxury fibre. Sea Island cotton, an ancestor of pima, is highly susceptible to boll weevil attack and so is produced in much lower quantities.

The term Egyptian cotton is used to describe all cotton produced in Egypt, including giza and lower-quality types. Therefore the term does not guarantee consistently high quality.

Upland cotton (*G. hirsutum*) is of early South American origin and today makes up the vast majority of global production. There are several varieties, each of which yields a slightly different-length staple. The most popular hybrid yields a long-staple fibre of 22 to 24 mm (0.87–0.94 in).

Asiatic cotton, cultivated in India and central and eastern Asia, yields a short to medium staple ranging in length from 12 to 25 mm (0.47–0.98 in).

## SUSTAINABILITY

Industrially produced cotton uses vast quantities of pesticides, fertilizer and water, which together account for more than 10% of global agrochemical consumption. Add to that the water and chemicals required to bleach, scour, mercerize and dye cotton fabric – the production of a regular cotton t-shirt consumes a staggering 2.5 m³ (88 ft³) of water – and it is clear why cotton is considered the most unsustainable and environmentally damaging natural fibre. This is in stark contrast to other plant fibres – flax (page 400), ramie (page 408) and hemp (page 406), for example – whose cultivation can have a positive impact on the environment.

Genetically modified (GM) grades of cotton have been developed to try to reduce the reliance on pesticides. Modifying cotton with the *Bacillus thuringiensis* bacterial gene, referred to as Bt cotton, provides resistance to most pests, but not all. It has been widely adopted and as a result the use of pesticides has been reduced, while biodiversity in cotton fields has increased.

Fair trade and organic cotton is providing a sustainable alternative, albeit in smaller quantities and at a premium price. Each year, organic cotton production increases, and the quality and consistency are improved. Demand is driven largely by

**Versatile**
Cotton combines numerous desirable properties, including softness, drape, absorbency and ease of processing. While many well-known fabric constructions – terry, denim, corduroy and so on – have evolved around these attributes, cotton is used in place of more expensive natural fibres in a host of others.

**Colour**
It is naturally off-white, red, green or brown. Bleaching out the natural colour produces white cotton. It is virtually pure cellulose, which means that it takes dye very well and yields high-quality and consistent colour.

**Blends**
The desirable characteristics of cotton are combined with other fibres for a variety of end uses. For example, cotton is blended with linen (flax) to produce a stronger and more breathable fabric than is possible with cotton alone; or it is combined with man-made fibre to improve surface lustre and wrinkle resistance.

the popularity of organic cotton for baby clothes, diapers and underwear.

Naturally coloured cotton eliminates the need for bleaching and dyeing, thus significantly reducing the negative impacts of fabric production. However, one of the challenges of naturally coloured cotton is that it needs to be kept isolated from whiter grades, otherwise there is a chance of contamination.

Cotton fabrics can be recycled and it is estimated that around 20% of used garments are collected and processed for this purpose. Fabrics that contain cotton blended with other fibres are converted into cloths and industrial products.

By-products of cotton production include linters (fibres less than 3 mm [0.12 in] long), hulls and seeds. Linters are valuable raw materials used for batting (mattresses and upholstery), man-made fibres (see Viscose, page 252) and paper (page 268). The seeds are converted into fertilizer and animal feed.

## COTTON IN FASHION AND TEXTILES

Around three-quarters of cotton produced each year is converted into textile for apparel; the rest is used in home furnishing, beauty products, packaging and industrial applications. Over the years, a range of fabrics has evolved that take advantage of the unique qualities of cotton, and the combination has become inseparable. Well-known examples include denim, cambric, seersucker and pile fabrics (terry, velveteen and corduroy).

**Left**
**Cycling musette** A cycling bag featuring black graphics screen-printed onto custom-dyed cotton twill. Cotton has very good affinity to dyeing, in particular vat dyes, which can produce a wide range of colours with excellent fastness. Photo courtesy of Progress Packaging.

**Opposite**
**Leavers lace** This machine-woven lace is made up cotton warp yarns held in place by nylon (page 164) woven around at regular intervals. Unlike embroidery (see pages 87 and 95), complex patterns and figures are reproduced in the structure of the textile itself. Cotton is the predominant material used in decorative lace, but in practice all types of yarn are suitable.

page 420), but the pile lies flatter.

High-quality cotton goes through a series of treatments in preparation for use. Mercerizing is used to improve strength and brightness: the fibre is exposed to high-strength caustic acid (sodium hydroxide), which causes it to swell while under tension. It is almost always carried out in preparation for dyeing and printing, because it improves colour saturation and process efficiency.

Large quantities of water, heat and chemicals are required. Replacing the chemicals with enzymes helps to reduce the environmental impacts. Relatively small concentrations of enzymes are used to replace alkalis in chemical washing (known as bio-stonewashing); to replace acids, alkali or oxidizing agents in scouring and desizing (known as bio-scouring); and to produce a smoother and glossier cotton (known as bio-polishing).

Cotton fabrics, including blends, are pre-shrunk by compressive shrinking. This process, known widely under the trade name Sanforizing, is carried out to ensure that the fabric does not shrink during further processing or washing. After proper treatment, the fabric has a shrink-proof value of less than 1%.

Coatings are used to make longer-lasting and higher-quality items. Coatings that can be replaced or repaired, such as wax, increase the lifespan of the cotton fabric. And coatings that reduce the amount an item needs to be washed, such as polyurethane (PU) (page 202), save significant water and energy over the lifespan of an item.

Denim has the ideal balance of lightness, durability and pliability for use in workwear. Traditional indigo denim is twill-woven with a white-coloured weft and blue-dyed warp. This produces the familiar blue front and white back to the fabric. The indigo-coloured dye penetrates only the outside surface of the cotton warp, leaving the core uncoloured. Therefore, as the surface is gradually worn away by daily use, the denim fades to white. This patina has become so desirable that techniques have been developed to artificially age the surface in a controlled fashion, such as by abrasive or chemical washing.

Cambric and batiste are fine-woven French fabrics that were originally made from linen (see Flax), but are now more often produced in cotton. The smooth surface is improved with glazing, or calendering, which gives it a distinctive stiff and shiny appearance. It is traditionally used in shirts and handkerchiefs. Chambray is constructed in a similar fashion, but like denim, is produced using a mix of coloured warp and plain weft. It is not calendered and so retains a soft feel.

Seersucker is a lightweight – often striped – fabric typically used in warm weather clothing. It is woven in such a way that the surface puckers up to create a wrinkled texture. This has two key benefits: it means garments do not need pressing, and it helps keep the fabric away from the skin, which aids air circulation and heat dissipation.

Terrycloth makes use of cotton's affinity for water: loops of loosely twisted yarn produce a soft, insulating and absorbent layer with high surface area. This type of construction is used in towels, robes and other fabrics whose job it is to absorb moisture.

In the case of cut pile, such as velveteen and corduroy, the ends of the fibres are exposed to create a soft luxurious surface. While corduroy has distinctive wales (ridges) that run the length of the fabric, the floats (cut to produce pile) in velveteen are not arranged in a linear pattern. This gives it a similar appearance to velvet (see Silk,

# Coconut Coir

These hardy fibres are used for brush bristles, flooring, upholstery and horticulture. Coir is the least expensive plant fibre and offers superior resistance to microbes and water. It is extracted from the husk and processed into yarn or nonwoven. Or the husk is processed with fibre and pressed into sturdy fibreboard. Sustainability depends on the method of extraction.

| Types | Typical Applications | Sustainability |
|---|---|---|
| • Coir fibre: white (immature) and brown (mature) <br> • Husk (mix of fibre and pith) | • Bristles for brooms and brushes <br> • Upholstery padding, flooring and matting <br> • Rubberized coir and geotextiles | • Traditional retting techniques are highly polluting <br> • As a by-product it has very low embodied energy |

| Properties | Competing Materials | Costs |
|---|---|---|
| • Highly resistant to microbes and water <br> • Stiff and hardy <br> • Low strength | • Abaca, sisal, jute and wool <br> • Man-made fibres such as PP and PA <br> • Engineered timber | • Low material costs <br> • Inexpensive to process |

416

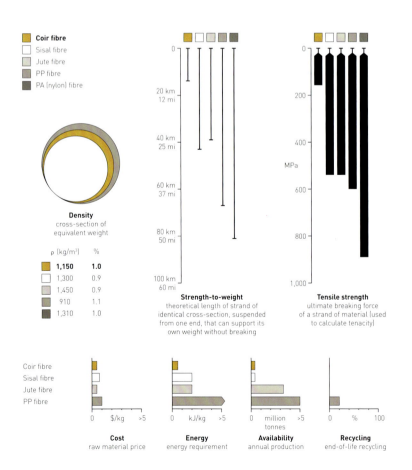

Coir fibre
Sisal fibre
Jute fibre
PP fibre
PA (nylon) fibre

**Density**
cross-section of equivalent weight

| ρ [kg/m³] | % |
|---|---|
| **1,150** | **1.0** |
| 1,300 | 0.9 |
| 1,450 | 0.9 |
| 910 | 1.1 |
| 1,310 | 1.0 |

**Strength-to-weight**
theoretical length of strand of identical cross-section, suspended from one end, that can support its own weight without breaking

**Tensile strength**
ultimate breaking force of a strand of material (used to calculate tenacity)

**Cost**
raw material price

**Energy**
energy requirement

**Availability**
annual production

**Recycling**
end-of-life recycling

## INTRODUCTION

Coconut coir is obtained from the husk of the coconut palm (*Cocos nucifera*). A great deal of coconut is grown for food (copra, milk and desiccated coconut) and coir fibre is a by-product of this.

Around one-third of the coconut's weight is husk and one-third of that is fibre; the remainder is pith. The amount of coir fibre on the market is likely only a small proportion of total production, because most is used locally.

## COMMERCIAL TYPES AND USES

The two main types are brown and white. Brown is harvested from mature coconuts and white is obtained from coconuts before they have ripened (known as green). Brown fibre is shorter, coarser and stiffer than white fibre. It is mainly utilized for brush bristles, flooring and upholstery padding. White fibre is spun into yarn suitable for twine or weaving.

The fibre is used in the production of nonwoven textiles, such as geotextiles and roof felt. Rubberized coir is produced using a latex (page 248) matrix and is used in mattresses, flooring and upholstery.

White fibre is made up of around one-third cellulose and an equivalent amount of lignin; brown fibre contains an even higher proportion of lignin. This makes it difficult to dye, except for black. Bleaching produces shades of cream through brown. With exposure to ultraviolet, bleached fibre will gradually darken.

Coir pith, a by-product of fibre production, is now considered a valuable resource and is an alternative to peat as a growing medium for horticultural purposes (from seed cells to grow bags).

It also provides the matrix in coir fibreboard, or coir binderless board. This strong and dense building material provides a low-impact alternative to wood panels (see Engineered Timber, page 296).

The husk is ground until the fibres reach the desired length; it is placed into a mold that is the shape of the final product, and formed under heat and pressure. The lignin in the pith forms cross-links (similar to thermosetting plastic) to provide a strong and stable binder.

## SUSTAINABILITY

As a by-product of coconut production, the impacts of coir are limited to extraction and processing, the embodied energy of which is negligible.

The method of extraction depends on available production technology and requirements of the application. Short fibres that will be spun into yarn or converted into nonwoven (mattresses, upholstery and so on) can be extracted by straightforward decortication, without the need for retting (see page 402). The husks may need to be soaked for a few months and the run-off from this is polluting if not properly managed.

Long and high-quality fibres, such as so-called golden fibres used in bristles, traditionally involve a lengthy retting process. This generally takes place in standing water, such as lagoons. Large amounts of organic matter are released,

**Scrubbing brush** This type of Japanese scrubbing brush is known as 'kamenoko tawashi', which translates as 'turtle scrubber'. The hardy and long-lasting brown coir fibres are quite abrasive, which means it is good for pots and pans, but not suitable for delicate items.

which is highly polluting and impacts directly on biodiversity.

While the rate of mechanization is increasing in some countries, in particular India, traditional methods continue to be employed elsewhere. Small-scale producers are often obliged to stick with polluting processes.

ANIMAL

5

# Silk

Luxurious, strong and the only natural monofilament, silk is a unique fibre. There are thousands of silk-producing insects; the most appropriate fibre for textiles is derived from the cocoon of the mulberry silkworm. Many attempts have been made to harness the potential of spider's silk, but for now and for various reasons, this incredible fibre remains just out of reach.

| Types | Typical Applications | Sustainability |
|---|---|---|
| • Mulberry silkworm<br>• Tussah (or tussore) silkworm | • Apparel textiles and linings<br>• Medical<br>• Interior fabrics | • Sericulture is hugely energy-intensive<br>• Filament production requires that the pupa be killed |

| Properties | Competing Materials | Costs |
|---|---|---|
| • High strength-to-weight<br>• Lustrous with high affinity for dyestuffs<br>• Fine and smooth | • Wool and hair<br>• Man-made alternatives, in particular viscose, cellulose acetate and PET | • High raw material price; filament is the most expensive and staples are less so<br>• Relatively expensive to process |

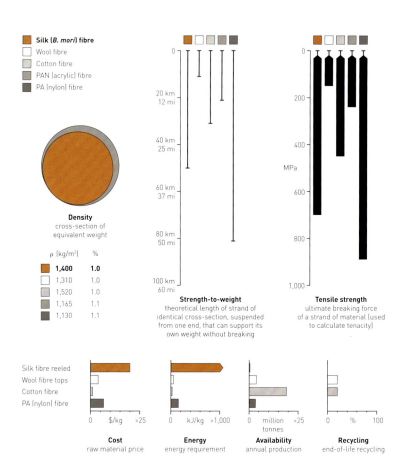

Silk (*B. mori*) fibre
Wool fibre
Cotton fibre
PAN (acrylic) fibre
PA (nylon) fibre

**Density**
cross-section of
equivalent weight

| ρ (kg/m³) | % |
|---|---|
| 1,400 | 1.0 |
| 1,310 | 1.0 |
| 1,520 | 1.0 |
| 1,165 | 1.1 |
| 1,130 | 1.1 |

**Strength-to-weight**
theoretical length of strand of
identical cross-section, suspended
from one end, that can support its
own weight without breaking

**Tensile strength**
ultimate breaking force
of a strand of material (used
to calculate tenacity)

Silk fibre reeled
Wool fibre tops
Cotton fibre
PA (nylon) fibre

**Cost**
raw material price

**Energy**
energy requirement

**Availability**
annual production

**Recycling**
end-of-life recycling

## INTRODUCTION

The superb mechanical properties of silk, as well as its outstanding qualities as a textile fibre, have been known since ancient times. The Chinese managed to keep sericulture, or silk production, secret for millennia. In the 3rd century BCE, around the time that the Silk Route from China to the Mediterranean became well established, knowledge about how to produce thread from domesticated silkworms spread to the rest of Asia and into Europe. Even so, the Chinese continued to dominate high-quality silk production for centuries.

Textile-processing innovations in 18th and 19th centuries, such as the development of the jacquard loom (to allow speedier production of highly figured fabrics), expanded the design opportunities of silk. More recently, silk has been used in medical applications, such as sutures. It is pliable, with excellent knot strength, and is biologically compatible with human tissue, so the immune system does not attack it. It is being explored for many other medical applications, including drug delivery systems and the creation of scaffolds for bone regeneration.

In 2011, the Institute of Materials Research and Engineering (IMRE) in Singapore published details of a technique they had developed for

**Digital printed scarf**
The smooth, uniform surface of woven silk, along with its white base colour, results in high-quality printed graphics. This scarf, from Silken Favours, London, combines lightweight woven silk with digital printing. With this process, multicolour files are transferred directly from computer to the substrate. This provides maximum flexibility; there are no minimums and turnaround is rapid. Screen-printing produces equally high-quality results, but is limited to larger volumes owing to the cost and complexity of set-up.

**Raw domesticated silk**
*(Bombyx mori)*

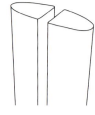

**Degummed domesticated silk filaments**

**Raw tussah silk**
*(genus Antheraea)*

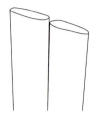

**Degummed tussah silk filaments**

### The structure of silk

Like wool, silk is a protein fibre made up of amino acids. Even though they consist of similar ingredients, they have some contrasting properties owing to the structure and strength of the chemical attachments. Caterpillars produce silk by mixing liquids from glands in their head. Raw silk thread is made up of fibroin (structural centre made up of insoluble protein) and sericin (adhesive gum that holds the fibroin filaments together). It is squeezed out through fibre-forming ducts and stretched, which causes the polypeptide chains that make up fibroin to become highly organized in a linear fashion (forming a highly crystalline structure, see page 166). With exposure to the atmosphere,

the fibre hardens. The adhesive makes up about one-third of the fibre by weight. In a process known as degumming, the fibre is soaked in water to dissolve the sericin and liberate the two strong filaments (each around 10 microns across). There are thousands of silk-producing insects; the characteristics of each has evolved to accommodate specific protective needs. Several species of moth larva produce a silk cocoon suitable for use in textile production, the most appropriate being the mulberry silkworm (*B. mori*). Once degummed, the filaments have a triangular cross-section that reflects light in all directions. Silk from tussah silkworms (genus *Antheraea*) is flatter, which gives a duller appearance.

producing coloured silk straight from the caterpillar. When fed dyed leaves a few days before it spins its cocoon, the silkworm produces intrinsically coloured filament, which could eliminate the energy, labour and waste associated with conventional dyeing. Still experimental, this innovation may need some time before making it into commercial textiles.

Over the years, several man-made fibres have been developed as an alternative to silk. The most successful include filaments extruded with the same triangular profile, such as polyamide (PA, nylon) (page 164), and viscose (page 252). These synthetic fibres are less expensive, highly controllable and potentially recyclable, and do not kill silkworms. Nevertheless, silk remains desirable and commands a high price.

As a protein fibre, it shares many similarities with wool (page 426). For example, silk is hydroscopic and can absorb around one-third of its weight in moisture before feeling damp (and gets weaker when wet); it is flame-retardant and self-extinguishes; and as a poor conductor it is inherently insulating. Thanks to the differences in chemical structure, and to the fineness of silk, it is stronger and smoother.

The role of the cocoon is to protect the larva during pupation. As a result, it has evolved some beneficially resistive properties, for example against alcohols, weak acids and water. The fibres are bonded together with sericin proteins excreted by the larva. These make up about a third of the cocoon once complete and are removed in the production of silk for textiles. Recent developments include combining this by-product with cosmetics, highly effective moisturizers, mixing with polymer foam to enhance moisture absorption properties, or simply using it as one part of a copolymer to make plastic film or sheet.

Spider's silk is considered to be one of the highest-performing fibres. Its combination of properties far exceeds any man-made material. It is not practical to farm spiders, so researchers have explored other ways to mass-produce or mimic the material. Since 2014, German company AMSilk has been producing a spider silk-inspired biopolymer manufactured from recombinant silk proteins. The new material, called Biosteel, is soft and, like natural silk, can be processed and dyed.

### COMMERCIAL TYPES AND USES

Modern sericulture involves traditional practices. A great deal of the work is done by hand, so production is limited to

countries where low labour costs make it economically viable.

Although there are many thousand species, the mulberry silkworm (*Bombyx mori*) is the most widely studied and cultivated. The eggs are hatched and fed leaves of mulberry (*Morus alba*) for around one month. After this time, they make their cocoon, which may contain up to 1.5 km (nearly 1 mi) of thread.

The cocoons are heated to kill the moths and the silk is soaked in water to dissolve the sericin. The filaments are carefully unravelled by hand. The filaments vary and so several are typically combined to produce a uniform thread.

Silk filament is utilized for its luxurious softness and lustre, as well as its practical benefits. It is converted into satin fabrics and velvet for fine garments and interior fabrics and used for embroidery. Its high absorbency and insulating properties mean that it is comfortable and lightweight in garments designed for both cold and warm weather conditions.

Tussah (or tussore) silk is derived from several types of moth in the genus *Antheraea*. It is typically around half the price of *B. mori*. Traditionally, this silk came from wild larvae. Nowadays, this is less common, because it is not so financially rewarding as sericulture. The larvae feed on a variety of leaf types, which means the colour of the filament ranges from pale cream to dark brown. Most commercial tussah silk comes from China (*A. pernyi*) reared on oak leaves, so the filament is honey-coloured. The fibres are around 30 microns wide, considerably coarser than silk from *B. mori*.

If the silkworm is allowed to complete its metamorphosis and hatch then the filament will be broken. These cocoons are converted into staple (short-fibre) silk. While not so valuable as filaments, staple

**Jacquard-woven**
Textile designer Victoria Richards works with silk to produce bright, bold and eye-catching patterns in her ties. In this example, the Dublin Big Wave, the pattern is jacquard-woven

and so integral to the fabric. The difference between jacquard and conventional looms is that the warp yarns are controlled individually. This means that they are more versatile and capable of producing any type of pattern.

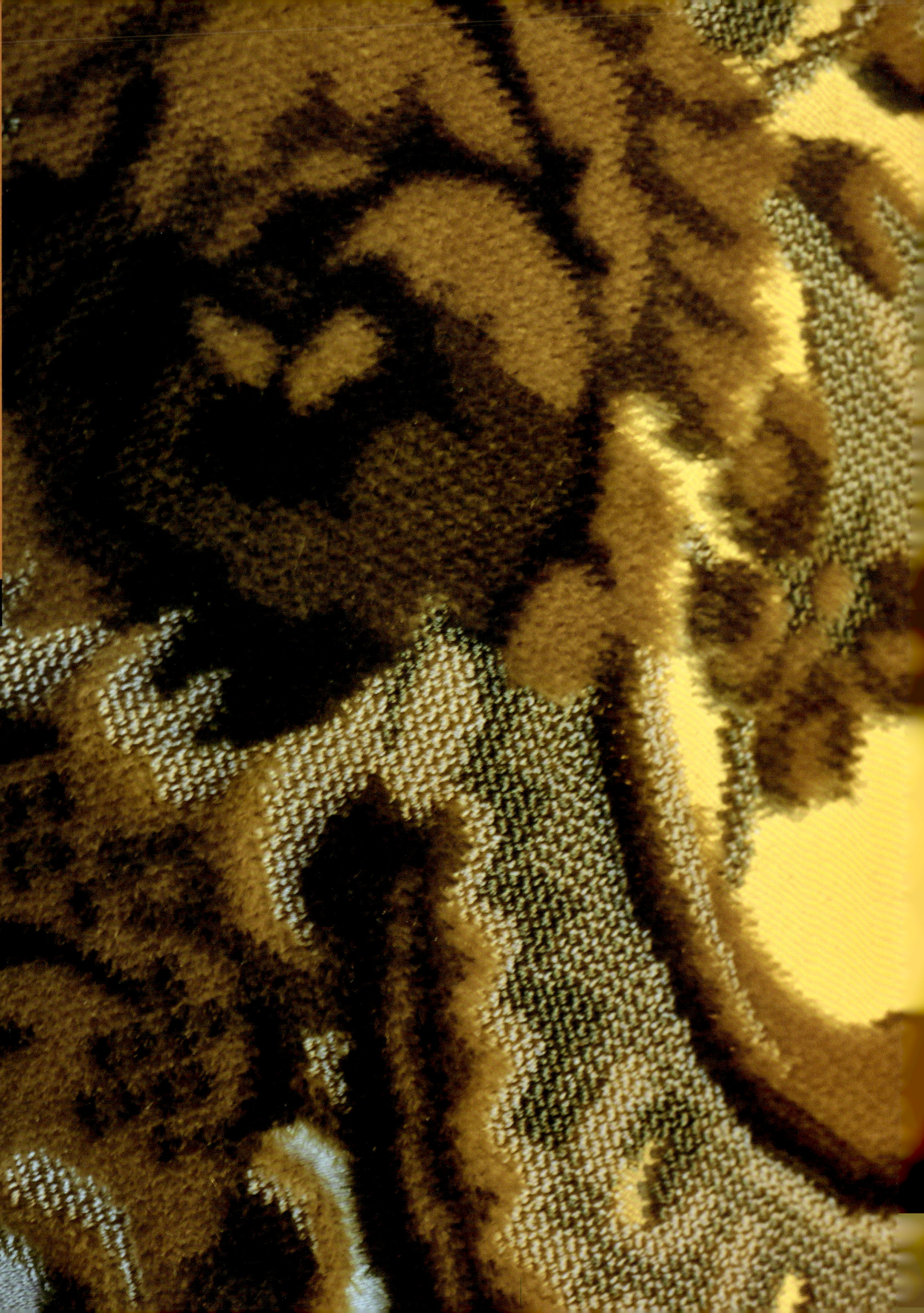

silk can be blended (to impart softness and strength) and processed using the same equipment as other natural fibres.

## SUSTAINABILITY
Silk production has changed little since the Industrial Revolution. While it may be considered sustainable in some ways, it is energy-intensive to produce. *B. mori* feeds exclusively on mulberry leaves and this presents a significant input, because growing mulberry requires water, energy, herbicides, pesticides and fertilizer.

It takes around 10 kg (22 lb) of cocoons to produce 1 kg (2.2 lb) raw silk. Reeling uses a lot of energy, as the cocoons need to be heated in water for a prolonged period at specific pH and hardness.

To make a continuous filament the pupa must be killed before it can turn into a moth and break out of the cocoon. Using farmed or wild staple silk means the caterpillar has been allowed to grow into a moth (although some staple comes from the waste of cultivated filament). By-products of sericulture include pupae, leaves and waste silk. These are typically used as fertilizer.

## SILK IN FASHION AND TEXTILES
Silk is unique among the natural fibres. It comes as one long filament, as opposed to staples (short fibres). The advantage of this is that silk fabrics can be woven very light (such as sheer chiffon), smooth or dense; more so than any other natural fibre. Now, modern man-made fibres offer far higher strength-to-weight. This reduced the demand for silk in non-essential applications and elevated its status as a luxury and exclusive fibre.

Choice of fabric is critical, because the full potential of silk is only realized when the fibre is floated (exposed on the surface) and allowed to shine. Therefore, the fine and lustrous properties of silk are best exploited in satin weaves (see page 240), whose long floating yarns catch the

**Figured velvet**
Complex figured velvet continues to be made by hand at Prelle, Lyon, France, assisted by the jacquard process. Using the over-wire method, loop and cut pile are combined with a satin-woven ground. Such is the complexity of this design that it takes about one day to weave just 300 mm (12 in).

Weft pile (corduroy and velveteen)

Over-wire (figured velvet and Wilton carpet)

Axminster (carpet)

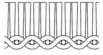

Double-cloth (velvet and faux fur and technical textiles)

Slack tension (terry, towel, cloth and seersucker)

Tufted cut pile (carpet, rugs, faux fur and artificial grass)

Tufted loop pile (carpet, rugs, faux fur and artificial grass)

**Woven pile fabric**
Material selection and technique depend on the application. Silk is used to make the highest-quality fabrics; cotton is used for its softness and high moisture absorption; wool provides insulation and padding; and man-made fibres are used in virtually all situations where pile fabrics are used. Corduroy and velveteen are constructed in the same way: wefts are woven with long floats, cut and brushed to open up the fibres.

Whereas corduroy has distinctive wales (ridges) that run the length of the fabric, velveteen does not follow an orderly linear fashion. Velvet, as well as some faux fur, is produced as double-cloth. Two layers of fabric are woven simultaneously, joined by lengths of warp, which are cut to form pile. The over-wire technique allows for figured designs (utilizing jacquard) to be produced with velvet-like quality. Weaving with the

warps held over wires forms the pile. Once the fabric is stable the wires are removed to leave loops; incorporating a blade at the end of the wire produces cut pile. Wilton, considered to be the finest carpet, is produced in this way. Terry and seersucker are produced with slack-tension weaving. This is a simple technique: the pile warps are left slack and the rest compacted, which causes loops to be formed. The pile can be on one side or both sides, depending on the warp arrangement. The

Axminster technique is used solely for carpet. The pile is inserted into a base fabric and held in place by the weft yarns. This allows for many colours to be used, and with computer-guided looms, one-offs and bespoke designs are possible. Tufting is similar, except that the pile is formed from a continuous yarn that is fed through a base layer or carrier fabric. It is carried out by hand using a tufting gun, or on a large loom with rows of needles.

light and show brilliant colour. Long floats allow for the fibres to be packed together very tightly, by reducing the number of interlacings, creating a dense fabric that enhances colour saturation.

Velvet, or silk pile, takes advantage of its fineness. As a filament, it can be woven with extremely dense pile, unrivalled among the natural fibres. Velvet is used in apparel and interiors, but is limited to applications that will not cause abrasion to the delicate surface. Flattening the

pile will affect the look and feel. Crushed velvet takes advantage of this, produced by twisting the fabric when wet.

Traditionally, silk was measured in terms of momme (mm), a measurement system developed in Japan. Momme weight is the weight in pounds of a piece of fabric 45 in (114 cm) wide and 100 yards (91.4 m) long. Thus, 15-momme silk is notionally silk that would weigh 15 lb (6.8 kg) if it were those dimensions. Heavier fabric has a higher momme weight.

# Wool

**Wool is a renewable fibre harvested from sheep. Ranging from coarse to fine, it has many desirable qualities, including water resistance, moisture absorption, fire resistance and good insulation properties, and dyes very well. These are the reasons why it has been so widely used for so long, even considering its relatively high cost; rearing animals is expensive.**

| Types | Typical Applications | Sustainability |
|---|---|---|
| • Virgin (new), reclaimed or salvaged<br>• Lamb (first shearing), hogget (first shearing from a sheep older than 7–8 months) and sheep (subsequent shearings) | • Apparel and undergarments<br>• Upholstery and interior fabrics<br>• Carpet, rugs and throws | • Renewable and compostable or recyclable<br>• Processing consumes energy, water and chemicals<br>• Can be a sensitizer |

| Properties | Competing Materials | Costs |
|---|---|---|
| • Highly resilient and insulating<br>• Fine to coarse and straight to crimped, depending on breed<br>• Water-resistant and fire-resistant | • Hair and silk<br>• PAN, PET, PA and similar man-made fibres<br>• Leaf fibres and grass | • Moderate to high raw material cost<br>• Low-cost to process from fabric |

**Also known as**
Yarn referred to as: worsted, woollen
Nonwoven referred to as: felt

## INTRODUCTION

Wool is an exceptionally versatile fibre available in many different guises. The raw fibre is used to provide insulation, felted to make a smooth and stiff fabric, or converted into yarn that is subsequently knitted or woven into high-quality textile. The properties of textile depend on the fibre – type and age of animal, and processing – through fabric construction. Wool offers many opportunities compared to other types of natural, as well man-made fibres. It is renewable, sustainable and, owing to the diversity of breeds farmed throughout the world, available in a range of different qualities.

As a natural protein fibre (see also Hair, page 434, and Silk, page 420), wool is inherently fire-resistant. To be precise, it will burn when in a flame, but self-extinguish once the flame is removed. This is in stark contrast to plant fibres, such as cotton (page 410) and hemp (page 406), which burn readily once they have been exposed to an open flame.

Protein, in the form of keratin, is vulnerable to environmental conditions; more so than cellulose, which makes up the aforementioned vegetable fibres. As a result, wool loses strength when wet, as well as becoming more flexible and supple. It returns to its full strength and stiffness once dry. This is handy for production, because reducing the

**Felt slipper** This is thought to be one of the earliest forms of textile; construction is simple and does not require a loom, like woven and knitted fabric. Subjecting layers of wool (or hair) to heat, moisture, pressure and oscillation causes the fibres to become entangled. The scales on the surface interlock, preventing the wool fibres from moving, resulting in a strong, dense fabric. It is utilized in applications ranging from Mongolian yurts (nomadic tents) to these Danish house slippers.

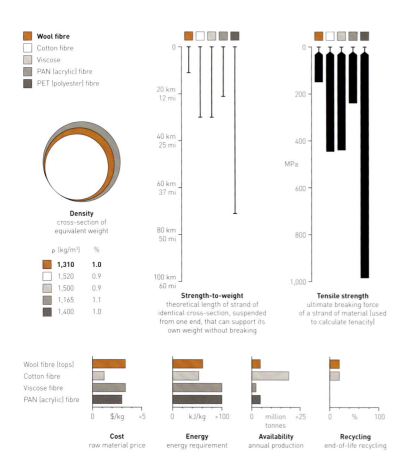

Wool fibre
Cotton fibre
Viscose
PAN (acrylic) fibre
PET (polyester) fibre

**Density**
cross-section of equivalent weight

| ρ (kg/m³) | % |
|---|---|
| 1,310 | 1.0 |
| 1,520 | 0.9 |
| 1,500 | 0.9 |
| 1,165 | 1.1 |
| 1,400 | 1.0 |

**Strength-to-weight**
theoretical length of strand of identical cross-section, suspended from one end, that can support its own weight without breaking

**Tensile strength**
ultimate breaking force of a strand of material (used to calculate tenacity)

Wool fibre (tops)
Cotton fibre
Viscose fibre
PAN (acrylic) fibre

**Cost**
raw material price

**Energy**
energy requirement

**Availability**
annual production

**Recycling**
end-of-life recycling

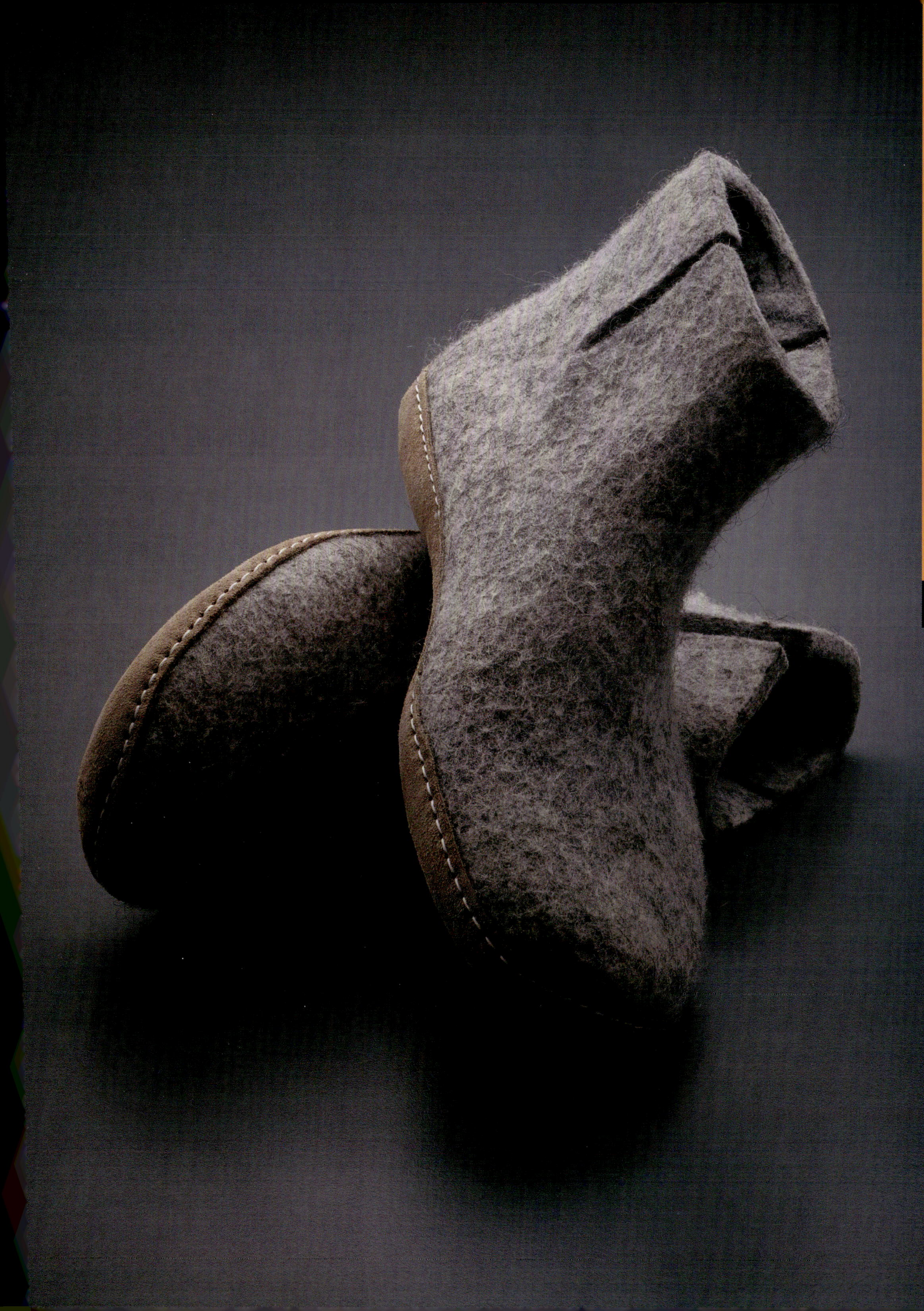

bending strength makes it easier to process into yarn.

## COMMERCIAL TYPES AND USES

Wool is graded according to strength, length, fineness, consistency and number of defects. Wool fibre diameter is measured in microns (a micron is a micrometre, one thousandth of a millimetre, or about 0.00004 inches), ranging from 10 to 50. There are different applications for wool, depending on its diameter. Fine wool up to 30 microns is typically used in items where softness and smoothness are important, such as apparel. The finest wool fibres are utilized in the production of high-quality garments, from formal suits to underwear. Work clothes and other more durable items tend to use mid-range fibres, which offer a more suitable balance of smoothness and durability. Coarser fibres are utilized in applications that will be subjected to even greater wear and tear, such as overcoats, rugs and carpet.

Wool grows from follicles in the sheep's skin and has a wavy structure. Known as crimp, the ripples are the result of its bilateral construction; the two halves have slightly opposing properties and so cause the fibre to twist and bend. This contributes to wool's elasticity and resilience. The number of crimps per unit length can be taken as a guide to fibre fineness: fine fibres tend to be highly crimped; mid-range fibres have what is known as coarse crimp; and the largest diameter fibres have very little crimp, if any.

Lambswool is obtained from sheep that are younger than seven months old. The first shearing produces the finest and softest wool because one end remains uncut. The superior qualities of this wool are utilized in fine products, including lightweight garments, baby clothes and scarves.

**Hand-knitted jumper**
A traditional Icelandic jumper constructed from local wool. The yarn is left untwisted (known as *plötulopi*), which makes it tricky to knit, but due to the long staples (fibres) it yields a particularly soft jumper that is also sturdy.

Hoggets are sheep that are older than seven or eight months, but less than two years (yearling). The wool may still be from the first shearing. In which case it retains the uncut end, but will be stronger (coarser) than lambswool.

Sheepswool comes from all subsequent shearings. The sheep's genes determine the fibre quality to a great extent, shaped by the environment that they have evolved to thrive in. There are several pure breeds of sheep whose wool is widely used, including Merino (fine, high crimp, bulky, high quality), Jacob (thick, low crimp, mixed colour, hardy), English Leicester (thick, low crimp with long staples) and New Zealand Romney (heavy and durable fibre). It is labelled 'virgin wool' when processed for the first time. Wool produced from recycled fibre is known as salvaged or reclaimed.

## SUSTAINABILITY

Wool is a by-product of the meat and milk industries; sheep are sheared to avoid them overheating or catching fly strike (maggot infestation) during the summer months. Of course, unlike leather (page 444) and fur (page 466), it does not require that the animals be killed. However, some wool will have been sheared from slaughtered animals.

Wool production begins on farms, where sheep graze grass or eat hay or feed. Other inputs include fertilizer, medicine and bedding. Once the fleece has been sheared, the fibres are washed – consuming approximately 4 litres (1 gallon) of water per 1 kg (2.2 lb) of finished wool – and processed using chemicals and energy. Even allowing for this, the production of wool has a lower environmental impact than the production of man-made fibres.

There are many incentives for buying wool. However, the animal proteins and oils can causes skin allergies in some people. For this reason baby clothes are more often produced from cotton.

## WOOL IN FASHION AND TEXTILES

Wool is a high-quality and high-performance fibre unrivalled by man-made alternatives. It is suitable for

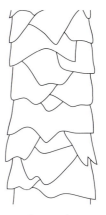

**Coarse wool**

**Fine wool**

**Wool fibre properties**
Wool, hair and fur (page 466) consist of keratin (a fibrous protein). The fibres are made up of a cortex (core) – a complex layered structure of spiralling microfibrils – wrapped in a protective layer of overlapping cuticle cells. These act like hooks, gripping the scaled surface of other fibres. This surface prevents the fibres slipping over one another and is the basis for felt. This property also makes wool products difficult to launder, as they tend to shrink and become stiffer. The scaly surface aids in the production of resilient yarn, as the entangled fibres are relatively difficult to pull apart. This attribute means wool is suitable for light openwork fabrics with good shape retention. Fibres range from very fine (10 microns) to coarse (50 microns). Fine wool with low-profile scales, such as Merino, will not grip together so well. Thus, yarn is twisted a little tighter to prevent the fibres slipping.

**Woollen**

**Worsted**

**Wool yarn configurations** In the construction of yarn, multiple fibres are twisted together. Woollen yarn is made from shorter staples (fibres) that are carded to remove tangles and debris. Yarns produced from this mix of fibres tend to be light and airy (bulky). Worsted yarn is produced from fibres that are combed to increase alignment and remove the shorter staples. The yarn is stiffer, stronger and harder. Bulkier woollen yarn has fewer twists per inch (TPI), because it contains more air between the fibres.

### Absorbency

Wool is highly absorbent and can take on around one-third of its weight in water before it feels wet or clammy. Unlike plant fibres and down, wool retains its insulating properties when wet, a quality that has been exploited in cold-weather clothing for millennia.

### Colour

Wool has an excellent affinity to dyestuffs. It can be produced in a range of colours, from muted to vivid. Even so, it is also often processed in its natural colour, which offers great variety, depending on the breed.

### Wrinkle resistance

Wool has excellent elastic recovery: it can be bent around 20,000 times before breaking, compared to just a few thousand for cotton and some man-made fibres. This resilience means that wool items are less likely to crease.

### Durability and resilience

The crimp allows wool fibres to be stretched considerably – up to 50% when wet and 30% when dry – before breaking. Once the pressure is released, the fibre springs back to its original shape; recovery is faster in a humid environment.

warm- as well as cold-weather clothing. This is mainly due to its hygroscopic nature: it absorbs both moisture from the atmosphere and sweat. This helps it to regulate temperature, providing protection in all weather conditions. However, the choice of fibre will be different depending on the intended end use. Cold-weather garments are bulky and insulating, providing the greatest possible barrier between the wearer and low temperatures. Warm-weather clothing, on the other hand, should be as light as possible. Garments produced from very fine Merino are sometimes referred to as Cool Wool, which is a sub-brand of Woolmark. This indicates the use of fibres with a mean diameter of 22.5 microns or less, and a maximum fabric weight of 190 g/m² (5.6 oz/yd²). Dating back to the 1980s, Cool Wool is so called to draw attention to the fact that lightweight wool garments are suitable for warm-weather clothing.

Owing to its natural crimp, wool is durable, resilient and elastic. It can tolerate a lot of abuse and bend many thousand times before breaking. However, it is vulnerable to felting. While this is advantageous in some situations (it is referred to as milling or fulling when used to produce a soft surface on wool textiles), it means that wool garments

**Left**
**Napped lambswool**
Woven wool fabrics are finished with a variety of processes to enhance the visual and textile qualities. Raising the nap creates a softer finish, increases cushioning and improves insulation. In the past, napping was done with dried teasel pods. Teasels are still used today to produce some of the finest woollen products, such as scarves and blankets; however, the majority of napping is now done with wire brushes. The two processes are essentially the same, except that the brushing is done with either a natural material or a wire brush.

**Opposite**
**Upholstery** Danish designer Finn Juhl created the Poeten (Poet) sofa for his own home in 1941. This example is upholstered in Kvadrat Remix (see overleaf). Its name is in reference to its appearance in the romantic Danish film *The Poet and his Wife*, (1959). The backrest is button tufted, creating a distinctive relief profile. Photo courtesy of House of Finn Juhl.

are not easy to care for. Treatments exist, such as Superwash (a chemical coating), that can reduce friction and entanglement, thus allowing garments to be machine-washed.

Wool fibres pass through extensive processing prior to being converted into yarn. Only about half the fleece

sheared from a sheep is usable. The rest includes lanolin (fatty substance that has many uses elsewhere), dirt and other contamination. Separating the usable fibres involves several washing stages, which are collectively referred to as scouring. Next, the fibres are carded, which removes tangles and any

**Light shade** Luceplan, Italy, produces the Silenzio suspension lamp clad in Kvadrat Remix fabric, which is 90% wool and 10% nylon. Designed by Monica Armani, 2013, the lamp may be

customized to fit with the decor thanks to the fabric selection. Another benefit of wool is that it is an efficient sound insulator, hence the name given to this design. Photo by Studio CCRZ.

remaining debris. This raw mix of fibres may be processed directly into felt. Layers of fibres are laid on top of one another and combined with moisture, heat, agitation and pressure. The fibres become entangled and the scales (see page 429) hold them together as a dense sheet.

Woollen yarn is produced from wool that has been carded but not combed. Combing removes the shorter staples and improves the alignment of the fibres, resulting in a superior-quality yarn (worsted) that is preferred for fine and formal garments. Fabrics woven from worsted yarn will be smoother with better shape retention. The weave pattern tends to be clearly visible (unless surface treatments have been carried out). Woollen yarn, on the other hand, is preferred for casual knitwear, because it yields a softer and bulkier garment.

Wool may be a natural fibre, but this does not exclude it from continual innovations and development in the mill. As an example, Australia's national science research agency, CSIRO, in a project funded by Australian Wool Innovation Ltd, developed a way to reduce the surface energy of wool and thus the ability of water to cling to fibres. As a result, the amount of water it can absorb is reduced while the speed with which it dries is increased. This finishing technology, labelled Quick-Dry Merino (QDM), increases the efficiency of washing and drying, and reduces water absorption in wet weather.

Another recent example is MerinoPerform WP, which is an innovative pure wool fabric constructed from Optim Max. This fibre has been stretched but not set. When wet-finished, the stretch is released, causing the fibre to contract and an extreme tightening of the fabric structure. The contracting results in a fabric with enhanced water resistance and reduced air permeability. This gives a textile suitable for sportswear and outdoor pursuits, hence the name. The fabric is crisp, resistant to wrinkles and resilient, providing an alternative to polyamide (PA, nylon) (page 164).

There are several man-made alternatives to wool that are suitable for use in garments. While they offer

**Resistant to flames**
Even without chemical treatment wool does not support combustion. It will burn in the presence of a flame, but self-extinguish as soon as the source of fire has been removed.

**Resistant to compression**
This determines its suitability for a range of applications. Fine fibres with a high level of crimp tend to have lower resistance and are used to make fine textiles, such as for garments. At the other end of the spectrum, hardy fibres with high resistance are suitable as padding in mattresses.

**Durability and wear resistance**
The surface of wool resists soiling and provides a durable surface that can tolerate heavy wear. This means wool is suitable for demanding situations, such as carpets and furniture in high-traffic areas. However, applications are somewhat limited by the relatively high initial cost compared to man-made alternatives.

cost savings and a host of design opportunities – colour, formability and so on – they cannot compete with wool's unique combination of high-performance attributes. As a result, wool is often combined with synthetics to take advantage of the benefits of both.

Polyacrylonitrile (PAN) fibre, also known as acrylic (page 174), is soft and lofty and commonly used as a wool substitute. Woven or knitted PAN pile is even used to mimic fur and fleece (see Sheepskin, page 452), dyed and painted to look as natural as possible.

The regenerated fibres, including cellulose acetate (CA) and viscose (page 252), are often used in combination with wool. Viscose has a lustrous surface, the properties of which can be controlled to come extent. This means it can be produced to look and feel like wool, as well as other natural fibres. CA is formed with heat and pressure. This thermoplastic quality allows for permanent pleats or embossing to be achieved with CA/wool blends.

## WOOL IN FURNITURE, LIGHTING AND INTERIORS
Wool fabrics are utilized extensively throughout the interior. They provide luxurious and durable upholstery; deep-pile and long-lasting carpet; cushioning; and insulation.

Wool is not a cheap fibre. The initial cost is, in some cases, several times higher than man-made alternatives. Of course, this is not always true, because high-quality, high-performance synthetics are not cheap either. Over time, wool tends to work out less expensive, because it is so long-lasting.

In the case of carpets, wool is used alongside durable man-made fibres such PA and polypropylene (PP) (page 98). Each has their unique advantages and, as a result, they are often combined to maximize the benefits. A mix of 80% wool and 20% synthetic is chosen for the places that will get the hardest wear, because the wool ages gracefully; 100% wool is used only for the most expensive domestic applications.

Wool is inherently anti-static, thanks to its high moisture absorption. This helps it to stay clean for longer – static energy attracts dirt and dust – which is useful for interior fabrics, such as carpet and upholstery. The anti-static properties are further improved by incorporating a small proportion of conductive fibres. Such fabrics are used in aircraft, workwear and packaging, for example.

Felt is used in a wide range of applications and is now more often produced from materials other than wool. A range of synthetics, as well as other materials, is used. Non-wool felts are produced with needle punching. This is a versatile production method: the fibres are entangled using barbed needles, which are passed back and forth through the raw material. As such, virtually any type of material may be combined, including wool. Choice depends on the application. For example, where absorbency is the primary concern, materials such as viscose, polyethylene terephthalate (PET, polyester) (page 152), wool and kenaf (page 404) are used; for fire-retardant items aramid (page 242), carbon, PAN and wool are preferred; and acoustic applications use wool, polyester and hemp, for example.

# Hair

**Also known as**
Softer types generically referred to as: wool
Cashmere also referred to as: pashmina

**These are sophisticated protein-based fibres that range from ultra-soft angora to rare vicuña. Animals that have evolved in cold climates grow fur coats that are highly insulating and provide a great deal of protection from the elements. We have been harvesting these fibres and converting them into fabric for millennia, taking advantage of their many useful properties.**

| Types | Typical Applications | Sustainability |
|---|---|---|
| • Goat: cashmere and mohair (angora)<br>• Rabbit: angora<br>• Camel, llama, alpaca, vicuña, guanaco<br>• Bovine: qiviut (muskox) and yak | • Apparel<br>• Throws, rugs and carpets<br>• Tents and ropes<br>• Brush bristles and wigs | • As with wool, hair is renewable and harvested from animals periodically; the source is critical to ensure high standards of animal welfare |
| **Properties** | **Competing Materials** | **Costs** |
| • Depends on type. Angora has the highest heat retention and best moisture wicking; alpaca is durable and lightweight; cashmere is luxuriously soft. | • Wool and silk<br>• Man-made fibres, such as viscose, cellulose and PAN<br>• Leather and fur | • Soft undercoat used in similar situations to wool tends to be more expensive, because it is produced in lower quantities<br>• Processing is similar to wool |

434

## INTRODUCTION

Hair is similar to wool (page 426) and like fur (page 466) includes a mix of guard hairs and undercoat. The role of the long stiff guard hairs is to protect the undercoat of fine downy fibres that insulate the animal. Short, brittle hairs, called kemp, may be intermingled with both types of fibre. During the conversion process, blowing or combing is used to separate the different types. The softest and most luxurious fabrics are produced from yarns that contain very little, if any, guard hairs or kemp. By contrast, tents, ropes and bristles rely on the relatively longer, stronger and stiffer hairs.

As protein-based fibres, they share many qualities with wool, such as moisture absorption, wicking and fire resistance. Generally, the soft undercoat is finer and the scales less pronounced than on wool, making them less prone to felting. Fibres from younger animals are superior and the first shearing or moulting produces the highest quality, because only one end is cut and the other remains naturally rounded. Expect the price of baby hair to be around double that of high-quality adult fibre.

Hair is mimicked using man-made fibres. The closest resemblance, in terms of physical and aesthetic properties, is achieved with polyacrylonitrile (PAN, acrylic) (page 180), as well as viscose and cellulose acetate (CA) (page 252). They are light and lustrous and the surface can be tailored to closely resemble the look and feel of animal hair.

## COMMERCIAL TYPES AND USES

Goat's hair includes cashmere and mohair. These fibres are generally superior to sheep's wool, though this will depend on the quality and age of the animal.

Mohair comes from the angora goat (*Capra hircus ancryrensis*). It is the closest

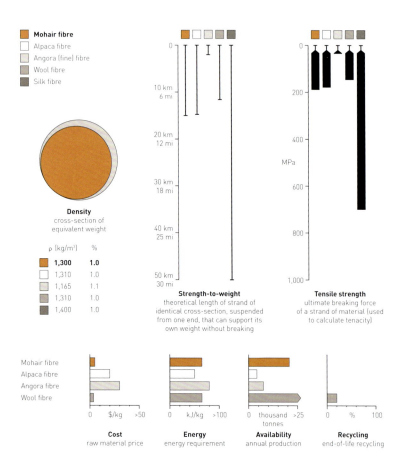

Mohair fibre
Alpaca fibre
Angora (fine) fibre
Wool fibre
Silk fibre

**Density**
cross-section of
equivalent weight

| ρ [kg/m³] | % |
|---|---|
| 1,300 | 1.0 |
| 1,310 | 1.0 |
| 1,165 | 1.1 |
| 1,310 | 1.0 |
| 1,400 | 1.0 |

**Strength-to-weight**
theoretical length of strand of
identical cross-section, suspended
from one end, that can support its
own weight without breaking

**Tensile strength**
ultimate breaking force
of a strand of material (used
to calculate tenacity)

**Cost**
raw material price

**Energy**
energy requirement

**Availability**
annual production

**Recycling**
end-of-life recycling

to wool, in terms of physical properties, and consumed in the largest quantities (around four times more than cashmere). The only significant differences are that it is longer, less crimped and has less pronounced scales; its smooth surface gives good lustre. Like wool, it is prized for its resilience, durability and strength (mohair works out stronger on average, because the fibres tend to be coarser). Fibres range in thickness from 20 to 40 microns, depending on the age of the goat, and have good insulation properties.

Smaller-diameter fibre is considered the best quality and is obtained from kids or young goats within their first few shearings. Typically, the kids are shorn at six months old (producing less than 1 kg [2.2 lb]), 12 months (around 2.5 kg [5.5 lb]) and every six months thereafter. There is little difference between the hair that grows from the primary and secondary follicles – high-quality fleece will contain very little medullated (kemp-type) hair – so the whole coat may be converted into yarn. Medullated fibres have a different texture and colour and affect the processing of the fibre, resulting in lower-quality yarn.

Mohair has very good wrinkle resistance, which when combined with its high stiffness produces a fabric well suited to warm-weather clothing. As a result, fine suits produced from mohair are popular in hot and humid climates, such as Japan. Its lightweight and insulating properties are equally desirable in cold-weather clothing, such as knitwear (this is likely the largest area of application) and blankets. Its durability and resilience are utilized in rugs and carpets. Today, the majority of mohair comes from South Africa.

**Knitted German angora long johns**
Angora is popularly used in the construction of medical and thermal underwear. These long johns contain just 25% German angora (75% cotton), which is enough to provide the comfort benefits of its thermal properties. Pure angora would be very warm and not so comfortable. Unlike wool, angora does not contain lanolin, which can cause skin irritation. Thus, combining it with cotton ensures a hypoallergenic garment.

Cashmere is the fine and downy hair obtained from the neck region of the cashmere goat (*Capra hircus laniger*). It makes up only about one quarter of a typical 125 g (4.4 oz) fleece. They take time and care to extract – the highest-quality fibre is obtained from the goat by combing over one or two weeks during the spring moulting season – making this an expensive fibre (costing several times more than mohair). This practice, which originated in the Kashmir Valley in northern India, has been carried out since ancient times. Nowadays, the majority of cashmere comes from China, as well as Mongolia, Turkey and Pakistan.

It is typically around 15 to 18 microns, which is comparable with the highest-quality Merino. The natural colour ranges from white through grey and brown. It can be dyed a range of colours and is often blended with wool, as well as man-made fibres, to keep the cost down. It is used to make a limited number of fine-quality

**Baby alpaca throw** The Inca were the first to exploit the fibre for textiles, around 5,000 BCE, and since then it continues to be used in luxury clothing, blankets and tapestries. Baby alpaca, which comes from the first shearing before the animal is a year old, is extremely soft and luxurious. It is thought the Inca reserved this fibre for royalty. The chevron throw by American designer Jonathan Adler is hand-woven by Peruvians, who reinterpreted classic patterns for this project.

items such as suits, sweaters, scarves, socks and blankets. Cashmere shawls are also known as pashmina (traditionally from northern India). The lower-value hairs – typically around 80 microns in diameter – from the rest of the fleece are used to make padding, among other things.

Angora is a luxuriously soft fibre obtained from the angora rabbit (genus *Oryctolagus*). There are four main breeds that grow a long coat much more quickly than other types – English is the silkiest; French is a little coarser with around one-third guard hairs; German (Giant) is the result of selective breeding and yields a high quantity of fine and soft fibre; and Satin is lighter. Intensive selective breeding over centuries has produced a very smooth and fine fibre, in the region of 15 microns. Ultra-fine angora, below 15 microns, has superior softness, but is not so durable, and is prone to shedding fibres and wearing out quickly.

All types of angora contain medullated hairs. They are partially hollow, which accounts for the low density and high insulation properties of the fibre, and this affects the dyeability and processibility of the fibre. The porosity increases the brittleness of the fibre, making them prone to break during processes and thus difficult to spin into yarn. It also affects how well they accept dyestuffs. Therefore, it is important that there is homogenous distribution of fibre diameter and medullation to ensure a high-quality end result.

Blending angora with other fibres, such as wool and cotton, yields superior fabrics than would be possible with angora alone. Fabric knitted or woven from pure angora would be very expensive, more likely to have irregularities and prone to shedding fibres. Colour ranges from white through brown and black. It is used in knitted and woven outer garments, as well as underwear, hosiery and hats.

Alpaca (*Lama pacos*), llama (*Lama guanicoe glama*), vicuña (*Vicugna vicugna*) and guanaco (*Lama guanicoe*) are closely related animals (members of the camel family) of South America. Compared to sheep's wool, these fibres tend to be stronger and finer. They are naturally antimicrobial and, unlike

wool, do not contain lanolin, which means they are lighter as well as being hypoallergenic. They yield long staples, which are converted into both woollen and worsted yarn (see page 429). The finer fibres, which tend to have much less pronounced scales, require a tighter twist to produce a resilient yarn. Fabrics woven from this yarn will be particularly smooth, stiff and strong.

Alpaca and llama have been domesticated since ancient times and

**Horsehair bristles** Not all hair is converted into fabric. The guard hairs, manes and tails of horses and yaks, for example, are utilized in ropes, wigs, brush bristles and fishing lures. This shaving brush features horsehair in a walnut (page 348) handle. Despite its strength and stiffness, the uncut end remains soft on the skin.

are sheared like sheep. They yield a soft and bulky fibre, which is partially hollow, making it a superior insulator. There are two principal domesticated breeds of alpaca: Huacaya and Suri. While the former has a fine, dense, uniform and curly coat, Suri hair is longer, silky and more lustrous (thanks to the long scales on its surface). The Suri is less common and so its hair tends to fetch a higher price. It is quite slippery and so often mixed with cotton (page 410), wool or silk (page 420) to make it easier to work.

The softest fibre is derived from the neck and chin area. The diameter ranges form 15 to 25 microns, making it a little coarser than cashmere. Alpaca have been reared and bred for their hair for so long that 22 natural shades have evolved, from creamy-white to black and including shades of grey and brown. These can, of course, be mixed to create intermediate shades, or dyed like wool.

Llamas are not traditionally bred for their hair – instead they are used as pack animals and to guard livestock – but yield a soft and insulating fibre. It is not as consistent or high-quality as alpaca and is produced in significantly smaller quantities; applications span rugged apparel (such as ponchos) through fine outerwear. The softest and finest hair comes from cria, or baby llamas.

Vicuña and guanaco are wild and are an endangered species. The vicuña is the rarest of all, because the animal was hunted almost to extinction by the 1960s and so is now governed by strict South American laws. Vicuña fibre is exquisite, very fine and around 12 microns in diameter. It is highly insulating and soft – it protects the animals from the very cold weather high up in the Andes. The coarser guard hairs are typically removed from the shorn fleece by hand. Guanaco fibre is coarser – around 15 microns – and considered lower quality, but is still a luxury fibre comparable with cashmere.

Vicuña hair grows very slowly and so, according to Peruvian law, they are caught, sheared and released no more than once every two years. This equates to just a few tonnes of fibre each year.

Camel hair is derived from the domesticated Bactrian camel (*Camelus*

*bactrianus*) or the dromedary camel (*Camelus dromedarius*), which is also called the Arabian camel. These breeds have served as pack animals since ancient times. The hair is collected by hand and is a by-product of keeping the camels that are used for transporting people and goods around the desert. In the wild, the Bactarian camel (*Camelus ferus*) is now critically endangered.

The coat is typically a shade of brown, but can be almost white. Both the strong, coarse outer hair and the soft undercoat are used to make textiles. The guard hairs can be up to 400 mm (15 in) long, while the downy hairs are 19 to 24 microns thick and up to 125 mm (5 in) long. It has good water-shedding properties and is highly insulating, as a result of having to keep the animal warm during the cold desert nights and cool during the hot days. Used mainly by local herders to make clothes and shelter, it is difficult to obtain a consistent supply.

Yaks (*Bos mutus*) live mainly in the Tibetan Plateau in the Himalayan region of south-central Asia. They are farmed for their meat and milk, and like cows their hide (page 444) and bone (page 442). In the wild they are endangered.

Their fleece contains three specific types of fibre: long straight guard fibres around 50 microns in diameter; mid-layer semi-crimped fibres between 25 and 50 microns; and soft undercoat fibres, which have irregular crimp and are highly insulating and very fine (typically less than 20 microns). In production the fibres are usually divided into undercoat and coarse fibres above around 35 microns. The undercoat feels similar to cashmere and camel, but has not reached the same level of popularity, although local weavers make luxurious fabrics from it.

Qiviut is the soft downy undercoat of the muskox (*Ovibos moschatus*), an Arctic animal in the same family as yak and cows. The undercoat fibres are very fine and typically only 10 to 18 microns in diameter, similar to Merino. It is highly prized for its softness and insulation properties, but is exceptionally rare and expensive. A full-grown animal yields around 3 kg (6.6 lb) of raw fibre, which converts into around 1 kg (2.2 lb) of qiviut.

## SUSTAINABILITY

The fibres are harvested from the animals by shearing or combing. In many cases, the hair is more valuable than the meat and milk (although this is not true for yak and llama). The implications of this depend on the animal. The larger animals are domesticated and farmed like cows and sheep, providing hair on an annual basis. Angora rabbits, on the other hand, are often kept in isolation to prevent their hair becoming tangled (matted); they are shorn, combed or plucked several times a year. As is the case with farming fur, this practice has raised some concerns, which were graphically brought to peoples attention by an undercover film produced by People for the Ethical Treatment of Animals (PETA). In 2013, they documented the grim reality of plucking fur, a technique employed in China, where the majority of angora now comes from. As a direct result, several large retailers halted orders of angora. Of course, angora fibre production does not have to be this cruel and there are many examples of good animal husbandry, where the rabbits are carefully sheared, or combed. As with all animal-related products, the source is critical to ensure high standards of animal welfare.

The conversion of hair into yarn follows much the same route as wool, including washing (scouring), carding, combing and twisting. The only significant difference is that it does not contain lanolin (which can cause an allergic reaction and skin irritation). It does contain grease and oil, so requires washing, but typically not as much as wool, by weight. Therefore, production typically consumes less water and fewer chemicals.

**Formal wear** The lustrous quality of mohair makes it an ideal suit fabric, in particular for evening garments. It is lightweight and offers very good crease resistance. Mohair is coarser and crisper than cashmere and so is rarely, if ever, used alone. To take advantage of its properties, while maintaining a comfortable and affordable fabric, it is often blended with a large proportion of wool. Mohair is typically off-white and dyed the desired colour, such as black. Through selective breeding, a range of natural colours has become available, from grey to red and brown.

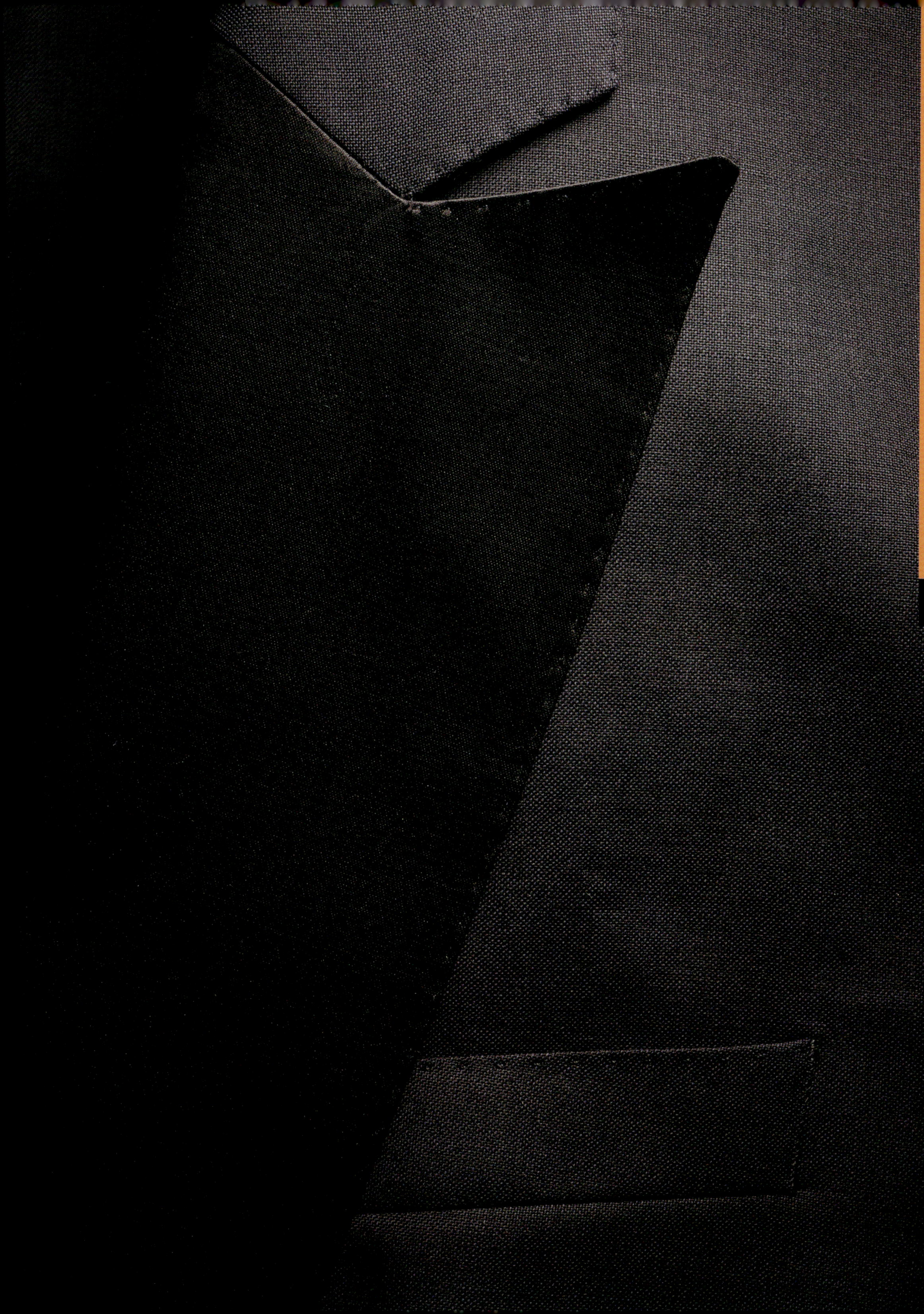

# Horn

Horn is a natural composite that has evolved to perform under extreme impact loads. Used since ancient times to make practical and decorative objects, the horns of cows, buffalo and sheep are today available as a by-product of the meat and milk industry. They continue to be used for adornment, in the form of eyewear frames and jewelry.

| Types | Typical Applications | Sustainability |
|---|---|---|
| • Buffalo, cow and sheep | • Jewelry and buttons<br>• Eyewear frames<br>• Handles and utensils | • A by-product of meat production<br>• Biodegradable end-of-life |

| Properties | Competing Materials | Costs |
|---|---|---|
| • Excellent toughness<br>• Thermoplastic behaviour<br>• Anti-static | • CA, PA and PC<br>• Bone and antler<br>• Bamboo | • Raw material is moderately expensive<br>• Handmade pieces range from small inexpensive items produced in the thousands to high-value one-offs |

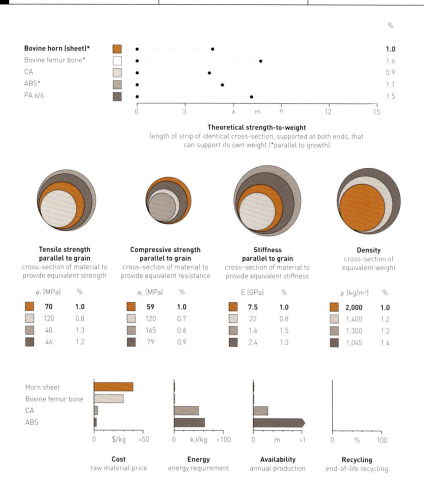

|  |  | % |
|---|---|---|
| Bovine horn (sheet)* | ▮ | 1.0 |
| Bovine femur bone* | ▯ | 1.6 |
| CA | ▯ | 0.9 |
| ABS* | ▮ | 1.1 |
| PA 6/6 | ▮ | 1.5 |

**Theoretical strength-to-weight**
length of strip of identical cross-section, supported at both ends, that can support its own weight (*parallel to growth)

| Tensile strength parallel to grain | | Compressive strength parallel to grain | | Stiffness parallel to grain | | Density | |
|---|---|---|---|---|---|---|---|
| cross-section of material to provide equivalent strength | | cross-section of material to provide equivalent resistance | | cross-section of material to provide equivalent stiffness | | cross-section of equivalent weight | |
| $\sigma_t$ (MPa) | % | $\sigma_c$ (MPa) | % | E (GPa) | % | $\rho$ (kg/m³) | % |
| 70 | 1.0 | 59 | 1.0 | 7.5 | 1.0 | 2,000 | 1.0 |
| 120 | 0.8 | 120 | 0.7 | 22 | 0.8 | 1,400 | 1.2 |
| 40 | 1.3 | 165 | 0.6 | 1.6 | 1.5 | 1.300 | 1.2 |
| 46 | 1.2 | 79 | 0.9 | 2.4 | 1.3 | 1,045 | 1.4 |

| | Cost | Energy | Availability | Recycling |
|---|---|---|---|---|
| Horn sheet | | | | |
| Bovine femur bone | | | | |
| CA | | | | |
| ABS | | | | |
| | $/kg >50 | kJ/kg >100 | m >1 | % 100 |
| | raw material price | energy requirement | annual production | end-of-life recycling |

## INTRODUCTION

Horn grows from birth and is permanent. It is not living tissue like bone (page 442), but made up of fibrous protein (keratin), which is also found in hair (page 434) and hooves. The composite structure is highly resistant to impact, superior among natural materials, rivalling the toughness of polycarbonate (PC) (page 144). Its strength-to-weight is comparable with cellulose acetate (CA) (page 252), a plastic used to make similar handcrafted items.

Horn has thermoplastic properties, which means heating softens it and makes it malleable. It can be bent, shaped and molded into a variety of shapes.

## COMMERCIAL TYPES AND USES

Horn appears on several different animals, including bovines, such as cow and buffalo, as well as other families, such as sheep and goat.

Domesticated cattle (*Bos* genus) have been selectively bred so they no longer grow horns. Cow horn tends to come from places such as Nigeria, where the cattle have kept their horns. Both sexes have horns, although the males' tend to be larger. They comprise two parts: a core of living tissue (bone) surrounded by a layer of horn. The tip is solid.

Colour is highly variegated and no two pieces will look the same. It is typically a mix of light and dark including brown, yellow, black and white; the lighter areas may be translucent. It is used to make utensils, handles and eyewear.

Buffalo horn tends to come from the Asian water buffalo (*Bubalus* genus) from India and Thailand. These draft animals are domesticated and not a protected species like African buffalo (*Syncenrus* genus). The horn resembles cow horn, but the outer layer is thicker and the solid tip extends further along. This means they produce more usable material. It is almost entirely black and can be polished to a fine finish. They are used in similar situations to cow horn, including eyewear, gun stocks and umbrella handles.

Domesticated sheep (*Ovis* genus) produce helical-shaped horns that taper towards the tip. Rams produce the largest horns; the dimensions depend on the breed and age of animal. Colour ranges from streaked translucent creamy-white to opaque black. It is used to make combs, buttons and knife handles.

In terms of mechanical properties, buffalo horn is superior, followed by cow and then sheep. Buffalo horn is stiffer and stronger, with a thick outer layer. The surface is quite rough and ridged, but can be polished to a very smooth finish.

## SUSTAINABILITY

The majority is a by-product of the meat industry. The source is critical, to ensure the animals were treated humanely.

Several types are traded illegally. Despite press coverage and campaigning, there is still demand for materials derived from vulnerable and endangered species. Rhino horn, for example, is today worth a staggering $65,000 per kg.

**Cross-section through horn lamella** Unlike bone, horn is not a living material. It is a composite made up of lamellae stacked radially around a hollow core. Each lamella consists of oriented strands of keratin, a fibrous structural protein, held together by a protein-based matrix. Tubules pass through the lamellae and run the length of the horn. As a result of this pattern, the material is anisotropic: strength and stiffness are greatest in-line with the direction of growth. Both porosity and density increase towards the outside edge, like bamboo (page 386), which helps to ensure high flexural strength-to-weight. The wall thickness varies from thin at the base to solid at the tip.

**Horn spoons** Using a technique that dates back to the Vikings, horn is cut open ('breaking') and heated to allow it to be unrolled into a flat sheet. Once pressed flat, it is cut into the desired shape and remolded, if necessary. The thinner the horn the easier it is to work with. Cow horn tends to be variegated (left). The buffalo horn spoon created by Sarah Petherick (right) features a bone handle.

# Bone and Antler

**These self-healing composites have some impressive properties as a result of the extreme loading they must be able to withstand. Like horn, they are utilized in both decorative and functional items. Nowadays, the raw materials are available as a by-product of the meat industry, or, as is the case with antler, foraged once they have been naturally shed.**

| Types | Typical Applications | Sustainability |
|---|---|---|
| • Bone: cow<br>• Antler: deer, elk (wapiti), moose (elk) and reindeer (caribou) | • Jewelry and buttons<br>• Utensils and handles<br>• Decorative inlay | • A by-product of meat production<br>• Biodegradable end-of-life |
| **Properties** | **Competing Materials** | **Costs** |
| • Excellent hardness<br>• Anisotropic with high strength-to-weight in direction of growth<br>• Antler has superior fracture toughness | • Bamboo, hickory and ash<br>• Horn<br>• CA, ABS and PA | • Raw material is moderately expensive<br>• Handmade pieces range from small inexpensive items produced in the thousands to high-value one-offs |

442

## INTRODUCTION

Aside from stone, these are some of the earliest materials fashioned into tools and other useful objects. They became so common in everyday life in the Middle Ages that their usefulness at the time could be compared to our relationship with modern plastics. They were carved to make cherished personal items, including combs and adornments, and their strength and hardness were utilized in tools such as needles and hooks. Today, they remain useful for both decorative and practical applications.

Bone is a living, growing tissue made up of calcium salts (minerals that provide hardness) and collagen fibres (a protein also found in skin that provides tensile strength; see also Cowhide, page 446). Bone grows in an efficient manner along the lines of anticipated stress, following instructions inherited from previous generations. But while its strength-to-weight is pretty good, it is its ability to self-repair that makes it such an efficient structural material. Its composite structure adapts to changes throughout the animal's life. Even though the processes are not fully understood, many attempts have been made to mimic its smart, self-healing ability.

Antler is a very fast-growing type of bone that is an appendage of the skull. Every year, new antlers grow and calcify to form a strong, hard structure. They are shed at the end of the breeding season, when they are no longer needed. Colour ranges from dark brown to creamy-white. Bone starts out milky-white and the surface may be polished to a glass-like finish. The surface is porous and suitable for staining. When used in jewelry and similar applications, natural-coloured bone gradually turns light yellow as it absorbs grease and oil from the skin.

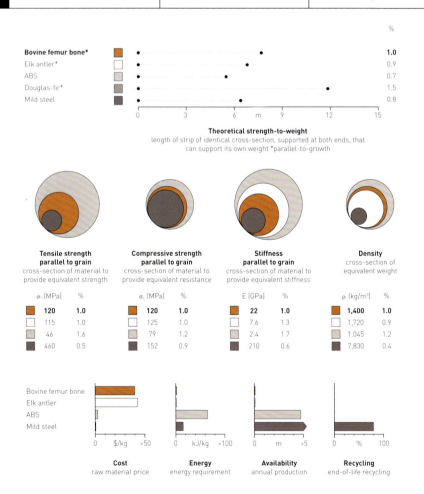

Theoretical strength-to-weight
length of strip of identical cross-section, supported at both ends, that can support its own weight *parallel-to-growth

| | % |
|---|---|
| Bovine femur bone* | 1.0 |
| Elk antler* | 0.9 |
| ABS | 0.7 |
| Douglas-fir* | 1.5 |
| Mild steel | 0.8 |

**Tensile strength parallel to grain**
cross-section of material to provide equivalent strength

| σₜ (MPa) | % |
|---|---|
| 120 | 1.0 |
| 115 | 1.0 |
| 46 | 1.6 |
| 460 | 0.5 |

**Compressive strength parallel to grain**
cross-section of material to provide equivalent resistance

| σ_c (MPa) | % |
|---|---|
| 120 | 1.0 |
| 125 | 1.0 |
| 79 | 1.2 |
| 152 | 0.9 |

**Stiffness parallel to grain**
cross-section of material to provide equivalent stiffness

| E (GPa) | % |
|---|---|
| 22 | 1.0 |
| 7.6 | 1.3 |
| 2.4 | 1.7 |
| 210 | 0.6 |

**Density**
cross-section of equivalent weight

| ρ (kg/m³) | % |
|---|---|
| 1,400 | 1.0 |
| 1,720 | 0.9 |
| 1,045 | 1.2 |
| 7,830 | 0.4 |

Bovine femur bone
Elk antler
ABS
Mild steel

**Cost**
raw material price

**Energy**
energy requirement

**Availability**
annual production

**Recycling**
end-of-life recycling

**Bone handle razor** The design of this Böker steel (page 28) bone-handled razor dates back to the early 20th century – Böker has been manufacturing blades in its German factory since 1869. The razor is relatively small, which makes it popular with professionals and, as a result, it became the best-selling razor for the company. The bone scales (handle sides) are comfortable and practical, providing a strong guard for the blade when not in use.

## COMMERCIAL TYPES AND USES

Historically, bone from several different animals would have been used, including horses, cows, sheep, pigs and birds. Nowadays, the majority comes from domesticated cows (*Bos* genus) slaughtered for meat. Thick pieces with a dense fine grain are required to make fine and detailed carvings. Cost depends on size and type.

Bone is cut and polished to make practical items, such as tools (folders and polishers), needles, spear tips and fishing hooks. Traditional ceremonial items, such as produced by the New Zealand Maori, are carved by hand. These hold significant cultural value and in the past would have been passed down through the generations along with the stories and myths of their tribe.

Cervids – including deer, moose (elk), elk (wapiti) and reindeer (caribou) – are the only animals that have antlers. It is only the males that grow antlers, except in the case of reindeer. As a raw material, antler has been used throughout history to make tools, weaponry, ornaments and gaming pieces. Even though the same material, antler has higher fracture toughness than bone, which is not surprising considering its role in combat. They are shed each year and collected for use, and are obtained from culled animals and those killed for their meat.

## SUSTAINABILITY

Like horn (page 440), bone is a by-product of the meat industry. The source of material is critical, to ensure that the animals were treated humanely. Antler, on the other hand, may be foraged for once shed by the animal, representing a renewable material that does not require the animal be killed.

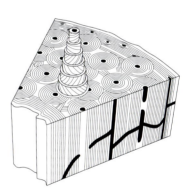

**Cross-section through compact bone** There are two types of bone: compact (or cortical) and spongy (or cancellous). As the names imply, they have different densities. Compact bone – the majority – consists of closely packed osteons interconnected by vascular canals (haversian system). Each osteon consists of a central canal called the osteonic canal, which is surrounded by a matrix of lamellae (sheets) spiralling in concentric rings. The osteonic canals contain blood vessels that are parallel to the long axis of the bone. These blood vessels interconnect, by way of radiating canals, with vessels on the surface of the bone. Spongy bone, which is found within an outer shell of compact bone, consists of many small cavities filled with bone marrow. The structure is made up of interconnected trabeculae (plates) and bars of bone that follow the lines of stress.

# Cowhide

Cowhide is functional and affordable; it is widely available and comes in a variety of grades and finishes. The visual quality is affected by the lifestyle of the animal and each one will be unique. The hide is sliced to make it lighter (thinner) and pliable. The top layer comprises densely packed fibres, making it the most hard-wearing and desirable.

| Types | Typical Applications | Sustainability |
|---|---|---|
| • Full grain, split or pelt (hair-on hide)<br>• Chrome-, vegetable-, synthetic- or combination-tanned | • Apparel, footwear, bags and accessories<br>• Upholstery and automotive interiors<br>• Sports products | • Tanning consumes large amounts of water and chemicals<br>• Leather is a by-product of meat and milk production |
| **Properties** | **Competing Materials** | **Costs** |
| • Flexible and durable<br>• High-quality leather burnishes over time<br>• Soft and breathable | • Horse, sheep, kangaroo and pig<br>• Synthetic leather (e.g. PU- or PVC-based)<br>• Bonded leather<br>• Bark and wicker | • Moderate raw material price, but depends on animal and tanning process<br>• Calfskin is up to around twice the price, depending on quality |

## INTRODUCTION

This section sets out the properties of leather generally, as well as the characteristics unique to bovine hides. Leather from cattle (*Bos* genus) is highly consistent, in terms of weight (thickness) and usable area, which minimizes waste. It is also widely available and accounts for around two-thirds of global leather output. Quality ranges from soft and lightweight calfskin to heavy hard-wearing buffalo (*Bison* genus) hide.

Leather has a characteristic odour and, as a natural material, each piece will be different. Over time, it will gradually become suppler as the fibres become looser. The highest-quality leather will improve with time: it adapts to the shape of use and the surface gradually becomes burnished, taking on a unique patina.

Cowhide covers a wide range of different leathers, but they can generally be considered durable with high resistance to tearing, puncturing and stretching. The mechanical properties are highly variable and the strength depends on several factors, including the animal (steer, bull and buffalo are generally stronger than heifer and calf), tanning process (vegetable-tanned leather is superior) and from where on the hide it was taken (shoulders and back are typically the toughest).

Compared to horsehide (page 458), cowhide tends to be more consistent and finer-grained, but with inferior resistance to abrasion and moisture. Compared to kangaroo (page 460), cowhide is heavier, stiffer and not nearly as strong or durable.

There are several synthetic alternatives

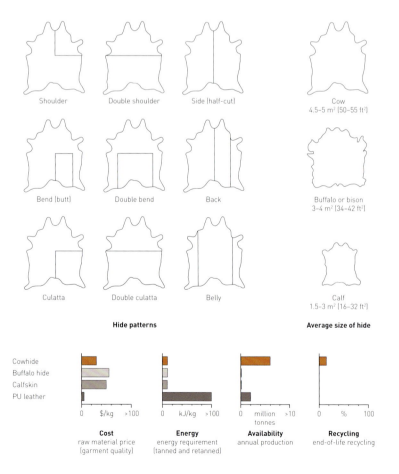

Shoulder · Double shoulder · Side (half-cut) · Cow 4.5–5 m² (50–55 ft²)

Bend (butt) · Double bend · Back · Buffalo or bison 3–4 m² (34–42 ft²)

Culatta · Double culatta · Belly · Calf 1.5–3 m² (16–32 ft²)

**Hide patterns** · **Average size of hide**

Cowhide
Buffalo hide
Calfskin
PU leather

| 0 | $/kg | >100 | 0 | kJ/kg | >100 | 0 | million tonnes | >10 | 0 | % | 100 |

**Cost**
raw material price (garment quality)

**Energy**
energy requirement (tanned and retanned)

**Availability**
annual production

**Recycling**
end-of-life recycling

**Calfskin handbag**
Designed by Sofia Coppola in collaboration with Louis Vuitton, this handbag is made using highest-

quality full-grain calfskin. It is soft and lightweight, making it a practical material for an everyday bag, albeit a pricy one.

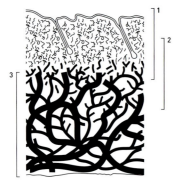

**Cross section through cowskin** Skin acts as a defensive shield, protecting the rest of the body from weather, dirt, bacteria and so on. The outermost layer is the epidermis, which consists mainly of keratin (tough protein cells also found in wool, page 426, hair, page 434, and horn, page 440). This is bonded to a thick layer of tangled collagen (protein) fibres, known as the dermis (or corium). Below this is flesh and fat. In preparation for tanning, the fleshy matter is removed and the hide is cut to thickness and split into layers to make them lighter (thinner) and more pliable. The top layer, which is the outside surface (grain side), has densely packed fibres, making it the most durable and water-resistant. The highest-quality leather, known as 'full grain' (1), or simply 'grain', has all the appearance of the original skin with hair follicles and blemishes; the surface is left intact. This cut is used in jackets, shoes, bags and upholstery. Over time, the leather will burnish and become more beautiful. 'Top grain' (2) refers to leather taken from the upper layer of – often blemished – hides that have been shaved and buffed to produce a uniform finish free from natural imperfections. Lower-quality hides that are split and buffed to a smooth finish on the top side are known as 'corrected grain'. They are usually heavily coloured or embossed. The inner layers (3) are known as 'split' leather. They are not as smooth as top grain and are less wear-resistant, because the fibres have been cut through. It is also loosely referred to as 'genuine leather' and embossed or buffed and painted to create a more durable finish. It is used in bags, upholstery and stationery, for example.

to cowhide, which are generally less expensive and considered inferior. However, they do have some advantages: they are more durable, stable, controllable, waterproof and colourful, and can be molded. In some ways they can be considered more ethical, because they do not contain any animal products.

Plastic-coated canvas, also known as leatherette or pleather, is inexpensive and utilized widely in bags, apparel, upholstery, car interiors, shoe uppers and sports goods. It typically consists of polyurethane (PU) (page 202) or polyvinyl chloride (PVC) (page 122) applied to cotton or polyethylene terephthalate (PET, polyester) (page 152) fabric. The surface is embossed to mimic leather.

Nonwoven synthetic leather and suede are made by needle punching polyester or thermoplastic polyurethane (TPU) (see Thermoplastic Elastomer, page 194) microfibres. They mimic the fibrous structure of skin, which gives them some advantages over plastic-coated types. Recent technological developments have created finer fibres. This has led to improvements in quality, density, firmness and breathability. They are utilized in footwear, linings, bags and sports goods, for example.

Bonded leather, or reconstituted leather, is produced from offcuts that are ground up, mixed with PU and molded. It is of inferior quality and much less expensive than virgin leather. It is used in the production of footwear, stationery and book covers, for example.

## COMMERCIAL TYPES AND USES
Bovine leather is categorized according to the type of animal, tanning and finishing processed. The source of hide determines the ultimate quality that can be achieved. Skins are derived from calves, heifers, steers and bulls, and also buffalo.

Calfskin is the softest of the bovine leathers and has a fine grain. They are smaller and lighter (thinner) than those from older animals; the finest calfskin comes from slinks (stillborn calves) or young animals that have fed on milk alone. As the cow gets older the leather becomes tougher. Kipskin comes from young or small animals that fall somewhere between calf and cow.

Vellum, a high-quality parchment, is traditionally made from calfskin (or sheep or goat, page 452). Its use predates paper in Europe and the USA, and it has traditionally been the material of choice for important documents, religious texts and public laws.

Heifers are females that have not yet borne a calf, or have had only one calf. As a result, the belly region tends to be heavier, and less spongy and elastic than that of a cow. The hides of older animals tend to be more heavily marked.

Steers, also known as bullocks, are male cattle that have been castrated and are raised for meat. They yield heavy (thick) and strong hides. Bull hides are heavier still, larger and are often wrinkled around the shoulders. Like cows, they tend to live longer than steers and so will be more marked and damaged. These are further categorized into heavy Holstein steer, heavy branded steer, fed heavy native cow, branded bull and so on.

The hides of buffalo, also known as bison, are quite different from those of cattle owing to the shape of the animal and way they are raised. The skin is less uniform; it has thinner areas and tends to have more striations, wrinkles and texture. They are often not stretched, so as to retain the texture, which results in a smaller hide on average.

The appearance is controlled by the choice of tanning, retanning, dyeing and finishing processes. The quality of ingredients and time taken at this stage are critical to ensure high-quality leather. Thus some leather will be significantly less expensive but sacrifice long-term flexibility, durability, weather resistance and, in extreme cases, safe ingredients.

Tanning is used to preserve the skin. It is a curing process, whereby a chemical agent forms cross-links between the strands of protein (collagen) in the skin. This makes the leather durable, water-resistant and non-perishable. Tanning agents are derived from mineral (chrome, aluminium or zirconium), synthetic (syntans) or vegetable sources.

Chrome is by far the most common; it is fast (taking around 20 hours) and results in highly consistent leather. It turns the leather grey-blue, which is why semi-finished leather processed in this way is also referred to as 'wet blue'. The tanning agent is typically trivalent chromium (chromium III), which is a natural, non-toxic element thought to have the least environmental impact of all tanning agents. Hexavalent chromium (chromium VI) is banned in many countries, because it is known to be carcinogenic. However, traces of it have

been found in some leathers as a result of the oxidization of trivalent chromium.

Modern chrome-free tanning processes have been developed. 'Wet white' leather is produced using a mix of synthetic (such as phenol and naphthalene) and mineral (such as aluminium and zirconium) agents. Demand for chrome-free leather is increasing, especially in the automotive industry. End-of-life vehicle (ELV) directives in the EU have placed the burden of waste

on the manufacturers to incentivize them to make better material selections. Chrome-free leather, unlike chrome-tanned leather, is biodegradable and may be safely incinerated.

In addition, it is lighter in colour and so suitable for dyeing white through pastel shades. It has good softness and a pleasant touch. However, it is a little more expensive. As well as automotive interiors, it is also commonly used in clothing and shoes for babies.

**Steerhide holster**
Leather is heated with steam to make it suitable for molding. The combination of heat and moisture loosens the fibres and means they can slide over one another. This allows the leather to stretch (it is much more difficult to compress), and pulling the leather taut over a mold takes advantage of this. Lighter leathers form more readily than heavy types. In situations where the shape is too deep or complex for a single piece, multiple panels are joined.

Vegetable tanning uses bark (page 280), wood (see Chestnut, page 346, and Oak, page 342), fruits and leaves. The tannins naturally present in these materials are extracted, and the skins soaked in them for a year or so (minimum 60 days). This process results in stronger and more hard-wearing leather, but it will not be as long-lasting, stain-resistant or heat-resistant. Unlike chrome-tanned leather, it may be left in its natural colour, so each piece will be unique. As it ages, the colour will darken and become richer. This traditional process is on the decline, except for in Italy, where it is supported by the fashion industry. When both processes are employed in the same piece it is known as 'combination leather'.

The age, lifestyle and breed of the animal all contribute towards the quality of leather. Physical and mechanical properties, such as thickness, suppleness, elasticity and strength, are determined by where the leather was cut from on the hide. The side and back provide long lengths of leather, useful for bag bodies, belts, straps and harnesses. The shoulder covers around 1.8 m² (19 ft²). It is high-quality, close-grained, supple and easy to work. Molded items, such as cases and holsters, are produced from this part.

The bend (butt) yields the thickest and strongest leather. Parts cut from this region are used to make bridle leather, belts and other items that require high strength. It is also commonly used to make shoes and boots. The culatta is the rear part of the hide, comprising the butt,

**Pre-distressed calfskin boot** Leather is durable and breathable, which makes it ideal for footwear; around half of all bovine hides go into the production of shoes and boots. The upper is formed over a last (mold), using a technique that has been practised for generations. The finest shoes, such as these Paul Smith chukka boots, are produced from calfskin (horse and kangaroo are also popular, but more expensive). The leather is mechanically treated, prior to molding, to give a distressed and broken-in quality without affecting its integrity. The highest-quality calfskin comes from France and the best finishing comes from Italy. While the processes and techniques used have been exported worldwide, these countries have been practising the art for longer and, for now, remain leaders.

### Longevity
Bovine leather has remained a practical and desirable material for many generations. It is hard-wearing and suitable for demanding applications, from shoes to upholstery.

### Supple
The flexibility and pliability depend on the animal, from soft calfskin through stiff bull and buffalo hide.

### Efficient
Calf and cowhides are relatively consistent in terms of thickness and quality, which helps to minimize waste compared to other types of leather.

### Colour and finish
Leather is produced in a broad range of colours and finishes. Each year, leather suppliers launch new colours and combinations that are available off-the-shelf. Of course, if the volumes are sufficient, then bespoke colour and finish are feasible.

### Affordable
Cowhide provides an affordable and durable material that is widely available. The price will depend on the choice of animal and tanning process, because while some types are inexpensive, the finest vegetable-tanned slink calfskin fetches a very high price.

### Luxury
The process of converting leather into finished goods requires skill and experience; the combination of materials and processes results in items that are worth more than the sum of their parts.

the belly middles and the hind shanks. It is used in a range of items, including belts, shoes and handbags. This cut incorporates leather of varying quality. Therefore, items made from it can take advantage of the transition in properties, such as from soft belly to stiff back.

The belly region is thicker and fuller and not very strong. It is soft and stretchy, which is useful for molding deep profiles. It is not considered particularly high quality and so is generally used for shoe linings and other secondary uses. The size of the hide will depend on the animal and typically measures no more than 2.5 m (8 ft) from neck to butt by 1.8 m (6 ft) across the middle. This equates to around 4.5–5 m² (48–54 ft²), depending on the shape. Of course, every skin is different and the cutting area is typically in the region of 1.8 x 1.5 m (6 x 5 ft).

## SUSTAINABILITY
Animal skins were once a practical material fundamental to our ancestors' way of life. Nothing was wasted when an animal was killed and the skins provided a versatile material used to make shelter, bedding, clothing and footwear. Today, leather is a by-product of the meat and milk industries. In the case of cattle, the sale of leather contributes to the growth and development of the industry.

There are concerns about the negative impacts of the livestock industry as a whole, including freshwater consumption, overuse of antibiotics, energy consumption and greenhouse gas emissions. The impacts depend on location, as there is tremendous variation in agricultural practices around the world.

Immediately after slaughter, bacteria will begin to break down the skin. It is preserved by adding salt or by refrigeration. The best option is to use locally sourced refrigerated hides because salting can cause pollution, for example by increasing chloride levels in rivers.

Processing the skins in the tannery consumes large quantities of chemicals and water. There has been significant improvement in recent years. Even so, most tanneries consume more than 350 litres (77 gal) water per 1 m² (11 ft²)

**Pigmentation and effects** Specific qualities are given to the leather during retanning, such as adding colour and enhancing softness, tear-strength and elasticity. The additives penetrate deeply, giving a high-quality and durable finish. In the case of Ecco Leather's Kromatafor, the skin is tanned to produce a heat-sensitive effect; the colour shifts and morphs through bright hues. Unlike a laminate or coating, the effect runs throughout. Photo courtesy of Ecco Leather.

of leather. This is significant considering that a typical sofa requires around 28 m² (300 ft²) of leather to be upholstered. The majority of tanning takes place in China, India and Bangladesh, where labour costs are low and worker protection is virtually non-existent.

All three tanning techniques – mineral, synthetic and vegetable – are damaging to people and to the environment when carried out on an industrial scale. Each has its drawbacks: for example, chrome tanning waste is dangerous and polluting; synthetic tanning uses large quantities of nasty chemicals such as formaldehyde and naphthalene; and vegetable tanning consumes a lot of

water, even though it is, in most cases, the least damaging overall.

## COWHIDE IN FASHION AND TEXTILES

Leather is one of those materials that cross tradition with modern technology. It is punched, stitched, embossed and ironed using techniques that have evolved over generations to make the most of the character and quality of the material.

It all starts with the conversion of tanned leather into a material suitable for application. A range of finishes and colours is available, from natural-looking aniline to glossy plastic-looking patent. Each has its own unique set of qualities and characteristics, and items have evolved around these properties to take advantage of the benefits of the material in all its guises.

Full- and top-grain leathers are finished with dyes and coatings. They are referred to as aniline when they have been dyed but left uncoated. This means the leather retains the hide's natural finish, grain and blemishes; it is the most natural-looking and so typically only the highest-quality full-grain leather is produced with this finish. It is used in everything from footwear, bags, jackets and upholstery to industrial belts.

Nubuck leather, or grain-suede leather, is buffed on the top side to produce a roughened, more hard-wearing surface. It is typically used in high-quality work boots (the quintessential Timberland, for example), bags, gloves and outerwear.

Semi-aniline leather has a thin protective topcoat, which makes the surface more durable and resistant to wear and staining. Pigmented leather is coated with plastic, making it even more resistant to wearing, staining and fading. These leathers are utilized for upholstery (commercial and practical) and car interiors, for example.

Glossy leather is produced in two ways: ironing, or laminating (coating) with a thin film of plastic. To be classified as patent, the plastic coating (typically PU or PVC) must be no more than 0.15 mm (0.01 in). If the coating is greater than this, but less than half the total thickness of the finished material, it is classified as patent laminated leather. This finish is combined with embossing to create imitation exotic leather (page 462), such as crocodile.

Apparel, footwear and bags are made using leather finished in this way. The surface appears striking when new – gloss enhances colour saturation – but will fade as it becomes scratched and scuffed.

Suede is produced from split leather, which is napped (abraded with emery sandpaper) to pull up the fibres. The appearance can vary, but it will not be as fine or tough as nubuck owing to the looser fibre structure. It is applied in linings, for comfort and away from rain and dirt, such as in footwear and bags.

Leather patterns are punched out by mechanical means (scissors and dies) or with laser cutting. While die cutting (or clicking) offers a low-cost and high-speed solution suitable for producing a large volume of identical parts, laser cutting is more versatile and suitable for creating one-offs as well as repeats. In all cases, the uniqueness of each piece of leather means flexibility is required, because no two patterns will be cut in quite the same way if imperfections are to be avoided. Modern systems allow for the operator to position laser-guided cutting paths over a hide, finding the best position for each before starting the cutting process.

The weight, also referred to as thickness or substance, is an important consideration when specifying leather. It is generally sold in ounces (oz) or mm, with 1 oz equal to around 0.4 mm (0.02 in) of thickness. The scale is based on increments of 0.5 oz or 0.2 mm (0.01 in). Calfskin is typically 1.5–3 oz or 0.6–1.2 mm (0.03–0.05 in), and steerhide around 5–14 oz or 2–5.6 mm (0.08–0.2 in). They can be sliced to make lighter (thinner) sheets. There will always be slight variation in thickness, which is why leather is often sold as a weight range. For example, upholstery uses 2.5–3 oz; footwear uppers are typically constructed from 5–5.5 oz (soles are heavier and around 12–14 oz); bags, purses and small cases use up to 6–7 oz; and belts and holsters are produced from 8–9 to 9–10 oz.

The amount of leather required depends on the application. In the case of upholstery, a typical sofa needs 28 m² (300 ft²) and an armchair 18.5 m² (200 ft²). Looser-fitting styles require more leather.

**Hardy sole-leather grip** The heads and handles of Estwing hammers are forged from a single billet of steel. This version features a traditional handle grip fabricated from washers made of shoe-sole leather, which have been compressed together and riveted. It is polished and the surface protected with two layers of lacquer.

# Sheepskin and Goatskin

**Also known as**
Skins also referred to as: nappa, chamois, hide
Fleece also referred to as: shearling, woolskin

These skins are prized for their soft, buttery quality; chamois and nappa are good examples. Sheepskin fleeces are tanned with the wool intact, which provides excellent insulation and is anti-static, perfect for lining cold-weather garments and footwear. The colour and softness of the fleece and suppleness of the skin depends on the breed and age of the animal.

| Types | Typical Applications | Sustainability |
|---|---|---|
| • Full grain, split, fleece (sheep) and pelt (hair-on goat hide) <br> • Chrome-, vegetable-, synthetic- or combination-tanned | • Gloves and garments <br> • Footwear <br> • Throws and spreads | • Tanning consumes large amounts of water and chemicals <br> • Leather is a by-product of meat and milk production |
| **Properties** | **Competing Materials** | **Costs** |
| • Soft and pliable (slightly stretchy) <br> • Fleeces are highly insulating <br> • Highly variegated wool and hair, depending on the breed | • Calf, deer, kangaroo and pig <br> • Fur and wool <br> • PAN, pile fabrics and synthetic leather | • Sheepskin and goatskin are cost-effective leathers <br> • Lambskin and kidskin are more expensive, depending on the age and breed |

452

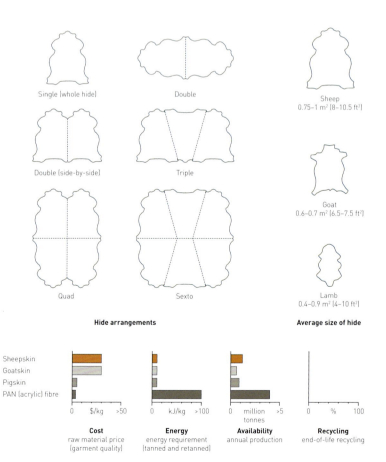

Single (whole hide)

Double

Double (side-by-side)

Triple

Quad

Sexto

**Hide arrangements**

Sheep
0.75–1 m² (8–10.5 ft²)

Goat
0.6–0.7 m² (6.5–7.5 ft²)

Lamb
0.4–0.9 m² (4–10 ft²)

**Average size of hide**

Sheepskin
Goatskin
Pigskin
PAN (acrylic) fibre

| 0 | $/kg | >50 |
| 0 | kJ/kg | >100 |
| 0 | million tonnes | >5 |
| 0 | % | 100 |

**Cost**
raw material price
(garment quality)

**Energy**
energy requirement
(tanned and retanned)

**Availability**
annual production

**Recycling**
end-of-life recycling

## INTRODUCTION

Like cowhide (page 444), the skin is a by-product of meat production. However, breeds that yield very high-quality fleece may be reared mainly for their wool (page 426) and skins. Sheep account for 15% of global leather production and goats provide only around half that; they are in shorter supply owing to the prevailing farming practices.

During the tanning process, after the flesh and fatty tissue has been removed, the decision is made whether the skin will be converted into leather or fleece. Producing leather requires that all the wool be removed and follows much the same process as for cowhide. The skin is relatively smooth and suitable for a range of finishing processes, including laser cutting and digital printing. Designers exploit this versatility to create intriguing aesthetics and tactile experiences with leather, as well as to mimic more expensive (rare or endangered, see Exotics, page 462) skins.

If the fleece is left on, then tanning follows a slightly different route. The main difference is that with wool (and hair-on hide), chromium is mixed with aluminium sulphate. This helps to preserve the natural colour of the skin and wool. A suppleness agent is added to enhance the skin's flexibility. They are relatively inexpensive and, as a result, are often found printed, sprayed or dyed to imitate the skin and fur (page 466) of other animals, such as badger and leopard.

Adult sheepskins range from 0.75 to 1 m² (8–10.5 ft²). Lambskins are smaller; the size range depends on the breed and is typically in the region of 0.4 to 0.9 m² (4–10 ft²). Goatskins fall somewhere in between, averaging 0.6 to 0.7 m² (6.5–7.5 ft²). They are joined together to make large areas of material suitable for upholstery

and apparel. Of course, if the various parts of an item – gloves and footwear, for example – are smaller than the skin then no additional joins are required.

Synthetic fleece (as well as wool and fur) is produced from polyacrylonitrile (PAN, acrylic) (page 180). It provides a low-cost alternative free from natural inconsistency. Fine fibres yield a soft and dense pile, which is dyed and sprayed to look like natural material.

## COMMERCIAL TYPES AND USES

Skins from domesticated sheep (*Ovis aries*) and lambs, as well as goats (*Capra aegagrus hircus*) and kids, are converted into soft and supple leather suitable for a range of applications. The quality of the leather, and thus the range of applications, depends on the animal.

Sheepskin leather provides a soft all-purpose material suitable for a range of applications. It is manufactured into casual, loose-fitting gloves, footwear and outerwear through to skinny-fit trousers. It is applied as bare leather, or with the fleece intact, providing a layer of insulation.

The colour, texture and pattern of fleece depend on the breed. Merino is

**Suede court shoes**
Kidskin provides soft, smooth leather suitable for footwear, gloves and apparel. Suede is produced from the underside of the skin, abraded to produce a soft velvety nap. It does not have the durability of full-grain leather and the textured surface is prone to picking up dirt. These heels are manufactured by Dune, London.

perhaps the best known (mainly for its use in wool garments). Originally from Spain, they are now mainly reared in Australia and New Zealand. The fleece is very fine, dense, soft and bright white. The skins are large and often used as rugs, throws and upholstery. When used

**Fleece quality**
Depending on type, breed and environment, the quality ranges from coarse and resilient to fine and insulating. Sheep's wool has many desirable properties: it is water-resistant, fire-resistant (it will burn in a flame, but self-extinguish when no longer in the flame), a good insulator (it traps air), absorbs water without feeling wet, and dyes well. The length of fleece depends on the age of animal and can be more than 70 mm (2.8 in), ranging from straight (top image) to highly crimped. Shearling refers to the pelt of a lamb up to a year old that has been shorn after tanning to a uniform length. Lambskin (middle image) refers to fleece from a young animal that has never been sheared; the softest fleece comes from slink (stillborn) lambs. The hides of cows, horses and most goats (bottom image) are covered with straight, short and brittle hair. Without the dense undercoat the hairs lie flat against the skin to produce a smooth surface with a distinctive grain. Breeds that have evolved in cold climates have developed a softer and more pronounced undercoat, including cashmere and angora (mohair) goats.

for medical and nursing applications, the wool is shorn to a uniform 25 mm (1 in) or thereabouts.

Toscana sheepskin, from Spain, is prized for its long, soft fleece. The wool ranges from tight curls to loose ripples, making it an excellent substitute for fur. Icelandic is another breed of sheep that provides high-quality fleece. Their coat has evolved two layers to help keep the animal warm in the harsh Icelandic climate: a long outer coat of highly crimped fleece and a soft dense underlayer. They are mostly white, but come in a range of colours.

There are many other breeds used, each with its own distinctive characteristics. For example, Jacob sheep have light-coloured wool covered with black or brown spots, known as piebald. The wool is medium soft with little kemp (coarse under-fibres). Herdwick are hardy sheep from the Lake District in England. The fleeces of lambs are black and gradually lighten, as they get older. The typical Herdwick fleece is mottled grey, brown and white with a coarse texture.

Hair sheep leather, also known as cabretta leather, is considered to be one of the finest glove-making materials. It provides a unique combination of strength with fineness, softness and elasticity; this helps gloves to fit and be long-lasting. The sheep come from Nigeria and Ethiopia and grow hair, as opposed to wool, thanks to the environment.

Napa, or nappa, is full-grain un-split leather from sheep, lamb, goat or kid (although it seems the name has spread to cover any soft leather). It is named after Napa Valley in California, where the tannery in which it was first produced is situated. It is tanned in a way that makes it particularly soft and pliable, yet strong and durable. It is commonly used to make items of clothing (trousers, jackets and so on), as well as speciality goods, such as bags, wallets and footwear. It is often coated or printed for decorative effect.

Lambskin is softer and lighter (thinner) than sheep leather. Compared to calfskin, it offers more stretch and pliability, which means it is better suited to items of clothing, because it more readily conforms to the shape of the body.

Calfskin is used in handbags, coats and other items that require greater durability and shape retention.

Slink lambskin, used to make some of the most expensive formal gloves, is very fine leather derived from stillborn lambs, in particular from New Zealand.

Goat leather is similar quality to sheep, but it is typically a little coarser and harder-wearing. It too, is used to make bags, wallets, gloves, apparel and footwear. Kidskin, like lambskin, is softer and lighter than goat. It is used for small, high-value items, such as dress gloves and shoes.

Goatskin pelt, or hair-on hide, is used in similar applications to fleece, including upholstery, rugs and throws. There exists a huge range of colours and patterns, from white through brown and black. The best-known breeds are cashmere and angora (mohair); although mainly used to produce yarn (see Hair, page 434), their fleeces are soft and valuable.

Goat pelt tends to have pronounced patterns of different lengths of hair and the hair itself ranges from straight to wavy and may lie flat or stick out from the pelt. In some cases, the guard hairs are removed, known as 'pulled goat', to produce a softer fleece predominantly made up of undercoat. The length and coarseness of hair will depend on the breed and source: goats from colder climates have thicker coats.

## SUSTAINABILITY

Sheep and goats are reared for their meat, milk and wool (or hair). Raw material quality is therefore variable and depends on the abattoir. As they become more valuable, the meat becomes a by-product of the hide.

Sheep and goats are available locally across much of the globe. The source of the hide is critical to ensure that adequate social, environmental and animal welfare standards have been met.

**Working gloves** Like sheepskin, goat leather is light (thin) and pliable; which is ideal for gloves. The advantage of goat is that it is a little tougher and more hard-wearing, and so suitable for working gloves, such as these produced by US-based Filson.

# Pigskin

Pigskin is versatile, soft and relatively easy to work. Quality ranges from inexpensive shoe lining, produced from skins that are a by-product of the meat industry, to the finest wild pig leather. Pigskin is typically full-grain. Split leather, known as pigsplit and used in shoe and trainer uppers, is produced with suede or glazed finish.

| Types | Typical Applications | Sustainability |
|---|---|---|
| • Grain (pigskin) and split leather (pigsplit)<br>• Chrome-, vegetable-, synthetic- or combination-tanned | • Gloves and apparel<br>• Footwear uppers and linings | • Tanning consumes large amounts of water and chemicals<br>• Pigskin is a typically a by-product of meat production |
| **Properties** | **Competing Materials** | **Costs** |
| • Soft and lightweight<br>• Pliable and flexible, but not very elastic so will gradually lose its shape<br>• Deep hair follicle pattern | • Sheep, goat and deer<br>• Synthetic leather, such as PU- and PVC-based | • While split leather is very low-cost, full grain is more expensive<br>• Peccary is rare and expensive |

456

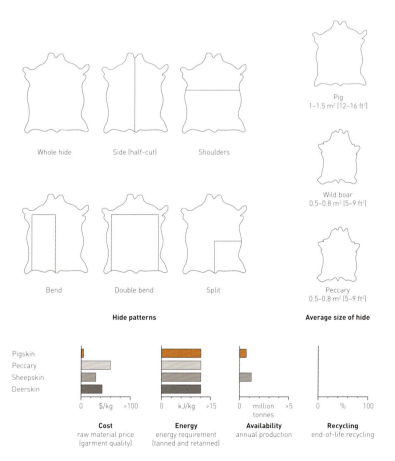

Whole hide    Side (half-cut)    Shoulders

Bend    Double bend    Split

**Hide patterns**

Pig
1–1.5 m² (12–16 ft²)

Wild boar
0.5–0.8 m² (5–9 ft²)

Peccary
0.5–0.8 m² (5–9 ft²)

**Average size of hide**

Pigskin
Peccary
Sheepskin
Deerskin

| 0    $/kg    >100 | 0    kJ/kg    >15 | 0    million tonnes    >5 | 0    %    100 |
|---|---|---|---|
| **Cost**<br>raw material price (garment quality) | **Energy**<br>energy requirement (tanned and retanned) | **Availability**<br>annual production | **Recycling**<br>end-of-life recycling |

## INTRODUCTION

Pigskin accounts for around 10% of leather production, nearly equivalent to sheepskin (page 452). While a huge amount of pig meat is consumed (around one billion pigs are slaughtered each year), only around one-fifth of the skins are converted into leather. The remainder are left intact and cooked with the meat, or the collagen is used as a raw material, such as in the production of gelatine.

Pigskin is the least expensive leather and has many beneficial properties; as with the other animals the best-quality leather comes from the back (bend). It is porous, which means it provides good breathability (used in shoe lining). It is soft, and after getting wet it returns to its original softness (similar to deerskin, page 460). It is typically sold as lightweight leather in the region of 1–2 oz (0.4–0.8 mm [0.02–0.03 in]) (see page 451).

Pigskin is not tolerated in certain religions, in particular Islam. Jews also consider pigs to be unclean, but according to Jewish law the skin of an animal does not transmit impurities, especially if it has been tanned, and so is suitable for use in garments and footwear.

There are several synthetic alternatives to pigskin. As with other common leathers, full grain is mimicked by textile coated with polyurethane (PU) (page 202) or polyvinyl chloride (PVC) (page 122). Suede is reproduced in synthetics using nonwoven microfibre (see Polyamide, page 164). Typically polyethylene terephthalate (PET, polyester) (page 152) mixed with PU, synthetic suede is commonly referred to by trademark names, such as Ultrasuede and Alcantara.

## COMMERCIAL TYPES AND USES

There are many different breeds of pig, including domesticated animals and wild boar (*Sus* genus). The skins from domesticated pigs are inexpensive and widely available in many forms and finishes, whereas the skins from boar and peccary are rare and expensive.

Pigskin is popularly utilized as a lining material, such as in the production of footwear, gloves and books. It is light, supple and durable. It is relatively porous, which provides good breathability compared to other types, a quality that is particularly useful in footwear.

Synthetic shoe lining is often PU-based. Such is the popularity of leather that synthetic types are often embossed with pigskin's grain and characteristic hair follicle pattern. This provides an easy way to tell pigskin from synthetic mimics: the hair follicles pass right through pigskin, but will only be embossed (or printed) on one side of synthetic leather.

Peccary is a small pig-like mammal that closely resembles wild boar and is classified in the same suborder (*Suina*). Peccary yields particularly soft, strong and supple leather. The best-quality hides come from wild animals from Central and South America, where they are harvested under strict CITES regulations. Its unsurpassed combination of softness and durability is utilized in the highest-quality hand-sewn gloves and watchstraps, for example. It is identifiable by its distinctive hair follicles, grouped in threes. This is often mimicked in lower-quality leather and punched right through, which can make it hard to distinguish.

Other than the more conventional applications, pigskin is used for medical purposes, such as the treatment of burns, and as a practice medium for tattoo artists. Living pigs have even been tattooed and turned into works of art whose skins are worth huge sums of money once they are slaughtered.

American footballs are sometimes referred to as pigskin, but they are actually pebble-embossed cowhide or rubber (page 248). They were never made of pigskin; the name probably derives from the use of inflated pig's bladders.

## SUSTAINABILITY

In many countries pigs have become an important farmed animal. The skin comprises only around 3% of the total weight, and only a small proportion of them are converted into leather. Absolutely nothing goes to waste. The entire animal – meat, bones, organs, blood and so on – is utilized in some shape or form. For example, gelatine is used in sweets and beer, fatty acids go into fabric softener and shampoo, heart valves are used in transplants, the internal organs are used to make musical instruments, and the collagen is used as a raw material in wood adhesive.

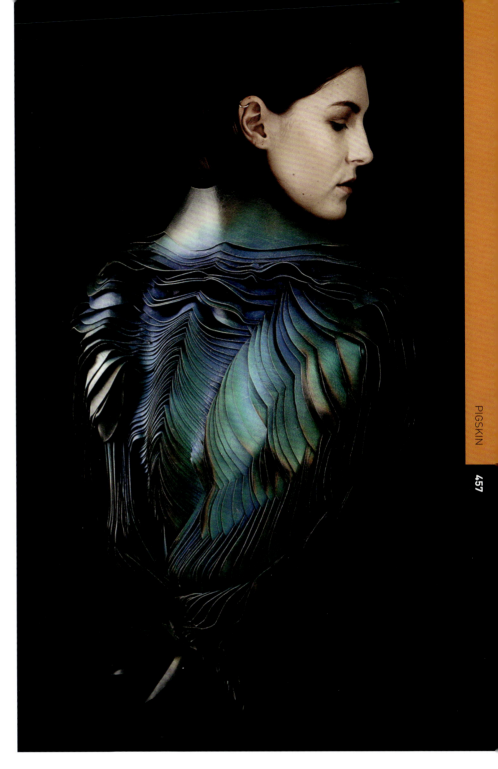

**Coated pigskin** This sculptural garment is built-up from layers of pigskin lining leather coated with a form of pressure-sensitive ink. Its combination of workability and suppleness proved ideal for this application. Created by The Unseen, London, and first shown at the Barbican, London, 2014, the garment uses reactive ink that changes colour on contact with changing air pressure to reveal the invisible turbulence and airflow that surround us. Photo by Jonny Lee Photography and The Unseen.

# Horsehide

Horsehide is renowned for its dense grain, durability and water resistance. The front half of the horse is used in situations similar to cowhide, from hair-on hide upholstery to hard-wearing gloves. The shells (butt) are the most expensive part of the hide. Unrivalled in terms of longevity and toughness, they are used almost exclusively in the production of shoe uppers.

| Types | Typical Applications | Sustainability |
|---|---|---|
| • Grain, split and pelt (hair-on hide)<br>• Chrome-, vegetable-, synthetic- or combination-tanned | • Jackets, gloves and footwear<br>• Throws and upholstery | • Tanning consumes large amounts of water and chemicals<br>• The hides are a typically a by-product of meat production |
| **Properties** | **Competing Materials** | **Costs** |
| • Close-grained with low porosity<br>• Durable<br>• Shell cordovan folds and ripples instead of creasing | • Cow, kangaroo and deer<br>• Synthetic leather such as PU- and PVC-based | • Horsehide is generally comparable with cowhide (although can be more); pony and donkey are more expensive<br>• The shells are the most expensive |

458

## INTRODUCTION

Horsehide is comparable with cowhide (page 444) in many ways. However, it is far less widely available, as horsemeat is consumed in lower quantities than beef. In some countries there is resistance to using horses for meat and leather, because they are often kept as pets.

Horsehide is generally not as consistent as cowhide; the thickness is much more varied and light colours are best avoided, because they are less likely to be uniform. It is close-grained with a dense fibre structure. As a less porous material than cowhide, it is inherently more water-resistant. Owing to the way horses are reared and employed, the skins are often more varied and marked.

## COMMERCIAL TYPES AND USES

Domesticated horses (*Equus caballus*) are raised for meat in many parts of the world. The skins are processed in much the same way as cowhide: the hair is removed and the leather is split to the correct thickness prior to tanning. Or, the hair is left intact and the hide is processed whole, so that it retains the colours and markings of the horse. The hair length varies from skin to skin. Animals raised in colder climates, such as the famous wild Icelandic horses, have long, soft coats that are highly sought after. They are used as throws, rugs and upholstery.

Horsehide used as leather is typically divided into three parts: front (shoulders), strip (croup) and shells (butt). The front and shoulders are used to make jackets, gloves, and upholstery, for example.

The shells have higher density than the rest of the hide. They provide leather with superior wear and finish characteristics. They are not large areas of leather and are very expensive, which limits their use to shoes, wallets and watchstraps. The non-creasing characteristics of shell cordovan

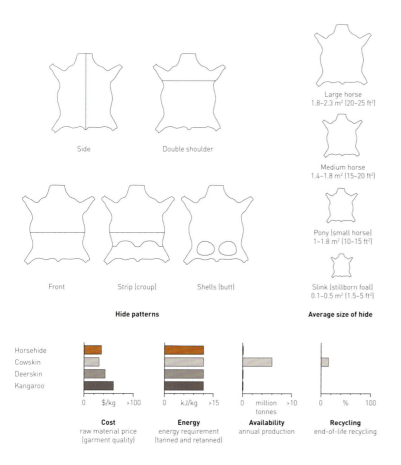

Side     Double shoulder

Large horse
1.8–2.3 m² (20–25 ft²)

Medium horse
1.4–1.8 m² (15–20 ft²)

Pony (small horse)
1–1.8 m² (10–15 ft²)

Slink (stillborn foal)
0.1–0.5 m² (1.5–5 ft²)

Front     Strip (croup)     Shells (butt)

**Hide patterns**     **Average size of hide**

Horsehide
Cowskin
Deerskin
Kangaroo

| 0 | $/kg | >100 |
| 0 | kJ/kg | >15 |
| 0 | million tonnes | >10 |
| 0 | % | 100 |

**Cost**
raw material price
(garment quality)

**Energy**
energy requirement
(tanned and retanned)

**Availability**
annual production

**Recycling**
end-of-life recycling

mean that it will survive much longer than calfskin and other leathers used in similar applications. 'Cordovan' originally referred to leather produced in Córdoba, Spain, from goatskin (page 452). Now, it is used for horse hide produced by a certain artisanal tanning technique (see caption).

Pony skin comes from smaller or younger horses, and is softer and suppler than leather derived from larger and older animals. However, today, it can be difficult to know if it is actually pony, or cow printed to look like pony, since it has become such a popular look to mimic. Slink horse leather comes from stillborn foals. It is rare and accounts for only a very small fraction of horse leather production.

The hides of donkeys (*Equus asinus*) are converted into shoe and sole leather. Once inexpensive, this type of leather is becoming progressively harder to find.

## SUSTAINABILITY

Most of this leather comes from horses raised in countries where they are farmed for meat. It is not common in the UK or the USA. There are few abattoirs in these countries capable of dealing with horses and obtaining high-quality skins. This means the animals must be transported great distances to be slaughtered, presenting many challenges for their welfare. Recent protests will hopefully lead to improvements in treatment.

**Shell cordovan shoes**
Shell is cut from the hindquarters of the horse and each one measures around 450 mm (18 in) in diameter. The top layer is removed and the surface compacted to produce a very smooth, grain-free finish. There are only a few tanneries in the world capable of producing shell cordovan. US-based Horween have been doing it the longest (since 1905) and their leather is considered the best. Their shell cordovan is vegetable-tanned and goes through an extensive retanning process, whereby fats, greases and oils are 'hot stuffed' (rolled in heated drums) to nourish the skin fibres. This defines the leather's physical, aesthetic and sensory characteristics. The process takes several months and is worth it; the end result has acquired legendary status among shoemakers.

# Deerskin and Kangaroo Hide

**Also known as**
Deer also known as: elk, moose
Kangaroo also known as: roo
Kangaroo hide also referred to as: K-leather

These two animals, which occupy opposite sides of the world, yield leather with an unrivalled combination of softness and strength. Deerskin, which has long been associated with Native American clothing, continues to be utilized in the production of practical, as well as elaborate, garments. Kangaroo is used to make motorcycle racing leathers and football boot uppers.

| Types | Typical Applications | Sustainability |
|---|---|---|
| • Full grain, split and pelt (hair-on hide)<br>• Chrome-, vegetable-, synthetic- or combination-tanned | • Gloves, footwear and apparel<br>• Protective clothing and sports equipment | • Tanning consumes large amounts of water and chemicals<br>• In some cases, but not all, leather is a by-product of meat production or culling |
| **Properties** | **Competing Materials** | **Costs** |
| • Deerskin is soft, elastic, strong and hard-wearing<br>• Kangaroo is the strongest of all leathers | • Cow, horse, pig, goat and sheep (in particular cabretta or hairsheep)<br>• Synthetic leather such as PU- and PVC-based | • Deer is moderately priced, depending on the source<br>• Kangaroo is one of the most expensive leathers and in relatively short supply |

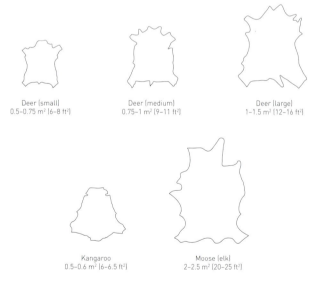

Deer (small)
0.5–0.75 m² (6–8 ft²)

Deer (medium)
0.75–1 m² (9–11 ft²)

Deer (large)
1–1.5 m² (12–16 ft²)

Kangaroo
0.5–0.6 m² (6–6.5 ft²)

Moose (elk)
2–2.5 m² (20–25 ft²)

**Average size of hide**

Deerskin
Elk hide
Kangaroo hide
Horse hide

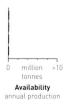

| 0    $/kg    >100 | 0    kJ/kg    >15 | 0    million    >10<br>tonnes | 0    %    100 |
|---|---|---|---|
| **Cost**<br>raw material price<br>(garment quality) | **Energy**<br>energy requirement<br>(tanned and retanned) | **Availability**<br>annual production | **Recycling**<br>end-of-life recycling |

## INTRODUCTION

Kangaroo (*Macropus* genus) hide has the highest strength-to-weight of all leathers. Compared to cowhide (page 444), the collagen fibre bundles in kangaroo are highly oriented parallel to the epidermis and it has far lower fat content (fat is removed during tanning and so leaves voids, which weakens the fibrous structure). This means that for the same thickness, kangaroo leather is stronger and the skin retains much more of its strength when split. Other types of leather, by contrast, are strongest on the outside edge. Thus, when split, the underside will be weaker and more easily torn than full grain.

Deer (Cervidae family) leather is high-quality, comfortable and long lasting. It is softer and suppler than most other types, yet strong and hard-wearing.

## COMMERCIAL TYPES AND USES

Deer are farmed for meat and fur, and wild animals are culled or hunted. The size of the skin depends on the species: a large deer will yield up to 1.5 m² (16 ft²) and a small deer may produce as little as half that. Skins from wild deer are typically blemished with insect bites, scrapes and scratches. Therefore, it is most commonly dyed a light colour. Tanned leather is used for gloves, handbags, garments, wallets and moccasins.

The hides of some species are processed as pelts (with the hair intact) to preserve the markings, and are used as rugs, throws and floor coverings. Examples include reindeer (caribou in the USA) (*Rangifur tarandus*), which are various shades of grey; axis deer (*Cervus axis*), with a white-spotted fawn coat; and red deer (*Cervus elaphus*), which have a rich red-brown summer coat and white rump. The coats are, in many cases, different in winter and summer.

There are four species of kangaroo harvested commercially in Australia and two species of wallaby harvested in Tasmania. There are thought to be 15 to 50 million of these animals, depending on seasonal conditions. Around 15 to 20% are culled each year; the quota is based purely on numbers and not market demand. The leather is used in horse-riding gear, protective motorcycle apparel, belts, bags, football boots (cleats) and whips.

## SUSTAINABILITY

These animals are considered pests in their native countries and are culled in large numbers. They have provided an important source of meat and skin for the indigenous peoples for millennia. None of the species culled are threatened or endangered, and the industries provide employment in many rural communities. There are many environmental benefits to consuming leather (and meat) from wild animals, as opposed to farmed livestock.

However, Australia's kangaroo industry has been subjected to considerable scrutiny over the years with regard to animal welfare. The Royal Society for the Prevention of Cruelty to Animals (RSPCA), which audited welfare outcomes in the kangaroo harvest, believed that it was one of the most humane forms of animal slaughter when carried out correctly. But the Vegetarians International Voice for Animals (Viva) claims that while culling is legal, it is often done using inhumane methods. In response to their campaign, several high-profile football players stopped using boots made from kangaroo leather, and this prompted manufacturers to follow suit.

**Kangaroo leather upper**  Kangaroo leather was used by Adidas in the Copa Mundial football boot (cleat), launched 1979. This became the world's best-selling football boot, and all the major manufacturers went on to produce high-performance boots using kangaroo leather. This is the Adidas Ace 15.1, a more recent design with kangaroo leather upper and dual-density molded thermoplastic polyurethane (TPU) (see TPE, page 194) outsole to maximize agility and traction on firm ground. Following pressure from animal welfare groups and ethical investors, manufacturers are now cutting down on their use of kangaroo leather.

# Exotics

The skin of any animal can be turned into leather. As a decorative addition, exotic leathers tend to be selected according to their colour, texture and pattern. While some are available as a by-product of meat production, most – such as alligator, snake and ostrich – are considered so valuable that they are farmed and killed primarily for their skin.

| Types | Typical Applications | Sustainability |
|---|---|---|
| • Stingray, eel, salmon, wolffish, perch, cod and shark; ostrich and chicken; snake, lizard, alligator and crocodile | • Apparel, belts, bags, wallets, purses and footwear<br>• Upholstery and car interiors | • Many animals are farmed for their skins; others are taken from the wild<br>• Fish skins may be the by-product of meat production |
| **Properties** | **Competing Materials** | **Costs** |
| • Generally strong and hard-wearing<br>• Range of scale configurations, patterns and colours | • Fur<br>• Commodity leathers (e.g. cow, sheep, pig)<br>• Synthetic leather, such as PU- and PVC-based | • Expensive, but with a great deal of variation, depending on the age of animal, type and quality<br>• There are fees associated with export |

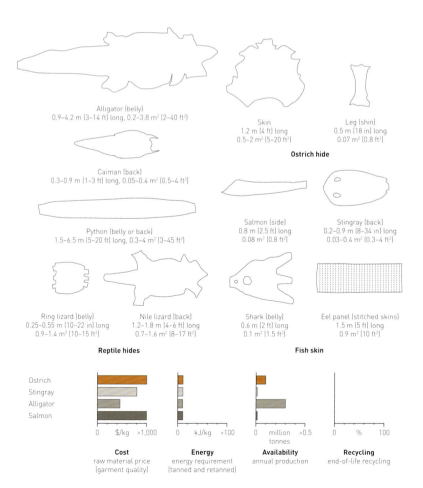

Alligator (belly)
0.9–4.2 m (3–14 ft) long, 0.2–3.8 m² (2–40 ft²)

Caiman (back)
0.3–0.9 m (1–3 ft) long, 0.05–0.4 m² (0.5–4 ft²)

Python (belly or back)
1.5–6.5 m (5–20 ft) long, 0.3–4 m² (3–45 ft²)

Ring lizard (belly)
0.25–0.55 m (10–22 in) long
0.9–1.4 m² (10–15 ft²)

Nile lizard (back)
1.2–1.8 m (4–6 ft) long
0.7–1.6 m² (8–17 ft²)

**Reptile hides**

Skin
1.2 m (4 ft) long
0.5–2 m² (5–20 ft²)

Leg (shin)
0.5 m (18 in) long
0.07 m² (0.8 ft²)

**Ostrich hide**

Salmon (side)
0.8 m (2.5 ft) long
0.08 m² (0.8 ft²)

Stingray (back)
0.2–0.9 m (8–34 in) long
0.03–0.4 m² (0.3–4 ft²)

Shark (belly)
0.6 m (2 ft) long
0.1 m² (1.5 ft²)

Eel panel (stitched skins)
1.5 m (5 ft) long
0.9 m² (10 ft²)

**Fish skin**

Ostrich
Stingray
Alligator
Salmon

| 0 | $/kg | >1,000 |
| 0 | kJ/kg | >100 |
| 0 | million tonnes | >0.5 |
| 0 | % | 100 |

**Cost**
raw material price (garment quality)

**Energy**
energy requirement (tanned and retanned)

**Availability**
annual production

**Recycling**
end-of-life recycling

## INTRODUCTION

Today, leather is distinguished as either commodity – that is, mammals including cow (page 444), sheep (page 452) and pig (page 456), among others – or exotic. The second group includes several genera of fish, bird and reptile. While they may be practical, in some cases more so than commodity types, they are significantly more expensive and so typically reserved for luxury goods.

The skins are converted into leather using similar tanning processes to mammal hides (see Cowhide), but they require a lot more work in preparation and this is often done by hand, further contributing to their luxury status. Such is the worth of the skins and the importance of how to raise the animals and convert their skins into high-quality leather that the luxury brands have been buying up farms to ensure consistent supply.

As a result of the relatively high cost of exotic leather, as well as animal rights issues, several imitations have been developed using synthetic materials. Alternatively, less expensive leathers, such as sheep and pig, are finished to mimic the appearance of exotics.

## COMMERCIAL TYPES AND USES

While there are countless different types of exotic leather, the most popular include reptiles, fish and ostrich. The skins are used in the fashion industry for similar applications, including footwear, bags, wallets, purses, watchstraps and accessories, for example.

**Toad skin**
Demonstrating that almost any animal skin can be converted into leather, this hide comes from a large toad (*Bufo* genus). Small skins are typically joined together to make large panels suitable for a broader range of applications.

Reptile leathers come from alligator (*Alligator* genus); crocodile (*Crocodylus* genus), such as the freshwater (*C. johnstoni*), saltwater (*C. porosus*) and caiman (subfamily Caimaninae); lizards (*Varanus* genus) such as the ring lizard (*V. salvator*) and Nile monitor lizard (*V. niloticus*); and snakes including reticulated python (*Python reticulatus*), short tail python (*Python brongersmai*) and anaconda (*Eunectes notaeus*).

Their skins are tough, but are mainly used for their decorative colour, pattern and texture. This varies, but is characterized by overlapping scales, the size of which depends on the species. They are bone-like and protect the animal during its life.

Python leather has long been valued for its elegance. Each year, more than 300,000 python skins are traded. As a result of their desirability, strict rules have been established and are enforced by CITES (the Convention on International Trade in Endangered Species of Wild Fauna and Flora).

Cost depends on many factors. In the case of crocodiles, the freshwater variety from New Guinea is considered the most desirable and is thus the most expensive. Caiman is less so, because the skins are usually inferior quality with imperfections that affect dyeing. As the size of the skin increases, the cost per square metre rises. This is because as the animal grows it consumes significantly more food per body weight, and the larger it is the greater the demand from the fashion industry. For example, an animal that yields a hide suitable for a 400 mm (16 in) wide handbag takes three years to grow, which drives the price up.

Saltwater stingrays (*Dasyatis* genus) native to Southeast Asia have evolved a tough skin covered with bony plates, and tanneries have methods for softening the hard-wearing hides. Stingray is perhaps the most durable of all leathers and is widely available. Polished or sanded stingray is commonly referred to as shagreen. It is considerably more expensive, owing to the wastage that occurs as part of the process.

Shark (subclass Elasmobranchii) leather is known for its rough and coarse texture (against the grain). Once tanned, the high oil content yields soft fabric-like leather. It is relatively heavy (thick) compared to popular exotics, such as alligator and stingray. However, its high resilience means that it will maintain its quality and appearance for many years. It is used for accessories (wallets and bags, for example), upholstery and car interiors (trim, seats and so on). There are several non-endangered and non-threatened species – the species varies according to the season and availability – available as a by-product of the fishing industry.

The skin of eels (order Anguilliformes) yields soft, stretchy leather and is also a by-product of fishing. Typically, several of the long thin hides are sewn together to make large panels suitable for bags and wallets, for example.

Ostrich (*Struthio camelus*) is the only bird commonly used to make leather. The skin of farmed chicken (*Gallus gallus domesticus*) is also available as leather, but to a much lesser extent.

Ostriches are farmed – mainly in South Africa, where around 200,00 birds are slaughtered annually – and their meat and eggs are a by-product of leather production. They yield three distinctive types of leather: body leather, which is partly (one-third to two-thirds) covered with characteristic raised bumps as a result of the large quill follicles; and shin leather. When the ostrich is around 14 months old the leather is strong enough, without being too damaged, and the birds are slaughtered.

Ostrich is one of the strongest and most flexible leathers and so is desired as much for its durability as for the distinctive markings. It is a little lighter than sheepskin, although this depends on where the leather is derived from, because the sides are softer than the back and shins. It is often mimicked with embossed cow or pig leather.

A new type of exotic leather has emerged in recent years, produced as a by-product of the fishing industry and based on the Icelandic tradition of fish skin shoes. The skin of salmon, perch (*Perca* genus), wolffish (*Anarhichas* genus) and cod (*Gadus* genus) is tanned to make decorative, patterned leather.

For its svelte and flexible qualities, fish leather is reasonably strong. The Icelandic tannery Atlantic Leather produces these leathers in a range of finishes and colours, including machine-washable salmon leather. This capacity greatly expands the potential of leather as a decorative feature in garments.

The surface of fish skin varies from coarse to smooth, depending on the species; the scales are typically removed during tanning. For example, cod has finer scales than salmon, perch is rough, and wolffish is the only one that yields smooth leather (it is a deep-sea fish free from scales). The dark spotted pattern gives wolffish a unique and distinctive appearance, something that will always be visible unless the skin is dyed black.

## SUSTAINABILITY

As with fur (page 466), killing animals primarily for their skin is considered unethical by many. The exotic leather trade is carefully regulated by international government wildlife organizations, such as CITES, in addition to the government requirements of individual countries.

Many animals that yield exotic leather are endangered or threatened and so trapping in the wild is banned or controlled. Certain species are entirely banned in other countries (even if they have the correct paperwork), such as the Siamese crocodile in the USA and Malaysian snakeskin in the European Union. As a result, the vast majority of exotic leather comes from animals farmed for their skins. CITES requires that commercial farms demonstrate a viable second generation and so are not reliant on new stock from the wild.

**Fish skin dress** Fish skin is a by-product of the fishing industry. Converting it into leather creates a desirable product from something that would otherwise be of little value. It is often processed using vegetable tanning and dyeing methods. This dress, created by Milan-based British eco-designer Bav Tailor, is constructed from Nile perch skin sourced from lake Victoria in Africa. Photo courtesy of Bav Tailor.

# Fur

The soft and insulating properties of fur have long been used to keep us warm and comfortable in cold weather. Considered a luxury, the fur of some animals is so valuable that they are farmed primarily for their pelt, which many people consider to be unethical. There are several renewable natural alternatives and man-made materials that offer equivalent properties.

| Types | Typical Applications | Sustainability |
|---|---|---|
| • Rabbit, chinchilla, coypu (nutria), Asiatic raccoon dog, mink, sable, fox, wolf and coyote | • Apparel and footwear<br>• Scarfs, trims and linings<br>• Rugs and throws | • Rabbit fur is, in some cases, a by-product of meat production<br>• Many animals are farmed for their furs; others are taken from the wild |

| Properties | Competing Materials | Costs |
|---|---|---|
| • Soft and highly insulating undercoat<br>• Long and variegated guard hairs<br>• Some furs have no grain and so feel soft in all directions | • Fleece and pelts (hair-on hide)<br>• Fake fur produced by knitting, weaving, tufting and flocking<br>• PAN, PA, PET and viscose | • Tens of dollars per kg for rabbit; hundreds for fox, wolf and coyote; and thousands for mink and sable<br>• Converting furs is and expensive |

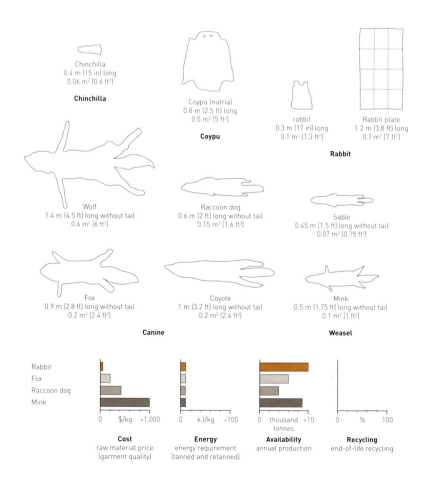

Chinchilla
0.4 m (15 in) long
0.06 m² (0.6 ft²)

**Chinchilla**

Coypu (nutria)
0.8 m (2.5 ft) long
0.5 m² (5 ft²)

**Coypu**

rabbit
0.3 m (17 in) long
0.1 m² (1.3 ft²)

Rabbit plate
1.2 m (3.8 ft) long
0.7 m² (7 ft²)

**Rabbit**

Wolf
1.4 m (4.5 ft) long without tail
0.6 m² (6 ft²)

Raccoon dog
0.6 m (2 ft) long without tail
0.15 m² (1.6 ft²)

Sable
0.45 m (1.5 ft) long without tail
0.07 m² (0.75 ft²)

Fox
0.9 m (2.8 ft) long without tail
0.2 m² (2.4 ft²)

Coyote
1 m (3.2 ft) long without tail
0.2 m² (2.4 ft²)

Mink
0.5 m (1.75 ft) long without tail
0.1 m² (1 ft²)

**Canine**

**Weasel**

Rabbit
Fox
Raccoon dog
Mink

| 0 | $/kg | >1,000 | 0 | kJ/kg | >100 | 0 | thousand tonnes | >10 | 0 | % | 100 |

**Cost**
raw material price
(garment quality)

**Energy**
energy requirement
(tanned and retanned)

**Availability**
annual production

**Recycling**
end-of-life recycling

## INTRODUCTION

The fur trade is a global industry, but it is not nearly as significant now as it was two centuries ago. Mammals and rodents from cold climates, in particular beaver, were so highly sought after in Europe prior to the 19th century that the fur trade fuelled the development of North American cities including New York, Edmonton and Winnipeg. Prior to the colonization of the Americas, Russia was an important source of pelts, and trappers established many new settlements in Siberia.

The industry has changed dramatically over the centuries for many reasons, in particular our changing attitude towards animals as a material source. Improvements in domestic heating, such as the organized distribution of coal in the 19th century, reduced the need for fur as a practical item of clothing. Meanwhile, the price of high-quality alternatives – wool (page 426) and cotton (page 410), for example – decreased thanks to efficiency improvements. More recently, fur has been replaced by less expensive, and less controversial, man-made imitations.

Fake fur, or faux fur, is typically knitted or woven from polyacrylonitrile (PAN, acrylic) (page 180), viscose (page 252) or polyethylene terephthalate (PET, polyester) (page 152). Elaborate techniques have evolved to create fabrics with exceptionally realistic appearance and texture, including the formation of multilayered pile that resembles pelage (the complete fur) in all but the keratin. Even so, as a mimic, they are of course considered inferior. And it should not be forgotten that synthetics have environmental implications of their own.

Fur maintains its status as a luxurious and desirable material and there continue to be many active trappers in northern areas of Canada and Russia. Animals

that cannot be taken from the wild are farmed in countries where it continues to be legal, including Denmark, Finland and China.

Owing to the inevitable variation of furs, and their restricted size, multiple pelts are often combined to make larger and more practical panels. The softest furs tend to come from small animals, such as chinchilla and mink, and stitching techniques have evolved to convert their small pelts into garments without creating obvious seams on the fur side.

Alternatively, strips of fur are combined into larger pieces by weaving. This technique is used to produce lighter and less expensive items such as hats, scarves and jackets.

## COMMERCIAL TYPES AND USES
The principal furbearers are rabbit (Leporidae family); chinchilla (*Chinchilla* genus); coypu (the fur of which is referred to as nutria; *Myocastor* genus); mink (Mustelidae family) and other types of weasel, namely the marten (*Marten*

**Parka** The hoods of cold-weather parkas, such as this model from Spiewak, are lined with fur – coyote in this case, but raccoon is also popular – to keep a warm pocket of air around the face and stop the skin freezing.

genus), including Russian sable; and the canines, such as Asiatic raccoon dog (*Nyctereutes procyonoides*), fox (*Vulpes* and *Alopex* genera), wolf and coyote (both *Canis* genus).

Rabbits grow a fine winter coat that reaches up 20 mm (0.8 in) in length; the ground is around half that. The quality varies and depends on the species. For example, the Rex has the fewest guard hairs and so produces dense and soft fur, and the angora produces a particular fine fur that is often converted into yarn (see Hair, page 434). Their hair is not very strong and prone to abrasion.

Their natural colour ranges from white through brown. Apart from angora, the pelts are relatively cheap and often used to mimic the appearance of more exotic and expensive furs, such as mink, through a combination of dyeing and spraying.

Chinchilla (a type of rodent that originates from the Andes in South America) yields an incredibly soft fur. Many hairs grow from each follicle to create a highly insulating coat, which in turn produces a particularly desirable pelt. It is a distinctive grey-blue-black colour and is often used in its natural state, because dyeing weakens the fibres. They are small and so a hundred or more are required for a long coat, for example. All chinchilla comes from farmed animals, because they are endangered in the wild as a result of being hunted for their pelts.

Coypu (another rodent from South America) fur resembles beaver, with a soft ground and stiff guard hairs. Ranging from light to rich dark brown, the fur is often dyed. And it is typically sheared or plucked to produce a softer and more velvety pelt. The majority comes from farmed animals. However, there has been a concerted effort to try to raise awareness of the potential of wild fur. Considered an invasive species in parts of North America, they are killed and the majority disposed of. Organizations such as the Barataria-Terrebonne National Estuary Program are promoting its potential as a more 'ethical' source for fur.

Furs from weasels, such as mink and sable, are considered to be some of the finest of all. Their winter coat is long, soft and lustrous. Shearing the fur to a uniform length (in particular removing coarse guard hairs) produces an even more luxurious pelt. Sable furs have the added quality of feeling smooth in all directions; the coat does not have a distinctive grain. The majority comes from Russia. A cheaper version of sable comes from Canadian farms, but is generally considered inferior.

The Asiatic raccoon dog is a popular fur-bearer. It has a distinctive pelage made up of long sleek guard hairs over a short, dense ground. Fox, wolf and coyote yield lustrous fur up to around 70 mm (2.75 in) in length. Similar to raccoon, the fur is thick and so stands upright on the skin. Pelts from animals from the northern climates, such as Siberia, have the highest insulating properties.

Their natural colour varies according to the breed and climate. Foxes range from silver, white and red to black. Red is the most common and least expensive, silver and white are more valuable. Wolves are shades of white, brown, grey and black. Coyotes have less colour variation and are typically greyish-fawn with dark tips to the guard hairs. The pelts may be dyed, but the highest-quality fur is used in its natural colour.

Several of the leather-bearing mammals – cow (page 444), sheep and goat (page 452) – yield soft hair, or wool, that is converted into pelt suitable for similar applications. They are not as soft as the coats of the aforementioned fur-bearers, but are much larger and often quite durable, making them suitable for a broad range of applications.

## SUSTAINABILITY

Rabbit fur (except angora) is available as a by-product of meat production. A huge number are slaughtered each year and only some of the skins are converted into fur. All other types of fur are derived from animals farmed or trapped solely for their pelt (fox, chinchilla, mink, coypu and sable). Some furs come from the wild (wolf, fox and sable for example), but this is becoming increasingly rare and now accounts for only around 15%. Strict laws are in place to protect wild animal populations and their welfare. Buying products that have been certified helps to ensure that animals have been treated properly. The Humane Care Certification scheme by the Fur Commission USA was put in place to protect animals farmed for their fur; the Agreement on International Humane Trapping Standards (AIHTS) sets standards for wild animal trapping techniques; and the Convention on International Trade in Endangered Species of Wild Fauna and Flora (CITES) is set out to protect endangered and monitored species.

**Hair structure and types** Pelage is made up of two types of hair, which grow from different follicles: guard hair and ground hair (also known as down or undercoat). Both are made up of fibrous keratin (a type of protein, see also Wool, and Horn, page 440), but serve different purposes. The guard hairs are typically long, straight and hollow. They protrude from the undercoat to create a layer of protection against rain, dirt and sunlight, as well as providing much of the visible colour. The shorter undercoat is curly, soft, dense and water-shedding. It keeps the animal dry and warm by trapping a layer of air next to the skin. The difference between these two is not always clear, because some fibres have the properties of both. The proportion, length and density affect the quality of pelt. A densely packed and fine undercoat feels soft and luxurious. Long and brittle guard hairs can detract from the downy undercoat. In some cases, the guard hairs are plucked or sheared to produce a more uniform and velvety material.

**Opposite**
**The quality and character of fur** This depends on the animal and environment that it has had to adapt to. Rabbit (top) pelage is typically homogenous with a uniform distribution of silky guard hairs and undercoat. Chinchilla, sable, mink and coypu have similar coats that can be cut to produce a soft and uniform texture. Raccoon dog fur (bottom) consists of guard hairs that protrude from the soft and densely tangled undercoat (this is the natural colour). This creates a distinctive texture and appearance, and the fur will feel different against the grain. The same is true for fox, wolf and coyote.

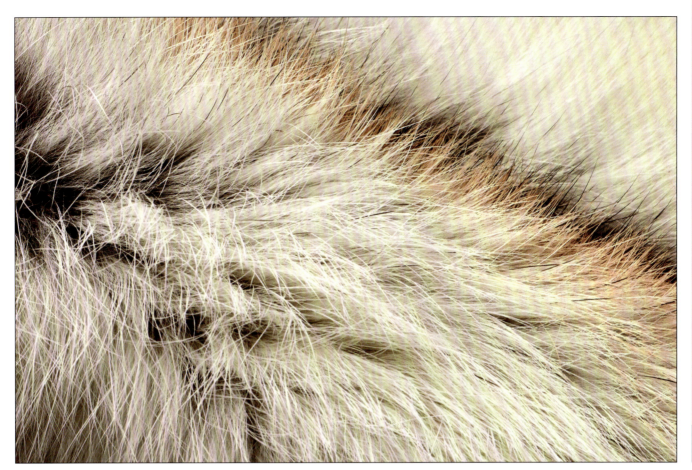

# MINERAL

# 6

# Stone

**From the first man-made tools to high-performance composites, the inherent strength and durability of stone has proved immensely valuable. Rough stone blocks are cut or split from rocks that have been formed by heat and pressure over the course of millennia. They are shaped and dressed, by hand and machine, or melted and extruded as heat-resistant fibre.**

| Types | Typical Applications | Sustainability |
|---|---|---|
| • Sedimentary: limestone, sandstone, soapstone<br>• Metamorphic: marble, slate<br>• Igneous: granite, gabbro, basalt | • Dimensional stone: construction and monuments<br>• Interiors and furniture<br>• Products and tableware | • The largest impacts come from mining and transportation |
| **Properties** | **Competing Materials** | **Costs** |
| • Extremely hard and durable<br>• High heat resistance and incombustible<br>• Resistance to chemicals depends on the stone | • Clay, plaster and cement<br>• Engineered timber<br>• Glass, carbon and aramid | • Although cost per unit weight is low, they are heavy and used in thick sections, making cost per unit area moderate to high |

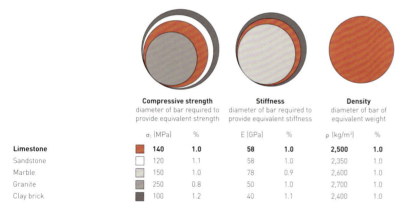

| | Compressive strength<br>diameter of bar required to provide equivalent strength | | Stiffness<br>diameter of bar required to provide equivalent stiffness | | Density<br>diameter of bar of equivalent weight | |
|---|---|---|---|---|---|---|
| | $\sigma_c$ (MPa) | % | E (GPa) | % | $\rho$ (kg/m³) | % |
| Limestone | 140 | 1.0 | 58 | 1.0 | 2,500 | 1.0 |
| Sandstone | 120 | 1.1 | 58 | 1.0 | 2,350 | 1.0 |
| Marble | 150 | 1.0 | 78 | 0.9 | 2,600 | 1.0 |
| Granite | 250 | 0.8 | 50 | 1.0 | 2,700 | 1.0 |
| Clay brick | 100 | 1.2 | 40 | 1.1 | 2,400 | 1.0 |

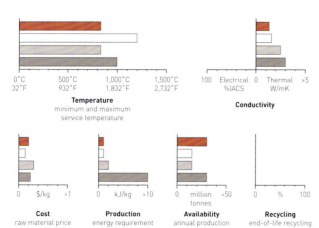

## INTRODUCTION

In Europe, the Bronze Age (see also Copper, page 66) superseded the prehistoric period known as the Neolithic (New Stone Age) during the 4th and 3rd millennia BCE. But the practical use of stone has prevailed for many reasons. It is abundant in the earth's crust and often easily accessible on the surface. Extracting it is relatively straightforward and it can be shaped, dressed and applied without any further processing. Compressed below ground, it is incredibly hard and dense, which makes it a durable and hard-wearing material. Porosity depends on the type of rock, but is generally far less than man-made alternatives, such as cement (page 496).

## COMMERCIAL TYPES AND USES

There are three principal types of rock: sedimentary, metamorphic and igneous. The properties of each are determined by mineral composition and formation.

Sedimentary rock is composed of the shells of aquatic creatures and minerals deposited there by erosion and weathering. It forms a thin layer over mostly metamorphic and igneous rock. Over time and as a result of the pressure of new material deposited, the particles

**Basalt fibre** Basalt is heated and extruded – using a similar process to glass fibre – to produce high-performance fibre. It has exceptional tensile strength, comparable with other high-performance textile fibres, and very good stiffness. Unlike carbon, it is non-conductive and so does not interfere with radio waves. This means it is useful for applications that require higher stiffness than glass can offer, without the electrical interference of carbon. Its main attribute though, is its fire-resistance: basalt fibre is incombustible and can tolerate very high temperatures. As such, it offers an alternative to asbestos, a mineral once used in large quantities until it was discovered that the fine fibres have a propensity to cause fatal illnesses when inhaled.

compress and fuse together. Fossils are most commonly found in this type of rock, because the temperature and pressure is not sufficient to destroy them.

Common types of sedimentary stone include limestone, sandstone and soapstone. Limestone mainly consists of calcium carbonate – formed on the bottom of lakes and seas from calcareous skeletons and bones – with impurities such as clay (page 480), sand and iron. Stone with a higher proportion of magnesium carbonate is graded as dolomite or dolostone.

Limestone is an important material used in a variety of applications as well as building stone, including construction aggregate, cement and plaster (page 492). Outside the construction industry, it is an

important raw material in the production of iron (page 22), steel (page 28), glass (page 508) and sugar; and provides mineral fill in paper (page 268), paint and plastic.

Limestone ranges from soft (chalk) to hard. The type suitable for use as a building block, flooring or counter consists of a very high percentage of calcium carbonate. This makes it hard enough to polish. It is typically white, but can range from black to grey to brown.

Sandstone, as the name suggests, mainly consists of quartz (silica, which is used in glass production, page 508) along with feldspar and lithic fragments (from other rocks). The percentage of each ingredient varies and this is commonly referenced in the name. Sandstone is

hard, compact and fine-grained. As a result of the high proportion of silica, it is very resistant to acids and alkalis. It is typically a shade of light brown or red. It is used in paving, fire hearths and as a load-bearing building block. Its inertness makes it particularly useful for flooring in facilities that deal with chemicals.

Soapstone is comprised primarily of talc (hydrated magnesium silicate). This makes it soft enough to carve. Like sandstone, it is unaffected by liquids, acids and alkalis and so suitable for kitchen and laboratory countertops. However, it is vulnerable to wear and tear and so best avoided in situations where it might receive rough treatment.

Colour often includes shades of grey, green and brown. Its decorative properties

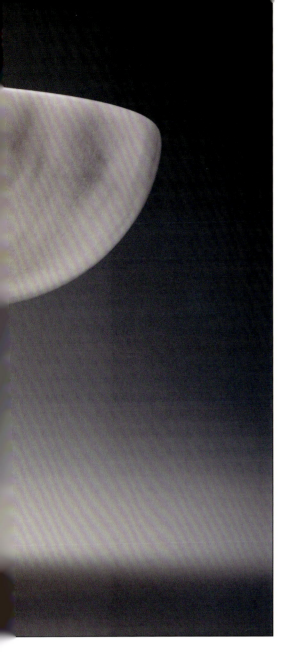

**Carved marble** Using diamond-tipped (see Diamond and Sapphire, page 476) cutting tools, stone may be shaped just like wood and metal. This French fruit bowl is cut from semi-translucent white marble. Stone will hold fine details and sharp edges. However, it is brittle and so care must be taken to ensure that parts are not vulnerable to tensile stress or blunt impact.

are used in construction and sculpture. A notable example is the *Christ the Redeemer* statue that overlooks the city of Rio de Janeiro, which is made of reinforced concrete clad with soapstone. The surface has become pitted and weathered from decades of exposure.

It has high heat capacity, which means that it will retain heat, or cold, for a prolonged period. Combined with its superior temperature resistance, this makes it useful for fire hearths, cooking pots and cooking stones, for example.

There are several types of event that can lead to the formation of metamorphic rock – a pre-existing rock is converted into metamorphic rock through exposure to extreme heat and pressure – such as tectonic movement or the intrusion of hot molten magma. This process results in a refined grain structure. As the minerals in these types of rock are only those formed at high temperature and pressure the stone is typically hard and dense and so can be polished to a very smooth finish. Examples include marble and slate.

Marble is formed from limestone; over time the carbonate minerals go through a process of recrystallization. This results in the formation of large, coarse, interlocked grains of principally calcite or dolomite. The final qualities depend on the impurities present and conditions of formation. Pure limestone produces translucent white marble; variegated colour comes from the presence of impurities. As a result, marble from different quarries will have a different appearance. It is named after its place of origin, such as Bianco Carrara (white with grey veins, Italy), Parian (translucent white, Greece), Vermont (variegated white and grey, USA) and Nero Marquina (black with white veins, Spain).

Marble has long been prized for its beauty and durability. It featured heavily in Greek and Roman architecture and sculpture: Michelangelo famously used high-quality Carrara marble in many of his sculptures; the Greek Parthenon is extravagantly carved from high-quality Greek marble; and the Taj Mahal is clad in various types of bright white marble. Blocks are cut and carved to make bricks, pillars, floors and counters. Crushed marble is used as aggregate, such as to enhance the whiteness of concrete.

Slate is formed from mud: clay, shale and other particles are compressed into a moderately hard and compact rock. It is predominately composed of quartz and mica. Colour is typically dark grey, but various shades of grey-green and grey-blue exist. The crystals form in thin flat layers, which may be split to make sheets.

As a result of its durability and weather resistance, these sheets are applied as paving, roof shingles (tiles) and cladding.

Igneous rock is formed from volcanic material, namely magma. Minerals mix with the hot molten lava, resulting in a variety of compositions with or without crystallization. The magma cools within the earth's crust, or outside as volcanic rock. They are referred to as intrusive and extrusive, respectively.

Granite is an example of intrusive rock made up of quartz, feldspar and potassium. Within the earth's crust, the magma cools slowly and so forms coarse-textured rock. This gives granite its granular appearance. As the hardest of building stones, it has exceptional durability and can be polished to a mirror finish. It is used in a variety of interior and exterior applications, including floors, countertops, hearths and monuments.

'Black granite' is typically gabbro, another type of intrusive rock. It is considered too fragile to use for construction purposes, but provides a valuable decorative material, such as for interiors and façades.

Basalt is an extrusive rock. It cools quickly, which results in a fine grain and crystalline structure (see page 516). It is typically dark-coloured and can be cut and polished like granite. It is used in buildings and monuments. Perhaps its most important application is as a fibre. It is strong, stiff and incombustible. Patented in 1923, it has been explored for a range of applications, primarily military and aerospace. Consumer applications have emerged too. For example, Gitzo manufactures a camera tripod from basalt fibre, offering good mechanical properties at a lower price than carbon.

## SUSTAINABILITY

Mining has impacts on the local environment and stone is a heavy material that is transported all over the world. Even so, these materials have very low embodied energy, because all of the work required to form a strong and durable material was completed prior to extraction. Slate has particularly low energy, because the material is generally split, rather than cut.

# Diamond and Corundum

These gemstones are rare mineral formations prized for their beauty and durability. Predominantly used in jewelry, they are available in a range of striking colours, or may be colourless, in which case lustre and refraction become a measure of its beauty. As industrial materials, these minerals are utilized for their superior hardness, optical properties and chemical resistance.

| Types | Typical Applications | Sustainability |
|---|---|---|
| • Diamond: natural or synthetic<br>• Corundum (ruby and sapphire): natural or synthetic | • Jewelry and accessories<br>• Industrial: abrasives and coatings | • Low embodied energy<br>• Conflict minerals, in particular diamonds, are mined in areas of armed conflict and traded illegally to finance the fighting |
| **Properties** | **Competing Materials** | **Costs** |
| • Very hard and resistant to abrasion<br>• Good chemical resistance<br>• Bright and lustrous; colour depends on impurities | • Stone, glass, clay and technical ceramics<br>• Gold, silver, platinum and titanium<br>• PMMA, PC and ionomer | • Depends on the type and rarity: diamond and ruby are the most valuable<br>• Synthetic minerals are, in some cases, less expensive |

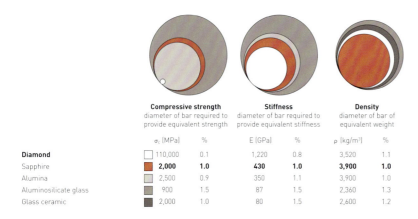

| | Compressive strength<br>diameter of bar required to provide equivalent strength | | Stiffness<br>diameter of bar required to provide equivalent stiffness | | Density<br>diameter of bar of equivalent weight | |
|---|---|---|---|---|---|---|
| | $\sigma_c$ [MPa] | % | E [GPa] | % | $\rho$ [kg/m³] | % |
| Diamond | 110,000 | 0.1 | 1,220 | 0.8 | 3,520 | 1.1 |
| Sapphire | 2,000 | 1.0 | 430 | 1.0 | 3,900 | 1.0 |
| Alumina | 2,500 | 0.9 | 350 | 1.1 | 3,900 | 1.0 |
| Aluminosilicate glass | 900 | 1.5 | 87 | 1.5 | 2,360 | 1.3 |
| Glass ceramic | 2,000 | 1.0 | 80 | 1.5 | 2,600 | 1.2 |

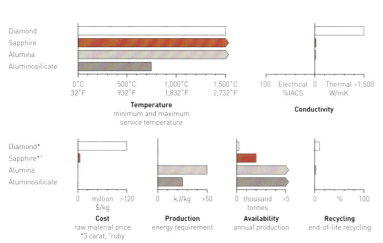

**Temperature**
minimum and maximum service temperature

**Conductivity**

**Cost**
raw material price
*3 carat, ⁺ruby

**Production**
energy requirement

**Availability**
annual production

**Recycling**
end-of-life recycling

## INTRODUCTION

These rare materials have been a source of fascination ever since their discovery. Such is their beauty and mystery that they have been endowed with meaning and symbolism. Diamond, for example, was thought to give strength and fortitude to its wearer in battle; it is a symbol of wealth and power; and in modern times it has become a gift of people in love.

They are valuable industrial materials, too. Along with technical ceramics (page 502), gemstone minerals are some of the hardest and most wear-resistant materials, making them efficient industrial abrasives and additives in protective coatings.

Gemstones synthesized in laboratories provide some unique qualities and are, in some cases, less expensive. Sapphire, for example, is optically transparent, extremely hard-wearing and scratch-resistant, and can be grown as very large, clean crystals. As well as in jewelry, laboratory-grown sapphire is utilized in super-tough windows, such as for watches, phones, sensors and lasers.

Gemstones are sold by the carat (a unit of weight equal to one-fifth of a gram or one-fortysecond of an ounce). However, the price per carat depends on the size of stone. Large stones will be significantly more expensive per carat, because they are much less common than small ones.

## COMMERCIAL TYPES AND USES

There are hundreds of minerals, but only a handful have come to be regarded as gemstones. The most important of these, for decorative and industrial applications, are diamond and corundum (sapphire and ruby).

Diamond is formed of pure carbon in a uniform and compact arrangement that yields the most durable material known. It is believed to be formed from

carbon-containing minerals deep within the mantle, tens of kilometres below the surface of the earth, under extreme pressure and heat, and delivered to the surface by volcanic activity. Other processes thought to be responsible for diamond formation, such as asteroid impacts, are a far less common source.

Diamond is the hardest of all materials and so defines the upper limit of the Mohs scale (a relative measure of hardness based on one mineral's ability to scratch, or be scratched by, another). The same bonds that make it very hard also provide very good chemical resistance and extremely high thermal

conductivity (more than three times that of copper, page 66).

Gemstones sold for their beauty and clarity are colourless; tinted yellow, red, orange, green, blue or brown; or opaque black. The colour comes from impurities in the carbon structure. Industrial diamond may be of very high quality but too small to use for jewelry, or derived from diamond with a high level of impurities. These are ground up into small particles and bonded onto saw blades, drill bits and other tools. They provide a very hard cutting edge or abrasive surface, capable of grinding any other rigid material.

Polished to a mirror finish, diamond

**Sapphire crystal window** Synthetic sapphire is hard-wearing, resistant to chemicals, transparent across the visible spectrum and stronger than high-strength glass for the same thickness. However, it is relatively expensive to produce and this limits applications. As well as laser systems and optical sensors, in the last few decades it has become very popular in high-end watches. The Bell &

Ross BR 126 Heritage, features a domed sapphire window held within a steel case. The matt black finish on the machined steel is produced by physical vapour deposition (PVD) – essentially a thin-film ceramic coating (see Technical Ceramic). This combination of materials yields a very beautiful, durable and high-quality watch that can comfortably stand up to the demands of aviation pilots. Photo courtesy of Bell & Ross.

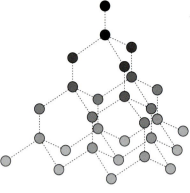

The carbon arrangement forms
a tetrahedral structure

Cubic close-packed
arrangement

Tetrahedral structure
inscribed in a cube

**Diamond** Owing to the arrangement of carbon atoms and strong covalent bonds, diamond is the hardest of all materials. Each carbon atom is joined to four neighbours. The close-packed arrangement forms a giant tetrahedral structure. It is based on the face-centred cubic structure (see page 68) with four extra atoms (pictured as grey balls). Compare this to the structure of graphite (see page 238), another type of giant covalent structure, with each carbon atom joined to three others to form planes. The weak points in the structure of diamond and graphite are along the faces, where fewer bonds exist. At this point, the material can be split with a blunt impact. Because the bonds elsewhere are so strong, diamond can be cut only by using another diamond, or a laser.

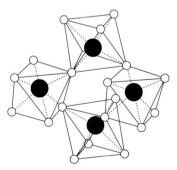

Corundum crystal structure

**Sapphire and ruby** These crystals are both made up of corundum. Also known as aluminium oxide or alumina, it crystallizes with each aluminium atom surrounded by six oxygen atoms, forming an octahedral shape. This forms a trigonal crystal system and is normally described using hexagonal axes. It is an exceptionally hard, tough and stable structure: it is the third hardest mineral.

exhibits a high lustre (it reflects a high percentage of the light that strikes the surface). Colourless and tinted diamond has very high dispersion, which means light waves are separated into their component colours. These qualities combine to produce dazzling aesthetic properties highly sought after in jewelry and accessories. While colourless diamonds free from flaws and inclusions (particles) are traditionally the most valuable, those with impurities that cause colour distortions are becoming popular as a result of their uniqueness.

Synthetic diamonds have the same chemical composition, crystal structure and properties. Indeed, they can be impossible to tell apart from natural ones. Two principal methods are used. The first forms diamond from graphite by placing it under intense pressure and heat. Known as high-pressure high-temperature (HPHT), it is limited by what is physically possible with modern machinery and so only capable of producing very small diamonds. These are typically used for industrial purposes. The second, developed more recently, uses chemical vapour deposition (CVD) and results in perfect diamond crystal formation. Carried out in a vacuum chamber at high heat and under precisely controlled conditions, carbon-containing gas (usually methane and hydrogen) is decomposed and deposited onto a surface. Diamond is used to seed the process: the carbon atoms build on the existing diamond lattice. CVD is used to form stones as well as apply coatings. The majority is used in industrial applications, such as lenses, cutting tools and wear-resistant components.

Diamond-like carbon (DLC) is a different material produced by plasma enhanced CVD (PECVD). It is created by bombarding a surface with carbon particles and yields a hard and chemically stable material. In this case, the carbon atoms form an amorphous (random) network, not a crystalline structure. In other words, not diamond. However, it yields a desirable and high-quality finish utilized in jewelry and watches, as well as for industrial applications.

Corundum consists of alumina (aluminium oxide) (see Technical Ceramic) and the colour is determined by impurities in the crystal structure: chromium produces red (ruby); and trace amounts of iron and titanium produce blue (sapphire). Of course, many other colours are possible (green, yellow, orange and purple), but in its purest form, corundum is colourless. It provides excellent optical clarity, because it is transparent to the entire visible range of light. Combined with its impressive durability, this is what makes it such a valuable window material, such as for watches and industrial equipment.

Sapphire melts to form a liquid with the same composition. This makes it a relatively straightforward mineral to grow in the laboratory. There are many techniques available; the two principal types are flame-fusion (Verneuil process) and melt growing (Czochralski process).

Developed in 1902, flame-fusion is the oldest method and continues to be used today in the production of industrial gemstones and seed for other processes to grow larger crystals from. Finely ground ingredients are heated to their melting point (around 2,000°C [3630°F] for sapphire) in a crucible and the droplets combine to form a very pure boule atop a support rod. Slowly lowering the support rod and continuously feeding raw material allows for the growth of very long single crystals.

Melt growing also produces single crystals, which can be very large. It is used in the production of semiconductors, such as silicon and geranium; metals, including platinum and gold; and synthetic gemstones. The process involves melting the ingredients together in a crucible. A seed crystal on a carefully positioned rod is inserted into the mix. Through a combination of localized freezing (cooling) and pulling (raising of the rod), a perfect, large crystal is formed. By pulling the sapphire melt through a shaped die, a range of geometries is possible, including tube, sheet and bespoke shapes.

There have been many developments on these techniques. The Kyropoulos process, for example, first applied to sapphire in 1980s, is used to produce very large (tens of kilos) high-quality crystals.

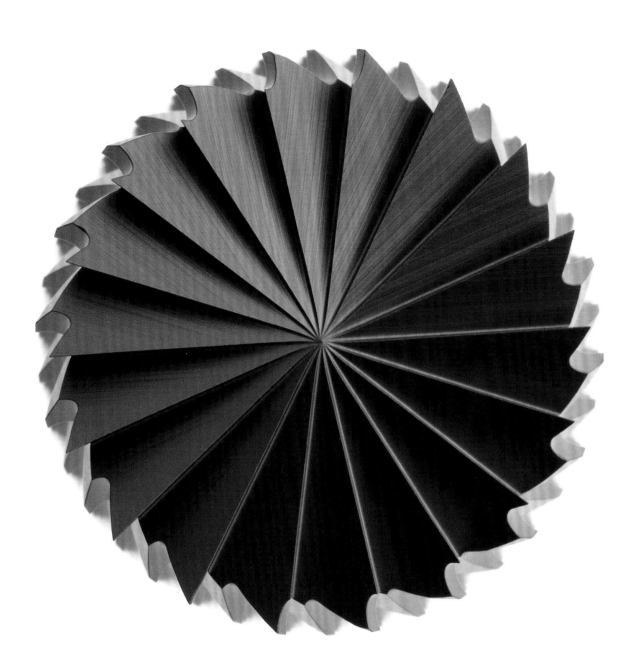

## SUSTAINABILITY

As with other mined materials, the process of digging a hole and taking stuff out is clearly not sustainable. It is possible to manage the ecological impacts of mining, to a point, and minimize loss of habitat and biodiversity. However, what is challenging to manage is how the very high economic value of these minerals can negatively affect the local community.

Conflict minerals are materials derived from parts of the world where armed warfare is taking place and the mining and trading of those materials helps to finance the fighting. These are predominantly columbite-tantalite, also known as coltan (from which tantalum is derived), cassiterite (tin), gold, and wolframite (tungsten), which are mined in the Democratic Republic of Congo. The term 'conflict diamond', or 'blood diamond', was coined in the 1990s in response to how sales of the mineral helped fund civil wars in such places as Angola and Sierra Leone. In response, a joint governments and industry initiative was established to stem the flow of conflict diamonds. However, only a small portion of the world's diamonds is traceable. Those derived from banned sources are easily smuggled across borders and sold into the global market.

**CVD diamond coating**
Synthetic diamond is chemically, physically and visually identical to natural diamond. One of the main advantages is that it can be produced in a range of formats. Adding a thin-film diamond coating to cutting tools makes them extremely hard, which decreases wear and improves cutting performance. The Jabro JC800 tungsten carbide (see Technical Ceramics) cutters produced by Seco Tools feature a CVD diamond coating. These exceptionally high-performance cutters are specifically designed for machining composite parts. The combination of design and materials yields a high-quality edge finish with reduced fibre break-out and delamination. Photo courtesy of Seco Tools.

# Clay

Clay is a humble material dug from the ground that, with careful processing, becomes fine porcelain, structural building material, hygienic sanitaryware or aesthetic dental repair. The final properties – strength, temperature resistance, colour, water absorption and so on – are realized with high-temperature firing and depend on the type and proportion of mineral ingredients.

| Types | Typical Applications | Sustainability |
|---|---|---|
| • Pottery: earthenware, stoneware and porcelain<br>• Structural: brick and tile | • Tableware<br>• Dental<br>• Bricks, pavers, tiles, pipes and so on<br>• Sanitaryware | • Clay is derived from open mines<br>• It has low embodied energy<br>• It is recycled as aggregate |

| Properties | Competing Materials | Costs |
|---|---|---|
| • Brittle and hard<br>• Compressive strength is typically ten times tensile strength<br>• Colour depends on ingredients | • Construction materials such as steel, glass, PVC, cement, plaster and timber<br>• Cookware materials such as cast iron, steel and aluminium | • Raw material price depends on material quality<br>• Processing is relatively inexpensive |

## Also known as

Earthenware: terracotta, redware, creamware, pearlware, delftware, jackfield, lustreware, ironstone
Stoneware: jasperware, caneware, basaltware
Porcelain: china, bone china, parian, hard-paste, soft-paste

## INTRODUCTION

Traditional ceramics – earthenware, stoneware, porcelain, bricks and tiles – are manufactured from consolidated sediment, of different geological ages and composition, which has been mined, processed, molded and fired at high temperature. Since it is impractical to remove impurities from clay, the raw material tends to undergo very little processing. In the past, this meant the quality and properties were determined largely by geographical location. This is why regions became renowned for a certain quality of pottery or colour of building. Nowadays, clay minerals are carefully mixed and blended to yield more predictable properties, regardless of location.

There are many different minerals involved and each plays its role in the physical and aesthetic properties of the final material. Clays are residual and found where they were deposited; or sedimentary, which means they have been moved as a result of weathering. Residual, or primary, clays yield a material of higher purity, but are quite rare. Sedimentary, or secondary, clays typically have smaller particle size and contain a

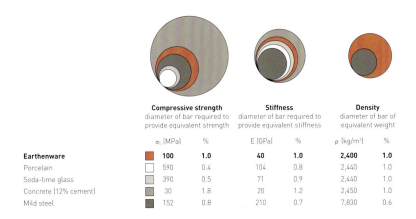

| | Compressive strength<br>diameter of bar required to provide equivalent strength | | Stiffness<br>diameter of bar required to provide equivalent stiffness | | Density<br>diameter of bar of equivalent weight | |
|---|---|---|---|---|---|---|
| | σ_c [MPa] | % | E [GPa] | % | ρ [kg/m³] | % |
| Earthenware | 100 | 1.0 | 40 | 1.0 | 2,400 | 1.0 |
| Porcelain | 590 | 0.4 | 104 | 0.8 | 2,440 | 1.0 |
| Soda-lime glass | 390 | 0.5 | 71 | 0.9 | 2,440 | 1.0 |
| Concrete (12% cement) | 30 | 1.8 | 20 | 1.2 | 2,450 | 1.0 |
| Mild steel | 152 | 0.8 | 210 | 0.7 | 7,830 | 0.6 |

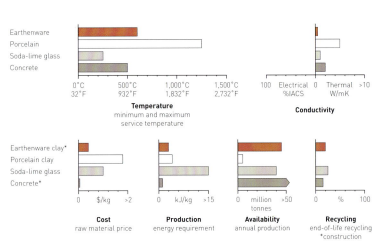

**Temperature**
minimum and maximum service temperature

**Conductivity**

**Cost**
raw material price

**Production**
energy requirement

**Availability**
annual production

**Recycling**
end-of-life recycling
*construction

**Thrown stoneware**
Glaze is poured, dipped, sprayed or brushed onto the surface of clay. It is used to provide colour, decoration and protection from water. It consists of glass (silica or boron), stiffener (such as clay), colour (metal oxides), and opacity and melting agents (such as soda). Decorative techniques evolved over centuries range from colour and texture effects to sagging and crazing. This stoneware jug is by British ceramicist Clive Davies. Renowned for his painterly style, he buys powdered glaze and mixes ingredients. His unique designs are created by dipping in plain-coloured glaze and then decorating over the surface with various methods, such as wax resist, brushing and sgraffito (scratching through the top layer to reveal colours beneath).

**Above**
**Hand-thrown porcelain**
This Japanese bowl demonstrates the quality and finesse that can be achieved with porcelain. It is the finished appearance, not the workability, that determined the choice of material. As the strongest pottery clay,

porcelain will tolerate the thinnest wall sections. However, it is not easy clay to work by hand and requires a great deal of skill owing to the very fine particle size, which means it has very little plasticity and is prone to collapsing during shaping.

**Opposite**
**Partially glazed terracotta**
Earthenware is porous and requires a glaze to be applied if it is to be watertight. This cazuela dish is glazed on the inside surface.

Leaving the outside unglazed retains the clay's inherent porosity. This allows hot moist air to circulate through the material, helping to promote slow and even cooking.

more diverse mix of ingredients. In both cases, the key component is kaolinite (hydrated aluminosilicate). The chemistry and arrangement of its stacked crystal structure, along with the other minerals, is fundamental in determining the physical properties of the clay.

Named after the hill in China (Gao Ling) from where it was first derived, kaolin, or china clay, is composed of 75% or more kaolinite. Kaolin is found throughout Europe, the Americas and Asia, although material from different mines will have markedly different properties. Its commercial value is determined by purity, fineness and whiteness. The majority is used in paper making (page 268), where it helps to reduce cost and improves printability. In the case of ceramics, kaolin forms the principal ingredient in the highest-quality sanitaryware and porcelain.

Ball clay is another class of material. As well as kaolinite, it contains mica and quartz (silica). It is added to other clays to enhance the plasticity and robustness of the unfired material, allowing it to

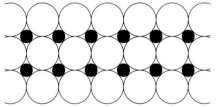

**Atomic bonding and arrangement** Ceramics consist of metallic and nonmetallic elements, held together by ionic and covalent bonds. Ionic bonds are formed by the electrostatic attraction of oppositely charged ions. Thus, the strength depends on the size of the charge. Covalent bonds are formed by atoms sharing electrons; the greater the number of electrons being shared, the stronger the bond. Various structures and arrangements exist, depending on the composition. Ceramics may be entirely crystalline (see page 516) or contain regions

with amorphous (glassy) arrangement. The ductility of metal is due to weaker bonds between the atoms – positive metal ions are held together by a mass of delocalized electrons, allowing freer movement than is the case with ceramics – which means they can be bent and squeezed without breaking. Ceramics have greater propensity to fracture as a result of their brittleness combined with porosity. Tiny flaws act as stress concentration points, thus focusing loads onto a very small area, forcing the atomic bonds apart.

be more easily shaped and molded. As a result, it often makes up only a small percentage of clay body.

Fireclay is a sedimentary mudstone, so-called thanks to its ability to resist heat and its original use in firebricks (such as for lining furnaces). It has similar composition to ball clay. The difference comes from the greater geological age of fireclay, which means it is not as plastic (moldable) and requires firing at a higher temperature. It contains relatively little iron and so produces a buff-coloured

ceramic, which is now mainly utilized in bricks and pipes.

Red clay is normal sedimentary clay that is so-called because it fires to a reddish-brown colour. This is a direct result of iron in the clay, which oxidizes during firing to form red-coloured ferrous oxide. Firing in a reducing atmosphere (without oxygen, also called flashing), produces dark grey through black. Other metal oxides result in different colours. Carbonate minerals, such as calcite and dolomite, yield paler-coloured ceramic.

**Extruded brick** Clay is the oldest structural man-made building material; the ancient Egyptians sun-dried mud bricks and the Romans produced vast quantities of kiln-fired brick. The advantage of brick construction, and why its fundamental design has changed so little over the course of millennia, is its impressive flexibility in application. Many different shapes and sizes exist including molded and extruded types. One attribute they all share, is that a single mason can lay and manipulate them, one by one, to form a sturdy structure.

### Local materials

The differences in traditional architectural forms can be attributed to a combination of the properties of clay found nearby and local needs. This house in Haarlem, the Netherlands, is constructed from earthenware brick. Renowned for its durability, Dutch brick is sometimes a washed-out yellow, but more typically dark brownish-red. This humble building block has a long and rich history in the Netherlands and remains a fundamental part of the architecture. Intricate and crafted brickwork dominates the façades of its towns and cities.

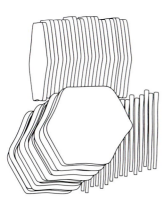

### Crystal arrangement

Kaolinite forms a structure made up of thin hexagonal plates stacked together. Water is able to penetrate between the thin plates, reducing the friction between them and thus allowing them to slide over one another. This provides clay with its plasticity (moldability). As well as water content, the workability of clay depends on particle size and composition – a broad range of minerals and particles is intermingled with the kaolinite. A balance is required to ensure the clay is soft enough to be formed with ease while being sturdy enough to retain its shape. Increasing the percentage of water forms a slurry, or water suspension, that is suitable for slip casting or coating. Drying the clay produces a rigid, but brittle material. When fired in a kiln at high temperature, permanent physical and chemical changes occur, resulting in a hard, durable ceramic.

White to off-white is only possible if the clay has a very low iron content.

These clays, along with several other mineralogical ingredients, are mixed to give clay bodies the properties required for production and use.

## COMMERCIAL TYPES AND USES

Earthenware, also called terracotta, is the earliest-known form of pottery – with evidence dating back 9,000 years – and remains popular. Widely available, it is used to make a huge variety of

items, from cookware to brick and sculpture to pipe.

Naturally occurring, it consists of kaolinite and quartz, among other sedimentary materials. The iron and other impurities act as flux (substance that lowers the melting point), which means it can be fired at relatively low temperature. Other low-fire flux materials include talc, frit and nepheline syenite (similar to feldspar). It is bisque fired (see page 488) to temperatures between 1,000 and 1,150°C (1,830–2100°F). The colour of red earthenware is affected by firing temperature and atmosphere: lower temperatures produce terracotta and higher temperatures with reduced

oxygen levels turn the clay brown or even black. White earthenware does not occur naturally. It is manufactured from kaolin and other clay minerals that allow it to be low-temperature fired.

During firing, the minerals fuse, but do not vitrify, so the clay remains porous and 'soft'. Therefore, it must be glazed in order to be watertight.

It has good plasticity, which makes it easy to shape by hand or machine. It can be produced as thin as porcelain, but owing to its poor mechanical properties and ease of chipping, relatively thick wall sections are required. It is used in cookware and has sufficient temperature resistance to move from the freezer to the

oven without failing. Another attribute is its low shrinkage, which means it can be formed into sculpture with thick sections.

Stoneware is also based on kaolinite, but owing to its slightly different composition it has a higher firing temperature. Bisque firing is typically around 1,000°C (1,830°F) followed by glaze firing of 1,200 to 1,300°C (2,190–2,370°F), depending on the flux content. At this temperature, stoneware becomes vitreous (glass-like), or semi-vitreous, resulting in a more durable material with very low porosity. Glaze becomes integral to the ceramic, forming a glaze-clay interlayer. However, stoneware is completely watertight once fired and does not

**Stoneware** Pottery has long been a highly valued part of the tea ceremony in Japan; every detail is purposeful and there is a great synergy between practicality and beauty. This stoneware teapot derives from Tokoname, a city that has been central to Japanese ceramic production since the 12th century. The iron-oxide-rich clay is left unglazed, because it is believed the alkalinity of the ceramic enhances the flavour and body of the tea by removing the bitterness. The colour of fired clay depends on chemical composition and firing temperature. In this case, the iron-rich clay was reduction fired, causing the clay to turn dark grey.

## PRODUCTS, FURNITURE AND LIGHTING

**Versatility**
Clay provides the ceramicist with countless opportunities for experimentation and artistic expression. At the other end of the spectrum, it provides the raw material for mass-produced flatware, cookware and sanitaryware.

**Durability**
Once fired, clay has the most impressive longevity of all man-made materials. It is inert and the surface will remain unchanged for millennia if left alone. The only way to destroy it is to crush or break it into smaller pieces.

**Inert**
The surface of non-absorbent ceramic – porcelain, stoneware and glaze – is hygienic and easy to keep clean. If ceramics are to be used in food-contact applications, then appropriate glazes must be selected that are safe, tolerate washing and resist abrasion.

require glazing; this is done purely for decorative purposes.

Body colour ranges from white to buff and light to dark grey, depending on the impurities. It may have a speckled appearance as a result of the inclusion of particles of stone and flint, making each piece unique. Its added robustness makes it more forgiving during manufacture, although this depends on the stoneware.

Applications are similar to earthenware, with the addition of light-coloured bricks and chemical storage vessels. A broad range of glaze colours is possible on light-coloured stoneware, because it has a lower firing temperature than porcelain.

Porcelain, or china, is produced from the highest-quality kaolin-rich clay, which is mixed with selected ingredients to increase plasticity and reduce the firing temperature. It was developed in medieval China and did not feature in European pottery until the 18th century.

As a result of the fine particle size, porcelain can be produced bright white, with thin walls and a very smooth surface. The hot firing temperature – between 1,200 and 1,400°C (2,190–2,550°F) – results in a strong and translucent ceramic of fine quality. At this temperature, promoted by the inclusion of flux (such as feldspar), porcelain becomes vitreous. The kaolinite becomes glassy and mullite (aluminosilicate, see High-Performance Glass, page 522) crystals develop, which greatly strengthens the ceramic structure. Porcelain has the lowest porosity of the clay ceramics and absorbs less than 3% moisture, but typically closer to zero. By contrast, stoneware absorbs up to 5% and earthenware up to 10%.

Porcelain is used in all forms of pottery, from sculpture and vases to teacups and wall tiles. Its very low porosity means that it will not absorb fats, odour or bacteria. It is tough, and suitable for the freezer, fridge and oven. It is an important industrial material and applied as an electrical insulator and enamel coating on metal (such as for baths, sinks, ovens, stoves and white goods).

True porcelain is also referred to as hard-paste. So-called soft-paste porcelain, first produced in Europe in an attempt to mimic Chinese porcelain, comprises clay and frit (a mixture of silica and fluxes, such as feldspar) among other ingredients. It can be fired at significantly lower temperature than hard-paste, which means that a much wider range of coloured glazes is available. However, it does not yield such a strong, vitreous ceramic, thus remaining somewhat porous and of inferior quality. It continues to be used in the production of tableware, such as plates, cups and bowls.

Bone china, first produced in England during the 18th century, combines calcinated bone ash with kaolin and feldspar. High-quality bone china may contain as much as half bone ash, by weight. It is prized for its strength, chip resistance and high levels of whiteness and translucency. Like soft-paste porcelain, it is mainly used in tableware. As a result of its animal content, it is avoided in some cultures.

The durability, biocompatibility and aesthetic qualities of porcelain-like materials are utilized in dental restoration work, such as crowns and veneers. Dental ceramics are mainly comprised of feldspar with only a little kaolin to act as binder, which results in a large proportion of glass after firing. With advances in 3D scanning, it is now possible to create milled ceramic parts that fit patients very precisely. Alternatives to porcelain include technical ceramic (such as alumina and zirconia, see Technical Ceramic, page 502), glass ceramic (see High-performance Glass) and polymethyl methacrylate (PMMA, acrylic) (page 174).

## SUSTAINABILITY

Clay is an abundant material, but requires mining, which has an impact on the surrounding environment. Management of the land is governed by local laws, which typically require that the site be re-landscaped once mining is complete. Open-pit mines are often allowed to fill with water and become lakes.

Clay has very low embodied energy; natural forces have, over the course of the many millennia, done most of the work. Production of the raw material used to be located close by the mine, but this is now not always the case. The mined material is pulverized, sieved and washed and major impurities are removed (where possible). It is either mixed wet, or dried and mixed in powder form. Factories mass-producing wares, such as sanitary items, commonly mix their own batches of material from powdered clay at the start of each shift. Studios and potteries, on the other hand, tend to purchase premixed clay.

In the production of ceramic wares, the firing process accounts for the majority of the energy consumed. Transportation is a significant contributor too, because ceramic is heavy, bulky, fragile and shipped all over the world.

Ceramic may contain a host of recycled material and by-products from other industries. Bricks may contain pulverized fuel ash (PFA), which is a by-product of coal-fuelled power stations. Other types of waste material – including sawdust, straw and expanded polystyrene (EPS) (page 132) – may also be incorporated in the mix. As well as reducing the amount of mined material required, waste materials may yield benefits for production (such as lowering firing temperature) or affect the appearance of the finished article.

Ceramics are durable and able to survive for thousands of years. While this is desirable for building materials and handmade items, other types of ceramic waste require disposal. It is impossible to recycle ceramic directly, but it may be broken up and used as aggregate or gravel, or bonded together with resin, such as in the production of countertops.

## CLAY IN PRODUCTS, FURNITURE AND LIGHTING

Whether clay is used in one-off artwork or mass-produced by the million, the end result is defined by a combination of material, process and finish.

There are many variations on the three principal materials – earthenware, stoneware and porcelain – and the boundaries between them can become somewhat blurred. Material selection comes down to a number of factors: processability, finishing options, physical properties and cost.

Clay is formed in its plastic state, green, by powder forming or suspended in water as slip. The range of design opportunities depends on how well the clay performs at the desired consistency.

Plastic forming is the most widely used and includes manual (hand building, throwing and carving), semi-automated (jiggering and jolleying) and mass-production (ram pressing and extrusion) techniques. The plasticity, or formability, of clay depends on particle size and water content. Workability is a combination of plasticity and wet strength. Thus, it is possible to increase workability without affecting plasticity, such as by adding grog (crushed unglazed ceramic) or sand. This allows for the production of tall and slender items without fear of collapse.

Fine or dry clays lack plasticity, which means that they are stiffer and less forgiving to work by hand. Fine-grained porcelain is particularly difficult to work into thin-walled vessels, requiring a great deal of skill and experience. Earthenware is much more forgiving and suitable for thick- and thin-walled vessels of all shapes and sizes.

Jiggering and jolleying are an extension of wheel throwing. Both of these processes are limited to the production of rotationally symmetrical parts (although of course, they can be manipulated off the wheel). In the case of jiggering and jolleying, the ceramicist's fingers and tools are replaced with a mold and former. This means that every piece will be the same. They are suitable for semi-automated or fully automated production, but because the clay is left to dry on the mold, high-volume production is somewhat limited.

Fully mechanized processes, such as ram pressing and extrusion, use much stiffer clay than is suitable for handwork. This ensures that the part holds its shape throughout the rapid forming cycle and is less prone to shrink and distort.

Ram pressing is carried out in plaster

**Clay body**

**Ceramic**

### Drying and firing

Water is held between the plates of the crystal structure. Clay will gradually dry out as surface water evaporates and draws water from inside out. The clay body shrinks as a result, until the plate faces are in contact with one another and maximum density is reached. At elevated temperatures inside the kiln, the water that is chemically bonded within the clay minerals is released. The temperature is gradually increased, so that all the water can escape before turning into steam. If pressure builds up then it is likely the soft clay will crack. Warpage occurs as a result of uneven shrinkage. In other words, if water is able to escape more quickly from one part or side than another, the item will bend. As the rest catches up, it will be too stiff to return to its intended shape.

Once dry, the clay particles begin to fuse. Known as sintering (solidifying), the process of clay becoming a hard ceramic is irreversible. Bisque, or biscuit, firing fuses the particles without vitrifying the ceramic. This allows glazes to adhere. Once the surface has been decorated the ceramic is returned to the kiln for a second firing. Called glaze or glost firing, the ceramic is heated to the point at which the minerals begin to melt and vitrify (convert into glass-like material). At maturation temperature, the porous structure is converted into a strong, watertight material. The temperature at which this occurs depends on the clay and its composition. Higher temperature will result in more vitreous ceramic, but if the temperature is too high the clay will melt and slump.

(page 492) molds, which help to draw moisture from the clay. The process is typically run at high temperature, further accelerating the drying process. This allows for the part to be handled straight out of the mold. It is used to produce flatware and in particular non-symmetrical parts, which are not suitable for jiggering and jolleying.

Greenware is a general term used to describe shaped clay that has not been fired. Clay that is described as leather-hard is partially dry, but remains slightly pliable; and clay referred to as bone-dry is brittle. At the leather-hard stage, the clay is firm enough to tolerate being handled and pierced, incised or carved – adding delicate features that would not be

**Porcelain** This Royal Copenhagen teapot is part of the service designed by Arnold Krog, artistic director of the Royal Copenhagen Porcelain Manufactory from 1885. Krog relaunched the Blue Fluted pattern that emulated the quintessential blue-and-white Chinese porcelain of the Ming and Qing dynasties, which had become very popular in Europe. The blue glaze is painstakingly hand-painted, requiring more than a thousand strokes of the brush.

## ARCHITECTURE AND CONSTRUCTION

**Longevity**
The durability of clay makes it an ideal building material. Brick buildings are reused, repointed and redecorated. Porous earthenware is vulnerable to absorbed water freezing and causing frost damage and spalling (fragments breaking away), but formulations have emerged to overcome this problem.

**Versatility**
The full range of traditional ceramics is utilized as building materials. Choice is determined by a combination of aesthetics, performance and cost.

**Low cost**
Earthenware is a low-cost building material available in a range of formats – bricks, tiles, pavers, pipes and so on. Stoneware and porcelain provide greater strength, durability and heat resistance, which are useful in some cases, but come at a higher price.

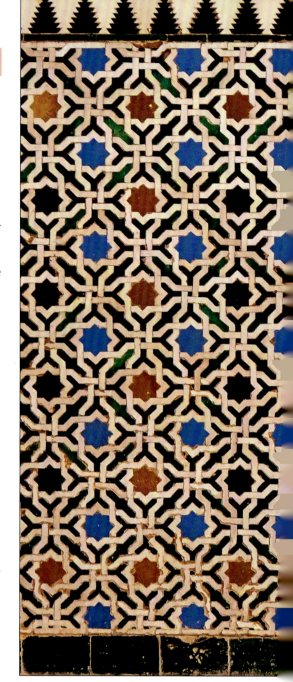

possible on wet clay – without deforming the item or depressing the surface.

Powder forming, or dry pressing, is a mass-production technique used mainly for flatware, such as plates, bowls and cups. It eliminates drying, which presents many advantages: quicker turnaround, reduced shrinkage and less warpage. Molds are typically two-part and so suitable for low-profile shapes. In the case of technical ceramics, complex three-dimensional items are shaped with multi-part molds or by isostatic pressing.

Liquid clay, also called slip or slurry, is used for casting and coating. Casting is economic for large volumes and allows for the production of complex designs. A plaster mold is created that is a representation of the outside surface. The slip is poured into the cavity and the water is drawn out by the plaster, causing clay particles to collect on the inside surface of the mold. Once the desired wall thickness is achieved, excess slip is poured out and the part is ready to be removed from the mold. Reproduction is precise and fine surface details are faithfully reproduced. It is a widely used process and applications span studio work, such as teapots and lamp bases, through to mass-produced sanitaryware.

The next step in the making process is firing, which offers a staggering range of design opportunities. The typical procedure, as mentioned previously, involves two stages. The first stage is bisque firing, which takes the clay up to the point at which it becomes ceramic without going through vitrification. This is to allow for glazes to be applied without damaging the item. The temperature is raised slowly to reduce the chances of items cracking or exploding.

Once glazed, items are put back into the kiln for a second firing, known as glaze or glost firing. This time, the materials are taken to their vitrification temperature. This causes chemical changes within the glaze and clay, forming a glossy and durable item.

'Once firing' (or single firing) eliminates the bisque and goes straight to the vitrification temperature. It is possible with any type of clay (although the glazes are limited), but requires careful temperature control, because it is more stressful on the clay. Developed in China, the technique is rarely used in studios. However, it is popular in mass production because of the labour and energy savings. Parts are loaded onto a conveyor at one end of a tunnel kiln and their temperature raised gradually as they progress through. By the time they reach the far end the firing process is complete. High volumes of tableware, sanitaryware and industrial ceramics are commonly produced in this way.

### CLAY IN ARCHITECTURE AND CONSTRUCTION

Brick structures dating back to Roman times are testament to the durability and versatility of this unique building material. Modern brick, tile, pipe and similar items are molded or extruded; the fundamental processes and ingredients have changed little over the centuries.

Before the development of suitable transport systems, most buildings were constructed from local materials. The mineralogical composition of clay is different depending on location; and as a result, many different strengths and colours of clay building material have evolved over the years.

Traditional bricks and tiles are still handmade. It is a straightforward process, whereby a wet clay mix is pressed into molds by hand. To prevent the clay from sticking, the inside surface is coated with sand (sand-struck) or water (water-struck). Owing to the nature of the process and handwork involved, the size and shape of items produced in this way may be slightly irregular.

Over the years, hand processes have been largely replaced by machine molding, which helps to reduce cost and improve consistency. In the production of bricks, tiles and similar items, clay (wet or powdered) is pressed into steel molds

with significant force. The finished article is precise and includes all the ribs, fixing nibs and so on.

Extrusion, or the 'stiff mud' process, produces a long length of clay, which is cut to the desired size. Core holes are incorporated to reduce weight, without affecting strength. The process is fast and efficient; bricks, pipes and similar items will be more consistent than molded types and less expensive. As a result, the majority of clay building products are now produced using this method.

The extruded billet is cut, scratched, rolled or brushed to roughen the surface and, in some cases, remove evidence of

the extrusion process. Bricks can be given an antique-looking finish by tumbling before or after firing.

Coatings include slip (or slurry) and glaze. Slip fired onto the ceramic body provides colour and hardness without affecting the water absorption. Glaze, on the other hand, is impervious to water. It is applied onto the green clay and once fired, or processed using the more conventional two-stage firing technique. While once firing saves on labour and energy, the advantage of using a two-stage process is that a greater range of colours is achievable because of the lower kiln temperature.

**Glazed tiles** This colourful tessellation of glazed tiles at the Alhambra palace in Granada, Spain, demonstrates the architects' concern with covering every conceivable surface with decoration. In addition to the countless number of tiles, there is a great deal of carved stucco (see Plaster) and wood. Glazed tiles offer many practical benefits, too, such as providing a hygienic and durable surface resistant to fading, staining and scratching.

# Plaster

**Plaster enhances the durability and cleanliness of buildings, as well as providing a means of artistic expression. Based on clay or calcium minerals, it transforms from a wet and pliable material to stone-like when dry. It is an ancient medium – synonymous with sculpture, stucco and fresco – that has found modern application in the form of precision 3D printing.**

| Types | Typical Applications | Sustainability |
|---|---|---|
| • Clay<br>• Lime<br>• Gypsum | • Interior and exterior walls, and ceilings<br>• Sculpture, model making and mold making<br>• Medical casts | • Clay has the lowest impact; gypsum and lime have higher embodied energy<br>• Widely available from local sources<br>• Non-renewable |
| **Properties** | **Competing Materials** | **Costs** |
| • Gypsum is fast-setting and does not shrink or crack<br>• Lime is strong with very good resistance to weathering | • Concrete and stone<br>• Lining materials, such as paper and PVC | • Inexpensive raw materials<br>• Straightforward to process |

## INTRODUCTION

Plaster is traditionally used to coat the walls and ceilings of buildings. As well as providing a smooth, clean surface, it enhances the durability of masonry (see Clay, page 480) and provides passive fire protection. It has been utilized in this way for thousands of years; pyramids built by the Egyptians more than 4,000 years ago feature plastered walls that remain intact to this day. The gypsum formulation used then is almost identical to modern plaster. The ancient Greeks continued the use of plaster and covered the inside and outside walls and ceilings of temples. They used plaster casting in the reproduction of sculpture and objects.

As well as providing a smooth covering for walls, plaster is molded and modelled into relief profiles. Known as stuccowork, it is used to decorate buildings as well as for free-standing sculpture. This practice has a long history in the Mediterranean and was employed extensively by the Greeks and Romans. It became popular in 18th-century Europe, as can be seen in many elaborately stuccoed monuments and terraced houses of major cities.

The original method of three-dimensional printing technology

**Hand-modelled stucco**
This stucco by architectural sculptor Geoffrey Preston is located in the dining hall of a new Palladian-style villa in Wiltshre, England, designed by George Saumarez Smith of Adam Architecture. They are a work of art, reflecting the Italian character of the house with long curling leaf forms reminiscent of Baroque and Rococo plasterwork. The four panels, each measuring 2.3 x 1.2 m (7.5 x 4 ft), took several months to complete. The stucco consists of a combination of lime, gypsum, aggregate and binder. This gives a putty-like consistency with just the right setting time for hand modelling. To achieve the deep profile each section was built up in layers: a core is laid down followed by a fine finishing coat. Photo by Nick Carter; courtesy of Geoffrey Preston.

| | Compressive strength<br>diameter of bar required to provide equivalent strength | | Stiffness<br>diameter of bar required to provide equivalent stiffness | | Density<br>diameter of bar of equivalent weight | |
|---|---|---|---|---|---|---|
| | $\sigma_c$ (MPa) | % | E (GPa) | % | $\rho$ (kg/m³) | % |
| **Hydrated lime** | 5 | 1.0 | 3 | 1.0 | 480 | 1.0 |
| Gypsum | 9 | 0.8 | 5 | 0.9 | 1,130 | 0.7 |
| Earthenware clay (brick) | 100 | 0.2 | 40 | 0.5 | 2,400 | 0.5 |
| Concrete (12% cement) | 30 | 0.4 | 20 | 0.6 | 2,450 | 0.4 |
| Stone, marble | 540 | 0.1 | 54 | 0.5 | 2,770 | 0.6 |

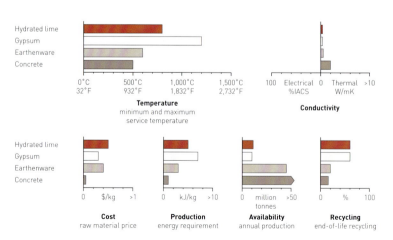

(3D printing) – a form of additive manufacturing (rapid prototyping) developed at Massachusetts Institute of Technology (MIT) in 1993 and commercialised by Z Corporation – used a mix of gypsum-based plaster and water. The plaster is engineered to precise consistency and particle size, and mixed with additives that maximize strength and quality of surface finish. The printed structure is infiltrated with resin – cyanoacrylate (superglue) or epoxy (page 232), for example – to fill the pores and create a robust part.

Applying the same methodology as 2D printing, it is now possible to create multicoloured 3D-printed plaster parts. The water binder is dyed and applied according to the colour of the 3D CAD model. Thus, the colour becomes permanently embedded in the material.

## COMMERCIAL TYPES AND USES

Natural plaster is bound with clay, gypsum or lime. In recent years, cement (page 496) has become popular too, thanks to its low cost and high strength. Clay is dug from the ground and applied as it is, or processed to a more uniform material. Either way, it has very low embodied energy, proving a sustainable solution. It has the highest breathability, but lacks strength. Available in a range of earthy colours, it is typically left uncoated, providing a low-maintenance finish.

Lime plaster is derived from limestone: calcium carbonate mineral is heated to over 900°C (1,650°F) to drive off the carbon dioxide and produce calcium oxide, known as quicklime. This is, in turn, reacted with water to form hydrated lime (calcium hydroxide). After application, the water evaporates and the lime absorbs carbon dioxide to become calcium carbonate once again. Known as carbonization, the process relies on water and so the lime must be kept wet during application. The process is long, but once set it will not react with water (unlike gypsum). As a result, it is very durable and suitable for use outdoors.

There are two principal types of lime plaster: pure (also known as non-hydraulic or air lime) and hydraulic (also known as bagged lime). The main

difference is consistency: pure lime is mixed with less water and so forms a putty-like material. Hydraulic lime – modern dry-hydrated hydraulic lime is marketed as 'natural hydraulic lime' (NHL) and graded according to compressive strength after 28 days – is a powder that after mixing with water cures more quickly. They are both strong and flexible enough to cope with the expansion and contraction of buildings. Lime is more expensive and not as common as gypsum for several reasons: it takes a long time to harden (days or weeks), it is sensitive to working conditions (requiring just the right weather conditions, humidity and so on) and it is prone to shrinkage.

Lime provides an excellent balance of strength and flexibility. It is porous and allows water vapour to pass through, which helps to prevent natural materials rotting. It also helps to stabilize the humidity of the building by absorbing and releasing moisture. This results in a comfortable living environment.

Fresco painting combines fresh lime-based plaster with water-based pigments. Famously employed by Michelangelo in the decoration of the Sistine Chapel, the pigments are absorbed into the plaster as it dries and retained by the material. It is very durable and unlike painting on dry plaster (known as fresco secco), cannot be rubbed from the surface. This means mistakes and changes cannot simply be painted over, but must be chipped from the wall and rebuilt.

Gypsum is produced by dehydration of calcium sulphate. Heating the mineral to between 150°C (300°F) and 165°C (330°F) releases the chemically bound water, resulting in molding plaster (plaster of Paris). Heating to over 190°C (375°F) fully dehydrates the mineral, resulting in a material with superior resistance to moisture and weathering.

It sets by rehydration with water (an almost indefinitely repeatable process) in an exothermic reaction. One of the main advantages is that this process is rapid. It does not shrink or crack as it dries, which is why it is suitable for making molds, accurate reproductions and casts to immobilize broken bones. Its temperature resistance is sufficiently high to be used

for molding non-ferrous metals, such as aluminium alloys (page 42) and copper alloys (page 66).

Drywall, or plasterboard, panels are produced from powdered gypsum pressed between sheets of paper (page 268). Used to make interior walls and ceilings, it revolutionized the building industry. Prior to drywall, lath and plaster was the predominant finishing method. The technique involved decking out the interior with lath (strips of wood), onto which plaster was applied.

## SUSTAINABILITY

Mined from the ground, clay goes through the least processing of all. It is often available locally, which helps to minimize transportation. At the end of the building's life, it can be recycled or put back in the ground. Lime and gypsum require kiln firing, which means they have relatively high embodied energy and cause more greenhouse gas emissions

Lime was a very commonly used material up until the development of cement. Since evidence of the damage done by cement has emerged, the use of lime has witnessed a resurgence. However, it is quite an aggressive material: frequent handling can cause skin sensitization leading to eczema.

Gypsum powder may be derived as a by-product of coal-fired power stations. This material, known as synthetic gypsum, is the result of desulphurization of flue gases; its chemical structure is almost identical to that of mined gypsum and it has higher purity (96%). In some countries, it provides a significant proportion of overall gypsum production. But this is likely to change as our reliance on coal-fired power stations is reduced.

**3D printing with colour**
Family vase by Studio Droog was created as part of the New Originals Project, 2013. The colour comes from the analysis of antique Chinese vases: the exact percentage of each colour on a vase is calculated and reproduced as a gradient in the 3D model. The data is translated directly as 3D-printed coloured plaster. Rachel Harding produced four vases to represent the traditional colour families: yellow, black, green and pink. Photo by Mo Schalkx.

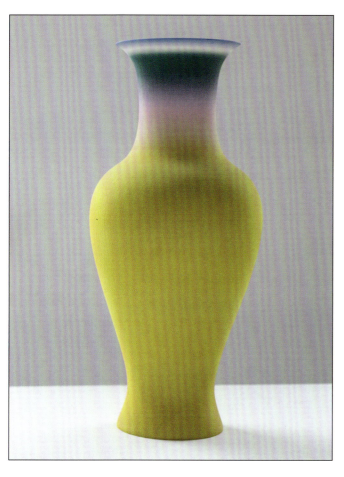

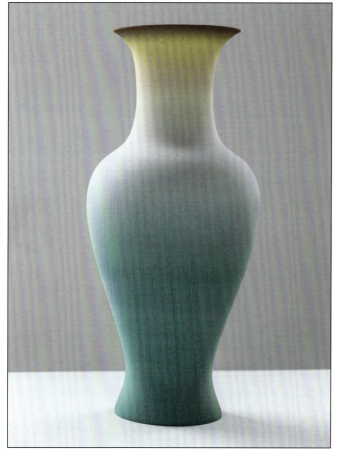

# Cement

**Cement provides the binder in concrete, mortar and render. Via chemical reactions, the mineral ingredients convert from a plastic material when wet into a rock-like mass when hardened. This transformation provides cement with immense versatility. Since its invention in 1824, Portland cement has shaped modern architecture and civil engineering more than any other material.**

| Types | Typical Applications | Sustainability |
|---|---|---|
| • Cement: volcanic or man-made (Portland) <br> • Cement composite: concrete, masonry (bricks and mortar), stucco and terrazzo | • Concrete buildings, infrastructure, interiors and furniture <br> • Masonry | • Cement is energy-intensive and polluting to produce <br> • It is alkaline and so potentially hazardous and a sensitizer |

| Properties | Competing Materials | Costs |
|---|---|---|
| • Good compression strength <br> • Resistant to weathering, but porosity means it is prone to spalling and flaking <br> • Passive fire protection | • Plaster, clay and stone <br> • Steel, iron and glass <br> • Engineered timber, wood and bamboo | • Very low cost, thanks to the availability of raw materials <br> • Economical to process <br> • Performance concretes are more costly |

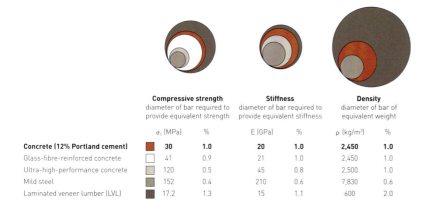

|  | Compressive strength <br> diameter of bar required to provide equivalent strength | | Stiffness <br> diameter of bar required to provide equivalent stiffness | | Density <br> diameter of bar of equivalent weight | |
|---|---|---|---|---|---|---|
|  | $\sigma_c$ (MPa) | % | E (GPa) | % | $\rho$ (kg/m³) | % |
| Concrete (12% Portland cement) | 30 | 1.0 | 20 | 1.0 | 2,450 | 1.0 |
| Glass-fibre-reinforced concrete | 41 | 0.9 | 21 | 1.0 | 2,450 | 1.0 |
| Ultra-high-performance concrete | 120 | 0.5 | 45 | 0.8 | 2,500 | 1.0 |
| Mild steel | 152 | 0.4 | 210 | 0.6 | 7,830 | 0.6 |
| Laminated veneer lumber (LVL) | 17.2 | 1.3 | 15 | 1.1 | 600 | 2.0 |

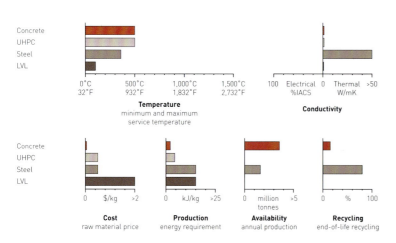

## INTRODUCTION

The vast majority of cement is mixed with aggregate and water to make concrete. As iconic now as it was in Roman times, concrete is consumed in huge quantities – it is the most widely used man-made material. Evidence of the Romans' mastery of early concrete exists in the form of large temples (the roof dome of the Pantheon in Rome is the largest unreinforced concrete structure in existence), multi-storey coliseums, sea defences and vast aqueducts.

From these engineering triumphs until relatively recently, there was no significant progress. This all changed with the development of modern Portland cement. As with iron (page 22), steel (page 28) and glass (page 508), today's architecture and civil engineering is intrinsically linked to the properties and behaviour of this material. It is the glue that binds masonry, supports skyscrapers, spans ravines and decorates the front of buildings. Its combination of strength, durability and low cost are what makes it such a valuable material.

Performance is defined by composition and importantly, ratio of water to cement. A balance must be struck to ensure that enough water is used so that all of the cement particles are coated, but not too much so that strength and durability are compromised. Every desirable physical property is adversely affected by adding water. Each country has its own standards

**Ultra-high-performance concrete (UHPC)** The Ydin stool, created by Franck Divay of Inoow Design, combines Italcementi UHPC with oiled oak (page 342). The high-quality ingredients and short strands of glass-fibre reinforcement ensure that the cast seat is very strong and resistant to cracking and abrasion. Avoiding the use of steel bar makes production easier and allows for a more slender design. Photo courtesy of Inoow Design.

for cement; there is no international standard. Each uses different criteria for measuring properties and defining physical characteristics, which means they are virtually non-translatable.

## COMMERCIAL TYPES AND USES

The Romans produced concrete by mixing limestone with volcanic ash and water. Volcanic ash from sites such as Campi Flegrei near the city of Pozzuoli outside Naples is rich in siliceous and aluminous minerals (aluminosilicate). In the presence of water, it reacts with calcium hydroxide, derived by heating limestone to around 900°C (1,650°F) (see also Plaster, page 492), and through a series of chemical reactions forms calcium-aluminium-silicate-hydrate (C-A-S-H), an incredibly strong and stable binder.

One of the advantages of the chemical process, known as hydration, is that it will take place even if the material is submerged underwater. The many ancient concrete structures that remain standing to this day, such as Roman harbours that have tolerated being submerged in the sea for millennia, are testament to its impressive durability.

Portland cement, a recent invention by comparison, is comprised of similar ingredients: limestone-derived calcium minerals, aluminosilicate, shale, sand and iron ore. It is formed by heating the mixture to around 1,450°C (2,640°F) to drive off the chemically combined water and carbon dioxide. The calcinated pellets of material, or clinker, are finely ground to produce cement. Manufacturers often add gypsum or limestone to give the desired working properties.

Mixed with water, the powder becomes plastic and moldable and, like Roman cement, forms into a hard ceramic through a process of hydration. The resulting compound of calcium, silicates and hydrates (C-S-H) is made up of around 85% lime and silica. This is far higher than the Roman version and partly why Portland is not as strong, durable or weather-resistant. Indeed, modern concrete has a much shorter lifespan.

There are eight principal types of Portland cement: type I is general-

**Relief pattern** Concrete faithfully reproduces the surface of the mold or formwork that it is cast within. Fine details, patterns and graphics may be applied in this way. Graphic Concrete has developed a novel technique that allows photographs, illustrations and text to be reproduced as a relief pattern on the surface of precast concrete. The image is applied as a retarder to the membrane used in the casting process. Once the concrete has cured, the retarder is washed away to reveal the image, which is created by the contrast between the smooth finish and exposed aggregate. This is the façade of Tähystäjä, a 13-storey apartment block in Ulappatori, Finland, designed by Petri Rouhiainen. Photo courtesy of Graphic Concrete.

purpose; type II is suitable for structures in water or soil containing moderate amounts of sulphate, or when heat build-up is a concern; type III gets strong faster than the others and so allows forms to be removed sooner; type IV gives off less heat during curing, which is useful for massive structures, such as dams; type V resists chemical attack by soil and water high in sulphates; and types IA, IIA and IIIA are the same as types I, II and III, with the addition of air bubbles, caused by the inclusion of air entraining agents. Several other admixtures are used, such as to enhance workability, or to slow or accelerate the curing process.

The majority of concrete is provided ready mixed. It is produced in centralized plants and delivered to the construction site by the familiar cement-mixer lorries.

Precast concrete is produced in a factory environment. This helps to ensure consistent physical properties and accurate dimensions. Examples include masonry (bricks, blocks and pavers), countertops and structural components (beams, girders and wall panels). Autoclaved cellular concrete (ACC), also known as autoclaved aerated concrete (AAC), is a lightweight precast concrete produced under elevated pressure in an autoclave. The mix of ingredients – including cement, limestone, aluminium, silica (such as from fly ash) and water – go through a chemical reaction that releases a mass of tiny hydrogen bubbles. This results in a foam-like material that more than doubles in size before curing and is around one-quarter the weight of conventional concrete.

The compressive strength of concrete is typically in the region of 48 MPa (7,000 psi). By refining the ingredients and optimizing the ratios, manufacturers have been able to produce concrete with compressive strength in the region of 100 MPa (14,500 psi). Admixtures, such as fly ash and silica fume (similar to the Romans' volcanic ash), impart additional strength. This has enabled taller structures to be built than previously thought possible with concrete.

Reinforced concrete combines the high tensile strength of steel (page 28) with the bulk and compressive strength of concrete. The resulting composite is able to resist tensile stresses that would cause conventional concrete to fail. In other words, when bent the steel prevents the edge that is under tension from cracking. Without the use of reinforcement, modern large-span structures would not exist. Pre-stressed, or post-stressed (also called pre-tensioned and post-tensioned), concrete is embedded with steel held under tension. This balances the tensile loads imposed on the member in service

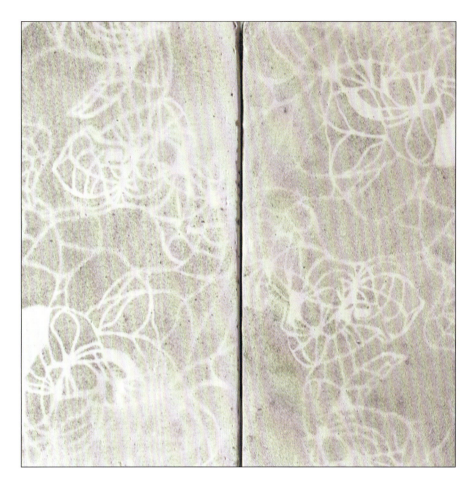

and thus means that lighter and more slender structures are possible.

Fibre-reinforced concrete (FRC) provides a less expensive and more versatile alternative. However, while strength is increased many times compared to conventional concrete, it will not be as strong as steel bar reinforced. Fibre selection depends on the requirements of the application. Examples include carbon (page 236), glass (page 508), super fibres (see PBO, page 246), polypropylene (PP) (page 98) and natural fibres (see Bamboo, page 386, and Leaf Fibre, page 394). In the past, a range of natural materials was used, such as horsehair (page 434) and straw (see Grass, page 392). Asbestos was very common until the health risks were recognized.

Within the last few decades, a new class of concrete emerged, known as ultra-high-performance concrete (UHPC) or reactive powder concrete (RPC), whose mechanical properties and durability far surpass those of conventional concrete. A mixture of Portland cement, silica fume, quartz, water and fibre reinforcement

**Functional coating**
This concrete has been selectively coated so that, over time and with exposure to airborne pollution, a motif emerges. Alessia Giardino screen-printed paint mixed with a photocataytic additive (titanium dioxide) onto bare concrete. The pattern emerges as a result of the self-cleaning effect of the titanium dioxide. With the help of the sun, surface dirt is broken down into molecules such as oxygen, carbon dioxide, water and so on. Gases evaporate and the rain washes surface debris away, but only where the coating has been applied. Photo courtesy of Alessia Giardino.

(typically steel) produces concrete with compressive strength of 120 to 150 MPa (17,000–22,000 psi). So far, it has been used in the construction of bridges and lightweight roof structures. It holds great potential for producing lighter, taller and longer unsupported structures.

A broad range of decorative finishes exists. Concrete shaped within formwork (see also Engineered Timber, page 296), will reproduce exactly the surface of the panels. So, for example, if wood grain is present, it will appear on the surface of the finished concrete.

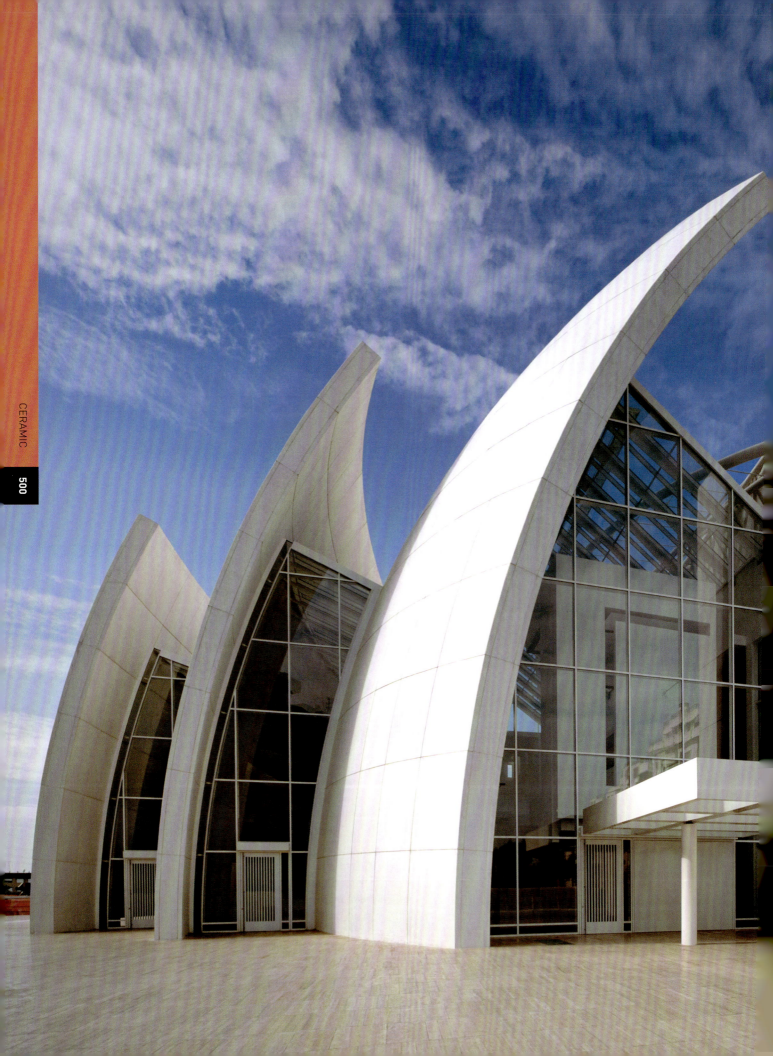

White cement, produced with modified ingredients, provides the most satisfying ground for colour pigments (liquid or powder). Colour may be applied in situ using chemical stains, painting or screen printing or by exposing the embedded ingredients on the surface (gravel, glass and so on). Chemical stains react chemically with the concrete. Metallic salts in the water-based solution react to form shades of blue, green, brown or black. Brighter colours are achieved with dye.

Other cement-based materials that share many of the qualities of concrete but are classed differently include mortar, grout and stucco (plaster). They consist of similar ingredients and their consistency and working properties are tailored to their different roles in construction.

## SUSTAINABILITY

Cement and concrete have seen massive development over the years. Concrete has become lighter, stronger and more durable. The amount of energy required in production has decreased, but still, the production is polluting and responsible for around 5% of industrial carbon dioxide emissions. A remarkably low-cost material, it is consumed in vast quantities and this amplifies its negative impacts.

The cement industry consumes a lot of waste. The very high firing temperature means that waste with high embodied energy – car tyres, chemicals and other hazardous materials – can be safely incinerated. In addition, concrete may include fly ash (or volcanic ash) from coal-burning power stations. Ultimately, it is preferential to reduce waste rather than burn and trap it in concrete. But for now, cement provides an alternative to landfill.

**Precast concrete**
Richard Meier designed the Jubilee Church (Chiesa del Dio Padre Misericordioso), Rome, 2003. The expanse of precast Italcementi concrete – its whiteness enhanced with the addition of Carrara marble (see Stone, page 472) and titanium dioxide – is protected from air pollution through the self-cleaning effect of the impregnated titanium dioxide (see also Functional coating, previous page). Through the same process, titanium dioxide breaks down pollution in the air it comes into contact with, so the surrounding air is cleaner. Photo by Scott Frances/OTTO.

# Technical Ceramic

**Also known as**
Also referred to as: advanced ceramics, engineering ceramics, high-performance ceramics
Zirconia trademark names include: Nilcra, Zyranox

The ceramics in this class are hard, durable and resistant to chemicals; some remain stable at temperatures in excess of 2,000°C (3,600°F). As well as providing the grit in abrasives, they are used for some of the most demanding engine, aircraft, military and industrial projects. Consumer products, such as watches and kitchenware, take advantage of their durability.

| Types | Typical Applications | Sustainability |
|---|---|---|
| • Powder: alumina; zirconia; silicon nitride: tungsten carbide; silicon carbide; boron carbide<br>• PVD and CVD (various nitrides) | • Ballistic armour<br>• Automotive and aerospace engine, brake and exhaust pads<br>• Watches, jewelry, consumer electronics | • High embodied energy as a result of the high temperatures and energy used in production<br>• Impractical to recycle in most cases |
| **Properties** | **Competing Materials** | **Costs** |
| • High-temperature resistance<br>• Hard and resistant to abrasion<br>• Stiff and brittle | • Stone, gemstone and high-performance glasses<br>• Steel, titanium, palladium, rhodium and gold | • Moderate to high raw material cost, depending on the type and quality<br>• Expensive to process, although ceramic injection molding (CIM) is less so |

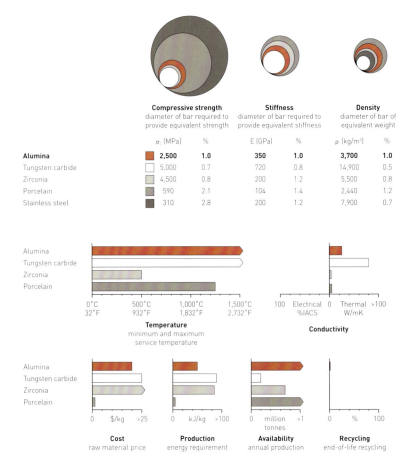

| | Compressive strength diameter of bar required to provide equivalent strength | | Stiffness diameter of bar required to provide equivalent stiffness | | Density diameter of bar of equivalent weight | |
|---|---|---|---|---|---|---|
| | $\sigma_c$ [MPa] | % | E [GPa] | % | $\rho$ [kg/m³] | % |
| Alumina | 2,500 | 1.0 | 350 | 1.0 | 3,700 | 1.0 |
| Tungsten carbide | 5,000 | 0.7 | 720 | 0.8 | 14,900 | 0.5 |
| Zirconia | 4,500 | 0.8 | 200 | 1.2 | 5,500 | 0.8 |
| Porcelain | 590 | 2.1 | 104 | 1.4 | 2,440 | 1.2 |
| Stainless steel | 310 | 2.8 | 200 | 1.2 | 7,900 | 0.7 |

Alumina
Tungsten carbide
Zirconia
Porcelain

| 0°C 32°F | 500°C 932°F | 1,000°C 1,832°F | 1,500°C 2,732°F | 100 Electrical %IACS | 0 | Thermal W/mK | >100 |

**Temperature**
minimum and maximum service temperature

**Conductivity**

Alumina
Tungsten carbide
Zirconia
Porcelain

| 0 | $/kg | >25 | 0 | kJ/kg | >100 | 0 | million tonnes | >1 | 0 | % | 100 |

**Cost**
raw material price

**Production**
energy requirement

**Availability**
annual production

**Recycling**
end-of-life recycling

## INTRODUCTION

These non-metallic, inorganic materials are built from the ground up. The ingredients are selected according to specific performance requirements, including mechanical, electrical, optical, biomedical and chemical properties. Three-dimensional parts are shaped from powder, which is pressed and sintered – fused at very high temperature, just below the material's melting point but hot enough to bond the particles – to become a solid, functional part. Alternatively, the ceramic is formed as a coating. This is achieved by mixing the ingredients as a gas, which condenses to form the ceramic.

Technical ceramics are available in a huge variety of formulations and formats. The industry is growing rapidly as the processes are refined and more potential applications are found. Regardless of whether an ordinary abrasive medium or part of a missile, they all share some common properties: a hard and inert surface, dimensional stability at high temperature, and high compressive strength; but heavy with low fracture toughness as a result of their inherent brittleness. To overcome some of these flaws, technical ceramics are combined with metal or fibre reinforcement. Known as metal matrix composite (MMC), or cermet, and ceramic matrix composite (CMC), respectively, these materials offer some exceptional properties. Fracture

**Precision-machined alumina** An industrial seal ring produced from high-purity alumina. To ensure precise dimensions, the cold isostatic pressed powder part is machined prior to sintering. Surface quality depends on the finishing process and type of abrasive media. Alumina is available in a variety of colours, depending on the composition, from white through tan, pink and red.

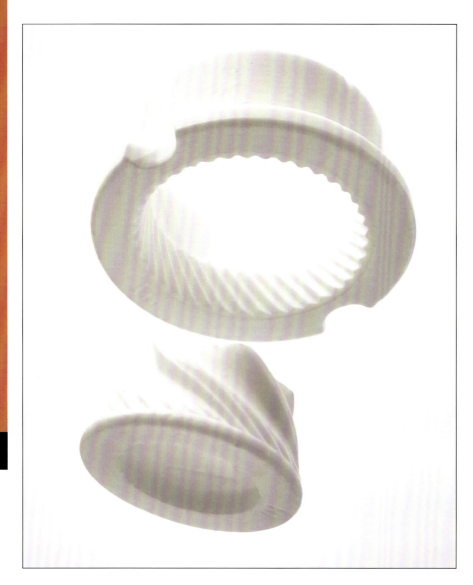

**Injection-molded alumina** High volumes of identical parts, such as these salt grinder components (from a Cole & Mason salt mill), are produced by ceramic injection molding (CIM). Similar to conventional plastic injection molding, complex design details are achieved in a single operation.

toughness, shock resistance and strength-to-weight are all improved compared to unreinforced ceramic. They are expensive and the design is very restricted, so applications have remained limited: MMCs are utilized in cutting tools, armour and automotive engine and brake parts; and CMCs are used in so-called hot zones, such as fighter jet exhaust nozzles and high-performance car disc brakes.

## COMMERCIAL TYPES AND USES

Alumina (aluminium oxide, AlO) is an important industrial material, as well as occurring as a single crystal gemstone (see Diamond, page 476) in the form of sapphire. It is also responsible for the durability and longevity of aluminium alloy (page 42) – anodizing enhances the naturally occurring oxide layer on the surface to give a tough and passive film.

As a ceramic, it is relatively inexpensive and offers a range of useful properties. The most beneficial of these are its exceptional hardness, resistance to temperatures up to 1,650°C (3,000°F), resistance to chemicals and low conductivity (both thermal and electrical). It is available in a range of purities, from around 60% to 99.7%. Lower-purity grades are used as refractories. Higher-purity types are utilized for applications that are subject to high wear or impact, such as industrial seal rings, prostheses, armour and abrasive.

Zirconia (zirconium dioxide, ZrO) is another popular ceramic that is hard and tough (at room temperature). Its hardness combined with a very fine grain enables an excellent surface finish. These are the reasons why zirconia is used to make blades (knives, peelers and slicers): it will take and hold a sharp edge, and will flex without breaking. Other applications include dental repairs (see also Clay, page 480), watches, bearings and gears.

Even though its melting point is above 2,500°C (4,530°F), zirconia on its own is susceptible to cracking when heated to above 500°C (930°F). Adding a stabilizer, such as yittria (yittrium oxide) or magnesia (magnesium oxide, MgO), reduces thermal expansion and thereby increases toughness at elevated temperatures.

Tungsten carbide (WC) is exceptionally hard and wear-resistant. However, it is very heavy, which limits applications. So, it is more often found in combination with cobalt or nickel as a MMC, or cermet. The metal provides the binder and when sintered, strong bonds are formed between the different materials. This results in a very stiff and hard material that is more versatile than plain WC. It is often known as 'hard metal', because it is much harder and more wear-resistant than other types. Applications range from the balls in ballpoint pens to high-speed cutters (see image, page 479) and dies.

Silicon nitride (SiN) offers very high temperature resistance, excellent resistance to wear and good resistance to oxidization. These properties are utilized in some niche applications, such as in automotive engines and gas turbines. As a coating it provides the antireflective surface on solar panels, which helps to boost efficiency. As a result, its distinctive blue colour is becoming an increasingly familiar site.

Silicon carbide (SiC), also known as carborundum, occurs naturally and very rarely in the form of crystal moissanite. It has a Mohs hardness of 9 (see page 477), which is close to diamond. As a result, it has become an important abrasive. It is strong for its weight, highly conductive of heat and can operate in conditions up to 1,600°C (2910°F). Therefore, like SiN, it has found application in engine, turbine and rocket components.

SiC is combined with carbon fibre (page 236) in the production of high-performance composites for disc brakes, aerospace and chemical processing. This CMC, known as C/SiC, exhibits high fracture toughness (resistance to cracking is dramatically improved), stability at high temperature, low density and exceptional hardness. The fibre reinforcement used may be short or long strand, woven or felt.

Boron carbide (BC) is an exceptionally hard ceramic that ranks just behind diamond on the Mohs scale. This makes it a valuable material for abrasive media, nozzles for abrasive slurries and wear applications. For its hardness, BC is relatively light and tough; its density is around one-sixth and elastic modulus (stiffness) is around half that of WC. These properties are utilized in ballistic armour protection, for example.

There are other powdered ceramics, but these are the principal types in use today. They are shaped by five methods. Die pressing is used to produce high volumes of simple-geometry parts. The predetermined measure of ingredients is combined – including ceramic and binders – and pressed to consolidate the powder into a solid. Long parts with a continuous cross-section are produced by extrusion. Powder is compacted in a chamber and forced through a shaped die. Prior to sintering, the parts are quite fragile and must be handled with care.

Ceramic injection molding (CIM), uses a similar mix of ingredients, but in this case the binder melts to form a liquid

**Dry-pressed and hot isostatic pressed (HIP) zirconia** Ceramic blades are typically produced from zirconia, because it is the least likely to shatter on impact or bending. However, as a brittle material, it is likely to chip. The blade is dry pressed from black zirconia powder. In the case of this Kyocera blade, toughness and density are improved by passing the formed part through an additional hot isostatic pressing (HIP) process. The razor-sharp edge is applied by hand, using a diamond-encrusted grinding wheel. The hardness of the material means that it will retain its edge for longer than steel and will rarely need sharpening. However, if the blade does dull, it requires professional resharpening.

medium that carries the powder into the die cavity when injected. In the die the binder cools and solidifies. Similar to conventional plastic injection molding, the tools may be single- or multi-cavity. Indeed, many of the same design tools used with plastic injection molding may be applied, such as mold flow analysis and simulation. It is suitable for higher volumes and more complex parts than die pressing. The part is around one-third larger than its end dimensions in its 'green' state and passes through a two-stage firing process. First, the binder is melted out, and then the part is sintered.

Cold isostatic pressing (CIP), developed in the 1950s, is used to shape metals, plastics and composites, as well as ceramics. Powder is loaded into a flexible mold (membrane or hermetic container) and uniform pressure is applied by gas or liquid. Compacting the powder in this way reduces the geometry limitations of die forming. Parts are around 60 to 70% dense and strong enough to be machined in their green state prior to sintering.

The sintering process causes the parts to shrink by up to around 20%. Careful process control is essential to ensure consistent parts of uniform density. Once fully hardened, the parts may be machined and polished to be very precise. However, this is expensive and time-consuming, typically requiring diamond cutting tools (see Diamond).

Hot isostatic pressing (HIP) is carried out at very high temperature and pressure. This produces a fully dense part, with improved mechanical properties and surface finish. As such, it does away with a separate sintering step and may be applied as a post-forming operation, such as to die-pressed or injection-molded parts.

Ceramics are applied as a coating by physical vapour deposition (PVD) or chemical vapour deposition (CVD). This is typically onto another ceramic, or metal (such as steel, page 28, or titanium, page 58), to enhance durability and resistance to corrosion and abrasion. Ceramic is brittle. So, if the substrate being coated is too 'soft', such as aluminium, then the ceramic will offer limited protection.

The parts to be coated are loaded into a heated vacuum chamber and the atmosphere evacuated. A suitable powder, or target material, is vaporized (with heat or bombardment of ions) and nitrogen, hydrocarbon or silicide is introduced. The gases mix and condense as a precise layer of ceramic on the surface of the part. Coating thickness of up to 30 microns is possible, although it is typically just a few microns. In some cases, multiple layers are built up, which can include different properties, to provide enhanced protection.

A range of coatings exists for different applications. As well as augmenting mechanical properties, these coatings provide colour, which is used for both decorative and practical purposes. Titanium nitride (TiN) is perhaps the most well known and recognized. It produces a bright gold colour familiar on high-speed steel and WC cutters. It is used to improve wear resistance and thus extend the life of the cutting tool. Its metallic gold colour is utilized in jewelry, consumer electronics and automotive applications. It has been superseded in many cases by alternative compositions, as follows.

Titanium aluminium nitride (TiAlN) is a more recent development. The colour depends on the ratio of ingredients and ranges from black to bronze. It has mostly been used in place of TiN on cutters and to protect the surface of dies and punches. It provides equivalent wear resistance, but offers superior high temperature resistance (800°C [1,470°F] versus 500°C [930°F]).

Titanium carbon nitride (TiCN) is an excellent all-purpose coating that appears blue-grey. It is tough and hard-wearing with a low coefficient of friction – properties utilized in tooling, such as for injection molding, punching and cutting. However, it is not a direct replacement for the aforementioned coatings, owing to its relatively low maximum operating temperature. It is non-toxic and biocompatible, which means it is suitable for medical devices and implants.

Chromium nitride (CrN) is silver-coloured and hard and has good resistance to oxidization and chemicals; it outperforms conventional hard

chrome plating. Compared to TiN, it is not quite as hard, but it offers greater temperature resistance and performs well in corrosive environments and sliding wear applications. As a result, it is often used to protect tooling, such as for plastic molding. It bonds very well to the substrate, so will not chip or flake, and is non-toxic. This combination of properties is essential for food processing equipment. Outside industrial applications, the bright metallic silver appearance is often used in jewelry, automotive and consumer products.

Zirconium nitride (ZrN) is combined with small amounts of carbon to produce gold or brass colour. It is used in many of the same situations as TiN, providing superior toughness, hardness and corrosion resistance. A major advantage of this material is that it can be deposited at relatively low temperature. Therefore, it is suitable for temperature-sensitive substrates. It is biocompatible and commonly used for medical equipment. Additionally, its combination of mechanical properties and gold colour is utilised in jewelry, taps (faucets) and door hardware.

## SUSTAINABILITY

These are energy-intensive to produce, but remain irreplaceable in many situations, in particular renewable energy production. Owing to the high cost of the raw materials and difficulty of processing, they tend to be used only in the most demanding applications.

As a result of their limited use and the wide range of formulations available, recycling is virtually non-existent. In some cases, abrasive media may be reused. But because of contamination, this is often not practical.

Ceramic coatings offer many advantages. They reduce material consumption by extending the life of the materials they protect. In the case of coated steel and WC cutters, for example, the use of ceramic reduces wear, improves efficiency and prolongs the life of the tool. Compared to protective metal coatings, such as chrome plating, PVD is much less harmful and consumes significantly less material.

**PVD coatings on stainless steel** Colour is determined by a combination of ceramic type – black (TiAN), bronze (ZrN), metallic silver (CrN) and blue (SiN) – and film thickness. Some are more sensitive to film thickness than others, which makes achieving consistent colour difficult. In other words, different batches may not look the same. Glossiness is determined by the surface texture of the base metal. These four samples show PVD coatings on stainless steel. The steel was prepared by polishing and one half has been abrasive blasted to a matt texture. This type of finish is popular in the watch industry, because it offers a high-quality, colourful and durable finish without the aesthetic limitations of painting.

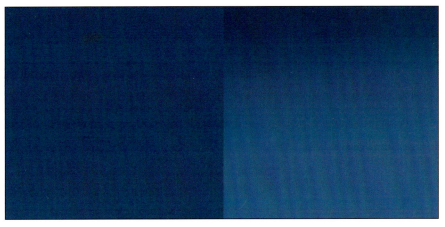

# Soda-Lime Glass

**Glass provides an unrivalled combination of transparency and durability. The most common is soda-lime, which has been in commercial production since the mid-19th century. With developments in manufacturing, this once precious material has been transformed into a widely used commodity. Tempering and chemical strengthening enhance mechanical properties.**

| Types | Typical Applications | Sustainability |
|---|---|---|
| • Float (sheet) glass<br>• Container glass | • Packaging<br>• Glazing<br>• Glassware, light bulbs, products, furniture and lighting | • Fully recyclable and collected in significant quantities<br>• Low embodied energy compared to other transparent materials |
| **Properties** | **Competing Materials** | **Costs** |
| • Hard, wear-resistant and inert<br>• Transparent or coloured<br>• High compressive strength, but poor under tension | • Transparent plastics such as PC, PMMA, PS and ionomer<br>• Clay, technical ceramic, stone and gemstone<br>• Steel and aluminium | • Low raw material price<br>• Low processing costs |

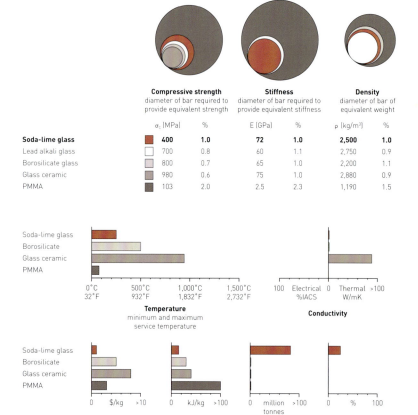

| | Compressive strength<br>diameter of bar required to provide equivalent strength | | Stiffness<br>diameter of bar required to provide equivalent stiffness | | Density<br>diameter of bar of equivalent weight | |
|---|---|---|---|---|---|---|
| | $\sigma_c$ [MPa] | % | E [GPa] | % | $\rho$ [kg/m³] | % |
| Soda-lime glass | 400 | 1.0 | 72 | 1.0 | 2,500 | 1.0 |
| Lead alkali glass | 700 | 0.8 | 60 | 1.1 | 2,750 | 0.9 |
| Borosilicate glass | 800 | 0.7 | 65 | 1.0 | 2,200 | 1.1 |
| Glass ceramic | 980 | 0.6 | 75 | 1.0 | 2,880 | 0.9 |
| PMMA | 103 | 2.0 | 2.5 | 2.3 | 1,190 | 1.5 |

**Temperature**
minimum and maximum service temperature

**Conductivity**

**Cost**
raw material price

**Production**
energy requirement

**Availability**
annual production

**Recycling**
end-of-life recycling

## INTRODUCTION

Glass is hard, impervious to air and water, and chemically stable. Combined with the range of visual qualities available these properties set it apart from plastic, metal and wood. It was once considered a very precious material: the Egyptians viewed it as a valuable alternative to gemstones (see Diamond, page 476) and began to produce large quantities from silica sand, lime and soda around the 2nd and 1st millennia BCE. These ingredients became the basis of modern commercial glass.

Glassblowing developed with the Roman Empire. While the tools and techniques have changed little, glass production developed massively during the 19th and 20th centuries. First came mechanical pressing in 1825, which led to the first mass-produced glassware. This was followed in 1903 by Michael Owens' automatic bottle-blowing machine. In the 1950s, Alastair Pilkington revolutionized architecture and design with the invention of the float glass process. This is the method by which most sheet glass is manufactured today.

## COMMERCIAL TYPES AND USES

Soda-lime glass is the most common and lest expensive type of glass. It is suitable for the majority of applications where the properties of glass are required. A range of other glasses exists, which are used for specialist applications. For example, lead glass (page 518) has superior optical properties, and high-performance glasses (page 522) – such as borosilicate, aluminosilicate and glass ceramic – are employed for their superior strength, toughness and thermal shock resistance.

Soda-lime glass is produced from a mix of widely available materials – silica (silicon dioxide, SiO), soda ash (sodium carbonate, NaCO) and lime (calcium oxide, CaO). The soda ash acts as a flux, reducing

the temperature of fusion. However, silica and soda alone do not produce a stable glass. Therefore, lime is added to counter the soda ash. Magnesia (magnesium oxide, MgO) and alumina (aluminium oxide, AlO) are used to enhance specific properties. The exact ingredients are adjusted according to the method of production and application requirements. Heated in a furnace to around 1,600°C (2,900°F), the minerals form a viscous mass of molten glass ready for shaping. As with steel production (page 28), the furnaces run continuously.

Once formed, glass is annealed by heating and gradual cooling to remove internal stresses in the molecular structure. If glass is allowed to cool quickly then it will be highly strained at room temperature. In other words, it will easily break if placed under load.

Tempered glass, also known as safety or toughened glass, is produced by heat treatment. Soda-lime glass is heated to

**Colour and finish**
These low tables by Oki Sato, founder of Japanese design studio Nendo, were launched at Milan's Salone del Mobile 2015. Produced by Italian manufacturer Glas Italia, each box is made from five sheets of flat glass. The vivid gradients come from printed colour on the mitred join. The backside of the frosted glass is also printed with a gradient, which continues the colour across the surfaces. Printing the joins is an impressive technical achievement and results in a beautiful, soft colour, contrasting elegantly with the hard, sharp glass forms. Photo by Kenichi Sonehara.

approximately 650°C (1,200°F) and then quenched in blasts of cool air. This forces the surface of the glass to cool more rapidly than the core and thus forms a structure under compression. This means the glass is able to tolerate higher tensile loads, because as the load is applied the pre-compression force counteracts it. As a result, the tensile strength of tempered glass is 120 to 200 MPa, compared to only 40 MPa for annealed glass. Compressive strength remains the same.

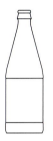

**Blow and blow**          **Press and blow**

### Hollow containers

Packaging is produced from soda-lime glass containing a lower proportion of magnesia than float glass (to reduce viscosity). Hot glass (gob) is channelled from the furnace to the mold via guide rails. Blow and blow is used to form narrow-neck containers, such as bottles. The gob drops into the mold cavity and the neck is formed by a plunger. The glass cools and solidifies on contact with the mold. This allows it to be transferred to another mold, where it is blown

to the final shape. As it is transferred, the heat retained within the glass re-melts the surface, allowing it to be blown. Press and blow is used to form wide-necked containers, such as jars. It is identical to blow and blow, except that in the first stage, the plunger that forms the neck pushes up into the molten glass to form a larger diameter opening. Next, it is transferred to the blowing mold and follows the same process as blow and blow.

### Cosmetic packaging

Oils and fragrances were perhaps some of the earliest items to be stored in glass. Alongside the production of glass jewels and decorative objects, it is thought the ancient Egyptians produced small containers for such luxuries. Even though glass is primarily used for practical reasons,

its optical properties and mass maintain it as a form of high-value packaging. These qualities are enhanced through design. This Issey Miyake perfume bottle incorporates facets to highlight optical qualities. In addition, the heavy base, produced by incorporating extra glass in the gob, enhances gravitas.

Once tempered, it cannot be modified or machined. When it breaks, the fragments tend to be small and blunt as a result of the modified structure, so it is used in safety applications such as door glazing, car windscreens and dinnerware.

Heat strengthening is similar except that the cooling is slower. This means it provides only around twice the tensile resistance of annealed glass. This type of glass is used where the additional strength required, such as to resist wind pressure or thermal shock, does not justify tempering. However, it is not suitable where safety glass is required, because it fractures in the same way as annealed glass, forming long sharp fragments.

Chemical strengthening produces a similar effect to toughening except it does not thermally strain the glass and so results in superior flatness and optical quality. However, it cannot be considered safety glass, because it shatters like annealed glass. The surface is put under tension through an ion exchange process, whereby sodium ions are replaced by relatively larger potassium ones. This results in a glass six to eight times stronger than annealed glass. It has been used in the production of canopies for fighter jets and helicopters, for example. The most widespread use of this technique is strengthening aluminosilicate glass (see High-Performance Glass).

Glass sheets are laminated together for safety, security and decorative effect. Laminated safety glass is produced by bonding together sheets of glass with a polyvinyl butyral (PVB) film. Combining the strength and durability of glass with the toughness of plastic results in a composite that is more difficult to penetrate (break through) and is proven to reduce noise transmission. When broken, the shards or pieces of glass are held in place by the adhesive. The process uses heat and pressure to remove any air bubbles so the sheet appears solid.

Depending on the design requirements, laminated glass may be produced with annealed, tempered, heat-strengthened or chemically strengthened glass. This product is primarily used in automotive and construction

applications. Bullet-resistant and bulletproof glass is produced from three or more layers of glass with two or more polycarbonate (PC) (page 144) interlayers. The composition and thickness of the laminate will determine its effectiveness.

Armoured glass is produced with a wire mesh encapsulated between two layers of glass. The non-oxidizing wire is introduced while the glass is semi-molten and laminated under pressure.

### SUSTAINABILITY

Glass is produced directly from readily available materials, which eliminates the inefficiencies associated with widely distributed production, such as is the case with plastics and metals. It is inert, non-toxic and completely food safe.

Production is continuous and the temperature in the furnace is maintained every day, all year round. This is more efficient than producing material in batches, which means soda-lime has only around one-sixth of the embodied energy of polymethyl methacrylate (PMMA, acrylic) (page 174), for example.

Glass is fully recyclable and loses none of its strength during reprocessing. In fact, cullet (recycled glass) plays an important role in glass production by lowering the firing temperature required. This provides the economic incentive for collection and recycling. Glass bottle recycling is in the region of 50 to 80%. For the manufacture of green glass bottles up

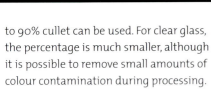

to 90% cullet can be used. For clear glass, the percentage is much smaller, although it is possible to remove small amounts of colour contamination during processing.

Owing to the differences in composition, it is important that different types of glass are separated during recycling. This is true even for different grades of soda-lime, such as float and container glass (although small amounts of contamination may not present a problem if properly mixed in).

## SODA-LIME GLASS IN PACKAGING

Before the development of semi-automated glassblowing in the mid-19th century and later Michael Owens' fully automated machine, containers – bottles, jars and so on – were produced by hand blowing. Nowadays, all containers are produced by one of two methods: blow and blow, or press and blow. The machines operate at high speed and are capable of outputting in excess of 600 containers every minute. It is no surprise then that the majority of glass production goes into containers.

The production of colourless glass, known as 'flint' (see also Lead Glass, page 518), is made with the highest-purity and -quality raw ingredients. Even so, it is inevitable that some impurities exist, such as iron oxide and chromium, which result in the familiar yellow-green hue of commercial glass. Other colours are carefully added to produce a grey, which appears colourless. Optical glass (see Lead Glass), produced using lead oxide or barium oxide, offers superior transparency over conventional soda-lime.

The most common colour of container glass is amber (or brown), which is produced with a mix of iron, sulphur and carbon. It is popularly used to package beer and pharmaceuticals, because the amber absorbs a high proportion of the ultraviolet spectrum. Chromium produces green. It does not offer the same level of protection as amber glass (although dark antique green does), but can absorb a lot of recycled content, making it a relatively inexpensive product. Blue glass is produced in very low quantities and is made by adding cobalt. Either

**Curtain wall** This north-facing curtain wall in a sports centre designed by Explorations Architecture in the French commune of Arpajon, near Paris, provides daylight for the gymnasium. Photo by Michel Denance.

the whole furnace of glass is coloured, or it is coloured between the furnace and molding. Only a few colours are commercially available, because it tends to be expensive and complicated to do.

Soda-lime glass containers are not usually tempered, because this adds considerable processing cost. Where additional strength or thermal shock resistance is required, such as glass packaging destined for the oven, borosilicate glass is used.

Glass packaging is decorated in a number of ways. Square (flat) and cylindrical containers are screen-printed. It is a versatile process suitable for small batches in the studio and mass production in the factory. Irregular-shaped containers are tampo printed (also called pad printing).

The most commonly used colours are supplied as a glaze, or frit, which is made up of powdered glass and pigment. It is printed onto the glass and permanently bonded to the surface by firing in a kiln at between 500°C (930°F) and 600°C (1110°F).

Metallic colours are produced in the same manner and are very durable, because they become integral to the structure of the glass. Precious metals, such as gold (page 90) and platinum, may also be applied by screen printing. Powdered metal is deposited onto the surface and forms a foil after firing that can be polished to its natural lustre. It will not be as durable as pigmented colour, because the metal is not integrated into the glass. Durability is important, especially if the packaging contains aggressive chemicals, such as vinegar.

A frosted, or matt, finish is produced by chemical etching or painting. Chemical etching involves the use of harmful chemicals and a great deal of water (around 10 litres [2.2 gal] per bottle). It is also important that there is no contamination on the inside of the bottle.

## ARCHITECTURE AND CONSTRUCTION

### Transparency
There exists a huge range of tints, colours, coatings and films that provide glass with enhanced functionality. Visible light is permitted into buildings and heat is reflected out using a variety of techniques; selection depends on the technical and visual requirements.

### Formability
While the majority of glass is used flat, it is possible to bend and drape glass into three-dimensional curves. In addition, the surface may be textured or produced with a relief profile by blasting, etching or rolling.

### Energy and cost
The initial cost is high, because adding windows is expensive. Over the lifetime of a building, glass has a significant impact on energy use and the environmental impacts of buildings. Bringing in natural light reduces the use of artificial lighting. Furthermore, functional coatings significantly reduce solar gain and heat loss, which helps to maximize a building's efficiency.

This is achieved by placing a rubber stopper in the mouth. However, this is not 100% effective and so generally this type of frosting is not taken right up to the top.

Chemical frosting is being phased out and replaced with painting, which is less environmentally damaging. This process yields high-quality results, but is around three times more expensive. The paint is applied as an electrostatically charged powder and cured in an oven at approximately 200°C (390°F). Translucent paints tend to be more durable than opaque colours. If the bottle is to be printed, then inks with a lower firing

temperature are required. The results will be different from printing on untreated glass and the finish a lot less durable.

Production lines typically run continuously, producing duplicate graphics. Drinks company Absolut, in the 2012 Unique collection, demonstrated that this need not be the case. Featuring a complex interaction of human and mechanical elements, the production line used splash guns, 38 colours, 51 pattern types and computerized pattern algorithms to create complete randomness in the graphic outcomes. It followed this up in 2013 with the

Originality collection. In this case, it added a drop of cobalt to the molten glass to form a unique blue streak in every bottle. The marketing impact was deemed to outweigh the added cost of production.

## SODA-LIME GLASS IN ARCHITECTURE AND CONSTRUCTION

Sheets of soda-lime glass are produced using the float-glass method. This is an ingenious technique for producing very large and perfectly flat sheets of glass. The hot molten glass leaves the furnace at around 1,000°C (1,830°F) and is floated on a bath of molten tin in a controlled atmosphere of hydrogen and nitrogen to prevent the tin from oxidizing. The glass cools with a mirror finish on both sides.

The glass is cut to size by scoring and breaking. Introducing a tiny flaw in the surface, typically with a diamond-tipped tool, produces a fault line that breaks readily when the glass is flexed. Edge finish depends on the application requirements. Exposed edges are typically ground and polished. Bevelling provides a couple of benefits: it reduces the sharpness of the angles and provides a crisp, aesthetic edge.

The curtain wall method of glazing allows for large, uninterrupted areas of glass. While it does not carry any weight other than its own, the difficulty with glass is its brittleness; tiny flaws can lead to catastrophic failure if the structure is bent. This drawback is easily overcome by fixing the glass to an existing load-bearing structure, but this is not much different from installing a window. With developments in steel and reinforced concrete (see Cement, page 496) structures, the outside walls of a building no longer need to be load-bearing. However, it was not until Foster & Partners pioneered the 'patch fitting' (bolted corner fitting) in the headquarters of Willis Faber and Dumas

**Hand-blown glass**
Harri Koskinen designed Cosy in Grey for Muuto, Copenhagen. It is hand-blown using a smoked-grey soda-lime glass. It is made up of two parts, which are individually blown into molds. This ensures consistency, even if they each have unique qualities. The bulb is supported by a concealed plastic structure.

in Ipswich, UK, 1975, that large expanses of suspended glazing became possible. With this system, they were able to create the 15 m (49 ft) tall glass façade virtually uninterrupted. It is not just for decoration; curtain walls allow light to penetrate deep into buildings, thus providing an improved working environment.

Laminating is commonly used in glazing, because it provides many functional benefits. In addition, the PVB layer may be tinted, coloured or printed. It is also possible to incorporate non-plastic materials, such as wire mesh, fabric and wood veneer between the glass sheets. Fusing two layers of glass with pre-cut coloured glass produces multicoloured patterns.

Ceramic frit – a combination of powdered glass and pigment – is screen-printed onto the surface and permanently bonded to the glass by kiln firing. A wide range of colours and tints is possible similar to packaging, from white to metallic silver. The amount of sunlight that is blocked depends on the coverage of the pattern. Manufactures tend to offer standard patterns, such as dots and lines, to reduce the cost to the consumer.

The majority of glass is produced clear. It is possible to produce coloured and tinted glass. However, it is only feasible in very large volumes and this limits what is on offer. Tinted glazing is designed to reduce solar gain. The glass absorbs the sun's rays and reduces light transmission. As a result, it will gradually warm up, and this can affect the interior temperature, offsetting the overall solar heat gain benefits. Of course, tinting will reduce the brightness of the outward view. The colour – traditionally grey and bronze – is carefully chosen to maximize absorption whilst minimizing the view of the outside. Recently, compositions have been developed that have less effect on visible light, while absorbing more of the light at the near-infrared part of the spectrum. So-called spectrally selective glazing is typically blue-green and much more effective than conventional grey and bronze tints at reducing solar gain.

Metal oxides and nitrides (see Technical Ceramic, page 502) are applied as thin-film coatings onto the

surface of sheet glass to provide a range of technical benefits, as well as for decoration. Alternatively, they are applied to transparent plastic film – polyethylene terephthalate (PET, polyester) (page 152) – and retrofitted. However, this will not be nearly as efficient or effective.

Self-cleaning coatings are typically based on titanium dioxide (TiO) and are photocatalytic. In other words, with the help of the sun's ultraviolet rays, nanoparticles of TiO break down dirt and pollution into its basic ingredients, such as water and carbon dioxide. Gases evaporate and rain washes dirt away. This ensures a low-maintenance surface (especially useful on buildings) while optimizing light transmission. The same technology is used to help keep painted surfaces and concrete dirt-free.

Low-emissivity glass (low-e glass), also called solar-control glass or heat-reflective glass, is produced by physical vapour deposition (PVD). A multilayered coating, which typically consists of very fine layers of metal oxide and nitride, reflects the ultraviolet rays from the sun while allowing most of the visible light to pass through. Thus, the heat is reflected, helping to keep the interior cool and without reducing the natural light within the building. Likewise, infrared radiation coming from internal heat sources is almost entirely reflected back into the building, maximizing efficiency. They are typically only suitable for multilayered windows (double or triple glazing, for example), whereby the coating can be protected from chemicals and abrasion.

A more durable coating is achieved when the metal oxide is deposited on the glass during production, while it is semi-molten. Applied by chemical vapour deposition (CVD), the coating is baked on to the surface of the glass and so not as vulnerable to cleaning and chemicals.

Mirrored glass coatings consist of a thin layer of metal oxide and come in various colours – silver, gold and bronze – that reflect virtually all of the visual light. They are used for security and to reduce daylight transmission in very hot climates. Based on reflection, the mirror effect will work only on the side that is brighter. At night when it is dark outside

**Durability**
Glass is suitable for eating from, working on and storing in. It is unaffected by chemicals, weathering and most types of wear. Even after centuries of use it remains as if it had just emerged from the factory.

**Formability**
The amorphous structure of glass means that it remains moldable across a wide temperature range and so is compatible with plastic-forming techniques, including blowing, pressing and bending.

**Versatility**
Very high-quality results can be achieved working with glass by hand as one-offs, batch-produced using molds and mass-produced in factories. It offers a great deal of design freedom ranging from a medium for artistic expression to engineering solutions.

glass is treated to reduce the surface energy and produce a hydrophobic and, in some cases, oleophobic effect. Instead of spreading across the surface, water droplets group together and build up enough mass to run off the surface, taking dirt and debris with them. Unlike non-stick plastics (see PTFE, page 190), these treatments may be entirely transparent and so do not affect the appearance of the glass.

and the lights are on inside the building, the effect is reversed. Also, the impact of reflective coatings on the outside should be carefully considered, because it can intensify the sun's effects and so impact on the building's surroundings.

Anti-reflective glass, by contrast, is coated inside and out to reduce light reflectance to 2% or less. For comparison, conventional float glass has around 8% light reflectance. Views from inside and out are improved.

Acid etching and sandblasting are used to produce textures and relief patterns. The rough surface scatters light and so diminishes transparency. It is known as carving when abrasive blasting is used to produce deep and multilayered surface designs. Alternatively, semi-molten glass is passed between profiled rollers, which leave behind a relief imprint.

## SODA-LIME GLASS IN PRODUCTS, FURNITURE AND LIGHTING

While this sector accounts for only a small percentage of total glass production, it includes the widest range of interpretations of glass as a medium. Applications stretch from lavishly coloured ornaments to delicate lighting and transparent furniture. In all cases, glass provides an enduring, hygienic and low-maintenance solution.

Glasses, light bulbs, storage jars and similar hollow vessels are all produced using the same processes as for packaging. They are manufactured in high volumes and so tend to follow standard shapes and sizes.

Of course, these and other similar items are also suitable for hand blowing and lampworking. The advantage of studio glassblowing over factory-based production is that there exists a huge

range of techniques, colours and styles. Free from the constraints of mechanized production, artists are able to produce multilayered, textured and decorated forms that would not be practical in any other material. The finest stemware is hand blown from crystal (see Lead Glass).

Mouth blowing into a mold allows for the production of shapes that would be impractical with glassblowing alone. The glass is partially inflated and the blowing is completed within the confines of a mold. This technique is also useful for producing multiples, because the outside surface (that comes into contact with the mold) remains consistent, even if the wall thickness varies.

Glass molding is used to produce items that have features that make them impractical to blow. Dishes, lampshades and lemon juicers, for example, are all manufactured in this way.

Large items, such as tables, chairs and shelving, are typically fabricated from sheet glass. Using a process similar to that used in the production of car windscreens, shaped furniture may be molded from a single sheet.

In addition to the finishes and decorations that can be borrowed from architecture and packaging, some are particularly useful for products and interiors. For example, glass items for use in bathrooms and other humid environments where condensation can be a problem are finished with an anti-fogging coating. Available in many forms and guises, anti-fogging coatings and surface treatments create a hydrophilic surface on the glass. This causes the water to form a thin film, rather than water droplets. As a result, it remains invisible.

The opposite is true for easy-to-clean and anti-wetting surfaces. In this case,

Amorphous          Crystalline

**Glass structure** What differentiates glass from other types of ceramic (see Clay, page 480, Technical Ceramic, Cement, Stone, page 472, and Diamond, page 476) is its amorphous structure. Glass is predominantly made up of oxides, primarily silica (silicon dioxide, SiO) which does not crystallize when cooled slowly. The resulting material has random atomic arrangement, which means it is transparent. Unlike crystalline ceramics, the bonds in glass show a range of strengths. Thus, as it is heated, they break over a wide temperature range, causing the glass to gradually soften and become viscous. This phenomenon creates many opportunities for forming. Impurities in the matrix, principally metal oxides, result in various colours. For example, the distinctive green hue of commercial glass is the result of iron oxide; green is also produced by chromium, blue by cobalt, pink through red by selenium, and yellow by graphite. A crystalline structure results in a lighter, stronger, denser and harder material. It is possible to convert an amorphous glass into a crystalline ceramic through heating. These materials, called glass ceramics (see High-Performance Glass), are formed as glass, but once heat treated, exhibit the behaviour of a crystalline ceramic.

**Layered colour** Alvar Aalto created his series of glass vases in 1936. The elegant design has become an icon of Finnish design and remains in production to this day. The vases are blown by hand into a mold. Various colours are combined at different thicknesses; with hand blowing each one may include a different configuration. This example is produced with a layer of red and then white encapsulated within a transparent outer.

# Lead Glass

Replacing the lime in soda-lime glass with lead results in a glass with superb clarity and brilliance. The amount of lead varies from only a small proportion in crystal glass to more than half in radiation shielding. It is heavy and robust, but 'soft' enough to be cut and engraved into items ranging from precision lenses to delicate stemware.

| Types | Typical Applications | Sustainability |
|---|---|---|
| • Full lead crystal: more than 30% lead<br>• Lead crystal: more than 24% lead<br>• Crystal glass: metal oxide greater than 10% | • Lenses, prisms and lighting<br>• Tableware and glassware<br>• Jewelry | • Glass has relatively low embodied energy<br>• Fully recyclable<br>• Lead is poisonous |

| Properties | Competing Materials | Costs |
|---|---|---|
| • High refractive index and chromaticity<br>• Dense<br>• Not as hard as other common glasses, making it easier to cut and scratch | • Soda lime, borosilicate glass and fused silica<br>• PMMA, PC and ionomer | • Low to medium, depending on the type<br>• Cutting and polishing by hand is time-consuming and expensive |

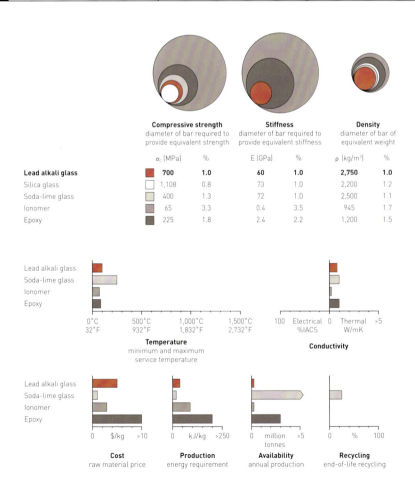

|  | Compressive strength<br>diameter of bar required to provide equivalent strength | | Stiffness<br>diameter of bar required to provide equivalent stiffness | | Density<br>diameter of bar of equivalent weight | |
|---|---|---|---|---|---|---|
|  | σ_c (MPa) | % | E (GPa) | % | ρ (kg/m³) | % |
| Lead alkali glass | 700 | 1.0 | 60 | 1.0 | 2,750 | 1.0 |
| Silica glass | 1,108 | 0.8 | 73 | 1.0 | 2,200 | 1.2 |
| Soda-lime glass | 400 | 1.3 | 72 | 1.0 | 2,500 | 1.1 |
| Ionomer | 65 | 3.3 | 0.4 | 3.5 | 945 | 1.7 |
| Epoxy | 225 | 1.8 | 2.4 | 2.2 | 1,200 | 1.5 |

## INTRODUCTION

Lead alkali glass is often referred to as crystal (see Diamond, page 476), because of its brilliance. The structure is amorphous (see page 516) and, like soda-lime glass (page 508), it is based on silica (silicon dioxide, SiO). The difference in optical quality comes from replacing lime (calcium oxide, CaO) with lead oxide (PbO).

As well as the optical enhancements, the inclusion of PbO results in a useful and complementary set of properties. It becomes more workable, because the PbO acts a flux and thus reduces the temperature at which the glass softens. This makes it relatively easy to blow and press with varying complexity.

It increases the density of glass. This quality is often emphasized in the design of decorative objects, by giving generous thickness at the bottom, because adding weight contributes to the item's gravitas. The added density also helps to ensure a high quality and flaw-free surface finish.

Surface hardness is reduced, along with stiffness, which allows for a range of mechanical treatments to be used to great effect, such as cutting, grinding and polishing. When used in applications that benefit from added sparkle – stemware, decanters, jewelry and lighting – the glass is cut and faceted. Increasing the surface area and number of edges enhances the internal refraction and light-dispersive properties. Acid polishing is traditionally used to enhance the brilliance of the glass while maintaining the design details. This finishing technique has been shown to reduce the concentration of lead at the surface and so reduce the potential for lead to migrate into stored contents.

## COMMERCIAL TYPES AND USES

According to an EU directive, a traditional full lead crystal contains at least one-third

PbO, but any glass containing at least one-quarter PbO can be described as lead crystal. Glass containing less than that is known simply as crystal glass.

Glass with even higher levels of PbO (more than half) may be used as radiation shielding, because of the ability of lead to absorb gamma rays and other forms of harmful radiation. It is used for this purpose in hospitals and laboratories.

Ranging from heavily crafted tumblers and decanters to delicate stemware,

lead glass provides unrivalled brilliance in items of glassware. All of the forming techniques that are used with soda-lime glass may be applied. There tends to be a greater level of opulence in lead glassware, from added cutting, polishing and use of precious metals (see Gold, page 90). Soda-lime is less expensive, is used in higher quantities for such things as tableware, and can be high-quality 'colourless' glass. Lead glass tends to be reserved for high-end and bespoke wares.

**Sparkle** The close tolerances permitted in the production of consumer electronics would seem to conflict with the craftsmanship involved in cutting and polishing lead glass. In this case, Swarovski combined its expertise in crystal jewelry with Philips' experience in lifestyle electronics to create luxurious and innovative headphones. The glass does not contribute to the performance of the headphones; it is purely for added sparkle.

Glass items that are likely to be subjected to thermal shock are produced in borosilicate or glass ceramic (see High-Performance Glass, page 522).

For optical applications – lenses and prisms – the quality of transparency is measured according to refractive index (N) and Abbe number (V). The refractive index is a comparison of the speed of light in a vacuum with the speed of light through the transparent material. The Abbe number is a measure of dispersion (the separation of white light into colours); a material with a high V value produces less chromatic aberration than one with a low V value.

Lead glass has a refractive index of 1.7 and Abbe of 30.9. 'Flint' glasses are arbitrarily defined as having an Abbe number of 55 or less. Common soda-lime glass has a refractive index of 1.5 and Abbe of 58.6; glasses with an Abbe number of between 50 and 85 are, in optical applications, referred to as crown glass. This explains why the two types of glass have such different visual quality. Lead glasses separate the light and so appear more colourful, the same quality that makes them a good prism.

Chromatic aberration in a lens causes wavelengths of light to have different focal lengths. German physicist Ernst Abbe developed the achromatic lens to overcome the problem. It works by combining two types of glass, flint and crown, which partially compensate for one another, resulting in reduced chromatic aberration. Achromatic lenses bring two of the three colour wavelengths (red and blue) into common focus. Bringing all three colours together (including green) requires three elements. These lenses, known as apochromatic (APO), are used in cameras and telescopes that capture very sharp images.

Modern glass lenses are manufactured to extremely close tolerances; there has been significant progress in the materials and processes in recent years. The ingredients are mixed and melted in batches. The molten mass is poured into a tray and allowed to cool. Once solidified, it is crushed and re-melted, mixed and carefully homogenized to remove all of the air bubbles. The fusing and cooling processes are controlled to ensure high-quality optical properties. It is produced as a sheet, which is cut and pressed to the desired shape and size. Small popular lenses are pressed on automated machines. Larger and specialist lenses, on the other hand, are pressed by hand. The shaped glass is annealed to relieve internal stresses and optimize optical qualities. Finally, the surface is ground and polished to very precise dimensions. The finished lens is coloured and coated according to application requirements.

The majority of eyewear lenses are now plastic, because it is significantly lighter and less expensive to produce; glass is still used where thinness is critical (high prescription or design). There are several types available, each with varying refractive index and quality of colour. One of the most popular plastics for eyewear lenses is CR-39, a thermoset (allyl diglycol carbonate, ADC) with a refractive index of 1.5 and Abbe of 56.8. It has very good resistance to abrasion and is only around half the weight of glass. Polymethyl methacrylate (PMMA, acrylic) (page 174), has values similar to soda-lime glass: refractive index is 1.49 and Abbe is 57. For comparison, polycarbonate (PC) (page 144), another popular transparent plastic, has a refractive index of 1.6 and Abbe of 30. It is generally only used for children's eyewear and for safety glasses, because the surface durability is poor.

As well as plastic alternatives, there are reduced-lead and lead-free glasses that offer some of the optical quality of lead. These compositions are typically based on replacing some or all of the PbO with an alternative oxide, such as from zinc (ZnO), barium (BaO) or potassium (KO). While they may not be as brilliant as lead glass, they have good optical quality. Barium glass, for example, has a refractive index of 1.58 and Abbe of 52.1. However, as a heavy metal, BaO presents similar challenges to PbO. Several of the high-performance glasses are colourless. They tend to be more expensive than lead glass though, and a lot more difficult to work.

## SUSTAINABILITY
Like soda-lime glass, lead glass is fully recyclable. However, it is much more likely to be reused and passed down as an heirloom than re-melted and manufactured into new glassware. The quality and purity of ingredients is very important, so unless the source of glass is known, it is not practical to recycle.

The use of lead dates back 5,000 years and is thought to be linked to its likeness to silver (page 84). As well as being used alone in the production of ornaments and jewelry, it has provided a valuable raw material in the manufacture of ceramic glazes (see Clay, page 480), petrol and as a whitener in paint and make-up. It has since been replaced in the majority of applications, because it is a toxic and heavy metal. Prolonged exposure to the element is potentially very harmful, especially for babies and children. As part of the EU REACH (Registration, Evaluation, Authorization and Restriction of Chemicals) regulation, the lead content of jewelry and similar items is restricted.

Rather ironically, this poisonous material provides shielding from harmful radiation. As well as its use in hospitals and laboratories, lead glass was utilized in cathode ray tubes in televisions and monitors. Each of the glasses used – screen, cone and neck – contained varying amounts of PbO and BaO.

In the case of glass, the lead is locked into the structure. Minute amounts will leach out over prolonged periods through diffusion controlled ionic exchange with the stored ingredients, but the levels are considered too small to have an adverse affect on health. Indeed, lead glass is exempt from the REACH regulation. However, the use of lead in production is problematic, because it is volatile and so the workplace and environment are likely to be exposed to lead vapours.

**Blown, cut and polished** The artisans at Cumbria Crystal produce traditional full lead crystal wares (content of at least 30%). They mix state-of-the-art furnaces and equipment with wooden tools and techniques that have changed little, if at all, over the centuries. Cutting is a two-stage process: the cut is made on a diamond wheel and then smoothed over on a sandstone wheel. The glass is acid polished to enhance its brilliance while maintaining the detail of the design. Photo courtesy of Cumbria Crystal.

# High-Performance Glass

These glasses are used where other materials fail; they maintain their transparency, stability and durability even when exposed to the harshest environments, chemicals and thermal shock. As well as playing a crucial role in technological development, their properties are utilized in some very familiar items including composites, fibre optics, stovetops and phone cover glass.

| Types | Typical Applications | Sustainability |
|---|---|---|
| • Borosilicate; aluminosilicate; fused silica and glass ceramic | • Lab equipment and kitchenware<br>• Composites and fibre optics<br>• Phone, tablet and computer cover glass | • Fully recyclable, but impractical to separate from mixed waste streams<br>• Moderate embodied energy |

| Properties | Competing Materials | Costs |
|---|---|---|
| • Hard-wearing and impermeable<br>• High resistance to abrasion, chemicals and thermal shock<br>• Some are colourless, others are translucent | • Soda-lime and lead glass<br>• Technical ceramic and gemstone<br>• Carbon, aramid, PBO and basalt | • Moderate to high raw material price<br>• Expensive to process |

## INTRODUCTION

High-performance glasses account for only a fraction of total glass production; the majority is soda-lime (page 508). However, as a group, they offer some exceptional properties unrivalled among the engineering materials. They are unique in that they can be formed like commercial glass and perform like technical ceramic (page 502). But above all, they are transparent.

Since the start of the 20th century there has been significant development in glass technology. As a window material, high-performance glasses offer a view into extreme environments and this makes them fundamental in technological fields including chemistry, automotive and alternative energy.

Their impact on the domestic environment and consumer products has been no less profound. While borosilicate glass provides transparency in the kitchen, aluminosilicate glass has helped touch-screen interaction to become the dominant means of communication between people and the Internet. Glass-fibre-reinforced composites have helped to improve the safety and efficiency of transportation, and silica fibre optics provide the cables along which telecommunications can travel faster and with fewer interruptions than

**Laboratory glass**

Borosilicate was developed at the start of the 20th century to satisfy the demand for glass with high thermal resistance. This property, combined with is low coefficient of thermal expansion and excellent chemical durability, makes it an ideal material for laboratory equipment and cookware alike. It is compatible with all of the same processing and finishing as soda-lime glass and lead glass. Labware such as this volumetric flask is shaped from extruded tube by lampworking. Labware that will be exposed to higher temperatures is produced from glass ceramic or silica.

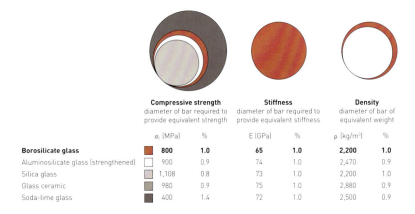

| | Compressive strength<br>diameter of bar required to provide equivalent strength | | Stiffness<br>diameter of bar required to provide equivalent stiffness | | Density<br>diameter of bar of equivalent weight | |
|---|---|---|---|---|---|---|
| | $\sigma_c$ (MPa) | % | E (GPa) | % | $\rho$ (kg/m³) | % |
| Borosilicate glass | 800 | 1.0 | 65 | 1.0 | 2,200 | 1.0 |
| Aluminosilicate glass (strengthened) | 900 | 0.9 | 74 | 1.0 | 2,470 | 0.9 |
| Silica glass | 1,108 | 0.8 | 73 | 1.0 | 2,200 | 1.0 |
| Glass ceramic | 980 | 0.9 | 75 | 1.0 | 2,880 | 0.9 |
| Soda-lime glass | 400 | 1.4 | 72 | 1.0 | 2,500 | 0.9 |

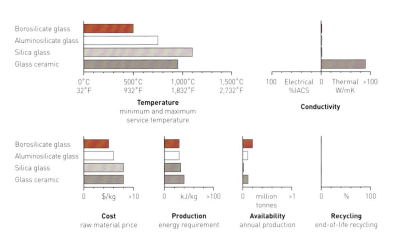

+20
+15
+10
+5
725ml

−5
−10
−15
−20
−25
−30
−35
−40

725ml
IN 20°C
AVERAGE SYSTEM
JayTec
Made In England
1634

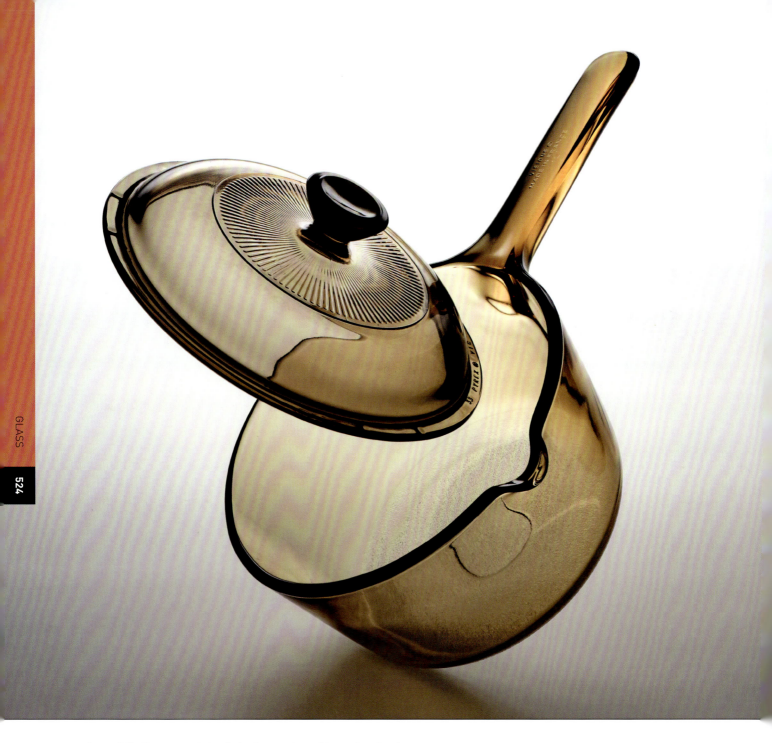

copper (page 66). Glass ceramic is a hybrid that combines the forming benefits of glass with the mechanical benefits of crystalline ceramics (see Technical Ceramic). As a result of its extreme properties – high strength, ultra-high temperature resistance and near-zero thermal expansion – entirely new areas of application for glass have emerged.

## COMMERCIAL TYPES AND USES
There are several types of high-performance glass and selection depends on the application requirements.

Borosilicate glass has become very familiar as a result of its use in ovenware and is more often known by its trademark names Duran, Simax and Pyrex (although the Pyrex consumer brand no longer uses borosilicate glass in North America). It contains up to 15% boric oxide (BO) and small amounts of other alkalis (sodium and potassium oxides) and alumina (aluminium oxide, AlO).

Its low alkali content gives it excellent chemical resistance and thermal shock resistance, superior to soda-lime glass. It has low thermal expansion, which means

**See-through cookware**
In 1958 CorningWare glass ceramic was launched. Dr Donald Stookey, a scientist working at Corning who also developed photochromic glass (darkens in response to light), developed the material by accident. Thinking he had broken the furnace, he pulled out a glass sample, which slipped from his tongs onto the floor. In his account he said that not only did it bounce rather than break, but 'it sounded like steel hitting the floor'. Glass ceramic is the only see-through material capable of tolerating the high temperatures and thermal shocks involved with cooking directly on the hob. Indeed, it can go directly from freezer to stovetop. In this case, the pan is glass ceramic and the lid is borosilicate.

almost no tension is built up in the glass when the temperature changes. It is suitable for use at up to 500°C (930°F) and down to -70°C (-95°F), although types exist that can tolerate the maximum possible negative temperature (-273°C) (-459°F).

Its low coefficient of expansion also means it can be manufactured with relatively thick walls, giving it good mechanical properties. As a result of its versatility and moderate price, it is used in diverse application, spanning kitchenware, laboratory apparatus and chemical processing equipment. It is suitable for ovenware, but cannot be placed directly onto the hob, because the temperature difference would be too great. In this case, glass ceramic is used.

It is available in a range of formats, including rod, tube and vessel, as well as sheet. It also extruded as glass fibre (GF). While glassfibre building insulation (glass wool) is typically soda-lime glass, borosilicate is preferred for textiles because it is more durable and resistant to chemicals.

Injection-molded engineering plastics, such as polyamide (PA, nylon) (page 164), are reinforced with short-strand GF to improve strength-to-weight and stiffness. This general-purpose composite is utilized in diverse situations, from under-the-bonnet automotive parts to mobile phone and power-tool housings. Continuous-strand GF is utilized as unidirectional (UD) fabric, woven textile or chop strand mat (nonwoven) in high-performance composites (see UP Resin, page 228). They are used in applications that demand very high strength-to-weight and stiffness, from boat hulls and racing cars to furniture and construction materials.

Aluminosilicate consists of 20% alumina, often including small amounts of calcium oxide (CaO), magnesia (magnesium oxide, MgO) and BO, and a small proportion of soda or potash. It is able to withstand severe thermal shock and temperatures up to 750°C (1,380°F). Technical applications include halogen-tungsten lamps and combustion tubes.

In recent years, aluminosilicate glass has exerted a formative influence on the development of electronic devices, such as laptops and mobile phones.

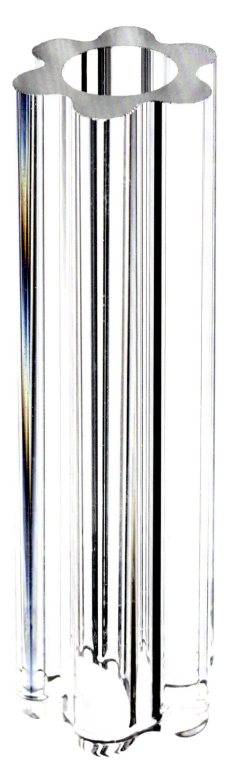

**Extruded glass**
Borosilicate is extruded as long lengths of rod, tube and a multitude of other profiles; a huge range exists as stock shapes. It is applied as it is, or cut and manipulated to make laboratory glassware and lighting, for example. Hand working tubes of glass is known as lampworking. The glass is heated locally, allowing it to be bent, drawn out and joined into a range of configurations.

**Braided glass** It was not until the 1930s that continuous glass fibre was produced at commercial scale. Since then it has become a valuable industrial material utilized in composites, cables and insulation. The exact composition of the fibre depends on the requirements of the application and they are labelled accordingly: E (low electrical conductivity); S (high-strength); C (chemical durability); M (high stiffness); A (soda-lime glass); and D (low dielectric constant).

In this industry it is more commonly referred to by trademark names, such as Gorilla (Corning), Xensation (Schott) and Dragontrail (Asahi). Even though it has been in commercial use for decades, Apple was the first to introduce it to mobile phones (iPhone, 2007) and later to laptops and tablets. The improved strength, toughness and durability of aluminosilicate, compared to soda-lime glass, reduce the likelihood of breakage through bending and blunt force impact. As a result, aluminosilicate cover glass is today considered industry standard for portable devices.

A chemical treatment is used to enhance the strength, durability and resistance to impact, abrasion and thermal shock. The process works by ion exchange on the surface and creates a deep compression layer. As with toughening (see Soda-Lime Glass), forming a surface under compression greatly improves the amount of tensile and bending load that the glass is able to withstand. As load is applied the glass does not come under tension until the force exceeds that of the pre-compressed surface. Another benefit of chemical strengthening is that the surface is hardened. This reduces the likelihood of abrasion creating flaws that would cause the glass to fail under tension.

Aluminosilicate sheet glass is produced using the fusion-draw method. This is different from float glass (see Soda-Lime Glass). An isopipe (trough) is filled with molten glass until it spills over each side. Glass runs downward and the two sides meet underneath, fusing to form a single sheet that is drawn as it cools.

Its properties have been optimized to make the most of the chemical strengthening process. Once formed into the final shape, it is placed into a potassium salt bath, where the small sodium ions in the glass are replaced with larger potassium ions. As the glass cools and shrinks the surface becomes highly compressed. The depth of penetration, or depth of layer (DoL), greatly affects overall performance and this is what differentiates the various types. Corning claims that Gorilla has the greatest DoL and provides superior strength.

There is great potential for chemically strengthened aluminosilicate glass in many applications beyond consumer electronics. BMW used Gorilla glass in the i8 and testing is under way to enable it to be used more widely. While it is more expensive than soda-lime glass, it has the potential to save weight and thus reduce fuel consumption.

Fused silica, also called vitreous silica, is a hard and high-temperature resistant glass. Unlike the other glasses, it does not contain any other ingredients. As a result, it has very high working temperature (up to around 1,000°C [1,830°F]) coupled with exceptional optical, thermal and mechanical properties. There are several commercial grades, which are broadly divided into those produced from natural quartz and synthetic types.

It has excellent transparency to a wide range of wavelengths, from ultraviolet to near-infrared, and this is utilized in fibre optics. Communication fibres typically comprise two glasses: a core of highly refracting glass with a sheath of glass or plastic with a lower refractive index. While a range of materials can be used, the core is typically silica and the sheath borosilicate. The surface is protected from damage by a plastic coating.

Glass ceramic is a fascinating material. It is shaped like conventional glass and then converted by heat treatment to a predominantly crystalline material. Its unique combination of properties has opened up entirely new areas of application for glass, from transparent furnace linings to missile nose cones transparent to radar.

A unique manufacturing advantage of these materials is their compatibility with all the shaping processes used for conventional glass (pressing, bending and blowing). Once formed, the crystalline structure is propagated through the inclusion of nucleating agents, which are melted into the glass. The properties of the material in application depend on the bulk composition and microstructure.

It has near-zero thermal expansion and can operate at temperatures in excess of 950°C (1,740°F) and tolerate sudden temperature changes of 800°C (1,470°F) or more without difficulty. As

manufacturers like to demonstrate, very hot glass ceramics can be submerged directly in cool water. The water responds dramatically and the glass remains intact. It is compatible with all cooking and heating technologies, including electric, gas and induction. It is transparent – revealing the heating element enhances usability – and hygienic. In electric cookers, the high thermal conductivity of the material ensures most of the energy reaches the pot. The same quality means this material is suitable for infrared heaters, wood stoves and fireplaces.

It is available in a range of colours, including white, black, grey, tinted and colourless. Sheet thickness typically ranges from 2 to 8 mm (0.08–0.3 in).

## SUSTAINABILITY

A wide range of ingredients goes into the production of high-performance glasses. Essentially, they are all based on silica with varying amounts of other ingredients, except for pure silica glass. Many of them are mined and some are potentially harmful; they are comparable with technical ceramic.

All glass materials are recyclable. While it is practical to reuse scrap generated during production, it is not so straightforward to collect and distinguish the many different types end-of-life. Therefore, very little will be recycled and if it does get into the mix with commercial glass, then it causes problems further down the production line.

**3D cover glass**  Prior to the success of the iPhone, many argued that plastic offered superior properties for large phone cover glass. Plastic has become the predominant material in eyewear lenses; it is lighter and tougher than glass; it is inexpensive and compatible with a wide range of forming processes. The reason why chemically strengthened aluminosilicate glass has become the norm in phones is that it offers a superior touch-screen experience. It is not as tough as plastic, but it is exceptionally strong and hard-wearing. It has proved so successful that it is now being used for shaped windows, something previously possible only with plastic. This cover glass from the Samsung Curve follows the shape of the display, which is wrapped around the sides of the device. This reduces width and allows for on-screen interaction along the side of the device for the first time.

# Glossary and Abbreviations

## Common material abbreviations, acronyms and generic names

### METAL

**Ag** silver
**AHSS** advanced high-strength steel
**Al** aluminium
**Au** gold
**CGI** compacted graphite iron
**Cu** copper
**duplex alloy** alloy that contains a mix of two molecular structures, or phases (e.g. alpha-beta) (see Silver, page 88)
**Fe** iron
**ferrous** containing or consisting of Fe (iron)
**HSLA** high-strength low-alloy steel
**MAG** magnesium
**Mg** magnesium
**MMC** metal matrix composite
**non-ferrous** not iron or steel
**SHG** special high-grade zinc
**sterling** silver alloy that contains 7.5% copper
**Ti** titanium
**Zn** zinc

### PLASTIC

**ABS** acrylonitrile butadiene styrene
**acetal** POM
**acetate** CA fibre
**acrylic** PMMA or PAN
**ADS** air-dried sheet, in reference to natural rubber and latex
**AFRP** aramid-fibre-reinforced plastic
**aramid** Aromatic PA
**ASA** acrylic styrene acrylonitrile
**bioplastic, biopolymer** Plastic derived from biological sources (made without petrochemicals) including starch plastic, PLA, PHA, PHB
**block rubber** TSR
**BMC** bulk molding compound based on UP, also known as DMC
**BOPET** biaxially-oriented PET (film)
**BOPP** biaxially-oriented PP (film)
**BR** polybutadiene rubber
**CA, CAB, CAP** cellulose acetate, CA butyrate, CA propionate
**CF, CFRP** carbon fibre, carbon-fibre-reinforced plastic
**COPA** copolyamide elastomer, see TPA
**COPE** copolyester elastomer, see TPC
**CR** polychloroprene rubber, neoprene
**DMC** dough molding compound based on UP, also known as BMC
**EAA** ethylene acrylic acid
**EEA** ethylene ethyl acrylate
**elastane** TPU fibre
**elastomer** a natural or man-made material that exhibits elastic properties and has the ability to deform under load and return to its original shape once the load has been removed. For example, TPE, PU, silicone and rubber.
**EMA** ethylene methyl acrylate
**EMMA** ethylene methacrylic acid
**EnBA** ethylene n-butyl acrylate
**EPDM** ethylene propylene diene, synthetic rubber
**epoxy** polyepoxide resin
**EPR** ethylene propylene rubber
**EPS** expanded PS
**ePTFE** expanded PTFE, fluoropolymer
**ETFE** ethylene tetrafluoroethylene, fluoropolymer
**EVA** ethylene vinyl acetate
**EVOH** ethylene vinyl alcohol
**FEP** fluorinated ethylene propylene, fluoropolymer
**FRP** fibre-reinforced plastic
**fluoropolymer** PTFE, ePTFE, ETFE, PFA, FEP or other fluorine-containing polymer
**GF, GFRP** glass fibre, glass-fibre-reinforced plastic
**GPPS** general-purpose PS
**HDPE** high-density PE
**Hevea crumb** SMR
**HIPS** high-impact PS
**HM** high-modulus, typically in reference to CF, aramid or other super fibre
**HNBR** hydrogenated NBR
**HT** high-tensile, typically in reference to CF
**HTV** high-temperature vulcanizing, typically in reference to silicone
**HWM** high-wet-modulus, in reference to viscose fibre
**IIR** isobutylene isoprene rubber
**IM** intermediate-modulus, typically in reference to CF
**IR** polyisoprene rubber
**LCP** liquid crystal polymer
**LDPE** low-density PE
**LLDPE** linear low-density PE
**LSR** liquid silicone rubber
**lyocell** viscose fibre produced by a modified wet-spinning process
**m-aramid** meta-aramid
**MF** melamine-formaldehyde-based thermosetting plastic
**modal** modified version of HWM
**NBR** acrylonitrile butadiene rubber, nitrile rubber
**neoprene** CR, synthetic rubber
**nitrile rubber** NBR
**nylon** PA
**olefin** typically PP or PE
**PA** polyamide, nylon
**PAEK** polyaryletherketone
**PAN** polyacrylonitrile, acrylic fibre
**p-aramid** para-aramid
**PBO** polyphenylene benzobisthiazole
**PBT** polybutylene terephthalate, polyester
**PC** polycarbonate
**PE** polyethylene
**PEBA** TPA
**PEEK** polyetheretherketone
**PEK** polyetherketone
**PEL** PET
**PES** PET
**PET, PETE** polyethylene terephthalate, polyester
**PETG** PET modified with glycol
**PF** phenol-formaldehyde-based thermosetting plastic
**PFA** perfluoroalkoxy, fluoropolymer
**PHA, PHB** polyhydroxyalkanoate, polyhydroxybutyrate
**PLA** polylactic acid
**plastisol** PVC
**pleather** synthetic leather, typically PVC
**PMC** molding compound based on UP
**PMMA** polymethyl methacrylate, acrylic
**poly** typically PE or PET
**polyester** PET, PTT, PBT or UP
**POM** polyoxymethylene, acetal
**PP** polypropylene
**PPA** polyphthalamide
**PPC PP** copolymer
**PPH PP** Homopolymer
**PS** polystyrene
**PTFE** polytetrafluoroethylene, fluoropolymer
**PTT** polytrimethylene terephthalate, polyester
**PU, PUR, PUL** polyurethane (thermoset)
**PVC** polyvinyl chloride
**RSS** ribbed smoked sheet, in reference to natural rubber and latex
**RTV** room-temperature vulcanizing, typically in reference to silicone
**SAN** styrene acrylonitrile
**SBR** styrene butadiene rubber
**SEBS, SEPS** styrenic block copolymer, see TPS
**SHT** super-high-tensile, typically in reference to CF
**silicone** polysiloxane
**SMC** sheet molding compound based on UP
**SMR, SIR** Standard Malaysian Rubber, Standard Indonesian Rubber; types of TSR
**spandex** TPU fibre
**super fibre** synthetic fibres differentiated from common types by their superior strength-to-weight, including UHMWPE, p-aramid, CF, PBO and ePTFE
**synthetic rubber** man-made thermosetting elastomers: SBR, BR, CR (neoprene), NBR, IIR and IR
**thermoplastic** polymer that becomes soft and pliable when heated. Whereas amorphous types soften gradually, semi-crystalline thermoplastics have a more clearly defined melting point.
**thermosetting** Commonly referred to as thermoset, this group of materials is formed by heating, catalysing or mixing two parts to trigger a one-way polymeric reaction. Unlike most thermoplastics, thermosets form cross-links between the polymer chains that cannot be undone.
**TPA** polyamide-based TPE
**TPAE** TPA
**TPC, TPC-ET** copolyester-based TPE
**TPE** thermoplastic elastomer, including TPS, TPC, TPU, TPA, TPO and TPV
**TPE-ES, TPE-EE** TPC
**TPE-S** TPS
**TPO** PP- or PE-based TPE
**TPS** styrene-based TPE or thermoplastic starch (bioplastic)
**TPU** urethane-based TPE
**TPV** PP-based TPE with the addition of cross-linked elastomer
**triacetate** CA fibre
**TSR** technical specified rubber, in reference to natural rubber and latex
**UF** urea-formaldehyde-based thermosetting plastic
**UHM** ultra-high-modulus, typically in reference to CF
**UHMWPE** ultra-high-molecular-weight PE
**ULDPE** ultra-low-density PE
**UP** unsaturated polyester (thermosetting) resin
**uPVC** unplasticized PVC
**vinyl** PVC
**viscose** CA fibre
**WPC** wood-plastic composite
**XNBR** NBR with the addition of carboxylic acid groups
**XPS** extruded foamed PS

### WOOD

**D fir-L, DF-L** Douglas-fir–larch
**ER** European redwood (pine)
**EW** European whitewood (spruce)
**glulam** glued laminated timber
**HEM, HEM-FIR, HEM-TAM** hemlock, hemlock and fir, hemlock and tamarack (North American larch)
**LSL** laminated strand lumber
**LVL** laminated veneer lumber
**MEL** machine-evaluated lumber
**MSR** machine stress-rated
**OSB** oriented strand board, sterling board
**PSL** parallel strand lumber
**SPF** spruce-pine-fir
**TMT** thermally modified timber
**WPC** wood-plastic composite

### PLANT

**cane** stems of bamboo and rattan; used in basketry
**China grass** ramie
**ELS** extra-long staple cotton
**Natural Blend** blend containing 60% or more cotton
**reed** rattan core used in basketry
**sinamay** abaca
**Supima** a type of ELS
**wicker** flexible weaving material, such as from rattan, bamboo or willow

### ANIMAL

**kip** leather from young or small animals somewhere between calf and cow
**qiviut** hair from the muskox

### MINERAL

**AlO** aluminium oxide, corundum
**alumina** AlO
**BC** boron carbide
**carborundum** SiC
**cement** CMC
**CMC** ceramic matrix composite, cement
**CrN** chromium nitride
**crystal** lead glass with more than 10% metal oxide
**gypsum** man-made plaster
**lead crystal, full lead crystal** lead glass with more than 24% lead, lead glass with more than 30% lead
**Portland cement** man-made cement
**SiC** silicon carbide, carborundum
**SiN** silicon nitride
**TiAlN** titanium aluminium nitride
**TiCN** titanium carbon nitride
**TiN** titanium nitride
**UHPC** ultra-high-performance concrete
**WC** tungsten carbide
**zirconia** ZrO
**ZrN** zirconium nitride
**ZrO** zirconium dioxide

## Physical property symbols and abbreviations

**E** modulus of elasticity (Also known as Young's modulus) Material rigidity (stiffness) is defined as a ratio of stress versus strain. It is a constant value used to characterize materials: for example, whereas aramid (page 242) has a high modulus (rigid), rubber (page 248) has a low modulus (flexible).

**ρ ('rho') density** The quantity of mass per unit volume of a material (e.g. kg/m³ or lb/ft³). Thus, soda-lime glass (page 508), which weighs 2,500 kg/m³ (156 lb/ft³) has a density 2.1 times greater than polymethyl methacrylate (PMMA, acrylic) (page 174), which weighs only 1,190 kg/m³ (74 lb/ft³).

**σ$_c$ ('sigma c') compressive strength** The ability of a material to resist loads tending to reduce its size and defined as the force (see also Pa) required to cause deformation or crushing. For brittle materials, such as concrete (see cement, page 496), the point of failure is clear, because these materials fracture suddenly. However, ductile materials, such as steel (page 28), become gradually distorted as the compressive load is increased, and there is no clear point of failure. In this case, compressive strength is somewhat arbitrary and defined as the point at which the material reaches the maximum permanent deformation that can be accepted.

**$\sigma_T$ ('sigma t') tensile strength**
Also referred to as ultimate strength or breaking force, it is a measure of the resistance of a material to break under tension and thus the force (see also Pa) required to break it apart. It depends, to some extent, on the format of the material. For example, molded polyethylene terephthalate (PET, polyester) (page 152) has a tensile strength of 60 MPa, which is only around 16% of the tensile strength of PET fibre (985 MPa).

**IACS international annealed copper standard**
Used to compare the electrical conductivity (a measure of how well a material accommodates the movement of an electrical charge) of materials, in particular metals, 100% IACS is equivalent to a conductivity of 58 MS/m (megasiemens per metre), the same as annealed copper (page 66). So for example, cast iron (page 22), which has a conductivity of 10 MS/m, is reported as 18% IACS.

**Shore A, Shore D Shore durometer scale**
The hardness of a plastic, rubber or elastomer is measured by the depth of indentation of a shaped metal foot on a measuring instrument known as a durometer. The depth of indentation is measured on a scale of 0 to 100; higher numbers indicate harder (less flexible) materials. These tests are generally used to denote the flexibility of a material. The two most popular are Shore A and Shore D. Indenter feet with different profiles are used in each case, and so each process is suitable for different material hardnesses. Soft materials are measured on the Shore A scale, and hard materials are measured on the Shore D scale. There is not a strong correlation between different scales. Shore hardness is also known as durometer hardness.

**Tg glass transition temperature**
The temperature at which the amorphous regions (see page 166) in a plastic become pliable. While some plastics have a low Tg (elastomers, for example, feel rubbery, because the amorphous regions are

mobile), others are stiff at room temperature (structural plastics, for example, rely on a high Tg so that they maintain their structural integrity above room temperature). A plastic with a high Tg is made pliable at room temperature by adding plasticizer.

**W/mK thermal conductivity**
Also known as the U value and lambda (λ), it is the rate at which heat passes through a material, independent of its thickness. It is measured in W/mK, which is calculated as W per m² surface area for a temperature gradient of 1 K for every 1 m of thickness. In other words, a material with a value of 1 W/mK and a surface area of 1 m² will allow 1 W (1 J/s) to transfer through it when one side is 1 degree warmer than the other.

**Units of measurement**

**GPa gigapascal**
Denotes 10⁹ (one billion) Pa

**J joule**
The SI unit of energy, equal to the work done by 1 N to move an object 1 m. It is equivalent to 3,600th of a W-hour

**K kelvin**
The SI base unit of thermodynamic temperature, with an equivalent magnitude to degrees Celsius (°C), but with a different zero

**kJ kilojoule**
Denotes 10³ (one thousand) J

**micron micrometre**
A unit of length equal to one millionth of a metre (0.000039 in); symbol: μm

**MPa megapascal**
Denotes 10⁶ (one million) Pa

**MS megasiemens**
Denotes 10⁶ S

**N newton**
The SI unit of force; it is equal to the force needed to give an object with a mass of 1 kg an acceleration of 1 m/s² (metre per second per second). It is equivalent to 100,000 dynes.

**Pa pascal**
The SI unit of pressure, equal to 1 N per m² (0.000145 psi).

**psi pounds per square inch**
A unit of pressure (pounds-force per in²) equal to 6894.76 Pa

**S siemens**
The SI unit of electrical conductance, equal to the reciprocal of 1 ohm; also referred to as the mho.

**W watt**
The SI unit of power equivalent to 1 J/s (joule per second). It is used to express the rate of energy consumption in an electrical circuit.

# GLOSSARY OF TERMS
Words in **bold** refer to terms that have their own entry.

**3D printing** The original form of **additive manufacturing**, three-dimensional printing (3D printing) was developed at Massachusetts Institute of Technology (MIT) in 1993 and commercialized by Z Corporation. In operation, layers of gypsum-based (page 492) plaster powder are deposited and rehydrated with water to form a rigid structure. Once the build is complete, the model is infiltrated with resin to create a robust part.

**additive manufacturing** Also known as rapid prototyping, **3D printing** and digital manufacturing, a process by which three-dimensional objects are built up layer by layer. The principal methods are based on fusing powder (laser **sintering** is suitable for certain plastics and metals), curing resin (epoxy), or melted filament (plastic, chocolate and any other material that can be softened at relatively low temperature). There are many variations on these three themes, and new approaches to additive manufacturing are continually emerging and developing.

**air knife** Also known as a floating knife, it is used to apply coatings and adhesives to textiles, and so called because the textile is unsupported as it passes under the blade; pressure is applied by holding the textile under tension.

**aliphatic** A **polymer** structure that comprises carbon atoms in open chains (not **aromatic**) (see also Polyamide, page 166). They may be saturated or unsaturated. Examples include polyamide (PA, nylon) and polyethylene terephthalate (PET, polyester) (page 152), two common plastics.

**alpha-beta (α-β) alloy** See **duplex alloy**.

**alpha-olefin (α-olefin)** Primarily used as co-**monomers** in the production of polyethylene (PE) (page 108), alpha-olefins are alkenes with a double bond between the first and second carbon atom (alpha position).

**amine** Derived from ammonia, amines are produced by replacing one or more of the hydrogen atoms with organic groups. It is utilized as a hardener to cure epoxy resin (page 232).

**anisotropic** A material whose properties are different widthways and lengthways. For example, wood is stronger in the direction of growth (along the grain) as opposed to across the grain; fibre-reinforced composites (FRP) are strongest in line with the fibres; and loom-woven textiles tend to be stronger in the direction of warp (machine direction), because the warp yarn has to be strong enough to withstand the loads applied

during weaving. See also **isotropic**.

**anneal** A heat-treatment utilized in the production of metal and glass. In the case of metal, controlled heating and cooling allows the crystal structure to find its equilibrium (see Steel, page 38, Aluminium, page 44, and Silver, page 88). The same methodology is used to remove internal stresses in formed glass: heating and gradually cooling reduces the build-up of tension in the molecular structure at room temperature (see Soda-Lime Glass, pages 509 and 511, and Lead Glass, page 520).

**anodize** An electrochemical process used to build up the naturally occurring oxide (AlO) layer on the surface of aluminium (see page 44). As well as providing protection – AlO is among the hardest materials known (see also Diamond and Corundum, page 476, and Technical Ceramic, page 502) – it may be coloured, and as a result has became very popular in design, featuring in a wide range of sectors and applications.

**aromatic** A **polymer** structure that contains unsaturated rings of atoms (not **aliphatic**). In the case of synthetic plastics, this property means that during polymerization the **monomers** join together into longer unbroken chains (higher strength) with highly oriented crystal structure. As an example, aramid (page 242), which is an aromatic polyamide, has higher strength, stiffness and dimensional stability compared to aliphatic polyamide (PA, nylon) (page 164). Polymers with a partially aromatic structure – see, for example, polyetheretherketone (PEEK) (page 188) – are known as semi-aromatic.

**bast fibre** Long, durable fibres extracted from the stems of certain tall-growing plants. Those extracted from flax (page 400), hemp (page 406) and ramie (page 408) are the strongest and stiffest of all plant fibres.

**biocompatible** Not harmful or toxic to living tissue (typically in reference to materials used in surgery or for surgical implants). See also **cytotoxic**.

**bicomponent fibre** Fibres co-extruded and spun together in various configurations to combine the properties of two or more material types. See Polyamide (PA, nylon) (page 173).

**blowing agent** A substance used to produce a cellular structure in plastics, metals and ceramics. It is mixed with the material in its liquid state and forms pockets of gas via a foaming process. The material converts from a liquid to a solid via hardening or phase transition, exactly as it would without blowing agent, thus fixing the cellular

structure. Density is controlled by restricting the expansion of the material, such as within a mold. Well-known examples include expanded polystyrene (EPS) (page 132) packaging and building insulation, and polyurethane foam (PU foam) (page 202) upholstery and building insulation.

**blow molding** A group of processes used to mass produce hollow plastic packaging containers. There are two principal methods: extrusion blow molding (EBM) and injection blow molding (IBM). In both cases, a hot plastic **parison** is placed within a mold and compressed air is blown into it, forcing it to conform to the internal shape of the mold. Whereas EBM is less expensive to set up and more widely used, IBM allows for more complex and precise details to be achieved. See also polyethylene (PE) (page 112).

**brazing** Process used to form permanent joins in metal by melting a filler material between adjacent parts. The melting temperature of the filler material determines whether the process is known as soldering, which is below 450°C (840°F), or brazing, which is above.

**breathable** Used to described materials that allow atmosphere and vapour to pass through but typically do not allow liquids to penetrate. This includes natural materials such as leather (page 444), and man-made materials such as ePTFE (page 190).

**CAD** Computer-aided design, a general term used to cover computer programs that assist with the design and engineering of an item.

**calendering** A mechanical finishing technique used to change the appearance and feel of textile. The unfinished material is passed between metal cylinders under high pressure. As a result, the surface profile of the roller is imparted onto the surface, or right through the structure, of the textile. It is used to smooth the surface and improve lustre, or to reproduce a three-dimensional pattern. Depending on the material and technique, it may be semi-permanent or last the lifetime of the fabric.

**CAM** Computer-aided manufacturing, a term used to cover software required to drive computer-guided processes, such as **CNC** milling and laser cutting.

**carbon black** Virtually pure elemental carbon produced by the incomplete combustion of hydrocarbons. It is added to natural and synthetic rubber (page s248 and 216) to enhance physical properties, such as strength and durability.

**cathodic protection, action** A technique used to reduce the corrosion of a metal surface. The metal to be protected is turned into the cathode of an electrochemical cell by placing a more readily corroded metal (sacrificial) – the anode – in the vicinity. A common application of this technique is galvanized steel, whereby the steel (page 28) is protected by a sacrificial layer of zinc (page 78). The rate at which metals are corroded depends on their **nobility**: metals with a lower **galvanic number** will be eroded more quickly than those with a higher number. See also **galvanic corrosion**.

**CIM** Ceramic injection molding, which is similar to **injection molding** plastic, is used in the production of high volumes of identical parts. A mix of ceramic powder and plastic binder is injected into the die cavity. Afterwards, the binder is melted out and the part is **sintered** to fuse the ceramic particles. See Technical Ceramic, page 504. See also **MIM**, which is a very similar process used to shape metal powders.

**CIP** Cold isostatic pressing. See **isostatic pressing**.

**CITES** The Convention on International Trade in Endangered Species of Wild Fauna and Flora is an international treaty drawn up in 1973 to protect species against overexploitation. Checking the CITES status helps to ensure the suitability of plant and animal products, in particular exotics (pages 374 and 462 respectively).

**CNC** Machine equipment operated by a computer is known as 'computer numerical control' (CNC). See also **machining**.

**coefficient of friction** A value that represents the friction between two surfaces by showing the relationship between the force of friction between the materials and the normal force between them. It is not based on units. Instead, a low number indicates that there is little friction (0 is the theoretical lower limit), and a high number (typically up to 1) indicates that there is a high degree of friction.

**compression modulus** Used to indicate the ease with which a material can be crushed, it is defined as the ratio of compressive stress applied to a material compared to the resulting compression.

**compression molding** This process is used to manufacture high volumes of thermosetting plastic and rubber parts. Plastic powder (such as phenolic, page 224), rubber (such as silicone, page 212) or dough (such as unsaturated polyester, page 228) is squeezed into the die cavity under pressure. The metal mold is heated to accelerate the curing process. Once solidified, the part is de-molded. It is not as rapid as injection molding and the scrap cannot be recycled.

**copolymer** A **polymer** made up of long chains of two repeating

monomers, for example EPR (page 216).

**covalent bond** Chemical bond formed by the sharing of electrons between the atoms. It helps to enhance the physical properties of certain **polymers** (see Acid Copolymers and Ionomers, page 130), to provide a strong mechanism of adhesion (see Polysiloxane, Silicone, page 214) and, in combination with neatly packed carbon atoms, to make diamond the hardest of all materials (page 478). See also **ionic bond**.

**creep** A measurement of the permanent elongation (**stretch**) of a material after prolonged load. Low creep is particularly important for fibres and rope used in critical structural applications.

**cure** To polymerize rubber or resin (solid, coating, adhesive or composite matrix) to form a thermosetting plastic. The reaction may be stimulated using a catalyst or heat.

**CVD** Chemical vapour deposition: a group of processes used to deposit a solid material from gaseous phase onto a substrate; similar in some ways to **PVD**. The object to be coated is placed into a reaction chamber and the atmosphere evacuated. Precursor gases are fed into the chamber and react, or decompose, to form a solid material on the surface of the substrate. Compatible materials include metals and ceramics (such as carbide, nitrides and oxides). It is a versatile process, capable of producing very precise coatings (just a few microns thick) through to entire diamonds (page 476).

**cyclic load** Regularly repeating stress, which is of particular concern in structural applications, because cyclic loads below the ultimate tensile strength of a material can result in premature failure. For example, whereas steel can tolerate cyclic loads up to around 10% of its strength, aluminium alloy cannot and so is unsuitable for applications that involve vibration or rotation and require a long lifespan.

**cytotoxic** Toxic to living tissue (typically in reference to materials used in surgery or for surgical implants). See also **biocompatible**.

**damping** Reducing vibration in a system (in particular automotive and machine applications), whereby the mechanical energy is converted into heat.

**debossing** A pattern depressed into the surface of a material, as opposed to raised up (**embossing**). Designs are applied under pressure, such as with **calendering** or press molding.

**deep drawing** A cold metal pressing technique (see also Steel, page 34), it is known as deep drawing when the

relationship between depth and diameter means that controlled drawing is required, which slightly reduces the material's thickness during forming. For example, two-piece aluminium beverage cans (see page 44) are produced using this technique.

**die casting** A range of techniques used to form molten metal, including high- and low-pressure die casting and gravity die casting. High-pressure die casting is the most rapid way of forming non-**ferrous** metal parts: molten metal is forced at high pressure into the die cavity to form the part. The high pressure means that small parts, thin wall sections, intricate details and fine surface finishes can be achieved. The tooling and equipment are very expensive. In low-pressure die casting, molten material is forced into the die cavity by low-pressure gas. There is very little turbulence as the material flows in and so the parts have good mechanical properties. This process is most suitable for rotationally symmetrical parts in low melt temperature alloys. A good example would be an alloy wheel (see Magnesium, page 55). Gravity die casting is also known as permanent mold casting; steel molds are the only feature that differentiate it from **sand casting**. Reduced pressure means that tooling and equipment costs are lower, so gravity die casting is often used for short production runs, which would not be economical for other die casting methods. See also **investment casting**, **MIM** and **Thixomolding**.

**die cutting** This process, also referred to as clicking or blanking, is a high-speed pattern-cutting operation. It is utilized to process suitably soft materials including textiles, paper (page 268) and plastic sheet materials. It is rapid and used to cut out small and medium-sized parts, as well as for kiss cutting (in which the top layer is cut through and the support layer is left intact), perforating and scoring.

**dielectric strength** An indication of the voltage that can be applied to an insulating material before it begins to break down. Thus materials with high dielectric strength are good insulators.

**diffusion bonding** This metal welding technique, suitable for joining both similar and dissimilar materials, operates on the principal of solid-state diffusion: under pressure the atoms at the join interface intermingle over time.

**dip molding, coating** A low-cost method of manufacturing thermoplastic products, it is used to produce hollow and sheet geometries in flexible and semi-rigid materials. The

tool is preheated and dipped into liquid plastic – typically polyvinyl chloride (PVC) (page 122), polyurethane (page 202) or latex (page 248) – which gels on the surface of the tool to form a uniform layer of material. The side that comes into contact with the tool is precise; **embossed** details and textures will be reproduced on the tool-side of the molding exactly. It is possible to revert the part after molding, so that textures are on the outside. It can easily be converted into a coating process by exchanging the release agent for a primer: a thick, bright, insulating and protective layer is built up on metal parts.

**drawing** The process of stretching **filament** yarns during production to align the **polymer** chains and so increase strength. See also, polyethylene terephthalate (PET, polyester) (page 154).

**ductile, ductility** The ability of a material to be deformed without sacrificing toughness. This property is utilized in the production of steel wire (page 28) and gold leaf (page 90), for example.

**elastic deformation** A temporary change in shape of a solid material, which is reversed once the applied load is removed; contrast **plastic deformation**.

**elastic modulus** See **E, modulus of elasticity**.

**electron beam welding, melting (EBM)** A metal welding technique capable of producing coalesced joints in steels (page 28) up to 150 mm (5.9 in) thick and aluminium (page 42) up to 450 mm (17.7 in) thick. Heat produced by the concentration of energy in the power beam (electrons are energized using a cathode heated to above 2,000°C [3,632°F] and up to two-thirds the speed of light) is focused on the join interface, which causes the materials to melt and coalesce. The focused electrons create power densities as high as 30,000 W/mm$^2$ (46.5 W/in$^2$) in a localized spot, which results in very high-integrity welds. The process has been adapted for **additive manufacturing**: using a technique known as electron beam melting (EBM), titanium (page 58) powder is fused together into fully dense three-dimensional parts.

**electrolysis** The decomposition of ionic substances into simpler substances using electricity. The otherwise non-spontaneous chemical reaction relies on the free movement of **ions**. In other words, the substance must be liquid – molten or dissolved in an **electrolyte** – for the process to work.

**electrolyte** An **ion**-containing substance that is electrically conductive when in solution (e.g. salty water); used in **electrolysis** and promotes

galvanic corrosion of dissimilar metals.

**elongation at break** Also known as fracture strain, it is defined as the ratio between changed length and initial length after the material has broken under tension. It illustrates the ability of a material to resist changing shape without cracking of failing.

**embossing** Forming a relief (raised) pattern on the surface of a material, as opposed to **debossing**. Designs are applied by cutting or carving excess away, or by pressing.

**engineering material, metal, plastic** A material suitable for structural application, with clearly defined physical properties.

**extrusion** Material is forced through a die to form long lengths with a continuous profile, a little like squeezing toothpaste from the tube. Several of the material groups are compatible: thermoplastic is heated, mixed and squeezed through (plastic extrusion); continuous fibre reinforcement is coated with resin and cured as it is drawn through a heated die (pultrusion); fine fibres of plastic, glass or basalt are drawn out (spinning); aluminium is heated and forced through under phenomenal pressure (metal extrusion); and clay is pressed through prior to firing (stiff mud process).

**fibrillation** The splitting or breaking apart of the separate fibres or elements, such as plastic yarn used in tufted artificial grass (page 117), or the degradation of regenerated fibres (see Cellulose Acetate, Viscose, page 252).

**figured** Artwork or natural patterns that represent human or animal forms, such as those produced by jacquard weaving (see Silk, page 420) or found in wood veneer (page 290).

**filament** A continuous yarn. The only naturally occurring example is silk (page 420). Man-made fibres, such as viscose (page 252) and polyethylene terephthalate (PET, polyester) (page 152), are spun as filament (see also **monofilament** and **multifilament**) or **bicomponent fibre**, which may subsequently be cut into short lengths, called **staples**.

**flux** A substance added to the raw ingredients in metal smelting, glass making and ceramic firing to lower the melting temperature and thus improve production efficiency. It combines with other impurities to form slag, which may be skimmed from the surface.

**forging** A metal slug is put under considerable pressure between mold halves causing it to flow (plastically) into the die cavity. Complex shapes and deep profiles are formed progressively. The amount of shaping that can be achieved in each step depends on the metal: for example, aluminium is much 'softer' than steel and so considerably easier and more cost-effective to forge.

**friction-stir welding** A metal welding technique: the join is formed by a rotating non-consumable probe (tool), which progresses along the joint mixing the material at the interface. It is a relatively new development and provides a great deal of potential in the design of aluminium (page 42) assemblies, because no heat is added, which makes it particularly well suited to long joins in parts with thin wall section (thermal processes tend to cause distortion).

**galvanic corrosion, number** A process that occurs when metals of contrasting nobility are placed together and in contact with an **electrolyte** (such as salty water): the least noble will become the anode and thus corrode preferentially. As well as presenting a challenge in engineering applications (galvanic corrosion can lead to catastrophic failure), this electrochemical process can lead to discolouration, which is of particular concern in architecture and cladding. See also **cathodic protection**.

**geotextile** Permeable textiles used outdoors to improve the strength of soil. Synthetic examples include polypropylene (PP) (page 98) and polyethylene terephthalate (PET, polyester) (page 152), and natural fibres used in this way include hemp (page 406), flax (page 400) and coir (page 416).

**homopolymer** A **polymer** made up of a single type of **monomer**, such as polypropylene (PP) (page 98).

**HIP** Hot isostatic pressing. See **isostatic pressing**.

**hydrophilic** Propensity to absorb or attract water: for example, natural plant fibres, such as cotton (page 410) and flax (page 400). The opposite of **hydrophobic**.

**hydrophobic** Repels water and similar liquids: for example, silicone (page 212) and polytetrafluoroethylene (PTFE) (page 190), which are applied as coatings. The opposite of **hydrophilic**.

**injection molding** One of the leading processes used for manufacturing plastic products, and ideal for high-volume production of identical products. Plastic is melted with heat and injected under pressure and at high speed into a die cavity. The least expensive injection molding tooling consists of two halves, known as the male and female tool. In this case, the part geometry is limited to the so-called 'line-of-draw', because it must be removable from both sides of the tool in a straight line. For more complex shapes

a multi-part tool is required – each part of the tool retracts in sequence – to allow conflicting angles to be achieved in a single part. Variations on conventional molding include multi-shot (two or more materials combined in a single, seamless part), glass assisted (a small amount of gas is blown in during molding to produce long, hollow profiles) and in-mold decoration (printed film is placed into the mold prior to the plastic, so that after injection the graphics and colour become integral to the object). It is also possible to injection mold certain ceramics (ceramic injection molding or **CIM**; see also Technical Ceramic, page 504) and metals (metal injection molding or **MIM**; see also Aluminium, page 48). While these processes follow a similar principal to plastic injection molding, the design considerations are quite different.

**interference fits** Also known as a press fit or friction fit, this type of join relies on the friction at the interface to hold the two parts together. Typically, the external dimension of one part is greater than the internal dimension of the part into which it fits.

**intumescent coating, paint, seal** A coating or sealant that is designed to swell when heated (creating a foam barrier) and so protect the materials beneath in case of fire. See Polyacrylonitrile (PAN), page 180.

**investment casting** Also known as lost-wax casting. Liquid metal is formed into intricate shapes using non-permanent (friable) ceramic molds. The shape to be made in metal is first formed in wax, or other suitable medium that can be melted. This is coated with ceramic, which is built up in layers until the mold is strong enough to withstand the casting process. This wet dipping and dry stuccoing process, known as investing, is repeated 7 to 15 times with progressively coarser refractory materials. The mold is heated to melt out the wax and fired. While still hot, molten metal is poured in, filling the cavity left by the wax pattern. Once the metal has solidified the ceramic is broken away to reveal the finished part.

**ion, ionic bond** An atom or molecule that has a net positive or negative charge as a result of having respectively more or fewer electrons than protons. Positive and negative ions bind together via electrostatic attraction, forming an ionic bond; a type of chemical bond (see also **covalent bond**). They play an important role in plastics (forming the cross-link in ionomers, which provides several advantageous properties, see page 130)

and minerals (see Clay, page 483).

**isostatic pressing** Used to shape metals, plastics, composites and ceramics, powder is compacted in a flexible mold (membrane or hermetic container) and pressure is applied by gas or liquid. After compacting, the powder is **sintered** (heated to fuse the particles). Forming parts in this way reduces the geometry limitations of pressing in a metal mold. It is carried out cold (CIP) or hot (HIP). The difference is that with very high temperature and pressure, HIP results in fully dense parts, which have improved mechanical properties and surface finish compared to those formed by CIP.

**isotropic** A material with uniform physical properties in all directions, such as steel (page 28) and soda-lime glass (page 508). These materials behave in a very predictable manner, regardless of the direction and type of force applied, which is advantageous for engineering applications. It is referred to as quasi-isotropic when the properties are almost uniform. See also **anisotropic**.

**jacquard** A system invented by Joseph M. Jacquard in the 19th century that uses punched cards to facilitate weaving and knitting intricate patterned fabrics (see Silk, page 420). Originally developed for handlooms, jacquard looms nowadays are **CNC** and able to produce any type of pattern.

**laser sintering** See **sintering**.

**lignin** A strong and stiff natural **polymer** found in the cell walls of plants and trees. Along with polysaccharides (cellulose and hemicellulose), it provides plant stems with the strength to stand upright. Woods that contain a low proportion of lignin, such as hickory (page 352), exhibit relatively higher elasticity. Paper with a high proportion of lignin (such as newsprint produced from mechanical pulp, page 268) will yellow over time and so is not suitable for high-quality or long-lasting applications.

**lightweighting** Typically used in reference to the automotive industry, this is the process of designing vehicles with reduced weight to help improve efficiency and handling. For example, magnesium (page 54) is progressively being used in critical applications thanks to the benefits associated with weight reduction, even though it is relatively expensive.

**lost-wax casting** See **investment casting**.

**machining (milling)** Material is removed from the workpiece by a cutter rotating at high speed. Any hard material can be cut, as long as the cutter material is harder. For example, wood is cut with steel, which is in turn cut with tungsten

carbide. Computer-guided machining is capable of producing very precise and complex shapes. The number of axes determines the geometry that can be achieved: from 3-axis machines used to cut sheet materials to 7-axis machines capable of carving a lifelike bust from a solid.

**matrix** The substance used to bind together particles or fibres in a composite structure. For example, epoxy resin (page 232) is commonly applied as the matrix in CFRP (page 236).

**medullated** The hollow structure of certain wool (page 426), hair (page 434) and fur (page 466), caused by the deterioration of a specific group of cells that make up the core. It is known as partially medullated if the hollow structure does not run the full length of the fibre.

**metal spinning** The process of forming rotationally symmetrical sheet metal profiles. It is carried out on a single-sided tool, as progressive tooling or – in a process known as spinning 'on-air' – without tooling at all. A disc of metal is placed in contact with the tool and they are spun together. With a roller, or metal tool, the sheet is gradually formed onto the surface of the tool. Two metals commonly formed in this way are aluminium (page 42) and copper (page 66).

**MIG welding** Metal inert gas welding forms a strong join between similar metals (typically steel, page 28, aluminium, page 42, or magnesium, page 54). An arc is formed between the consumable electrode and the workpiece, protected by a plume of inert gas. The electrode is continuously fed from a spool and the shielding gas is supplied separately, which means it is possible to semi-automate the process; as a result it has been adopted by the automotive industry and accounts for around half of all welding operations. See also **TIG welding**.

**MIM** Metal injection molding (MIM) is a powder process and similar in principle to **injection molding** plastic. Powdered metal is mixed with a resin binder and injected into the die cavity. Once molded, the part is heated to remove the binder and **sintered** to fuse the metal particles. It is suitable for the production of small parts in steel (page 28), stainless steel, bronze (page 66), nickel alloys and cobalt alloys. See also **pressure die casting**, **Thixomolding** and **CIM**, which is a similar process used to shape powder ceramic.

**Mohs hardness** A relative measure of hardness based on one mineral's ability to scratch, or be scratched by, another, from talc (see Stone, page 472) to diamond (page 476).

**moisture-wicking** The ability of certain fibres to draw moisture

away from the wearer's skin to the garment's outer layer to facilitate faster drying. Animal fibres are inherently wicking (see Wool, page 426, and Hair, page 434); and synthetic fibres produced with this ability include polyamide (PA, nylon) (page 164), polyethylene terephthalate (PET, polyester) (page 152), polyacrylonitrile (PAN, acrylic fibre) (page 180) and polylactic acid (PLA) (page 262).

**molecular weight** A unit of measure of the length of **polymer** chain, such as in synthetic plastic. Higher molecular weight creates denser and higher-strength plastics, because there are more overlaps between the polymer chains. For example, ultra-high-molecular-weight polyethylene (UHMWPE) is several times stronger than commodity polyethylene (PE) (page 108).

**monofilament** A single thread of silk (page 420) or man-made fibre. See also **filament** and **multifilament**.

**monomer** A small, simple compound with low molecular weight, which can be joined with other similar compounds to form **polymers**. Multiple identical monomers are joined to form a homopolymer, two different types form a copolymer and three form a terpolymer.

**multifilament** Cord or yarn consisting of multiple **filaments** twisted together. See also **monofilament**.

**net shape** The final shape of an object, after all of the processes have been carried. For example, whereas zinc (page 78) die castings are considered to be net shape, because they require little or no machining, aluminium (page 42) die castings are only near-net shape, because cutting and finishing is likely required post-forming.

**nobility, noble metals** Metals with low voltage potential, such as magnesium (page 54) are described as less noble and identified by a low **galvanic number**. They are vulnerable to **galvanic corrosion** when placed together with a substance of high nobility (such as carbon fibre, page 236) and in contact with an **electrolyte**.

**non-polar plastic** See **polar plastic**.

**offset lithographic** A printing process often simply referred to as offset litho. It is the most commercial of the printing techniques for magazines, catalogues and books, including this one, because it is a very rapid and low-cost method of reproducing high-quality images and text. A print is created as a result of the basic principle that oil and water do not mix: the non-image areas on the printing plate absorb water, whereas the image areas repel water (**hydrophobic**). During printing, the printing plates are kept wet and so the ink, which is oily, only sticks to the image areas that remain dry. The ink is transferred to a rubber surface on the blanket cylinder, which is pressed against the paper as it rotates, creating a sharp and well-defined print. This indirect method of printing is known as 'offset'. It is most commonly associated with mass-production lithographic printing, but is also utilized for other printing techniques.

**overmolding** An **injection molding** technique, whereby an object is integrated into a plastic part during the molding cycle. It is used to integrate metal parts (such as handles, see page 167) and electronics (such as wearable electronics, see page 195), as well as combine two types of plastic for functional (such as composites, see page 237) or decorative (such as graphics, see page 131) purposes: the objects to be overmolded are placed into the mold and held securely, then the molten plastic is injected over the top.

**parison** A rounded mass of glass or plastic tube that is subsequently formed by glassblowing or blow molding respectively.

**patina** Surface layer, or pattern, developed over time with use, such as seen on leather (page 444).

**phase, crystal phase** In the context of metals, crystal formations are known as phases. A single-phase alloy consists of one type of crystal structure and a two-phase alloy (see **duplex alloy**) consists of a mix of two crystal types. The advantage of duplex alloys is that they are highly susceptible to heat treatment (see **quenching** and **precipitation hardening**).

**phthalates** A group of chemicals (esters of phthalic acid) used to make synthetic plastics such as polyvinyl chloride (PVC) (page 122) more flexible (in this application they are known as **plasticizers**). They are restricted in many countries owing to the potential harm they pose to people and the environment.

**plain-sawn** Tangential sawing, producing plain-sawn timber, is the most efficient and economic method for cutting up a log to make lumber. The tree is sliced along its length into parallel planks. See also **quarter-sawn**.

**plastic deformation, plasticity** Permanent deformation of a material in its solid or semi-solid state (i.e. not just plastics); contrast **elastic deformation**.

**plasticizer** A substance added to plastic to make it more flexible and less brittle. It works by spacing out the **polymer** chains, which gives them room to slide past one another. It has a similar effect to heating an amorphous plastic beyond its **Tg**. The problem with plasticizers is that over time, they migrate to the surface and evaporate; this contributes to the way new cars smell and is why flexible polyvinyl chloride (PVC) (page 122) has such a strong odour. Plasticizers are, in some cases, potentially harmful substances, such as the **phthalates** commonly used in PVC. Non-toxic stabilizers (such as calcium-zinc) and non-phthalate plasticizers are available for sensitive applications, such as toys, packaging and medical devices.

**ply** Single layer of a laminated construction, such as in the case of laminated fabric, wood veneer (page 290) or high-performance composite (see Carbon-Fibre-Reinforced Plastic, page 236).

**Poisson's ratio** The ratio of proportional change in width to length when a material is stretched or compressed. In other words, when compressing a material, it expands laterally; the less it expands then the lower the Poisson's ratio.

**polar plastic** These plastics – see polyamide (PA, nylon) (page 164), polycarbonate (PC) (page 144), polyvinyl chloride (PVC), (page 122) and acrylonitrile butadiene styrene (ABS) (page 138) – contain molecules in which the electrons are distributed asymmetrically. This is caused by the nuclei being made up of atoms that do not share the electrons equally. As a result, the molecule will have a positive and negative pole (dipole). Areas of polarity will oscillate when exposed to an electric field (a property utilized in **RF welding** to generate the heat necessary to melt the plastic). Polarity affects the attractive forces between the **polymer** chains (solubility) and thus permeability; polar plastics are generally more permeable than non-polar ones. Examples of non-polar plastics include silicone (page 212), natural rubber (page 248), polypropylene (PP) (page 98) and polyethylene (PE) (page 108); all of which exhibit excellent resistance to solutions. The affect on attraction between molecular chains means polar plastics are vulnerable to loss of strength, in particular impact strength, when high concentrations of additive are used.

**polymer** a natural or synthetic compound made up of long chains of **monomers**.

**precipitation hardening** Also known as age hardening, it is a heat treatment process used to enhance the yield strength of certain structural metals, such as steel (page 28), aluminium (page 42), copper (page 66) and titanium (page 58). Through controlled heating over a prolonged period of time, beta-phase particles cluster within the alpha-phase **matrix** (see Silver, page 88). These clusters restrict the movement of the crystal lattice, which results in a stronger, stiffer and harder alloy. See also **duplex alloy** and **quenching**.

**prepreg lamination, prepregging** Pre-impregnating with resin, abbreviated to prepregging, is the process of embedding resin **matrix** into continuous fibre reinforcement for application in composite laminating or **compression molding**. The role of the matrix is to support and bond the fibres, transferring applied loads and protecting them from damage. Composite parts are typically made up of multiple layers of prepreg, which are laminated together with heat and pressure. The number and orientation of the layers greatly affects the performance of the part, because fibres are much stronger along their length than across their width.

**pressure die casting** See **die casting**. See also **MIM** and **Thixomolding**.

**PVD** In physical vapour deposition, similar to **CVD**, thin film coatings of nitrides and oxides (see Technical Ceramic, page 502) are created on the surface of three-dimensional objects. It takes place in a vacuum chamber, whereby elements are vaporized in the presence of a gas and condensed onto the surface of the object. It is used for both functional and decorative purposes (interference colour).

**quarter-sawn** Cutting a tree into lumber in a pattern radiating from the centre of the log. Compared to **plain-sawn** lumber, quarter-sawn lumber has a more even grain pattern and hard-wearing surface and is less liable to twist and warp as it dries and shrinks (timber is prone to greater shrinkage across the grain).

**quenching** The process of rapidly cooling metal (in particular **duplex alloys**) from red-hot to cold in water or oil. At high temperature, the beta-phase particles are dissolved and distributed within the alpha-phase **matrix**. Rapidly cooling the metal does not give the beta-phase particles a chance to re-cluster and so maintains the malleability of the metal. This presents many advantages for production. Once forming is complete, the metal may be subjected to **precipitation hardening** to accelerate the process of age hardening, creating a stronger, stiffer and harder metal (see Silver, page 88).

**resilience** The ability of a material to spring back to its original shape once load has been removed.

**RF welding** Radio frequency welding: a plastic joining technique also known as high-frequency or dielectric welding, which uses high-frequency electromagnetic energy. This process is limited to polar materials (see **polar plastic**), mainly polyvinyl chloride (PVC) (page 122). The electric fields causes molecules in these materials to oscillate, **plasticize** and mix at the joint interface

**rapid prototyping** Another term for **additive manufacturing** processes.

**rotation molding** A plastic forming process that yields hollow forms with a constant wall thickness. In a cost-effective process, **polymer** powder is tumbled around inside the heated mold to produce virtually stress-free parts. Recent developments include in-mold graphics and multi-layered wall sections.

**sand casting** A manual metal casting technique: molten metal is cast in expendable sand molds, which are broken apart to remove the solidified part. The sand molds are formed around a reusable pattern, compacted and sometimes bonded to ensure they remain stable throughout the casting process. It relies on gravity to draw the molten material into the die cavity and so produces rough parts that have to be finished. For one-off and low-volume production this is relatively inexpensive and suitable for casting a range of **ferrous** metals and **non-ferrous** alloys. See also **die casting**.

**semi-crystalline** A **polymer** structure that contains both crystalline (highly organized, see page 166) and amorphous (random) regions, for example polyethylene terephthalate (PET, polyester) (page 152).

**semi-synthetic** A group of synthetic plastics manufactured from naturally occurring **polymers**, including cellulose and protein, and converted into fibre, for example viscose and acetate (page 252).

**service temperature** The temperature range an engineering material can function within without breaking down or becoming permanently deformed. The upper limit is known as the maximum service temperature and the lower limit the minimum service temperature.

**shape memory** The ability of a material to be heavily manipulated and then return to its original shape (such as elastomers, including thermoplastic elastomer, page 194, polyurethane, page 202, silicone, page 212, and natural rubber, page 248), sometimes with the application of heat or electricity.

**shear** Strain produced in a substance when its layers are laterally shifted against one another. As well as occurring between the individual components in an assembly, compressive and torsional (twisting) forces cause shear strain to occur between the crystals or lattices in solid materials. For example, under compression, aluminium (page 42) fails suddenly and dramatically as a result of shear. It occurs in liquids, too, and is utilized to generate frictional heat within a mass of material and thus accelerate melting in preparation for molding.

**SI units** The International System of Units, abbreviated as SI units, is the modern form of the metric system and has been adopted by the majority of developed countries. The named units (such as Pascal, Newton, Watt and so on) are derived from the SI base units (length, mass, time and so on).

**sintering** Powder materials – including metals (such as titanium, page 58), plastics (such as polyamide, page 164, and fluoropolymers, page 190) and ceramics (such as technical ceramic, page 502) – are coalesced into a solid or porous mass by fusing the particles together with heat (such as laser, electron beam or kiln). The material does not pass through a liquid phase and this opens up a range of forming options. For example, powder is compatible with **MIM**, **CIM**, **isostatic pressing** and **additive manufacturing**.

**slip** The plastic deformation of single crystals. It is the reason why metals can be formed in their solid state, because while a very great deal of force is required to break all of the atomic bonds, the movement of dislocations allows atoms in a crystal plane to slide past one another at much lower stress levels. **Ductile** metals are more easily formed than brittle ones (such as aluminium, page 42, and magnesium, page 54, respectively) because they contain slip planes in many directions. Slip begins when the external force causes stress in a slip plane and slip direction to reach the critical resolved shear stress.

**SLS** Selective laser sintering: a technique used in **additive manufacturing** to bind layers of powder. See also **sintering**.

**snap fit** An assembly method that relies on the elasticity of one of the materials to springback, thus interlocking with the other parts of the structure. There are several different geometries possible, including cantilever, torsional and annular. The advantage compared to other types of mechanical fastening, is that snap fits may be integrated into one or more parts of the assembly, thus reducing the overall number of parts and, in some cases, materials.

**soldering** See **brazing**.

**specular** Mirror-like, as opposed to transmissive.

**springback** The speed and force with which a material returns to its original shape following **elastic deformation**.

**spring tension** The ability of

a material to resist **elastic deformation** and thus maintain its shape as the applied load is increased.

**staple fibre** Short lengths of fibre, which may occur naturally, such as cotton (page 410) and wool (page 426), or may be man-made **filament** cut to length.

**strain** The deformation experienced by a material when force is exerted upon it, measured as the change in dimension divided by the original dimension.

**stress** The internal force associated with **strain**.

**stretch** The amount a material deforms when tension is applied. It manifests as elastic behaviour (the material returns to its original shape once the load is removed, for example silicone, page 517), permanent or **creep**.

**superplastic, superforming** A metal alloy (aluminium, page 42, in particular grades 5083, 2004 and 7475; and titanium, page 58) capable of extreme **plastic deformation** (more than 1,000%) when heated to a specific temperature. The superforming process, which is a similar process to **thermoforming** plastic, exploits this unique property.

It requires less pressure than conventional techniques and can form deep complex parts with tight radii from a single sheet. As a result, it has had a major impact in the automotive, aerospace and rail industries.

**tear-out** The delamination of fibrous materials – such as wood, in particular those with an interlocked grain (see page 368), and **FRP** – during mechanical cutting. The problem occurs along the cutting path and is exasperated by a blunt blade.

**tempering** A heat-treatment process used in the manufacture of metal and glass. In the case of metals, it is the process of heating the material to a specific temperature (below that of **quenching** to allow the crystal phases to reach an equilibrium without becoming finely distributed) and allowing it to cool in the atmosphere. Thus, a higher temperature will yield a relatively softer material with higher toughness, and a cooler temperature will result in a harder and more brittle material. In glassmaking, the heat-treatment process is used in conjunction with quenching to create surface

and edge compression: the outside surfaces cool more quickly than the core and this results in a structure under compression. Tempered glass, also known as toughened or safety glass, has greater tensile strength than non-heat-treated glass (see Soda-lime Glass, page 508).

**tenacity** A measure of the strength of a fibre or yarn calculated for a specific density (denier or decitex) of yarn. See also $\sigma_T$ **tensile strength**.

**terpolymer** A **polymer** made up of long chains of three repeating **monomers**, such as ABS (page 138).

**thermoforming** Thermoplastic sheet materials are formed with the use of heat and pressure, including vacuum forming, pressure forming, plug-assisted forming and twin-sheet thermoforming. Vacuum forming is the simplest and least expensive: a sheet of hot plastic is blown into a bubble and then sucked onto the surface of the tool. In pressure forming the hot softened sheet is forced into the mold with pressure, so more complex and intricate details can be molded, including surface

textures. For deep profiles the process is plug assisted. The role of the plug is to push the softened material into the recess, stretching it evenly. Twin-sheet thermoforming combines the qualities of these processes with the production of hollow parts. In essence, two sheets are thermoformed simultaneously and bonded together while they are still hot.

**Thixomolding** Trade name for a magnesium forming process (page 57) that works on similar principle to **injection molding**.

**TIG welding** Tungsten inert gas welding: a precise and high-quality metal joining technique ideal for thin sheet materials and intricate geometries. Unlike **MIG welding**, it does not use a consumable electrode; instead, it has a pointed tungsten electrode. The weld area is protected with a shielding gas and filler material is added separately.

**vacuum deposition, vacuum metallizing** Materials are coated with a plume of vaporized metal in a vacuum chamber. With high pressure and an electrical discharge, almost pure metal (typically aluminium, page 42) is

vaporized and condenses onto the surfaces of any objects contained within the chamber. It is used for functional (such as providing electromagnetic interference [EMI] or radio frequency [RF] shielding, improved wear resistance, heat deflection, light reflection, an electrically conductive surface or a vapour barrier) well as decorative purposes. As well as three-dimensional objects, it is suitable for coating plastic films, such as polyethylene terephthalate (PET, polyester) (page 152).

**van der Waals bonds** The electrostatic attractive (or repulsive) forces found between certain molecules or atomic groups. They differ from **covalent** and **ionic bonds** in that the forces are intermolecular, relatively weak and short-range.

**vermicular** Worm-like in form or nature: used to describe the graphite microstructure in CGI (see Cast Iron, page 22).

**wicking** See **moisture-wicking**.

**work hardening** See **precipitation hardening**.

# Featured Designers, Artists and Manufacturers

**24gramm Architektur**
Vienna, Austria
www.24gramm.com

**66°NORTH**
Garðabær, Iceland
www.66north.com

**Aberrant Architecture**
London, UK
www.aberrantarchitecture.com

**Aesop**
Melbourne, Australia
www.aesop.com

**Alberto Meda**
Milan, Italy
www.albertomeda.com

**Alessi**
Crusinallo, Italy
www.alessi.com

**Alessia Giardino**
London, UK
www.alessiagiardino.com

**Alexir Packaging**
Edenbridge, UK
www.alexir.co.uk

**Alfredo Häberli**
Zürich, Switzerland
www.alfredo-haeberli.com

**Alias**
Bergamo, Italy
www.alias.design

**Amorim Cork Composites**
Mozelos, Portugal
www.amorimcorkcomposites.com

**AMSilk**
Munich, Germany
www.amsilk.com

**Ananas Anam**
London, UK
www.ananas-anam.com

**Anastasiya Koshcheeva**
Berlin, Germany
www.anastasiyakoshcheeva.com

**Anish Kapoor**
London, UK
www.anishkapoor.com

**Apple**
Cupertino, USA
www.apple.com

**Arcam**
Mölndal, Sweden
www.arcam.com

**Arian Brekveld**
Rotterdam, The Netherlands
www.arianbrekveld.com

**ARJUNA.AG**
New York, USA
www.arjuna.ag

**Arketipo**
Calenzano, Italy
www.arketipo.com

**Artek**
Helsinki, Finland
www.artek.fi

**Aston Martin**
Warwick, UK
www.astonmartin.com

**Atelier Shinji Ginza**
Tokyo, Japan
www.ateliershinji.com

**ATL**
Milton Keynes, UK
www.atlltd.com

**Atlantic Leather**
Sauðárkróki, Iceland
www.atlanticleather.is

**Audi AG**
Ingolstadt, Germany
www.audi.com

**Aven**
Ann Arbor, USA
www.aventools.com

**Banshu Hamono**
Hyogo Prefecture, Japan

**BAS Castings**
Pinxton, UK
www.bascastings.co.uk

**BASF**
Ludwigshafen, Germany
www.basf.com

**Bav Tailor**
Milan, Italy
www.bavtailor.com

**Bell & Ross**
Paris, France
www.bellross.com

**Bing Thom Architects**
Vancouver, Canada
www.bingthomarchitects.com

**Blackbird Guitars**
San Francisco, USA
www.blackbirdguitar.com

**Black Diamond**
Salt Lake City, USA
www.blackdiamondequipment.com

**Böker**
Solingen, Germany
www.boker.de

**Bond-Laminates**
Brilon, Germany
www.bond-laminates.com

**Caimi Brevetti**
Nova Milanese, Italy
www.caimi.com

**Casa Constante**
Valencia, Spain
www.casaconstante.com

Cassina
Meda, Italy
www.cassina.com

Clements Engineering
Bedford, UK
www.clementsengineering.co.uk

Clive Davies
Bungay, UK
www.daviesceramics.co.uk

Cole & Mason
Farnborough, UK
www.coleandmason.com

Colnago
Cambiago, Italy
www.colnago.com

Corning
New York, USA
www.corning.com

Cumbria Crystal
Ulverston, UK
www.cumbriacrystal.com

DANZKA Vodka
Copenhagen, Denmark
www.danzka.com

Darkroom
London, UK
www.darkroomlondon.com

Design House Stockholm
Stockholm, Sweden
www.designhousestockholm.com

Dissing + Weitling
Copenhagen, Denmark
www.dw.dk

Divertimenti
London, UK
www.divertimenti.co.uk

Don Chadwick
Los Angeles, USA
www.donchadwick.com

Dune
London, UK
www.dunelondon.com

DuPont
Wilmington, USA
www.dupont.com

Ecco Leather
Bredebro, Denmark
www.ecco.com

Elisa Strozyk
Berlin, Germany
www.elisastrozyk.de

Ercol
Princes Risborough, UK
www.ercol.com

Eric Parry Architects
London, UK
www.ericparryarchitects.co.uk

Established & Sons
London, UK
www.establishedandsons.com

Estwing
Rockford, USA
www.estwing.com

Eva Solo
Måløv, Denmark
www.evasolo.com

Explorations Architecture
Paris, France
www.explorations-architecture.
com

Fast + Epp
Vancouver, Canada
www.fastepp.com

Filson
Seattle, UK
www.filson.com

Finn Juhl
Copenhagen, Denmark
www.finnjuhl.com

Fiskars
Helsinki, Finland
www3.fiskars.com

Formway Design
Lower Hutt , New Zealand
www.formway.com

Foster + Partners
London, UK
www.fosterandpartners.com

Frank Gehry
Los Angeles, USA
www.foga.com

Futures Fins
Huntington Beach, USA
www.futuresfins.com

G. Cova & C
Milan, Italy
www.panettonigcovaec.it

Gautier+Conquet & associés
Paris, France
www.gautierconquet.fr

Geoffrey Preston
Ide, UK
www.geoffreypreston.co.uk

Gestalten
Berlin, Germany
www.gestalten.com

Google
Mountain View, California,
USA
www.google.com/about/

Graphic Concrete
Helsinki, Finland
www.graphicconcrete.com

Greece is for Lovers
Athens, Greece
www.greeceisforlovers.com

Grimshaw Architects
London, UK
www.grimshaw-architects.com

Guillem Ferrán
Barcelona, Spain
www.guillemferran.com

H&M
Stockholm, Sweden
www.hm.com

H&P Architects
Hanoi, Vietnam
www.hpa.vn

Hancock
Cumbernauld, UK
www.hancockva.com

Hand & Lock
London, UK
www.handembroidery.com

Harri Koskinen
Helsinki, Finland
www.harrikoskinen.com

HAY
Copenhagen, Denmark
www.hay.dk

Hayashi Cutlery
Gifu, Japan
www.allex-japan.com

Herman Miller
Zeeland, USA
www.hermanmiller.com

Hood Jeans
Attleborough, UK
www.hoodjeans.co.uk

Hopkins Architects
London, UK
www.hopkins.co.uk

Horween
Chicago, USA
www.horween.com

Hot Block Tools
Pittsburgh, USA
www.hotblocktools.com

Hyperlite Mountain Gear
Biddeford, USA
www.hyperlitemountaingear.com

Ian Lewis
Ivybridge, UK
www.handmadefishingfloats.co.uk

Iittala
Helsinki, Finland
www.iittala.com

Inntex
Florence, Italy
www.inntex.com

Inoow Design
Landavran, France
www.inoowdesign.fr

Institute for Composite Materials
Kaiserslautern, Germany
www.ivw.uni-kl.de

Irwin Industrial Tools
Huntersville, USA
www.irwin.co.uk

Issey Miyake
Tokyo, Japan
www.isseymiyake.com

Italcementi
Bergamo, Italy
www.italcementigroup.com

Jacob Plastics
Wilhelmsdorf, Germany
www.jacobplastics.com

Jaguar
Coventry, UK
www.jaguar.co.uk

Jasper Morrison
London, UK
www.jaspermorrison.com

Jo Nagasaka
Tokyo, Japan
www.schemata.jp

Jonathan Adler
New York, USA
www.jonathanadler.com

Jürgen Mayer H. Architects
Berlin, Germany
www.jmayerh.de

Karimoku New Standard
Chita, Japan
www.karimoku-newstandard.jp

Kartell
Milan, Italy
www.kartell.com

Kawasaki
Tokyo, Japan
www.kawasaki.com

Kenzo
Paris, France
www.kenzo.com

KGID
Munich, Germany
www.konstantin-grcic.com

KitchenAid
Benton Harbor, USA
www.kitchenaid.com

Knauf and Brown
Vancouver, Canada
www.knaufandbrown.com

Knoll
London, UK
www.knoll-int.com

Knoll, Inc
East Greenville, USA
www.knoll.com

KraussMaffei
Munich, Germany
www.kraussmaffei.com

Kvadrat
Ebeltoft, Denmark
www.kvadrat.dk

Kyocera
Kyoto, Japan
www.kyocera.co.jp

LaCie
Paris, France
www.lacie.com

Lanxess
Mannheim, Germany
www.lanxess.com

Larke
London, UK
www.larkeoptics.com

Layer
London, UK
www.layerdesign.com

Leslie Jones Architects
London, UK
www.lesliejones.co.uk

Lexon
Boulogne-Billancourt, France
www.lexon-design.com

LINDBERG
Aabyhoj, Denmark
www.lindberg.com

Lockheed Martin Aeronautics
Fort Worth, USA
www.lockheedmartin.co.uk

Louis Vuitton
Paris, France
www.louisvuitton.com

Luceplan
Milan, Italy
www.luceplan.com

M+R
Wöhrmühle, Germany
www.moebius-ruppert.com

MadeThought
London, UK
www.madethought.com

Makita
Anjo, Japan
www.makita.co.jp

Marc Berthier
www.marc-berthier.com

Marcel Wanders
Amsterdam, The Netherlands
www.marcelwanders.com

Mario Bellini
Milan, Italy
www.bellini.it

Marucci
Baton Rouge, USA
www.maruccisports.com

Maruni Wood Industry
Hiroshima, Japan
www.maruni.com

Matceramica
Mamede, Portugal
www.matceramica.com

Mau
New York, USA
www.marianschoettle.org

Mauviel
Normandy, France
www.mauviel.com

Mazzucchelli 1849
Castiglione Olona, Italy
www.mazzucchelli1849.it

Metsä Wood
Espoo, Finland
www.metsawood.com

Mike Draper
Wyoming, USA
www.draperknives.info

Moooi
Breda, The Netherlands
www.moooi.com

Moose Racing
www.mooseracing.com

Muji
Japan
www.muji.com

Muuto
Copenhagen, Denmark
www.muuto.com

Naoto Fukasawa
Japan
www.naotofukasawa.com

Nendo
Tokyo, Japan
www.nendo.jp

Nervous System
Somerville, USA
www.n-e-r-v-o-u-s.com

Newtex Industries
New York, USA
www.newtex.com

Nigel Cabourn
London, UK
www.cabourn.com

Nike
Beaverton, USA
www.nike.com

No. 22 Bicycle Company
Toronto, Canada
www.22bicycles.com

Nokia
Espoo, Finland
www.nokia.com

Normann Copenhagen
Copenhagen, Denmark
www.normann-copenhagen.com

Oliver Tolentino
Beverly Hills, USA
www.olivertolentino.com

Omi Tahara
Milan, Italy
www.omitahara.com

OneSails GBR (East)
Ipswich, UK
www.onesails.co.uk

Palm Equipment
Clevedon, UK
www.palmequipmenteurope.com

Panasonic
Kadoma, Japan
wwww.panasonic.jp

PaperFoam
Barneveld, The Netherlands
www.paperfoam.com

Paul Smith
London, UK
www.paulsmith.co.uk

Pelican
Torrance, USA
www.pelican.com

Philippe Starck
Paris, France
www.starck.com

Philips
Amsterdam, The Netherlands
www.philips.com

Plank
Ora, Italy
www.plank.it

Plus Minus Zero
Tokyo, Japan
www.plusminuszero.jp

POC
Stockholm, Sweden
www.pocsports.com

PP Møbler
Lillerød, Denmark
www.pp.dk

PRAUD architects
Boston, USA
www.praud.info

Prelle
Lyon, France
www.prelle.fr

Pringle Richards Sharratt
London, UK
www.prsarchitects.com

Prodrive
Banbury, UK
www.prodrive.com

Progress Packaging
Huddersfield, UK
www.progresspackaging.co.uk

Puma
Herzogenaurach, Germany
www.puma.com

Rachel Harding
London, UK
www.rachelharding.co.uk

Reiko Kaneko
Stoke-on-Trent, UK
www.reikokaneko.co.uk

Reiss
London, UK
www.reiss.com

Renzo Piano
Genova, Italy
www.rpbw.com

Richard Meier
Newark, USA
www.richardmeier.com

Richard Rogers
London, UK
www.rsh-p.com

Rosendahl
Copenhagen, Denmark
www.rosendahl.com

Rossignol
Isère, France
www.rossignol.com

Roundel
London, UK
www.roundel.com

Royal Copenhagen
Glostrup, Denmark
www.royalcopenhagen.com

Royal VKB
Delft, The Netherlands
www.royalvkb.kempen-begeer.nl

Samsung
Suwon, South Korea
www.samsung.com

Scholten & Baijings
Amsterdam, The Netherlands
www.scholtenbaijings.com

Sebastian Cox
London, UK
www.sebastiancox.co.uk

Seco Tools
Fagersta, Sweden
www.secotools.com

Securency International
Craigieburn, Australia
www.innoviasecurity.com

Silk & Burg
London, UK
www.silkandburg.com

Silken Favours
London, UK
www.silkenfavours.com

Sirch
Böhen, Germany
www.sirch.de

Sony
Tokyo, Japan
www.sony.jp

Spiewak
New York, USA
www.spiewak.com

Squire and Partners
London, UK
www.squireandpartners.com

Stanley Tools
New Britain, USA
www.stanleytools.co.uk

Stelton
Copenhagen, Denmark
www.stelton.com

Steve Cayard
Wellington, Canada
www.stevecayard.com

Stine Bülow
Luxembourg
www.stinebulow.com

Structurflex
Auckland, New Zealand
www.structurflex.co.nz

Studio Droog
Amsterdam, The Netherlands
www.droog.com

Suzuki
Hamamatsu, Japan
www.suzuki.com

Swarovski
Wattens, Austria
www.swarovski.com

Taylor Trumpets
Norwich, UK
www.taylortrumpets.com

The Unseen
London, UK
www.seetheunseen.co.uk

Thomas Ferguson
County Down, UK
www.fergusonsirishlinen.com

Thonet
Frankenberg, Germany
www.thonet.de

TigerTurf
Kidderminster, UK
www.tigerturf.com

Tom Dixon
London, UK
www.tomdixon.net

Topshop
London, UK
www.topshop.com

Torafu Architects
Tokyo, Japan
www.torafu.com

Uniqlo
Yamaguchi, Japan
www.uniqlo.com

Vector Foiltec
London, UK
www.vector-foiltec.com

Victionary
North Point, Hong Kong
www.victionary.com

Victoria Richards
London, UK
www.victoriarichards.com

Vitra
Birsfelden, Switzerland
www.vitra.com

Vortice
Milan, Italy
www.vortice.com

Woven Image
Sydney, Australia
www.wovenimage.com

Yamakawa Rattan
Tokyo, Japan
wwww.yamakawa-rattan.com

Yana Surf
Lake Oswego, USA
www.yanasurf.com

Zhik
Artarmon, Australia
www.zhik.com

# Selected Bibliography

Addington, Michelle and Daniel L. Schodek, *Smart Materials and Technologies: For the Architecture and Design Professions* (Burlington: Architectural Press, 2004)

Antonelli, Paola, *Objects of Design from the Museum of Modern Art* (New York: Museum of Modern Art, 2003)

Ashby, Mike, *Materials and the Environment* (Oxford: Butterworth-Heinemann, 2013)

Ashby, Mike, Hugh Shercliff and David Cebon, *Materials: Engineering, Science, Processing and Design* (Oxford: Butterworth-Heinemann, 2010)

Ashby, Mike and Kara Johnson, *Materials and Design: The Art and Science of Material Selection in Product Design* (Oxford: Butterworth-Heinemann, 2002)

*ASM Metals Handbook*, Desk Edition, 2nd edn (London: EDS Publications, 1998)

Ball, Philip, *Made to Measure: New Materials for the 21st Century* (Princeton: Princeton University Press, 1997)

Ballard Bell, Victoria and Patrick Rand, *Materials for Architectural Design* (London: Laurence King Publishing, 2006)

Beukers, Adriaan and Ed van Hinte, *Flying Lightness: Promises for Structural Elegance* (Rotterdam: 010 Publishers, 2005)

Beukers, Adriaan and Ed van Hinte, *Lightness: The Inevitable Renaissance of Minimum Energy Structures* (Rotterdam: 010 Publishers, 2001)

Beylerian, George M., Andrew Dent and Anita Moryadas (eds), *Material Connexion: The Global Resource of New and Innovative Materials for Architects, Artists and Designers* (London: Thames & Hudson Ltd., 2005)

Black, Sandy, *Eco-Chic The Fashion Paradox* (London: Black Dog Publishing Ltd, 2008)

Braddock, Sarah E. and Marie O'Mahony, *Techno Textiles: Revolutionary Fabrics for Fashion and Design* (London: Thames & Hudson, 1998)

Brownell, Blaine (ed.), *Transmaterial: A Catalogue of Materials, Products and Processes that Redefine Our Physical Environment* (Princeton: Princeton University Press, 2006)

Carvill, James, *Mechanical Engineer's Data Handbook* (Oxford: Butterworth-Heinemann, 1993)

Croft, Tony and Robert Davison, *Mathematics for Engineers: A Modern Interactive Approach*, 2nd edn (Boston: Prentice Hall, 2003)

Denison, Edward and Guang Yu Ren, *Thinking Green: Packaging Prototypes 3* (Hove: RotoVision, 2001)

Hara, Kenya and Takeo Co. Ltd., *Haptic: Tokyo Paper Show 2004* (Tokyo: Masakazu Hanai, 2004)

Harper, Charles A., *Handbook of Materials for Product Design*, 3rd edn (Columbus: McGraw-Hill, 2001)

Hoadley, R. Bruce, *Understanding Wood: A Craftsman's Guide to Wood Technology* (Newtown, CT: The Taunton Press, 2000)

Joyce, Ernest, *The Technique of Furniture Making*, 4th edn, revised by Alan Peters (London: Batsford, 2002)

Kula, Daniel and Élodie Ternaux, *Materiology: The Creative Industry's Guide to Materials and Technologies* (Amsterdam: Frame, 2009)

Leydecker, Sylvia, *Nano Materials in Architecture, Interior Architecture and Design* (Basel: Birkhäuser, 2008)

Lupton, Ellen, *Skin: Surface, Substance + Design* (London: Laurence King Publishing Ltd., 2002)

Mason, Daniel, *Experimental Packaging* (Crans-Près-Céligny: RotoVision, 2001)

McDonough, William and Michael Braungart, *Cradle to Cradle: Remaking the Way We Make Things* (New York: North Point Press, 2002)

McQuaid, Matilda, *Extreme Textiles: Designing for High Performance* (London: Thames & Hudson, 2005)

Mori, Toshiko (ed.), *Immaterial Ultramaterial: Architecture, Design and Materials* (New York: Harvard Design School/ George Braziller, 2002)

Mostafavi, Mohsen and David Leatherbarrow, *On Weathering: The Life of Buildings in Time*, 2nd edn (Massachusetts: MIT Press, 1997)

Mullins, E. J. and T. S. McKnight (eds), *Canadian Woods: Their Properties and Uses*, 3rd edn (Toronto: University of Toronto Press, 1981)

Müssig, Jörg, *Industrial Application of Natural Fibres: Structure, Properties and Technical Applications* (Chichester: John Wiley & Sons, Ltd, 2010)

O'Mahony, Marie, *Advanced Textiles for Health and Wellbeing* (London: Thames & Hudson, 2011)

Onna, Edwin van, *Material World: Innovative Structures and Finishes for Interiors* (Amsterdam/Basel: Frame Publishers/Birkhäuser, 2003)

Rossbach, Ed, *Baskets as Textile Art* (Toronto: Studio Vista, 1973)

Roulac, John W., *Hemp Horizons: The Comeback of the World's Most Promising Plant* (Vermont: Chelsea Green Publishing Company, 1997)

Rowe, Jason (ed.), *Advanced Materials in Automotive Engineering* (Oxford: Woodhead Publishing, 2012)

Sen, Ashish Kumar, *Coated Textiles: Principles and Applications* (2nd edn) (New York: CRC Press, 2008)

Stattmann, Nicola, *Ultra Light Super Strong: A New Generation of Design Materials* (Basel: Birkhäuser, 2003)

*The Best of Fine Woodworking* (Newtown, CT: The Taunton Press, 1995)

Wilkinson, Gerald, *Epitaph for the Elm* (London: Arrow Books Ltd, 1979)

Wright, Dorothy, *Baskets and Basketry* (London: B. T. Batsford Ltd, 1959)

# Illustration Credits

Martin Thompson photographed the objects, buildings and apparel in this book. The authors would like to thank the following for permission to reproduce their photographs.

## Introduction
Page 16 (The limits of possibility): Alberto Meda
Page 17 (Reinterpreting materials): Photo by Masayuki Hayashi; courtesy of Nendo
Page 19 (Advanced materials): Bell & Ross

## Cast Iron
Page 27 (Sand-cast ductile iron): BAS Castings

## Aluminium
Page 51 (Aluminium alloy architecture of the Jaguar XE): photo by FP Creative, London; courtesy of Jaguar

## Titanium
Page 59 (Lightweight titanic glasses): LINDBERG
Page 61 (Titanium alloy road bike): No. 22 Bicycle Company
Page 63 (Airframe): Lockheed Martin Aeronautics
Page 65 (Custom lattice skull implant): Arcam

## Copper, Brass, Bronze and Nickel Silver
Page 74 (Brass dress): photo by Mike Nicolaassen; courtesy of Inntex
Page 75 (Bronze cladding): Gautier+Conquet & associés

## Zinc
Pages 82–83 (Zinc cladding): photo by Kyungsub Shin; courtesy of PRAUD

## Silver
Page 86 (Silver-plated clothing): ARJUNA.AG

## Polypropylene (PP)
Page 99 (Printed tote): Progress Packaging
Page 101 (Lightweight, stackable one-piece chair): Knoll, Inc.

## Ethylene Vinyl Acetate (EVA)
Page 120 (Frosted-film carrier bag): Progress Packaging

## Polyvinyl Chloride (PVC)
Page 126 (PVC tensile structure): Structurflex

## Polyethylene Terephthalate (PET), Polyester
Page 155 (Laminated PET composite sails): OneSails GBR (East)
Page 160 (PET mesh upholstery): Alberto Meda
Plage 161 (PET acoustic panel): Caimi Brevetti
Page 162 (Electronic paper FES watch): Sony
Page 163 (One-piece PBT cantilever chair): Plank

## Polyamide (PA), Nylon
Page 169 (Additive-manufactured structure): Nervous System

## Polymathy Methacrylate (PMMA), Acrylic
Pages 176–77 (Cast transparent table): photo by Masayuki Hayashi; courtesy of Nendo

## Fluoropolymer
Page 193 (Ultralight ETFE cladding): Vector Foiltec

## Thermoplastic Elastomer (TPE)
Page 199 (Flex back task chair): Knoll, Inc.

## Polyurethane (PU)
Page 206 (Machined coffee table): photo by Masayuki Hayashi, courtesy of Nendo
Page 207 (Molded floor lamp): Luceplan

## Synthetic Rubber
Page 222 (Thermal long john): Palm Equipment

## Polyepoxide, Epoxy Resin
Page 233 (Cast resin tabletop): photo by Peter Guenzel; courtesy of Schemata Architects.

## Carbon-Fibre-Reinforced Plastic (CFRP)
Page 238 (Composite bicycle frame): Colnago

## Natural Rubber and Latex
Page 249 (Rubber-bonded cotton jacket): Hancock

## Wood Pulp, Paper and Board
Page 276 (Three-dimensional washi): photo by Akihiro Yoshida; courtesy of Nendo
Page 277 (Three-dimensional washi): photo by Hiroshi Iwasaki; courtesy of Nendo

## Bark
Page 284 (Bark upholstery): photo by Crispy Point Agency; courtesy of Anastasiya Koshcheeva
Page 285 (Birch bark canoe): Steve Cayard

## Veneer
Page 291 (Wooden textile): Elisa Strozyk
Page 295 (Laminated maple chair): Knoll

## Engineered Timber
Page 298 (Oak veneer lounge chair): Moooi
Pages 302–03 (Curved whitewood glulam superstructure): photo by Airey Spaces

## Spruce, Pine and Fir
Page 307 (Spruce glulam and steel hybrid structure): photo by Hufton+Crow; courtesy of Leslie Jones Architects

## Larch
Page 311 (Larch folding chair): Knauf and Brown
Page 312 (Curved glulam arches): photo by Peter Mackinven; courtesy of Pringle Richards Sharratt
Page 313 (Untreated larch cladding): photo by Martin Weiss; courtesy of Judith Benzer of 24gramm

## Douglas-Fir
Page 315 (Truss roof structure): Fast + Epp
Pages 316 (Wood, steel and glass): photo by Michel Denance; courtesy of Explorations Architecture
Page 317 (Weathered wood cladding): photo by Michel Denance; courtesy of Explorations Architecture

## Cypress Family
Page 322 (Western red-cedar shiplap): Hopkins Architects

## Maple
Page 331 (Compact and lightweight stool): Scholten & Baijings

## Beech
Page 340 (Dance studio floor): photo by Michel Denance; courtesy of Explorations Architecture
Page 341 (Carved furniture): photo by Yoneo Kawabe; courtesy of Maruni Wood Industry

## Oak
Page 343 (Veneered packaging): Scholten & Baijings
Page 344 (Solid wood table): Vitra

## Chestnut
Page 347 (Chestnut-clad cabinet): Sebastian Cox

## Walnut
Page 350 (Walnut straight-backed chair): Knoll

## Ash
Page 355 (Bentwood easy chair): photo by Jens Mourits Sørensen; courtesy of PP Møbler
Page 356 (Traditional sled): Sirch

## Cherry, Apple and Pear
Page 363 (Solid cherry wood chair): photo by Katja Kejser and Kasper Holst Pedersen, courtesy of PP Møbler

## Iroko
Page 367 (Outdoor furniture): Thonet
Page 369 (CNC-carved box): photo by Nikos Alexopoulos; courtesy of Greece is for Lovers

## Balsa
Page 379 (Hollow blast surfboard): Yana Surf

## Rattan
Page 383 (Curved upholstery): photo by Lorenzo Nencioni; courtesy of Omi Tahara

## Bamboo
Page 389 (Modular construction): H&P Architects

## Grass, Rush and Sedge
Page 393 (Diagonal cross pattern weave): Guillem Ferrán

## Leaf Fibres
Page 396 (Nonwoven pineapple fibre): Ananas Anam
Page 397 (Piña lace dress): Oliver Tolentino

## Flax, Linen
Page 403 (Bio-fibre-reinforced composite): Blackbird Guitars

## Hemp
Page 407 (Acoustic partition system): Layer

## Cotton
Page 412 (Ventile): Nigel Cabourn
Page 414 (Cycling musette): Progress Packaging

## Wool
Page 431 (Upholstery): Finn Juhl
Page 432 (Light shade): photo by Studio CCRZ; courtesy of Luceplan

## Cowhide
Page 449 (Pigmentation and effects): Ecco Leather
Page 450 (Hair-on-hide upholstery): Cassina

## Pigskin
Page 457 (Coated pigskin): photo by Jonny Lee Photography and The Unseen

## Exotics
Page 465 (Fish skin dress): Bav Tailor

## Diamond and Corundum
Page 477 (Sapphire crystal window): Bell & Ross
Page 479 (CVD diamond coating): Seco Tools

## Plaster
Page 493 (Hand-modelled stucco): photo by Nick Carter; courtesy of Geoffrey Preston
Page 495 (3D printing with colour): photo by Mo Schalkx; courtesy of Studio Droog

## Concrete
Page 497 (Ultra-high-performance concrete [UHPC]): Inoow Design
Page 498 (Relief pattern): Graphic Concrete
Page 499 (Functional coating): Alessia Giardino
Pages 501–02 (Precast concrete): photo by Scott Frances/OTTO

## Soda-Lime Glass
Page 509 (Colour and finish): photo by Kenichi Sonehara; courtesy of Nendo
Pages 512–13 (Curtain wall): photo by Michel Denance; courtesy of Explorations Architecture

## Lead Glass
Page 521 (Blown, cut and polished): Cumbria Crystal

# Sources

## GENERAL

**AZoM** www.azom.com
Information about a broad range of materials and processes, including suppliers' and manufacturers' details.

**Design inSite** www.designinsite.dk
Examples of materials, processes and products where they are applied.

**Engineering ToolBox**
www.engineeringtoolbox.com
Resources, tools and basic information for engineering and design of technical applications.

**Engineers Edge**
www.engineersedge.com
Useful database of information, charts and tables for making calculations in product development.

**Goodfellow** www.goodfellow.com
Leading supplier of materials, including metals, plastics, glasses and ceramics; providing a wealth of information online.

**Institute of Materials, Minerals and Mining (IOM3)**
www.iom3.org
London-based organization that produces a monthly publication called Materials World and holds periodic competitions.

**MakeItFrom** www.makeitfrom.com
A database of engineering material properties that emphasizes ease of comparison. It covers metals, plastics, ceramics and some natural materials.

**Matbase** www.matbase.com
A free and independent online materials properties resource covering ceramics and glasses, metals, natural and synthetic polymers, natural and synthetic composites, and a range of other materials (liquids, fuels and gases).

**Materials Research Society**
www.mrs.org
A diverse organization, which publishes monthly bulletins and journals with information about a broad range of materials.

**MatWeb** www.matweb.com
A comprehensive database that includes tens of thousands of metals, plastics,

composites and ceramics. It is also possible to search via trade name.

**MIT Technology Review**
www.techreview.com
Bimonthly technology magazine published by Massachusetts Institute of Technology (MIT).

**Modern Plastics Worldwide**
www.modplas.com
US-based magazine and online resource dedicated to plastic news, markets, technology and trends.

**O Ecotextiles**
www.oecotextiles.com
A resource for sustainable textiles.

**Recycling Today**
www.recyclingtoday.com
US-based news and information concerning recycling.

**Society for the Advancement of Material and Process Engineering** www.sampe.org
A global professional member society, that provides information on new materials and processing technology.

**Swicofil** www.swicofil.com
Leading supplier of high-performance fibres.

**Total Materia**
www.totalmateria.com
Comprehensive materials database that subscription offers access to more than 10 million material records. Owned by Key to Metals.

**Transstudio** www.transstudio.com
Research and publications covering new materials and research from companies and institutions.

**United Nations Environment Programme (UNEP)**
www.unep.org
Global environmental authority that sets the global environmental agenda, promotes the coherent implementation of the environmental dimension of sustainable development within the United Nations system and serves as an authoritative advocate for the global environment. Online database with a lot of useful articles and information.

**Waste and Resource Action Programme (WRAP)**
www.wrap.org.uk
UK-based promotion campaign working with companies to help create better awareness of the economic advantages of a sustainable approach to materials, backed up by a useful online resource.

**Waste Management World**
www.waste-management-world.com
The latest products and technology, as well as policy and legislation affecting the waste management industry.

## METAL

**Aerodyne Alloys**
www.aerodynealloys.com
Supplier of high-temperature speciality alloys of nickel, cobalt, titanium and stainless steel.

**Alcoa** www.alcoa.com
World leader in lightweight metals technology, providing a wealth of technical information online.

**AlcoTec** www.alcotec.com
The world's largest producer of aluminium welding wire; they provide lots of useful technical application articles online.

**All About Aluminium**
www.aluminiumleader.com
Russian promotional campaign that presents lots of useful information about aluminium and its application.

**Aluminium Federation**
www.alfed.org.uk
Uk-based trade association, which has an online technical library, educational material, database of supplier and other useful information about aluminium and related alloys.

**Aluplanet** www.aluplanet.com
Lots of information about aluminium, its applications and recycling.

**American Foundry Society**
www.afsinc.org
Metal casting society that produces a range of useful publications that cover the materials, processes and developments associated with metal casting.

**American Galvanizers Association**
www.galvanizeit.org
Trade association that provides

a wealth of information useful for architects and designers.

**American Iron and Steel Institute**
www.steel.org
Industry association representing US-based iron and steel manufactures with lots of useful information online.

**Austral Wright Metals**
www.australwright.com.au
Australian distributer of metals that provides a lot of useful technical information online.

**Foundry Trade Journal International**
www.foundrytradejournal.com
Useful news and information about many types of metals.

**British Stainless Steel Association (BSSA)** www.bssa.org.uk
Promotional campaign that provides lots of useful information about stainless steel and its uses.

**Carpenter** www.cartech.com
Manufacturer of several speciality metals, including stainless steel and titanium, with a large online technical library.

**Cast Metals Federation (CMF)**
www.castmetalsfederation.com
Promotional campaign for the UK casting industry; a good place to start if looking for a foundry.

**European Aluminium Association**
www.european-aluminium.eu
Provides a range of useful information about aluminium and suppliers across Europe.

**European Copper Institute**
www.copperalliance.eu
European-based promotional campaign that provides a lot of useful education and technical information about copper and its alloys.

**Farmers Copper**
www.farmerscopper.com
Metal supplier that provides a lot of useful technical information about copper and its alloys online.

**International Aluminium Institute**
www.world-aluminium.org
Useful information about the mining of bauxite, and the production, use and recycling of aluminium and its alloys.

**International Copper Study Group (ICSG)** www.icsg.org
Intergovernmental organization that provides a lot of useful and educational information about copper and its alloys.

**International Iron Metallics Association (IIMA)**
www.metallics.org.uk
Industry association that provides useful information about iron and related material developments online.

**International Magnesium Association** www.intlmag.org
Promotional campaign that provides lots of useful educational and technical information about magnesium and its alloys.

**International Stainless Steel Forum (ISSF)** www.worldstainless.org
A non-profit research organization, which provides lots of useful information about stainless steel and various aspects of the international stainless steel industry.

**International Zinc Association**
www.zincworld.org
Information about the benefits or zinc in a wide range of applications.

**Iron Casting Research Institute**
www.ironcasting.org
Promotional campaign that provides lots of useful information about iron casting.

**Key to Metals**
www.key-to-metals.com
Comprehensive database that with subscription provides information about metals, suppliers and manufacturers globally.

**London Metal Exchange**
www.lme.com
Centre for the trading of industrial metals with information on market prices.

**LTC Thixomolding**
www.ltc-gmbh.at
A Thixomolding component supplier, with lots of useful information about the process online.

**Magnesium** www.magnesium.org
Lots of useful information about magnesium and its alloys.

**Mining Facts** www.miningfacts.org
A resource for Canadian mining information.

**Minor Metals Trade Association**
www.mmta.co.uk
Promotional campaign focused on the minor metals, such as cobalt, zirconium and titanium; providing a lot of useful information online.

**Morgo Magnesium**
www.magnesiumsquare.com
Lots of useful information about magnesium and its alloys including production, processing, forming and recycling.

**Silver Institute**
www.silverinstitute.org
Promotional campaign that provides a lot of useful information about silver, related developments and its uses.

**SteelConstruction**
www.steelconstruction.info
Free encyclopaedia of UK steel construction information.

**Steel Recycling Institute**
www.recycle-steel.org
Information about the collection and recycling of steel.

**Supra Alloys** www.supraalloys.com
Titanium supplier that provides a lot of useful technical information online.

**Titanium Industries**
www.titanium.com
Titanium supplier that provides a lot of useful technical information online.

**Titanium Information Group (TIG)**
www.titaniuminfogroup.co.uk
A subsidiary of IOM3, which provides lots of useful information about titanium.

**Unified Number System (UNS)**
www.unscopperalloys.org
A database of the UNS relating of copper and its alloys.

**World Steel Association**
www.worldsteel.org
Industry association that runs a promotional campaign for steel, which provides lots of useful information about materials properties, applications and recycling. It produces many educational publications.

**PLASTIC**

**AKSA** www.aksa.com
Leading manufacturer of acrylic fibre.

**American Plastics Council**
www.plastics.org
Trade association representing many leading plastic manufacturers.

**Association of Rotation Molders International**
www.rotomolding.org

US-based organization that provides information about rotation molding and manufacturers from around the world.

**BASF** www.basf.de
Leading plastics manufacturer.

**Bio-Plastics** www.bio-plastics.org
Guide to bioplastic materials, processes, uses and developments.

**Bisphenol-A** www.bisphenol-a.org
A comprehensive resource for environmental, health and safety information about bisphenol A (BPA).

**Boedeker** www.boedeker.com
US-based supplier of plastic sheet, rod, tube and machined parts; with lots of useful material data on the website.

**Borealis** www.borealisgroup.com
Leading plastics manufacturer.

**British Plastics Federation (BPF)**
www.bpf.co.uk
Trade association that provides an overview of a range of plastic materials and processes, each one sponsored by a manufacturer.

**Castoroil** www.castoroil.in
Promotional campaign dedicated to the expansion of castor oil, such as a providing a starter material for plastics.

**Center for Polyurethanes Industry**
www.polyurethane.org
US-based promotional campaign for polyurethane in a wide range of industries.

**CES Silicones Europe**
www.silicones.eu
Promotional campaign dedicated to silicones.

**Distrupol** www.distrupol.com
European plastics distributor that provides a wealth of materials information online and in print.

**Dow Corning**
www.dowcorning.com
Leading plastics manufacturer.

**DuPont** www.dupont.com
Leading plastics manufacturer.

**EMS Grivory** www.emsgrivory.com
Leading plastics manufacturer.

**Ensinger**
www.ensinger-online.com
Leading supplier of engineering plastics.

**EPDM Roofing Association (EPA)**
www.epdmroofs.org
Promotional campaign that provides a lot of useful information about ethylene propylene diene, synthetic rubber, for architecture.

**Epoxy Resin Committee (ERC)**
www.epoxy-europe.eu
Promotional campaign dedicated to epoxy resin materials and uses.

**Essential Chemical Industry** www.essentialchemicalindustry.org
Reference library of the principal chemicals hosted by the University of York, UK.

**Expanded Polystyrene Australia**
www.epsa.org.au
National industry body providing lots of useful information.

**Exxon Mobil** www.exxonmobilchemical.com
Leading plastics manufacturer.

**Fibersource** www.fibersource.com
Guide to man-made fibres.

**Fluoropolymers**
www.fluoropolymer-facts.com
Guide to fluoropolymers.

**Global Silicones Council (GSC)**
www.globalsilicones.org
Promotional campaign dedicated to silicones.

**Green Dot Bioplastics**
www.greendotpure.com
Leading supplier of bioplastics and wood–plastic composites.

**Gore** www.gore.com
Leading supplier of fluoropolymer-based fabrics.

**Huntsman** www.huntsman.com
Leading plastics manufacturer.

**Injection Molding Magazine**
www.immnet.com
US-based monthly magazine that provides information about the latest developments in molding and associated materials.

**Innovia** www.innoviafilms.com
Leading plastic films manufacturer.

**International Institute of Synthetic Rubber Producers (IISRP)**
www.iisrp.org
Trade association offering lots of useful information concerning synthetic rubber and its uses.

**JEC Composites**
www.jeccomposites.com
Promotional campaign for composite materials, including an annual trade fair.

**J. J. Short Associates**
www.jjshort.com
Leading US-based supplier of molded rubber parts; provides lots of useful information online.

**LyondellBasell**
www.lyondellbasell.com
Leading plastics manufacturer.

**Medical Plastics News (MPN)** www.medicalplasticsnews.com
Publication dedicated to biocompatible plastics, processes and associated developments.

**Miliken Chemical**
www.millikenchemical.com
Leading plastics manufacturer.

**National Association for PET Container Resources (NAPCOR)**
www.napcor.com
US- and Canada-based trade association for the polyethylene terephthalate (PET, polyester) plastic packaging industry.

**NatureWorks**
www.natureworksllc.com
Leading supplier of bioplastic.

**Net Composites**
www.netcomposites.com
Leading supplier of composite materials.

**Pebax** www.pebax.com
Guide to polyether block amide (TPA), a type of TPE.

**PET Resin Association (PETRA)**
www.petresin.org
Promotional campaign that provides a lot of useful information about polyethylene terephthalate (PET, polyester) materials and uses.

**Plasticker** www.plasticker.de
Latest plastic news and prices.

**Plastics Europe**
www.plasticseurope.org
Leading European trade association, with a comprehensive information and education centre.

**Plastics Foodservice Packaging Group** www.polystyrene.org
US-based promotional campaign that provides a range of useful information about polystyrene and its environmental impacts.

**Plastics Technology**
www.ptonline.com
Monthly magazine providing information about plastics, processing and developments.

**PMMA Acrylic Sustainable Solutions**
www.pmma-online.eu
Promotional campaign providing lots of useful information about polymethyl methacrylate (PMMA), its uses and manufacturers.

**PolyOne** www.polyone.com
Leading plastics manufacturer.

**Polyurethane Foam Association (PFA)** www.pfa.org
Promotional campaign with lots of useful information about polyurethane foam and its uses.

**PVC** www.pvc.org
Promotional campaign including lots of useful information about polyvinyl chloride materials and uses.

**Rubber Manufacturers Association**
www.rma.org
US-based trade organization that represents manufacturers of rubber and elastomers.

**Society of Plastics Engineers**
www.4spe.org

Organization that promotes the use of plastic through publications and trade fairs.

**Syntech Fibres**
www.syntechfibres.com
Polypropylene fibre manufacturer, providing lots of useful information.

**Tenara Architectural Fabrics**
www.tenarafabric.com
Leading manufacturer of fluoropolymer-based architectural fabrics.

**Vector Foiltec**
www.vector-foiltec.com
Leading manufacturer of fluoropolymer-based architectural fabrics.

**Vinyl** www.vinyl.org
Promotional campaign that provides a lot of useful information about polyvinyl chloride and its uses.

**Vortex** www.victrex.com
Leading plastics manufacturer.

**Xantar** www.xantar.com
Polycarbonate produced by Mitsubishi.

**WOOD**

**100% Cork**
www.100percentcork.org
Promotional campaign with lots of useful information about cork materials, production and recycling.

**American Hardwood Information Centre**
www.hardwoodinfo.com
US-based promotional campaign that provides useful information about a range of American hardwood species, their properties and uses.

**American Hardwood Export Council (AHEC)**
www.americanhardwood.org
Trade association for the US hardwood industry, providing information and marketing.

**Amorim Cork**
www.amorimcork.com
Leading cork manufacturer.

**APA** www.apawood.org
Information about engineered wood products.

**Associated Timber Services**
www.associatedtimber.co.uk
Leading European timber supplier.

**Bark Cloth** www.barktex.com
Leading supplier of bark-based products and materials.

**Brooks Bros**
www.brookstimber.com
Leading UK-based timber merchant.

**Canadian Wood Council (CWC)**
www.cwc.ca
Association representing manufacturers of Canadian wood products used in construction.

SOURCES

**Catalyst** www.catalystpaper.com
Leading paper manufacturer.

**Classical Chinese Furniture**
www.chinese-furniture.com
Guide to Chinese wood species
for furniture making.

**CorkLink** www.corklink.com
Leading cork manufacturer.

**English Woodlands Timber** www.
englishwoodlandstimber.co.uk
Leading UK wood supplier.

**Forestry Innovation Investment
(FII)**
www.naturallywood.com
Resource promoting British
Columbia as a global supplier
of quality, environmentally
responsible forest products.

**Forest Stewardship Council (FSC)**
www.fsc.org
International, non-profit
organization that promotes
forest management systems
that are sustainable, economic
and beneficial to people and
the environment.

**Gymnosperm Database**
www.conifers.org
Source of information on
conifers and their allies.

**J. S. Wright**
www.cricketbatwillow.com
Leading willow cricket bat
wood and blade supplier.

**Kew Royal Botanical Gardens**
www.kew.org
Guide to wood species.

**Make it Wood**
www.makeitwood.org
Australian promotional
campaign dedicated to wood
as a construction material.

**Meyer** www.meyertimber.com
Leading wood-based panel
supplier.

**Musterkiste** www.musterkiste.com
Information and samples on
wood-based materials.

**PaperOnWeb**
www.paperonweb.com
Guide to pulp and paper
materials and uses, including
manufacturers, converters,
recyclers and so on.

**Pure Timber** www.puretimber.com
Manufacturer of custom
bentwood curved parts,
components and fabrications
and also sells engineered cold-
bend hardwood.

**ReCORK** www.recork.org
North America's largest
natural cork recycling
programme.

**Southern Forest Products
Association (SFPA)**
www.southernpine.com
US-based promotional
campaign providing lots of
useful information about
Southern Pine.

**Sustainable Forestry Initiative (SFI)**
www.sfiprogram.org
US-based forest certification
scheme: the SFI label certifies
the percentage of certified
wood content, recycled wood
content, source of wood and
chain of custody.

**Timbersource**
www.timbersource.co.uk
Leading UK supplier of
sustainable timber.

**Timber Trade Federation**
www.ttf.co.uk
UK-based promotional
campaign that provides a lot
of useful information about
buying wood from certified
sources.

**Timber Trades Journal**
www.ttjonline.com
UK-based magazine that
contains a lot of useful
information about wood,
manufacturers and a buyer's
guide.

**Timcon** www.timcon.org
Timber packaging and pallet
confederation.

**Trada** www.trada.co.uk
An international membership
organisation dedicated to
inspiring and informing best
practice design, specification
and use of wood in the built
environment.

**Wester Forest Products**
www.westernforest.com
Leading supplier of Canadian
coastal wood.

**Western Wood Products
Association** www.wwpa.org
Association that represents
softwood lumber
manufacturers in the 12
Western states and Alaska;
providing lots of useful
technical information.

**Weyerhaeuser**
www.woodbywy.com
Leading engineered timber
manufacturer.

**Wisa Plywood**
www.wisaplywood.com
Leading wood-based panel
manufacturer.

**Wood Based Panels International
(WBPI)** www.wbpionline.com
Information about wood-
based panel materials and
manufacturing developments,
including all the MDF,
particleboard and OSB mills in
the world with their capacities.

**Wood Database**
www.wood-database.com
Guide to thousands of
species of wood, including
their appearance, physical
properties, working properties
and uses.

**Wood Explorer**
www.thewoodexplorerfe.com
Extensive database covering
many species of commercial
wood; including photographs

of the appearance and lists of
properties.

**Wood for Good**
www.woodforgood.com
UK promotion campaign
aimed at maximizing the
awareness of the benefits
and sustainability of wood for
architecture.

**Wood Magazine**
www.woodmagazine.com
Publications dedicated to
wood for furniture making.

**WoodSolutions**
www.woodsolutions.com.au
Provides details about the
timber species and materials
available for building in
Australia

**Wood Works** www.wood-works.org
Promotion campaign operated
by the Canadian Wood Council.

**WoodWorkWeb**
www.woodworkweb.com
Lots of useful information
about wood species and
properties.

**Woodweb** www.woodweb.com
Online directory of wood-
related books, suppliers,
forums and other useful
resources.

**WRA** www.woodrecyclers.org
Association representing wood
recyclers; provides information
about recycling processes and
companies.

**PLANT**

**Agriculture Marketing Resource
Center (AgMRC)**
www.agmrc.org
A US-based information
resource for value-added
agriculture.

**Center for International Forestry
Research (CIFOR)** www.cifor.org
A non-profit, scientific facility
that conducts research on
the most pressing challenges
of forest and landscape
management around the
world.

**European Industrial Hemp
Association** www.eiha.org
Promotional campaign with
lots of useful information
about hemp fibre and by-
products.

**Flax Council of Canada**
www.flaxcouncil.ca
A national organization that
promotes Canadian flax and
flax products for nutritional
and industrial uses in
domestic and international
markets

**Food and Agriculture Organization
of the United Nations**
www.fao.org
Lots of useful information
about plant-based materials
and products.

**Global Organic Cotton Community
Platform**
www.organiccotton.org
Online platform of the organic
cotton community worldwide,
where knowledge about
organic and fair trade cotton
is exchanged and relevant
information made available.

**Guadua Bamboo**
www.guaduabamboo.com
Leading supplier of bamboo
construction materials.

**HempFarm** www.hempfarm.org
Blog dedicated to the benefits
of hemp in all its guises.

**J. H. Velthoven**
www.jhvelthoven.com
Leading suppliers of dressed
raw materials to the brush
industry worldwide.

**Lineo** www.lineo.eu
Leading flax fibre
manufacturer for composite
applications.

**National Cotton Council**
www.cotton.org
US-based promotional
campaign providing lots of
useful information about
cotton types and uses.

**Panama Hat Company**
www.brentblack.com
Guide to Panama hat materials
and making.

**Ventile** www.ventile.co.uk
Information about Ventile, the
inherently waterproof apparel
fabric.

**Wigglesworth Fibres**
www.wigglesworthfibres.com
Leading manufacturer of sisal.

**Wild Fibres** www.wildfibres.co.uk
Supplier of plant-based and
animal fibres.

**ANIMAL**

**Abbeyhorn** www.abbeyhorn.co.uk
Leading UK supplier of horn
and bone.

**APLF** www.aplf.com
Trade association serving the
global leather and fashion
industries.

**Arctic Quiviut**
www.arcticqiviut.com
Leading supplier of muskox
wool, with information about
the material.

**BLC Leather Technology Centre**
www.all-about-leather.co.uk
Guide to leather types and
uses.

**Born Free USA**
www.bornfreeusa.org
Non-profit organization that
campaigns against the use of
animal fur in fashion.

**Chichester** www.chichesterinc.com
Leading supplier of exotic
natural products, from skins to

taxidermy, antler to horn and
animal parts.

**Crocodile Leather**
www.crocodileleather.net
Guide to crocodile leather,
including images and a buyer's
guide.

**Dents** www.dents.co.uk
Leading UK manufacturer of
fine leather gloves.

**Horween** www.horween.com
Leading US leather supplier.

**J Hewit** www.hewit.com
Leading UK-based leather
supplier.

**Khunu** www.khunu.com
Sustainable yak wool sweaters,
with information about the
material.

**KIAA** www.kangarooindustry.com
Australia-based promotion
campaign dedicated to
kangaroo products.

**Leather International**
www.leathermag.com
Magazine that covers the
leather industry, from raw
material sourcing through to
the influence of fashion on
end-user markets.

**Mohair South Africa**
www.mohair.co.za
Online resource dedicated
to mohair, with information
about the material, designers,
manufacturers, retailers and
wholesalers.

**Moore & Giles**
www.mooreandgiles.com
Leading leather supplier.

**Packer Leather**
www.packerleather.com
Leading supplier of kangaroo
leather.

**Pan American Leathers**
www.panamleathers.com
Leading suppliers of American
exotic leather and leather
goods.

**Rojé Exotics** www.rojeleather.com
Leading suppliers of American
exotic leather and leather
goods.

**Silvateam** www.silvateam.com
World leader in the production,
commercialization and sale of
vegetable extracts, tannins and
their derivatives.

**SLC** www.twslc.com.tw
Leading Taiwanese cowhide
supplier.

**Urbanara** www.urbanara.co.uk
UK retailer with a useful
animal fibre buying guide.

**Vanderburgh** www.
vanderburghhumidors.com
Supplier of high-quality
leather and hand-crafted
leather products.

**Woolmark** www.woolmark.com
Brand and promotion
campaign that promotes
Australian wool.

**MINERAL**

**American Ceramic Society**
www.ceramics.org
Provides useful information
about ceramics and publishes
a monthly magazine.

**Brick Development Association**
www.brick.org.uk
Promotional campaign
dedicated to brick as a building
material.

**Brick Directory**
www.brickdirectory.co.uk
Lots of useful information
about bricks and the history of
brickmaking.

**British Glass** www.britglass.org.uk
Representing the UK glass
industry, the website contains
a wealth of information about
all types of commercial glass
and production techniques.

**Ceramic Arts Daily**
www.ceramicartsdaily.org
Online community serving
active potters and ceramic
artists worldwide, including
publishing magazines.

**Clay Times** www.claytimes.com
Quarterly magazine covering
clay forming, decorating, firing,
studio maintenance, health
and safety, events and contests.

**Concrete Joint Sustainable
Initiative**
www.sustainableconcrete.org
Promotion campaign about
concrete with lots of useful
information.

**Concrete Society**
www.concrete.org.uk
A leading provider of
information serving the
needs of architects, engineers,
specifiers, suppliers and users
of concrete, with emphasis on
quality and competitiveness.

**Corning Museum of Glass**
www.cmog.org
The museum is based in New
York, and the website provides
a lot of useful information

about glass and the history of
glassblowing.

**CVD Diamond**
www.cvd-diamond.com
A comprehensive resource
for this process, including
properties, processing and
applications.

**European Cement Association**
www.cembureau.be
Promoting the use of cement
with useful information about
the material.

**GIA** ww.gia.edu
Lots of useful information
about gems, including an
encyclopaedia.

**Glass Magazine**
www.glassmagazine.net
US-based monthly publication
that serves the architectural
glass market.

**Glass on Web**
www.glassonweb.com
Online directory of glass
supplies and manufacturers
from around the world.

**Glass Pac** www.glasspac.com
Operated by British Glass, the
website provides information
about and promotes the use of
glass in packaging.

**Glass Packaging Institute**
www.gpi.org
Trade association representing
the North American glass
container industry.

**Gypsum to Gypsum**
ww.gypsumtogypsum.org
Promotion campaign focused
on the uses and benefits of
gypsum.

**National Glass Association**
www.glass.org
US-based organization that
represents glass suppliers
to architecture, including
publications.

**Performance Materials** www.
performance-materials.net
Online directory with
information about new
material developments, in
particular high-performance
ceramics and composites.

**Portland Cement Association (PCA)**
www.cement.org
Promotion campaign about
cement and concrete with lots
of useful information.

**Potter's Friend**
www.pottersfriend.co.uk
Online pottery advice.

**Saint-Gobain**
www.saint-gobain-glass.com
Leading glass manufacturer.

**Schott** www.schott.com
Leading glass manufacturer.

**Society of Glass Technology (SGT)**
www.societyofglasstechnology.
org.uk
Website provides useful
information about books,
publications and events
relating to glass technology.

**US Glass** www.usglassmag.com
US-based glass magazine
covering architectural glass
materials, uses and trends.

# Index

Page numbers in **bold** refer to
property comparison charts and
those in *italics* refer to captions.

**#**
24gramm Architektur *313*, 533
3D printing 142, 247, 494, *494*, see
also additive manufacturing
66°NORTH 157, 533

**A**
abaca **394**, 396, *397*, *399*;
papermaking 271; see also
cellulose acetate (CA)
Aberrant Architecture *333*, 533
acacia 16, 358, 364, **364**, 365, 366,
374, 377
acetal, see polyoxymethylene (POM)
acetate, see cellulose acetate (CA)
acrylic, for fibre, see
polyacrylonitrile (PAN) and
for sheet, see polymethyl
methacrylate (PMMA)
acrylonitrile butadiene rubber
(NBR) 199, *216*, **216**, 218, 221, see
also synthetic rubber
acrylonitrile butadiene styrene
(ABS) 98, 107, *108*, 124, 132, **132**,
137–38, *138*, **138**, 140, *140*, 142, *142*,
144, 149, *166*, 180, 200, 228, 264,
*300*, *407*, **440**, 442; PC/ABS 146,
150, *150*, 187
additive manufacturing 65, 142, 164,
170, 188–89, 264, 494, see also
3D printing
Aesop 45, 533
Alberto Meda *16*, *160*, 533

Alessi 35, *168*, 533
Alessia Giardino *499*, 533
Alexir Packaging *273*, 533
Alfredo Häberli *207*, 533
Alias *16*, *160*, 533
aliphatic *165*, *166*, 242
alpaca **434**, 437–38; baby *436*; see
also hair and wool
alligator leather *462*, **462**, 464; see
also exotic leather
alumina (AlO) 11, **476**, 478, *478*,
488, *502*, **502**, 504, *504*, 509,
524; additive in glass 509,
524–25; protective oxide
layer 11, 44, 69; see also
corundum and technical
ceramic
aluminium 8, 11, **22**, 24, 27, 30, 32,
34, 37, 38, 40, 42, *42*, **42**, 44–48,
*45–46*, *48*, 50–56, *50–53*, **54**,
*55*, **58**, 58–60, *60*, 62, 66, 72, 77,
78, **78**, 80, 88, 90, 100, 110, *124*,
127, 142, *144*, **144**, 150, 157, 158,
160, 164, 170, 176, *188*, **188**, 188–89,
230, 234, *234*, 239, 240, 273,
274, 301, *322*, 329, 356, 377, *407*,
494, 504, 506; aluminium
bronze **66**, 68–69, *69*, *75*, 76;
aluminium zinc 83; concrete
498–99; extrusion 38, 42, 48,
*48*, 51, 50, 52–53, *52*, see also
impact extrusion; oxide, see
alumina (AlO), corundum
and anodizing; tanning
agent 446–47, 452; titanium
aluminium nitride (TiAlN) 506;
vacuum-deposited coating 86,

*158*, *158*, 178, see also vacuum
metallizing
aluminizing, see vacuum
metallizing
aluminosilicate glass 178, **476**,
508, 511, 522, **522**, 525, 526;
mineral 483, 487, 498
Alvar Aalto 301, 334, *336*, 516
Amorim Cork Composites *288*, 533
AMSilk 422, 533
Ananas Anam 396, 533
angora (rabbit) **434**, 434–35, *435*,
437–38, 454, *454*, 468; see also
hair and wool
Anastasiya Koshcheeva *284*, 533
Anish Kapoor 126
anneal steel 38; aluminium 44;
silver 88; glass 509, 511, 520
anodize 8, 11, 46, 54, *234*
antimicrobial metal 13, 66, 68, 72, 75,
*75*, 84, 86, *86*, 88, 173; wood 286;
plant 406; hair 437
antler 442–43, **442**; see also bone
and horn
Apple (technology company) 48,
58, 149, *149*, 526; wood 360, *360*,
362, *532*
aramid (para-) 13, 48, 108, 117, 142,
164, *166*, **190**, 208, 228, 234, **236**,
237, 241–42, **242**, 243–44, 244,
246–47, **246**, 433; (meta-) 189,
241–42, **242**
Arcam **65**
Arian Brekveld *108*, 533
ARJUNA.AG *86*, 533
Arkana 377, 533
Arketipo *207*, 533

aromatic (polymer structure)
*146*, 166, *166*, 242, 244, 246;
(polyamide) see aramid; semi-
aromatic 170, 188
Artek *337*, 533
ash (wood) 16, 324, 330–31, **330**, *332–
33*, 336, 338, 347, 352–58, **354**, *355–
57*, **360**, *368*, 377; heat-treated
296; veneer 292, 294, 302
Asiatic raccoon dog **466**, 467–68,
*469*; see also fur
aspen 324, 326, *326*, 328; see also
poplar
Aston Martin *55*, *241*
Atelier Shinji Ginza *92*
ATL *208*
Atlantic Leather 464
Audi AG 170
Aven *189*

**B**
Bakelite, see phenolic (PF)
balsa *324*, 374, 378–79, **378**, *379*
bamboo wood 328, *329*, *332*, 352,
**352**, 354, 382, **382**, *385*, 386,
*386*, **386**, 388, 388–89, 391,
*391*, **392**, 393, *394*, 499; fibre
252, 254, 258, **386**, 391; bast fibre
**386** see also viscose
Banshu Hamono 13, 533
bark 14, 280, *283*, 283–88, *288*,
319–20, 391; birch 280, **280**,
*283–85*, 334, 336, 354, **382**;
cherry 280; cloth (including
tapa) *283*, 283–84; rattan 382,
*385*; tanning 309, 342, 448;
willow 328

BAS Castings 27, 533
basalt 475; fibre 472; see also stone
BASF *163*, 533
Bav Tailor *465*, 533
beech *15*, 16, 308, 332, 336, 338, *338*,
**338**, 340, *340*, 343, 348–49, 357,
*358*, *359*; veneer 292, 294, *296*,
302, 334
Bell & Ross *19*, 477, 533
biaxial-oriented film, see
polyethylene terephthalate
(PET) and polypropylene (PP)
bicomponent fibre 173, 200
Bing Thom Architects *315*, 533
biocompatible 13, 58, 60, 65, 118, 189,
196, 506
bioplastic (including biopolymer)
13, 262, 264–65, 265, 302, 422
Biosteel 422
birch 16, 82, **324**, 330–32, *332*, 334,
*334*, **334**, 336, *336*, 338, 357, 391;
laminated (including plywood)
*226*, *296*, 299; fibre (pulp) 268;
veneer 292; see also bark
Blackbird Guitars *403*, 533
Black Diamond (equipment
manufacturer) 52, 533
blackwood *362*, 364, 375; see also
exotic timber
block rubber, see technically
specified rubber (TSR)
blow molding *108*, 110, 112, *112*, 114,
120, 128, 131, 137, 138, 146, 150, 154,
157–58, *157*, 168, 192, 194, 264;
blown film 123, 261, 264
blown glass, see glassblowing
board, see paper

bocote *376*; see also exotic timber
Böker 443, 533
Bond-Laminates *170*, 533
bone (animal) 438, 440, **440**, *441*, **442**, 442–43, *443*, 457; repair 58, 64–65, 189, 420, 494; structure *388*, *441*, *443*; tool *332*; see also antler and horn
bone china *90*, 487; see also porcelain
boron carbide (BC) 505; see also technical ceramic
borosilicate glass 508, **508**, 512, 520, **522**, 523–26, *523–25*
bossé 368, 372–73; see also mahogany
brass **22**, 24, 66, *66*, **66**, 68, 70, *70*, 72, 76, 78, 80; patinated *333*; textile 72, *75*; see also copper
brazing 76; see also soldering
breathable 112, 128, 157, 196, 200, *200*, 211, *396*, *413*, *448*
bronze 66, 68–70, *69*, 72, *72*, 75, 76, *77*, **90**; see also copper
bubinga **374**, 376; see also exotic timber
buffalo hide 444, **444**, 446; horn 440–41; see also cow
bull hide 444, 446; see also cowhide
butyl rubber, see isobutylene isoprene rubber (IIR)

C
Caimi Brevetti 160, 533
calendering textile 128, *211*, 250, 414; paper 270
calfskin 444, *444*, **444**, 446, *448*, 451, 454, 459; see also cowhide
camel 437–38; see also hair and wool
carbon fibre (CF) 117, *155*, 170, 180, *182*, *189*, 192, 234, 236, **242**, *244*, **400**; crystal structure *238*; reinforced composite (CFRP) 14, *16*, 52, **58**, 60, 62, *62*, 106, 150, 232, **232**, 236–37, **236**, *238–40*, 239–40, **242**, 407
Casa Constante *393*, 533
cashmere 434–38, *438*, 454, *454*; see also wool and hair
Cassina *450*, 534
cast iron **22**, 22–24, *24*, 26–27, 28, 46, 50, 72, 80, 170, 350; see also iron
cathodic protection, action 82–83; see also galvanic corrosion, action
cedar 82, 285, *285*, 294, 309, 310, **310**, 313–14, 318–21, **318**, *321–22*, **346**, *347*, 379; bark cloth 283; Lebanese *292*; Spanish- 373, see also mahogany; see also cypress family
cellulose (plant-based) 14, 16, 254, 258, 260, 283, 286, *385*, *388*, 391, 394, 399, *402*, 408, *409*, *413*, 416, 426
cellulose acetate (CA) 13, *14*, 164, 252, *252*, **252**, 254, *254*, 258, 440, **440**; butyrate (CAB) 254; fibre (paper) 268, 278; fibre (textile) *173*, 252, **252**, 256–57, 258, *258*, 391, 433–34; film 256, *257*, see also lyocell and viscose; propionate (CAP) 254
cement 11, 472, 474, 494, 496, **496**, 498–99, 501, 515, *516*; see also concrete
ceramic injection molding (CIM) *504*, 505
Charles and Ray Eames *231*, 301, 334, 349
Charlotte Perriand *450*
chemical vapour deposition (CVD) 32, 478, *479*, 506, 515; plasma-enhanced (PECVD) 478; see also physical vapour deposition (PVD)
cherry (wood) 16, 333, 348, 357–58, **358**, 360, *360*, **360**, 362, *362*; veneer *292*, 302, *334*; see also bark
chestnut (wood) 82, 240–41, **338**, 342–43, **346**, *347*, 353, 356; tanning 448; veneer *292*, 347
chicken leather 464; see also exotic leather
chinchilla **466**, 467–68, *469*; see also fur
Chinese-fir 321; see also cypress family
chipboard, see particleboard
CITES 374, 457, 464, 468
clay 18–19, 24, *90*, 226, 474, 480, *480*, *483*, 483–92, *485*, 494, 504, *516*, 520; brick 18, **472**, 480, 484–88, *484–85*, 490–91; see also earthenware, stoneware, porcelain and pottery
Clements Engineering *69*, 534
Clive Davies *480*, 534
cod leather 464; see also exotic leather
coir 416–17, **416**, *417*
cold isostatic pressing (CIP), see isostatic pressing
Cole & Mason *504*, 534
Colnago *238*, 534
compression molding 117, *129*, 192, *216*, 221–22, 226, 230, *231*, 234, *237*, 238, 250, *274*, 288, *350*
concrete *11*, 236, 388, 391, 399, 475, **480**, 496, *496*, **496**, 498–99, *498–99*, 501, *501*, 515, 528–29; formwork *296*, 299, 303, **492**, *498*; replacement 306, *313*, 386; Roman 11, 498; ultra-high-performance (UHPC) **496**, *496*, 499, 528; see also, cement
copper *14*, 24, 34, 44, 46, 50, 56, 66, *66*, **66**, 68–70, 72, *72*, 75–78, *75–76*, 80, *85*, 87, 92, *319*, 342, 346, 472, 477, 494, 524; alloy in silver 84–85, 88, see also sterling silver; alloy in steel 30, *30*; alloy in zinc 80; antimicrobial 66, 68, 72, 75, 86, 173; coating 162; plastic pigment and additive 142, 264; see also brass, bronze and nickel silver
cork 14, 280, 286–87, *286*, **286**, 288, *288*, **378**, 379
Corning *524*; Gorilla 526, 534
corundum 11, 239, 478, *478*; see also gemstone, sapphire and ruby
cotton 18, 129, 157, 164, 173, *173*, 180, 182, 200, 224, 252, 254, 258, **268**, 284, 394, *397*, 399, 400, 402, **404**, 404–05, *405*, 407–09, **408**, **410**, 410–11, *411*, 413–14, *413–14*, **420**, *425*, 426, **426**, 429, 446, 466; blend 173, 180, 182, 252, 256, 399, 405, 409, 413–14, *435*, 437–38; cellulose-yielding 252, 254, 391; extra long staple (ELS) 411, *413*; paper 268; pima 411, 413; rubber-bonded *248*
cottonwood 324, 326, *326*, 328; see also poplar
covalent bond 18, 130, *214*, *478*, *483*
cow bone 438, 440, **440**, *441*, 442–43, **442**, *443*; hair-on-hide *450*, *454*; hide 128, 208, **280**, 442, 444, **444**, 446, *450*, 452, 457–58, 460, 462; skin *446*; horn **440**, 440–41, *441*; see also bull, calf, kip and steer
coyote **466**, *467*, 468, *469*; see also fur
coypu (nutria) **466**, 467–68, *469*; see also fur
crocodile 450, 464; see also exotic leather
crystal glass **130**, 516, 518–19, *519–20*; imitation 131, *175*; see also lead glass
Cumbria Crystal *521*, 534
cypress family 313–15, 319, *319*, 321, 322, 370, *373*; see also cedar, redwood and Chinese-fir

D
DANZKA Vodka *42*, 534
Darkroom *252*, 534
debossing metal *36*; paper 278; coating on wood *296*
deep drawing 34, *34*, 38, *38*, 44, *44*, 46, 50, 62, 68, 72
deer antler 443; skin 456, 460, **460**, see also moose
Design House Stockholm *386*, 534
diamond 18–19, 476–79, **476**, *478–79*, 504–05; cutting tool 50, *475*, *505*, 506, 515, *520*; diamond-like carbon (DLC) 32, 478; synthetic 19, 478, *479*; see also gemstone
die casting 48, 56, 72, 80, *80*
die cutting *273*, 294, 299, 451
diffusion bonding 62
dip molding 124, *125*, 222, 250, *250*; coating *125*, *211*, 250
Dissing + Weitling *59*, 534
Divertimenti *46*, 534
Don Chadwick *101*, 534
donkey 459; see also, horse
Douglas-fir 16, **28**, **122**, 124, *232*, **296**, 300, **304**, 306, 308–09, **314**, 314–16, *315–16*, **318**, **342**, **386**, **442**
Dune *453*, 534
DuPont 164, 184, 190, 192, 218, 534; Corian 176; Hytrel RS *199*; Kevlar 243; Nomex 242; Sorona 158; Surlyn *131*; Teflon 190, 192; Tyvek *104*, 112, *117*, 278
Dyneema, see polyethylene (PE), ultra-high-molecular-weight (UHMWPE)

E
earthenware 480, **480**, **483**, 485, *485*, 486–88, **492**; see also clay
ebony *362*, 374–76, **374**, *375–76*; veneer *292*; see also exotic timber
Ecco Leather *449*, 534
eel **462**, 464; see also exotic leather
Eero Saarinen *377*
elastane *129*, 200, 222; see also spandex and thermoplastic urethane (TPU)
electron beam welding 62; melting (EBM) 65
Elisa Strozyk *290*, 534
elk, see moose
elm 16, 336, 357–59, **357**, *359*, 368
embossing metal *36*, *44*; plastic 128, 182, *205*, *211*; paper 278; veneer; 294; textile 433; leather 446, *446*, 450, 457, 464
engineered timber 11, *11*, 14, *231*, 290, 294, 296, 298, 301–03, 304, 306, 315–16, 326, *336*, 368, 386, 388–89, 391; see also fibreboard, glued laminated timber (glulam), hardboard, laminated strand lumber (LSL), laminated veneer lumber (LVL), oriented strand board (OSB), parallel strand lumber (PSL), particleboard and plywood
epoxy 14, *16*, **28**, *204*, 211, **224**, 228, *228*, 230, 232, **232**, 234, 238, 240, 379, 494, **518**; biobased 234, *403*; casting 204, *234*; coating 146, 232, 234
Ercol *359*, 534
Eric Parry Architects *30*, 534
Established & Sons *120*, *232*, *343*, 534
Estwing *451*, 534
ethylene propylene diene (EPDM) 99, 199, *216*, 218; see also synthetic rubber
ethylene propylene rubber (EPR) 99, 218; see also synthetic rubber
ethylene tetrafluoroethylene (ETFE) 192, *193*; see also fluoropolymer
ethylene vinyl acetate (EVA) 102, 110, **108**, 118, *118*, **118**, 120, 124, 157, **202**, 216, 287; foam 110, 118, 120, 158, **286**
ethylene vinyl alcohol (EVOH) 118, 120
Eva Solo *37*, 534
exotic leather 128, 450, 452, 462, 464, 468, see also alligator, chicken, cod, crocodile, eel, lizard, ostrich, perch, salmon, snake and wolfish; timber *292–93*, 294, 313, 348, 357, 360, 365, 375, see also blackwood, bocote, bubinga, ebony, greenheart, kadalox, lacewood, macacauba, padauk, pink ivory, rosewood, wengé, zebrawood, ziricote
expanded polystyrene (EPS), see polystyrene (PS)
Explorations Architecture *316*, *340*, *512*, 534
extrusion, see aluminium

F
Fast + Epp *315*, 534
fibreboard 226, *296*, 299–300, *299*, *326*, 336, *389*; coir 416; see also engineered timber
Filson *454*, 534
Finn Juhl *430*, 534
fir (cypress family) 16, 82, **286**, 304, 306, 308–09, 314, 321, 368, 390; see also cypress family
fish leather, see stingray, eel, salmon, wolfish, perch, cod and shark
Fiskars *167*, 534
flax 18, **394**, 399–400, **400**, 402–07, *402–03*, **404**, **406**, **408**, 413; paper production 268; see also linen
fleece, see sheepskin
fluorinated ethylene propylene (FEP) 192; see also fluoropolymer
fluoropolymer 127, 130, 190, *190*, **190**, 192, 196, *209*, *214*, 218, 238, 242; see also, ethylene tetrafluoroethylene, fluorinated ethylene propylene, perfluoroalkoxy, polytetrafluoroethylene
forging 11, 22, *32*, 34, 38, 52, *55*, 56, 59, 60, 68, 76, 80, 94, *166*, *256*, *451*
formaldehyde 184, 186, 224, 226, 228, 294, 301, 391, 449; see also melamine (MF), phenolic (PF) and urea (UF)
Formway Design *199*, 534
Foster & Partners *18*, *53*, 515, 534
fox **466**, 468, *469*; see also fur
Frank Gehry 62, *294*, 534
friction-stir welding 50
fur 18, 309, 429, *429*, 434, 438, 460, 464, 466–68, *467–68*; alternatives *182*, *425*, 433, 452–54; farming 438; see also rabbit, chinchilla, coypu (nutria), Asiatic raccoon dog, mink, sable, fox, wolf and coyote
fused silica glass **518**, **522**, 526
Futures Fins *239*, 534

G
G. Cova & C *272*, 534
galvanic corrosion, 40, 56, 62, 77, 82, 239; number 77
galvanize, see zinc
Gautier+Conquet & associés *75*, 534
gemstone, see diamond and corundum
Geoffrey Preston 492, 534
George Nakashima 349, *350*
geotextile (man-made) 106, 154; (natural) 404–05, 407, 416
Gestalten *290*, 534
glass, see soda-lime, lead and high-performance
glass ceramic **476**, 488, 508, **508**, 520, *522*, **522**, 524–26, *524*
glass fibre (GF) **98**, 106, 244, **246**, **400**, 472, 525, *525*; long (LGF) 106, **228**; paper production 271; reinforced concrete **496**; reinforced plastic (GFRP) **28**, *170*, 224, **236**; short (SGF) 14, **78**, 100, 106, 132, 140, **144**, 146, *146*, 149, 162, **164**, 169, **184**, 187, 192, **228**
glued laminated timber (glulam) *299*, 300, *303*, *306*, 313, *313*, *357*, 368; see also engineered timber
goatskin 452, **452**, 454, 459; see also kidskin
gold 11, 84, **84**, *85*, *87*, 87, 90, *90*, **90**, 92–94, *92*, 478–79, 513, 519; embroidery 94, *94*; leaf 90, 92, *93*, 94; plated *66*, 94; textile 47
Google 534; Nexus One *48*
granite **472**, 475; see also stone
Graphic Concrete *498*, 534
grass 16, 354, *385*, 386, 392–93, 399, 402, *405*; artificial *117*, *425*; see also rush, sedge and straw
Greece is for Lovers *368*, 534
greenheart 376; see also exotic timber
Grimshaw Architects *193*, 534
guanaco 437–38; see also hair and wool
Guillem Ferrán *393*, 534

H
H&M *258*, 534
H&P Architects *389*, 534
hair 18, 426, *426*, *429*, 434–35, *437*, 438, 440, *446*; fur 468, *468*; imitation *182*; hair-on-hide *450*, 452, 454, *454*, 458, 460; see also cashmere, mohair, angora, camel, llama, alpaca, vicuña, guanaco, qiviut and yak
Hancock *248*, 534
Hand & Lock *87*, *94*, 534
Hans Wegner 349, *355*, 356, *362*
hardboard 300–01, 316; see also engineered timber
Harri Koskinen *515*, 534
HAY *271*, *338*, 534
Hayashi Cutlery *190*, 534
hemlock 16, 308–09, **308**, *309*, 314–15
hemp 18, 391, 393, 396, 399–400, **400**, *402*, *405*, **406**, 406–07, *407*, **410**, 413, 426, 433; fibre-reinforcement 285, 403; imitation 104; paper 268
Herman Miller 200, *231*, 534
hickory 16, 328, *336*, 342, 348, *350*, **352**, 352–53, *353*, **354**, 356–58, 386
high-density polyethylene (HDPE), see polyethylene (PE)
high-performance glass, see aluminosilicate, borosilicate, fused silica and glass ceramic
Hood Jeans *319*, 534
Hopkins Architects *303*, *322*, *345*, 534
horn 440–43, **440**, *441*, *446*; see also antler, bone and cow
horse bone 443; hair *437*, 499; hair-on-hide *454*; hide 444, *448*, 458–59, **458**; slink **458**
Horween *459*, 534
Hot Block Tools *360*, 534
hot isostatic pressing (hot), see isostatic pressing
Hyperlite Mountain Gear *110*, 534

I
Ian Lewis *287*, 534
Iittala *24*, 534

impact extrusion *43*, 44, *45*; see also aluminium extrusion
injection molding 48, 100–01, *102*, 106, *106*, 110, 114, 122, 134, 136, *137*, 138, 140, 146, 149–50, *150*, *163*, 175, *175*, 178, *187*, 188–89, 192, 194, 196, 204, 208, 214, 226, *231*, 237, 244, 250, 258, 260, 262, 264, *300*, *350*, 506; depth effect 149, *149*; foam 100, *101*, 106, *150*, 170; gas-assisted 170; multishot 149; overmolding 101, 131, *131*, 137, *166*, *194*, 200, 208, 214, 226, *237*; reaction (RIM) *150*, 204, 207
Inntex *75*, 534
Inoow Design *496*, 534
Institute for Composite Materials *170*, 534
intumescent coating 26; paints and seals 180
investment casting 22, 62, 72, 92, 94
ion exchange (glass strengthening) 511, 526
ionic bond 18, 130, *214*, *483*
ionomer 8, 110, 130–31, **130**, *131*, **518**
iroko 16, 322, *336*, 357, **364**, 366, *366*, **366**, 368, *368*, **370**, 371, 374
iron 28, 30, 56, 82, 342, 474, 478, 484, 486, 496, 498; oxide *30*, 512, *516*; see also cast iron
Irwin Industrial Tools *256*, 534
isobutylene isoprene rubber (IIR) **216**, 218, 221, 222; see also synthetic rubber
isostatic pressing 490; hot (HIP) *62*, *505*, 506; cold (CIP) 506
Issey Miyake *122*, 158, *511*, 534
Italcementi *496*, *501*, 534

J
Jacob Plastics *170*, 534
jacquard 420, *422*, *425*
Jaguar *51*, 534
Jasper Morrison *34*, 534
Jean Prouvé *344*
Jo Nagasaka *232*, 534
Jonathan Adler *436*, 534
Jürgen Mayer H. Architects *11*, 534
jute *102*, 391, *397*, 404–06, **404**, *405*, **406**, **416**; fibre-reinforcement 403; paper 104; see also kenaf

K
katalox 376; see also exotic timber
kangaroo hide 444, *448*, 460–61, **460**, *461*
Karimoku New Standard *331*, 534
Kartell *140*, *175*, 534
Kawasaki *106*, 534
Kay Bojesen *371*
kenaf 404–05, 406, 433; see also jute
Kenzo *131*, 534
KGID *163*, 534
khaya, see mahogany, African
kidskin 453, *453*, 454; see also goatskin
kipskin 446; see also cowhide
KitchenAid *80*, 534
Knauf and Brown *310*, 534
Knoll *101*, *198*, *294*, *350*, *377*, 534
koa, see acacia
KraussMaffei *170*, 534
Kvadrat *430*, *432*, 534
Kyocera *505*, 534

L
lacewood 377; see also exotic timber
LaCie *274*, 534
lambswool 429, *430*; lambskin 452–54, **452**, *454*; see also sheepskin
laminated strand lumber (LSL) 301; see also engineered timber
laminated veneer lumber (LVL) **296**, *299*, 300–01, *302*, *326*, **496**; see also engineered timber
Lanxess *170*, 534
larch 16, 82, 300, *303*, **304**, **308**, 309, 310, *310*, **310**, 313–15, *313*, **314**, **318**, 322, *336*, **346**, 370; untreated *313*
Larke *252*, 534
laser sintering 58; selective laser sintering (SLS) *169*, 170, 189
latex 216, 221, 248, 250, *250*; rubberized coir 416; see also natural rubber
Layer *407*, 534
Le Corbusier *450*
leaf fibres 394, 397, 399, 403, 406; papermaking 271; see also pina, sisal, abaca and panama
lead glass 508, **508**, 512, 518–20, **518**, *519–20*, 522; see also crystal
Leslie Jones Architects *306*, 534
Lexon *214*, 534
lignin 14, 271–72, *253*, 283, *285*, 286, *388*, 391–92, 399, *402*, 404–05, 406, 416–17
limestone **472**, 474–75, see also stone; concrete 498–99; feedstock 221; flux 24; plaster 494
LINDBERG *59*, 534
linen 129, 156, 164, 396, 400, *400*, 402, 406, 408–09, 414; see also flax
lizard **462**, 464; see also exotic leather
llama 437–38; see also hair and wool
Lockheed Martin Aeronautics *62*, 534
lost-wax castings, see investment casting
Louis Vuitton *444*, 534
low-density polyethylene (LDPE), see polyethylene (PE)
Luceplan *207*, 534
lyocell 257–58, *258*; see also cellulose acetate (CA) and viscose

M
M+R *70*, 534
macacauba 376; see also exotic timber
machining (milling) metal 27, *32*, 48, *48*, 66, 68, *69–70*, 72, 90, 94, *477*; plastic 116, 164, 168, 176, *178*, *187*, 189, *207*; wood 309, *309*, 318, *331*, 350, 352, *365*, 366, 370, 372; ceramic 472, *502*, 506; glass 511
MadeThought *120*, 534
magnesium 40, 50, *51*, 54, 54–56, *55–56*, 58, **58**, 62, 88, 234, 239, 256; additive 24, 38, 44; oxide (MgO) 504, 509, 525
mahogany **290**, 294, 357, 364, *368*, 372–74, *373*; African (khaya) 348, **348**, **366**, **370**, **372**, 373; American 362; true (Honduran, Mexican, Cuban) 372–73, **372**; veneer *292*; see also sapele, bossé and cedar, Spanish-
Makita *146*, 534
maple **290**, 294, *304*, 330–32, **330**, *331–33*, 334, *334*, **334**, 336, *336*, **352**, **354** 356–57, 362, *362*, *368*; bird's eye (sugar) *292*, 330; rock *285*; veneer 302
Marc Berthier *314*, 534
marble 77, **472**, 475, **492**, *501*; see also stone
Marcel Wanders *298*, 534
Mario Bellini *140*, 534
Marucci *332*, 534
Maruni Wood Industry *340*, 534
Masonite, see hardboard
Matceramica *288*, 534
Mau *117*, 534
Mauviel *72*, 534
Mazzucchelli 1849 *14*, *254*, 258, 534
melamine (MF) 224, **224**, 226; surface 300; adhesive *326*; see also formaldehyde
Merino 429, *429*, 430, 433, 436, 438, 453; see also wool
metal spinning 46, 50, *66*, 68, 72, *72*
Metsä Wood *302*, 534
metal inert gas (MIG) welding 50; see also tungsten inert gas (TIG) welding
Mike Draper *64*, 534
mink **466**, 467–68, *468*; see also fur
modal 257; see also viscose
mohair 434–36, **434**, *438*, 454, *454*; see also hair and wool
moisture-wicking 155, 173, *173*, 182, 264, 434
Moooi *298*, 534
moose antler 443, **442**; (hide) **460**, see also, deerskin
Moose Racing *254*, 534
Muji *14*, 101, *279*, 534
Muuto *515*, 534
Mylar, see polyethylene terephthalate (PET, polyester) film

N
Naoto Fukasawa *14*, *144*, *340*, 534
natural rubber 13, **118**, 126, **202**, **216**, 248, *248*, **248**, 250, **280**, **286**, 287, 457; rubberized coir 416; see also latex
Nendo *16*, *177*, *207*, *276*, *509*, 534
neoprene 218; see also polychloroprene rubber (CR)
Nervous System *169*, 535
Newtex Industries *47*, 535
nickel silver 66, *66*, 68–70, 76, 86, 88; see also copper
Nigel Cabourn *413*, 535
Nike *152*, *194*, 200, *200*, *237*, 535
nitrile rubber, see acrylonitrile butadiene rubber (NBR)
No. 22 Bicycle Company *61*, 535
Nokia *149*, 535
Normann Copenhagen *224*, 535
nylon, see polyamide (PA)

O
oak 16, 82, **308**, **310**, 313, **314**, **318**, 322, 332, *336*, 338, **338**, *340*, 342–47, **342**, *344–45*, **346**, *347*, 348, **348**, 353, 354, **354**, 357–58, **358**, 360, **360**, 362, 368, *368*, 370, 372, 375, 377, 388, *496*; bog *293*, 342, 375; burr *293*; cork 288; grain and rays *344*; tanning 448; veneer 294, *298*, 302, *334*, *343*
offset lithographic 37, 45, *99*, 158, *272*
Oliver Tolentino *397*, 535
Omi Tahara *383*, 535
OneSails GBR (East) *155*, 535
optical glass 512, see also lead glass
oriented strand board (OSB) 299, *299*, 301, *326*; see also engineered timber
ostrich leather 462, **462**, 464; see also exotic leather
overmolding, see injection molding

P
padauk *368*, **374**, 376, *376*; veneer *293*; see also exotic timber
Palm Equipment *222*, 535
panama 394, *394*, 397, 399; see also leaf fibres
Panasonic *56*, 535
paper 14, 268, *268*, 271–73, *274*, *276*, 278, *379*, 494; alternative *104*, 112, *116*, *162*, 283–84, *285*, *288*, 446; -based 131, 224; packaging board 182, 268, 270–73, *273*, 278, *278*; cord *355*; decorating 182; kraft **268**, 382, 270, 272, *274*, **280**, 382, 392, **392**; mineral-fill 474, 483; newsprint **268**, 270, *274*, 531; papyrus 393; printing 155, 157, 162, see also offset lithography; pulp 306, 316, 334, 336, 364, 386, 388, 391–92, 396, 399, 400, 402, 405, 407, 413; types 270
PaperFoam *274*, 535
parallel strand lumber (PSL) 301; see also engineered timber
particleboard 226, 299, 302, 313, 392, 400; see also engineered timber
Paul Smith *448*, 535
peccary **456**, 457; see also, pig
Pelican *102*, 535
perch leather 446, *446*; see also exotic leather
perfluoroalkoxy (PFA) 192; see also fluoropolymer
phenolic (PF) 13, 224, **224**; adhesive 296, 301; finish 302, 336; see also formaldehyde
Philippe Starck *168*, 535
Philips *519*, 535
phthalates 136, 154, 258
physical vapour deposition (PVD) 32, *477*, 506, *507*; see also chemical vapour deposition (CVD)
Pierre Jeanneret *450*
pig leather 456–57, **456**, *457*, 462, 464; imitation 128
piña 394, 397, *397*, 399; see also leaf fibres
Piñatex *396*
pine 16, 82, **286**, **290**, **304**, 306, 308–09, **308**, 310, **310**, 313–15, 318, 321–22, 324, 368, 391, 393; papermaking 268; rosin *285*; veneer **290**, *293*, 294, 299; see also cypress family
pink ivory *376*, 376; see also exotic timber
Plank *163*, 535
plaster 492, *492*; gypsum **492**, 494; lime 476, **492**, 494; molds 488, 490; see also 3D printing
pleather 128–29, 446; see also polyurethane (PU) and polyvinyl chloride (PVC)
Plus Minus Zero *144*, 535
plywood 211, 226, *226*, *231*, *292*, *296*, 298–302, *299*, 308, *315*, 324, *326*, 334, 336, 338, *345*, *366*; see also engineered timber
POC *142*, 535
polyacrylonitrile (PAN, acrylic fibre) 180, *180*, **180**, 182, **420**, **426**, 433–34, 453, 446; precursor to carbon fibre 182, 236, *238*
polyamide (PA, nylon) 14, *37*, **42**, 48, 54, 75, **78**, 80, 102, 124, 133, 138, **138**, 144, **144**, **152**, 164–66, **164**, *165–66*, 168–70, *168–70*, 172, 175, 184, **184**, **188**, 190, **228**, 230, **232**, 234, 252, 260, 356, 425, **440**; castable 204; elastomer 192, **194**, 196, *196*, 199–200, *199*, see also thermoplastic polyamide elastomer (TPA); fibre *86*, **152**, **164**, 173, *173*, 180, **180**, 189, 200, *208*, 238, 242, **242**, **252**, *255*, 258, *265*, 400, **416**, **420**, 422, 433; film 112
polybutadiene rubber (BR) 134, 216, 250; see also synthetic rubber
polycarbonate (PC) 48, **54**, 55, *62*, 80, 99, 100, **130**, 131, *133*, 136, **136**, 138, **138**, 140, 142, 144, *144*, **144**, 146, *146*, 149–50, *149–50*, 166, 168, 170, 174, **174**, 178, 208, 258, 440, 511, 520; PC/ABS 140, *142*, 146, 150, *150*, 187
polychloroprene rubber (CR, neoprene) *208*, **212**, 216, **216**, 250; see also synthetic rubber
polyester, see polyethylene terephthalate (PET) and unsaturated polyester (UP)
polyetheretherketone (PEEK) 50, 166, *166*, 169, 188–89, **188**, 230, 234; carbon-fibre-reinforced *189*
polyethylene (PE) 48, 98, 100, 102, 104, 108, 110, *110*, 112, *115*, 117–18, *117*, 120, *120*, 124, 127–28, 130–32, 134, 150, 154, *154*, 157, *157*, 158, 166, *166*, 190, 192, 199–200, 214, 218, *257*, 260, **262**, 264, 272, 278, 301, *301*, 368, 379, 383; high-density (HDPE) **98**, *104*, 108, *108*, 110, *110*, 112, 114, *114*, 117, *117*, **122**, **152**, **262**, 278, **382**; low-density (LDPE) **108**, 110, *110*, 112, 117, **118**, 130–31, **130**, **260**, **268**; ultra-high-molecular-weight (UHMWPE) 104, 108, **108**, 110, *110*, 112, 114, 117, 158, 169, 189, 236, 242, 244, *244*, *247*
polyethylene terephthalate (PET, polyester) 11, 37, 70, 100–02, **108**, 112, 128, 132, 146, 150, *150*, 152, **152**, 154–55, *154–55*, 157, 158, 160, 164, *165–66*, 166, 168–69, **184**, 200, **228**, 230, 260, **260**, **262**, 264; film (including biaxially-oriented [BOPET]) 70, 94, 104, *110*, 154, 157, *158*, 162, *162*, 244, *244*, 278, 515; fibre and textile 48, 94, 117, 120, *122*, 124, 126, 128, *129*, **152**, *160*, **164**, 180, **180**, 182, *186*, *211*, 222, *239*, 252, **252**, 271, 410, **410**, **426**, 432, 446, 456, 466
polyhydroxyalkanoates (PHA) 152, *166*, 260–61, 262, **262**, 264; see also polylactic acid (PLA)
polyisoprene rubber (IR) 218, 248; see also synthetic rubber
polyhydroxybutyrate (PHB) 152, *166*, **262**, 264; see also polylactic acid (PLA)
polylactic acid (PLA) 142, 152, *166*, 260–61, **260**, 262, **262**, 264–65, *264–65*, 302; see also polyhydroxyalkanoates (PHA) and polyhydroxybutyrate (PHB)
polymethyl methacrylate (PMMA, acrylic) 136, **136**, **144**, 146, 166, *166*, 174–76, **174**, *175*, 178, *177–78*, **232**, 234, 488, **508**, 511, 520
polyoxymethylene (POM, acetal) *166*, 168–69, 184–87, **184**, *185–87*
polyphenylene benzobisthiazole (PBO) 13, **190**, 236, 244, 246–47, **246**, *247*, 499
polypropylene (PP) *9*, 14, 80, 98–101, **98**, 104, 106, *106*, 108, 110, 124, 128, 132, **132**, **136**, **138**, 144, 146, **164**, *166*, 168, **184**, 187, **188**, *194*, 200, *214*, 218, **228**, 230, 234, 238, 264, 301, 302, 368, 379; elastomer *196*, 199; fibre and textile 18, **98**, 104, 112, 117, 154, *154*, 164, 180, **180**, 182, 272, **394**, 396, 400, **400**, 404–05, **404**, **406**, **416**, 433, 499; film (including biaxially-oriented [BOPP]) 37, *99*, 102, 104, *104*, 106, 112, 120, 127, 157, 166, 252, *257*, 264, **268**, 278; foam 100, *100–01*, *103*, 104, *278*,
polystyrene (PS) 102, 130, **130**, 132, **132**, *133*, 134, 136, 138, *166*, 174, **174**, 200, 218, **260**, **262**, 264–65, 379; expanded (EPS) 104, **132**, 134, *134*, 211, *274*, 278, *326*, 488; high-impact (HIPS) **130**, **132**, 134, **138**, 142
polytetrafluoroethylene (PTFE) 142, 166, 169, 184, *189*, 190, *190*, **190**, 192; expanded (ePTFE) 157, 192, 211; fibre **190**, 192; non-stick coating 46, 516; see also fluoropolymer
polyurethane (PU) 14, 101, 120, 127, 130, 134, 149, 194, 202, **202**, 204, *204*, 207–08, *207–08*, 211, 216, 226, 234, 244, 287; coating 149, *211*, *350*, 414; synthetic leather 200, *204*, 208, 446, 456, see also pleather; foam *101*, 120, 134, 202, *202*, 204, 207–08, *207*, 211, 226, **286**, **378**, 379, *379*; see also

thermoplastic polyurethane (TPU)

polyvinyl chloride (PVC) 53, 102, 112, 118, **118**, 122, 122, **122**, 124, 124–29, 126–29, 137, 140, 142, 157–58, 166, 190, 196, 202, 216, **248**, 301, 301, 302; coating 160, 204, 209, 209, 211, 211, 221, 446, 450, 456; see also pleather; film 200; unplasticized (uPVC) 122, **122**, 124, 127, **296**, **342**

pony **458**, 459; see also horse

poplar 82, 264, 324, 324, **324**, 326, 326, 328–29, **334**, 336, **338**, 346–47, 357, 360, **378**, 379; plywood 299, 301; thermally modified timber (TMT) 357, 377; see also aspen and cottonwood

porcelain 480, **480**, 483, 483, 486–88, **489**, **502**; see also clay

Portland cement, see cement

pottery 19, 480, **483**, 485, 487, 487; see also clay

PP Møbler 355, 363, 535

PRAUD architects 82, 535

precipitation hardening 30, 88, 88

Prelle 425, 535

prepreg 234, 237, 238, 241, 241

pressure die casting, see die casting

Pringle Richards Sharratt 313, 535

Prodrive 55, 241, 535

Progress Packaging 99, 120, 414, 535

Puma 120, 535

python **462**, 464; see also snakeskin

**Q**

qiviut 438; see also hair and wool

quenching steel 40; aluminium 60; copper 69, 70; silver 88, 88; soda-lime glass 511

**R**

rabbit fibre 437, 438, see also angora; fur **466**, 467–68, 468, see also angora and fur

Rachel Harding 494, 535

radio frequency (RF) welding 124

ramie **386**, **394**, 400, 403, 404, **408**, 409–09, 409, 413

rapid prototyping, see additive manufacturing

rattan 382–83, **382**, 383, 385–86, 385, 391, **392**, 393

reaction injection molding (RIM), see injection molding

redwood 306, 321; see also pine and cypress family

Reiko Kaneko 90, 535

Reiss 178, 535

Renzo Piano 40, 535

Richard Meier 501, 535

Richard Rodgers 322, 535

Rosendahl 371, 535

rosewood 362, 364, 368, 373, **374**, 375, 376, 377; veneer 293, 294; see also exotic timber

Rossignol 199, 535

rotation molding 114, 115, 124, 125, 146, 168, 368

Roundel 99, 535

Royal Copenhagen 489, 535

Royal VKB 108, 535

rubber, see synthetic rubber and natural rubber

ruby 476, 478, 478; see also corundum

rush 392–93, 399; see also grass and sedge

**S**

sable fur **466**, 468; see also fur

safety glass, see toughened glass

salmon leather **462**, 464; see also exotic leather

Samsung 526, 535

sand casting 22, 27, 56, 69, 72

sandstone 472, 474, 520; see also stone

sapele 290, **364**, 368, **370**, **372**, 373; veneer 293, 302, 334; see also mahogany

sapphire 19, 19, 475, 476, **476**, 477–78, 478, 504; see also corundum

Scholten & Baijings 331, 343, 535

Sebastian Cox 347, 535

Seco Tools 479, 535

Securency International 104, 535

sedge 392–93, 399; see also grass and rush

selective laser sintering (SLS), see laser sintering

sheepskin 128, 446, 452–54, **452**, 454, 462, 464, 465, 468; see also lamb and wool

silica glass, see fused silica

silicon carbide (SiC) 504; see also technical ceramic

silicon nitride (SiN) 504; see also technical ceramic

silicone 14, 202, 204, 212–14, **212**, 213–14, 216, 222, **248**; coating 28; TPSiV 196, 200, 214; see also synthetic rubber

silk 18, 87, 173, 258, **394**, 397, 399, 420, 420, **420**, 422, 422, 425, **434**, 438; imitation 155, 164, 252

Silk & Burg 226, 535

Silken Favours 420, 535

silver 32, 66, 84–88, 84, 85–88, **90**, 520; alloy in gold 92, 94; coating (plating) 75, 86, 162; wire and textile 47

sintering metal 58; plastic 117, 169, 170, 189, 190, 192; ceramic 488, 502, 502, 504–06

Sirch 356, 535

sisal **394**, **394**, 396, 399, 399, **404**, **416**; papermaking 271; see also leaf fibres

slate 475; see also stone

slink, see calfskin, lambskin and horsehide

snakeskin 462, **462**, 464; see also exotic leather and python

soapstone 474; see also stone

soda-lime glass 174, **174**, 178, **480**, 508–09, **508**, 511–12, 511, 515–16, 515, 518–20, **518**, 522, **522**, 524–26; see also toughened glass

soldering 36, 70, 75–77, 88; see also brazing

Sony 162, 535

spandex 157, 200; see also elastane and thermoplastic polyurethane (TPU)

Spiewak 467, 535

spinning (man-made fibre) 102, 172–73, 173, 182, 188, 200, 243, 244, 247, 256, 258

spruce 16, 82, 285, **286**, 304, 304, **304**, 306, 306, 308, 313, **314**, 315, 324, 324, 326, **334**, 368, 373, 391; engineered timber 294, 296, 299–300, 303, 303; papermaking 268; see also cypress family

Squire and Partners 178, 535

**T**

tapa cloth, see bark

Taylor Trumpets 66, 535

teak 294, 348, 356, **364**, **366**, 368, **370**, 370–71, 371, 372, **372**, 374, 376, 377; plantation-grown 16, 371

technical ceramic 11, 19, 32, 34, 476,

Stanley 99E 78, 535

starch plastic 258, 260–62, 261, 302; see also thermoplastic starch (TPS)

steel 11, 13–14, 18, 22, **22**, 24, 26–27, 27, 28, **28**, 30, 32, 34, 36–38, 40, 40, 42, **42**, 46, 48, 50, 52–54, 52–53, 56, 58–59, **58**, 60, 62, 62, 66, 72, 78, **78**, 80, 82–83, 85, 86–87, 88, **98**, 100, 106, 110, 124, 126, 150, 164, 166, 189, 230, 231, 240, 256, 284, **296**, 301, 306, 306, 310, 313, 314, 316, 322, 342, **342**, 346, 350, 352, 356, 366, **382**, 383, **386**, 388, 390, 406, **442**, 443, 450, 474, 477, **480**, 496, **496**, 499, 505, 506, 507, 509, 515, 524; duplex 30; high-carbon 30, 34, 70; high-strength low-alloy (HSLA) 11, 30, 30, 38, 40; laminated 28, 34; stainless 11, 28, 30, 32, 32, 34, 34, 37, 40, 52, 54, 58, 62, 66, 69, 72, 72, 78, **84**, 86–87, 176, 189, 357, 386, **502**, 507; tinplate 36, 36; weathering 11, 30, 40; wire 221, 246–47;

steer hide 444, 446, 451; see also cowhide

Stelton 137, **138**, 138, 300, 535

sterling board, see oriented strand board (OSB)

Steve Cayard 285, 535

Stig Ahlstrom 386

Stine Bülow 88, 535

stingray **462**, 464; see also exotic leather

stone 18, 26, 442, 472, 474–75; see also basalt, marble, limestone, sandstone, soapstone, granite and slate

stoneware 480, 480, 486–88, 486; see also clay

straw 392, 393, 399, 402, 488, 499; see also grass

stucco 491, 492, 492, 501; see also cement and plaster

Structurflex 126, 535

Studio Droog 494, 535

styrene acrylonitrile (SAN) 100, 132, 136–38, **136**, 137, 146, 166, **174**, 180, 200

styrene butadiene rubber (SBR) 216, **216**, 218, 221, 25, 528; see also synthetic rubber

superplastic 62; forming 62, 64

Suzuki 150, 535

Swarovski 519, 535

synthetic rubber 14, 100, 106, 120, 124, 128, 132, 134, 137, 138, 194, 199, 202, 204, 209, 216, 221, 244, 250; rubberized cork 288; see also acrylonitrile butadiene rubber (NBR), ethylene propylene diene (EPDM), ethylene propylene rubber (EPR), isobutylene isoprene rubber (IIR) polybutadiene rubber (BR), polychloroprene rubber (CR), polyisoprene rubber (IR), styrene butadiene rubber (SBR)

477, 502, 515, 516, 522, 524, 526; see also alumina (AlO), boron carbide (BC), silicon carbide (SiC), silicon nitride (SiN), tungsten carbide (WC), zirconia (ZrO)

tempered glass, see toughened glass

tempering metal 40, 69, 76, 88; glass 508, 511

terracotta, see earthenware

The Unseen 457, 535

thermoforming 100, 120, 127, 131–32, 134, 157, 157, 166, 170, 176, 178, 194, 214, 237, 254, 261, 264

thermoplastic elastomer (TPE) 14, 100, 118, 120, **146**, 166, 166, 194, 194, 196, 200, 216, 221, 264; copolyester (TPC) **194**, 196, 196, 199, **199**, 200; polyamide (TPA) 192, **194**, 196, 196, 199–200, 199; polyolefin alloy (TPV) 199, **202**, 214; polyolefin blend (TPO) **194**, 199, 199; styrenic (TPS) **194**, 196, 196, 200; urethane (TPU) 52, 124, 142, 157, **194**, 196, **202**, 214, 237, 441

thermoplastic polyurethane (TPU), see thermoplastic elastomer (TPE)

thermoplastic starch (TPS) 244–45, **260**; see also starch plastic

Thixomolding 56

Thomas Ferguson 400, 535

Thonet 340, 366, 535

TigerTurf 117, 535

titanium 13, **42**, 48, 52, **54**, 58–60, 58, **58**, 60, 62, 62, 64–65, 64, 76, 80, **90**, 150, 234, **236**, 239–40; alloying element 30, 78, 80; aluminium nitride (TiAlN) 506; carbon nitride (TiCN) 506; coating 13; dioxide (TiO) 127, 218, 499, 501, 515; heat treatment 88; nitride (TiN) 506

Tom Dixon 70, 115, 535

Topshop 180, 535

Torafu Architects 268, 535

toughened glass 174, 509, 533; see also, soda-lime glass

triacetate 256; see also, cellulose acetate (CA)

tropical hardwood 16, 321, 358, 364, 368, 368, 372, 374–77; plywood 299; see also exotic timber

tungsten carbide (WC) 479, **502**, 504, 515; see also, technical ceramic

tungsten inert gas (TIG) welding 50; see also metal inert gas (MIG) welding

**U**

ultra-high-molecular-weight polyethylene (UHMWPE), see polyethylene (PE)

Uniqlo 165, 535

unsaturated polyester (UP) 14, 37, 106, 152, 176, **224**, 228, **228**, 230–31, 232, **232**, 237–38, 528

urea (UF) 224, **224**, 528; adhesive 294, 301; see also, formaldehyde

**V**

vacuum metallizing (including aluminizing) 47, 48, 94, 159

van der Waals bonds 110, 533

Vector Foiltec 193, 535

Ventile™ 413, 540; see also, cotton

Victionary 127, 535

Victoria Richards 422, 535

vicuña 437–38; see also hair and wool

vinyl, see polyvinyl chloride (PVC)

viscose 18, 164, 252, **252**, 256–58, 258, 386, 391, **408**, 410, 413, 422, **426**, 433–34, 466, 528; polyamide (PA, nylon) blend 173; carbon fibre production 236; paper production 271; see also lyocell and cellulose acetate (CA)

Vitra 344, 535

Vortice 140, 535

**W**

walnut (wood) 16, 313, 332, 333, **338**, 340, 344, 348–50, **348**, 349–50, 353, 358, 360, **360**, 362, 364, 372, 375, 377, 437; veneer 293, 294, 302, 334

wengé 313, 368, 375; veneer 293; see also, exotic timber

wicking, see moisture-wicking.

willow 324, 328–29, **328**, 329, 336, 347, **382**, 382, 391, **392**, 393, 528; cricket bat 328–29

wolffish leather 464; see also, exotic leather

wolf fur **466**, 468; see also, fur

wood-plastic composite (WPC) **296**, 298, 300–01, 301–02, 528; see also, engineered timber

wood pulp: bamboo 386, 391; cellulose acetate (CA) production 256–57, 258; molded 274, 276; paper production 268, 271–73, 278, 304, 306, 316, 324, 334, 336, 364

wool 18, 155, 157, 157, 173, **180**, **280**, **408**, 410, 411, 420, 422, 422, 426, 426, **426**, 429–30, 429–30, 432–38, 432, **434**, 435, 438, 446, 452–54, 464, 466, 468, 468, 531, 533; alternative 180, 182, 252; blend 173, 256, 258, 409; pile 425

work hardening, see precipitation hardening

Woven Image 407, 535

**Y**

yak 437, 438; see also hair and wool

Yamakawa Rattan 383, 535

Yana Surf 379, 535

**Z**

zebrawood 376, 377; see also, exotic timber

Zhik 222, 535

zinc 66, 72, 76, 78, 78, **78**, 80, 80, 82–83, 82–83, 346, 528, 531–32; alloying element 44, 55, 66, 66, 68, 92; galvanizing 32, 38, 40, 78, 80, 82–83, 342, 530; galvanic corrosion 40, 77; oxide in glass production 520,

zirconia (ZrO) 11, 488, **502**, 504, 505, 528; see also, technical ceramic

ziricote 376, 376; see also, exotic timber

Zylon, see polyphenylene benzobisthiazole (PBO)